Interstate Compact Law: Cases & Materials

Jeffrey B. Litwak
Adjunct Professor
Lewis & Clark Law School

ISBN 978-1-943689-11-8

Semaphore Press

www. semaphorepress.com

Interstate Compact Law: Cases & Materials

Jeffrey B. Litwak

Printing A Paper Copy

If you would like to have a printed copy of the book in addition to the electronic copy, you are welcome to print out a copy of any part, or all, of the book. Please note that you will find blank pages throughout the book. We have inserted these intentionally to facilitate double-sided printing. We anticipate that students may wish to carry only portions of the book at a time. The blank pages are inserted so that each chapter begins on a fresh, top-side page.

Finding Aids and Annotations

Finally, please note that the book does not include an index, a table of cases, or other finding aids that are conventional for printed books. This is because a Semaphore Press book, in pdf form, can be searched electronically for any word or phrase in which you are interested. With the book open in Adobe Reader, simply hit control-f (or select the "find" option in the "Edit" pull-down menu) and enter the search term you want to find. We also enable Reader's commenting features in our pdf books, so you can highlight text, insert comments, and personally annotate your copy in other ways you find helpful. If your copy of Reader does not appear to permit these commenting features, please check to make sure you have the most recent version; any version numbered "8" or higher should permit you to annotate a Semaphore Press book.

Table of Contents

PREFACE

Ask any legal professional about interstate compacts, and he or she might respond with a vague memory from a constitutional law class. Ask a state legislator to name three compacts in his or her own state, and with some prompting, you might get one. Ask a person on the street about compacts, and you will get a blank stare. Compacts are not one of the traditional local, state or federal governments, but they are pervasive in the governance of the United States. The more than 200 current interstate compacts address subjects as varied as social services delivery; child placement; education policy; emergency and disaster assistance; corrections, law enforcement, and supervision; professional licensing; water allocation; land use planning; environmental protection and natural resources management; and transportation and urban infrastructure management.

In the United States Constitution, the states reserved their right to enter into agreements with each other subject only to the restriction for congressional consent. The Compact Clause, art. I, § 10, cl. 3, reads: "No State shall, without the Consent of Congress, . . . enter into any Agreement or Compact with another state, or with a foreign Power . . . ." The very text of this clause has historically raised questions such as what constitutes consent of Congress; when is consent necessary; and whether the term "states" also includes U.S. territories. Existing jurisprudence readily answers these questions and they hardly deserve the attention of a casebook. More interesting are the questions about whether consent is required for the compact to bind the states; whether Congress may alter, amend, or repeal consent; federalism, preemption, and conflict of laws problems created by congressional consent; and the nature, treatment, and governance of interstate compact agencies. This book raises these and many other interesting questions, only some of which are illustrated in the case law.

In 1970, one compact scholar noted a "paucity of significant interstate compact law," and that "the imperfect state of compact law has not been widely lamented; in fact, it even has not been generally recognized." David E. Engdahl, *Interstate Urban Areas and Interstate "Agreements" and "Compacts": Unclear Possibilities*, 58 GEO. L.J. 799, 803 (1970). Compact law has developed greatly since 1970, but is still largely undeveloped. Compacts and compact agencies generate few cases relative to the number of federal and state laws and federal and state agencies that generate tens of thousands of cases each year; there are few practitioners and scholars interested in this area of law, and thus few law review articles and books; and few lawyers or law students have even studied compacts. *See* Michael L. Buenger & Richard L. Masters, *The Interstate Compact on Adult Offender Supervision: Using Old Tools to Solve New Problems*, 9 ROGER WILLIAMS U. L. REV. 71, 72 (2003). Some legal questions surprisingly arise only infrequently in court, and some of the reasoning and logic in those cases is slim. This undeveloped state of the law makes compacts a fun study because there are unique opportunities to discuss differing theories and reasoning with few already established jurisprudential sideboards. Many of the case excerpts in this book are long to illustrate the breadth and complexity of interstate compacts, and the political and legal disputes that arise when creating and administering them. The notes and questions challenge readers to think about the material in the broader context of compacts as unusual but important government actions that require special attention different from typical federal and state laws and agencies.

Despite the dearth of precedent, courts have created legal maxims, and scholars have suggested principles that address the unique nature of interstate compacts. This book is my attempt to summarize those maxims and principles, and create tidy and distinct chapters. Each chapter builds on the prior materials, but inevitably, early chapters mention some concepts that are covered more comprehensively in later chapters. The choice and division of the materials is entirely my work. Disagreements with my choices, the flow of the book, where certain materials fit, my interpretation of how the law has developed, and my projections for how the law should continue to develop can only enrich the study of this area of law. I welcome your comments.

This fourth edition retains the same overall organization as the first two editions, while adding and reorganizing some specific materials. New materials and discussion in this edition include new primary cases, updated notes and questions with new case law, scholarly work, and administrative and legislative actions; and a new chapter on compacts between states and foreign governments that consolidates and significantly expands on those materials in the third edition. As with the prior editions, astute readers will glean familiar principles of constitutional law, administrative law, conflict of laws, contract law, and statutory construction in these materials.

Chapter 1 begins with an overview of interstate problems, the many forms in which states and other levels of government cooperate, and the compact solution. Chapter 2 jumps right into the constitutional requirement for consent. While not all compacts require consent, most of the compacts that have generated law for our study have received consent. Consent is not a formula; it is intricate legislation based on political judgment that establishes rights and limitations for the federal government and party states. The Constitution and constitutional jurisprudence establish an enormously complex set of rules about the roles of the federal government and the states, but say very little about compacts and compact agencies.

Chapter 3 looks at the authority of states to enter into compacts and the political concept of compacts as states regain pieces of their sovereignty back from the federal government, but at the same time sharing that sovereignty with sister states. Chapter 4 considers the special nature of compact agencies as independent entities, and how courts have struggled to define just what is a compact agency.

Chapter 5 analyzes the primarily Supreme Court jurisprudence that treats compacts with congressional consent as federal law and the implications of this jurisprudence. Chapter 6 studies jurisdiction in the federal and state courts to address compact disputes and review compact agency actions, and the complexities not found in typical challenges to federal or state legislation and agency action.

Chapter 7 focuses on the related topic of the application of the Eleventh Amendment. This is one of the few aspects of compact law that is largely settled; however, the development of the Supreme Court's jurisprudence is an interesting study.

Chapter 8 introduces the multi-faceted relationship between a compact and state law. While conceptually simple, this is one of the least-settled aspects of compact law, and many current court decisions show judicial discomfort with deciding whether state law conflicts with a compact and resolving that conflict in favor of a compact. Chapter 9, concerning interpretation of compacts, starts with parallels between interpreting international treaties and interpreting interstate compacts. It then covers some of the judicial methods and overarching considerations that courts use when interpreting compacts.

Chapter 10 looks at many governance issues not typically found in compact text or federal consent legislation, such as when compacts become effective, oversight of compacts, and administrative procedures used by a compact agency. Chapter 11 discusses problems that party states, compact agencies, and third parties must consider when seeking to enforce compacts. Enforcement illustrates many of the compact issues studied in the earlier chapters. The final chapter, Chapter 12, concludes the book with an introduction to interstate compacts that also involve Canadian provinces and agreements between a state and a foreign power where there is no domestic interstate compact.

Few attorneys will work closely with interstate compacts. So why study compacts? One reason is that compact law principles are transferable. Studying this most formal type of intergovernmental agreement provides a framework for thinking about all forms of intergovernmental cooperation and more common agreements between state administrative officials, between municipal officials, and between municipalities through various state law authorities. Every state authorizes non-compact agreements using terms such as intergovernmental, intermunicipal, interagency, interlocal or administrative agreements. No matter the term used, these agreements may be intrastate or between entities in different states and they share many of the same legal issues as interstate compacts, including their ability to bind future governing boards; formation and drafting problems; administration of the agreement by the parties or a separate entity; liability under the agreement; withdrawal from and termination of the agreement; and enforcement of the agreement. Many of the notes and questions throughout this book address links between compacts and non-compact intergovernmental agreements.

Another reason to study compacts is to reflect on governmental structure free from many existing legal constraints. Because compacts and compact agencies are independent of the federal and state governments, many of the existing procedural and transparency laws do not apply, or they apply only in the manner specified in the compact. Developing good governance of compacts and within compact agencies often requires constructing unique approaches that address problems foreign to federal and state laws and agencies.

These materials have evolved over more than 15 years of teaching Interstate Compact Law at Lewis & Clark Law School and more than 20 years of practice and study. Past students' express and subtle input into which subjects and materials are interesting, where the materials best fit, and how to present them has been invaluable. Special thanks goes to the Columbia River Gorge Commission, which continues to treat ongoing fluency with this most interesting area of law and thinking about the big picture of compact law as one of my general counsel priorities. Another special thanks goes the American Bar Association Section of Administrative Law and Regulatory Practice, which asked me to write and has published an annual chapter on new development in interstate compact law since 2008 in its annual *Developments in Administrative Law and Regulatory Practice* book. Still another special thanks goes to the Council of State Governments National Center for Interstate Compacts, which has generously shared staff time and documents in response to questions, and has invited me to be part of the National Center's work since 2004. Finally, more special thanks go to the many people around the country that have been my professional network; together we have thought through many esoteric compact questions, you have reviewed my writing, and you have provided me with dozens of pages of topics for students to consider for their course papers.

This fourth edition is dedicated to the memory of William S. Morrow, Jr., Executive Director and General Counsel of the Washington Metropolitan Area Transit Commission and one of the true scholars and practitioners of interstate compact law. Bill argued the *Old Town Trolley* case at the D.C. Circuit in 1998 (excerpted in Chapter 8) and used that decision to start the ABA's (and consequently my own) study of the administrative law applicable to interstate commissions. Bill, you invited me to be part of the ABA Administrative Law Section and mentored me for many years. We should have had many more years to collaborate. I miss you.

Editing & Citation Notes

Case Excerpts: In editing cases, this book does not indicate omitted footnotes or citations; the book does, however, retain footnote numbering from the cases as reported. Where the book omits substantive discussion, it notes the omission with an ellipsis.

Citations to Interstate Compacts: There is no standard form for citing interstate compacts. Neither the Bluebook, nor the ALWD Citation Manual discuss interstate compacts or their citation form. This book cites to the name of the compact and the appropriate article, section, or paragraph. This book does not cite to the states' and federal government statutes enacting compacts or federal actions granting consent to compacts because the citations would become unwieldy. This book cites to those state or federal actions when discussing them specifically. Copies of compacts and citations to the states' enactments and federal actions granting consent are available on the website for The Council of State Governments. http://apps.csg.org/ncic/.

Interstate Compact Titles: Some compacts do not have a popular name or have a generic name using only the party states. In these instances, this book refers to the interstate agency that the compact creates followed by "compact" in lowercase. For example, this book uses "Port Authority of New York and New Jersey compact" to refer to the 1921 amendments to the New York-New Jersey Compact of 1834 that created the Port Authority of New York Harbor (now Port Authority of New York and New Jersey).

Interstate Compact Agency Names: Interstate agencies that compacts create have many different names, including bi-state, multistate, interstate, agency, entity, commission, council, authority, etc. When discussing interstate agencies generally, this book uses the generic term "compact agency," unless the context suggests otherwise. References to specific compact agencies use the same terminology as the compact.

Citations to Federal and State Statutes: This book does not cite to the year of federal and state statutes that were current as of July 1, 2020. For statutes that are no longer current, this book cites to the last hard-published version for the code where those statutes were codified. Citations to state statutes were verified using the online code available through links on each state legislature or state court website as of July 1, 2020.

Citations to Internet Sources: All internet citations were verified as of July 1, 2020. This citation note is a substitute for adding a "last visited" notation to each internet citation in the text.

About the Author

Jeffrey B. Litwak has been Counsel to the Columbia River Gorge Commission, the interstate compact agency for the Columbia River Gorge National Scenic Area, since 1999 and an adjunct professor of law at Lewis & Clark since 2004, where he teaches interstate compact law, land use law, and administrative law. Jeff is currently an advisory board member for The Council of State Governments National Center for Interstate Compacts, and has previously been a council member of the American Bar Association Section of Administrative Law and Regulatory Practice, the Oregon State Bar Real Estate and Land Use Section Executive Committee, the Oregon State Bar Administrative Law Section Executive Committee, and the Washington State Bar Association Administrative Law Section Board of Trustees. Jeff has written several chapters in Oregon and Washington State Bar legal publications, written the Intergovernmental Relations chapter in the ABA Administrative Law Section's annual *Developments in Administrative Law and Regulatory Practice* book since 2008, co-authored the second edition of *The Evolving Law and Use of Interstate* Compacts (ABA Publ'g 2016), written the Intergovernmental Agreements chapter for the *Municipal Law Deskbook* (ABA Publ'g 2015), and edited the second edition of *A Guide to Federal Agency Adjudication* (ABA Publ'g 2012).

CHAPTER 1: FORMS OF INTERSTATE COOPERATION

I. INTRODUCING INTERSTATE COOPERATION

A probationer wishes to move to another state. How will he or she continue to be managed by a probation officer, under what law, at which state's expense, and to which correction facility is he or she returned after violating probation?

Eight states and two Canadian provinces border the Great Lakes. How should this binational water resource and watershed be managed to avoid depletion of water, ensure efficient transportation, provide for hydroelectric power, and combat pollution, soil erosion and flooding?

Rivers flow through states and form many of the boundaries between the states. Which state may properly claim new land resulting from accretion or lose land through reliction? How should these rivers be managed to ensure downstream water supply or avoid upstream pollution? How should river crossings be financed, maintained, and managed? How can individual ports on these rivers cooperate to better compete in the global economy?

Metropolitan areas cross state boundaries. How can the states undertake regional land use planning or provide efficient transportation and other urban services throughout a two-state or multistate region? How can municipalities cooperate rather than compete for economic development or share support for cultural institutions?

The United States is a mobile society. How can professionals move from state to state or practice in neighboring states without going through laborious professional licensing requirements? How can licensed professionals provide emergency assistance in other states? How can insurance companies provide single products that do not need multiple state approvals and that insured persons can take with them when they move to a new state?

Education is a primary responsibility of states. How can states collectively study, develop policy alternatives, collect and disseminate information, and stimulate innovation in education?

Military families move many times during a service member's career. How can states address educational transition issues such as enrollment, attendance, eligibility, and graduation requirements for service members' school-age children?

Interstate issues exist wherever you look and interstate cooperation takes many forms, from state officials who simply make the effort to work together to very formal interstate compacts that create new interstate agencies and require new statutes and regulations and specific means of judicial intervention.

A. Interstate Cooperation and Dispute Resolution in the U.S. Constitution

This first excerpt looks at tools for state-to-state cooperation and dispute resolution specified in the U.S. Constitution, and tools that have evolved over time outside the text of the Constitution. This seminal piece is surprisingly still current in its political thought and legal concepts, and scholars, courts, and practitioners continue to cite it nearly 100 years after its publication.

Felix Frankfurter & James M. Landis, *The Compact Clause of the Constitution—A Study in Interstate Adjustments*, 34 Yale L.J. 685 (1925)*

The Constitution is naturally acclaimed as the creative achievement of statesmen bent on maintaining the co-operation of the States and on forming "a more perfect Union." But in the creation lurked the seeds of inevitable contest between the new Union and its constituent members. Controversy over the spheres appropriate for action by States or Nation began in 1789; it is rife today....

...

We must face, therefore, two sets of legal authorities—the individual States and the United States—with their respective fields of action not definitively delimited by law and yet constantly interacting in fact, particularly in crucial legislative areas. The challenge of the situation is to make legal accommodations of these practical impingements. Inasmuch as there are these two categories of law-making agencies, State and Nation, the solution of the problem has usually been conceived in terms of exclusive duality. Evils calling for legislative redress, recognized subjects of administrative control, governmental promotion of social ends, have throughout our history divided men into two hostile camps, those seeking relief through State action and those appealing for national intervention. As a result legal inventiveness has been curbed and its resources largely confined to an untrue antithesis. The combined legislative powers of Congress and of the several States permit a wide range of permutations and combinations for governmental action. Until very recently these potentialities have been left largely unexplored. Political energy has been expended on sterile controversy over supposedly exclusive alternatives instead of utilized for fashioning new instruments adapted to new situations.... The exclusiveness of the traditional choice in governmental intervention is becoming correspondingly inadequate. Creativeness is called for to devise a great variety of legal alternatives to cope with the diverse forms of interstate interests.

Intimations of fruitful direction are furnished by new technique and new machinery devised during recent years in the settlement of problems which transcend State lines. Since 1890 the National Conference of Commissioners on Uniform State Laws has promoted uniformity of State legislation on subjects beyond the power of Congress and where, from the nature of the case, diversity of treat-

---

ment is an interstate evil. By this method a vast domain of the commercial transactions of the country which do not respect State lines are sought to be brought under common legal control. The scheme of reciprocal legislation has been resorted to whereby the capacity of one State to harm or advantage another, when conflicting interests need adjustment, is exercised by creating immunities or handicaps conditioned upon like treatment by sister States. The importance of a policy of common action in certain fields of legal control is again reflected in the conscious practice of courts to base decisions in these fields on grounds of needed harmony between jurisdictions legally independent of each other. Conferences of governors and other State officials, partly initiated by and partly in collaboration with Federal authorities, have more or less stimulated common State action and have served as a fruitful interchange on State policies essential to an understanding of common interests. Again, the States have been enabled to control more effectively matters predominately the concern of State legislation by auxiliary Federal legislation. Following the English device of grants in aid, the Federal government has latterly sought to stimulate through financial assistance State action in matters subject to State control by involving an interest common to the whole country. Another method is seen in the regulation of interstate preserves through the practical fusion of distinct State administrative agencies by means of joint sessions and joint action in order to deal as a unit with legally separate parts of a common interest. These six instances illustrate extra-constitutional forms of legal intervention for the solution of problems touching more than one State. They were neither contemplated nor specifically provided for by the Constitution.

Two other modes of adjustment have their source in constitutional provisions. Through jurisdiction over "Controversies between two or more State" the Supreme Court is building up a body of law for the settlement of interstate problems susceptible of judicial disposition. Finally, the Constitution authorizes a State to "enter into any Agreement or Compact with another State" with "the Consent of Congress." . . .

. . . .

Notes & Questions

1. Referring to the federal government and state government, Frankfurter and Landis stated, "The exclusiveness of the traditional choice in governmental intervention is becoming correspondingly inadequate." Similarly, in their conclusion (not excerpted here), Frankfurter and Landis also argue, "The overwhelming difficulties confronting modern society must not be at the mercy of the false antithesis embodied in the shibboleths 'States-Rights' and 'National Supremacy.'" 34 YALE L.J. at 729. Many other scholars have highlighted the realm between states and the federal government with similar statements. One book describes this realm as "sub-federal, supra-state." MICHAEL L. BUENGER, ET AL., THE EVOLVING LAW AND USE OF INTERSTATE COMPACTS 1 (2d ed. 2016). Another scholar asked, "[H]ow are [interstate compacts] to fit into a doctrinal reality based on a federalist conception of dual—but no more than dual—sovereignty?" Note, *Charting No Man's Land: Applying Jurisdictional and Choice of Law Doctrines*

to Interstate Compacts, 111 HARV. L. REV. 1991, 1996 (1998). And another noted, "Unless Congress or the courts establish a special classification specifically for compact law, an event that seems unlikely, the compact somehow must be forced into the 'state or federal' mold." L. Mark Eichorn, *Cuyler v. Adams and the Characterization of Compact Law*, 77 VA. L. REV. 1387, 1411 (1991).

The Supreme Court has also discussed how compacts fit within our federalist system, stating, "Compact entities formed to deal with 'broad, region-wide problems' should not be regarded as 'an affirmation of a narrow concept of state sovereignty,' but as 'independently functioning parts of a regional polity and of a national union.'" *Hess v. Port Auth. Trans-Hudson Corp.*, 513 U.S. 30, 40 (1994). Other courts have similarly noted that compact agencies differ from traditional levels of government. For example, in *State ex rel. Trimble v. Ryan*, 745 S.W.2d 672 (Mo. 1988), the dissent noted, ". . . that Bi-State was a new kind of agency, not readily fitted into existing concepts such as 'political subdivision.'" *Id.* at 677. This question of how compacts fit into the traditional federal-state distinction underlies many political and legal issues, disputes and legal arguments relating to compacts.

2. Elsewhere in their article, Frankfurter and Landis describe an example that gives some perspective on where compacts may belong within our federal system.

> Specifically, may a regional group of States especially affected by a project for electric power development enter into an agreement, with the consent of Congress, for the effective utilization of such energy generated in one State and transmitted for distribution to neighboring States? All aspects of this problem, as we have seen, are not included within the conception of interstate commerce. But to the extent that the process of electrification crosses State lines we are in a field open to Federal regulation. If it chooses, Congress may act and pre-empt State control. Even without Federal action, no State may discriminate against, or obstruct, the transactions in interstate commerce. *Between these limits—what Congress may do and the States obviously may not do—lies the field in which compact would operate.* Its availability, as a matter of law, depends on whether the constitutional grant to Congress of power to regulate commerce among the several States, however unused, excludes all State action, however reasonably conceived and restricted to the interests of a region of States immediately affected.

34 YALE L.J. at 718 (emphasis added). Throughout this book, you will read that Congress encourages states to enact compacts concerning subjects that are within the authority of the federal government to control. Similarly, states enact compacts with the specific reason of demonstrating to the federal government that they are competent to resolve interstate problems without federal control. Section II in this chapter discusses specific factors that lead states to enact compacts.

3. One method of interstate cooperation that Frankfurter and Landis did not mention is multistate litigation. Examples of prominent multistate litigation include the 1998 Master Settlement Agreement between 46 states and several tobacco companies, and the antitrust case, *New York, et al. v. Microsoft Corp.* 29 F.

Supp. 2d 132 (D.D.C. 2002). The web site for the National Association of Attorneys General contains information about hundreds of multistate antitrust litigation matters. *See* http://www.naag.org (search for "multistate task force"). One cigarette manufacturer challenged the 1998 Master Settlement Agreement as violating the Compact Clause; however, the court held that the agreement did not require consent pursuant to the Compact Clause. *Star Scientific, Inc. v. Beales*, 278 F.3d 339, 357–60 (4th Cir. 2002). Materials relating to when consent is required are in Chapter 2, Section III.

4. Scholars have long suggested subjects for compacts. States have enacted (and terminated) several compacts involving subjects that one early scholar suggested; however, it is usually impossible to know whether a scholar's suggestion was the impetus for states to enact a compact. For example, in the 1930s, one scholar suggested,

> The possibilities are unlimited. Compacts may be used to regulate interstate transportation. A controversy, for example, which had been going on for some time between Pennsylvania and New Jersey over the regulation of motor vehicles, could undoubtedly be ironed out to the satisfaction of both states by an interstate compact.
>
> Some years ago, Vermont and New Hampshire made provision for a joint state penitentiary to serve both states. If this can be done it would seem feasible that two or more states could join together for the purpose of consolidating their educational systems, including their state universities, the underlying advantage being economy and the raising of educational standards.
>
> Interstate public health regulation, standardization of commodities, taxes such as gasoline, liquor corporation, income, and inheritance levies, relief, public works, social security, improvement of educational facilities, regulation of air traffic, motor truck regulation, insurance, exchange system of supervising persons on parole, taxation of mail order houses, uniform divorce, unemployment insurance, drought and flood control, eradication of pests, child labor, establishment of standards of safety in certain industries, establishment of regional health and sanitation authorities in contiguous states, irrigation, timber, game, public welfare, and many other purely interstate and sectional questions could be adjusted by the use of compacts insuring mutual interstate accord coupled with federal acquiescence in accordance with the Constitution.

Alice Mary Dodd, *Interstate Compacts*, 70 U.S. L. REV. 557, 572–73 (1936). *See also* Leonard J. Feldman, *The Interstate Compact: A Cooperative Solution to Complex Litigation in State Courts*, 12 REV. LITIG. 137 (1992) (suggesting a "Multistate Complex Litigation Interstate Compact" to create a system of multistate complex litigation courts and designate a single choice of law doctrine); Frank P. Darr, *Electric Holding Company Regulation by Multistate Compact*, 14 ENERGY L.J. 357 (1993) (discussing regional planning for electric utility companies); Jerome C. Muys, et al., *Utton Transboundary Resources Center Model Interstate Water Compact*, 47

NAT. RES. J. 17 (2007); Byron Schlomach, et. al., *Multilateral Disarmament: A State Compact to End Corporate Welfare*, MACKINAC CENTER FOR PUBLIC POLICY (2019); Lisa Hansmann & Ganesh Sitaraman, *Designing an Interstate Compact for a Pandemic Testing Board*, EDMOND J. SAFRA CENTER FOR ETHICS (MAY 4, 2020).

5. Sometimes state legislators introduce a new compact text to test the waters and see if other states express interest in that compact. For example, in 2019, one legislator introduced a "Company-Specific Subsidy Interstate Compact Act" with a bill section stating, "This legislation is a first version of such an interstate compact and intends to be replaced in 2020 after input from experts and organizations from all sides of the political spectrum." S.B. 643, § 12-9-1(8), 2019 Reg. Sess. (W. Va. 2019).

6. Trade and professional associations have also become active in promoting and drafting interstate compacts, principally to facilitate interstate professional licensing. These associations produce a draft with a working committee from the states and then introduce the compact text to state legislators and lobby for its adoption.

The materials below introduce three of the methods that Frankfurter and Landis mentioned: administrative agreements, uniform and model laws, and original jurisdiction in the U.S. Supreme Court for disputes between states. These subjects appear many times throughout this book.

B. Administrative Agreements

An agreement between state agencies or officials (the administrative branch of government) is an administrative agreement. Unfortunately, there is no single set of objective factors that distinguish an administrative agreement from an interstate compact. Typically, state legislatures enact compacts whereas state executive officials enact administrative agreements. This distinction works much of the time; however, as discussed below and in Chapter 3, legislatures may authorize agency officials to enact a compact and the text of some compacts allow for officials to enact the compact. For example, article XII of the Nonresident Violator Compact specifically provides that the compact may be entered into force "by resolution of ratification, executed by authorized officials of the applying jurisdiction."

Another distinction between compacts and administrative agreements is the source of authority for their enactment. As discussed in Chapter 3, states have inherent authority to enact compacts. In contrast, the source of authority for administrative agreements comes from a state's constitution or statute that generally authorizes agencies, general municipal governments, and special districts to enter into administrative agreements. Other common sources of authority for administrative agreements include organic statutes creating policy programs or administrative agencies and specific subject matter statutes. Constitutional and statutory provisions may also grant authority for administrative agreements between entities and officials in different states. These non-compact administrative agreements have many different names, including interlocal, intergovernmental, intermunicipal, and interagency.

As discussed throughout this book, interstate compacts are supposed to contractually bind the party states to the terms of the agreement. Like compacts, courts often conclude that administrative agreements are binding. For example, the Georgia Supreme Court interpreted GA. CONST. art. IX, § III, ¶ 1(a), which authorizes intergovernmental agreements for a period "not exceeding 50 years," to mean that an agreement for a term exceeding the terms of the governing officials that entered into the agreement binds later governing officials. *Greene Cty. Sch. Dist. v. Greene Cty.*, 278 Ga. 849, 850 (2005). Another court concluded that a voter initiative could not abrogate a prior administrative agreement because it would violate the Contracts Clause in the state constitution. *Tri-Cty. Metro. Transp. Dist. v. Clackamas Cty.*, No. CV13030258, slip op. at 5–6 (Or. Cir. Ct. Clackamas Cty., July 1, 2013).

Unlike compacts, administrative agreements cannot bind a state legislature to prevent that legislature or future legislatures from changing the substantive law that is the subject of an administrative agreement. This is because administrative agreements are not contracts between states in their sovereign capacity. The Iowa Supreme Court described a test for whether an agreement is a valid state contract as "whether [the administrator] has been empowered to bind his jurisdiction and whether the specific terms of his offer for an agreement are those which he had been directed or authorized to make by the empowering statute." *Gen. Expressways v. Iowa Reciprocity Bd.*, 163 N.W.2d 413, 419 (Iowa 1968) (citing FREDERICK L. ZIMMERMAN & MITCHELL WENDELL, THE LAW AND USE OF INTERSTATE COMPACTS 8 (1961)).

Of course, not all agreements fit neatly into being a "compact" or an "administrative agreement." For example, many scholars have opined whether the northeast states' Regional Greenhouse Gas Initiative, started in December 2005, is really a compact, and if so whether it needs congressional consent. *See, e.g.*, Claire Carothers, *United We Stand: The Interstate Compact as a Tool for Effecting Climate Change,* 41 GA. L. REV. 229 (2006). The Unified Carrier Agreement is another example. Two courts have mentioned that it is compact, but without any analysis. *12 Percent Logistics, Inc. v. Unified Carrier Registration Plan Bd.*, 282 F. Supp. 3d 190 (D.D.C. 2017); *Midwest Crane & Rigging, LLC v. Kansas Corp. Comm'n*, No. 114,168, 2016 Kan. App. Unpub. LEXIS 649 (Kan. Ct. App. Aug. 5, 2016), *rev'd on other grounds*, 306 Kan. 845 (2017). But the text of the Unified Carrier Registration Act of 2005, Pub. L. No. 109-59, §§ 4304 *et seq.*, 119 Stat. 1763, which authorizes the interstate agreement is not so clear. That Act contains several sections expressing consent for states to create compacts relating to transportation policy, but the Act does not give consent in the Unified Carrier Registration section. Perhaps this suggests that Congress did not intend the states to create a compact when enacting the UCR agreement. Additionally, the U.S. Secretary of Transportation appoints the members of the board. Only one-third of the board may be from the states; the other members come from the Department of Transportation and the motor carrier industry. *Id.* at § 4305(d)(1)(B), 119 Stat. at 1767. While compact jurisprudence does not establish any membership standard indicating the presence or absence of a compact, no compact has a board in which a single federal official appoints the members.

Many cases have involved a question whether a particular state action constitutes an interstate compact, some other type of agreement, or no agreement at all. For example, the Illinois Supreme Court concluded that a reciprocity provision of a state act that "merely empowers the Secretary of State to ascertain which States grant reciprocity to Illinois residents and to embody his findings in the official form of a reciprocity agreement" was not a compact between states. *Bode v. Barrett*, 412 Ill. 204, 231–33 (1952). More recently, state courts have split on whether the Smarter Balanced Assessment Consortium (SBAC) was an illegal compact because it did not have congressional consent. States created the SBAC to take advantage of federal funding (which required consortia of at least 15 states). After federal funding ended in 2014, SBAC moved its administration to the University of California at Los Angeles, and states enacted memoranda of understanding with the Regents of the University of California to continue their membership. A Missouri trial court judge concluded that the SBAC violated the Compact Clause. *Sauer v. Nixon*, No. 14AC-CC00477, 2015 WL 4474833 (Mo. Cir. Ct. Cole Cty. Feb. 24, 2015), *appeal dismissed as moot*, 474 S.W.3d 624 (Mo. Ct. App. 2015). In contrast, the South Dakota Supreme Court expressed doubt that the state's memorandum of understanding with the U.C. Regents constituted a compact. *Mauricio v. Daugaard*, 895 N.W.2d 358, 363 (S.D. 2017). *See also Regan v. Otter*, No. 1:15-cv-00455-BLW, 2016 U.S. Dist. LEXIS 49547 (D. Idaho Apr. 11, 2016) (dismissing a challenge to the SBAC because the taxpayer plaintiffs did not have standing).

Some legislatively enacted compacts authorize administrative agreements. An example of a compact authorizing interstate administrative agreements is the Interstate Library Compact, enacted by approximately two-thirds of the states. For example, Oregon's codification of the Library Compact, OR. REV. STAT. §§ 357.330–.370, authorizes public officials to cooperate and share library resources or establish a joint library district across state lines. The states' Attorneys General must approve the resulting agreement, but the legislatures do not need to enact it as state law. The Interstate Compact on Mental Health, art. XI, similarly authorizes the states to enact supplementary administrative agreements.

State agencies, municipalities, and special districts may also enact non-compact intergovernmental agreements to implement or ensure compliance with an interstate compact. *See, e.g.*, *Estermann v. Bose*, 296 Neb. 228, 231 (2017) (describing four natural resource districts enacting an interlocal agreement "to regulate and manage water to assist the State with compliance with the Republican River Compact").

Interstate compact agencies may also participate in administrative agreements. For example, the Delaware River Basin Commission, the Susquehanna River Basin Commission, and the Tahoe Regional Planning Agency all use intergovernmental agreements with local governments and their departments and state and federal agencies to help establish their relationship to those other governments and responsibilities for administering the compact. Copies of the Tahoe Regional Planning Agency memoranda of understanding are available at http://www.trpa.org/permitting/mous/.

As of mid-2020, eleven states have statutes authorizing administrative agreements between an agency (broadly defined to include state officials and local governments too) in the home state and an agency in another state, and which specify the agreements have the status of an interstate compact.[1] These "status of an interstate compact" provisions originated with The Council of State Governments[2] in its 1957 suggested Interlocal Cooperation Act. COMM. OF STATE OFFICIALS ON SUGGESTED STATE LEGISLATION, THE COUNCIL OF STATE GOV'TS, SUGGESTED STATE LEGISLATION PROGRAM FOR 1957 93 (1956) (suggested act at § 5). Subsequently, the Advisory Commission on Intergovernmental Relations recommended this provision in its 1967 suggested legislation. ADVISORY COMM'N ON INTERGOVERNMENTAL RELATIONS, A HANDBOOK FOR INTERLOCAL AGREEMENTS AND CONTRACTS 27 (1967) (suggested act at § 5). One law review article notes that surprisingly, there is no case law about these "status of an interstate compact" provisions, because they raise two problems. The first problem is that state legislatures enact compacts; there is no case law addressing whether a state statute can, by operation of law, convert administrative agreements into interstate compacts. The second problem is that an administrative agreement cannot have the status of an interstate compact unless all the states in which the parties to the agreement are located intend an agreement to have the status of an interstate compact. Of all the state borders in the United States, only six are between states where both states have such a provision, and three of the states with a "status of an interstate compact" provision do not border any other state that has such a provision. *See* Jeffrey B. Litwak, *State Border Towns and Resiliency: Barriers to Interstate Intergovernmental Cooperation*, 50 IDAHO L. REV. 193, 210–17 (2014).

C. Uniform and Model Laws

States also cooperate by enacting uniform and model laws on specific topics. The Uniform Law Commission has been drafting uniform and model laws since 1892 and has adopted more than 250 uniform and model acts. The first uniform law to be enacted by every state and the District of Columbia was the Negotiable Instruments Act, adopted by the Commission in 1896. *See* JOSEPH F. ZIMMERMAN, HORIZONTAL FEDERALISM: INTERSTATE RELATIONS 184 (State Univ. of N.Y. Press 2011). In the Uniform Law Commission's drafting process, each

---

[1] ARK. CODE ANN. § 25-20-105; IND. CODE § 36-1-7-8; IOWA CODE § 28E.9; KAN. STAT. ANN. § 12-2905; KY. REV. STAT. ANN. § 65.290; NEV. REV. STAT. § 277.160; OKLA. STAT. tit. 74, § 1005; R.I. GEN. LAWS § 45-40.1-5; TENN. CODE ANN. § 12-9-105; WASH. REV. CODE § 39.34.040; WIS. STAT. § 66.0303(4).

[2] The Council of State Governments is a non-partisan organization. Its members are all elected and appointed state and territorial officials in the United States. For more information about CSG, see www.csg.org.

model or uniform law goes through a thorough evaluation before any drafting begins, then gets developed over months or years with one or more drafting committees with vetting from the American Bar Association and other entities with an interest in the subject matter of a particular law. The commission is a nonprofit unincorporated association made up of uniform state law commissions from each state, the District of Columbia, Puerto Rico, and the U.S. Virgin Islands. State commissions vary in size and in the length of the commissioners' terms. The only requirement is that commissioners must be active members of a state bar.

A variation on drafting model or uniform laws is The Council of State Governments (CSG) annual book of "Suggested State Legislation," which contains text of existing state laws that CSG believes would be a good model for other states to consider. CSG may recommend variations on the existing state law but does not develop model or uniform laws like the Uniform Law Commission.

Uniform and model laws are recommended legislation; states may choose whether to enact uniform or model laws completely or in part and may modify their enactments without restriction or consequence. *See, e.g.*, *Bushard v. Reisman*, 334 Wis. 2d 571 (2011) (noting that while the Uniform Law Commission suggested changes to the Uniform Partnership Act, the Wisconsin legislature chose not to enact the changes); *E & J Lounge v. Liquor Comm'n of Honolulu*, 174 P.3d 367, 375 n.21 (Haw. Ct. App. 2007) (noting that there are distinct differences between Hawaii's administrative procedures act and the Model State Administrative Procedure Act).

Scholars have long explained that interstate compacts are not uniform or model laws. *See, e.g.*, Note, *A Reconsideration of the Nature of Interstate Compacts*, 35 COLUM. L. REV. 76, 77 n.8 (1935) (stating, "it has never been suggested that a compact results from the enactment of uniform laws . . . The absence of an interstate promise is a primary distinction between repealable reciprocal legislation and a compact" and citing sources); Elmer Wollenberg, *The Columbia River Fish Compact*, 18 OR. L. REV. 88, 96 n.2 (1939) (noting, "The Columbia River Fish Compact is a stage beyond the uniform law in interlegislative cooperation. It tends in the direction of a confederation region.").

One uniform act, the Revised Uniform Athlete Agents Act (Unif. Law. Comm'n 2015), contains two recommended alternatives for registering athlete agents—either the states would enact reciprocal legislation or an interstate compact. As of mid-2020, ten states have enacted the revised law and none have opted for the interstate compact alternative.

As you study the elements of a compact in Section IV below and throughout this book, keep in mind how the Uniform Law Commission describes uniform laws and model laws:

(1) An act is designated as a uniform act if:

(A) there is a substantial reason to anticipate enactment in a large number of states; and

(B) uniformity of the provisions of the proposed enactment among the states is a principal objective.

(2) An act is designated as a model act if:

(A) uniformity is a desirable objective, although not a principal objective;

(B) the act may promote uniformity and minimize diversity, even though a significant number of states do not enact the act in its entirety; or

(C) the purposes of the act can be substantially achieved even though it is not adopted in its entirety by every state.

Statement of Policy Establishing Criteria and Procedures for Designation and Consideration of Uniform and Model Acts, sec. 2.e, https://www.uniformlaws.org/projects/overview/newprojectcriteria.

In the following case, the Supreme Court addressed the constitutionality of uniform state laws. In doing so, the Court gave an expansive reading of the Constitution to facilitate cooperation between the states.

New York v. O'Neill
359 U.S. 1 (1959)

FRANKFURTER, JUSTICE:

This case is before us to determine the constitutionality of a Florida statute entitled "Uniform Law to Secure the Attendance of Witnesses from Within or Without a State in Criminal Proceedings." Respondent, a citizen of Illinois, had traveled to Florida to attend a convention. In accordance with the Florida statute, the Circuit Court of Dade County, Florida, responded to a certificate executed by a judge of the Court of General Sessions, New York County by summoning respondent before it to determine whether he was to be given into the custody of New York authorities to be transported to New York to testify in a grand jury proceeding in that State. The Circuit Court, ruling that the Florida statute violated the Florida and the United States constitutions, refused to grant New York's request. The Supreme Court of Florida affirmed this decision on the ground that the statute violated the United States Constitution. We granted certiorari inasmuch as this holding brings into question the constitutionality of a statute now in force in forty-two States and the Commonwealth of Puerto Rico....

The Uniform Act as enacted by the Florida Legislature in 1941 was formulated by the National Conference of Commissioners on Uniform State Laws in its present form in 1936. The Uniform Act is reciprocal. It is operative only between States which have enacted it or similar legislation for compelling of witnesses to travel to, and testify in, sister States.

....

In *Commonwealth of Kentucky v. Dennison*, 24 How. 66 [1861], Mr. Chief Justice Taney, speaking of the obligation imposed by the Constitution upon the Governor of Ohio to deliver to Kentucky one accused of violation of the criminal laws of Kentucky, called attention "to the obvious policy and necessity of this provision to preserve harmony between States, and order and law within their respective borders * * * ." 24 How. at 103. The same "policy and necessity" underlie the measure adopted by Florida and forty-two other jurisdictions. Unless there is some provision in the United States Constitution which clearly prevents States from accomplishing this end by the means chosen, this Court must sustain the Uniform Act. The absence of a provision in the United States Constitution specifically granting power to the States to legislate respecting interstate rendition of witnesses presents no bar. To argue from the declaratory incorporation in the Constitution, Art. IV, 2, of the ancient political policy among the Colonies of delivering up fugitives from justice an implied denial of the right to fashion other cooperative arrangements for the effective administration of justice, is to reduce the Constitution to a rigid, detailed and niggardly code. In adjudging the validity of a statute affecting a new form of relationship between States, the search is not for a specific constitutional authorization for it. Rather, according the statute the full benefit of the presumption of constitutionality which is the postulate of constitutional adjudication, we must find clear incompatibility with the United States Constitution. The range of state power is not defined and delimited by an enumeration of legislative subject-matter. The Constitution did not purport to exhaust imagination and resourcefulness in devising fruitful interstate relationships. It is not to be construed to limit the variety of arrangements which are possible through the voluntary and cooperative actions of individual States with a view to increasing harmony within the federalism created by the Constitution. Far from being divisive, this legislation is a catalyst of cohesion. It is within the unrestricted area of action left to the States by the Constitution.

. . . .

In any event, to yield to an argument that benefiting other States is beyond the power of a State would completely disregard the inherent implications of our federalism within whose framework our organic society lives and moves and has its being—the abundant and complicated interrelationship between national authority and the States and between the States *inter sese*. To yield to this argument would foreclose to the States virtually all arrangements which increase comity among the States. These extra-constitutional arrangements are designed to solve "problems created by a constitutional division of powers without disturbance of the federal nature of our government." [Jane Perry] Clark, *Joint Activity Between Federal and State Officials*, 51 POL. SCI. Q. 230, 269 [1936]. Reciprocal legislation, such as the Uniform Law to Secure the Attendance of Witnesses from Within or Without a State in Criminal Proceedings and the Acts providing reciprocal periods of grace in the registration of out-of-state automobiles is one such arrangement. The uniform laws proposed by the National Conference of Commissioners on Uniform State Laws and adopted by individual States have (among other benefits) increased ease of interstate commercial relationships by providing uniformity in commercial laws through uniform Acts governing sales and negotiable instruments. Uniform laws have frequently been concerned with enforcement of criminal laws. Thus, the Uniform Criminal Extradition Act provides for rendition of alleged criminals whose conduct does not bring them within the constitutional extradition provision. . . .

. . . .

Notes & Questions

1. The Court's citation to *Kentucky v. Dennison* is curious. That was an 1861 case involving a federal statute that administered the Extradition Clause of the U.S. Constitution, which states, "A person charged in any State with treason, felony, or other crime, who shall flee from justice, and be found in another State, shall, on demand of the Executive authority of the State from which he fled, be delivered up, to be removed to the State having jurisdiction of the crime." U.S. CONST. art. IV, § 2, cl. 2. The Court cited *Kentucky v. Dennison* for the purpose of illustrating the need for interstate cooperation; however, in 1861, the Court emphasized the need for federal legislation to guard against different state requirements.

> This duty of providing by law the regulations necessary to carry this compact into execution, from the nature of the duty and the object in view, was manifestly devolved upon Congress; for if it was left to the States, each State might require different proof to authenticate the judicial proceeding upon which the demand was founded.

Kentucky v. Dennison, 65 U.S. (24 How.) 66, 104 (1861). The Court may have emphasized the need for federal law simply because uniform laws would have been unfamiliar to the Court. The Uniform Law Commission did not exist for another 30 years, and there may simply have been no conscious work to create a system of uniform laws in 1861. Today, there are many uniform laws and interstate compacts that facilitate transfer of persons between states for various criminal proceedings.

The Supreme Court had heard several compact cases by 1861 and had upheld the compacts. Consider whether in 1861, the Court might have recognized and upheld uniform laws as another form of state-developed and managed processes.

2. Reread the Supreme Court's quote in note 1 from *Dennison*. The Court used the term "compact," but *Dennison* did not involve a compact between the states as we think of a compact today. Earlier in that decision, the Court stated:

> When the thirteen colonies formed a Confederation for mutual support, a similar provision was introduced, most probably suggested by the advantages which the plantations had derived from their compact with one another. But as these colonies had then, by the Declaration of Independence, become separate and independent sovereignties, against which treason might be committed, their compact is carefully worded so as to include treason and felony . . . .

65 U.S. (24 How.) at 101. In 1861, the Supreme Court was referring to the U.S. Constitution as a compact between the states. This was not a novel concept; many of *The Federalist Papers* referred to the Constitution as a compact.

3. In *O'Neill*, did the Supreme Court seem easily convinced to uphold laws that promoted comity and cooperation between the states? Many of the cases excerpted and cited in this book have a similar theme of supporting state attempts at cooperation and discouraging non-cooperative state-versus-state problems.

4. Uniform laws present obvious problems of ensuring uniform interpretation and application by the myriad responsible state officials and state and federal courts, and of keeping the states from unilaterally amending their enactments of the uniform laws in a manner that would destroy the benefits of uniformity. Interstate compacts share these same issues. Keep these issues in mind as you study compacts and consider whether these issues are at the heart of many of the principles of compact law.

D. Original Jurisdiction

Frankfurter and Landis mentioned original jurisdiction in the U.S. Supreme Court as one of the two methods under the Constitution for settling controversies between the states. Original jurisdiction in the Supreme Court has its basis in Article III, Section 2 of the U.S. Constitution. The federal statute is 28 U.S.C. § 1251(a), which states, "The Supreme Court shall have original and exclusive jurisdiction of all controversies between two or more States." U.S. Supreme Court Rule 17 governs original jurisdiction procedure. A state must file a motion for leave to file the matter with its initial pleading. The Court will typically use a special master to hear motions, determine questions of fact and make a recommendation. The Court must approve special master reports. Chapter 6 looks at original jurisdiction in more detail; but the following case gives a taste of the complexity and tenacity of such cases. The Supreme Court frequently laments its role in original jurisdiction cases and encourages the states to seek an alternative resolution. When reading the excerpt of *Vermont v. New York* below, consider whether the dispute raises a legal or political question, and whether that may have informed how the Supreme Court resolved the matter.

Vermont v. New York
417 U.S. 270 (1974)

PER CURIAM:

On April 24, 1972, after oral argument, we granted Vermont's motion to file a bill of complaint against New York and the International Paper Co. which alleged that as a result of discharge of wastes, largely from International's mills, that company and New York are responsible for a sludge bed in Lake Champlain and Ticonderoga Creek that has polluted the water, impeded navigation, and constituted a public nuisance. Issue was joined and the Honorable R. Ammi Cutter was appointed Special Master. Later the United States sought leave to intervene, stating it had numerous interests in these waters under federal statutes. We referred the motion to the Special Master, who granted intervention. During the year 1973, 75 days of testimony were received, Vermont presenting substantially all of its direct case. New York has put in about half of its direct case. Neither International nor the United States up to now has offered any evidence.

The Report of the Special Master dated April 24, 1974, states that he suggested that the parties might adjust their differences less expensively than by litigation. He reports that the United States succeeded in bringing about serious negotiations which resulted in a settlement that the Special Master commends to the Court for approval. The proposed settlement is represented by a Proposed Consent Decree and a stipulation that the Decree may be entered by the Court without further argument or hearing.

The settlement "contemplates that no findings shall be made" and it provides that "it shall not constitute an adjudication on any issue of fact or law, or evidence, or any admission by any party with respect to any such issue." The Special Master reports, "In my opinion, no settlement would be possible if this report were to contain any findings." He adds that in his opinion "it reaches a reasonable result, consistent with the public interest, and acceptable on the basis of the evidence thus far presented."

[The Decree recommends appointment of a special South Lake Master to resolve controversies and who would be authorized to order inspections of International Paper's mills. The Decree also specifies specific actions required of International Paper to reduce pollutants in, and overall amounts of water discharges and air emissions.]

The Special Master has done a very difficult task well and with distinction; we are indeed grateful for the professional services he has rendered. But we have concluded not to approve the Proposed Decree or appoint a South Lake Master.

In *Wisconsin v. Illinois*, 281 U.S. 696 [1930], the Court on the report of a Special Master enjoined the Sanitary District of Chicago from withdrawing through the Chicago drainage canal more than a stated number of cubic feet of water per second. That was on April 21, 1930. On May 22, 1933, on application of the States for a "commissioner or special officer" to execute the decree, the Court ordered Illinois to take certain steps respecting the diversion, but it denied the request to appoint the commissioner.

Wyoming v. Colorado, 259 U.S. 419 [1922], 260 U.S. 1 [1922], involved an allocation of the waters of the Laramie River. The parties were once more before the Court in 1936, 298 U.S. 573. This time the Court entered an injunction against continuing diversions contrary to the prior decrees. The Court refused to order measuring devices at places of diversion or to appoint a water master to keep the records, the Court saying, "While the problem of measuring and recording the diversions is a difficult one, we entertain the hope that the two States will by cooperative efforts accomplish a satisfactory solution of it." *Id.* at 586. In time the two States, policing themselves, resolved the controversy.

We noted in *Nebraska v. Wyoming*, 325 U.S. 589 [1945], that continuing Court supervision over decrees of equitable apportionment of waters was undesirable.

New Jersey v. New York, 283 U.S. 805 [1931], is not an exception. It involved a dispute between New Jersey, New York, New York City, and Pennsylvania over the waters of the Delaware River. The decree was an equitable apportionment of the water coupled with protective provisions, first, for a sewage disposal plant at Port Jervis, New York, that met prescribed cleansing standards; second, the banning of the discharge of untreated industrial wastes into the Delaware and Neversink Rivers; and third, the treatment of industrial wastes practically to free them "from suspended matter and [to render them] nonputrescent." That decree, entered May 25, 1931, was modified June 7, 1954 when a Special Master's Report was approved. The prior equitable apportionment was altered, and new and somewhat different formulae to measure and control the diversions were provided. A River Master was to be selected by the Chief Hydraulic engineer of the U.S. Geological Survey to administer the decree. He was authorized to measure the actual diversions, compile data, collect and correlate stream-flow gauging, make periodic reports, and make designated changes in the volume of daily releases.

But it is a rare case where we have appointed a Water Master. The one appointed in *New Jersey v. New York* was given only ministerial acts to perform, such as reading gauges and measuring the flow. In that case (1) the rights of the parties to the water had been determined by the Court and (2) the sewage and industrial waste problems had been adjudicated and resolved. All that remained was to supervise the application of the various formulae which the Court had decreed, based on findings of fact.

Wisconsin v. Illinois, 281 U.S. 179 [1930], involved the use of Lake Michigan waters by a sanitary district in Illinois to operate sewage treatment plants. The Court had ordered Illinois to restrict its use of Lake Michigan waters and to build certain facilities to allow treatment without the use of a great deal of lake waters. Illinois was given certain timetables for completion of the new facilities. The Special Master recommended either the appointment of a commission to supervise the construction or the filing of progress reports by the sanitary commission with the Clerk of this Court. The Court chose the option of not appointing a commission, and instead ordered the district to file semi-annual compliance reports with the Court. Masters were appointed at several points in this litigation for specific short-term purposes, but no quasi-permanent master to oversee general compliance was appointed. After the district was ordered to construct the facilities, Illinois impeded progress by withholding necessary state funds. The parties asked for a master to police compliance with the decree. The Court appointed a Master to investigate but he was relieved after the receipt of his report. Illinois was ordered to supply the necessary funds and to report its compliance with the Clerk of the Court.

In the instant case no findings of fact have been made; nor has any ruling been resolved concerning either equitable apportionment of the water involved or the questions relative to whether New York and International are responsible for the creation of a public nuisance as alleged by Vermont.

The proposed South Lake Master would police the execution of the settlement set forth in the Decree and pass on to this Court his proposed resolution of contested issues that the future might bring forth. Such a procedure would materially change the function of the Court in these interstate contests. Insofar as we would be supervising the execution of the Consent Decree, we would be acting more in an arbitral rather than a judicial manner. Our original jurisdiction heretofore has been deemed to extend to adjudications of controversies between States according to principles of law, some drawn from the international field, some expressing a "common law" formulated over the decades by this Court.

The proposals submitted by the South Lake Master to this Court might be proposals having no relation to law. Like the present Decree they might be mere settlements by the parties acting under compulsions and motives that have no relation to performance of our Art. III functions. Article III speaks of the "judicial power" of this Court, which embraces application of principles of law or equity to facts, distilled by hearings or by stipulations. Nothing in the Proposed Decree nor in the mandate to be given the South Lake Master speaks in terms of "judicial power."

The parties have available other and perhaps more appropriate means of reaching the results desired under the Proposed Court Decree. An interstate compact under Art. I, § 10, cl. 3, is a possible solution of the conflict here. Vermont and New York (along with Connecticut, Maine, Massachusetts, New Hampshire, and Rhode Island) are already parties to the New England Interstate Water Pollution Control Compact, Pub. L. No. 80-292, 61 Stat. 682 (1947).

A settlement of this interstate dispute by agreement of the parties is another alternative. Once a consensus is reached there is no reason, absent a conflict with an interstate compact, why such a settlement would not be binding. And such a settlement might be the basis for a motion to dismiss the complaint.

Notes & Questions

1. Special masters may serve many different roles in the judicial system. Judges may appoint a special master to assist in complex or technical litigation, oversee a settlement, or ensure judicial orders are carried out. The President and other high officials also appoint special masters. For example, several Attorneys General have appointed Special Masters to oversee the victim compensation fund following the 9/11 attacks. *See* https://www.justice.gov (search for "September 11 Victim Compensation Fund").

The Supreme Court typically appoints a special master in its original jurisdiction cases because those cases usually involve trial-like proceedings and the taking of evidence. Original jurisdiction proceedings can go on for years and, as in *Vermont v. New York*, trials can last for weeks or months, an amount of time the justices do not have. Appointment of a special master also solves a practical problem of nine justices ruling on trial-like motions and objections. The special master in original jurisdiction cases typically submits a report and proposed resolution to the Supreme Court, which the Supreme Court then adopts unless a party objects to the report. If a party files objections, the Supreme Court resolves the objections in its more familiar appellate role.

Special masters may be distinguished or retired judges or attorneys with special knowledge. The Special Master in *Vermont v. New York*, R. Ammi Cutter, was a legendary jurist in Massachusetts. When the U.S. Supreme Court appointed him in 1972, he had just reached the mandatory retirement age and retired from

16 years as an Associate Justice of the Massachusetts Supreme Judicial Court. His memorial, published in the Massachusetts Reports at 418 Mass. 1603 (1994), notes that as a justice, he authored 630 opinions, of which only 14 elicited a dissent. Following his service as Special Master in *Vermont v. New York*, he served another 10 years as a judge on the Massachusetts Appeals Court.

2. In *Vermont v. New York*, why was the Court unwilling to accept Special Master Cutter's recommendations? If the Supreme Court has jurisdiction over "adjudications of controversies between States according to principles of law," then why should it not consider proposals that may merely apply the law? Civil litigants in federal district court commonly submit settlement decrees for the court to accept, which makes the settlement decree enforceable as a court order, not just as a contract. What is different about original jurisdiction in the Supreme Court?

3. *Vermont v. New York* involved a dispute between states where there was no compact—indeed at the end of the opinion, the Supreme Court suggested the states could enact a compact. The existence of a compact, however, does not necessarily make the Court more willing to resolve a dispute. *See, e.g.*, *Texas v. New Mexico*, 462 U.S. 554 (1983), an often-cited case in which the Court refused to adopt a Special Master's recommendation because doing so would have granted relief inconsistent with the compact. The Court concluded its opinion stating, "It is within this Court's power to determine whether New Mexico is in compliance with Art. III(a) of the Pecos River Compact, but it is difficult to believe that the bona fide differences in the two States' views of how much water Texas is entitled to receive justify the expense and time necessary to obtain a judicial resolution of this controversy." *Id.* at 576. Chapter 11 contains an excerpt of this case.

4. Four months after issuing *Vermont v. New York*, the Supreme Court dismissed the case following a settlement. The settlement required International Paper to eliminate air pollution and make improvements in its wastewater treatment system. New York gave high priority to a new sewage treatment plant. The agreement did not require dredging or cleaning the sludge bed. The Supreme Court also awarded the special master $50,000 in compensation plus $5,150 in costs. Vermont's share was $20,000 and International Paper's share was $35,150. *See Vermont v. New York*, 419 U.S. 961 (1974). The states did not enact a compact; however, the states and Québec cooperate on environmental efforts through a Memorandum of Understanding (last renewed in 2015) and joint funding for a Lake Champlain Basin Program.

II. Why Do States Use Compacts?

A. The Case for Compacts

In the next to last paragraph of *Vermont v. New York*, the Supreme Court encouraged the states to settle their dispute through an interstate compact. The Supreme Court has never been shy about recommending that states resolve their disputes through a compact. In an early case involving the location of the Washington-Oregon border within the Columbia River, the Court wrote:

> It must be borne in mind that an inquiry of this kind is attended with much difficulty. Here is a river of great width, three miles or so at certain places, whose bed is largely of sand, and whose channels have been naturally affected by the flow of the water, and also of late years by the jetties constructed by the Government in order to facilitate navigation. . . .
>
> We may be pardoned if, in closing this opinion, we refer to the following:
>
> > "Joint Resolution To enable the States of Mississippi and Arkansas to agree upon a boundary line and to determine the jurisdiction of crimes committed on the Mississippi River and adjacent territory.
> >
> > 'Resolved by the Senate and House of Representatives of the United States of America in Congress assembled, That the consent of the Congress of the United States is hereby given to the States of Mississippi and Arkansas to enter into such agreement or compact as they may deem desirable or necessary, not in conflict with the Constitution of the United States, or any law thereof, to fix the boundary line between said States, where the Mississippi River now, or formerly, formed the said boundary line and to cede respectively each to the other such tracts or parcels of the territory of each State as may have become separated from the main body thereof by changes in the course or channel of the Mississippi River and also to adjudge and settle the jurisdiction to be exercised by said States, respectively, over offenses arising out of the violation of the laws of said States upon the waters of the Mississippi River.
> >
> > "Approved January 26, 1909."
>
> Similar ones have passed Congress in reference to the boundaries between Mississippi and Louisiana and Tennessee and Arkansas. We submit to the States of Washington and Oregon whether it will not be wise for them to pursue the same course, and, with the consent of Congress, through the aid of commissioners, adjust, as far as possible, the present appropriate boundaries between the two States and their respective jurisdiction.

Washington v. Oregon, 214 U.S. 205, 217–18 (1909). Washington and Oregon did enact a border compact, albeit nearly 50 years later. *See* WASH. REV. CODE § 43.58.060; OR. REV. STAT. § 186.520.

In another case involving apportionment of the North Platte River, a non-navigable stream in Nebraska, Wyoming and Colorado, the Court recognized that, although it prefers judicial caution, it must resolve states' disputes when negotiation and agreement pursuant to the Compact Clause fails.

> There is some suggestion that if we undertake an apportionment of the waters of this interstate river, we embark upon an enterprise involving administrative functions beyond our province. We noted in *Colorado v. Kansas*, [320 U.S. 383, 392 (1943)], that these controversies between States over the waters of interstate streams "involve the interests of quasi-sovereigns, present complicated and delicate questions, and, due to the possibility of

> future change of conditions, necessitate expert administration rather than judicial imposition of a hard and fast rule. Such controversies may appropriately be composed by negotiation and agreement, pursuant to the compact clause of the federal Constitution. We say of this case, as the court has said of interstate differences of like nature, that such mutual accommodation and agreement should, if possible, be the medium of settlement, instead of invocation of our adjudicatory power." But the efforts at settlement in this case have failed. A genuine controversy exists. The gravity and importance of the case are apparent. The difficulties of drafting and enforcing a decree are no justification for us to refuse to perform the important function entrusted to us by the Constitution.

Nebraska v. Wyoming, 325 U.S. 589, 616 (1945). *See also Florida v. Georgia*, 138 S. Ct. 2502, 2510–11 (2018) (noting the Court's preference for states to settle their own disputes, that the states in this case enacted a compact to develop an allocation formula, but failed to develop that formula, and the compact expired, and thus the Court granted leave to Florida to file its complaint). Most recently, Justice Breyer suggested states could enact interstate compacts to guarantee reciprocal sovereign immunity from suit in each other's state courts. *Franchise Tax Board v. Hyatt*, 139 S. Ct. 1485, 1506 (2019) (Breyer, J., dissenting). Chapter 6 discusses the discretionary nature of the Court accepting state-versus-state cases under its original jurisdiction.

State courts have also recommended states enact an interstate compact. For example, in *Grant Cty. Dep't of Soc. Servs. v. Unified Bd. of Grant & Ia. Counties (In re Jane E.P.)*, 283 Wis. 2d 258 (2005), the dissent wrote, "In my view, the majority opinion creates what amounts to a statute for the interstate transfer of guardianships and protective placements. While some type of an interstate compact may be helpful, that is a task that the constitution set out for the legislature. . . . When it does so, it has the ability to consider and address the financial impact of the agreements Wisconsin makes with other states. The majority opinion has not evaluated the financial impact of a transfer of Jane to Wisconsin." *Id.* at 289 (Roggensack, J, dissenting).

When is a compact the right solution versus federal or individual state legislation? One scholar concisely explained the relationship between the geographic scope of a problem, the varying sizes of states that the problem affects, and the choice between a federal, state, or regional solution.

> [I]t would be a rare genius indeed, who could divide the functions of government . . . between the national government and states varying in size as do the forty-eight states. The area of Rhode Island is 1,067 square miles, an area less than that of most counties in western states, while Texas covers an area of 262,398 square miles, or an area equal to the combined areas of Belgium, Holland, Denmark, Austria and Germany. A problem quickly spills over state boundary lines in Rhode Island, whereas problems of vast magnitude remain local problems as far as Texas is concerned. What may be a county affair in the West becomes an inter-state affair in New England,

> while Texas can successfully regulate a problem which in Europe would require international action.

Amry Vandenbosch, *Regions v. States*, 21 KY. L.J. 432, 433 (1933).

Does encouragement from the Supreme Court or a recognition of a regional problem explain why states join compacts? Two political science scholars studied several factors to explain differences in states' participation in compacts. Ann O'M. Bowman & Neal D. Woods, *Strength in Numbers: Why States Join Interstate Compacts*, 7 ST. POL. & POL'Y Q. 347 (2007). Using 33 compacts that are national in scope, they reached several conclusions. Consider a few: "[S]tates with weaker fiscal and institutional capacity participate in compacts more frequently, suggesting that compact membership is used to mitigate those problems." *Id.* at 363. "States respond to their neighbors' increased participation in national compacts by joining more themselves, a process which may be indicative of policy learning. *Id.* "[I]solated states show a preference for compacts that harmonize policies, while more proximate states are more likely to join compacts that exceed simple harmonization." *Id.* Professors Bowman and Woods also noted an irony in their findings.

> While much of the discussion about intergovernmental relations focuses on the states' felt needs to preserve their sovereignty against national government encroachment, in general states do not appear to be using compacts for this purpose. In fact, many states voluntarily enter into compacts that have the effect of eroding their autonomy by granting the compact supersessive legal authority. In particular, reciprocal compacts allow a state's peers to extend their influence into its borders. The cumulative effect of membership in a series of these compacts could thus be a meaningful reduction in state sovereignty through a series of horizontal and voluntary, rather than vertical and preemptive, process. Many states, especially those that are geographically proximate to one another, appear willing to sacrifice this autonomy in an effort to mitigate social problems.

Id. at 364. Another conclusion noted that:

> States' compacting decisions also appear to respond to actions of the national government. While some observers have speculated that states may use interstate compacts to preempt federal encroachment into their affairs, our results indicate a different pattern of intergovernmental policy adjustment. Rather than embracing compacts as a defense against federal incursion, the states in our dataset actually join fewer new compacts during periods of national policy centralization. This implies that states use compacts to fill the void left by national government retrenchment, in effect as an alternative means to coordinate national policy from the bottom up.

Id. Can you make arguments about both perspectives? The Council of State Governments notes that through compacts, states can avoid federal intervention. *See* http://www.csg.org/NCIC/about.aspx. Some states also enact legislation entitled "compacts" in efforts to negate existing federal law or address politically charged subjects at a state level. Recent examples include health care reform, interstate firearm sales, the balancing of the federal budget, immigration, border security, "prosperity," and the ownership of public lands. These politically charged "compacts" will likely never become effective compacts, but the states' intent is clear. Chapter 2 discusses that Congress retains its authority to legislate in policy areas where states have enacted a compact and has done so many times, so enacting a compact does not completely insulate states from federal policy action.

Do Professors Bowman and Woods's findings surprise you? As you study compact law, consider whether the cases (the parties' arguments and the courts' resolutions) suggest that the states really are willing to sacrifice some of their sovereignty. Chapter 10 discusses reasons that compacts fail, many of which suggest that the states may not be so willing.

B. Critiques of Using Compacts

There have been many critiques of compacts, but few as scathing as the following, which responded to the development of a minimum wage compact in the mid-1930s.

> Defenders of State action have tried to get round its competitive obstacles by the device of interstate compacts. If one State cannot achieve a certain object alone or if it fears competition of other States when it raises the costs of its own business concerns, it can, like an independent nation, make a treaty with the other States concerned, by which all agree to take the desired action. If ratified by Congress this treaty has the force of law.
>
> But interstate compacts present difficulties. They are a clumsy attempt to duplicate the Federal government itself, when the Federal government is prevented from acting. The States originally got together and formed a national government to serve their common needs. Now they are obliged to come together again and make treaties with one another, instead of having the legislature of their Federal government pass the desired laws. The negotiation of a treaty is a delicate and difficult matter. It has to be ratified by the separate legislatures. In order to be effective, it requires the unanimous consent of the States involved; whereas in legislatures a majority is sufficient. No government anywhere ever worked well by unanimous consent. Twelve manufacturing States, let us say, employ child labor; nine wish to abolish it and propose an interstate compact; three will not agree and so threaten the others with the competition of their cheap labor; the [nine] that are progressive and contain the majority of children and of voters are forced to choose between continuing to permit child labor or suffering from the competition of low standards in the others. In a case like this the interstate compact is even more clumsy and difficult than a Constitutional amendment, which can be ratified by three-quarters of the States. If the people of this country must rely on separate Constitutional amendments for every addition to important economic legislation, we are sunk. To rely on interstate compacts is even more hopeless than that.

Critical of Interstate Compacts, 25 AM. LAB. LEGIS. REV. 131 (1935) (reprinted from George Soule, *Back to States Rights*, 171 HARPER'S MAGAZINE 484 (1935)). More recent critiques echo similar complaints, but also point out, for example, "an arduous negotiation process, uneven adoption results, and disparate implementation . . . (and the difficulty of amending compacts)." Bill Mariano, et al., *A Case for Federal Regulation of Telemedicine in the Wake of the Affordable Care Act*, 16 COLUM. SCI. & TECH. L. REV. 274, 289 (2015). In congressional hearings on the Great Lakes Basin Compact, Congressman Barratt O'Hara from Illinois, stated

> What we are doing in these compacts is more and more relegating the authority of the States to a second place to regional governments. Of course, there is a reason for it. River that serve a number of States cause the States to get together in compacts, but despite the need in some cases, the wholesome trend toward compacts Is whittling down the authority of State government. It may not happen in my lifetime, but we may someday have regional governments supplanting State governments, so I take these compacts very, very seriously.

Granting the Consent of Congress to a Great Lakes Basin Compact and for Other Purposes: Hearing on H.R. 937, H.R. 12294, H.R. 12299, H.R. 12692, H.R. 13359, H.R. 14192, and H.R. 15042 Before the H. Comm. on Foreign Affairs, 89th Cong. 36 (Sept. 27, 1966). Throughout this book, many of the notes and questions mention concerns and critiques of specific elements of compacts and compact law.

III. Compacts in History

Frankfurter and Landis's seminal article, which is excerpted at the beginning of this chapter, provides a brief history of how the colonies resolved disputes prior to the Articles of Confederation and why the Articles of Confederation and U.S. Constitution needed to include a Compact Clause. Felix Frankfurter & James M. Landis, *The Compact Clause of the Constitution—A Study in Interstate Adjustments*, 34 YALE L.J. 685, 691–95 (1925). In short, the colonies were created by colonial charters from the Crown, which Frankfurter and Landis describe as "necessarily vague and expansive" and "had to be applied to strange and ill-surveyed territory." *Id.* at 692. Disputes over the boundaries of these charters were resolved through joint commissions or by appeal to the Privy Council in England. Frankfurter and Landis continued,

> The Revolution found a large number of these disputes still undetermined. The Articles of Confederation were framed by statesmen deeply alive to these contentions and familiar with the colonial methods for their adjustment. But the framers of these Articles were also familiar with the New England Confederacy of 1643, the Temporary Congress of 1690, the Plan of Union of 1754; they were in the midst of a political struggle against the might of Great Britain, which could be successfully carried on only through the united political action of the Thirteen Colonies. While, therefore, provision had to be made for the settlement of boundary and other disputes, which now emerged between the new independent States, in case of failure

> of direct negotiations between them, it was perhaps even more important to protect the new Union of States established by the Articles of Confederation, from the destructive political combination of two or more States. The Articles, therefore, specifically provided for an appeal to Congress "in all disputes and differences now subsisting or that hereafter may arise between two or more states concerning boundary, jurisdiction or any cause whatever." At the same time, they endeavored to secure the authority of the Confederacy against political rivalry by the following limitation upon the "sovereignty, freedom and independence" "retained" by each State.

Id. at 693. The Compact Clause in Article VI of the Articles of Confederation read, "No two or more states shall enter into any treaty, confederation or alliance whatever between them, without the consent of the United States in Congress assembled, specifying accurately the purpose for which the same is to be entered into, and how long it shall continue." The U.S. Constitution retained this clause in remarkably similar form as Frankfurter and Landis explain,

> . . . The records of the Constitutional Convention furnish no light as to the source and scope of the compact provision of Article I, Section 10. Nor does the Federalist help. But the history of the times furnishes an ample commentary. "It is a part of the public history of the United States . . . that at the adoption of the Constitution there were existing controversies between eleven states respecting their boundaries, which arose under their respective charters, and had continued from the first settlement of the Colonies." [*See Rhode Island v. Massachusetts*, 37 U.S. (12 Pet.) 657, 723 (1838)] In addition, the States had resorted to agreements among themselves, adjusting controversies other than boundary disputes. The framers were familiar with the modes of settlement prior to the Revolution—that controversies were determined partly through agreements confirmed by the Crown, and partly by litigation on appeal to the Privy Council. The Philadelphia Convention wrote both methods practised by the Colonies into the Constitution. Controversies between the Colonies which came before the Privy Council were, in effect, precursors of the types of litigation over which the Supreme Court assumed jurisdiction under Article III extending "the judicial Power" to "Controversies between two or more States." The power to negotiate settlements between the Colonies, subject to the sanction of the royal prerogative, was written into Article I, Section 10.
>
> Historically the consent of Congress, as a prerequisite to the validity of agreements by States, appears as the republican transformation of the needed approval by the Crown. . . .

Frankfurter & Landis, 34 YALE L.J. at 694. Frankfurter and Landis also listed nine colonial boundary disputes that the colonies resolved and submitted to the Privy Council for approval, and four acts of consent under the Articles of Confederation. *Id.* at 730–34. In addition, the Privy Council resolved at least three American colonial boundary disputes: Rhode Island and Connecticut (initiated in 1721, resolved in 1727). Order of Feb. 8, 1727, *reprinted in* 3 ACTS OF THE PRIVY COUNCIL

OF ENGLAND: COLONIAL SERIES 16 (W.L. Grant et al. eds., 1910); New Hampshire and Massachusetts (initiated in 1734, resolved in 1746), Order of May 28, 1746, *reprinted in* 3 ACTS OF THE PRIVY COUNCIL 601; and Rhode Island and Massachusetts (initiated in 1738, resolved in 1746), Order of May 28, 1746, *reprinted in* 3 ACTS OF THE PRIVY COUNCIL 449. Not surprisingly, the Supreme Court has had to resolve on-going disputes in most, if not all of the states' early negotiated boundaries, Privy Council resolutions, and compacts that received consent under the Articles of Confederation.

For an interesting discussion of the first boundary dispute that the colonies resolved through negotiation (between Connecticut and New Netherland), see Ronald D. Cohen, *The Hartford Treaty of 1650-Anglo-Dutch Cooperation in the Seventeenth Century*, 53 N.Y. HIST. SOC. Q. 311 (1969). Giving a sense of its ratification, which did not include England's approval, Cohen noted,

> The Dutch West India Company immediately accepted [the Hartford Treaty of 1650], but, through a careless oversight, it was not ratified by the States General [the body of delegates representing the Dutch Republic] until 1656. In the meantime, however, the Dutch government had instructed its ambassadors in England to obtain Parliament's assent or Lord Protector Cromwell's signature, a fruitless endeavor as it turned out. This was not because, as some historians have asserted, "to have recorded the line of 1650, or any other boundary, would have recognized the legal existence of New Netherland, and this the English government was resolved to avoid. Rather, there is no evidence to suggest that the confederation ever bothered to send the treaty to England for approval in the first place, and probably did not even give a hint to the mother country of its acceptance. This neglect is understandable, although somewhat startling to the Dutch at the time, when one considers that the New England colonies saw absolutely no need of submitting the treaty to England. Once they had approved it, what more could be necessary? In New Haven and Connecticut this attitude was probably reinforced by the belief that the treaty would be easier to violate if it remained an agreement between colonies instead of becoming internationally recognized.

Id. at 331–32.

IV. Elements of a Compact

An interstate compact is an agreement between two or more states in their capacity as sovereigns. Note that this definition uses the term "states." Most often, state legislatures enact compacts, which differentiates compacts from the myriad cooperative arrangements between state administrative officials. When a legislature enacts a compact, the compact typically becomes part of that state's statutory laws. Thus, compacts are often statutes and contracts at the same time. As noted above in the introduction to administrative agreements, a few compacts exist in which a legislature specifically authorizes the compact, but a state official, board or commission takes the formal action to enact the compact and the compact exists outside of state statutes.

As a contract between the states, you might expect courts to describe compacts in the familiar terms of a contract—offer, acceptance, and consideration. However, for more than 100 years, the Supreme Court described compacts merely as reciprocal and concurrent agreements. *E.g.*, *Virginia v. West Virginia*, 78 U.S. (11 Wall.) 39, 63 (1871) (Davis, J., dissenting) ("reciprocal and concurrent consent" of the parties to the compact); *Wharton v. Wise*, 155 U.S. 153, 163 (1894) ("mutual consent" of the parties); *Tennessee v. Virginia*, 190 U.S. 64, 65 (1903) ("concurrent laws of the states"). In 1904, the Supreme Court first mentioned the concept of offer in compacts, referring to the first state's enactment of a compact as "a continuing offer." *Wedding v. Meyler*, 192 U.S. 573, 583 (1904). A 1961 publication of The Council of State Governments was the first to describe an offer, acceptance, "meeting of the minds" and consideration in states' enactment of compacts. FREDRICK L. ZIMMERMANN & MITCHELL WENDELL, THE LAW AND USE OF INTERSTATE COMPACTS 8–10 (1961). Although courts commonly refer to compacts as statutes and contracts, they only occasionally describe compacts in terms of offer, acceptance, "meeting of the minds," and consideration. *See, e.g., Doe v. Pa. Bd. of Probation and Parole*, 513 F.3d 95, 105 (3d. Cir. 2008)

One scholar colorfully described the congressionally approved multi-state compact as a "'centaur of legislation' which is an offspring of both state and federal law," Comment, *Federal Question Jurisdiction to Interpret Interstate Compacts*, 64 GEO. L.J. 87, 110 (1975), a description the Ninth Circuit once adopted, *Jacobson v. Tahoe Reg'l Planning Agency*, 566 F.2d 1353, 1359 n.8 (9th Cir. 1977).

As you might expect, compacts take many forms. The Columbia River Compact is one of the shortest.

> All laws and regulations now existing, or which may be necessary for regulating, protecting or preserving fish in the waters of the Columbia River,[*] over which the States of Oregon and Washington have concurrent jurisdiction, or any other waters within either of said states, which would affect the concurrent jurisdiction, shall be made, changed, altered and amended in whole or in part, only with the mutual consent and approbation of both states.

OR. REV. STAT. § 507.010; WASH. REV. CODE § 77.75.010. Oregon and Washington enacted this compact in 1915, and Congress granted its consent in 1918. Act of April 8, 1918, Pub. L. No. 65-123, 40 Stat. 515. Most compacts, however, contain much more structure and detail, with many pages of text divided into articles, sections, and subsections, very much like other complex statutes. For example, one of the most recently enacted compacts, the Gateway Development Commission Compact, 2019 N.J. Laws c 195; 2019 N.Y. Laws c 108, is more than 40 pages

---

[*] [*Ed. Note*: Washington's enactment of the compact adds the phrase "or its tributaries" at this point in the text of the compact.]

long with 30 sections, and creates a compact commission, with rulemaking authority, authorizes subsidiaries of the Commission, provides for an inspector general and other government transparency standards, and specifies details on contracts of the Commission.

The Council of State Governments maintains the most complete database of compacts: http://apps.csg.org/ncic/. Take a few minutes to scroll through the compacts in the database to see the number and variety of subject matters of compacts and get a sense of compact language and structure.

As you read above in the section introducing administrative agreements, interstate cooperation may take many forms and courts sometimes struggle with determining when state action constitutes an interstate compact. In the first of the two case excerpts below, *Northeast Bancorp,* the Supreme Court questioned whether similar statutes in Massachusetts and Connecticut were a compact. In the second excerpt, *Seattle Master Builders,* the Ninth Circuit focused on the states' creation of the Pacific Northwest Electric Power and Conservation Planning Council because there is no "compact" document. The majority quickly concluded that the Council satisfied the *Northeast Bancorp* factors; however, we read the strong dissent to the contrary. As you read these excerpts, look for the essential elements of a compact and compare them to the elements of a contract.

Ne. Bancorp, Inc. v. Bd. of Governors of the Fed. Reserve Sys.
472 U.S. 159 (1985)

REHNQUIST, JUSTICE:

Respondents Bank of New England Corporation (BNE), Hartford National Corporation (HNC), and Bank of Boston Corporation (BBC) are bank holding companies which applied to the Federal Reserve Board to obtain approval for the acquisition of banks or bank holding companies in New England States other than the ones in which they are principally located. Petitioners Northeast Bancorp, Inc., Union Trust Company, and Citicorp opposed these proposed acquisitions in proceedings before the Board. The Board approved the acquisitions, and the Court of Appeals for the Second Circuit affirmed the orders of the Board. Petitioners sought certiorari, contending that the acquisitions were not authorized by the Bank Holding Company Act of 1956, and that, if they were authorized by that Act, the state statutes which permitted the acquisitions in each case violated the Commerce Clause and the Compact Clause of the United States Constitution. . . .

. . . .

The Board will evaluate the proposed transaction for anticompetitive effects, financial and managerial resources, community needs, and the like. In addition, § 3(d) of the Act, known as "the Douglas Amendment," prohibits the Board from approving an application of a bank holding company or bank located in one State to acquire a bank located in another State, or substantially all of its assets, unless the acquisition "is specifically authorized by the statute laws of the State in which such bank is located, by language to that effect and not merely by implication." Pursuant to the Douglas Amendment, a number of States recently have enacted statutes which selectively authorize interstate bank acquisitions on a regional basis. This case requires us to consider the validity of these statutes.

....

Beginning with Massachusetts in December 1982, several States have enacted statutes lifting the Douglas Amendment ban on interstate acquisitions on a reciprocal basis within their geographic regions. The Massachusetts Act specifically provides that an out-of-state bank holding company with its principal place of business in one of the other New England States (Connecticut, Maine, New Hampshire, Rhode Island, and Vermont), which is not directly or indirectly controlled by another corporation with its principal place of business located outside of New England, may establish or acquire a Massachusetts-based bank or bank holding company, provided that the other New England State accords equivalent reciprocal privileges to Massachusetts banking organizations. In June 1983, Connecticut followed suit by adopting a substantially similar statute.

The other New England States have taken different courses or have not acted. ...

....

Petitioners maintain that the Massachusetts and Connecticut statutes constitute a compact to exclude non-New England banking organizations which violates the Compact Clause, U.S. Const., Art. I, § 10, cl. 3, because Congress has not specifically approved it. We have some doubt as to whether there is an agreement amounting to a compact. The two statutes are similar in that they both require reciprocity and impose a regional limitation, both legislatures favor the establishment of regional banking in New England, and there is evidence of cooperation among legislators, officials, bankers, and others in the two States in studying the idea and lobbying for the statutes. But several of the classic indicia of a compact are missing. No joint organization or body has been established to regulate regional banking or for any other purpose. Neither statute is conditioned on action by the other State, and each State is free to modify or repeal its law unilaterally. Most importantly, neither statute requires a reciprocation of the regional limitation. Bank holding companies based in Maine, which has no regional limitation, and Rhode Island, which will drop the regional limitation in 1986, are permitted by the two statutes to acquire Massachusetts and Connecticut banks. These two States are included in the ostensible compact under petitioners' theory, yet one does not impose the exclusion to which petitioners so strenuously object and the other plans to drop it after two years.

....

Notes & Questions

1. Should the presence or absence of the term "contract" be an important consideration in determining whether a compact exists? In *I.B.M. v. Dep't of Treasury*, No. 306618, 2012 Mich. App. LEXIS 2293 (Mich. Ct. App. Nov. 20,

2012), *rev'd on other grounds*, 496 Mich. 642 (2014), the Michigan Court of Appeals concluded that the Michigan Legislature did not create a binding contract because it did not use specifically use the words "contract" or "covenant."

2. The issue in *Northeast Bancorp* was whether the Massachusetts and Connecticut statutes were unconstitutional in the absence of consent. The parties and amici argued that the indicia were relevant to determining whether the statutes increased the power of the states relative to the federal government or other states, which as Chapter 2 covers, is the test for whether a compact requires consent. But in the past few years, several courts have latched on this "classic indicia of a compact" phrase and have applied *Northeast Bancorp* for determining whether a compact exists (regardless of consent) and whether a compact is binding on the states—neither of which the *Northeast Bancorp* parties argued. *See, e.g., U.S. v. California*, No. 2:19-cv-02142 WBS EFB, 2020 U.S. Dist. LEXIS 43422 (E.D. Cal. Mar. 12, 2020); *Waterfront Comm'n of N.Y. Harbor v. Murphy*, No. 18-650 (SDW)(LDW), 2018 U.S. Dist. LEXIS 92148 (D.N.J. June 1, 2018); *Health Net, Inc. v. Dep't of Revenue*, 362 Or. 700 (2018), *Graphic Packaging Corp. v. Hegar*, 538 S.W.3d 89 (Tex. 2017); *Mauricio v. Daugaard*, 895 N.W.2d 358 (S.D. 2017); *Kimberly-Clark v. Comm'r of Revenue*, 880 N.W.2d 844 (Minn. 2016); *Gillette Co. v. Franchise Tax Bd.*, 62 Cal. 4th 468 (2015). As you read the notes and questions in this section, consider whether the *Northeast Bancorp* indicia are fair indicia of whether a compact exists or is binding.

3. *Northeast Bancorp* noted that the question of reciprocity is "most important," but does not explain why. The Court may have been reflexively reacting to the attention that the parties gave reciprocity in their briefing. Northeast Bancorp and Union Trust Company argued: "This Court has held that where two or more state statutes are reciprocal in nature, that fact alone mandates an inquiry as to whether the interstate arrangement intrudes upon the concerns embodied in the Compact Clause." Brief of Petitioners Northeast Bancorp and Union Trust Co. at 31, *Ne. Bancorp, Inc. v. Bd. of Governors of the Fed. Reserve Sys.*, 472 U.S. 159 (1985) (No. 84-363). This brief cited *U.S. Steel Corp. v. Multistate Tax Comm'n*, a 1978 case excerpted in Chapter 2; however, courts have long suggested that reciprocal state statutes require consent. *E.g.*, *Massachusetts v. Klaus*, 130 N.Y.S. 713 (N.Y. App. Div. 1911) (Laughlin, J., dissenting).

The 1961 publication of The Council of State Governments discussed above gives some explanation of the need for reciprocity, comparing the concept of reciprocity in a compact to the concept of consideration in a contract.

> The basic principle of consideration is probably applicable to compacts, but it has far less practical meaning than in the field of private contracts. While it is quite possible to have a compact which places entirely different sets of obligations on each of the parties, such cases so far have been rare, or perhaps even nonexistent. Almost invariably the compact represents either the settlement of a dispute or an undertaking to be associated in a joint or common activity. In the former instance, the acceptance of the agreed solution and the attendant abandonment by each of the parties of its inconsistent

> claims constitutes the consideration. The situation is analogous to an agreement to submit to arbitration and to be bound by the award, or to a settlement out of court. In such an instance the consideration is the settlement of the dispute. Where the compact provides for a joint or common undertaking or for cooperation in a reciprocal fashion, the existence of consideration would be difficult to avoid. Even if no other element is present, it is to be found in the reciprocal obligation to perform or in the contribution to the enterprise.

FREDERICK L. ZIMMERMANN & MITCHELL WENDELL, THE LAW AND USE OF INTERSTATE COMPACTS 9–10 (1961).

In contrast, consider *Landes v. Landes*, 1 N.Y.2d 358 (1956) in which the Court of Appeals of New York (New York's highest court) concluded that reciprocity in a uniform law did not necessary suggest a compact between the states). Do you agree that reciprocity is a defining element of an interstate compact? What constitutes reciprocal statutes?

4. Consider whether the presence or absence of a joint organization is a "classic" indicator of a compact. As with the reciprocity indicator discussed in the note above, several parties argued in *Northeast Bancorp* that there was no increase in the power of the states that interferes with federal supremacy because the Connecticut statute did not create an independent commission or other administrative body. Brief of Respondent, State of Connecticut at 30; Brief of Bank of New England, et al. at 41. Similarly, the federal respondent argued that the presence of an interstate entity may suggest expanded political powers. Brief of Federal Respondent at 29. These arguments about the increase in the power of the states are applying the Supreme Court's test for when Congress must consent to a compact; they are covered in Chapter 2.

Numerous compacts do not create a joint organization. For example, boundary compacts do not typically require an on-going joint organization. Similarly, several law enforcement compacts, such as the Interstate Agreement on Detainers, a national compact, and the Boating Offense Compact between Oregon and Washington, operate without a joint organization. The Interstate Compact on the Placement of Children, perhaps the most often-used compact applicable in all 50 states, the District of Columbia and the U.S. Virgin Islands, operates without a compact-required joint organization, but has an association of state administrators of the compact. In another example, a federal court referred to the United Carrier Registration Plan as an interstate compact, *12 Percent Logistics, Inc. v. Unified Carrier Registration Plan Bd.*, No. 17-cv-02000 (APM), 2019 U.S. Dist. LEXIS 17160 (D.D.C. Feb. 4, 2019). The federal legislation authorizing the Registration Plan requires the U.S. Secretary of Transportation to appoint the members of the Plan Board. 49 U.S.C. § 14504a(d)(1)(B). Does this federally appointed board indicate an interstate compact?

5. Additionally, in *Northeast Bancorp*, New York argued that the Connecticut and Massachusetts statutes were a compact within the meaning of the Compact

Clause because they enacted virtually identical reciprocal and exclusive legislation within a six-month period. Brief of New York in Support of Petitioners at 6–7. Citicorp, Northeast Bancorp and Union Trust Company argued that the Connecticut and Massachusetts laws constituted a compact requiring consent because the states enacted reciprocal discriminatory legislation and enacted their laws close in time, imposed virtually identical geographical limitations, and coordinated their efforts. Brief of Petitioner Citicorp at 40–41; Brief of Ne Bancorp and Union Trust Co. at 33–35.

Should close-in-time enactments be a reliable indicator of whether the states have created a compact? There are many compacts in which the states have enacted the compact over a period of decades. For example, the Interstate Wildlife Violator Compact became effective in 1989 when the first two states enacted it. As of mid-2020, there were 49 member states. New Jersey and Nebraska were the latest states to enact it in 2017. Similarly, the Interstate Oil and Gas Compact became effective in 1935 when the first six states enacted it. As of mid-2020, there were 31 full-member states. Idaho was the latest to become a full member in 2017.

6. Over the years, scholars have suggested many "model" interstate compacts, most of which focus on a specific issue, but do not necessarily include the "elements" from *Northeast Bancorp*. *See, e.g.*, Jerome C. Muys, George William Sherk & Marilyn C. O'Leary, *Utton Transboundary Resources Center Model Interstate Water Compact*, 47 NAT. RES. J. 17 (2007) (model compact including suggested provisions and commentary with citations). Non-legal sources also issue suggestions for drafting compacts. *See, e.g.,* Am. Soc'y of Civil Eng'rs, ASCE/EWRI 60-12, *Guideline for Development of Effective Water Sharing Agreements* (2013).

7. Reread the first sentence of the last paragraph of the *Northeast Bancorp* excerpt: "Petitioners maintain that the Massachusetts and Connecticut statutes constitute a compact to exclude non-New England banking organizations which violates the Compact Clause, because Congress has not specifically approved it." Are the petitioners implying that Congress may permit compacting states to exclude others? Some multi-state matters only concern a limited number of states; for example, the Tahoe Regional Planning Compact concerns only California and Nevada. However, where there is no obvious limit on interests, should some states be able to act to the specific exclusion of others? The next case excerpt considers whether three states should be able to enact a compact concerning a subject for which there are eight potentially interested states.

Seattle Master Builders Ass'n v. Pac. Nw. Elec. Power & Cons. Planning Council
786 F.2d 1359 (9th Cir. 1986)

BEEZER, JUDGE, DISSENTING:

. . . .

Over half a century ago, Felix Frankfurter and James Landis argued that interstate compacts could provide an effective means for allowing coordinated federal-state control of electric power. The Council, joined by the four Pacific Northwest states and the National Governors' Association as *amici curiae*, argues that the [Pacific Northwest Electric Power Planning and Conservation] Act created an interstate compact. The petitioners, joined by the Pacific Legal Foundation as amicus curiae, argue that the Council is a federal agency.

In form, the creation of the Council resembles the creation of an interstate compact. After listing the purposes of the Council, the Planning Act states: "To achieve such purposes and facilitate cooperation among the States of Idaho, Montana, Oregon, and Washington, and with the Bonneville Power Administration, the consent of Congress is given for an agreement described in this paragraph and not in conflict with this chapter * * * ." 16 U.S.C. § 839b(a)(2). The Planning Act also states that the appointment of members by three states "shall constitute an agreement by the States establishing the Council and such agreement is hereby consented to by the Congress." *Id.*

On the other hand, the Council lacks several of the classic indicia of an interstate compact. For example, the Supreme Court recently noted that two reciprocal state statutes were unlike an interstate compact because "[n]either statute is conditioned on action by the other State, and each State is free to modify or repeal its law unilaterally." *Northeast Bancorp, Inc. v. Board of Governors*, 472 U.S. 159 (1985). None of the Pacific Northwest states conditioned their agreement to participate in the Council on action by the other states. All four states are free to repeal their statutes unilaterally.

More significantly, the Planning Act authorized the creation of the Council on the consent of only three of the four states. The Planning Act does not, however, limit the geographical scope of the Council's responsibilities in such a case. Suppose, for example, that Idaho, Montana, and Oregon had joined the Council, but that Washington had declined to join. The Council, composed of members from Idaho, Montana, and Oregon, would have been responsible for preparing a plan for all four states. In that case, the Council would have taken action that could have substantive effects in a nonmember state. If the Council is truly an interstate compact agency, that result would not be possible.

In fact, the "region" serviced by the [Bonneville Power Administration (BPA)] includes portions of Nevada, Utah, Wyoming, and California. To the extent the Council has authority over BPA actions, the Council also exercises authority affecting electric utility consumers living outside the four states from which the Council members were appointed. The four states involved have therefore agreed to participate in establishing policy and standards, not for each other, but for a federal agency with regional authority extending beyond those states. This is strong evidence that Congress did not intend the establishment of an interstate compact.

Finally, the Council lacks the most important indicia of an interstate compact agency: a state purpose. While it is apparent that the Pacific Northwest states have a strong interest in obtaining representation in regional policy making by the BPA, the purpose of the Council is not representative in nature. Instead, the purpose of the Council is to guide the actions of the BPA. Because the states have no right to exercise control over the BPA, that is not a state purpose. If the Council was responsible for coordinating energy and conservation planning at the state level, it would have a state purpose. The Council has no such responsibility.

It is true that interstate compacts by their very nature have federal law implications and provide a vehicle for states to act in a manner in which a state may not act without congressional consent, thus altering a state's sphere of authority. *See* L. Tribe, *American Constitutional Law* Sec. 6-31, at 402 (1978). Congressional consent does "transform an interstate compact * * * into a law of the United States," *Cuyler v. Adams*, 449 U.S. 433, 438 (1981), in that federal judicial interpretation of a compact under the Supremacy Clause controls over a state's application of its own law. *See West Virginia ex rel. Dyer v. Sims*, 341 U.S. 22 (1951) (Reed, J., concurring). However, granting a body of state-appointed officials the power to constrain the actions of a federal executive agency is quite another thing. That is not a legitimate function of an interstate compact agency.

While it is difficult to characterize the Council as an interstate compact agency, it is easy to characterize the Council as a federal agency. The classic definition of an "agency" is "a governmental authority, other than a court and other than a legislative body, which affects the rights of private parties through either adjudication or rulemaking." 1 K. Davis, *Administrative Law Treatise* § 1.01, at 1 (1st ed. 1958). The Council is a "governmental authority," and its plan constitutes "rulemaking." *See* 16 U.S.C. § 839b(a)(4) (stating that the Council is subject to the same general administrative rules as the BPA and the Federal Energy Regulatory Commission). As this case demonstrates, the Council's plan "affects the rights of private parties." The Council is thus an agency. Because the Council has a federal purpose and receives its authority from federal law, the Council is a federal agency.

. . . .

Notes & Questions

1. The state statutes creating the Pacific Northwest Electric Power and Conservation Planning Council (now called the Northwest Power and Conservation Council) do not use the term "compact." Each state enacted a statute stating, "The State of [Oregon] agrees to participate in the Pacific Northwest Electric Power and Conservation Planning Council pursuant to the Pacific Northwest Electric Power Planning and Conservation Act." OR. REV. STAT. § 496.803; WASH. REV. CODE § 43.52A.010; IDAHO CODE ANN. § 61-1201; MONT. CODE ANN. § 90-4-401. Are these statutes "reciprocal"?

2. In the case excerpt, Judge Beezer cited *Northeast Bancorp* in pointing out that the compact does not prohibit the states from unilaterally modifying or repealing their laws. Should such an express prohibition be an important factor to consider in determining the existence of a compact? Should a compact permanently bind states? Many compacts are silent about repeal and modification. The compacts that include terms allowing the states to modify the compact typically require concurrent action by the other states, and the compacts that allow states

to withdraw simply require repealing an enabling statute, after giving notice to the other states and a short waiting period. Chapters 2 and 8 discuss modifying and repealing compacts in more detail.

3. Judge Beezer also pointed out that the Council could be created by action of three of the four states, but the Council must prepare its plan for all four states, even if one state chose not to participate. BPA's region (for which the Plan would guide BPA's actions) includes four other states that are not eligible to participate in the compact. Does authority for three states to bind BPA's actions in four or eight states demonstrate cooperation between the states?

Judge Beezer argued that if the Council were truly an interstate compact agency, substantive effects on non-member states would not be possible. Recall that this issue arose in *Northeast Bancorp*, in which the Supreme Court suggested that congressional consent might authorize such substantive effects. Should the possibility of affecting a non-member state be a relevant in determining whether a compact exists?

4. What do you think about Judge Beezer's point that the Council does not serve a state purpose? Was he suggesting that a compact may not do more than act in harmony with federal administration of federal law? What about his next paragraph, in which he points out that a compact that has the consent of Congress becomes a federal law? Chapter 5 looks at the relationship between a compact and federal law.

An example of the Northwest Power and Conservation Council's control over BPA action is described in *Nw. Envtl. Def. Ctr. v. Bonneville Power Admin.*, 477 F.3d 668 (9th Cir. 2007). In 2005, BPA transferred funding and functions of the Fish Passage Center, a program called for by the Council that provides technical assistance and information to fish and wildlife agencies, to a private laboratory and, ironically, to another compact agency, the Pacific States Marine Fisheries Commission. In 2007, the Ninth Circuit set aside BPA's transfer, reasoning in part that because the Council's fish and wildlife plan expressly called for continuation of the Fish Passage Center, BPA acted inconsistently with the Planning Act by transferring funding and functions.

Not all compacts give a compact agency authority to direct federal agencies or actors. For example, the Fourth Circuit noted that the Atlantic States Marine Fisheries Commission (ASMFC) cannot as a matter of law "endow the Secretary of Commerce with some form of power over federal waters." *U.S. v. Saunders*, 828 F.3d 198, 205 (4th Cir. 2016). The court reasoned the Secretary is a member of the President's cabinet who derives her authority from acts of Congress and the inherent Article II powers of the Executive Branch. In contrast, the court noted that the ASMFC "is the creature of an interstate compact that only binds the states that are parties to it," *id*, and is not a federal agency within the meaning of the federal APA, and the fact that Congress approved the compact does not change this analysis. Quite succinctly, the Fourth Circuit stated, "The Secretary of Commerce needs nothing further and the Commission has nothing to bestow on her." *Id.* at 206.

5. *Seattle Master Builders* was much more than a compact case. It involved the extent to which state officials could administer cooperative federalism programs without being subject to presidential appointment under the Appointments Clause of the U.S. Constitution. One article from the Oregon Attorney General who co-authored the compact states' amicus brief and presented oral argument noted:

> [if the Master Builders had prevailed,] it would have transformed countless state officials into federal officers subject to presidential appointment. Governors often exercise federally-conferred powers. Attorneys General administer federally-funded child support programs. State transportation officers and state unemployment compensation law administrators carry out federal policies largely with federal dollars. The cooperative federal-state medicaid program is heavily enmeshed in mutual regulation and funding arrangements agreed upon between governments.

Dave Frohnmayer, *The Compact Clause, The Appointments Clause and the New Cooperative Federalism: The Accommodation of Constitutional Values in the Northwest Power Act*, 17 ENVTL. L. 767, 782 (1987). Other cases rejecting Appointment Clause arguments and other appointment and removal issues are discussed in Chapter 10.

V. Other Types of Compacts

The word "compact" does not exclusively refer to interstate compacts. Another type of compact is Tribal-State compacts authorized under the 1988 Indian Gaming Regulatory Act, 25 U.S.C. §§ 2701, *et seq.* These compacts are unrelated to interstate compacts, although a few courts have used interstate compact law principles to resolve legal issues in gaming compacts. *See, e.g.*, *Pueblo of Santa Ana v. Kelly*, 104 F.3d 1546 (10th Cir. 1997); *Flathead Irrigation Dist. v. Jewell*, 121 F. Supp. 3d 1008, 1024 (D. Mont. 2015). For an introduction to analogies and differences between interstate compacts and tribal-state gaming compacts, see Rebecca Tsosie, *Negotiating Economic Survival, The Consent Principle and Tribal-State Compacts Under the Indian Gaming Regulatory Act*, 29 ARIZ. L.J. 25 (1997). This book does not cover tribal-state gaming compacts.

Throughout this book, you will also see references to agreements between U.S. states and Canada and Canadian provinces. Chapter 12 covers these bi-national compacts.

CHAPTER 2: CONGRESSIONAL CONSENT

The Frankfurter and Landis article excerpted in Chapter 1 noted that interstate compacts have their source in the U.S. Constitution. Frankfurter and Landis were referring to the Compact Clause, which is quite brief and appears deceptively simple: "No State shall, without the consent of Congress, . . . enter into any agreement or compact with another State or with a foreign Power. . . ." U.S. CONST. art. I, § 10, cl. 3.

Only approximately half of the compacts that exist today have received consent; Section III in this chapter discusses when consent is needed. Additionally, there is some debate about whether specific compacts received consent by a broadly applicable consent statute. Section I discusses broad consent statutes.

Much of the compact jurisprudence involves compacts with consent so congressional consent, once given, forms the basis for much of the overall body of compact law. As you read through this chapter, consider whether the special attributes of compacts with consent make consent a litmus test for questions such as whether a compact is binding on the parties, whether the states must interpret the compact uniformly, or whether a state may enact new state law or apply pre-compact state law that conflicts with the compact.

This chapter looks at how Congress gives its consent, when Congress must give its consent, and limits on Congress's authority after it gives its consent. Concepts covered in later chapters, such as the federal law nature of compacts; conflict of laws questions; jurisdiction in state and federal courts; the relationship between a compact and the Commerce Clause; the state, federal, or hybrid nature of compact agencies; immunity under the Eleventh Amendment; and governance, all have some basis in the need for congressional consent.

Consent is a political judgment. As discussed in Section III of this chapter, Congress is fully within its authority to withhold consent when, in its sole judgment, such consent would lead to imprudent combinations, dangerous joint action, or intrusion on traditional federal matters. But Congress can also grant its consent even when it would result in one of these concerns. The granting of consent is a gratuity, not a right that the states possess under the Constitution. *Coll. Sav. Bank v. Fla. Prepaid Postsecondary Educ. Expense Bd.*, 527 U.S. 666, 686 (1999); *See also* MICHAEL L. BUENGER, ET AL., THE EVOLVING LAW AND USE OF INTERSTATE COMPACTS 76 (2d ed. 2016). Consistent with this notion of political judgment, one recent article argued that "presidential presentment is not necessary for Congress to exercise its consent power under the Compact Clause." James F. Blumstein & Thomas J. Cheeseman, *State Empowerment and the Compact Clause*, 27 WM. & MARY BILL RTS. J. 775 (2019). Congress is also not obligated to inquire into the validity of a compact under state law before granting consent. *Detroit Int'l Bridge Co. v. Gov't of Canada*, 192 F. Supp. 3d 54 (D.D.C. 2016), *aff'd on other grounds*, 883 F.3d 895 (D.C. Cir. 2018) (finding that the International

Bridge Act, granting general consent to cross-border bridges does not require such an inquiry and no clear error by the Secretary of Transportation).

I. Forms of Consent

The Supreme Court has consistently held a generous view of what type of congressional action constitutes consent. The Supreme Court's first case involving an interstate compact, *Green v. Biddle* in 1823, was also the first time it considered this question.

Green v. Biddle

21 U.S. (8 Wheat.) 1 (1823)

STORY, JUSTICE:

. . . .

The first objection is founded upon the allegation, that the compact was made without the consent of Congress, contrary to the tenth section of the first article, which declares, that 'no State shall, without the consent of Congress, enter into any agreement or compact with another State, or with a foreign power.' Let it be observed, in the first place, that the constitution makes no provision respecting the mode or form in which the consent of Congress is to be signified, very properly leaving that matter to the wisdom of that body, to be decided upon according to the ordinary rules of law, and of right reason. The only question in cases which involve that point is, has Congress, by some positive act, in relation to such agreement, signified the consent of that body to its validity? Now, how stands the present case? The compact was entered into between Virginia and the people of Kentucky, upon the express condition, that the general government should, prior to a certain day, assent to the erection of the District of Kentucky into an independent State, and agree, that the proposed State should immediately, after a certain day, or at some convenient time future thereto, be admitted into the federal Union. On the 28th of July, 1790, the convention of that District assembled, under the provisions of the law of Virginia, and declared its assent to the terms and conditions prescribed by the proposed compact; and that the same was accepted as a solemn compact, and that the said District should become a separate State on the 1st of June, 1792. These resolutions, accompanied by a memorial from the convention, being communicated by the President of the United States to Congress, a report was made by a committee, to whom the subject was referred, setting forth the agreement of Virginia, that Kentucky should be erected into a State, upon certain terms and conditions, and the acceptance by Kentucky upon the terms and conditions so prescribed; and, on the 4th of February, 1791, Congress passed an act, which, after referring to the compact, and the acceptance of it by Kentucky, declares the consent of that body to the erecting of the said District into a separate and independent State, upon a certain day, and receiving her into the Union.

Now, it is perfectly clear, that, although Congress might have refused their consent to the proposed separation, yet they had no authority to declare Kentucky a separate and independent State, without the assent of Virginia, or upon terms variant from those which Virginia had prescribed. But Congress, after recognising the conditions upon which alone Virginia agreed to the separation, expressed, by a solemn act, the consent of that body to the separation. The terms and conditions, then, on which alone the separation could take place, or the act of Congress become a valid one, were necessarily assented to; not by a mere tacit acquiescence, but by an express declaration of the legislative mind, resulting from the manifest construction of the act itself. To deny this, is to deny the validity of the act of Congress, without which, Kentucky could not have become an independent State; and then it would follow, that she is at this moment a part of the State of Virginia, and all her laws are acts of usurpation. . . .

Notes & Questions

1. The Supreme Court noted that the Constitution makes no provision regarding form of consent. The Court asked, "has Congress, by some positive act, in relation to such agreement, signified the consent of that body to its validity"? How did Congress grant its consent to the Virginia-Kentucky compact?

In *U.S. Steel Corp. v. Multistate Tax Comm'n,* 434 U.S. 452, 464 n.14 (1978), the Supreme Court stated that *Green v. Biddle* held consent could be implied. What was "implied" about Congress's consent?

2. What do you think about the last sentence in the *Green v. Biddle* excerpt? Was the Court indicating it felt obligated to find that Congress properly gave its consent? Is this a type of "laches" conclusion—had the states sufficiently relied on the compact such that the Court was loathe to disturb it?

3. *Green v. Biddle* involved a boundary compact. Broadly speaking, there are two types of boundary compacts. The first type simply establishes the boundary between existing states. While these compacts may sound like one-time deals, courts must continually interpret them. For example, the 1834 compact establishing the border between New Jersey and New York placed Ellis Island in New York State, but subsequently, the federal government placed several acres of fill to construct the immigration receiving facility there. In 1998, the Supreme Court held that the filled lands were part of New Jersey. *New Jersey v. New York*, 523 U.S. 767 (1998). Similarly, in 2014, Maryland's highest court interpreted a provision of Maryland and Virginia's 1785 boundary compact and a subsequent 1877 arbitration award establishing the boundary at the low-water mark on the south side of the Potomac River to mean that the boundary shifts as the low water mark shifts through accretion, erosion and reliction, all of which are natural processes that occur over time. *Potomac Shores, Inc. v. River Riders, Inc.*, 219 Md. App. 29 (2014). Despite ongoing interpretive disputes, states continue to enact boundary compacts. For example, in 1990, Missouri and Nebraska negotiated a boundary compact to address state-line issues following changes in the channel of the Missouri River, and in 2000, Texas and Oklahoma negotiated the Red River Boundary Compact that set a portion of the boundary between states as the vegetation line on the south bank of the Red River, except for a specific area, where the compact specified a process to determine the boundary.

Green v. Biddle involved the second type of compact, which relates to the creation of new states from land that was part of an existing state. Typically, the existing state enacted legislation authorizing the creation of the new state conditioned upon preserving the rights of the landowners in the new state as they existed in the former state. The compact in *Green v. Biddle* had such a provision. Article VII of the compact between Virginia and Kentucky states, "that all private rights and interests of lands, within the said District, derived from the laws of Virginia, shall remain valid and secure under the laws of the proposed State, and shall be determined by the laws now existing in this State." 21 U.S. at 11. Subsequently, in 1797 and 1812, Kentucky enacted new laws that changed landowner rights from Virginia law. *Green v. Biddle* involved Green's claim that the new Kentucky laws thus violated the compact.

4. *Robinson v. Campbell*, 16 U.S. (3 Wheat.) 212 (1818), similarly involved a provision in another Virginia compact preserving private rights under the former state's law. The Court observed, "By the compact settling the boundary line between Virginia and Tennessee, and the laws made in pursuance thereof, it is declared that all claims and titles to lands derived from the governments of Virginia, or North Carolina, or Tennessee, which have fallen into the respective states, shall remain as secure to the owners thereof, as if derived from the government within whose line they have fallen, and shall not be in any wise prejudiced or affected in consequence of the establishment of the said line." *Id.* at 218.

5. Real property law has obviously evolved since *Green v. Biddle* and *Robinson v. Campbell.* How long can or should a compact preserve law in an unchanged state? At what point in time should a new state no longer be tied to real property law as it existed in the original state at the time of the split? What factual or legal circumstances would justify the new state changing its law? In *Hawkins v. Barney's Lessee*, 30 U.S. (5 Pet.) 457 (1831), the Supreme Court concluded that the Virginia-Kentucky Compact at issue in *Green v. Biddle* did not make Virginia law perpetual and unrepealable. In this adverse possession case, Virginia law had a 20-year period of open, hostile, notorious use. Kentucky waited more than 20 years to enact a 7-year period. The Court concluded that Kentucky did not violate the compact because "she literally gave her citizens the full benefit of twenty years to prosecute their suits before she enacted the law now under construction." *Id.* at 466.

State v. Faudre, 54 W. Va. 122 (1903), involved a different provision of the Virginia-Kentucky Compact. *Faudre* was a criminal case involving a ferry operator who charged a passenger ten cents for passage across the Ohio River from Ohio to West Virginia contrary to a West Virginia order fixing the price at five cents. The West Virginia Supreme Court reversed the conviction reasoning in part that the Virginia-Kentucky Compact declared the states had concurrent jurisdiction over the use of the Ohio River and thus West Virginia could not fix the ferry price from the Ohio shore.

There are myriad variations on how Congress may give its consent to interstate compacts. Most obviously, Congress may give consent after the states enact the agreement. Surprisingly, this issue arose in a case, but unsurprisingly, the court concluded that states may enact a compact prior to seeking consent. *State ex rel. Baird v. Joslin*, 116 Kan. 615, 618 (1924). More common was the question whether Congress may give consent to a compact before the states enact the compact. In *Virginia v. Tennessee*, 148 U.S. 503 (1893), the Supreme Court observed that the timing of consent is unimportant, stating, "In many cases the consent will usually precede the compact or agreement . . . . But where the agreement relates to a matter which could not well be considered until its nature is fully developed, it is not perceived why the consent may not be subsequently given." *Id.* at 521. Nearly 100 years later, the Supreme Court reaffirmed that holding in *Cuyler v. Adams*, 449 U.S. 433, 442 (1981), noting that advance consent is valid provided Congress intended its act to be consent. An example of advance consent to a specific compact is Congress's consent to the Columbia River Gorge Compact: "To achieve the purposes of . . . this title and to facilitate cooperation among the States of Oregon and Washington, and with the United States of America, the consent of Congress is given for an agreement described in sections 544 to 544p of this title . . . ." 16 U.S.C. § 544c(a)(1). In this example, Congress had not seen the actual text of the compact, but the consent statute is quite detailed—nearly 20 pages in the U.S. Code.

Often, Congress gives its consent to a general type of compact without first seeing the compact text and without specifying any detail for a compact. For example, the Amtrak Reform and Accountability Act of 1997 states:

> Congress grants consent to States with an interest in a specific form, route, or corridor of intercity passenger rail service (including high speed rail service) to enter into interstate compacts to promote the provision of the service . . . .

Pub. L. No. 105-134, tit. IV, § 410, 111 Stat. 2570, 2587 (1997). This barebones grant of consent with no conditions or terms seems to have been added to the Amtrak legislation with little thought as to the complexity of the administration and regulatory system that goes along with a compact, which you will study throughout this casebook.

Congress gave slightly more direction in the Federal Power Act when it granted consent to interstate compacts establishing regional siting transmission agencies. The Federal Power Act states:

> (1) The consent of Congress is given for three or more contiguous States to enter into an interstate compact, subject to approval by Congress, establishing regional transmission siting agencies to –
>
> > (A) facilitate siting of future electric energy transmission facilities within those States; and
> >
> > (B) carry out the electric energy transmission siting responsibilities of those States.

(2) The Secretary [of Energy] may provide technical assistance to regional transmission siting agencies established under this subsection.

(3) The regional transmission siting agencies shall have the authority to review, certify, and permit siting of transmission facilities, including facilities in national interest electric transmission corridors (other than facilities on property owned by the United States).

(4) The [Federal Energy Regulatory] Commission shall have no authority to issue a permit for the construction or modification of an electric transmission facility within a State that is a party to a compact, unless the members of the compact are in disagreement and the Secretary makes, after notice and an opportunity for a hearing, the finding described in subsection (b)(1)(C) of this section.

16 U.S.C. § 824p(i). This grant of consent still does not address basic questions such as when the regional transmission siting agencies must follow state law; the relationship between section 3 and the Federal Energy Regulatory Commission; authority for the regional agencies to write regulations; the administrative procedures for the regional agencies to follow when writing regulations or reviewing, certifying, and permitting facilities; or jurisdiction and standards for judicial review of the regional agencies' decisions. Later chapters consider these questions and the problems resulting from sparsely detailed compacts and consent statutes.

In some legislation, Congress has given advance consent to a general type of compact, but also required subsequent approval of the final agreement. An example of this is in the Clean Air Act.

The consent of the Congress is hereby given to two or more States to negotiate and enter into agreements or compacts, not in conflict with any law or treaty of the United States, for (1) cooperative effort and mutual assistance for the prevention and control of air pollution and the enforcement of their respective laws relating thereto, and (2) the establishment of such agencies, joint or otherwise, as they may deem desirable for making effective such agreements or compacts. No such agreement or compact shall be binding or obligatory upon any State a party thereto unless and until it has been approved by Congress.

42 U.S.C. § 7402(c). This would seem to solve problems caused by non-detailed advance consent because Congress retains the ability to ensure that the compacts address important issues before granting subsequent approval. What then would be the purpose of the advance consent? Recall the Bowman and Woods article cited in Chapter 1 giving factors that suggest when states are more likely to enact compacts: another conclusion in the article suggests that states are more likely to enact compacts when Congress encourages states to do so through advance consent. Ann O'M. Bowman and Neal D. Woods, *Strength in Numbers: Why States Join Interstate Compacts*, 7 ST. POL. & POL'Y Q. 347, 364 (2007). Despite this conclusion, no states have developed compacts pursuant to the Clean Air Act or Amtrak legislation. What might account for this—the subject matter; the lack of detail; the lack of an immediate problem; the lack of a carrot or stick?

The Patient Protection and Affordable Care Act, Pub. L. No. 111-148, 124 Stat. 119, 206–07 (2010), authorizes two or more states to enact an interstate compact to allow a health plan to be offered in all the party states. The Act requires the Secretary of Health and Human Services to develop regulations for the creation of compacts in consultation with the National Association of Insurance Commissioners (NAIC). 42 U.S.C. § 18053(a)(1). Interestingly, the Secretary, not Congress, must approve the compacts. In the early 2000s, NAIC helped envision, draft, and promote the Interstate Insurance Product Regulation Compact, which did not require consent.

Congress may also give consent for a specific duration. An example of this is the Northeast Interstate Dairy Compact for which Congress gave consent for a period of five years. The Dairy Compact became inactive in 2001 after Congress did not renew its consent and had an interesting winding up situation that is discussed in Chapter 10.

The above are examples of express consent. As noted above, the Supreme Court has also concluded that implied consent is valid. *Virginia v. Tennessee*, 148 U.S. 503 (1893) (the same case discussed above holding that the timing of consent is unimportant), involved a suit to establish by judicial decree the location of the boundary between the states. The Court reviewed nearly 200 years of charters, claims, grants, and negotiation between the states, reciprocal 1803 legislation to establish the boundary, and Joseph Story,* *Commentaries on the Constitution of the United States*, § 1403. Regarding Story's treatise, the Court stated:

> Story says that the consent may be implied and is always to be implied when Congress adopts the particular act by sanctioning its objects and aiding in enforcing them; and observes that where a State is admitted into the Union, notoriously upon a compact made between it and the State of which it previously composed a part, there the act of Congress, admitting such State into the Union, is an implied consent to the terms of the compact.

The Court observed that Congress had treated the boundary established in the compact as the true boundary for the purpose of federal court districts, revenue collection, federal elections and federal appointments, and thus concluded, "The approval by Congress of the compact entered into between the States upon their ratification of the action of their commissioners is fairly implied from its subsequent legislation and proceedings." 148 U.S. at 521–22.

The creation of West Virginia is also an interesting example of implied congressional consent. A Virginia statute authorized 39 counties to create West Virginia and allowed other counties to join West Virginia if approved by the voters in those counties. Subsequently, after Congress granted its consent and the other counties voted to join West Virginia, the new smaller Virginia repealed its statute approving the creation of West Virginia. One issue in *Virginia v. West Virginia*, 78

---

*Joseph Story was an Associate Justice of the U.S. Supreme Court at the time he wrote his still-influential commentaries on the Constitution. He also authored the *Green v. Biddle* majority excerpted above in this chapter and in later chapters.

U.S. 39 (1870), was whether Congress's consent was valid because it predated the other counties' votes. The Supreme Court concluded that the congressional act expressly consenting to a compact creating West Virginia by 39 counties was, "an inference clear and satisfactory that Congress by that statute intended" its consent to include the other counties as well. *Id.* at 60.

Finally, some general authorizations for compacts specifically deem that the consent of Congress is granted to a compact after a specified period from the date the states transmit the compact to Congress. For example, in 1994, Congress authorized emergency preparedness compacts and deemed consent to be granted 60 days after transmittal to Congress. 42 U.S.C. § 5196(h)(3). Deemed consent seems to have been around for a long time. Nearly 40 years before the emergency preparedness legislation, in 1958, the American Bar Association adopted a recommendation from its Standing Committee on Commerce to support a bill in Congress that the ABA explained, "contemplates that the consent of the Congress shall be deemed to have been granted to a compact if, within a specified period of time following its transmittal to the Congress (a copy thereof having also been transmitted to the President of the United States), the Congress or either House thereof shall not have passed a resolution stating in substance that consent is not granted." Report and Recommendation of the Standing Committee on Commerce, 83 ANN. REP. A.B.A. 327–28 (1958) (adoption of report and recommendation at 83 ANN. REP. A.B.A. 195 (1958)).

One scholar noted that Congress has "historically consented to submitted agreements almost automatically." Jill Elaine Hasday, *Interstate Compacts in a Democratic Society, The Problem of Permanency*, 49 FLA. L. REV. 1, 13–14 (1997). She further noted,

> 'President Roosevelt's 1942 veto of the Republican River Compact on the grounds that it would limit national control over a navigable waterway and 'restrict the authority of the United States to construct irrigation works and to appropriate water for irrigation purposes in the basin,' 88 Cong. Rec. 3286 (1942), was a rare exception to this perfunctoriness. The agreement was subsequently revised and approved a year later. *See* ch. 104, 57 Stat. 86 (1943).

Hasday, *supra*, at 14 n.59. Another example of a difficult consent process is the original consent to the Atlantic States Marine Fisheries Commission, in which President Roosevelt vetoed the initial bill "because the original compact did not expressly require that the compact should be brought back to Congress for approval." *A Bill Granting the Consent and Approval of Congress to an Interstate Compact Relating to the Better Utilization of the Fisheries (Marine, Shell, And Anadromous) of the Atlantic Seaboard and Creating the Atlantic States Marine Fisheries Commission: Hearing on H.R. 6020 Before the H. Comm. on the Merchant Marine and Fisheries*, 77th Cong. 43 (1942) (Statement of Frederick L. Zimmermann, Research Consultant of the New York Joint Legislative Committee on Interstate Cooperation). Congress granted consent again after additional committee hearings and markup. Act of May 4, 1942, Pub. L. No. 77-539, 56 Stat. 267.

Notes & Questions

1. In *Virginia v. Tennessee,* the Supreme Court suggested that advance consent to a compact is preferred. Why would this be? How specific can Congress be in giving advance consent? What would happen if the states enact terms that varied from Congress's intent? Does requiring Congress to take a second look at the compact such as in the Clean Air Act cure any potential problem? Does review by an agency official, such as in the Affordable Care Act, provide the same cure?

2. Are there some characteristics of compacts that might be of enough concern to Congress or the states, such that implied consent might not be appropriate? Consider Judge Beezer's concern in *Seattle Master Builders* where three states could create a compact that would affect other states.

3. The Safe and Timely Interstate Placement of Foster Children Act of 2006, Pub. L. No. 109-239, § 2, 120 Stat. 508 stated, "It is the sense of the Congress that—(1) the States should expeditiously ratify the revised Interstate Compact for the Placement for Children . . . ." The Ninth Circuit has stated that a "sense of Congress" provision and use of the term "should" indicates the language is merely precatory and does not bestow rights, but may be used to buttress interpretations of other mandatory provisions. *Chong v. Dep't of Soc. Servs*, 183 F.3d 953, 958–59 (9th Cir. 1999). Is the "sense of Congress" provision for the Interstate Compact for the Placement of Children an express act of consent? Is this provision a form of implied consent? What if Congress enacted a "sense of Congress" provision concerning a general type of compact instead of identifying a specific compact?

The Safe and Timely Interstate Placement of Foster Children Act of 2006 did more than encourage the states to enact the Interstate Compact for the Placement of Children (ICPC); it added a new statutory requirement for states to complete home studies for interstate placements within 60 days. 42 U.S.C. § 671(a)(26). The new ICPC contains a time requirement for completing home studies and returning those studies to the requesting state. Is this time requirement in the 2006 federal act a condition of Congress's consent such that the "sense of Congress" provision should be considered consent? Conditions of consent are discussed later in this chapter.

The new ICPC requires 35 states to enact it, which as of mid-2020 had not occurred. Is the federal 60-day requirement to complete a home study effectively an amendment to the current ICPC, to which Congress did not grant consent? The application of new federal law to a compact is discussed later in this chapter.

4. Some state statutes that authorize non-compact intergovernmental agreements require enacting the agreement in a specific form. For example, Pennsylvania law requires enactment by ordinance. 53 PA. CONS. STAT. § 2305. This requirement limits the ability of municipal officers to enter into "tacit" agreements. *See Commonwealth v. Bable*, 254 Pa. Super. 72, 76 (1978). Should the U.S. Constitution have required states enact compacts in a certain manner or Congress give consent in a certain manner to ensure that the states and Congress intend a compact rather than a non-binding agreement?

All the compacts discussed above were enacted after the U.S. Constitution. The case below, *Wharton v. Wise*, involved a 1785 compact between Virginia and Maryland enacted under the authority for compacts in the Articles of Confederation. Wharton, a Maryland resident, was convicted in Virginia for taking oysters in Virginia waters as a non-resident. He argued that under the 1785 compact, citizens of Maryland possessed and were entitled to fish and take oysters in common with the citizens of Virginia in the Pocomoke River. Ultimately, the discussion of the validity of the compact is *dicta* because the Court concluded that the rights preserved in the compact vis-à-vis the Pocomoke River extended only to navigation, and the right to fish under the compact covered only the Potomac River. Nevertheless, it contains a good explanation of the authority for states to enter into compacts under the Articles of Confederation and is the Supreme Court's clearest statement that it recognizes pre-Constitution compacts.

Wharton v. Wise
153 U.S. 155 (1894)

FIELD, JUSTICE:

. . . .

Previously to June, 1784, citizens of both Maryland and Virginia experienced great inconveniences from the want of established and recognized regulations between those States respecting the jurisdiction and navigation of the river Potomac, which constituted a boundary between the two States for over one hundred miles. In that month and year the general assembly of Virginia, reciting that such inconveniences resulted from want of some concerted regulations between the States, "touching the jurisdiction and navigation of the river Potomac," passed the following resolutions:

> "Resolved, That George Mason, Edmund Randolph, James Madison, Jr., and Alexander Henderson, Esquires, be appointed commissioners, and that they, or any three of them, do meet such commissioners as may be appointed on the part of Maryland, and in concert with them frame such liberal and equitable regulations concerning the said river as may be mutually advantageous to the two States, and that they make report thereof to the general assembly."
>
> "Resolved, That the executive be requested to notify the above appointment, with the object of it, to the State of Maryland, and desire its concurrence in the proposition."

The resolutions were communicated to the Executive of Maryland, and by him laid before the legislature of that State, which responded to the invitation by a resolution, passed on the 18th of January, 1785, appointing commissioners on her part to meet those of Virginia, but with powers somewhat enlarged. The resolution, as adopted by the Senate of Maryland, declared that Thomas Johnson, Thomas Stone, Samuel Chase, and Daniel of St. Thomas Jenifer (selected by the

House of Representatives two days before) should be commissioners for the State of Maryland to meet the commissioners appointed by the Commonwealth of Virginia, "for the purpose of settling the navigation and jurisdiction over that part of the bay of Chesapeake which lies within the limits of Virginia, and over the rivers Potomac and Pocomoke;" and that the commissioners, or any two of them, should have full power, on behalf of Maryland, "to adjudge and settle the jurisdiction to be exercised by the said States, respectively, over the waters and navigation of the same, the proceedings to be laid before the general assembly of the State to be ratified," etc.

The commissioners met at Mt. Vernon in the following year, and on the 28th of March a compact between the two States was mutually agreed upon by them.

. . . .

The compact provided that its articles should be laid before the legislatures of the two States and, their approbation being obtained, should be confirmed and ratified by a law of each State, never to be repealed or altered by either without the consent of the other. The articles were accordingly laid before the legislatures of those States and were approved, ratified, and confirmed by a law of each substantially identical in terms. The concluding clause of the act of ratification of the legislature of Virginia is as follows: "And whereas this general assembly are of opinion that the said compact is made on just and mutual principles for the true interests of both governments, and the same having been confirmed by the general assembly of the State of Maryland, be it therefore enacted that the said compact is hereby approved, confirmed, and ratified by the general assembly of Virginia, and that every article, clause, matter, and thing therein contained shall be obligatory on this State and the citizens thereof, and shall be forever faithfully and inviolably observed and kept by this government and all its citizens according to the true intent and meaning of this compact; and the faith and honor of this State are hereby solemnly pledged and engaged to the State of Maryland and the government and citizens thereof that this law shall never be repealed or altered by the legislature of this commonwealth without the consent of the State of Maryland."

A similar clause concludes the act of ratification by the State of Maryland, with a change only in the terms required to indicate it as the act of Maryland instead of that of Virginia.

The provisions of the compact were well designed to promote the peace, good neighborhood, and welfare of both States, and facilitate intercourse between their citizens, and it was clearly within their competency at the time to adopt them, if not restrained by the Articles of the Confederation, then in existence and in which they had joined. They were then sovereign States, possessing, unless thus restrained, all the rights and powers of independent nations over the territory within their respective limits, and could exercise any control and dominion over their navigable waters and make any regulations necessary for the protection of their navigation or to promote the commerce upon them of their respective States. Those articles expressly provided that each State composing the Confederation retained its sovereignty, freedom, and independence, and every power, jurisdiction, and right, which was not by them expressly delegated to the United States in Congress assembled. The Confederation was a league of friendship of the States with each other, so declared in the articles and entered into "for their common defence, the security of their liberties, and their mutual and general welfare, binding themselves to assist each other against all force offered to, or attacks made upon them, or any of them, on account of religion, sovereignty, trade, or any other pretence whatever." But its articles did not form a constitution or ordinance of government, with power to enforce its provisions upon each other, or even a compact having any coherence or binding force other than that of a league of friendship, which its members only claimed them to constitute.

The validity of the compact of 1785 has been questioned as in conflict with the second clause of the sixth article of the Confederation, which provided that no two or more States should enter into any treaty, confederation, or alliance whatever between them without the consent of the United States in Congress assembled, specifying accurately the purposes for which the same was to be entered into, and how long it should continue; and also as having been superseded by the Constitution of the United States subsequently adopted. A few words upon each of these positions. The articles inhibiting any treaty, confederation, or alliance between the States without the consent of Congress were intended to prevent any union of two or more States, having a tendency to break up or weaken the league between the whole; they were not designed to prevent arrangements between adjoining States to facilitate the free intercourse of their citizens, or remove barriers to their peace and prosperity; and whatever their effect, such arrangements could not be the subject of complaint by the States making them until, at least, the Congress of the Confederation interposed objections to their adoption or enforcement, which was never done.

The provisions of the compact, so far as they were inconsistent with the Constitution of the United States, subsequently adopted, and to which Maryland and Virginia were parties, were of course suspended and superseded by it.

But as an operative agreement, binding the action of the two States upon the subjects embraced, where not inconsistent with the Constitution, its validity has often been recognized by their authorities. Neither of the governments has ever denied or repudiated its obligation, but, as in the present case and in all controversies between the States, it has been treated as of obligatory force.

. . . .

. . . [L]ooking at the object evidently intended by the prohibition of the Articles of Confederation, we are clear they were not directed against agreements of the character expressed by the compact under consideration. Its execution could in no respect encroach upon or weaken the general authority of Congress under those articles. Various compacts were entered into between Pennsylvania and New Jersey and between Pennsylvania and Virginia, during the Confederation, in reference to boundaries between them, and to rights of fishery in their waters, and to titles to land in their respective States, without the consent of Congress, which indicated that such consent was not deemed essential to their validity. Virginia and Maryland were sovereign States with no common superior and no tribunal to determine for them the true construction and meaning of its provisions in case of a conflict of opinion upon the subject. Each State was left to decide for itself as to their true construction and meaning, and to its own sense of the obligations of the compact for their enforcement. If, therefore, the Congress of the United States, which, as said above, never complained of the compact of 1785, had interposed objections to its adoption or enforcement as being within the meaning of the terms treaty or confederation, or as establishing an alliance within the prohibition of the articles mentioned, yet it would not lie in either of the States that were parties to the contract to allege its invalidity on the subject. As said by Mr. Steele, in his very able and elaborate opinion, upon the construction of provisions of the compact, given to the governor of Maryland, and which is referred to in the record, they cannot complain that there was in its adoption any breach of good faith towards themselves, and we may add, or any rupture by them of the league of friendship declared to be the object of the articles to establish.

In our judgment the compact of 1785 was not prohibited by the Articles of Confederation. It was not a treaty, confederation, or alliance within the meaning of those terms as there used, and it remained as a subsisting operative contract between them, in full force when the confederation went out of existence upon the adoption of the present Constitution of the United States. And it was not affected or set aside by the prohibitory clause of that instrument. Its prohibition extends only to future agreements or compacts, not against those already in existence, except so far as their stipulations might affect subjects placed under the control of Congress, such as commerce and the navigation of public waters, which is included under the power to regulate commerce.

As stated by counsel, stipulations as to riparian rights of fishery, and as to jurisdiction in and over waters lying between the two States, remained as they previously existed, neither suspended or impaired.

We are therefore of opinion that the compact continued in full force after the adoption of the Constitution, except so far as inconsistent with its provisions; and such we understand has been the clear declaration of the two States whenever they have been called upon to express their opinion upon the subject, and such is the concession of counsel. In the acts of both states, passed in 1874, designating arbitrators to ascertain and fix the boundary between them, the validity of the compact was affirmed in the declaration that "neither of the said states, nor the citizens thereof, shall, by the decision of the said arbitrators, be deprived of any of the rights and privileges enumerated and set forth in the compact between them, entered into in the year 1785, but that the same shall remain to and be enjoyed by the said states and the citizens thereof forever."

As justly observed, there could not be a more solemn and conclusive recognition and assertion—so far as the two states were concerned—of the continued existence and obligatory force of the compact than is contained in this language of both in appointing the arbitrators and designating the conditions upon which their award should be accepted. The states of Maryland and Virginia not only consented to the appointment of the arbitrators, upon the conditions mentioned, but their award was approved by both states and by an act of congress. That approval covered all the conditions and stipulations upon which the award was made, and renders the compact of 1785, the rights and privileges of which were to remain and be enjoyed by the states and the citizens thereof forever, thus consented to by congress, free from constitutional objections, if any that were valid had previously existed. The act of congress recited that arbitrators, duly appointed on the part of the states of Virginia and Maryland for the purpose of ascertaining and fixing the boundary between them, did proceed to examine into and ascertain the true line of said boundary, and had made their award, which was set forth, and that that award had been ratified and confirmed by the legislatures of those states, respectively; and then enacted that the consent of congress was given to the agreement or award, and to each and every part and article thereof. That consent, taken in connection with the conditions upon which the award was authorized, operated as an approval of the original compact, and of its continuance in force under the sanction of congress. The consent of congress to any agreement or compact between two or more states is sufficiently indicated, when not necessary to be made in advance, by the adoption or approval of proceedings taken under it. *Green v. Biddle*, 8 Wheat. 1, 85–87.

. . . .

Notes & Questions

1. In *Wharton v. Wise*, the Court held that a compact properly enacted under the Articles of Confederation would survive the transition to the Constitution, stating, "Its prohibition extends only to future agreements or compacts, not against those already in existence, except so far as their stipulations might affect subjects placed under the control of Congress." 153 U.S. at 171. Did the compact at issue in this case contain terms and conditions that might affect a subject placed under the control of Congress?

The Court noted a caveat with recognizing compacts made under the Articles of Confederation, "The provisions of the compact, so far as they were inconsistent with the constitution of the United States, subsequently adopted, and to which Maryland and Virginia were parties, were of course suspended and superseded by it." *Id.* at 167. Consider whether an amendment to the current Constitution might render modern compacts insecure.

2. The Court briefly addressed the need for consent (the need for consent is discussed later in this chapter). The Court stated, "[The compact under consideration] could in no respect encroach upon or weaken the general authority of Congress under those articles." 153 U.S. at 170. If the Court had concluded that the compact did affect Congress's authority, would Congress need to act to give consent, or might the Court have concluded that consent to pre-Constitution compacts is implied? How would you argue such an implied consent?

3. The Court also touched on an issue that courts have continued to struggle with to the present—differing interpretations of the compact: "Virginia and Maryland were sovereign States with no common superior and no tribunal to determine for them the true construction and meaning of its provisions in case of a conflict of opinion upon the subject. Each State was left to decide for itself as to their true construction and meaning, and to its own sense of the obligations of the compact for their enforcement." 153 U.S. at 171. This issue of differing interpretations of a compact appears in many of the cases throughout this book.

4. Reread this quote: "That approval covered all the conditions and stipulations upon which the award was made, and renders the compact of 1785, the rights and privileges of which were to remain and be enjoyed by the states and the citizens thereof forever, thus consented to by congress, free from constitutional objections, if any that were valid had previously existed." 153 U.S. at 172. Was the Supreme Court referring only to constitutional objections relating to the Compact Clause, or to other constitutional issues as well? Should congressional approval immunize a compact from other constitutional challenges? As mentioned in Chapter 1, consent immunizes compact from challenges under the Commerce Clause. However, other constitutional claims, such as challenges to compacts under the Property Clause or Takings Clause are still possible. *See, e.g.*, *Columbia River Gorge United v. Yeutter*, 960 F.2d 110 (9th Cir. 1992); *Suitum v. Tahoe Reg'l Planning Agency*, 520 U.S. 725 (1997).

II. Conditions of Consent

Congress has always had authority to attach conditions to its legislative direction to the states. These conditions may take the form of financial or other incentives to the states, or states having to choose between regulating in accordance with federal standards or having state law preempted by federal legislation or regulation. Other common conditions Congress has imposed include consent for only a limited time period, *e.g.*, Act of May 4, 1942, Pub. L. No. 77-539, 56 Stat. 267 (granting consent for "not more than fifteen years" to the Atlantic States Marine Fisheries Compact) and Act of Aug. 10, 1950, Pub. L. No. 81-721, § 2, 64 Stat. 467 (repealing time limit); abrogating Eleventh Amendment immunity for compact commissions and agencies, *see, e.g.*, *Petty v. Tennessee-Missouri Bridge Comm'n*, 359 U.S. 275 (1959); waiver of immunity from suit under specific federal statutes, *see, e.g.*, *Barbour v. Wash. Metro. Area Transit Auth.*, 374 F.3d 1161 (D.C. Cir. 2004) (waiver of immunity from suit under the Rehabilitation Act of 1973); and selection of jurisdiction for resolving disputes, *e.g.*, 16 U.S.C. § 544m(b) (condition of consent to Columbia River Gorge Compact specifying jurisdiction in state courts for actions involving Columbia River Gorge Commission). A good discussion of Congress's authority to condition its consent is found in *New York v. United States*, 505 U.S. 144, 166–69 (1992).

The following case, *Tobin v. United States*, suggested that there might be some limits to Congress's authority to impose conditions on its consent to a compact, questioning whether a specific congressional condition was proper. Here, the case involved the condition that Congress retains "the right to alter, amend or repeal" the compact. A different excerpt from this case appears in Chapter 10 for discussing the power of Congress to oversee and investigate compact agencies.

Tobin v. United States
306 F.2d 270 (D.C. Cir. 1962)

BASTIAN, JUDGE:

Austin J. Tobin, the Executive Director of the Port of New York Authority, was charged by information and convicted in the District Court of criminal contempt of Congress for refusing to produce certain documents called for by a subpoena issued by Subcommittee No. 5 of the Committee on the Judiciary of the United States House of Representatives.

The Port of New York Authority is a bi-state agency established in 1921 and 1922 by compacts between the States of New York and New Jersey to provide for the efficient administration of the New York harbor, which is divided geographically between the two states. Pursuant to the compact clause of the Constitution, Congress consented to the compacts but expressly retained, among other matters, "the right to alter, amend or repeal" its resolutions of approval. Over the years, the Port Authority has been remarkably successful in achieving its goals. As of 1959, it had investments of nearly one billion dollars and gross annual operating revenue in excess of one hundred million dollars.

In February of 1960, the Judiciary Committee initiated an investigation of the Authority on an informal basis. The Authority cooperated with the Committee investigators except as to disclosing certain documents alleged to relate exclusively to the internal administration of the Authority. After this refusal events moved swiftly to a climax.

On June 1, 1960, the Chairman of the Committee obtained from the House subpoena power in connection with matters "involving the activities and operations of interstate compacts." What little floor discussion there was preceding this grant of subpoena power was not very enlightening; it certainly provided no lucid analysis of what was soon to follow. On June 8, 1960, Subcommittee No. 5 of the Judiciary Committee instituted a formal inquiry into the Authority.

Appellant conferred with the Board of Commissioners of the Authority, as well as with the Governors of both New York and New Jersey, and the consensus of their opinion was that the investigation being attempted was too broad to be valid. The Subcommittee was informed of their objections and the reasons therefor. Discounting these objections, the Subcommittee issued the subpoena in question. Appellant requested postponement of the return date of the subpoena in order to give the Governors an opportunity to meet with the Subcommittee and discuss their objections but the Subcommittee refused the postponement.

After being denied the opportunity to appear before the Subcommittee, the Governors wrote identical letters to their respective representatives on the Board of Commissioners of the Authority, instructing them to direct appellant not to comply with the subpoena. The Board of Commissioners so directed appellant on June 27, 1960. Two days later, on June 29, 1960, the Subcommittee met to receive the return of the subpoena. It was against this background that appellant refused to comply with the demands of the subpoena and was ruled in default by the Chairman of the Subcommittee. Thereafter, the Subcommittee recommended to the full Committee that appellant be cited by the House for contempt. This recommendation was adopted by the Judiciary Committee, two members dissenting, and subsequently by the House itself. Charged by information, appellant waived his right to jury trial and was convicted of contempt of Congress by District Judge Youngdahl.

Appellant advances several arguments in support of the position that his conviction cannot stand. For present purposes, to illustrate the constitutional issues we would have to decide in order to affirm the conviction, we list but two of his arguments:

1. That Congress does not have the power, under the compact clause of the Constitution, to "alter, amend or repeal" its consent to an interstate compact, which was the stated purpose of the Subcommittee's investigation.

2. That "the subpoena issued by the Subcommittee, demanding documents relating to the internal administration of the Port Authority which the Governors of New York and New Jersey ordered appellant not to produce, [was] an unconstitutional invasion of powers reserved to the States under the Tenth Amendment to the Constitution."

Because of the view we take of this case, appellant's first contention demands some elaboration. In granting its consent Congress can attach certain binding conditions, not only to its consent to the admission of a new state into the Union, but also to its consent to the formation of an interstate compact. However, the vital condition precedent to the validity of any such attached condition is that it be constitutional. If Congress does not have the power under the Constitution, then it cannot confer such power upon itself by way of a legislative fiat imposed as a condition to the granting of its consent.

In the present case, therefore, Congress's express reservation of the right "to alter, amend or repeal" its initial consent to the creation of the Authority is meaningless unless Congress has the power under the Constitution "to alter, amend or repeal" its consent to an interstate compact. The compact clause of the Constitution does not specifically confer such power upon Congress. No case has been cited to us, nor have we been able to find any case through our own research, holding that Congress has such constitutional power. Nor do we find any to the contrary. Since no such power appears expressly in the compact clause, any holding that it exists and that Congress possesses it must be predicated on the conclusion that it exists as an implied power.

We have addressed ourselves at some length to this issue in order to show the gravity of passing upon even only one of the constitutional questions posed by this case. Moreover, in view of appellant's argument that the plenary powers specified in and by the Constitution are more than sufficient to enable Congress to protect, supervise and preserve all federal interests affected by the existence of interstate compacts, we are even less inclined to reach the constitutional issues involved here. We have no way of knowing what ramifications would result from a holding that Congress has the implied constitutional power "to alter, amend or repeal" its consent to an interstate compact. Certainly, in view of the number and variety of interstate compacts in effect today, such a holding would stir up an air of uncertainty in those areas of our national life presently affected by the existence of these compacts. No doubt the suspicion of even potential impermanency would be damaging to the very concept of interstate compacts.

Appellant argues that congressional consent becomes irrevocable once it is given under the compact clause since Congress thereby removes the constitutional ban against the formation of interstate compacts and thus, to that extent, restores the states to the inherent sovereignty they enjoyed prior to the adoption of the Constitution. This does not mean that once congressional consent is obtained the particular compact becomes a law unto itself, immune by reason of its autonomy from future congressional supervision. It simply means that the states are restored to that much of their original sovereignty as would permit them to enter into compacts with each other. To this extent, and to this extent alone, does congressional consent restore them to sovereignty—sovereign in the narrow sense of being free to conclude an interstate compact, not sovereign in the broad sense of being free of the Constitution.

Accordingly, if a particular compact happens to be operational in nature (as exemplified by the compact creating the Authority) as opposed to one static in nature (as exemplified by an agreement to settle a disputed boundary line, an *act* which necessarily dies at the moment of its birth), Congress is not without power to control the conduct of the former. Under our system of government the Constitution is paramount, and the Constitution gives to Congress certain plenary powers, as for example those in the field of interstate commerce and that of national defense. With the choice of acting pursuant to any or all of these plenary powers continuously available to it, Congress has at its disposal abundant authority to supervise and regulate the activities of operational compacts in such a way as to insure that no violence is done by these compacts to more compelling federal concerns.

Appellant argues, in short, that Congress can adequately protect every interest that needs such protection because of the existence of an operational compact without, in doing so, being forced to the extremity of rescinding its consent under the compact clause, an action which appellant contends Congress has no constitutional power to perform.

Appellant's assertion in this respect is not unpersuasive, since a holding that Congress has the constitutional power to "alter, amend or repeal" its consent under the compact clause can hardly be stated as a proposition of universal applicability. A line marking the boundary between two states, initially drawn by such states acting pursuant to an interstate compact, could hardly be erased at some later date by Congress's enactment of hindsight legislation purporting to repeal its consent to the compact by which such boundary was initially determined. See the discussion in *Hinderlider v. La Plata River Co.*, 304 U.S. 92 (1938) and cases cited therein.

In other words, appellant seeks to distinguish the ways in which congressional control over an operational compact may be properly exercised: he argues that control undertaken pursuant to the plenary powers is licit, whereas control attempted in the sense of withdrawing consent under the compact clause is illicit.

. . . .

Notes & Questions

1. The concept of Congress adding conditions to its consent dates back to the very first compacts. Frankfurter and Landis, in their 1925 law review article, noted, "[Compacts] may affect the interest of States other than those parties to the agreement: the national, and not merely a regional, interest may be involved. Therefore, Congress must exercise national supervision through its power to grant or withhold consent, or to grant it under appropriate conditions." Felix Frankfurter & James M. Landis, *The Compact Clause of the Constitution—A Study in Interstate Adjustments*, 34 YALE L.J. 685, 695 (1925).

2. Conditions of consent become integral parts of a compact. For example, in *Petty v. Tennessee-Missouri Bridge Comm'n*, 359 U.S. 275 (1959), the Supreme Court used a condition of consent to help interpret a provision of the compact that the states had negotiated and submitted to Congress. Consider this excerpt:

> Congress, under conditions specified in 33 U.S.C. § 525, *et seq.*, gave its consent to the construction of bridges over the navigable waters in the United States. Respondent is a "body corporate and politic" created by Missouri and Tennessee acting pursuant to the Compact Clause of the Constitution. Art. I, § 10, cl. 3. The compact prepared by the two States and submitted to the Congress provided in Art. I, §§ 1 and 2 that respondent should have the power to build a bridge and operate ferries across the Mississippi at specified points and in Art. I, § 3, that it should have the power "to contract, to sue and be sued in its own name." Congress granted its consent to the compact, stating in a proviso:
>
>> That nothing herein contained shall be construed to affect, impair, or diminish any right, power, or jurisdiction of the United States or of any court, department, board, bureau, officer, or official of the United States, over or in regard to any navigable waters, or any commerce between the States or with foreign countries, or any bridge, railroad, highway, pier, wharf, or other facility or improvement, or any other person, matter, or thing, forming the subject matter of the aforesaid compact or agreement or otherwise affected by the terms thereof.
>>
>> . . . .
>
> The States who are parties to the compact by accepting it and acting under it assume the conditions that Congress under the Constitution attached. So if there be doubt as to the meaning of the sue-and-be-sued clause in the setting of the compact prior to approval by Congress, the doubt dissipates

when the condition attached by Congress is accepted and acted upon by the two States.

3. Congress's consent to the Great Lakes Basin Compact stated that it was not granting consent to specific provisions in the compact that the states had drafted. Act of July 24, 1968, Pub. L. No. 90-419, § 2, 82 Stat. 414, 419. However, the states had already enacted the compact and had been implementing it for 13 years before Congress enacted Its consent statute. In earlier hearings in 1957, Congress questioned why the compact should have a paragraph that Congress did not consent to. One of the legislative assistants stated,

> Rather than backtrack and secure reratification and adoption by each of the several States who had already ratified, we felt the simple solution would be to adopt ratifying legislation to strike out the offending paragraphs.

Granting the Consent and Approval of Congress to a Great Lakes Basin Compact: Hearings on H.R. 4314, 4315, 4316, and S. 1416 Before the H. Comm. on Foreign Affairs, 85th Cong. 18 (July 30, 1957). Article XI in the Great Lakes Basin Compact specifies that compact provisions declared to be contrary to the U.S. Constitution are severable from the remainder of the compact. What is the effect of those paragraphs? Do they remain part of the compact, but don't enjoy the benefits of compact provisions with consent (discussed in Chapter 5)? Do they become inoperative or void?

Subsequently, in consent legislation hearings in 1966, one witness opposed to consent stated, "The consent bill amends the compact and the amended compact has never been before the legislature of any State. It just is not the same compact when you give consent to it because of the restrictions you place on it." *Granting the Consent of Congress to a Great Lakes Basin Compact and for Other Purposes: Hearing on H.R. 937, H.R. 12294, H.R. 12299, H.R. 12692, H.R. 13359, H.R. 14192, and H.R. 15042 Before the H. Comm. on Foreign Affairs*, 89th Cong. 108 (Oct. 4, 1966) (statement of James A. Fitzpatrick, Chairman, Power Authority of the State of N.Y.). Who is correct? Must the states reenact the compact after Congress strikes provisions in granting consent?

4. One type of condition that appears in many congressional grants of consent is a limit on the application of other federal laws. For example, Congress's consent to the Washington Metropolitan Area Transit Regulation Compact includes the following provision: "All laws or parts of laws of the United States and of the District of Columbia inconsistent with the provisions of Title III of this Act are hereby amended for the purpose of this Act to the extent necessary to eliminate such inconsistencies and to carry out the provisions of this Act and Title III ...." Pub. L. 89-774, § 5(a), 80 Stat. 1324, 1353 (1966).

5. In *Tobin*, when analyzing the constitutionality of Congress reserving its right to alter, amend or repeal its initial consent, the D.C. Circuit observed that the Compact Clause does not expressly grant authority for Congress to do so. Interestingly, however, the court did not continue its analysis to determine whether that power is implied. Could reserving the right to alter, amend or repeal consent to a compact be an implied power?

Early law review articles did not agree on whether Congress has the power to withdraw consent and the effect of a withdrawal of consent. Excerpts from two law review articles written nearly 30 years before *Tobin* illustrate the arguments. The first excerpt argues that Congress's withdrawal of consent would not affect the compact.

> Since the requirement of Congressional consent is phrased as a condition precedent to the validity of a compact, withdrawal of consent would not appear sufficient to invalidate the agreement[60] in the absence of fraud upon Congress or a change of circumstances.
>
> > Fn. 60. The requirement of assent was designed to prevent the formation of political alliances such as are absolutely forbidden by U.S. Const. Art. I, § 10, cl. 1 and, possibly, to protect in all cases the interests of states which are not parties to the compact. Consent is merely the removal of an impediment to the exercise of powers existing independently of the Constitution and Congress is nowhere given authority to abrogate valid existing agreements not in conflict with its own powers.

Note, *A Reconsideration of the Nature of Interstate Compacts*, 35 COLUM. L. REV. 76, 84–85 & n.60 (1935). The second excerpt argues that consent is a continuing concept that Congress must be able to withdraw at any time.

> It has been argued that since the consent of Congress is merely a condition precedent which is imposed upon the exercise of the power to contract inherent in sovereign states, once consent is given, the power can be exercised without further restriction. But it is just as defensible to treat the power of the Federal Government as one to give continuing consent subject to withdrawal, and there is supporting this interpretation the consideration that the policy requiring consent in the first place no less strongly demands the power in the Federal Government to withdraw the consent. A threat to the efficiency or supremacy of the Federal Government, or to the interests of other states, may develop or appear after a compact is put into effect as well as before; a "compact" may well assume the proportions of a prohibited "treaty, alliance, or confederation."

Note, *Legal Problems Relating to Interstate Compacts*, 23 IOWA L. REV. 618, 632 (1938). Another article written shortly after the *Tobin* decision argues that agreements between states are "valid but voidable," noting that even if Congress could not directly void a compact, it could choose to legislate in a manner that affected the compact. *Congress and the Port of New York Authority: Federal Supervision of Interstate Compacts*, 70 YALE L.J. 812, 815 (1961).

6. The Supreme Court's decision, *Louisville Bridge Co. v. United States*, 242 U.S. 409 (1917) concluded that Congress could require removal of a private bridge that it had previously authorized. The Court reasoned in part:

> We need not go so far as to say that Congress could not in any case by contract or estoppel prevent itself from modifying or revoking a regulation

> once made and substituting another in its place without compensation. But when private rights of an indefensible nature are sought to be derived from regulatory provisions established in the exercise of this power, the case is peculiarly one for the application of the universal rule that grants of special franchises and privileges are to be strictly construed in favor of the public right, and nothing is to be taken as granted concerning which any reasonable doubt may be raised.
>
> The absence of an express reservation of the right to alter or amend is not conclusive . . . Congress is not prevented by the Constitution from passing laws that impair the obligation of contracts, and in its enactments the presence or absence of such a reservation has not the same peculiar significance that it has in state legislation. It is no doubt a circumstance, but not by any means conclusive.

Id. at 417–18. Do interstate compacts raise the same considerations? If Congress may pass laws that impair the obligations of contracts, then isn't that an implied power to alter, amend, or repeal an interstate compact?

7. What are the ramifications of holding that consent is impermanent? Are there some compacts that Congress should have authority to alter, amend or repeal its consent without invoking these concerns?

In *Tobin*, the D.C. Circuit explained a distinction between compacts that are "operational" in nature and compacts that are "static" in nature. The court's example of a static compact is an agreement to settle a disputed boundary line, which the court noted, "necessarily dies at the moment of its birth." 306 F.2d at 273. An unsigned law review article, *Congressional Supervision of Interstate Compacts*, 75 YALE L.J. 1416 (1966), discussing *Tobin* and the Port Authority, similarly noted, "The differences between an 'authority' compact and a boundary agreement are apparent. Instead of neatly solving a dispute, the authority agreement creates a wealthy and powerful organization which can expand its activities and repulse efforts at political control." *Id.* at 1426.

Are boundary compacts, such as those you read about in *Green v. Biddle* and *Robinson v. Campbell*, "static"? Do they "neatly solv[e] a dispute"? Should they "necessarily die[] at the moment of their birth"? If so, then how could their preservation of prior state law continue to have any effect?

8. Since *Tobin*, Congress has only haphazardly conditioned its consent on having authority to investigate and to alter, amend or repeal its consent to compacts. In the 15 years after *Tobin*, Congress granted consent to 19 compacts (not including general consent statutes that did not result in a compact), but Congress only reserved Its rights to oversee and amend or repeal the compact in only four of those consent actions. Ross Caldwell, untitled, unpublished manuscript 7 (May 6, 2012) (on file with author). Below is an example of this condition from the Tahoe Regional Planning Compact:

> Sec. 6. The right is hereby reserved by the Congress or any of its standing committees to require the disclosure and furnishing of such information

and date by or concerning the Tahoe Regional Planning Agency as is deemed appropriate by the Congress or such committee.

Sec. 7. The right to alter, amend, or repeal this Act is hereby expressly reserved.

Pub. L. No. 96-551 §§ 6 & 7, 94 Stat. 3233, 3253 (1980). In another example, Congress's consent to low-level radioactive waste disposal compacts specifically provides that, "Each compact shall provide that every 5 years after the compact has taken effect that Congress may by law withdraw its consent." 42 U.S.C. § 2021d(d). Is the general "right to alter, amend, or repeal" in the Tahoe compact equivalent to the specific five-year period in the consent to low-level radioactive waste compacts, such that both conditions address the D.C. Circuit's concern with impermanence?

More than 20 years after *Tobin*, the Third Circuit followed the D.C. Circuit and expressed doubt that Congress has authority to alter, amend or repeal a compact. *Mineo v. Port Auth. of N.Y. & N.J.*, 779 F.2d 939, 948 (3d Cir. 1985). Neither *Tobin* nor *Mineo* actually decided whether Congress has such authority, and the U.S. Supreme Court denied certiorari in both cases. What do you think: are these provisions permissible? Did *Tobin* indicate some flexibility for Congress to expressly impose these conditions? Why wouldn't Congress add these conditions to all its grants of consent?

9. In *New York v. United States,* 505 U.S. 144 (1992), the Supreme Court held that Congress could not compel state action in its grant of general consent for states to create regional low-level radioactive waste compacts. The Court framed the issue as a question under the Tenth Amendment rather than the Compact Clause; nevertheless, this is an important limit on congressional power that the Compact Clause does not modify.

10. There is no generally applicable federal statute that requires compacts to contain specific provisions or address specific governance issues. In contrast, virtually all statutes that authorize non-compact intergovernmental agreements contain specific requirements for those agreements, much like Congress might require in a statute that preauthorizes a specific compact or type of compact. For example, Oregon law requires that intergovernmental agreements must specify apportionment of funding obligations and revenue; transfer of employees and the preservation of their benefits; transfer of or title to real property, duration of agreement, and rights of the parties to terminate the agreement. OR. REV. STAT. § 190.020. Washington's Interlocal Cooperation Act requires the agreement to specify, "The precise organization, composition and nature of any separate legal or administrative entity created thereby together with the powers delegated thereto . . . ." WASH. REV. CODE. § 39.34.030(3)(b). Should Congress require compacts to contain specific provisions or address specific governance issues before it consents to a compact? Chapter 10 discusses several governance issues.

III. When Consent is Needed

Despite the Constitution's use of the phrase "any agreement or compact," the Supreme Court has not interpreted that phrase to mean that every compact requires congressional consent. Historically, the Court has discussed two rationales for consent. As noted above, the issue of when consent was necessary arose briefly in *Wharton v. Wise*. The year before *Wharton v. Wise*, the Supreme Court had its first significant opportunity to discuss the issue in *Virginia v. Tennessee*, 148 U.S. 503 (1893). The case below, *U.S. Steel Corp. v. Multistate Tax Comm'n*, is a more recent case summarizing the early compact cases and discussing when consent is necessary in a much more readable form.

U.S. Steel Corp. v. Multistate Tax Comm'n
434 U.S. 452 (1978)

POWELL, JUSTICE:

.... The Multistate Tax Compact, which established the Multistate Tax Commission, has not received congressional approval. This appeal requires us to decide whether the Compact is invalid for that reason....

The Multistate Tax Compact was drafted in 1966 and became effective, according to its own terms, on August 4, 1967, after seven States had adopted it. By the inception of this litigation in 1972, 21 States had become members. Its formation was a response to this Court's decision in *Northwestern States Portland Cement Co. v. Minnesota*, 358 U.S. 450 (1959), and the congressional activity that followed in its wake.

In *Northwestern States*, this Court held that net income from the interstate operations of a foreign corporation may be subjected to state taxation, provided that the levy is nondiscriminatory and is fairly apportioned to local activities that form a sufficient nexus to support the exercise of the taxing power. This prompted Congress to enact a statute, which sets forth certain minimum standards for the exercise of that power. It also authorized a study for the purpose of recommending legislation establishing uniform standards to be observed by the States in taxing income of interstate businesses. Although the results of the study were published in 1964 and 1965, Congress has not enacted any legislation dealing with the subject.

While Congress was wrestling with the problem, the Multistate Tax Compact was drafted....

....

In 1972, appellants brought this action on behalf of themselves and all other multistate taxpayers threatened with audits by the Commission. They named the Commission, its individual Commissioners, and its Executive Director as defendants. Their complaint challenged the constitutionality of the Compact on four grounds: (1) the Compact, never having received the consent of Congress, is invalid under the Compact Clause; (2) it unreasonably burdens interstate commerce; (3) it violates the rights of multistate taxpayers under the Fourteenth

Amendment; and (4) its audit provisions violate the Fourth and Fourteenth Amendments. Appellants sought a declaratory judgment that the Compact is invalid and a permanent injunction barring its operation.

. . . [T]he District Court first rejected the contention that the Compact Clause requires congressional consent to every agreement between two or more States. The court cited *Virginia v. Tennessee,* 148 U.S. 503 (1893), and *New Hampshire v. Maine*, 426 U.S. 363 (1976), in support of its holding that consent is necessary only in the case of a compact that enhances the political power of the member States in relation to the Federal Government. The District Court found neither enhancement of state political power nor encroachment upon federal supremacy. Concluding that appellants' Commerce Clause, Fourth Amendment, and Fourteenth Amendment claims also lacked merit, the District Court granted summary judgment for appellees.

. . . .

Read literally, the Compact Clause would require the States to obtain congressional approval before entering into any agreement among themselves, irrespective of form, subject, duration, or interest to the United States. The difficulties with such an interpretation were identified by Mr. Justice Field in his opinion for the Court in *Virginia v. Tennessee*, *supra*. His conclusion that the Clause could not be read literally was approved in subsequent dicta,[9] but this Court did not have occasion expressly to apply it in a holding until our recent decision in *New Hampshire v. Maine*, *supra*.

Appellants urge us to abandon *Virginia v. Tennessee* and *New Hampshire v. Maine*, but provide no effective alternative other than a literal reading of the Compact Clause. At this late date, we are reluctant to accept this invitation to circumscribe modes of interstate cooperation that do not enhance state power to the detriment of federal supremacy. We have examined, nevertheless, the origin and development of the Clause, to determine whether history lends controlling support to appellants' position.

Article I, § 10, cl. 1, of the Constitution—the Treaty Clause declares: "No State shall enter into Any Treaty, Alliance or Confederation . . . ." Yet Art. I, § 10, cl. 3—the Compact Clause—permits the States to enter into "agreements" or "compacts," so long as congressional consent is obtained. The Framers clearly perceived compacts and agreements as differing from treaties. The records of the Constitutional Convention, however, are barren of any clue as to the precise contours of the agreements and compacts governed by the Compact Clause. This suggests that the Framers used the words "treaty," "compact," and "agreement" as terms of art, for which no explanation was required and with which we are unfamiliar. Further evidence that the Framers ascribed precise meanings to these words appears in contemporary commentary.

---

[9] E.g., *Wharton v. Wise*, 153 U.S. 155, 168–170 (1894); *North Carolina v. Tennessee*, 235 U.S. 1, 16 (1914).

Whatever distinct meanings the Framers attributed to the terms in Art. I, § 10, those meanings were soon lost. In 1833, Mr. Justice Story perceived no clear distinction among any of the terms. Lacking any clue as to the categorical definitions the Framers had ascribed to them, Mr. Justice Story developed his own theory. Treaties, alliances, and confederations, he wrote, generally connote military and political accords and are forbidden to the States. Compacts and agreements, on the other hand, embrace "mere private rights of sovereignty; such as questions of boundary; interests in land situate in the territory of each other; and other internal regulations for the mutual comfort and convenience of States bordering on each other." 2 J. Story, *Commentaries on the Constitution of the United States* § 1403. In the latter situations, congressional consent was required, Story felt, "in order to check any infringement of the rights of the national government."

The Court's first opportunity to comment on the scope of the Compact Clause, *Holmes v. Jennison*, 14 Pet. 540 (1840), proved inconclusive. Holmes had been arrested in Vermont on a warrant issued by Jennison, the Governor. The warrant apparently reflected an informal agreement by Jennison to deliver Holmes to authorities in Canada, where he had been indicted for murder. On a petition for habeas corpus, the Supreme Court of Vermont held Holmes' detention lawful. Although this Court divided evenly on the question of its jurisdiction to review the decision, Mr. Chief Justice Taney, in an opinion joined by Mr. Justice Story and two others, addressed the merits of Holmes' claim that Jennison's informal agreement to surrender him fell within the scope of the Compact Clause. Mr. Chief Justice Taney focused on the fact that the agreement in question was between a State and a foreign government. Since the clear intention of the Framers had been to cut off all communication between the States and foreign powers, he concluded that the Compact Clause would permit an arrangement such as the one at issue only if "made under the supervision of the United States * * * ." *Id.* at 578. In his separate opinion, Mr. Justice Catron expressed disquiet over what he viewed as Mr. Chief Justice Taney's literal reading of the Compact Clause, noting that it might threaten agreements between States theretofore considered lawful.

Despite Mr. Justice Catron's fears, courts faced with the task of applying the Compact Clause appeared reluctant to strike down newly emerging forms of interstate cooperation. For example, in *Union Branch R. Co. v. East Tennessee & G. R. Co.*, 14 Ga. 327 (1853), the Supreme Court of Georgia rejected a Compact Clause challenge to an agreement between Tennessee and Georgia concerning the construction of an interstate railroad. Omitting any mention of *Holmes v. Jennison*, the Georgia court seized upon Story's observation that the words "treaty, alliance, and confederation" generally were known to apply to treaties of a political character. Without explanation, the court transferred this description of the Treaty Clause to the Compact Clause, which it perceived as restraining the power of the States only with respect to agreements "which might limit, or infringe upon a full and complete execution by the General Government, of the powers intended to be delegated by the Federal Constitution * * * ." A broader prohibition could not have been intended, since it was unnecessary to protect the Federal Government. Unless this view was taken, said the court:

> "We must hold that a State, without the consent of Congress, can make no sort of contract, whatever, with another State. That it cannot sell to another state, any portion of public property, * * * though it may so sell to individuals. * * *
>
> "We can see no advantage to be gained by, or benefit in such a provision; and hence, we think it was not intended. *Id.* at 340.

It was precisely this approach that formed the basis in 1893 for Mr. Justice Field's interpretation of the Compact Clause in *Virginia v. Tennessee*. In that case, the Court held that Congress tacitly had assented to the running of a boundary between the two States. In an extended dictum, however, Mr. Justice Field took the Court's first opportunity to comment upon the Compact Clause since the neglected essay in *Holmes v. Jennison*. Mr. Justice Field, echoing the puzzlement expressed by Story 60 years earlier, observed:

> "The terms 'agreement' or 'compact' taken by themselves, are sufficiently comprehensive to embrace all forms of stipulation, written or verbal, and relating to all kinds of subjects; to those to which the United States can have no possible objection or have any interest in interfering with, as well as to those which may tend to increase and build up the political influence of the contracting states, so as to encroach upon or impair the supremacy of the United States, or interfere with their rightful management of particular subjects placed under their entire control." 148 U.S. at 517–518.

Mr. Justice Field followed with four examples of interstate agreements that could "in no respect concern the United States": (1) an agreement by one State to purchase land within its borders owned by another State; (2) an agreement by one State to ship merchandise over a canal owned by another; (3) an agreement to drain a malarial district on the border between two States; and (4) an agreement to combat an immediate threat, such as invasion or epidemic. As the Compact Clause could not have been intended to reach every possible interstate agreement, it was necessary to construe the terms of the Compact Clause by reference to the object of the entire section in which it appears:

> "Looking at the clause in which the terms 'compact' or 'agreement' appear, it is evident that the prohibition is directed to the formation of any combination tending to the increase of political power in the states, which may encroach upon or interfere with the just supremacy of the United States." *Id.* at 519.

Mr. Justice Field reiterated this functional view of the Compact Clause a year later in *Wharton v. Wise*, 153 U.S. 155 (1894).

Although this Court did not have occasion to apply Mr. Justice Field's test for many years, it has been cited with approval on several occasions. *Louisiana v. Texas*, 176 U.S. 1 (1900); *Stearns v. Minnesota*, 179 U.S. 223 (1900); *North Carolina v. Tennessee*, 235 U.S. 1 (1914). Moreover, several decisions of this Court have upheld a variety of interstate agreements effected through reciprocal legislation without congressional consent. E.g., *St. Louis & S. F. R. Co. v. James*, 161 U.S. 545 (1896); *Hendrick v. Maryland*, 235 U.S. 610 (1915); *Bode v. Barrett*, 344 U.S. 583 (1953); *New York v. O'Neill*, 359 U.S. 1, 79 (1959). While none of these cases explicitly applied the *Virginia v. Tennessee* test, they reaffirmed its underlying assumption: not all agreements between States are subject to the strictures of the Compact Clause. In *O'Neill*, for example, this Court upheld the Uniform Law to Secure the Attendance of Witnesses from Within or Without the State in Criminal Proceedings, which had been enacted in 41 States and Puerto Rico. That statute permitted the judge of a court of any enacting State to invoke the process of the courts of a sister State for the purpose of compelling the attendance of witnesses at criminal proceedings in the requesting State. Although no Compact Clause question was directly presented, the Court's opinion touched upon similar concerns:

> The Constitution did not purport to exhaust imagination and resourcefulness in devising fruitful interstate relationships. It is not to be construed to limit the variety of arrangements which are possible through the voluntary and cooperative actions of individual States with a view to increasing harmony within the federalism created by the Constitution. Far from being divisive, this legislation is a catalyst of cohesion. It is within the unrestricted area of action left to the States by the Constitution.

The reciprocal-legislation cases support the soundness of the *Virginia v. Tennessee* rule, since the mere form of the interstate agreement cannot be dispositive. Agreements effected through reciprocal legislation may present opportunities for enhancement of state power at the expense of the federal supremacy similar to the threats inherent in a more formalized "compact." Mr. Chief Justice Taney considered this point in *Holmes v. Jennison*, 14 Pet. at 573:

> Can it be supposed that the constitutionality of the act depends on the mere form of the agreement? We think not. The Constitution looked to the essence and substance of things, and not to mere form. It would be but an evasion of the constitution to place the question upon the formality with which the agreement is made.

The Clause reaches both "agreements" and "compacts," the formal as well as the informal. The relevant inquiry must be one of impact on our federal structure.

This was the status of the *Virginia v. Tennessee* test until two Terms ago, when we decided *New Hampshire v. Maine*, 426 U.S. 363 (1976). In that case we specifically applied the test and held that an interstate agreement locating an ancient boundary did not require congressional consent. We reaffirmed Mr. Justice Field's view that the "application of the Compact Clause is limited to agreements that are 'directed to the formation of any combination tending to the increase of political power in the States, which may encroach upon or interfere with the just supremacy of the United States.'" *Id.* at 369, quoting *Virginia v. Tennessee*, 148

U.S. at 519. This rule states the proper balance between federal and state power with respect to compacts and agreements among States.

Appellants maintain that history constrains us to limit application of this rule to bilateral agreements involving no independent administrative body. They argue that this Court never has upheld a multilateral agreement creating an active administrative body with extensive powers delegated to it by the States, but lacking congressional consent. It is true that most multilateral compacts have been submitted for congressional approval. But this historical practice, which may simply reflect considerations of caution and convenience on the part of the submitting States, is not controlling. It is also true that the precise interstate mechanism involved in this case has not been presented to this Court before. *New York v. O'Neill*, *supra*, however, involving analogous multilateral arrangements, stands as an implicit rejection of appellants' proposed limitation of the *Virginia v. Tennessee* rule.

Appellants further urge that the pertinent inquiry is one of potential, rather than actual, impact upon federal supremacy. We agree. But the multilateral nature of the agreement and its establishment of an ongoing administrative body do not, standing alone, present significant potential for conflict with the principles underlying the Compact Clause. The number of parties to an agreement is irrelevant if it does not impermissibly enhance state power at the expense of federal supremacy. As to the powers delegated to the administrative body, we think these also must be judged in terms of enhancement of state power in relation to the Federal Government. *See Virginia v. Tennessee, supra*, at 520 (establishment of commission to run boundary not a "compact"). We turn, therefore, to the application of the *Virginia v. Tennessee* rule to the Compact before us.

On its face the Multistate Tax Compact contains no provisions that would enhance the political power of the member States in a way that encroaches upon the supremacy of the United States. There well may be some incremental increase in the bargaining power of the member States *quoad* the corporations subject to their respective taxing jurisdictions. Group action in itself may be more influential than independent actions by the States. But the test is whether the Compact enhances state power *quoad* the National Government. This pact does not purport to authorize the member States to exercise any powers they could not exercise in its absence. Nor is there any delegation of sovereign power to the Commission; each State retains complete freedom to adopt or reject the rules and regulations of the Commission. Moreover, each State is free to withdraw at any time.

. . . .

We conclude that appellants' constitutional challenge to the Multistate Tax Compact fails. We affirm the judgment of the District Court.

WHITE, JUSTICE, DISSENTING (WITH JUSTICE BLACKMUN):

. . . .

The Compact Clause, however, is directed to joint action by more than one State. If its only purpose in the present context were to require the consent of

Congress to agreements between States that would otherwise violate the Commerce Clause, it would have no independent meaning. The Clause must mean that some actions which would be permissible for individual States to undertake are not permissible for a group of States to agree to undertake.

There is much history from the Articles of Confederation to support that conclusion. In framing the Constitution the new Republic was at pains to correct the divisive factors of the Government under the Articles; and among the most important of these were "compacts witht. the consent of Congs. as between Pena. and N. Jersey, and between Virga. & Maryd." James Madison, "Preface to Debates in the Convention of 1787," 3 M. Farrand, Records of the Federal Convention of 1787, p. 548 (1937). A compact between two States necessarily achieved some object unattainable, or attainable less conveniently, by separate States acting alone. Such effects were jealously guarded against, lest "the Fedl authy [be] violated." It was the Federal Government's province to oversee conduct of a greater effect than a single State could accomplish, to protect both its own prerogative and that of the excluded States.

Compacts and agreements between States were put in a separate constitutional category, and purposefully so.

. . . .

One aspect of the *Virginia v. Tennessee* test for congressional approval of interstate compacts requires specific emphasis. The *Virginia v. Tennessee* opinion speaks of whether a combination tends "to the increase of political power in the states, which may encroach upon or interfere with the just supremacy of the United States," 148 U.S. at 519, and later, whether a compact or agreement would "encroach or not upon the full and free exercise of federal authority." *Id.* at 520.

The majority properly notes that any agreement among the States will increase their power, and focuses on the critical question of whether such an increase will enhance "state power quoad the National Government." [434 U.S.] at 473. A proper understanding of what would encroach upon federal authority, however, must also incorporate encroachments on the authority and power of non-Compact States.

In *Rhode Island v. Massachusetts*, 12 Pet. 657 (1838), this Court held that the purpose of requiring the submission to Congress of a compact (in that case, regarding a boundary) between two States was "to guard against the derangement of their federal relations with the other states of the Union, and the federal government; which might be injuriously affected, if the contracting states might act upon their boundaries at their pleasure." *See also Florida v. Georgia*, 17 How. 478 (1855). There is no want of authority for the conclusion that encroachments upon non-compact States are as seriously to be guarded against as encroachments upon the federal authority, nor is that surprising in view of the Federal Government's pre-eminent purpose to protect the rights of one State against another. If the effect of a compact were to put non-Compact States at a serious disadvantage, the federal interest would thereby be affected as well.

The majority appears to recognize that allegations of harmful impact on other States is a cognizable challenge to a compact. *See* [434 U.S.] at 477–478, 462–463, n.12. The response the majority opinion provides is by now a familiar one: "Each member State is free to adopt the auditing procedures it thinks best, just as it could if the Compact did not exist." [434 U.S.] at 477–478. The criticism of this reasoning offered above, in the context of encroachment on federal power, is applicable here as well. Judging by effect, not form, it is obvious that non-Compact States can be placed at a competitive disadvantage by the Multistate Tax Compact.

. . . .

The Compact Clause is an important, intended safeguard within our constitutional structure. It is functionally a conciliatory rather than a prohibitive clause. All it requires is that Congress review interstate agreements that are capable of affecting federal or other States' rights. In the Court's decision today, a highly complex multistate compact, detailed in structure and pervasive in its effect on the important area of interstate and international business taxation, has been legitimized without the consent of Congress. If the Multistate Tax Compact is not a compact within the meaning of Art. I, § 10, then I fear there is very little life remaining in that section of our Constitution.

Notes & Questions

1. The majority recites the rule from *Virginia v. Tennessee* and *Wharton v. Wise*—that consent is necessary when a compact would "tend to the increase of political power in the states, which may encroach upon or interfere with the just supremacy of the United States." 434 U.S. at 467–68.

Note that the majority seemed to believe that the basis for the Supreme Court's decision in *Virginia v. Tennessee* came from *Union Branch R.R. Co. v. E. Tenn. & Ga. R.R. Co.*, 14 Ga. 327 (1853), in which the Georgia Supreme Court opined (without explanation) that "[the Compact Clause restrained] the power of the States only with respect to agreements 'which might limit, or infringe upon a full and complete execution by the General Government, of the powers intended to be delegated by the Federal Constitution.'" Are you surprised that a state Supreme Court may have been the first court to opine that the Compact Clause does not require consent for all compacts? Justice White's dissent, however, suggested that the basis for *Virginia v. Tennessee* came from *Rhode Island v. Massachusetts*, 37 U.S. (12 Pet.) 657 (1838).

2. Justice White's dissent also points out that a compact needs consent when the effect of the compact would put non-compacting states at a disadvantage. This rule also has a long history, but interestingly, is not often cited. Justice White cited *Florida v. Georgia*, 58 U.S. (17 How.) 478 (1855), in which the Court stated,

> And if Florida and Georgia had, by negotiation and agreement, proceeded to adjust this boundary, any compact between them would have been null and void, without the assent of congress. This provision is obviously intended to guard the rights and interests of the other States, and to prevent

> any compact or agreement between any two States, which might affect injuriously the interest of the others. And the right and the duty to protect these interests is vested in the general government."

Id. at 494. Reread the excerpt from the dissent in *Seattle Master Builders* in Chapter 1. Would Justice White have been concerned that the Northwest Power and Conservation Planning Council compact in that case could have been created by only three of four eligible states, or that the interstate Council makes plans that guide Bonneville Power Administration (a federal agency) actions in eight states?

In *Northeast Bancorp* (excerpted in Chapter 1), the Supreme Court also noted the need for consent when a compact could affect non-compacting states: "We do not see how the statutes in question either enhance the political power of the New England States at the expense of other States or have an "impact on our federal structure." *Ne. Bancorp, Inc. v. Bd. of Governors of the Fed. Reserve Sys.*, 472 U.S. 159, 176 (1985). Justice Rehnquist also mentioned this need in his dissent in *Cuyler v. Adams,* 449 U.S. 433 (1981), a case excerpted in Chapter 5: "As with the 'compact' in *Multistate Tax Comm'n*, any State is free to join the Detainer Agreement, so it cannot be considered to elevate member states at the expense of nonmembers." *Id.* at 451.

3. Many cases have considered whether a specific agreement between states constituted a compact that would need consent. For example, cases involving the Master Settlement Agreement (MSA) between 52 Attorneys General and several tobacco companies all concluded that the Agreement did not violate the Compact Clause. In *VIBO Corp. v. Conway*, 594 F. Supp. 2d 758 (W.D. Ky. 2009), the plaintiff argued, "The MSA encroaches on federal power by regulating interstate commerce through the establishment of a complex national tax and regulatory scheme; regulating access to the national cigarette market; and encroaching on federal supremacy with respect to antitrust laws. The plaintiff asserts that as a result of the MSA, the Settling States have enlarged their collective power and influence at the expense of the federal government." *Id.* at 785–86. The court applied *U.S. Steel* and concluded otherwise, stating,

> [just because] the effectiveness of each state's individual agreement is increased because fifty-one other states or territories made an identical agreement does not mean that the federal government's power has suffered a concomitant decrease. Such a conclusion implies that the amount of power and influence in the United States is fixed and that the increase of a state's power must necessarily imply a decrease in federal power.

Id. at 786. The court did not address whether the increase in the power of the states and territories that are parties to the agreement was at the expense of those that were not parties to the agreement such that the agreement might have needed congressional consent. In *PTI, Inc. v. Philip Morris, Inc.*, 100 F. Supp. 2d 1179 (C.D. Cal. 2000), the court concluded that the Master Settlement Agreement was not a compact that required congressional consent because it did not "purport to authorize the member States to exercise any powers they could not exercise in its absence." *Id.* at 1198. In *Star Scientific, Inc. v. Beales*, 278 F.3d 339 (4th Cir. 2002), the court concluded that the Master Settlement Agreement between states and tobacco companies did not implicate any political interests of the federal government in violation of the Compact Clause.

In *Dixie Wholesale Grocery, Inc. v. Martin*, 278 Ky. 705 (1939), the Court concluded, "A mere reading of [the Compact Clause] shows conclusively it has no application to such reciprocal agreement as has been entered into between Kentucky and Ohio in an effort to keep their respective [cigarette] tax laws from being evaded." *Id.* at 711. In *Bode v. Barrett*, 412 Ill. 204 (1952), the Court similarly concluded that a reciprocity provision in a motor vehicle tax statute did not constitute a compact with another state, noting

> that the Federal constitutional interdiction of 'interstate compacts' was written into the organic law of the land in order to protect a then nascent republic from such *ententes* among powerful States as would aggrandize their political power at the expense or the compromise of national sovereignty. The provision does not inhibit those purely fiscal interstate agreements that facilitate interstate commerce and aid in execution of internal revenue policies. This is particularly true when such agreements conduce to, rather than restrain, commerce among the several States.

Id. at 232–33. In *Gray v. North Dakota Game and Fish Dept.*, 706 N.W.2d 614, 622 (N.D. 2005), the North Dakota Supreme Court held that the Interstate Wildlife Violator Compact did not require congressional consent because it did not interfere with the just supremacy of the United States. In *State v. Kurt*, 802 S.W.2d 954, 955 (Mo. 1991), the Missouri Supreme Court concluded that the Nonresident Violator Compact regarding reciprocal enforcement of out-of-state traffic citations did not require congressional consent because it does not threaten an exclusive prerogative of the United States. In *Tichenor v. Missouri State Lottery Comm'n*, 742 S.W.2d 170, 176 (Mo. 1988) (the court concluded that a multistate gaming agreement did not require congressional consent). In *Town of Searsburg v. Town of Woodford*, 76 Vt. 370 (1904), the Vermont Supreme Court noted, "the running of a boundary may have no effect upon the political influence of either state; it may simply serve to mark and define that which actually existed before, but was undefined and unmarked." *Id.* at 373. In *Ham v. Maine-New Hampshire Interstate Bridge Auth.*, 92 N.H. 268 (1943), the court summarily concluded that the compact at issue authorizing a bi-state bridge authority did not encroach on federal authority and thus did not require consent.

4. Where courts conclude that a particular agreement is a compact that requires, but does not have, congressional consent, they may conclude the agreement is void. *See, e.g.*, *Sauer v. Nixon*, No. 14AC-CC00477, 2015 WL 4474833 (Mo. Cir. Ct. Cole Cty. Feb. 24, 2015), *appeal dismissed as moot*, 474 S.W.3d 624 (Mo. Ct. App. 2015).

5. Recall that reciprocity is one of the factors that the Supreme Court stated in *Northeast Bancorp* was a "classic indicia of a compact." The *Dixie Wholesale Grocery* and *Bode v. Barrett* cases in note 3 both involved fiscal reciprocal arrange-

ments, but the states' supreme courts specifically conclude those reciprocal arrangements were not compacts? Why would a fiscal arrangement not constitute a compact?

6. In *U.S. Steel*, the majority stated, "Agreements effected through reciprocal legislation may present opportunities for enhancement of state power at the expense of the federal supremacy similar to the threats inherent in a more formalized 'compact.'" 434 U.S. at 470. If the presence of a "more formalized compact" does not matter for the purpose of consent, then for what purpose does it matter? Is it related to reciprocity? Can states create a reciprocal obligation without creating a binding agreement?

Nearly 40 years after *U.S. Steel*, several state supreme courts concluded that the Multistate Tax Compact was not a binding compact in part because it did not involve a reciprocal obligation. *See Gillette Co. v. Franchise Tax Bd.*, 62 Cal. 4th 468, 478–79 (2015); *Graphic Packaging Corp. v. Hegar*, 538 S.W.3d 89, 102 (Tex. 2017); *Health Net, Inc. v. Dep't of Revenue*, 362 Or. 700, 716–17 (2018). Article VI(4)(b) of the Multistate Tax Compact requires the Multistate Tax Commission to present to member states a recommended assessment for each state to pay to maintain the commission. If the states refused to pay the assessment, then the commission could not function. Is this a reciprocal obligation? Is it a "purely fiscal arrangement" as discussed in note 5? Does not mandating payment in the compact suggest the Multistate Tax Compact is not binding? The Multistate Tax Compact, in articles III and IV, also specifies that the states must offer taxpayers (mostly multistate corporations) an election for determining how to apportion their multistate income. Is this a reciprocal obligation? Consider that one purpose of this election is to ensure that the member states do not compete for businesses by enticing them to move from state to state by offering lower tax formulas.

Interestingly, Proctor and Gamble (a co-plaintiff in the *Gillette* case) and I.B.M. were both plaintiffs in *U.S. Steel*. Recall *U.S. Steel* involved the question of whether the compact required consent. In that case, these companies argued that the compact was not enforceable because it required but had not received consent. Conversely, in the *Gillette* and *I.B.M.* cases, these companies argued that the compact is binding and enforceable despite not receiving consent.

7. Can coordinated action without any agreement between the states ever be considered an interstate compact? In *Abrams v. Trans World Airline, Inc.*, 728 F. Supp. 162 (S.D.N.Y. 1989), the court concluded that New York's application of guidelines adopted by the National Association of Attorneys General providing a recommended "safe harbor" for airline advertising did not fall within the Compact Clause because New York had independent authority to regulate airline advertising concurrent with federal regulation, and thus there was no encroachment on the authority of the federal government. The court did not discuss that there was no actual agreement between the states. In *Sauer v. Nixon*, No. 14AC-CC004477, 2015 WL 4474833 (Mo. Cir. Ct. Cole Cty. Feb. 24, 2015), the court concluded that the Smarter Balance Assessment Consortium "is an unlawful interstate compact to which the U.S. Congress has never consented [and] whose existence and operation violate the Compact Clause of the U.S. Constitution . . .

." On appeal, the Governor of Missouri argued that the Consortium is not an agreement between the states, but a research program housed at the University of California by which states participated through a memorandum of understanding between a state and the university. The Missouri Court of Appeals dismissed the case as moot after Missouri stopped funding its participation in the Consortium. *Sauer v. Nixon*, 474 S.W.3d 624 (Mo. Ct. App. 2015).

8. Should a compact need consent if the federal government is a party to the compact? Chapter 4 discusses several compacts in which the federal government has enacted a compact and is a voting member of a compact agency. Does the federal government's enactment of and participation in a compact constitute implied consent?

9. The Court rejected U.S. Steel's argument that, "history constrains us to limit application of [the *Virginia v. Tennessee*] rule to bilateral agreements involving no independent administrative body." How are bilateral compacts without independent agencies materially different from multilateral agreements or agreements that create independent agencies? The Court noted that most multilateral compacts have been submitted for congressional consent, but that practice, "may simply reflect considerations of caution and convenience on the part of the submitting States, [and] is not controlling." 434 U.S. at 471. Should parties seek consent regardless of whether consent is constitutionally required? Does the Constitution permit this? One party to the Southern Regional Education Compact suggested as much to Congress.

> I see, as I have said, no infringement of Federal prerogatives in any sense of the word in this educational objective. However, there is in the Federal Constitution, language which would tend to indicate that compacts of all kinds between the several States should be approved by the Congress.
>
> Now, the fact that the Supreme Court has subsequently said that that does not mean all compacts, that means those compacts which relate to Federal duties, powers, and prerogatives, raises the question in a number of minds, and we think the orderly and the sensible procedure is to comply with the letter of the Constitution and seek congressional approval of the compact. If would serve to identify this as an entity, and it would serve to set out the boundaries within which it may operate, and it will answer all questions. It is highly desirable that the Congress approve the compact.

Regional Education Interstate Compact: Hearing on S.J. Res. 191 Before a Subcomm. of the Comm. on the Judiciary of the U.S. Senate, 80th Cong. 6 (1948) (Statement of Millard F. Caldwell, Governor, State of Florida). What would be the effect of Congress giving consent to a compact when consent is unnecessary? Much of compact law and many "benefits" of compacts flow from consent, so there may be some incentives for states to seek consent. Chapter 5 considers this question.

In the congressional hearing cited above, some senators also argued that consent would be looked upon as an endorsement of segregated education. Congress never gave its consent, but also never rejected the compact. This debate was well known at the time, even garnering a mention in a law review book note. Book

Note, 68 HARV. L. REV. 567, 568 (1954) (reviewing Vincent V. Thursby, *Interstate Cooperation: A Study of the Interstate Compact* (1953)). Should Congress consider all compacts and affirmatively determine when one does not need consent?

10. The Court noted that the states did not delegate any of their sovereign power to the Multistate Tax Commission. The Multistate Tax Compact authorizes the Multistate Tax Commission to have only an advisory and administration role. But, as noted in note 6 above, articles III and IV of the Multistate Tax Compact also specify the states must offer taxpayers (mostly multistate corporations) an election for determining how to apportion their multistate income. Did the party states delegate some of their individual sovereign powers to each other in articles III and IV? Should Congress have to grant consent when states delegate some of their sovereign power to an interstate agency or to each other? Chapter 3 considers this concept of shifting sovereignty inherent in compacts.

11. Following the U.S. District Court decision in *U.S. Steel* in 1976, but prior to the Supreme Court decision in 1978, the Alabama Legislature deleted the requirement for consent from its codification of the Multistate Tax Compact. In a later case, the Alabama Department of Revenue argued that the deletion was not an effective repeal, the requirement for consent still existed, and the MTC was not effective in Alabama because there had been no consent. The Alabama Court of Civil Appeals disagreed, concluding that the repeal was effective, and the tax compact became effective without congressional approval. *Dep't of Revenue v. MGH Mgmt, Inc.*, 627 So. 2d 408 (Ala. 1993).

12. Scholars have suggested different tests for determining when compacts require congressional consent. One scholar suggested focusing on the subject matter of the compact and "that courts exempt from the requirement of congressional consent only compacts that lie squarely within the realm of traditional state concern." Matthew Pincus, *When Should Interstate Compacts Require Congressional Consent?*, 42 COLUM. J.L. & SOC. PROBS. 511, 537 (2009).

Another scholar suggested, "Once . . . a state agreement [between states in their official capacity as states, not in a proprietary or market participant capacity] has been shown to exist without congressional approval, a constitutional challenge for lack of congressional consent should succeed if the plaintiff makes a credible showing that the compact, reasonably construed, poses one of [four] risks—an exercise of powers concurrently possessed by the Congress; interstate externalities; cartelization; or agency problems, including a dilution of political accountability and a delegation of state legislative or executive power." Michael Greve, *Compacts, Cartels, and Congressional Consent*, 68 MO. L. REV. 285, 368 (2003). Note the first "risk" would hold compacts invalid if Congress could regulate the subject matter of the compact. How is this suggestion different from the suggestion in the Pincus article? Would either of these tests be easier to administer or more accurately reflect the relationship between the federal and state governments than the current test from *Virginia v. Tennessee* and *U.S. Steel*?

13. In the past, most compacts received consent; however, recently, states have been enacting many professional licensing compacts that do not. Consider

whether compacts that have not received consent could or should have a role in the states as broad as compacts that have received consent.

14. Is consent related to the binding nature of compacts? In *Health Net v. Dep't of Revenue*, 362 Or. 700 (2018), the Oregon Supreme Court suggested that the U.S. Supreme Court impliedly held in *U.S. Steel* that the Multistate Tax Compact was not a binding agreement.

> Although the Court's holding in *U.S. Steel Corp.* is limited to the Compact Clause, its reasoning reaches more broadly. As the Court described the rights and obligations created by the MTC, they resemble a uniform law rather than a contract among the states that enact it. As the Court recognized, the MTC does not create reciprocal obligations among the member states. . . .
>
> . . . Moreover, as the Court explained, in enacting the MTC, states do not delegate their sovereign power to a regulatory agency in return for binding rules that apply to multiple jurisdictions. Rather, the commission created by the MTC can only recommend rules, which member states are free to adopt or reject. In short, as the Court described the MTC, it resembles a uniform law, not a binding contract.

Id. at 713–14. Do you agree that the U.S. Supreme Court impliedly held the Multistate Tax Compact is not a binding agreement?

15. If the party states agree on a specific interpretation of a compact that received consent, should the states' interpretation of a compact require further congressional consent? Several cases have concluded not. In *North Carolina v. Tennessee*, 235 U.S. 1 (1914), the Supreme Court considered which of two determinations was the boundary between the states. The first, in 1790, was part of the cession act in which North Carolina ceded land to create the State of Tennessee. The second, in 1821, was pursuant to state acts appointing commissioners to settle the boundary line. In a subsequent dispute, Tennessee raised the issue of consent:

> But it is contended by Tennessee that if the commissioners located such line the location was a departure from the cession act and the act of Congress adopting it and that such line not having received the consent or sanction of Congress is invalid and in conflict with Article I, § 10, Clause 3 of the Federal Constitution providing that "No State shall, without the consent of Congress, . . . enter into any agreement or compact with another State," etc. If the fact of such departure could be conceded the conclusion might be disputed. *Virginia v. Tennessee*, 148 U.S. 503. But the fact cannot be conceded. The cession act is very general and necessarily demanded definition to satisfy the requirements of a boundary line, a line not only necessary to mark private property but political jurisdiction. This was realized and commissioners were appointed to run and settle the line exactly. Their work as executed was confirmed by the States.

Id. at 15–16. In *New Hampshire v. Maine*, 426 U.S. 363 (1976), the Supreme Court similarly concluded that a consent decree establishing the boundary line did not require consent, concluding, "neither State can be viewed as enhancing its power in any sense that threatens the supremacy of the Federal Government. The boundary defined by the proposed decree 'takes effect, not as an alienation of territory, but as a definition of the true and ancient boundary.'" *Id.* at 369–70.

16. The Compact Clause also requires congressional consent for agreements between a state and a foreign power. Yet, despite the apparent requirement for Congress to consent to all agreements between one of the United States and a foreign power, one scholar noted that Congress has consented to only few foreign compacts. Duncan B. Hollis, *The Elusive Foreign Compact*, 73 MO. L. REV. 1071, 1078 (2008). Professor Hollis further noted that

> . . . U.S. states have very active international agendas. Since North Carolina Governor Luther Hodges first led a gubernatorial trade mission to Western Europe in 1959, state engagements with foreign governments have risen dramatically. U.S. states now interact directly with foreign sovereigns and sub-national governments on a regular basis.
>
> These interactions have in turn produced hundreds of written agreements between U.S. states and foreign governmental entities. Finding these agreements poses a challenge; no centralized or coordinated reporting system exists and copies are often not made public. Still, the available evidence shows that in contrast with the limited scope of congressionally approved foreign compacts (cross-border bridges, fires, and emergencies), these foreign agreements cut a much broader swath in terms of parties, topics, and functions.

Id. at 1079. As one possible explanation why Congress acts on relatively few foreign compacts, Professor Hollis noted that the U.S. State Department, several scholars, and state officials invoke the *Virginia v. Tennessee* and *U.S. Steel* analysis for determining whether consent is needed, even though the U.S. Supreme Court has not applied that analysis for a foreign compact. *Id.* at 1088–91. Chapter 12 discusses compacts involving Canadian provincial governments and non-compact agreements between states and foreign powers.

17. The issue of consent has arisen in cases involving storied characters. For example, in *United States v. Flegenheimer*, 14 F. Supp. 584 (D.N.J. 1935), the court penned a strong statement explaining "the Constitution can have just nothing at all to do with a compact of extradition." *Id.* at 585. This case involved the notorious organized crime boss Dutch Schultz (born Arthur Flegenheimer), who had evaded a federal warrant issued by the U.S. District Court for the Southern District of New York by moving to (and not leaving) New Jersey for two years before turning himself in with his attorneys. Flegenheimer's attorneys informed the court that Flegenheimer was filing an affidavit of bias and prejudice because the court had made a record of the facts surrounding his surrender. The court rejected the bias and prejudice claim. The next day, "The Commission" (the organized crime governing body) shot and killed Flegenheimer at a tavern to prevent him from murdering a U.S. Attorney, which would have brought too much attention to organized crime. In an addendum to the original decision following his killing,

the court noted that the only reason Flegenheimer was in New Jersey was because his attorneys informed him that he could delay or avoid trial in the state where he was charged. The court referred an ethics complaint against Flegenheimer's attorneys to the American Bar Association and implored the states to ratify a compact or pass laws addressing extradition. In 1958, New Jersey became the first state to enact the Interstate Agreement on Detainers, a compact that facilitates interstate transfers of prisoners with warrants in other states and the federal government.

IV. Limits on the Federal Government After Consent

After Congress gives its consent to a compact, two questions commonly arise relating to the relationship between the compact and the federal government. The first question concerns whether consent limits the ability of the federal government to enact subsequent law that might affect the implementation of the compact. The first case excerpted below, *Riverside Irrigation Dist. v. Andrews*, contains a brief discussion of this question, and in doing so, demonstrates the importance of carefully framing arguments in a case. The second question concerns whether consent alters the responsibilities of the federal government under existing federal law that relates to the subject matter of the compact. The second case, *Universal Interpretive Shuttle Corp v. Wash. Metro. Area Transit Auth.*, tersely addressed this, but consider whether the facts in that case fairly presented the question.

Riverside Irrigation Dist. v. Andrews

568 F. Supp. 583 (D. Colo. 1983)

KANE, JR., JUDGE

This case involves the plaintiff's construction of an earth-fill dam on Wildcat Creek in Colorado. Wildcat Creek is a tributary of the South Platte River, which is a tributary of the Missouri River, a navigable water of the United States. Because the construction of the dam involves the placement of fill material into a tributary of navigable waters of the United States, § 404 of the Clean Water Act, applies.

. . . .

The plaintiff's final argument is that defendant's action was improper because of the South Platte Compact. They argue that congress could not pass a clean water act that would impair this previously approved compact. This argument should be rejected. It is true that congress cannot unilaterally reserve the right to amend or repeal an interstate compact. *Tobin v. United States*, 306 F.2d 270, 273 (D.C. Cir. 1962). This does not mean, however, that approving a compact limits congress's authority to enact federal laws. In *Pennsylvania v. Wheeling [Bridge Co.,* 59 U.S. (18 How.) 421, 433 (1856)], the court held:

> The question here is, whether or not the compact can operate as a restriction upon the power of congress under the constitution to regulate commerce among the several states? Clearly not. Otherwise congress and

the two States would possess the power to modify and alter the constitution itself.

A subsequent federal law of nationwide applicability will therefore be enforceable even if it affects a prior compact. Congress therefore did not limit its ability to enact the Clean Water Act when it approved the South Platte Compact.

Resolution of this case depends largely on its characterization. If the case is characterized as an attempt by the defendant to condemn the plaintiffs' Colorado water rights, then the plaintiffs should obviously prevail. On the other hand, if the case is characterized as an attempt by the defendant to exercise federal police power in a manner required by federal statutes, then the defendant should prevail, even if his actions affect the plaintiffs' exercise of their water rights. For the reasons set out above, I believe that the latter characterization is preferable, and that the defendant's actions were a proper exercise of federal police power, even though they will clearly affect the plaintiffs' exercise of their water rights. I must limit my decision to the propriety of the exercise of such power. Whether it is prudent to vest such power is a political question which must be addressed to congress not the courts.

Notes & Questions

1. Does the court's citation to *Pennsylvania v. Wheeling Bridge Co.* remind you of Judge Beezer's dissent in *Seattle Master Builders* (excerpted in Chapter 1)—questioning whether a compact agency can legitimately control the acts of a federal agency?

2. Note that the district court held that Congress could enact "a subsequent federal law of nationwide applicability" even if that law could affect a compact. Chapter 8 discusses restrictions on the states enacting legislation that conflict with a compact. If the states cannot enact new legislation that affects a compact, then should Congress be able to enact broadly applicable legislation that may have the effect of unilaterally amending or altering states' or its own obligations under a compact?

Riverside Irrigation does not follow the more commonly held understanding that Congress may legislate without restriction even when that legislation would conflict with a compact. *See* MICHAEL L. BUENGER, ET AL., THE EVOLVING LAW AND USE OF INTERSTATE COMPACTS 89–93 (2d ed. 2016) (citing *Arizona v. California*, 373 U.S. 546 (1963). In *Arizona v. California*, the Court concluded that Congress could create a comprehensive scheme for managing the Colorado River notwithstanding its prior consent to the Colorado River Compact, but also suggested there was no conflict between the federal legislation and the compact. *Id.* at 565–67.

Congress has enacted many laws that directly modify or effectively abrogate compacts. For example, in *Pennsylvania v. Wheeling Bridge Co.*, the Court upheld a federal statute that declared the bridges across the Ohio River to be lawful structures despite Congress's previous consent to the Virginia-Kentucky Compact (the same compact at issue in *Green v. Biddle*), in which the states agreed the river "shall be free and common to the citizens of the United States." In another example, the National Labor Relations Act mostly superseded the Compact for Establishing Uniform Standards for Conditions of Employment, Particularly with Regard to the Minimum Wage (also known as the "Concord Compact"). The text of the Concord Compact is reprinted in 8 SOC. SERV. REV. 597–602 (1934).

Federal agencies may also retain their regulatory authority in policy areas where states have enacted a compact. For example, in *Intermountain Municipal Gas Agency v. FERC*, 326 F.3d 1281 (D.C. Cir. 2003), a case involving Congress's express exemption of intrastate transactions from the coverage under the Natural Gas Act, the D.C. Circuit affirmed a determination by the Federal Energy Regulatory Commission that Utah and Arizona could not by interstate agreement create a mutual governing entity to avoid regulations under the Natural Gas Act.

3. Would a subsequent federal law aimed specifically at a compact violate the Tenth Amendment? In 2002, Congress enacted the Standards Act, Pub. L. No. 107-217, § 1, 116 Stat. 1291 (2002), the purpose of which was to adopt standards governing arbitrations "resolving disputes involving interstate compact agencies operating in the national capitol area in order to lower costs for public transportation in the Washington metropolitan area." 40 U.S.C. § 18301(b). Effectively, this applies only to the Washington Metropolitan Area Transit Authority created by the Washington Metropolitan Area Transit Regulation Compact. In *Wash. Metro. Area Transit Auth. v. Local 2, Office & Prof'l Emps. Int'l Union*, 965 F. Supp. 2d 13 (D.D.C. 2013), following a series of arbitrations in which the Transit Authority sought review of the arbitration awards, the unions argued that the Standards Act violated the Tenth Amendment by amending the Transit Compact without the consent or ratification of the signatory states. The court avoided this legal question. Chapter 3 discusses requirements to amend compacts. The Standards Act also changed how courts should apply the arbitrary and capricious standard of review in the federal APA. Does changing the manner in which courts review a compact agency's actions impermissibly modify the compact?

4. Note also that in *Riverside Irrigation Dist.*, the court cited to *Tobin*, stating, "It is true that congress cannot unilaterally reserve the right to amend or repeal an interstate compact." Was the D.C. Circuit's decision in *Tobin* so absolute?

5. Congress sometimes expressly specifies that a compact may not conflict with federal law. For example, Congress's broad consent to forest and water supply compacts states:

> Consent of the Congress of the United States is given to each of the several States of the Union to enter into any agreement or compact, not in conflict with any law of the United States, with any other State or States for the purpose of conserving the forests and the water supply of the States entering into such agreement or compact.

16 U.S.C. § 552. Should a conflict be evaluated only at the point in time that Congress grants its consent, or does the phrase, "not in conflict with any law of the United States," suggest that compacts enacted pursuant to this authorization

could become void if, in the future, Congress enacts a law that conflicts with those compacts?

6. Congress may also specify that new federal laws avoid conflicts with existing compacts to which Congress has previously granted consent. For example, in the Flood Control Act of 1960, Pub. L. No. 86-645, § 203, 74 Stat. 480, 493, Congress authorized the Army Corps of Engineers to construct the Middle Rio Grande Project and other projects and required that the operations of the project could not interfere with the Rio Grande Compact (and any deviation required the consent of the Rio Grande Compact Commission).

7. What do you think about the statement in *Riverside Irrigation Dist.* that resolution of the case depends on how the case is characterized? If courts routinely characterize cases as an exercise of federal police power, then wouldn't compacts always be susceptible to federal preemption? You will read more about conflicts between compacts and federal law in Chapters 5 and 8.

Universal Interpretive Shuttle Corp. v. Wash. Metro Area Transit Comm'n

393 U.S. 186 (1968)

WHITE, JUSTICE:

The Secretary of the Interior is responsible for maintaining our national parks, and for providing facilities and services for their public enjoyment through concessionaires or otherwise. In meeting this responsibility, he has contracted for petitioner to conduct guided tours of the Mall, a grassy park located in the center of the City of Washington and studded with national monuments and museums. Visitors to the Mall may board petitioner's open "minibuses" which travel among the various points of interest at speeds under 10 miles per hour. Guides on the bases and at certain stationary locations describe the sights. Visitors may debark to tour the museums, boarding a later bus to return to the point of departure.

Suit was brought by the Washington Metropolitan Area Transit Commission (hereafter WMATC) to enjoin petitioner from conducting tours of the Mall without a certificate of convenience and necessity from the WMATC. Carriers permitted by WMATC to provide mass transit and sightseeing services in the City of Washington intervened as plaintiffs, and the United States appeared as amicus curiae. The concessionaire and the United States contend that the Secretary's authority over national park lands, and in particular his grant of "exclusive charge and control" over the Mall dating from 1898, permit him to contract for this service without interference. The carriers and WMATC argue that the interstate compact which created the WMATC implicitly limited the Secretary's authority over the Mall, and gave rise to dual jurisdiction over these tours in the Secretary and the WMATC. One carrier, D.C. Transit System, Inc., also argues that its franchise limits the Secretary's power. In a detailed opinion the District Court dismissed the suit. The Court of Appeals reversed without opinion. We granted certiorari and, having heard the case and examined the web of statutes on which it turns, we reverse, finding the Secretary's exclusive authority to contract for services on the Mall undiminished by the compact creating WMATC or by the charter granted a private bus company.

That the Secretary has substantial power over the Mall is undisputed. The parties agree that he is free to enter into the contract in question. They also agree that he is free to exclude traffic from the Mall altogether, or selectively to exclude from the Mall any carrier licensed by the WMATC or following WMATC instructions. Moreover, the parties agree that the Secretary could operate the tour service himself without need to obtain permission from anyone. Yet the WMATC argues that before the Secretary's power may be exercised through a concessionaire, the consent of the WMATC must be obtained.

This interpretation of the statutes involved would result in a dual regulatory jurisdiction overlapping on the most fundamental matters. The Secretary is empowered by statute to "contract for services * * * provided in the national parks * * * for the public * * * as may be required in the administration of the National Park Service * * * ." 16 U. S. C. § 17b. Moreover, he is "to encourage and enable private persons and corporations * * * to provide and operate facilities and services which he deems desirable * * * ." 16 U. S. C. § 20a (1964 ed., Supp. III). [Through hearings on numerous bills,] Congress was well aware that the services provided by these national park concessionaires include transportation. In this case the Secretary concluded that there was a public need for a motorized, guided tour of the grounds under his control, and that petitioner was most fit to provide it.

The WMATC, however, also asserts the power to decide whether this tour serves "public convenience and necessity," and the power to require the concessionaire to "conform to the * * * requirements of the Commission" and the "terms and conditions" which it may impose. The Secretary's contract leaves the tour's route under his control, but the WMATC would in its certificate specify the "service to be rendered and the routes over which" the concessionaire might run within the Mall. Moreover, the WMATC might require the provision of additional service on or off the Mall and forbid the discontinuance of any existing service. The contract with the Secretary provides fare schedules, pursuant to statutory authority in the Secretary to regulate the concessionaire's charges. The WMATC would have the power to "suspend any fare, regulation, or practice" depending on the WMATC's views of the financial condition, efficiency, and effectiveness of the concessionaire and the reasonableness of the rate. And under the same section the WMATC could set whatever fare it found reasonable, although a profit of 6 1/2% or less could not be prohibited. The Secretary is given statutory authority to require the keeping of records by the concessionaire and to inspect those records, and the Comptroller General is required to examine the concessionaire's books every five years. The WMATC would also have the power to require reports and to prescribe and have access to the records to be kept. Finally, the Secretary is given by statute the general power to specify by contract the duties of a concessionaire; the WMATC would claim this power by regulation and rule.

We cannot ascribe to Congress a purpose of subjecting the concessionaire to these two separate masters, who show at the outset their inability to agree by presence on the opposite sides of this lawsuit. There is no indication from statutory language or legislative history that Congress intended to divest the Secretary partly or wholly of his authority in establishing the WMATC. When the WMATC was formed there was in the statute books, as there is now, a provision that the "park system of the District of Columbia is placed under the exclusive charge and control of the Director of the National Park Service." He was, and is, explicitly "authorized and empowered to make and enforce all regulations for the control of vehicles and traffic." And this extends to sidewalks and streets which "lie between and separate the said public grounds." The creation of the Public Utilities Commission—the predecessor of the WMATC was not intended "to interfere with the exclusive charge and control * * * committed to" the predecessor of the National Park Service.

In this context the WMATC was established. After World War II, metropolitan Washington had expanded rapidly into Maryland and Virginia. The logistics of moving vast numbers of people on their daily round became increasingly complicated, and increasingly in need of coordinated supervision. Congress therefore gave its consent and approval through a joint resolution to an interstate compact which "centralizes to a great degree in a single agency * * * the regulatory powers of private transit now shared by four regulatory agencies." These four agencies were "the public utility regulatory agencies of the States of Virginia, Maryland, and the District of Columbia and the Interstate Commerce Commission." The Secretary was not included in this listing. Moreover, Congress specifically provided that nothing in the Act or compact "shall affect the normal and ordinary police powers * * * of the Director of the National Park Service with respect to the regulation of vehicles, control of traffic and use of streets, highways, and other vehicular facilities * * * ." Finally, the House Report on the compact lists the federal legislation which was suspended to give effect to the compact, and the laws giving exclusive control of the Mall to the Secretary are not on the list.

There is thus no reason to ignore the principle that repeals by implication are not favored or to suspect that the Congress, in creating the WMATC, disturbed the exclusivity of the Secretary's control over the Mall either by extinguishing entirely his power to contract for transportation services or by burdening the concessionaire with two separate agencies engaged in regulating precisely the same aspects of its conduct. Congress was endeavoring to simplify the regulation of transportation by creating the WMATC, not to thrust it further into a bureaucratic morass. It therefore established the WMATC to regulate the mass transit of commuters and workers. A system of minibuses, proceeding in a circular route around the Mall at less than 10 miles per hour, and stopping from time to time to describe the sights before disgorging more passengers where it picked them up, serves quite a different function. The Mall is, and was intended to be, an expansive, open sanctuary in the midst of a metropolis; a spot suitable for Americans to visit to examine the historical artifacts of their country and to reflect on monuments to the men and events of its history. The Secretary has long had exclusive control of the Mall and ample power to develop it for these purposes. We hold that the WMATC has not been empowered to impose its own regulatory requirements on the same subject matter.

. . . .

We reverse the judgment of the Court of Appeals and reinstate the judgment of the District Court. If the Congress, which has the matter before it, wishes to clarify or alter the relationship of these statutes and agencies, it is entirely free to do so.

Notes & Questions

1. The Court observed that Congress's consent specifically provided that it does not diminish the Secretary of the Interior's authority over the Mall. Why wasn't this sufficient to resolve the case? Why did the Court exhaustively distinguish between the Secretary of the Interior's authority and the Transit Commission's authority?

2. The Court also stated, "There is no indication from statutory language or legislative history that Congress intended to divest the Secretary partly or wholly of his authority in establishing the WMATC. When the WMATC was formed there was in the statute books, as there is now, a provision that the 'park system of the District of Columbia is placed under the exclusive charge and control of the Director of the National Park Service.'" 393 U.S. at 186. If the Court considers text and legislative history, then should the Court entertain an argument that a compact could disturb federal law? The relationship between a compact and federal law is discussed in Chapter 5.

3. Are the facts of this case like the facts in *Seattle Master Builders*, in which Judge Beezer would have held that the compact agency should not oversee the actions of a federal agency?

4. Should courts review conflicts between a compact and federal law under traditional conflict of laws principles, such as whether the federal statute or the compact was later in time, or which was more specific? What other conflict of laws factors might be relevant?

5. *Riverside Irrigation* and *Universal Interpretive Shuttle Corp.* both involved cases framed as the relationship between a compact and federal legislation. Should compacts with consent supersede federal regulations? What principles of law would you use to evaluate such a claim? What principles would you use to evaluate a claim of a conflict between a compact agency's regulations and a federal agency's regulations? Chapter 10 discusses administrative procedures that compact agencies use. Few use the federal administrative procedure act. Would that suggest that federal regulations supersede compact agency regulations?

CHAPTER 3: STATE AUTHORITY & ACTION

Early court decisions described a state's authority to enter into a compact as inherent, that is, it exists as a sovereign power limited only by the U.S. Constitution's requirement for consent. Later decisions mostly stopped questioning state authority. This chapter looks at that authority and some of the restrictions and limits on states after enacting a compact.

I. AUTHORITY OF STATES TO ENTER INTO COMPACTS

The *Green v. Biddle* excerpt in Chapter 2 considered whether Congress properly consented to the Kentucky-Virginia compact. Here, we read another short excerpt from *Green v. Biddle* addressing the authority under which the states entered into the compact. Following that, we read another short excerpt, from *Poole v. Lessee of Fleeger* in which the Supreme Court discussed the inherent right of states to fix their boundaries subject only to the Compact Clause.

Green v. Biddle
21 U.S. (8 Wheat.) 1 (1823)

STORY, JUSTICE:

. . . .

The next objection, which is to the validity of the particular clause of the compact involved in this controversy, rests upon a principle, the correctness of which remains to be proved. It is practically opposed by the theory of all limited governments, and especially of those which constitute this Union. The powers of legislation granted to the government of the United States, as well as to the several State governments, by their respective constitutions, are all limited. The article of the constitution of the United States, involved in this very case, is one, amongst many others, of the restrictions alluded to. If it be answered, that these limitations were imposed by the people in their sovereign character, it may be asked, was not the acceptance of the compact the act of the people of Kentucky in their sovereign character? If, then, the principle contended for be a sound one, we can only say, that it is one of a most alarming nature, but which, it is believed, cannot be seriously entertained by any American statesman or jurist.

Various objections were made to the literal construction of the compact, one only of which we deem it necessary particularly to notice. That was, that if it be so construed as to deny to the legislature of Kentucky the right to pass the act in question, it will follow, that that State cannot pass laws to affect lands, the title to which was derived under Virginia, although the same should be wanted for public use. If such a consequence grows necessarily out of this provision of the compact, still we can perceive no reason why the assent to it by the people of Kentucky should not be binding on the legislature of that State. Nor can we perceive, why the admission of the conclusion involved in the argument should invalidate an express article of the compact in relation to a quite different subject. The agreement, that the rights of claimants under Virginia should remain as valid and secure as they were under the laws of that State, contains a plain, intelligible proposition, about the meaning of which, it is impossible there can be two opinions. Can the government of Kentucky fly from this agreement, acceded to by the people in their sovereign capacity, because it involves a principle which might be inconvenient, or even pernicious to the State, in some other respect? The Court cannot perceive how this proposition could be maintained.

. . . .

Poole v. Lessee of Fleeger
36 U.S. (11 Pet.) 185 (1837)

STORY, JUSTICE:

[This case involved a claim to land that Kentucky had granted to one party in 1796 and that Tennessee and North Carolina had granted to several parties between 1786 and 1814. In 1820, Tennessee and Kentucky enacted a compact resolving a dispute over the location of their common border, which placed the land in Kentucky. The Court held that the grants made by North Carolina and Tennessee were not rightfully made, because pursuant to the 1820 compact, they were originally beyond her territorial boundary.]

. . . It cannot be doubted, that it is a part of the general right of sovereignty, belonging to independent nations, to establish and fix the disputed boundaries between their respective territories; and the boundaries so established and fixed by compact between nations, become conclusive upon all the subjects and citizens thereof, and bind their rights; and are to be treated, to all intents and purposes, as the true and real boundaries. This is a doctrine universally recognized in the law and practice of nations. It is a right equally belonging to the states of this Union; unless it has been surrendered under the constitution of the United States. So far from there being any pretence of such a general surrender of the right, that it is expressly recognized by the constitution, and guarded in its exercise by a single limitation or restriction, requiring the consent of congress. The constitution declares, that "no state shall; without the consent of congress, enter into any agreement or compact with another state;" thus plainly admitting that, with such consent, it might be done: and in the present instance, that consent has been expressly given. The compact then, has full validity, and all the terms and conditions of it must be equally obligatory upon the citizens of both states.

. . . .

Notes & Questions

1. The Supreme Court has discussed state sovereignty and compacts in many cases. In *Green v. Biddle*, Justice Story asked, perhaps rhetorically, "was not the acceptance of the compact the act of the people of Kentucky in their sovereign character?" 21 U.S. at 88. In *Poole v. Lessee of Fleeger*, Justice Story just asserted that enacting a compact is a right of a state's sovereignty. The following year, the

Court reaffirmed this in *Rhode Island v. Massachusetts*, 37 U.S. (12 Pet.) 657 (1838), stating, "If Congress consented, then the States were in this respect restored to their original inherent sovereignty; such consent being the sole limitation imposed by the Constitution . . . ." *Id.* at 725.

More recently, in *Hess v. Port Auth. Trans-Hudson Corp.*, 513 U.S. 30, 42 (1994), the Court stated, "An interstate compact, by its very nature shifts a part of a state's authority to another state or states, or to the agency the several states jointly create to run the compact." (citing MARIAN E. RIDGEWAY, INTERSTATE COMPACTS: A QUESTION OF FEDERALISM 300 (1971)).

2. Justice Scalia's dissent in *New Jersey v. Delaware*, 552 U.S. 597 (2008) explained how he analyzed claims that one state has contracted away or cannot contract away one of its sovereign powers.

> . . . One of Delaware's principal arguments—an argument accepted by the [Special] Master and implicitly accepted by the Court—is that the 1905 Compact must not be construed to limit Delaware's pre-Compact (albeit at the time unrecognized) sovereign control over the Delaware River, because of the "strong presumption against defeat of a State's title" in interpreting agreements. . . .
>
> I have written of this presumption elsewhere that it "has little if any independent legal force beyond what would be dictated by normal principles of contract interpretation. It is simply a rule of presumed (or implied-in-fact) intent." *United States v. Winstar Corp.*, 518 U.S. 839, 920 (1996) (opinion concurring in judgment). It is a manifestation of the commonsense intuition that a State will rarely contract away its sovereign power. That intuition is sound enough in almost all state dealings with private citizens, and in some state dealings with other States. It has no application here, however, because the whole purpose of the 1905 Compact was precisely to come to a compromise agreement on the exercise of the two States' sovereign powers. Entered into at a time when Delaware and New Jersey disputed the location of their boundary, the Compact demarcated the authority between the two States with respect to service of civil and criminal process on vessels, rights of fishery, and riparian rights on either side of the Delaware River within the circle of a 12-mile radius centered on the town of New Castle, Delaware. There is no way the Compact can be interpreted *other than* as a yielding by both States of what they claimed to be their sovereign powers. The only issue is *what* sovereign powers were yielded, and that is best determined from the language of the Compact, with no thumb on the scales.

552 U.S. at, 629–30 (emphasis in original).

3. In the early 2000s, states became more aware of the implications of thinking of compacts as a means of shifting or sharing sovereignty and state power in the several cases challenging states' repeals of Articles III and IV of the Multistate Tax Compact (mentioned in the notes following the *Northeast Bancorp* excerpt in

Chapter 1 and following the *U.S. Steel* excerpt in Chapter 2). As taxpayers challenged the states' repeals as invalid violations of the compact and violation of the Contract Clause in the U.S. Constitution, the states argued that the repeals were valid because state power to tax is a sovereign power that can only be contracted away in unmistakable terms. In several of the cases, the states' supreme courts concluded that the Multistate Tax Compact did not satisfy the unmistakability doctrine. *Kimberly-Clark Corp. v. Comm'r of Revenue*, 880 N.W.2d 844, 850 (Minn. 2016); *Graphic Packaging Corp. v. Hegar*, 538 S.W.3d 89, 104–05 (Tex. 2017); *Health Net, Inc. v. Dep't of Revenue*, 362 Or. 700, 716–29 (2018).

These are the first cases in which all the party states and the interstate commission argued that a compact was not binding. The cost to the states of complying with the compact probably explains the states' argument. If the taxpayers had prevailed in these cases, each of the states would have needed to issue hundreds of millions of dollars in refunds. California estimated that its potential refund claim liability alone might have exceeded $750 million. *See* Petition for Writ of Certiorari at 29, *Gillette Co. v. California Franchise Tax Bd.*, 137 S. Ct. 294 (2016) (No. 15-1442) (cert. denied). Will these decisions empower states to argue that other compacts are similarly not binding?

4. The concept of shifting sovereignty has a long history. Emmerich de Vattel, a political thinker from the mid-1700s wrote in his treatise about international relations, "[A]s soon as a right is transferred by a lawful convention, it no longer belongs to the state that has ceded it." Emmerich de Vattel, *The Law of Nations* book II, § 192 (1758). Scholars and others have used Vattel's work to help interpret the Compact Clause of the U.S. Constitution and understand the political relationships created by multistate agreements. For example, one article argued that "the constitutional distinction between 'treaties' and 'agreements' or 'compacts' was taken directly from" Vattel. David E. Engdahl, *Characterization of Interstate Arrangements: When is a Compact Not a Compact?*, 64 MICH. L. REV. 63, 76–84 (1965). Another article used Vattel's work to try to explain distinctions between the terms "treaty," "compact," and "agreement," all of which appear in the Compact Clause. Andrew A. Bruce, *The Compacts and Agreements of States*, 2 MINN. L. REV. 500, 505–06 (1919). As well, the Supreme Court has relied on Vattel's work, *e.g., U.S. Steel Corp. v. Multistate Tax Comm'n*, 434 U.S. 452, 462 n.12 (1978).

5. Territories of the United States and the District of Columbia are members of several compacts. What is the authority of territories and the District to join interstate compacts? In *Kerpen v. Metro. Wash. Airports Auth.*, 260 F. Supp. 3d 567 (E.D. Va. 2017), the plaintiff claimed that the compact creating the MWAA was invalid because the compact includes the District of Columbia, which is not a "state." Citing long-established Supreme Court precedent, the district court concluded there is "little doubt that Congress delegated to the District the power to enter into agreements with states generally." *Id.* at 576. This is the first case to raise the question whether the District of Columbia has the authority to join interstate compacts and there are no cases addressing the authority of territories to join compacts.

6. Are there limits on the authority of a state to enact a compact? The next case excerpt considered whether the Colorado legislature could delegate authority to an interstate commission to approve insurance products that conflicted with Colorado statutes.

Amica Life Ins. Co. v. Wertz

2020 CO 29, 462 P.3d 51 (Colo. 2020)

GABRIEL, JUSTICE

This case requires us to answer the following certified question from the Tenth Circuit Court of Appeals:

> May the Colorado General Assembly delegate power to an interstate administrative commission to approve insurance policies sold in Colorado under a standard that differs from Colorado statute?

The certified question arises from a dispute in which plaintiff Amica Life Insurance Company seeks a declaratory judgment that it is not required to pay defendant Michael P. Wertz benefits under a life insurance policy naming Wertz as the beneficiary. The policy, which was issued in compliance with a standard enacted by the Interstate Insurance Product Regulation Commission (the "Commission"), contained a two-year suicide exclusion, and the insured committed suicide more than one year but less than two years after Amica had issued the life insurance policy to him. Wertz contends, however, that the policy's two-year suicide exclusion is unenforceable because it conflicts with a Colorado statute, section 10-7-109, C.R.S. (2019), which provides:

> The suicide of a policyholder after the first policy year of any life insurance policy issued by any life insurance company doing business in this state shall not be a defense against the payment of a life insurance policy, whether said suicide was voluntary or involuntary, and whether said policyholder was sane or insane.

Wertz asserts that the Colorado General Assembly could not properly delegate to the Commission the authority to enact a standard that would effectively override this statute.

....

B. The Non-Delegation Doctrine

Of our three branches of government, only the General Assembly has the power to make law. See Colo. Const. art. III ("The powers of the government of this state are divided into three distinct departments, —the Legislative, Executive and Judicial; and no person or collection of persons charged with the exercise of powers properly belonging to one of these departments shall exercise any power properly belonging to either of the others, except as in this Constitution expressly directed or permitted."); id. at art. V, § 1(1) ("The legislative power of the state shall be vested in the general assembly. "); id. at art. V, § 17 ("No law shall be passed except by bill, and no bill shall be so altered or amended on its passage through either house as to change its original purpose.").

Accordingly, it has long been settled that the legislature may not delegate its legislative power to another agency or person.

This so-called non-delegation doctrine derives from the constitutional separation of powers. . . .

. . . .

The question before us requires us to apply the foregoing principles to decide whether the legislature's delegation to the Commission of the authority to create uniform standards properly included the authority to adopt the Standard at issue, which effectively overrides Colorado statutory law precluding an insurer doing business in this state from asserting suicide as a defense to payment on an insurance policy after the first year of that policy. We turn next to that question.

. . . .

In our view, delegating to the Commission the authority to adopt a Standard that so circumvents the clear language of section 10-7-109 is to confer legislative powers on the Commission, and pursuant to the authorities discussed above, the General Assembly may not properly do this. And this is so even though, under the Compact, the Colorado Commissioner of Insurance is a member of the Commission and may have voted in favor of the Standard. If the Commissioner believes that the Commission should enact a regulation that conflicts with Colorado statutory law, then he must request action from the Colorado General Assembly because only that body may legislatively override one of its own enactments.

In reaching this conclusion, we are not persuaded by Amica's and its amici's various arguments to the contrary. We address these arguments in turn.

First, we disagree with Amica's assertion that because the Compact provided a means for the General Assembly to opt out of any Standard enacted by the Commission, the legislature did not improperly delegate its legislative authority to the Commission. As an initial matter, we note that the facts here present a legitimate question as to whether the Compact's opt-out provisions were effective, given that the Commission could give notice of a proposed Standard and the Standard could take effect while the legislature was not in session. We need not address this question, however, because even if the opt-out provisions were effective, we have seen no applicable authority excusing an improper delegation of legislative authority merely because the legislature could adopt or reject an administrative agency's legislative action after the fact, and neither Amica nor its amici cite any such authority. Indeed, in our view, the General Assembly's after-the-fact opt-out could not excuse the Commission's improper legislative action here because the opt-out would apply only prospectively, thus leaving in place the improper Standard in the period between its adoption and the General Assembly's decision to opt out.

. . . .

Third, we are not persuaded that because the Standard only applies to Commission-approved policies, whereas section 10-7-109 would continue to apply to policies approved by the Colorado Commissioner of Insurance, the Commission's suicide-exclusion Standard does not conflict with the statute. As noted above, section 10-7-109 applies to "any life insurance policy issued by any life insurance company doing business in this state." Accordingly, whether approved by the Commission or by the Colorado Commissioner of Insurance, the statute applies as long as the policy was issued by an insurer doing business here. The Commission's suicide-exclusion Standard therefore conflicts with section 10-7-109.

Fourth, we reject Amica's contention that the interstate nature of the Commission here distinguishes this case from the above-described authorities regarding intrastate delegations of authority to administrative agencies. Although, to be sure, regulations adopted pursuant to an interstate compact can at times override conflicting state law, the cases that have so concluded have involved interstate compacts that were approved by acts of Congress, and these cases have relied on federal preemption or supremacy clause principles. *See, e.g., Frontier Ditch Co. v. Se. Colo. Water Conservancy Dist.*, 761 P.2d 1117, 1123 (Colo. 1988) (noting that the Compact at issue was part of federal law, having been approved by an act of Congress, and was thus preemptive of any conflicting state law on the same subject). These cases do not assist Amica here, however, because Congress has not approved the Compact at issue, and Amica cites no law supporting its apparent position that any interstate compact can supersede conflicting state law. To the contrary, all of the cases on which Amica relies to support its argument involved congressionally approved compacts and thus implicated federal preemption principles. *See, e.g., Port Auth. Trans-Hudson Corp. v. Feeney*, 495 U.S. 299, 301 (1990) (concerning a congressionally approved compact between New York and New Jersey); *State ex. rel Dyer v. Sims*, 341 U.S. 22, 24–25 (1951) (concerning a congressionally approved compact among eight states to control pollution in the Ohio River); *Hinderlider v. La Plata River & Cherry Creek Ditch Co.*, 304 U.S. 92, 95 (1938) (concerning a congressionally approved river compact between Colorado and New Mexico); *Frontier Ditch*, 761 P.2d at 1123 (concerning a congressionally approved river compact between Colorado and Kansas). Thus, we are not persuaded that the legislature has the authority to delegate to interstate agencies powers that it cannot constitutionally delegate to intrastate agencies.

Finally, we are unpersuaded by Amica's argument that our conclusion here would limit the effectiveness of interstate compacts that are not approved by Congress. In this case, we conclude only that, in the context of an interstate compact that has not been approved by Congress, the Colorado legislature may not delegate to an interstate administrative agency the power to adopt regulations that conflict with Colorado statutory law because under longstanding Colorado law, such a delegation amounts to the improper delegation of legislative power. We express no opinion on any other form of interstate compact.

. . . .

Notes & Questions

1. The Colorado Supreme Court answered a certified question from the U.S. Court of Appeals for the Tenth Circuit. The U.S. District Court judge also certified the question to the Colorado Supreme Court, which declined at that time to accept the question. In certifying the question, the U.S. District Court judge explained:

> . . . It is not difficult to imagine the Colorado Supreme Court applying analogous reasoning—or pragmatism more generally—to the Insurance Compact. In that light, the Court notes the following arguments potentially in favor of the Compact.
>
> First, it is obvious from the structure and stated purposes of the Compact that the Interstate Commission will promulgate Uniform Standards that conflict with some member states' existing statutes. In other words, given the Compact's primary goal of uniformity, conflict with existing statutes is to be expected. One might even say that conflict is invited by any state legislature choosing to ratify the Compact, so that the desired uniformity will result. And if invited, the Compact might be viewed as a legislature's pre-approval of any conflict, functionally equivalent to the legislature's choice to repeal any conflicting statute to the extent of the conflict. Moreover, the Colorado Legislature appointed a Colorado state official (the insurance commissioner) to participate in the process of making those potentially conflicting standards. Perhaps this is enough under the Colorado Constitution to justify the Insurance Compact.
>
> Second, the Insurance Compact's promulgation procedures may be highly relevant. The Insurance Compact requires the Colorado Legislature to receive notice of a proposed Uniform Standard before it becomes enforceable, and the Colorado Legislature may opt out of that Standard at any time, both before and after it goes into effect. Colorado's insurance commissioner can do the same by regulation. This could be analogized to similar arrangements that have been deemed permissible in other jurisdictions, such as under the federal Rules Enabling Act, where amendments to the federal rules of court are submitted to Congress by May 1 and become effective on December 1 if Congress fails to reject them. *See* 28 U.S.C. § 2074(a). Perhaps the Colorado Legislature's continuing ability to opt out of any Uniform Standard is the functional equivalent of legislative consent to any standard that conflicts with an existing statute (although this would not account for the Governor's constitutional role in choosing whether to sign or veto legislation, *see* COLO. CONST. art. IV, § 11).
>
> Third, the Insurance Compact can be seen as establishing a statutory choice-of-law rule. In this view, Colorado and the Interstate Commission are viewed as different legal jurisdictions. Through the Insurance Compact, the Colorado Legislature has directed Colorado courts to apply "Interstate Commission law" to insurance policies that are "enforceable in the Interstate Commission," so to speak.

Amica Life Ins. Co. v. Wertz, 272 F. Supp. 3d 1239, 1254–55 (D. Colo. 2017).

2. Did you notice that the Colorado Supreme Court stated, "If the [Colorado State] Commissioner believes that the Commission should enact a regulation that conflicts with Colorado statutory law, then he must request action from the Colorado General Assembly because only that body may legislatively override one of its own enactments." How feasible is this solution? Under article VII.3 of the Insurance Compact, new uniform standards go into effect 90 days after the interstate commission promulgates them. Article VII.4 allows states to opt out of a uniform standard within 10 days after the commission promulgates the standard. Must Colorado opt out of every new standard from the interstate commission until the Colorado General Assembly enacts legislation allowing the new standard?

3. How should other states respond? Can Colorado continue to be a member of the Compact if it cannot observe the terms of the Compact? Should the interstate commission informally treat Colorado differently? Should the other states vote on allowing Colorado to act differently? How will other persons dissatisfied with an insurance product respond? Will there be copycat litigation in other party states? What does the decision mean for insurance policies in Colorado approved through the compact? The Interstate Insurance Product Regulation Commission's amicus curiae brief to the U.S. District Court case stated

> . . . a ruling that destabilizes the Insurance Compact calls into question a significant portion of in-force policies held by citizens of Colorado. The insurance policy issued in this case is approved for use in 45 other states. As of the end of September 2017, the Commission has approved more than 6,100 insurance products—78% of which were approved for use in Colorado—since it became operational in 2007. Insurance companies using the Commission represent more than 80% of the national market in the asset-based product lines.

Amicus Curiae brief of Interstate Insurance Product Regulation Comm'n at 3, *Amica Life Ins. Co. v. Wertz*, No. 15-cv-1161-WJM-CBS (D. Colo. Oct. 27, 2017), ECF No. 80-1. How would courts unwind the compact and some or all that volume in one or more states, or all 46 member states?

4. This question of authority underlies many compacts, not just compacts without congressional consent. The notes following the *West Virginia ex rel. Dyer v. Sims* case excerpt in the next section of this chapter discuss several cases that have held compacts with consent supersede limitations in the party states' constitutions. The Colorado Supreme Court's *Amica* decision distinguished these cases because a compact with consent becomes federal law, which supersedes state law. But consent does not mandate that states enact a compact; a compact only becomes "federal law" after the states choose to enact it. Do you agree that compacts without consent cannot supersede limitations in a state's own constitution?

5. There are many new interstate compacts involving professional licensing, all of which provide for a compact agency to enact binding regulation, and none

of which require congressional consent. Could this decision concluding that Colorado was without authority to enact the Insurance Compact affect those compacts as well?

Understanding the concept of state authority to enact compacts that binds future legislators can help understand similar concepts with more common non-compact intergovernmental agreements.

All states except Delaware broadly authorize non-compact administrative or "intergovernmental" agreements by statute or constitution, or both. For example, Oregon statutes authorize public agencies (defined as local governments, special districts, public corporations, boards, commissions, and state agencies) to enter into agreements with public agencies of other states with few limits. OR. REV. STAT. §§ 190.410–.440. Similarly, the Illinois State Constitution authorizes local governments and school districts to contract with other states and their units of local government and school districts "to obtain or share services and to exercise, combine, or transfer any power or function, in any manner not prohibited by law or by ordinance." ILL. CONST. art. VII, § 10(a).

Like in *Green v. Biddle*, in which the Supreme Court noted that the agreement was "binding" on the Kentucky Legislature, courts often hold that non-compact intergovernmental agreements are similarly binding. For example, in *City of Barling v. Fort Chaffee Redev. Auth.*, 347 Ark. 105, 115 (2001), the court stated, "By signing the Indenture, Barling agreed to be contractually bound by its language . . . ." Similarly, in *Greene Cty. Sch. Dist. v. Greene Cty.*, 278 Ga. 849, 850 (2005), the court interpreted GA. CONST. art. IX, § III, ¶ 1(a), which authorizes intergovernmental agreements for a period "not exceeding 50 years," to mean that an agreement for a term exceeding the terms of the governing officials that entered into the agreement binds later governing officials. Interestingly, GA. CODE. ANN. § 36-30-03(a) states, "One council may not, by an ordinance, bind itself or its successors so as to prevent free legislation in matters of municipal government." However, this statute has only limited effect. In *S. Airways Co. v. De Kalb Cty.*, 102 Ga. App. 850, 854 (1960), the court interpreted the former codification of this statute (former GA. CODE ANN. § 69-202) to apply only to governmental functions; a council may bind future councils when engaged in proprietary actions. The Georgia Supreme Court subsequently concluded that an intergovernmental agreement was valid for up to 50 years pursuant to the Georgia Constitution notwithstanding this statutory prohibition against binding successor councils. *Bldg. Auth. of Fulton Cty. v. State*, 253 Ga. 242, 249–50 (1984).

Even without such express constitutional authority suggesting the binding nature of intergovernmental agreements, courts hold that intergovernmental agreements are binding. For example, in *City of Whitefish v. Flathead Cty.*, 347 Mont. 490 (2008), the court concluded that a city was entitled to a preliminary injunction to preserve the status quo in its claim that a county improperly unilaterally rescinded an intergovernmental agreement. Similarly, in *Tri-County Metro. Transp. Dist. v. Clackamas Cty.*, No. CV13030258 (Or. Cir. Ct. Clackamas Cty.

July 1, 2013), the court's ruling on summary judgment concluded that a voter initiative could not abrogate a prior intergovernmental agreement.

Non-compact intergovernmental agreements also have authority issues that could be used to help understand similar issues with compacts that courts have not addressed. For example, the following excerpt of the "Interlocal Cooperation Act" suggests two issues of authority that are conceptually similar to issues of authority with compacts. The Interlocal Cooperation Act originated with The Council of State Governments in its 1957 suggested legislation book. Comm. of State Officials on Suggested State Legislation, The Council of State Gov'ts, *Suggested State Legislation Program for 1957* 93–97 (1956). In 1967, the U.S. Advisory Commission on Intergovernmental Relations (ACIR), a former federal agency, made a few changes to the 1957 suggested Act and adopted it as ACIR suggested legislation. As of mid-2020, eleven states still use the Interlocal Cooperation Act as their broadly authorizing statute for intergovernmental agreements, which, despite its name, applies to state agencies as well, and many other states still use portions of (or concepts from) it.

U.S. Advisory Comm'n on Intergovernmental Relations, *A Handbook for Interlocal Agreements and Contracts* (1967)

Suggested Legislation

. . . .

Section 1. Purpose. It is the purpose of this act to permit local governmental units to make the most efficient use of the powers by enabling them to cooperate with other localities on a basis of mutual advantage and thereby to provide services and facilities in a manner and pursuant to forms of governmental organization that will accord best with geographic, economic, population, and other factors influencing the needs and development of local communities

Section 2. Short Title. This act may be cited as the Interlocal Cooperation Act.

Section 3. Definitions. For the purposes of this act:

(1) The term "public agency" shall mean any political subdivision [insert enumeration, if desired] of this state; any agency of the state government or of the United States; and any political subdivision of another state.

(2) The term "state" shall mean a state of the United States and the District of Columbia.

Section 4. Interlocal Agreements. (a) Any power or powers, privileges or authority exercised or capable of exercise by a public agency of this state may be exercised and enjoyed jointly with any other public agency of this state [having the power or powers, privilege or authority], and jointly with any with any public agency of any other state or of the United States to the extent that laws of such other state or of the United States permit such joint exercise or enjoyment. Any agency of the state government when acting jointly with any public agency may exercise and enjoy all of the powers, privileges and authority conferred by this act upon a public agency.

. . . .

Section 5. Filing, Status, and Actions. Prior to its entry into force, an agreement made pursuant to this act shall be filed with [the keeper of local public records] and with the [secretary of state]. In the event that an agreement entered into pursuant to this act is between or among one or more public agencies of this state and one or more public agencies of another state or of the United States said agreement shall have the status of an interstate compact, but in any case or controversy involving performance or interpretation thereof or liability thereunder, the public agencies party thereto shall be real parties in interest and the state may maintain an action to recoup or otherwise make itself whole for any damages or liability which it may incur by reason of being joined as a party therein. Such action shall be maintainable against any public agency or agencies whose default, failure of performance, or other conduct caused or contributed to the incurring of damage or liability by the state.

. . . .

Notes & Questions

1. ACIR was a research agency that existed between 1959 and 1996. Act of Sept. 24, 1959, Pub. L. No. 86-380, 73 Stat. 703, created ACIR. The Treasury, Postal Service, and General Government Appropriations Act, 1996, Pub. L. No. 104-52, 109 Stat. 468, 480 (1995), terminated ACIR. As of 2020, the ACIR statutes remain in the U.S. Code. *See* 42 U.S.C. §§ 4271–4279. For a recent symposium on the history, accomplishments, and vision for a reconstituted Advisory Commission, see John Kincaid & Carl W. Stenberg, *Introduction to the Symposium on Intergovernmental Management and ACIR Beyond 50: Implications for Institutional Development Research*, 71 PUB. ADMIN. REV. 158 (2011), and the several articles that follow this introductory piece.

2. The bracketed phrase in section 4 did not exist in the 1957 CSG version of the suggested Act; ACIR added it. A state that adopted the Interlocal Cooperation Act *without* the bracketed text authorized municipalities to enter into an agreement if at least one of the parties had the power to undertake the subject of the agreement. ACIR's bracketed text restricted intergovernmental agreements to situations only where all municipalities to the agreement independently had authority to undertake the action. This more restrictive approach does not require independent authority to perform the subject activity in each of the other contracting parties' jurisdictions; it means that each party has the authority to perform the subject activity within its own jurisdiction. *E.g.*, MINN. STAT. § 471.59(1) (authorizing agreements where the powers "are the same except for the territorial limits within which they may be exercised"); *City of Medina v. Primm*, 160 Wash. 2d 268, 277 (2007) ("the question under [WASH. REV. CODE §] 39.34.080 is whether the city is authorized to perform the *type* of governmental activity that is the subject of the agreement" (emphasis in original)); *Durango Transp., Inc. v. City of Durango*, 824 P.2d 48, 49–53 (Colo. Ct. App. 1991) (same, citing several cases in accord). State intergovernmental cooperation statutes that do not directly descend from the suggested acts or have been amended such that

the suggested acts are no longer recognizable typically use language that suggests one or the other of these approaches.

ACIR's explanation for the bracketed text does not explain why ACIR added it:

> Alternative language is offered in section 4(a) which would provide a broad or narrow use of the joint agreement power. Without the language in parenthesis, the act permits two or more public agencies to exercise a power jointly or cooperatively as long as one of them possesses the power. For example, Community A which has the power to build and maintain a public water supply system and Community B which does not have such a power could enter into an agreement for the joint or cooperative construction and maintenance of such a facility. Some states may wish to enact a statute of this breadth. However, others may wish to limit the statute to use in situations where all agreeing public agencies can exercise the power separately. Inclusion of the language provided in parenthesis would accomplish this limitation if desired.

U.S. Advisory Comm'n on Intergovernmental Relations, *A Handbook for Interlocal Agreements and Contracts* 24–25 (1967). What are the benefits and drawbacks of using the narrow or broad approach authorized in section 4?

Consider again the notes following the *Amica Life Insurance* case excerpt. In essence, the federal district court in the *Amica* case was asking the Colorado Supreme Court the same question arising in the bracketed text of the Interlocal Cooperation Act—should a state have authority to enact a compact to do something that it has no independent authority to do? Colorado's intergovernmental relationships law requires each of the cooperating parties to have independent authority to perform the tasks specified in the agreement. COLO. REV. STAT. § 29-1-203(1) ("Governments may cooperate or contract with one another to provide any function, service, or facility lawfully authorized to each of the cooperating or contracting units . . . ."). Neither the federal district court nor the Colorado Supreme Court used Colorado's intrastate intergovernmental relationships law as helpful context in resolving the legal question.

3. Section 5 is identical in both "suggested" Acts, and as of mid-2020, all eleven states that still use the Interlocal Cooperation Act also have section 5 in their books. This provision, which declares an agreement between entities in different states to have the status of an interstate compact, is broadly applicable so that it includes agreements between two municipal governments or between a municipal government and a state agency. Some scholars also argue that the Compact Clause covers cities as well as states. *See, e.g.*, David E. Engdahl, *Interstate Urban Areas and Interstate "Agreements" and "Compacts": Unclear Possibilities*, 58 GEO. L.J. 799, 805–06 (1970) (comparing the Compact Clause to the Fourteen Amendment, which applies to cities); Duncan B. Hollis, *The Elusive Foreign Compact*, 73 MO. L. REV. 1071, 1093 n.92 (2008) (opining that the Compact Clause applies to municipalities to the extent they are component governmental units of a state).

As you study interstate compacts and non-compact intergovernmental agreements, consider whether states have authority to declare that an interstate interlocal agreement has the status of an interstate compact; whether common law or the federal or a state constitution requires that an interstate interlocal agreement must be a compact; and the many legal issues associated with declaring an interlocal agreement to be an interstate compact. One obvious problem is whether the agreement could be an interstate compact if one of the states does not have the section 5 provision. The eleven states that still use the Interlocal Cooperation Act have 48 borders with other states; only six of those state borders are between two states that both have a compact provision, and three states share no borders with another state that has the compact provision.

In reality, very few interlocal agreements between parties in different states address the compact issue in section 5. Why do you think parties remain silent about the "compact" issue?

II. Restrictions on States After Entering Into a Compact

The following case, *West Virginia ex rel. Dyer v. Sims*, is one of the most important compact cases the Supreme Court has decided. It involved the question whether a restriction in a state constitution allows a state to renege on a compact obligation. We read it here, almost in full, for its discussion of state authority to enter into compacts, and restrictions on states after entering into a compact.

West Virginia ex rel. Dyer v. Sims
341 U.S. 22 (1951)

FRANKFURTER, JUSTICE:

After extended negotiations eight States entered into a Compact to control pollution in the Ohio River system. See Ohio River Valley Water Sanitation Compact. Illinois, Indiana, Kentucky, New York, Ohio, Pennsylvania, Virginia and West Virginia recognized that they were faced with one of the problems of government that are defined by natural rather than political boundaries. Accordingly, they pledged themselves to cooperate in maintaining waters in the Ohio River basin in a sanitary condition through the administrative mechanism of the Ohio River Valley Water Sanitation Commission, consisting of three members from each State and three representing the United States.

. . . .

By Article X the States also agree "to appropriate for the salaries, office and other administrative expenses, their proper proportion of the annual budget as determined by the Commission and approved by the Governors of the signatory States * * * ."

The present controversy arose because of conflicting views between officials of West Virginia regarding the responsibility of West Virginia under the Compact.

The Legislature of that State ratified and approved the Compact on March 11, 1939. Congress gave its consent on July 11, 1940, and upon adoption by all the signatory States the Compact was formally executed by the Governor of West Virginia on June 30, 1948. At its 1949 session the West Virginia Legislature appropriated $12,250 as the State's contribution to the expenses of the Commission for the fiscal year beginning July 1, 1949. Respondent Sims, the auditor of the State, refused to issue a warrant upon its treasury for payment of this appropriation. To compel him to issue it, the West Virginia Commissioners to the Compact Commission and the members of the West Virginia State Water Commission instituted this original mandamus proceeding in the Supreme Court of Appeals of West Virginia. The court denied relief on the merits, and we brought the case here because questions of obviously important public interest are raised.

The West Virginia court found that the "sole question" before it was the validity of the Act of 1939 approving West Virginia's adherence to the Compact. It found that Act invalid in that (1) the Compact was deemed to delegate West Virginia's police power to other States and to the Federal Government, and (2) it was deemed to bind future legislatures to make appropriations for the continued activities of the Sanitation Commission and thus to violate Art. X, § 4 of the West Virginia Constitution.

Briefs filed on behalf of the United States and other States, as amici, invite the Court to consider far-reaching issues relating to the Compact Clause of the United States Constitution. Art. I, § 10, cl. 3. The United States urges that the Compact be so read as to allow any signatory State to withdraw from its obligations at any time. Pennsylvania, Ohio, Indiana, Illinois, Kentucky and New York contend that the Compact Clause precludes any State from limiting its power to enter into a compact to which Congress has consented. We must not be tempted by these inviting vistas. We need not go beyond the issues on which the West Virginia court found the Compact not binding on that State. That these are issues which give this Court jurisdiction to review the State court proceeding, 28 U.S.C. § 1257, needs no discussion after *Delaware River Joint Toll Bridge Comm. v. Colburn*, 310 U.S. 419, 427 [(1940)].

Control of pollution in interstate streams might, on occasion, be an appropriate subject for national legislation. But, with prescience, the Framers left the States free to settle regional controversies in diverse ways. Solution of the problem underlying this case may be attempted directly by the affected States through contentious litigation before this Court. Adjudication here of conflicting State interests affecting stream pollution does not rest upon the law of a particular State. This Court decides such controversies according to "principles it must have power to declare." But the delicacy of interstate relationships and the inherent limitations upon this Court's ability to deal with multifarious local problems have naturally led to exacting standards of judicial intervention and have inhibited the formulation of a code for dealing with such controversies. As Mr. Justice Holmes put it: "Before this court ought to intervene, the case should be of serious magnitude, clearly and fully proved, and the principle to be applied should be one which the court is prepared deliberately to maintain against all considerations on the other side." *Missouri v. Illinois*, [200 U.S. 496, 521 (1906)].

Indeed, so awkward and unsatisfactory is the available litigious solution for these problems that this Court deemed it appropriate to emphasize the practical constitutional alternative provided by the Compact Clause. Experience led us to suggest that a problem such as that involved here is "more likely to be wisely solved by cooperative study and by conference and mutual concession on the part of representatives of the States so vitally interested in it than by proceedings in any court however constituted." *New York v. New Jersey*, [256 U.S. 296, 313 (1921)]. The suggestion has had fruitful response.

The growing interdependence of regional interests, calling for regional adjustments, has brought extensive use of compacts. A compact is more than a supple device for dealing with interests confined within a region. That it is also a means of safeguarding the national interest is well illustrated in the Compact now under review. Not only was congressional consent required, as for all compacts; direct participation by the Federal Government was provided in the President's appointment of three members of the Compact Commission. Art. IV; Art. XI, § 3.

But a compact is after all a legal document. Though the circumstances of its drafting are likely to assure great care and deliberation, all avoidance of disputes as to scope and meaning is not within human gift. Just as this Court has power to settle disputes between States where there is no compact, it must have final power to pass upon the meaning and validity of compacts. It requires no elaborate argument to reject the suggestion that an agreement solemnly entered into between States by those who alone have political authority to speak for a State can be unilaterally nullified, or given final meaning by an organ of one of the contracting States. A State cannot be its own ultimate judge in a controversy with a sister State. To determine the nature and scope of obligations as between States, whether they arise through the legislative means of compact or the "federal common law" governing interstate controversies is the function and duty of the Supreme Court of the Nation. Of course every deference will be shown to what the highest court of a State deems to be the law and policy of its State, particularly when recondite or unique features of local law are urged. Deference is one thing; submission to a State's own determination of whether it has undertaken an obligation, what that obligation is, and whether it conflicts with a disability of the State to undertake it is quite another.

The Supreme Court of Appeals of the State of West Virginia is, for exclusively State purposes, the ultimate tribunal in construing the meaning of her Constitution. Two prior decisions of this Court make clear, however, that we are free to examine determinations of law by State courts in the limited field where a compact brings in issue the rights of other States and the United States.

Kentucky v. Indiana, 281 U.S. 163 [(1930)], dealt with a compact to build a bridge across the Ohio River. In an original action brought before this Court, Indiana defended on the ground that she should not be compelled to perform until the Indiana courts decided, in a pending case, whether her officials had been authorized to enter into the compact. Mr. Chief Justice Hughes, speaking for a unanimous Court, dismissed the argument: "Where the States themselves are before this Court for the determination of a controversy between them, neither can determine their rights *inter sese*, and this Court must pass upon every question essential to such a determination, although local legislation and questions of state authorization may be involved. A decision in the present instance by the state court would not determine the controversy here." 281 U.S. at 176–177.

In reaching this conclusion the Chief Justice could hardly avoid analogizing the situation to that where a question is raised whether a State has impaired the obligation of a contract. "It has frequently been held that when a question is suitably raised whether the law of a State has impaired the obligation of a contract, in violation of the constitutional provision, this Court must determine for itself whether a contract exists, what are its obligations, and whether they have been impaired by the legislation of the State. While this Court always examines with appropriate respect the decisions of state courts bearing upon such questions, such decisions do not detract from the responsibility of this Court in reaching its own conclusions as to the contract, its obligations and impairment, for otherwise the constitutional guaranty could not properly be enforced . . . ." 281 U.S. at 176.

Hinderlider v. La Plata River & Cherry Creek Ditch Co., [304 U.S. 92 (1938)], is the second of these cases. It also makes clear, if authority be needed, that the fact the compact questions reach us on a writ of certiorari rather than by way of an original action brought by a State does not affect the power of this Court. In the *Hinderlider* case, an action was brought in the Colorado courts to enjoin performance of a compact between Colorado and New Mexico concerning water rights in the La Plata River. The State court held that the compact was invalid because it affected appropriation rights guaranteed by the Colorado State Constitution. Mr. Justice Brandeis, likewise speaking for a unanimous Court, held that the relative claims of New Mexico and Colorado citizens could be determined by compact and reversed the decision of the State court.

The issue in the *Hinderlider* case was whether the Colorado Legislature had authority, under the State Constitution, to enter into a compact which affected the water rights of her citizens. The issue before us is whether the West Virginia Legislature had authority, under her Constitution, to enter into a compact which involves delegation of power to an interstate agency and an agreement to appropriate funds for the administrative expenses of the agency.

That a legislature may delegate to an administrative body the power to make rules and decide particular cases is one of the axioms of modern government. The West Virginia court does not challenge the general proposition but objects to the delegation here involved because it is to a body outside the State and because its Legislature may not be free, at any time, to withdraw the power delegated. We are not here concerned, and so need not deal, with specific language in a State constitution requiring that the State settle its problems with other States without delegating power to an interstate agency. What is involved is the conventional grant of legislative power. We find nothing in that to indicate that West Virginia may not solve a problem such as the control of river pollution by compact and by the delegation, if such it be, necessary to effectuate such solution by compact. If this Court, in the exercise of its original jurisdiction, were to enter a decree requiring

West Virginia to abate pollution of interstate streams, that decree would bind the State. The West Virginia Legislature would have no part in determining the State's obligation. The State Legislature could not alter it; it could not disregard it, as West Virginia on another occasion so creditably recognized. The obligation would be fixed by this Court on the basis of a master's report. Here, the State has bound itself to control pollution by the more effective means of an agreement with other States. The Compact involves a reasonable and carefully limited delegation of power to an interstate agency. Nothing in its Constitution suggests that, in dealing with the problem dealt with by the Compact, West Virginia must wait for the answer to be dictated by this Court after harassing and unsatisfactory litigation.

What Mr. Justice Brandeis said of the Colorado court decision in *Hinderlider v. La Plata River & Cherry Creek Ditch Co., supra*, applies to the decision of the West Virginia court: "It ignores the history and order of development of the two means provided by the Constitution for adjusting interstate controversies. The compact—the legislative means—adapts to our Union of sovereign States the age-old treaty-making power of independent sovereign nations. Adjustment by compact without a judicial or quasi-judicial determination of existing rights had been practiced in the Colonies, was practiced by the States before the adoption of the Constitution, and had been extensively practiced in the United States for nearly half a century before this Court first applied the judicial means in settling the boundary dispute in *Rhode Island v. Massachusetts*, 12 Pet. 657, 723–725." 304 U.S. at 104.

The State court also held that the Compact is in conflict with Art. X, § 4, of the State Constitution and for that reason is not binding on West Virginia. This section provides:

> "No debt shall be contracted by this State, except to meet casual deficits in the revenue, to redeem a previous liability of the State, to suppress insurrection, repel invasion, or defend the State in time of war; but the payment of any liability other than that for the ordinary expenses of the State, shall be equally distributed over a period of at least twenty years."

The Compact was evidently drawn with great care to meet the problem of debt limitation in light of this section and similar restrictive provisions in the constitutions of other States. Although, under Art. X of the Compact, the States agree to appropriate funds for administrative expenses, the annual budget must be approved by the Governors of the signatory States. In addition, Article V provides: "The Commission shall not incur any obligations of any kind prior to the making of appropriations adequate to meet the same; nor shall the Commission pledge the credit of any of the signatory States, except by and with the authority of the legislature thereof." In view of these provisions, we conclude that the obligation of the State under the Compact is not in conflict with Art. X, § 4 of the State constitution.

Reversed and remanded.

REED, JUSTICE, CONCURRING:

I concur in the judgment of the Court but disagree with the assertion of power by this Court to interpret the meaning of the West Virginia Constitution. This Court must accept the State court's interpretation of its own Constitution unless it is prepared to say that the interpretation is a palpable evasion to avoid a federal rule.

There is no problem concerning the binding effect upon this Court of state court interpretation of state law, under the Compact Clause such as there is under the clause against impairing the Obligation of Contracts. Under the latter clause, this Court, in order to determine whether the subsequent state law, constitutional or statutory, impairs the federal prohibition against impairment of contracts, has asserted power to construe for itself the disputed agreement, to decide whether it is a contract, and to interpret the subsequent state statute to decide whether it impairs that contract. Even then we accept state court conclusions unless "manifestly wrong." Examination here, under the Contract Clause, is to enforce the federal provision against impairment and is made only to decide whether under the Contract Clause there is a contract and whether it is impaired. This Court thus adjudges whether state action has violated the Federal Contract Clause. It does not decide the meaning of a state statute as applied to a state appropriation.

Under the Compact Clause, however, the federal questions are the execution, validity and meaning of federally approved state compacts. The interpretation of the meaning of the compact controls over a state's application of its own law through the Supremacy Clause and not by any implied federal power to construe state law.

West Virginia adjudges her execution of the compact is invalid as a delegation of state police power and as a creation of debt beyond her constitutional powers. Since the Constitution provided the compact for adjusting interstate relations, compacts may be enforced despite otherwise valid state restrictions on state action.

This, I think, was the basis of our holding in *Hinderlider v. La Plata River & Cherry Creek Ditch Co.*, 304 U.S. 92. The Supreme Court of Colorado held that compact invalid because it was an executive abandonment by Colorado of a citizen's previously acquired water rights. But we concluded:

> "Whether the apportionment of the water of an interstate stream be made by compact between the upper and lower States with the consent of Congress or by a decree of this Court, the apportionment is binding upon the citizens of each State and all water claimants, even where the State had granted the water rights before it entered into the compact." [304 U.S. at] 106.

For that conclusion reliance was placed upon *Rhode Island v. Massachusetts*, 12 Pet. 657, 725, where this Court, speaking of compacts, said:

> By this surrender of the power, which before the adoption of the constitution was vested in every state, of settling these contested boundaries, as in

> the plenitude of their sovereignty they might; they could settle them neither by war, or in peace, by treaty, compact or agreement, without the permission of the new legislative power which the states brought into existence by their respective and several grants in conventions of the people. If congress consented, then the states were in this respect restored to their original inherent sovereignty; such consent being the sole limitation imposed by the constitution, when given, left the states as they were before * * * whereby their compacts became of binding force, and finally settled the boundary between them; operating with the same effect as a treaty between sovereign powers.

I would uphold the validity of the compact and reverse the judgment of West Virginia refusing mandamus, with direction to that court to enter a judgment not inconsistent with an opinion based upon the Supremacy Clause.

JACKSON, JUSTICE, CONCURRING:

West Virginia officials induced sister States to contract with her and Congress to consent to the Compact. She now attempts to read herself out of this interstate Compact by reading into her Constitution a limitation upon the powers of her Governor and Legislature to contract.

West Virginia, for internal affairs, is free to interpret her own Constitution as she will. But if the compact system is to have vitality and integrity, she may not raise an issue of *ultra vires*, decide it, and release herself from an interstate obligation. The legal consequences which flow from the formal participation in a compact consented to by Congress is a federal question for this Court.

West Virginia points to no provision of her Constitution which we can say was clear notice or fair warning to Congress or other States of any defect in her authority to enter into this Compact. It is a power inherent in sovereignty limited only to the extent that congressional consent is required. *Rhode Island v. Massachusetts*, 12 Pet. 657, 725; *Poole v. Fleeger's Lessee*, 11 Pet. 185, 209. Whatever she now says her Constitution means, she may not apply retroactively that interpretation to place an unforeseeable construction upon what the other States to this Compact were entitled to believe was a fully authorized act.

Estoppel is not often to be invoked against a government. But West Virginia assumed a contractual obligation with equals by permission of another government that is sovereign in the field. After Congress and sister States had been induced to alter their positions and bind themselves to terms of a covenant, West Virginia should be estopped from repudiating her act. For this reason, I consider that whatever interpretation she may put on the generalities of her Constitution, she is bound by the Compact, and on that basis I concur in the judgment.

Notes & Questions

1. The majority opinion concluded there is inherent authority for states to enter into compacts: "That a legislature may delegate to an administrative body the power to make rules and decide particular cases is one of the axioms of modern government.... What is involved is a conventional grant of legislative power. We

find nothing in [West Virginia's constitution] to indicate that West Virginia may not solve a problem such as the control of river pollution by compact and by such delegation, if such it be, necessary to effectuate such solution by compact." 341 U.S. at 31. This should not surprise you. However, this case involved a purported conflict between the West Virginia Constitution and the compact. Did the Supreme Court effectively conclude that consent authorizes states to exercise powers not available without the agreement?

Consider Justice Jackson's concurrence, which stated, "West Virginia points to no provision of her Constitution which we can say was clear notice or fair warning to Congress or other States of any defect in her authority to enter into this Compact.... Whatever she now says her Constitution means, she may not apply retroactively that interpretation to place an unforeseeable construction upon what the other States to this Compact were entitled to believe was a fully authorized act." 341 U.S. at 35. What if West Virginia knew about the restriction in its own constitution, but ignored it when joining the compact? Should states be able to intentionally or knowingly avoid a state constitutional restriction by negotiating a compact that conflicts with the restriction? Recall that one common canon of statutory construction is that legislatures are deemed to know of other law.

Recall from the *Tobin* case in Chapter 2 that Congress cannot impose a condition in excess of limits in the federal constitution. If Congress is so limited, then should states be similarly limited to enter into compacts and take actions pursuant to compacts only to the extent authorized by their own constitutions? What should be the effect on a compact if a state later enacts a constitutional restriction?

Compare the ability of states to enact agreements that may conflict with their own constitution to the power authorized in the Interlocal Cooperation Act (excerpted above) for local governments to enact intergovernmental agreements to undertake tasks that only one of the parties has the power to do unilaterally. Should the power to enact a compact or non-compact intergovernmental agreement enlarge a government's authority?

2. Several years after *Dyer v. Sims*, the Washington State Supreme Court reached a similar conclusion as the West Virginia Supreme Court concerning the authority to enter into a compact.

> The state constitution is not a grant, but a restriction, of legislative power, and the power of the legislature to enact laws is unrestrained except where it is expressly or inferentially prohibited by the state or Federal constitution. Where there is no constitutional limitation upon the legislature to enter into compacts with sister states, all doubts must be resolved in favor of its power to do so. We do not find in the state constitution any limitation upon the power of the legislature to contract with its sister states. Art. I, § 10, of the Federal constitution, provides that states may enter into interstate compacts when authorized by Congress. Congress has approved the compact with which we are here concerned. Since there is no constitutional limitation upon the power of the legislature to contract in this regard, and Congress has consented thereto....

Washington ex rel. Tattersall v. Yelle, 52 Wash. 2d 856, 862 (1958). *Tattersall* was surprisingly similar to *West Virginia ex rel. Dyer v. Sims. Tattersall* was a taxpayer suit, in which the plaintiff questioned the right of the state auditor to transfer funds to the Western Interstate Commission for Higher Education. The Washington Supreme Court treated the case as one against a state agency, which enabled it to avoid *West Virginia ex rel. Dyer v. Sims* (however, we don't know whether the Court intended to avoid *West Virginia ex rel. Dyer v. Sims*). Chapter 4 considers the nature of compact agencies as state agencies.

3. The majority and one concurrence in *West Virginia ex rel. Dyer v. Sims* followed *Hinderlider v. La Plata River & Cherry Ditch Co.*, 304 U.S. 92, 106 (1938) holding that states may, with congressional consent, enact compacts even if those compacts would conflict with rights granted under a state constitution. Several lower federal courts have also held that obligations under a compact supersede restrictions in a state constitution. In *Wash. Metro. Area Transit Auth. v. One Parcel of Land,* 706 F.2d 1312 (4th Cir. 1983), the court held that Maryland may confer on an interstate agency federal quick-take condemnation powers not available to state agencies under Maryland's Constitution. The Fourth Circuit further explained that "the Maryland Constitution's prohibition against laws authorizing quick-take condemnation merely withdraws from the state the power of quick-take condemnation that, as a sovereign, it would otherwise possess; the prohibition does not, however, bar Maryland from exercising that power when delegated to it by the federal government." *Id.* at 1321–22. In *Jacobson v. Tahoe Reg'l Planning Agency*, 566 F.2d 1353 (9th Cir. 1977), the court held the "causes of action based on the state constitutional provisions must fail because the Compact, as federal law, preempts state law." *Id.* at 1358. In *Stephans v. Tahoe Reg'l Planning Agency,* 697 F. Supp. 1149, 1152 (D. Nev. 1988), the court held that the Tahoe Regional Planning Agency's regional plan preempts state law and state constitutional provisions and dismissed a taking claim based on the Nevada Constitution. Curiously, the Tahoe Regional Planning Compact, art. X(a), specifically severs provisions of the compact that conflict with the states' constitutions. In *Alcorn v. Wolfe,* 827 F. Supp. 47 (D.D.C. 1993), the court held that the Metropolitan Washington Airports Authority compact provision specifying that appointments are made for a specific term superseded the Virginia Constitution, under which political appointees are removable-at-will. In *Parkridge 6, LLC v. U.S. Dep't of Transp.*, No. 1:09CV1312(LMB/IDD), 2010 U.S. Dist. LEXIS 34182 (E.D. Va. Apr. 6, 2010), *aff'd on prudential grounds only*, 420 F. App'x 265 (4th Cir. 2011), the court dismissed claims against the Metropolitan Washington Airports Authority alleging that MWAA violated the Virginia Constitution and the Virginia Freedom of Information Act. The court succinctly stated that these claims "must also be dismissed because each count assumes, contrary to federal law, that the MWAA is required to follow state law or state constitutional provisions." The Court further stated, "[A]ny Virginia law or provision of the Virginia Constitution that conflicts with [MWAA's authority to levy tolls] is preempted under the Supremacy Clause of the United States Constitution." *Id.* at *18. In *Corr v. Wash. Metro. Airports Auth.*, 800 F. Supp. 2d 743, 758–59 (E.D. Va. 2011), the court concluded that the

compact creating the Washington Metropolitan Airports Authority preempted Article 1, Section 14 of the Virginia Constitution, which specifies, "no government separate from or independent of, the government of Virginia ought to be erected or established with the limits thereof."

4. State courts have similarly concluded that a compact obligation may supersede a provision of the state constitution. In *Alamosa-La Jara Water Users Prot. Ass'n v. Gould,* 674 P.2d 914, 922–23 (Colo. 1984), the Colorado Supreme Court concluded that state constitutional and statutory laws apply only to water that has not been committed to other states by interstate compact or United States Supreme Court decree. In another case, *Frontier Ditch Co. v. Se. Colo. Water Cons. Dist.*, 761 P.2d 1117 (Colo. 1998), the Court concluded, "Thus, to the extent that there might be some arguable conflict between [the compact's] Article VI B's grant of exclusive jurisdiction to Kansas and the Colorado water court's jurisdiction [granted in that state's constitution], Article VI B is the supreme law of the land and governs the rights of the parties in this case." *Id.* at 1124. In *State ex rel. List v. Cty. of Douglas*, 90 Nev. 272 (1974), the Nevada Supreme Court concluded that because of the nature of a compact, the legislature's enactment of the Tahoe Regional Planning Compact did not violate prohibitions in the Nevada Constitution against local or special laws and issued a mandate to Douglas County to pay its share of the Tahoe Regional Planning Agency's expenses. Two years later, in *State ex rel. List v. Douglas Cty.*, 92 Nev. 114 (1976), the Supreme Court had to issue another mandate to Douglas County, which had again refused to pay its share of the TPRA's expenses.

Courts also simply avoid resolving state constitutional questions. For example, in *Hill v. State of Nebraska*, 894 N.W.2d 208 (Neb. 2017), several water users sued the state alleging regulatory takings under the Nebraska Constitution after the Nebraska Department of Natural Resources (DNR) issued a "Compact Call" in the Republican River basin, which closed natural flows and precluded the release of storage water to the users. The Nebraska Supreme Court concluded that appropriators' right to use water is subject to the superior obligation of the State to ensure compliance with the Republican River Compact and thus that right is not a compensable property interest when limited to ensure Nebraska's compliance under the Compact.

Not surprisingly, courts have also applied state constitutions where they may seem to conflict with a compact, but consider whether there was an actual conflict. For example, in *Garey v. Nebraska Dep't of Nat. Res.*, 759 N.W.2d 919 (Neb. 2009), the Nebraska Supreme Court held that a property tax imposed by the state to fund its compact obligations (but not required by the compact) violated a state constitutional prohibition on property taxes. The court acknowledged the underlying compact as a valid agreement enjoying the consent of Congress, but held that state constitutional restrictions nevertheless applied to the state in enacting a supplemental statute to administer the compact. In *Pievsky v. Ridge*, 98 F.3d 730 (3d Cir. 1996), the court similarly concluded that a state constitution still applied to a compact: "The removal of state officers in Pennsylvania is governed by the Commonwealth's Constitution which provides that '[a]ppointed civil officers, other than the judges of the courts of record, may be removed at the pleasure of the power by which they shall have been appointed.' In the absence of statutory language providing otherwise this constitutional provision governs the removal of appointed officials. The legislature may 'impose such terms and limitations with reference to the tenure and removal of an incumbent [state official] as it sees fit.'" *Id.* at 738.

Other cases have considered whether a compact authority or action violates a state constitution, but did not expressly examined whether it was a proper claim. *See e.g., Miller v. Columbia River Gorge Comm'n*, 118 Or. App. 553 (1993); *Fairchild Corp. v. Metro. Wash. Airports Auth.*, 50 Va. Cir. 127 (1999) (but note that the MWAA Compact specifies application of Virginia law). Chapter 10 contains an excerpt of *Pievsky v. Ridge* and other material involving removal of compact agency officials.

5. In *Amica Life Ins. Co. v. Wertz*, 2020 CO 29, ¶ 40, the Colorado Supreme Court distinguished many of the cases cited above because those cases involved compacts with consent, whereas the Interstate Insurance Product Regulation Compact at issue in *Amica* does not have consent. Should consent matter? Do the same concerns that the concurrences in *West Virginia ex rel. Dyer v. Sims* arise in compacts without consent?

6. *Klickitat Cty. v. State*, 71 Wash. App. 760 (1993), involved a claim by a county seeking defense and indemnity from the State of Washington for inverse condemnation actions that might arise from the county's implementation responsibilities under the Columbia River Gorge Compact. The court found two principal reasons why the state was not responsible for defense and indemnity. First, consent transformed the compact into federal law, thus the compact was not a state program. Second, the county would be implementing regulations written by the compact agency, not the state, and thus would be acting as an agent of the compact agency. If a state has the inherent ability to enact a compact that creates an agency, should it be immune from liability for actions of that agency?

7. Some states require a supermajority of legislators to refer to voters a measure to amend a state constitution, or a double majority or supermajority of voters to approve an amendment to a state constitution. Should enacting a compact that has the effect of superseding a state constitution also require a double majority or supermajority vote?

8. In *Comm'r of Pub. Safety v. Freedom of Info. Comm'n*, 144 Conn. App. 821 (2013), two reporters requested NCIC information ("rap sheets"), from the Department of Public Safety pursuant to Connecticut's Freedom of Information Act. This information is accessible to the Department through the National Crime Prevention and Privacy Compact. The Freedom of Information Commission, a state entity that reviews appeals of denials for public records, concluded the Department had violated the Connecticut Freedom of Information Act, reasoning, in part "that the department could not lawfully avoid its obligation to disclose the NCIC printouts by 'contract[ing] away' the obligation, and that the state's entering into the compact constituted such a contract." *Id.* at 824–25. On

appeal, the Court of Appeals concluded, "'[A]n interstate compact is not just a contract; it is a federal statute enacted by Congress.' Accordingly, in the present case, the state is not 'contracting away' its obligations under the act but, rather, legislatively entered into a compact to participate in a federal program, which places limitations on the disclosure of NCIC printouts." *Id.* at 833.

9. Each of the *West Virginia ex rel. Dyer v. Sims* opinions seems uncomfortable with a state court having the final word on the meaning of a compact and that state's obligations under the compact. Do you think this reflected the specific dispute in this case? Is interpreting a state's obligation in a compact different from interpreting a state's obligation in a commercial contract?

10. The dispute in *West Virginia ex rel. Dyer v. Sims* began because Edgar B. Sims, the longest serving West Virginia Auditor, refused to issue a warrant for payment of compact expenses. He was first elected in 1932 and re-elected six times, and was not afraid of controversy. In one case, Sims refused to pay medical expenses for a West Virginia University football player injured in a game against Pitt. Sims claimed the state constitution did not permit the state to be responsible for debts and liabilities of corporations and individuals, arguing that the university was under the control of a board of governors, which West Virginia law specified was a corporation. The West Virginia Supreme Court disagreed. *State ex rel. Bd. of Governors v. Sims*, 134 W. Va. 428 (1960). The Pittsburgh Post-Gazette reported that Sims also argued that students are personally liable for the cost of private treatment of their injuries. *West Va. Court Airs Case to Fix Liability for Injury*, 34, Pittsburgh Post-Gazette (Apr. 25, 1950). The West Virginia Supreme Court did not address this latter argument in its opinion.

In another case, the IRS issued notices of levy directed to the State and served them on Sims. The levies seized the accrued salaries of state employees against whom the IRS had assessed income tax deficiencies. Sims refused to honor the levies and paid the employees their full salaries. The federal government sued Sims to recover from him personally the sums he had paid to the employees in disobedience of the government's levies. Sims lost at the district court, court of appeals and U.S. Supreme Court. *Sims v. United States*, 359 U.S. 108 (1959).

Sims apparently did not devise all his own controversies. The Charleston Gazette's obituary for Cleveland Monroe Bailey (July 16, 1965) wrote:

> Bailey's introduction to state politics came in 1933 when he came to Charleston as assistant to state Auditor Edgar B. Sims. The tall, lanky, tobacco chewing Sims, and the short, muscular, pipe smoking Bailey made a natural team.
>
> Sims prided himself in being the "watchdog of the treasury" and had a flair for gaining newspaper headlines by refusing to issue state checks for various reasons, usually on constitutional grounds, and a good record of winning his arguments. But what most people did not realize was that Cleve Bailey fashioned many of the political bullets that Edgar Sims fired. Bailey had a keen knack for interpreting the Constitution and a brilliant grasp of

> state finances, and he was constantly on the alert for projects that Sims could use to advantage and to the credit of his office.

http://www.wvculture.org/history/government/baileycleve01.html.

Another common dispute involving state authority and compacts is whether states and private parties may enforce state statutory or regulatory state law that conflicts with a compact. The next case is a brief introduction to when states may unilaterally impose requirements on a compact through legislation. Chapter 8 comprehensively covers the relationship between a compact and state law.

Kansas City Area Transp. Auth. v. Missouri
640 F.2d 173 (8th Cir. 1981)

STEPHENSON, JUDGE:

Kansas City Area Transportation Authority (the Authority) appeals from the district court's order denying its motion for summary judgment and granting summary judgment in favor of appellees. It also appeals from the denial of its motion to set aside the judgment. We affirm.

Appellant is a bi-state agency created pursuant to an interstate compact entered into by the States of Kansas and Missouri, adopted by the legislatures of those states, and approved by Act of Congress. The agency was established to "operate and maintain * * * passenger transportation systems and facilities" in the greater Kansas City area.

Mo. Rev. Stat. §§ 92.400–.421 provides that Kansas City may adopt an ordinance imposing a one-half of one percent sales tax for the benefit of the Authority. The City of Kansas City has provided for such a sales tax. The funding statute expires by its own terms every two years and the same or a similar statute has been re-enacted each time. In 1979, the Missouri legislature included the following provision:

> Transportation authorities operating a public mass transportation system under sections 92.400 to 92.420 shall provide for interior and exterior advertising on each vehicle for mass transportation purposes.

The Authority contends that this requirement is a unilateral act by the State of Missouri in derogation of the interstate compact, and therefore invalid. We disagree.

One party to an interstate compact may not enact legislation which would impose burdens upon the compact absent the concurrence of other signatories. *C. T. Hellmuth & Associates, Inc. v. Wash. Metro. Area Transit Auth.*, 414 F. Supp. 408, 409 (D. Md. 1976) (citing cases). However, as noted by the district court:

> It is within the competency of a State, which is a party to a compact with another State, to legislate in respect of matters covered by the compact so long as such legislative action is in approbation and not in reprobation of the compact.

Henderson v. Delaware River Joint Toll Bridge Comm'n, 362 Pa. 475[, 488] (1949).

We agree with the district court that the Authority has made no showing that the advertising provision imposes any burden on the operation of the compact. The only affidavit accompanying either motion for summary judgment is that of Richard Davis, the general manager of the Authority. The affidavit says only that a study by the staff led him to conclude that the placement of advertising on the interior of buses was undesirable from an economic standpoint.

The Authority also appeals from the denial of its subsequent motion for rehearing and to set aside the judgment. It argues that the affidavits supporting the motion establish that the advertising burdens the interstate compact. One exhibit was a study concluding that the exterior advertising mounts resulted in a fuel loss of between $66,775 and $131,550 per year. Another exhibit indicated the net advertising revenues in 1976 and 1977 were $3,084 and in 1978 was $5,692.

. . . .

Notes & Questions

1. Compare the Eighth Circuit's test whether a state law burdens a compact with the Supreme Court's discomfort in *West Virginia ex rel. Dyer v. Sims* with a state interpreting its own obligations under a compact and the application of its constitution to the compact. If a state supreme court cannot be the final word on the state's obligations under a compact, then should a state legislature be permitted to determine what constitutes a new burden on a compact?

2. Whether a state law burdens a compact is a fact-specific inquiry. Typically, courts will enforce state law that does not relate to the implementation of the compact, but not always. For example, in *E. Paralyzed Veterans Ass'n, Inc. v. City of Camden*, 545 A.2d 127 (N.J. 1988), the New Jersey Supreme Court noted, as an example, that compact agency employees from one state must observe state traffic laws while on agency business in another state, but concluded that the Delaware River Port Authority did not need to comply with New Jersey's Construction Code requiring it to install an elevator in a new terminal building. The Port Authority argued that compliance with the Construction Code would cause additional expense to the agency, as this would be the first elevator in its system. The Court questioned the policy behind the Port Authority's action, but ultimately concluded that it could not impose one state's law on the bi-state agency. In another elevator case, in *Delaware River Joint Toll Bridge Comm'n v. Oleksiak*, No. 19-2978, 2020 U.S. Dist. LEXIS 52312 (E.D. Pa. Mar. 26, 2020), a federal court in Pennsylvania declared that Pennsylvania could not, without the compact agency's consent apply state elevator and fuel storage regulations to the agency's administration building complex. The court did not question the policy behind the Bridge Commission's challenge to the application of such safety regulations.

III. How Does a State Enact a Compact?

In Chapter 1, we studied that states may enter compacts either by direct legislative action or through a specific delegation from the legislature to a state official or agency. States have tried other means to enact a compact. For example, in 1993, the Maine Legislature referred to its voters whether to enact the Texas Low-Level Radioactive Waste Disposal Compact. The question on the ballot was: "Do you approve of the interstate compact to be made with Texas, Maine and Vermont for the disposal of the State's low-level radioactive waste at a proposed facility in the State of Texas?" There was no challenge concerning whether this was proper. Other states also decided whether to join a low-level radioactive waste compact by direct vote, and there were legal challenges. For example, in 1984, the South Dakota Legislature passed a joint resolution referring the Dakota Low Level Radioactive Waste Management Compact to the voters. A taxpayer and a corporation wanting to operate a waste facility challenged the referendum as an unlawful delegation of legislative power under the South Dakota Constitution and a violation of the Supremacy Clause of the U.S. Constitution. The South Dakota Supreme Court held that the referral was proper and the election could proceed. *Wyatt v. Kundert*, 375 N.W.2d 186 (S.D. 1985).

Consider the next case involving the question whether Pennsylvania properly enacted the 1961 Driver License Compact when the Pennsylvania Legislature authorized the Secretary of the Department of Transportation to enter into the compact.

Sullivan v. Pennsylvania Dep't of Transp.
550 Pa. 639 (1998)

NEWMAN, JUSTICE:

The Commonwealth of Pennsylvania, Department of Transportation, Bureau of Driver Licensing (PennDOT) appeals from an Order of the Commonwealth Court that affirmed an Order of the Court of Common Pleas of Allegheny County (trial court) sustaining David J. Sullivan's (Sullivan) statutory appeal of a one-year license suspension [pursuant to Pennsylvania law]. We granted allocatur to decide the issue of whether, at the time of Sullivan's license suspension, PennDOT had the authority to suspend a driver's license based on an out-of-state conviction pursuant to the Driver License Compact of 1961 (Compact). Because we conclude that, at the relevant time, the Commonwealth had not enacted the Compact into law, we affirm the Order of the Commonwealth Court.

The Compact is a contractual agreement among states intended to promote compliance with each party state's driving laws and regulations. Besides Pennsylvania, the Compact has thirty-nine party jurisdictions (thirty-eight states and the District of Columbia), each of which has enacted the Compact into law by statute.

Article III of the Compact provides that "the licensing authority of a party state shall report each conviction [for an offense related to the use or operation of a motor vehicle] of a person from another party state occurring within its jurisdiction to the licensing authority of the home state of the licensee." Pursuant to Article IV(1) of the Compact:

> The licensing authority in the home state, for the purposes of suspension, revocation, or limitation of the license to operate a motor vehicle, shall give

> the same effect to the conduct reported, pursuant to Article III, as it would if such conduct had occurred in the home state, in the case of convictions for:
>
> . . . .
>
> (b) Driving a motor vehicle while under the influence of alcoholic beverages or a narcotic to a degree which renders the driver incapable of safely driving a motor vehicle;
>
> . . . .

On March 28, 1995, Sullivan, a resident and licensed driver of Pennsylvania, was convicted of driving under the influence (DUI) in Nebraska, which is a party to the Compact. Pursuant to the Compact, Nebraska reported Sullivan's conviction to PennDOT. By notice dated May 25, 1995, PennDOT informed Sullivan that his conviction for DUI in Nebraska was equivalent to a violation of [Pennsylvania law] and, accordingly, PennDOT was suspending his license for one year . . . . The notice, however, made no reference to the Compact.

Sullivan appealed to the trial court, arguing, *inter alia*, that he had not been convicted of a violation of [Pennsylvania law] and that PennDOT had no authority to suspend his license based on an out-of-state conviction. At the hearing on September 20, 1995, PennDOT for the first time cited the Compact as authority for its suspension of Sullivan's license . . . .

Although Sullivan's counsel did not address the issue of whether the Compact was effective as to the Commonwealth, he did argue that PennDOT improperly failed to notify Sullivan that the suspension of his license was based on the Compact. The trial court sustained Sullivan's appeal, and PennDOT appealed to the Commonwealth Court.

The Commonwealth Court considered Article VIII of the Compact, which provides as follows:

> (1) This compact shall enter into force and become effective as to any state when it has enacted the same into law.
>
> (2) Any party state may withdraw from this compact by enacting a statute repealing the same. * * *

The court concluded that the Commonwealth had not "enacted [the Compact] into law" as required by Article VIII(1), and, therefore, PennDOT lacked the authority to suspend Sullivan's license based on his conviction in Nebraska.

On appeal to this Court, . . . PennDOT next argues that the Commonwealth did enact the Compact into law pursuant to Section 6146 of the Vehicle Code, which provides as follows:

> The secretary may enter into agreements relating to the enforcement of this title, including, but not limited to:
>
> (1) the Driver License Compact and any other agreements to notify any state of violations incurred by residents of that state. * * *

According to PennDOT, the Secretary's exercising the authority conferred upon him by [Section 6146(1)] is sufficient to constitute enactment of the Compact into law. We regretfully disagree.

The Compact is a contract between states. Accordingly, we are bound to interpret its terms according to their plain meaning. Furthermore, this Court will not rewrite the terms of a contract, nor give them a meaning that conflicts with that of the language used. Pursuant to Article VIII(1) of the Compact, its provisions "enter into force and become effective as to any state when it has enacted the [Compact] into law." In the context of law making, the plain meaning of the term "enactment" is "the method or process by which a bill in the Legislature becomes a law."

The language of Article VIII(2) of the Compact supports this interpretation. It provides that, "any party state may withdraw from this compact by enacting a statute repealing the same. * * *"

If the passage of a statute were not also required for entry into the Compact, the withdrawal provision of Article VIII(2) would be incongruously burdensome. We cannot conclude that the Compact's drafters intended such a disparity between entry into and withdrawal from the Compact, nor are we empowered to give the terms of the contract a meaning inconsistent with the drafters' clear intent. Thus, we hold that the Compact becomes effective as to the Commonwealth only when the Legislature passes a statute adopting it. Any other construction would impermissibly strain the language of the contract beyond its plain meaning.

Notwithstanding the Compact's express language, PennDOT argues that, in passing Section 6146 of the Vehicle Code, the Legislature properly delegated to the Secretary of Transportation (Secretary) the authority to enter into the Compact. Overall, the Legislature may delegate policy making authority to an administrative agency, so long as the Legislature makes the "basic policy choices" and establishes "adequate standards which will guide and restrain the exercise of the delegated administrative functions." *Gilligan v. Pennsylvania Horse Racing Comm'n*, 492 Pa. 92, 96 (1980). Here, PennDOT asserts that Section 6141 of the Vehicle Code evinces the Legislature's basic policy choice to participate in interstate agreements regarding the regulation of drivers, and that Section 6146 adequately limits the Secretary's discretion in entering into such agreements, e.g., by specifically referring to the Compact. Thus, PennDOT concludes, by delegating to the Secretary the authority to enter into the Compact, the Legislature obviated the need to pass a statute enacting the Compact into law.

PennDOT's argument is unavailing, however, because it conflicts with the separation of powers mandated by the Pennsylvania Constitution. Article II, Section 1 provides that, "the legislative power of this Commonwealth shall be vested in a General Assembly, which shall consist of a Senate and a House of Representatives;" and Article III, Section 1 provides that, "no law shall be passed except by bill. * * *" In light of these constitutional provisions, "it is axiomatic that the Legislature cannot constitutionally delegate the power to make law to any other branch of government or to any other body or authority." *Gilligan*, 492 Pa. at 95.

In *Ruch v. Wilhelm*, 352 Pa. 586 (1945), this Court [has previously] held that the power of "substantive enactment" is vested in the Legislature alone. Thus, the Court determined that, "authority may be given to a government official or an administrative agency to make rules and regulations to cover mere matters of detail for the implementation of a statute, but where the statute itself is lacking in essential substantive provisions the law does not permit a transfer of the power to supply them, for the legislature cannot delegate its power to make a law." *Id.* at 592–93.

In this case, we view [Section 6146(1)] merely as a delegation of authority to implement the mechanics of the Compact in the Commonwealth. Pursuant to the Constitution's separation of powers, however, the Legislature could not delegate to the Secretary the power to enact the Compact into law as required by its terms. Thus, while not unconstitutional, Section 6146(1) is insufficient to render the Compact effective as to the Commonwealth.

Indeed, the Legislature seemed to concede as much in passing Act No. 1996-149 (Act). Although the Secretary had purported to enter into the Compact effective January 1, 1995, on December 10, 1996, the Legislature passed the Act, which, *inter alia*, added Section 1581 to the Vehicle Code. That section sets forth the full text of the Compact and provides that, "the Driver's License Compact is hereby enacted into law and entered into with all other jurisdictions legally joining therein. * * *" Had the Compact been enacted into law previously, the addition of [Section 1581] would have been unnecessary. Thus, in enacting [Section 1581], the Legislature anticipated our holding that the delegation of authority to the Secretary pursuant to [Section 6146] was insufficient to effectuate the Commonwealth's entry into the Compact, and that a statute enacting the Compact into law would be necessary.

In this case, however, PennDOT suspended Sullivan's license more than a year before the Legislature enacted the Compact into law pursuant to [Section 1581]. Consequently, PennDOT lacked the authority to suspend Sullivan's license based on his out-of-state DUI conviction. The Order of the Commonwealth Court is therefore affirmed.

Notes & Questions

1. Does the reasoning in this case surprise you? Do you think the case might have turned out differently if the compact did not allow a state to withdraw by enacting a law?

2. In this case, the Pennsylvania Supreme Court cited the state Vehicle Code, which specifically authorized the Commonwealth Transportation Secretary to enter into the Driver License Compact. The Court stated that PennDOT's argument relating to delegation of the authority to enter into the compact was unavailing because it conflicted with the separation of powers mandated by Pennsylvania's Constitution. Recall that *West Virginia ex rel. Dyer v. Sims* held that a state could not cite its own constitution as a disability in implementing a compact. Here, how is a conflict with the Pennsylvania Constitution relating to the form of

enactment a significantly different legal question such that the Pennsylvania Court did not need to follow *West Virginia ex rel. Dyer v. Sims*?

3. The former Interstate Compact for Supervision of Parolees and Probationers authorized governors to enter into the compact. Two compact scholars suggested, "This method, based on analogy to the role of the executive in the negotiation and ratification of international treaties, was designed to overcome any questions arising from the fact that the compact had not been negotiated by special commissioners appointed by the executive." FREDERICK L. ZIMMERMANN AND MITCHELL WENDELL, THE INTERSTATE COMPACT SINCE 1925 31 n.141 (1950). The former Parole compact was enacted in 1937. At that time, most compacts had been written by special commissioners appointed by state governors. The discussion in Chapter 1 about boundary compacts mentions such special commissioners. Chapter 9 includes materials on the analogy of compacts to international treaties. Do you agree with Zimmermann and Wendell's rationale? Are compacts that governors enact as binding as compacts that legislatures enact?

4. The form of enacting an agreement is important to the validity of enacting non-compact intergovernmental agreements as well. In *Schmoll v. Housing Auth. of St. Louis Cty.*, 321 S.W.2d 494 (Mo. 1959), the Missouri Supreme Court declared invalid an intergovernmental agreement between a county and a housing authority because the county enacted the agreement by order under authority of state statute, but the county's home rule charter required enactment by ordinance. However, most states authorize non-compact intergovernmental agreements in many different statutes, so an agreement enacted pursuant to one statute could be valid even if the agreement did not meet the requirements for another statutory authorization. For example, in *Utah Cty. v. Ivie*, 137 P.3d 797 (Utah 2006), the Utah Supreme Court held that a county and city had independent authority to undertake actions in an agreement, and thus the agreement was valid even though Utah's interlocal cooperation act did not authorize the agreement).

IV. Amendment of Compacts

The Constitution is silent about amending compacts, which leaves open the question whether states may amend compacts without further congressional approval. The *Tobin* case raised a related question, whether Congress may amend a compact without the states approving the amendment to their compact. Most compacts are also silent about their amendment. Compacts that do contain provisions regarding amendment allow amendment in various ways. For example, in several compacts, Congress consented to the states amending their compact by all the compacting states enacting the same new legislation. For example, the Tahoe Regional Planning Compact, art. X(b), states:

> The agency shall have such additional powers and duties as may hereafter be delegated or imposed upon it from time to time by the action of the legislature of either State concurred in by the legislature of the other.

The New York-New Jersey compact creating the Port Authority of New York and New Jersey, contains a substantially similar provision, N.J. STAT. ANN. 32:1-4;

McKinney's Unconsol. Laws of N.Y. § 6404 (as added by L. 1921 c 154, § 1). This language does not mention the need for congressional consent, but states and courts have treated this language to allow amendments without further consent. The "concurred in" provision of the Port Authority compact has been a source of much litigation. Chapter 8 covers the range of how courts have applied "concurred in" provisions.

In another example, the Washington Metropolitan Area Transit Regulation Compact creates two different compact agencies. Titles I and II of the compact create and relate to the Transit Commission. Title III creates and relates to the Transit Authority. The compact contains different ways of amending the titles. The portion of the compact relating to the Transit Commission states:

> This Compact may be amended from time to time without the prior consent or approval of the Congress of the United States and any amendment shall be effective unless, within one year, the Congress disapproves that amendment.

Washington Metropolitan Area Transit Regulation Compact, Pub. L. No. 101-505, tit. 1, art. VIII, § 1(a), 104 Stat. 1300, 1303 (1990). The portion of the compact relating to the Transit Authority, however, requires affirmative action by Congress.

> Amendments and supplements to this Title to implement the purposes thereof may be adopted by legislative action of any of the Signatory parties concurred in by all of the others. When one Signatory adopts an amendment or supplement to an existing section of the Compact, that amendment or supplement shall not be immediately effective, and the previously enacted provision or provisions shall remain in effect in each jurisdiction until the amendment or supplement is approved by the other Signatories and is consented to by Congress.

Washington Metropolitan Area Transit Regulation Compact, Pub. L. No. 104-322, art. XVI, ¶ 84, 110 Stat. 3884 (1996). In *Proctor v. Wash. Metro. Area Transit Auth.*, 412 Md. 691 (2010), the court considered whether the damages limit in the Maryland Tort Claims Act applied to the Washington Metropolitan Area Transit Authority. The Court cited to article 84 and concluded, "if the Maryland Legislature were to attempt to modify the extent to which WMATA has waived its sovereign immunity, such a modification would have no effect unless it were approved by all signatories and Congress." *Id.* at 723–24.

In another example, Congress amended its consent to the Atlantic States Marine Fisheries Compact to remove its initial fifteen-year time limitation for the life of the compact and approve addition of new states, and concurrently specified that the states did not need to submit their amendments to the compact for further consent. Act of Aug. 10, 1950, Pub. L. No. 81-721, § 2, 64 Stat. 467.

There is no direct authority concerning the implications of failing to receive congressional consent to an amendment to a compact; however, dicta in several cases suggest consent is necessary before an amendment to a compact is effective. In *Am. Sugar Refining Co. v. Waterfront Comm'n of N.Y. Harbor*, 55 N.Y.2d 11

(1982), the New York Court of Appeals observed that the name of the Waterfront Commission of New York Harbor was "changed by chapter 951 of the Laws of 1970 to the Waterfront and Airport Commission of New York and New Jersey. The change has never become effective, congressional consent to the additional Compact provisions never having been granted." *Id.* at 17 n.4. Subsequently, in *Leadbeater v. Port Auth. Trans-Hudson Corp.*, 873 F.2d 45 (3d Cir. 1989), the Third Circuit briefly considered whether a "sue and be sued" clause that New York and New Jersey enacted 30 years after the original compact pursuant to this article constituted Congress's abrogation of the states' Eleventh Amendment immunity. The Court stated, "any suggestion that Congress actually considered the implications of its approval of the compact here on the Port Authority's eleventh amendment immunity would be an obvious fiction." *Id.* at 50 n.6. And, in *Int'l Union of Operating Eng'rs, Local 542 v. Delaware River Joint Toll Bridge Comm'n*, 311 F.3d 273 (3d Cir. 2002), the Third Circuit noted that where a compact contains no provision for amendment, congressional consent to any modification would be necessary. *Id.* at 280 n.7.

How should states collectively amend an interstate compact when that compact has many member states? The Nurse Licensure Compact provides a good example. In 2015, the National Council of State Boards of Nursing approved a new "enhanced" Nurse Licensure Compact, which replaces the existing Nurse Licensure Compact initially approved in 1998. As of 2016, 25 states had enacted the original Nurse Licensure Compact and would need to transition to the revised compact. The enhanced Nurse Licensure Compact, art. X specifies the transition requirements:

> a. This Compact shall become effective and binding on the earlier of the date of legislative enactment of this Compact into law by no less than twenty-six (26) states or December 31, 2018. All party states to this Compact, that also were parties to the prior Nurse Licensure Compact, superseded by this Compact, ("Prior Compact"), shall be deemed to have withdrawn from said Prior Compact within six (6) months after the effective date of this Compact.

This provision provided the states approximately three years to adopt the new compact, which gave time for states with part-time or biennial legislatures to do so; it specifies alternative effective dates so that early-adoption states would know with reasonable certainty when the new compact becomes effective, and it terminates the states' participation in the original compact on a date certain to ensure states would only be members of one compact.

The Great Lakes Basin Compact provides an example of amending the states' obligations and compact agency's authority without amending the compact. Article VI(H) states the "Commission shall have power to . . . recommend amendments or agreements supplementary to" the Compact and to "assist in the formulation and drafting of such amendments or supplementary agreements." Article VI(L) states the Commission shall also "have power to . . . [c]ooperate with the governments of the United States and Canada, the party states and any public or private agencies or bodies having interests in or jurisdiction sufficient to affect the Basin or any portion thereof." In these provisions, the states authorized an adaptive governance role for the Commission that enables the Commission and the Compact to remain relevant over time through continued engagement with the states and other stakeholders, and authorized the Commission to recommend the most effective manner for its governance, which might not be an amendment to the Compact.

Chapter 4: Compact Entities

The preface noted that there are more than 200 interstate compacts. Many compacts operate under existing state and federal law structures without creating any new agency to administer the compact. For example, the Interstate Wildlife Violator Compact establishes a process for handling wildlife violations by a non-resident in the same manner as if the violator was a resident of the state where the violation occurred and for the home state to suspend the violator's license based on reciprocal recognition of another state's suspension. In another example, the Vermont-New Hampshire Interstate Water Supply Compact, authorized by Pub. L. No. 104-126, 110 Stat. 884 (1996), specifically states, "Nothing in this compact shall be construed to authorize the establishment of interstate districts, authorities, or any other new governmental or quasi-governmental entity." 110 Stat. at 884 (art. II).

Approximately two-thirds of the compacts, however, create some type of agency to administer the compact. The structure and authority of these compact agencies varies widely. Some compacts create a new board of existing state agency officials, many create an entirely new agency, board or commission with new officials. Some compacts, such as the Interstate Compact for Adult Offender Supervision create a new interstate commission and require each member state to set up an intrastate council to oversee, advocate, and develop policy concerning operations and procedures of the compact within that state.

Historically, where a compact did not provide for a strong compact agency, state administrators sometimes created an association of compact administrators to share information, best practices, and assist each other in administering the compact. This is not a common approach today. The Interstate Compact for the Placement of Children (ICPC) illustrates one of the potential legal authority issues of this model of governance. Article VII of the ICPC requires each state to appoint a general coordinator of activities within the state, and authorizes the coordinators to jointly promulgate rules. The coordinators established the Association of Administrators of the Interstate Compact on the Placement of Children (AAICPC) and provided it rulemaking authority; however, nothing in the compact specifically recognizes the AAICPC as an agency with rulemaking authority, leaving a question whether the coordinators could confer that authority on the association.

Some compact entities use other organizations for secretariat support. For example, the AAICPC is an affinity group of the American Public Human Services Association (APHSA) and receives secretariat services from APHSA. More recently, several professional associations have played key roles in the creation of new or revised interstate compacts and provided administration services to newly forming compact agencies before those commissions hired staff. For example, the National Council of State Boards of Nursing developed and promotes a revised

Nurse Licensure Compact. A recent book described benefits of using associations to support compact administration, but also noted potential risks:

> Using an association can also be risky when a compact has a high potential for disputes between member states because the association may be asked to take a position in support of one or more states that is contrary to other states. This can lead to disharmony within the association and conflict about the proper role of the association. This issue may also occur when an existing association creates and promotes a new compact where some states perceive a conflict between the compact and their individual state interests and may feel that the association no longer represents their particular interests when they raise issues with the compact or choose not to adopt the compact. Because associations are, by their nature, responsive to their member states, they may receive pressure to allow states to vary their enactments or implementation of the compact, which can lead to litigation over whether states are members of a compact and the proper interpretation and administration of a compact.

MICHAEL L. BUENGER, ET AL., THE EVOLVING LAW AND USE OF INTERSTATE COMPACTS 117–18 (2d ed. 2016).

This chapter looks at the variety of entities that compacts create and considers how courts and states characterize those entities. Are they governmental agencies? Are they agencies of each of the compacting states? Joint agencies of all the compacting states? Federal agencies? Separate entities? Chapter 10 covers governance issues of compact entities, such as appointment and removal and administrative procedure. This chapter focuses solely on the courts and legislatures' continuing struggle with the nature of the entities that compacts create.

I. The Many Descriptions of Compact Entities

As discussed in Chapter 1, courts, scholars, states, and individuals often characterize interstate compacts as either federal or state. However, you have already studied how compacts are different; compacts do not neatly fit into the federal or state molds. The characterization of a specific compact matters because it can anchor the analysis of legal issues such as whether sovereign immunity is available, the application of federal or state law (e.g., administrative procedure acts), and jurisdiction in federal or state court. The characterization of a compact can also affect uniform administration of a compact in the different member states.

Because courts start with the text when interpreting statutes, we will start our study of compact entities with the text of compacts. Compacts describe the entities they create using many different terms.

Separate or Independent Entities: A handful of compacts expressly pronounce that the compact agency is separate or independent of the states. For example, the Midwest Interstate Low Level Radioactive Waste Compact, art. III.m, describes the Midwest Interstate Low Level Radioactive Waste Commission as "a legal entity separate and distinct from the party states." Similarly, the Rocky Mountain Low-Level Radioactive Waste Compact, art. 6.A, states, "The Rocky

Mountain low-level radioactive waste board, which shall not be an agency or instrumentality of any party state, is created."

Body Corporate and Politic Entities: Approximately one-third of the compacts describe the compact agency as a "body corporate and politic." For example, the Bi-State Development Agency compact, art. III, states, "There is created The Bi-State Development Agency of the Missouri-Illinois Metropolitan District (herein referred to as The Bi-State Agency) which shall be a body corporate and politic." What is a "body corporate and politic"? The Virginia Supreme Court discussed the meaning of this term when considering whether the Washington Metropolitan Area Transit Authority was a corporation under a Virginia law. That Virginia law requires members of a county board of supervisors to disclose or recuse themselves from voting when they have a business and financial interest in or relationship with an applicant in a case before the board. The Court described the Transit Authority as:

> WMATA is a government agency created in corporate form by interstate compact between Virginia, Maryland, and the District of Columbia. The Washington Metropolitan Area Transit Regulation Compact of 1966, as amended by 2009 Acts chs. 771 and 828 ("the Compact") states:
>
>> There is hereby created, *as an instrumentality and agency of each of the Signatory parties hereto*, the Washington Metropolitan Area Transit Authority *which shall be a body corporate and politic*, and which shall have the powers and duties granted herein and such additional powers as may hereafter be conferred upon it pursuant to law.
>
> (Emphasis added.) The words "body corporate and politic" create a corporation. *See Dunningtons v. President & Dir. N. W. Turnpike Road*, 47 Va. (6 Gratt.) 160, 170 (1849); *Chapline v. Overseers of the Poor*, 34 Va. (7 Leigh) 231, 233 (1836). However, WMATA is also "an instrumentality and agency of" the Commonwealth. *See Short Pump Town Ctr. Cmty. Dev. Auth. v. Hahn*, 262 Va. 733, 742 & n.10 (2001) (language creating a "public body corporate and politic" or creating a "body corporate and politic" and a "political subdivision" creates a governmental agency).

Newberry Station Homeowners Ass'n v. Fairfax Cty., 285 Va. 604, 619 (2013).

Agency or Joint Agency of the Party States: Another handful of compacts describe the compact agency as a joint agency or instrumentality of the states. For example, the Great Lakes Basin Compact, art. 2, § 2.1, states, "There is hereby created an agency of the party states to be known as the great lakes commission . . . ." Similarly, the Mississippi-Louisiana-Alabama-Georgia Rapid Rail Transit Compact, art. III, states, "The states which are parties to this compact . . . do hereby establish and create a joint agency which shall be known as the Mississippi-Louisiana-Alabama-Georgia Rapid Rail Transit Commission."

As in the Washington Metropolitan Area Transit Regulation Compact discussed above in the *Newberry Station*, excerpt, many of the compacts that use the "body corporate and politic" description also use a "joint agency or instrumentality" description. Another example is the Palisades Interstate Park Compact, art. II.1, which states, "There is hereby created a body corporate and politic with the name and style of 'Palisades Interstate Park Commission' (for brevity hereinafter referred to as 'the commission') which shall be a joint corporate municipal instrumentality of both the state of New York and the state of New Jersey for the purpose of effecting the objects of this compact and which shall be deemed to be performing governmental functions of the two states in the performance of its duties hereunder."

Other variations: Approximately one-third of the compacts simply mention the name of the compact agency without any descriptive language, and a few compacts simply describe the compact agency as "interstate." Some compacts are governed through a more complex structure. For example, the Potomac Highlands Airport Authority Compact, sec. 2, authorized county and municipal governments to enter into intergovernmental agreements with each other and West Virginia and Maryland agencies to create the Airport Authority. Curiously, the Yellowstone River Compact creates an agency involving only two of the three compacting states, specifically rejecting the need to involve the third state in the agency. Article III.A of the Yellowstone River Compact states:

> It is considered that no Commission or administrative body is necessary to administer this Compact or divide the waters of the Yellowstone River Basin as between the States of Montana and North Dakota. The provisions of this Compact, as between the States of Wyoming and Montana, shall be administered by a Commission composed of one representative from the State of Wyoming and one representative from the State of Montana, to be selected by the Governors of said States as such States may choose, and one representative selected by the Director of the United States Geological Survey or whatever Federal agency may succeed to the functions and duties of that agency, to be appointed by him at the request of the States to sit with the Commission and who shall, when present, act as Chairman of the Commission without vote, except as herein provided.

Compacts involving international borders: How would you describe a compact that involves Canadian provinces or Mexican states? The Buffalo and Fort Erie Public Bridge Authority was created by legislative acts of the New York State and Canada, with the consent of Congress. 48 Stat. 662 (1934). The authority refers to itself as an "international compact entity." As you make your way through the remainder of the book, consider what law such an agency should use in its daily affairs: New York State law? U.S. federal law? Canadian law?

Non-government entities: Virtually all compact entities are government agencies, boards or commissions. However, some are not. For example, in *Franklin v. Callum*, 148 N.H. 199 (2002), the court held that an interstate entity created to implement a compact, but not specifically authorized by the compact, is an unincorporated association, not a separate legal entity. Why couldn't this entity still be a regional government agency under the states' non-compact intergovernmental cooperation statutes?

Some compact agencies have tried to organize themselves as not-for-profit corporations. For example, the Great Lakes Forest Fire Compact was registered with the Internal Revenue Service as a charity between 1996 and 2008. Similarly, in 2006, the Interstate Pest Control Compact applied to the Internal Revenue Service to become a tax-exempt public charity pursuant to Section 501(c)(3). The IRS issued an advance letter ruling approving the application for a period of five years ending in 2011. In 2010, the Compact noted that it was failing to meet the public support test for Section 501(c)(3) public charity status, and in 2011, the Compact concluded that should instead apply for status under Section 501(c)(5) for labor, agricultural, and horticultural organizations, which would still be tax-exempt, but private donations would not be tax deductible for donors. In 2012, the governing board voted to disband the compact and transfer its fund to the National Association of State Departments of Agriculture.

Courts sometimes use different terms than in the compact. For example, in holding that the Atlantic States Marine Fisheries Commission is not a federal agency as defined in the federal Administrative Procedure Act (5 U.S.C. § 551(1)), the Second Circuit referred to the commission as "an aggregation of states" and a "state cooperative agreement," even though the compact descries the commission as a "body corporate," *New York v. Atl. States Marine Fisheries Comm'n*, 609 F.3d 524, 532–33 (2d Cir. 2010).

Courts sometimes try to determine whether a compact agency is a federal or state agency to determine what law applies to the compact agency. For example, in *Allied Painting, Inc. v. Del. River Port Auth.*, No. Civ. A. 04-1032, 2005 U.S. Dist. LEXIS 5817 (E.D. Pa. Mar. 29, 2005), the court noted that it is unclear whether the DRPA is a federal agency governed by the federal APA or a state agency governed by state administrative law. More often, however, courts just recognize that compact entities are neither state nor federal agencies but treat them as they would a state or federal agency under a particular statute or regulation. For example, the U.S. District Court for the Western District of Washington allowed the Columbia River Gorge Commission to intervene in a case under Federal Rule of Civil Procedure 24(b)(2), which allows, "On timely motion, the court may permit a federal or state governmental officer or agency to intervene . . . ." The court noted that although the Commission is not a state or federal agency, the rule is intended to be inclusive. Order Granting Motion to Intervene, *GLW Ventures, LLC v. U.S. Dep't of Agriculture, U.S. Forest Service*, No. C14-05806-RBL (W.D. Wash. Dec. 16, 2014), ECF No. 25.

The same type-of-entity issues arise for entities created by non-compact intergovernmental agreements. For example, in *Single Source, Inc. v. Cent. Reg'l Tourism Dist.*, No. 08-40176-FDS, 2011 U.S. Dist. LEXIS 52784 (D. Mass. May 17, 2011), the court considered whether an intergovernmental entity can be a successor for debts and liabilities of municipal entities or state agencies. In *Burden-Meeks v. Welch*, 319 F.3d 897, 899 (7th Cir. 2003), the court implied that an intergovernmental entity is not an entity of one municipal party when concluding the attorney-client privilege over a document prepared by an attorney for the Intergovernmental Risk Management Agency was waived by disclosure to the mayor of one of the parties to the entity. In *Hervey v. Estes*, 65 F.3d 784, 791–92 (9th Cir. 1995), the court held that an intergovernmental task force composed of several local, county, and state governmental entities including several police departments, is not "a person or entity subject to suit under section 1983" because "it is only subject to suit if the parties that created [the association] intended to create a separate legal entity."

In *Heber Light & Power Co. v. Utah Pub. Serv. Comm'n*, 231 P.3d 1203 (Utah 2010), the court considered whether Heber Light and Power, a governmental entity created pursuant to Utah's interlocal cooperation act, was subject to the jurisdiction of the Utah Public Service Commission, which regulates utility providers. The ultimate question was whether this interlocal agency was a corporation, cooperative association, or person. The court concluded it was none of these. Most interestingly, the Utah Supreme Court concluded that Heber was not a corporation, which the public utility code defines as "towns, cities, counties, conservancy districts, improvement districts, or other governmental units created or organized under any general or special law of [Utah]." UTAH CODE ANN. § 54-2-1(5)(b). The court explained that Heber could not be a corporation because it was a governmental unit organized under the Interlocal Cooperation Act, but did not explain why the Interlocal Cooperation Act is not a general law of Utah, which would seem to have brought Heber under the definition of "corporation."

As you read the materials below, consider whether a compact agency should be treated like a state or federal agency, or an independent agency, or something altogether different. Consider whether a compact agency should be treated like one type of agency for certain purposes and treated as a different type of agency for other purposes, and the implications of doing so.

II. Compact Agencies as State Agencies

Courts often struggle to determine whether a compact agency is or should be treated like a state agency. Some of the courts' difficulties almost certainly come from the compact agencies themselves, which want to be treated like state agencies or local governments when they want to take advantage of favorable state law, but want to be treated otherwise to avoid other state law. But much of the confusion is likely the result of trying to figure out how to fit an unusual agency into familiar governmental structures.

Surprisingly, a compact's description of the agency is often not controlling. For example, in *Kansas City Area Transp. Auth. v. Ashley*, 478 S.W.2d 323 (Mo. 1972), the Missouri Supreme Court considered whether it had jurisdiction pursuant to Article V, Section 3 of the Missouri Constitution, which granted exclusive appellate jurisdiction to the Supreme Court "in all civil cases where the state or any county or other political subdivision of the state or any state officer as such is a party." The Missouri Supreme Court observed that the compact creating the Transit Authority describes it as a body corporate and politic and a political subdivision, but concluded that the compact did not delegate "governmental functions as would constitute that agency a governmental unit requiring our jurisdiction of suits involving it as a party." *Id.* at 324.

If courts don't take a compact's description at face value, then what do courts do? Case law involving Bi-State, the interstate compact transit agency for the Missouri-Illinois metropolitan area, provides an interesting illustration. Bi-State's compact describes it as a "political subdivision"; however, whether courts treat Bi-State as such seems to depend on the underlying law and analytical approach. Consider the following cases. In *Bi-State Dev. Agency v Dir. of Revenue*, 781 S.W.2d 80 (Mo. 1989), the Missouri Supreme Court concluded that Bi-State was not a political subdivision because the compact did not delegate traditional governmental functions. And, in *Hubble v. Bi-State Dev. Agency*, 393 Ill. App. 3d 1016 (2009), the Illinois Appellate Court held the Bi-State Development Agency is not a "local public entity" as that term is used in the Illinois Tort Claims Act. However, in contrast to the *Bi-State* and *Hubble* decisions, in *Barket, Levy & Fine, Inc. v. St. Louis Thermal Energy Corp.*, 948 F.2d 1084, 1087 (8th Cir. 1991), the Eighth Circuit stated, "state law treats Bi-State like a county or municipality. The compact characterizes Bi-State as 'a body corporate and politic,' which indicates Bi-State is a municipal corporation." The court thus concluded that Bi-State is not an arm of the states for the purpose of immunity under the Eleventh Amendment. In another case, the U.S. District Court for the Eastern District of Missouri concluded that Bi-State is a political subdivision of a state excluded from coverage under the federal Labor-Management Relations Act (LMRA). *Amalgamated Transit Union Div. 788 v. Bi-State Dev. Agency,* No. 4:15-CV-00455-AGF, 2015 U.S. Dist. LEXIS 74908 (E.D. Mo. June 10, 2015); *see also Vaught v. Bi-State Dev. Agency,* No. 4:15 CV 1499 CDP, 2016 U.S. Dist. LEXIS 45095 (E.D. Mo. Apr. 4, 2016). And in another case, the U.S. District Court for the Eastern District of Missouri concluded that Bi-State was "a local governmental entity rather than an arm of the state for the purpose of determining whether it is a 'person' subject to [False Claims Act] liability." *U.S. ex rel. Fields v. Bi-State Dev. Agency*, No. 4:14 CV 1321 RWS, 2015 U.S. Dist. LEXIS 116845, 30–41 (E.D. Mo. Sept. 2, 2015). Should the characterization of a compact agency differ depending on the underlying law that a plaintiff seeks to apply to that agency or different analytical methods that courts can use?

Should courts consider the geographic area that a compact agency serves in determining the form of the compact agency? In *Pac. States Marine Fisheries Comm'n v. Dep't of Revenue*, 346 Or. 117 (2009) the Oregon Supreme Court concluded that the Pacific States Marine Fisheries Commission, a five-state compact agency, was not entitled to a real property tax exemption that Oregon governmental entities could claim. Oregon law allows the exemption for "all public or corporate property used or intended for corporate purposes of the several counties, cities, towns, school districts, irrigation districts, drainage districts, ports, water districts, housing authorities and all other public or municipal corporations *in this state*." OR. REV. STAT. § 307.090(1) (emphasis added). The Court concluded that the Commission was a public corporation, but was not "in this state."

> . . . Pacific Fisheries is the creature of an interstate compact. It is not an Oregon public corporation. The geographic area it serves is not limited pri-

> marily to the State of Oregon; rather, under the terms of the interstate compact, it represents and serves a multistate area. The interests and geographic area served by Pacific Fisheries are regional, and Pacific Fisheries cannot be considered to be confined geographically within the State of Oregon. An organization that was created by and includes other states, is controlled by a board with equal representation from each state, and is charged with advising the several governments on issues concerning the region as a whole, is not "in this state"

Id. at 127. What do you think about the court's conclusion that the Commission is not a public corporation "in this state"? Why is the commission not "in" Oregon, "in" Washington, "in" California, "in" Idaho, and "in" Alaska? What would be the ramifications if the commission would be considered "in this state" in some, but not all the party states? While not the outcome the Commission sought, the Oregon Supreme Court's decision was helpful to the Commission in subsequent litigation.

Shortly after the Oregon Supreme Court's *PSMFC* decision, the Service Employees International Union, Local 1000 (SEIU) sought review at the California State Personnel Board of a series of contracts between the California Department of Fish and Game and the Pacific States Marine Fisheries Commission. SEIU argued that the contracts violated an implied civil service mandate in article VII of the California Constitution, which prohibits state agencies from contracting with private entities to perform work that the state has historically and customarily performed and can perform adequately and competently. SEIU argued that the PSMFC is not a bona fide public entity. The State Personnel Board concluded otherwise, reasoning in part that the Oregon Supreme Court's decision held that the PSMFC was a public entity, and the conclusion that PSMFC was not primarily "in this state" was solely for tax exemption purposes and did not cloud the PSMFC's status as a public entity. *In re Review of Contracts between Pac. States Marine Fisheries Comm'n and the Cal. Dep't of Fish and Game and Wildlife Servs. (Contract Nos. P0981007; P0660006-01; P0680067-03; P0981003; P0970005)*, No. 11-005(b) (Cal. State Pers. Bd. Letter Op. Dec. 2, 2011).

Courts typically treat a compact agency like a state agency, rather than hold that a compact agency is a state agency. *Washington ex rel. Tattersall v. Yelle*, 52 Wash. 2d 856 (1958), provides a rare example of a court holding that a compact agency is a state agency.

> We cannot agree with appellant's premise that the [Western Interstate Commission for Higher Education] is not a state agency.
>
> Article III of the compact provides that the commission "shall be a body corporate of each compacting state and territory and an agency thereof." Art. IX, § 1, of the state constitution, provides: "It is the paramount duty of the state to make ample provision for the education of all children residing within its borders, * * *"

> The commission performs a part of the obligation imposed upon the state by this constitutional mandate. In so doing, it is an agent of this state, and is not a private corporation having special powers and privileges.

Id. at 863. The Western Interstate Commission for Higher Education (WICHE) has 15 member states. If WICHE is a Washington state agency, then is it also an agency of the other 14 states? Which Washington state agency requirements must WICHE comply with? Must WICHE also comply with the myriad state agency requirements of the other 14 states? For example, if WICHE adopts regulations, must it file rulemaking paperwork in all 14 states? What if the states' requirements for drafting rules conflict or are duplicative?

With these concepts in mind, consider the next case, *Yancoskie v. Delaware River Port Authority*. There were four *Yancoskie* cases—two filed in different U.S. district courts, and one each in New Jersey and Pennsylvania state courts. Why would Yancoskie need to file four parallel actions? The New Jersey Court of Appeals held the DRPA fell within the definition of "agency" in the New Jersey Tort Claim Act, but Yancoskie did not comply with the act's notice requirements. The U.S. District Court for the District of New Jersey held that the matter raised a federal question, but the Third Circuit reversed, holding that the federal court had no jurisdiction. The Third Circuit's opinion is in Chapter 6. Here we look at the Pennsylvania Supreme Court decision, which discussed the status of the Port Authority.

Yancoskie v. Delaware River Port Auth.
478 Pa. 396 (1978)

POMEROY, JUSTICE:

The central question for decision in this case is whether the Delaware River Port Authority is immune from suit in trespass in the courts of this State. We hold that it is not.

Appellant's husband died as a result of injuries sustained on August 16, 1972, while employed in the construction of the Admiral Barry Bridge from Chester, Pennsylvania, to Bridgeport, New Jersey. A wrongful death and survival action against the appellee Authority and other defendants was brought by the administratrix of Yancoskie's estate and by his widow and child. Under the heading of new matter in its amended answer the Authority claimed that it was "a public corporate agency or instrumentality of the Commonwealth of Pennsylvania entitled to sovereign immunity" and that it was therefore immune from suit. The Authority's subsequent motion for judgment on the pleadings was granted by the court, and the Superior Court affirmed. The case is here upon our allowance of an appeal.

The courts below, in upholding the Authority's claim of immunity, did not have the benefit of our decision in *Specter v. Commonwealth*, 462 Pa. 474 (1975). In *Specter*, it was held that an answer to the question of whether the Pennsylvania Turnpike Commission was immune from suit depended upon whether the Commission was "part of the Commonwealth." *Id.* at 478. This issue in turn required "a scrutiny of [the entity's] status in the governmental framework of Pennsylvania" that focused on its "nature * * * and its relationship to other statewide governmental bodies." *Id.* at 479. We believe that an analysis of the legislative acts defining the purposes and powers of the Delaware River Port Authority, together with the relevant judicial decisions, requires a conclusion that, like the Turnpike Commission in *Specter*, the Authority is not "an integral part of the Commonwealth," and that it is therefore subject to suit, as are "political subdivisions or governmental entities other than the Commonwealth itself." *Id.* at 478.

In considering the Authority's statutory status some historical background is useful. Pennsylvania's recent involvement in the spanning of the lower Delaware River begins with the Act of July 9, 1919. Under this statute, the Commonwealth of Pennsylvania and the City of Philadelphia undertook to provide one half of the cost of construction of what is now known as the Benjamin Franklin Bridge from Philadelphia to Camden. A group known as the Pennsylvania Commission, consisting of four governmental and four non-governmental members, was created to supervise (in conjunction with a similar commission created by the State of New Jersey) the design, construction, and operation of the planned bridge.

Although the Pennsylvania Commission was granted extensive powers, including that of eminent domain, the General Assembly added important limitations. The enabling statute specifically provided:

> the * * * commission shall not proceed to exercise or carry out any authority or power herein or hereby given it to bind the Commonwealth of Pennsylvania beyond the extent to which the Commonwealth of Pennsylvania shall have appropriated or made available to said * * * commission the moneys hereinbefore stipulated as the share of the Commonwealth of Pennsylvania."

In addition, the appropriations to the Pennsylvania Commission were not grants but loans. The tolls agreed upon by the Pennsylvania Commission and its counterpart in New Jersey were to be collected at least "until such time as the State of New Jersey, the Commonwealth of Pennsylvania and the City of Philadelphia shall each have been fully reimbursed for all moneys expended to pay the cost of said bridge and the approaches thereto," with interest on such moneys to run at four per cent per annum. Finally, it was intended that the Pennsylvania Commission was to have a limited life; upon reimbursement in full to the governments that provided the funding, the bridge was to be turned over to local authorities.

By 1931, more ambitious plans for interstate cooperation in the economic development of the lower Delaware Valley required extensive statutory change. Accordingly, Pennsylvania and New Jersey created, by means of an interstate compact, a successor to the previously existing interstate body. That successor is now known as the Delaware River Port Authority, the appellee herein. Its purpose was expanded from the operation of a single interstate bridge to embrace the development and improvement of the lower Delaware port district from Philadelphia south to the Delaware border. In addition to its power to operate and maintain the bridges across the Delaware River from Philadelphia south to the Pennsylvania-

Delaware border, the Authority is charged with the development and improvement of port facilities in this area.

The powers granted the Authority by the compact are commensurate with its broad purposes. The Authority is designated as a "public corporate instrumentality of the Commonwealth of Pennsylvania and the State of New Jersey * * * exercising an essential governmental function * * * ." As such, it is granted power: to acquire, hold, use and sell real and personal property; "to exercise the right of eminent domain"; to enter into contracts; and to employ "counsel and such other officers, and such agents and employees, as it may require for the performance of its duties * * * and [to] fix and determine their qualifications, duties and compensation."

The powers granted to the Pennsylvania Turnpike Commission are similar in nature. The Authority's implied powers, however, are considerably broader than those of the Commission. Unlike the Turnpike Commission, the Authority is permitted

> generally to exercise, in connection with its property and affairs and in connection with property within its control, any and all powers which might be exercised by a natural person or a private corporation in connection with similar property and affairs.

The Authority differs from the Turnpike Commission in another important respect. Although it is contemplated that when all the Commission's financial obligations are paid or provided for the Commission will be dissolved and its assets vested in the Commonwealth's Department of Transportation, which will then operate the Turnpike system, the Authority is granted "perpetual succession."

In one critical particular, however, the Commission and the Authority possess precisely the same status, viz., both are financially independent of the Commonwealth of Pennsylvania. The Authority, like the Commission, raises revenue by means of bonds and satisfies these obligations by toll and other user charges. Moreover, and again like the Commission, the Authority's debts are not Commonwealth obligations. Article VII of the compact provides in full:

> Notwithstanding any provision of this agreement, the commission shall have no power to pledge the credit of the Commonwealth of Pennsylvania, or the credit of the State of New Jersey, or the credit of any county, city, borough, village, township or other municipality of said Commonwealth or said State, or to create any debt of said Commonwealth or of said State or of such municipality.

The interstate compact in question does not give an explicit answer to the question whether the Authority is an "integral part of the Commonwealth," but the structure of the authority strongly indicates that it is not. The Authority is declared to be a "public corporate instrumentality," and it is vested with the powers usually granted to a corporation operated for profit, e.g., perpetual succession. Although the Authority does possess the governmental power of eminent domain, it lacks an essential attribute of a true governmental body, the taxing power. Moreover, there is no close connection, such as that between the Pennsylvania Department of Transportation and the Turnpike Commission, between the Authority and Commonwealth agencies, and the financially separate status of the Authority is expressly provided. In sum, as this Court observed some forty years ago, the compact agreed upon by Pennsylvania and New Jersey in 1931 had the effect of "relinquishing the control theretofore exercised severally by the two states [over the predecessor commissions' property] and in turning the property over to [a] two-state corporation * * * ." *Commonwealth ex rel. Smith v. Clark*, 331 Pa. 405, 414–15 (1938) (dictum).[9]

Remaining for consideration are the judicial decisions in which the status of the Authority has been in issue.

In *Delaware River Joint Comm'n Case*, 342 Pa. 119, (1941), this Court stated that the Authority's predecessor in name "acts as the agent of the Commonwealth," *Id.* at 122, and that it was therefore not required to reimburse a telephone company for the cost of relocating certain lines. The Court had no occasion, however, to discuss the precise nature of the agency, and it was sufficient to observe that the grant of a franchise to the public utility in that case "was expressly subjected to municipal regulation * * * ." *Id.*

A comprehensive discussion of the Authority's status came one year later in *Souder v. Philadelphia Police Pension Fund*, 344 Pa. 286 (1942). In that case, payments from a pension fund were discontinued after plaintiff's decedent had gone to work for the Authority's predecessor in name; the Fund relied on a provision of its by-laws authorizing suspension of payment if a beneficiary should "enter the service of the State of Pennsylvania." This Court held that employment with the Authority did not constitute entering "the service of the State" and thus did not permit the suspension of benefits. In an opinion by Mr. Justice (later Chief Justice) Drew, we said:

> By directing the Governor to enter into this compact the legislature clearly indicated its intention to abandon the previous dependent administrative agency known as the 'Pennsylvania commission', and to establish in its

---

[9] Appellee argues that certain provisions of the compact require a conclusion that the Authority is an integral part of the Commonwealth. This is said to be the case because six of the eight Pennsylvania members of the Authority are appointed by the Governor (with the Auditor General and the State Treasurer filling the two remaining seats); because the Authority is required to submit annual reports to the legislatures of both states; and because new projects (with certain exceptions) must be approved by the legislatures of both states, and in some cases by the governors thereof.

We find these contentions unpersuasive. It should be noted that the members of the Turnpike Commission are also appointed by the Governor and, unlike his appointees to the Authority, must be confirmed by the Senate. In addition, there is nothing in the requirement that a public corporation submit reports to the legislatures of the compacting states that serves to make that corporation an integral part of either state, or of both. Finally, the requirement that legislative authorization be given for new projects is not dissimilar to the statutory authorizations for the various extensions of the Pennsylvania Turnpike System.

> stead the 'Delaware River Joint Commission' [i.e., the Authority] as a special public corporation. Upon the execution of the agreement on July 1, 1931, the Commission became a distinct entity, separate and apart from either State. * * *
>
> Its obligations were payable solely from its own revenues raised by it through the sale of its bonds and the collection of tolls. Its employees were not those of this Commonwealth or of the State of New Jersey, but of this public corporation, which hired them and paid their salaries.
>
> While the Delaware River Joint Commission acts as the agent of the Commonwealth, yet it is indeed similar in structure to the various Municipal Authorities authorized by statute to be created throughout the State. They are public corporations, being corporate agencies engaged in the administration of civil government." *Id.* at 291–92.
>
> . . . .

Notes & Questions

1. Why did the DRPA argue that it is a state agency? Why might a compact agency want to be considered a state agency? Why might it not?

2. What were the court's reasons for finding that the DRPA was not a state agency? Were these compelling reasons?

3. The court noted that the federal and New Jersey state courts dismissed the parallel cases filed there and Pennsylvania precedent already held the authority to be immune from damages. The court appears to have been aware that its holding in this case would provide the only possible hook for Yancoskie's suit against the authority. Do you think the Pennsylvania Supreme Court may have been thinking that if it dismissed the case, then no court would have jurisdiction?

4. The court observed that the DRPA is a "public corporate instrumentality of the Commonwealth of Pennsylvania and the State of New Jersey . . . deemed to be exercising an essential governmental function." What is a public corporate instrumentality that exercises an essential government function?

5. The court cited an interesting excerpt from *Souder v. Philadelphia Police Pension Fund*, which reasoned that the DRPA was a "distinct entity, separate and apart from either State" because it replaced a previous dependent administrative agency. Other compact agencies have taken over the responsibilities of prior state agencies. For example, the Columbia River Gorge Commission (created by Oregon and Washington when they enacted the Columbia River Gorge Compact in 1987) replaced the Oregon Columbia River Gorge Commission and Washington Columbia River Gorge Commission, both created in the 1950s. Is replacing prior state agencies compelling reasoning that a compact agency is not a state agency?

6. Chapter 7 covers the complex question when a compact agency may be considered an arm of the state for the purpose of Eleventh Amendment immunity. Chapter 10 considers the application of state administrative procedure and open

government requirements. Both are common situations in which courts have considered whether a compact agency is a state agency. For example, in *Parkridge 6 v. U.S. Dep't of Transp.*, 420 F. App'x 265 (4th Cir. 2011), the court stated, "The [Metropolitan Washington Airports Authority] is 'a political subdivision constituted to operate and improve the Metropolitan airports,' and it exists 'independent of Virginia and its local governments, the District of Columbia, and the United States Government.' 49 U.S.C. § 49106(a)(2)–(3) (2006). As such, it is not subject to Virginia's [Freedom of Information Act]." *Id.* at 268.

7. Chapter 3 discusses the suggested Interlocal Cooperation Act, which contains a provision specifying that agreements between local governments in different states are "interstate compacts." How would you describe an entity created through an agreement between local governments in different states?

III. Compact Agencies as Federal Agencies

Should congressional consent, the presence of a federal appointee on a compact agency's governing board, or federal membership in a compact cause courts to treat a compact agency like a federal agency? Reread Judge Beezer's dissent in the *Seattle Master Builders* case in Chapter 1, and then consider the following cases:

Brooklyn Bridge Park Coal. v. Port Auth. of N.Y. & N.J.
951 F. Supp. 383 (E.D.N.Y. 1997)

Raggi, Judge:

Plaintiff Brooklyn Bridge Park Coalition ("the Coalition"), a not-for-profit corporation comprised of approximately sixty civic associations, brings this action to challenge the decision of the Port Authority of New York and New Jersey ("the Port Authority") to lease Pier 3, a pier and warehouse located on the Brooklyn waterfront, to the Strober Organization ("Strober") for use as a building supply facility and corporate headquarters. The Coalition seeks declaratory and injunctive relief, specifically: (1) a declaration that the Port Authority is a "federal agency," which must comply with provisions of the National Environmental Protection Act ("NEPA") and the Coastal Zone Management Act ("CZMA") before leasing Pier 3 to Strober . . . .

. . . .

Since many of the legal issues in this case hinge on the structure and power of the Port Authority, the court briefly discusses the creation of this entity.

New York and New Jersey have a long history of cooperation regarding their shared port. For example, in 1834, the two states entered into "an agreement fixing and determining the rights and obligations of the two States" with respect to the "bay of New York and the Hudson River." As commerce in the port expanded, the states' legislatures, in 1917, authorized their respective governors to appoint members to a "New York, New Jersey Port and Harbor Development Commission," for the purpose of studying and making recommendations concerning the operation of the common port. The end result was an interstate compact signed on April 20, 1921 and ratified by Congress on August 23, 1921, creating the Port Authority.

In giving its consent to this compact, Congress acknowledged that the waterways common to the two states had "become commercially one center or district." It recognized that "better coordination of the terminal, transportation, and other facilities of commerce in, about, and through the port of New York will result in great economies, benefiting the Nation as well as the States of New York and New Jersey." It concluded that these ends could best be attained "through the cooperation of the two States by and through a joint or common agency."

By the terms of the compact, the Port Authority is defined as "a body corporate and politic, having the powers and jurisdiction hereinafter enumerated, and such other and additional powers as shall be conferred upon it by the legislature of either State concurred in by the legislature of the other, or by Act or Acts of Congress * * * ." The enumerated powers are broad. They include

> full power and authority to purchase, construct, lease, and/or operate any kind of terminal or transportation facility [in the port] district; and to make charges for the use thereof; and for any of such purposes to own, hold, lease, and/or operate real or personal property, to borrow money and secure the same by bonds or by mortgages upon any property held or to be held by it.

The compact further provides for the Port Authority to "have such additional powers and duties as may hereafter be delegated to or imposed upon it from time to time by the action of the legislature of either State concurred in by the legislature of the other."

With respect to fiscal matters, "the Port Authority was conceived as a financially independent entity, with funds primarily derived from private investors." *Hess v. Port Authority Trans Hudson Corp.*, 513 U.S. 30, 36 (1994). Any debts or obligations incurred by the Port Authority "are not liabilities of the two founding States, and the States do not appropriate funds to the Authority." Neither does Congress appropriate funds to the Port Authority. "Tolls, fees, and investment income account for the Authority's secure financial position." *Id.*

. . . .

The Coalition asks this court to declare the Port Authority a "federal agency," which must comply with both NEPA and CZMA before leasing Pier 3 to Strober. NEPA requires "all agencies of the Federal Government" proposing a "major Federal action[] significantly affecting the quality of the human environment" to prepare an environmental impact statement or assessment. This has not been done in connection with the proposed lease of Pier 3 to Strober. CZMA requires a "Federal agency activity" that affects a coastal zone to be carried out in a manner consistent with "approved state management programs." Plaintiff submits that the Port Authority has failed to ensure that the Strober lease of Pier 3 would be consistent with New York State's Waterfront Revitalization Plan. Defendants move for dismissal of these claims on the grounds that the Port Authority is not a "federal agency" within the meaning of either of these federal statutes. This court agrees.

On its face, NEPA applies only to "agencies of the Federal Government." While the statute does not define what qualifies as a "federal agency," guidance is provided in the accompanying regulations:

> Federal agency" means all agencies of the Federal Government. It does not mean the Congress, the Judiciary, or the President, including the performance of staff functions for the President in his Executive Office. It also includes for purposes of these regulations States and units of general local government and Indian tribes assuming NEPA responsibilities under section 104(h) of the Housing and Community Development Act of 1974.

The regulations pertaining to CZMA define "Federal agency" even more narrowly to mean "any department, agency, board, commission, council, independent office or similar entity within the executive branch of the Federal Government, or any wholly owned Federal Government corporation."

This court holds that the Port Authority is not a federal agency under either statutory scheme. Plainly, the Port Authority is not "within the executive branch of the Federal Government," nor is it "a wholly owned Federal Government corporation," as provided in the regulations for CZMA. Neither is it properly viewed as an "agency of the Federal Government" for purposes of NEPA. The Federal Government plays no role in the operation of the Port Authority. The agency is governed by commissioners appointed by the states of New York and New Jersey, whose actions are subject to the veto of their respective governors. Neither Congress nor the President participates in the agency's decision making. The federal government provides the agency with no financial support.

The Coalition nevertheless submits that the Port Authority should be treated as a federal agency because it was created with the approval of Congress under the Constitution's Compact Clause. This court is not persuaded. Compact Clause entities are hybrids, occupying a special position in the federal system. As the Supreme Court has observed, a Compact Clause entity is really the creation of multiple sovereigns: the compacting states whose actions are its genesis, and the federal government, whose approval is constitutionally required when the agency will operate in an area affecting the national interest. *See Hess v. Port Authority Trans-Hudson Corp.*, 513 U.S. at 40; *Lake Country Estates, Inc. v. Tahoe Regional Planning Agency,* 440 U.S. 391, 399 (1979). While congressional approval of a bistate compact makes it appropriate to treat the document's interpretation as a federal question, this "law of the Union" doctrine does not mean that Congress intends to subsume the Compact Clause agency within the federal government or to subject its operations to general federal regulatory schemes. Indeed, the Port Authority compact suggests the contrary. Congress specifically provided for the two founding states to amend the empowerment clauses of the Port Authority compact without further federal approval. Similarly, Congress contemplated that New York and New Jersey would formulate plans for the development of their common port district without consulting, much less seeking the approval of, the

Federal Government. These states, not Congress, would be responsible for enforcement of Port Authority rules. Port Authority annual reports would be made to the states' legislatures with no copy demanded by Congress.

Despite the close association between the Port Authority and the states of New York and New Jersey, the Supreme Court has ruled that the agency does not share the Eleventh Amendment immunity of its founding states. *Hess v. Port Authority Trans-Hudson Corp.*, 513 U.S. at 52. This ruling does not, however, support plaintiff's contention that the Port Authority is a federal agency. Indeed, if that had been the Supreme Court's view, the Eleventh Amendment claim in *Hess* could have been dismissed quite easily. Instead, the Court's analysis focused on the fact-specific test articulated in *Lake Country Estates, Inc. v. Tahoe Regional Planning Agency* for determining when Compact Clause agencies are entitled to Eleventh Amendment immunity: "we * * * presume the Compact Clause agency does not qualify for Eleventh Amendment immunity 'unless there is good reason to believe that the States structured the new agency to enable it to enjoy the special constitutional protection of the States themselves, and that Congress concurred in that purpose.'" *Hess v. Port Authority Trans-Hudson Corp.*, 513 U.S. at 43–44 (quoting *Lake Country Estates, Inc. v. Tahoe Reg'l Planning Agency*, 440 U.S. at 401). The Court proceeded to review numerous factors linking the Port Authority quite closely to its founding states. Nevertheless, it concluded that the financial independence of the agency removed any "good reason" for concern about New York's or New Jersey's solvency and dignity, the factors that underpin the Eleventh Amendment. There would simply have been no need to engage in this sort of balancing if the Port Authority were a federal agency.

Indeed, the Supreme Court denied Eleventh Amendment protection to another Compact Clause agency, the Tahoe Regional Planning Agency, in *Lake Country Estates v. Tahoe Regional Planning Agency*, 440 U.S. at 402, but in the same decision held that agency members were engaged in "state action" and, therefore subject to suit under 42 U.S.C. § 1983. Once again, such a ruling would not be consistent with any view of the Compact Clause entity as a "federal agency." Indeed, when *Lake Country Estates* was before the Ninth Circuit, that court, in a ruling not reviewed by the Supreme Court, upheld dismissal of the United States as a defendant in the lawsuit, in part on the ground that Congress's approval of a compact creating an interstate agency did not establish the entity as a federal agency. *See Jacobson v. Tahoe Regional Planning Agency*, 566 F.2d 1353, 1362 (9th Cir. 1977); *accord California Tahoe Regional Planning Agency v. Sahara Tahoe Corp.*, 504 F. Supp. 753, 763 (D. Nev. 1980) (Tahoe Regional Planning Agency not a "federal agency" subject to NEPA). Thus, Supreme Court rulings denying Eleventh Amendment immunity to Compact Clause agencies provide no support for plaintiff's claim that these entities are "federal agencies."

The claims for declaratory judgment based on non-compliance with NEPA and CZMA are dismissed.

. . . .

Notes & Questions

1. The court listed several factors it considered in determining that the Port Authority is not a federal agency for the purpose of NEPA. Many compacts have one or more of these characteristics. How many of these factors should a compact agency meet to be considered a federal agency for the purpose of NEPA or other federal statutes?

(a) Federal participation in the compact. The Delaware River Basin Compact, art. 2, § 2.2, and Susquehanna River Basin Compact, art. 2, § 2.2, each specify a federal member on their commissions, and require publishing their rulemaking notices in the Federal Register and their rules in the Code of Federal Regulations. The Arkansas River Basin Compact, art. VIII, gives the President or an authorized federal agency the option of designating a commissioner representing the United States. Many other compacts, such as the Apalachicola-Chattahoochee-Flint River Basin Compact, art. VI(a), and the Columbia River Gorge Compact, art. II.a, create a commission with a non-voting federal member.

(b) Federal financial support. The Delaware River Basin Compact, arts. 12.20 & 13.3, and the Susquehanna River Basin Compact, arts 13.20 & 14.3, specify that the signatory parties (which includes the federal government) will provide capital financing and annual current expense funding. Congress's consent to the Columbia River Gorge Compact authorizes the U.S. Secretary of Agriculture to provide technical assistance to the Columbia River Gorge Commission on a non-reimbursable basis. 16 U.S.C. § 544c(c). The Pacific States Marine Fisheries Commission receives and disperses federal moneys for its activities and projects of states and other organizations. *See* http://www.psmfc.org/psmfc-info/overview.

(c) Ability for the states to amend the obligations of the agency without further federal action. Chapter 3 discussed amendments to compacts and noted that most compacts do not specifically allow the states to amend their obligations without congressional consent.

(d) Development of plans without consulting or seeking approval from the federal government. Congress's consent to the Delaware River Basin Compact requires Congress approve water development projects. Pub. L. No. 87-328, Pt. II, art. 15.1(a), 75 Stat. 688, 713 (1961). Congress's consent to the Susquehanna River Basin Compact requires that Congress approve water development projects unless the funding is solely from the states. Pub. L. No. 91-575, § 2(a), 84 Stat. 1509, 1537 (1970). Congress's consent to the Columbia River Gorge Compact requires the U.S. Secretary of Agriculture to concur with a regional plan that the compact agency adopts; however, the compact agency can override the Secretary's denial of concurrence. 16 U.S.C. § 544d(f).

(e) Requirement to submit reports to Congress. Congress's consent statutes for the Delaware River Basin Compact and the Susquehanna River Basin Compact expressly require reporting when Congress requests. Pub. L. No. 87-328, Pt. II, art. 15.1(q), 75 Stat. 688, 715 (1961) (DRBC); Pub. L. No. 91-575, § 2(p), 84 Stat. 1509, 1539 (1970) (SRBC). The Tahoe Regional Planning Compact contains the same requirement for Congress to request reporting. Pub. L. No. 96-551 § 6,

94 Stat. 3233, 3253 (1980). Chapter 10 covers reporting requirements in more detail.

2. Another case, *Corr v. Metro. Wash. Airports Auth.*, 702 F.3d 1334 (Fed. Cir. 2012), used different factors to consider whether the Metropolitan Washington Airports Authority is a federal instrumentality for the purpose of federal court jurisdiction under the "Little Tucker Act," which gives concurrent jurisdiction to the Court of Federal Claims and U.S. District Courts for claims of improperly assessed tax or penalties and for claims under $10,000.

> Little Tucker Act jurisdiction "may be invoked whenever 'a federal instrumentality acts within its statutory authority to carry out [the government's] purposes' as long as no other specific statutory provision bars jurisdiction." *Auction Co. of Am. v. FDIC*, 132 F.3d 746, 749 (D.C. Cir. 1997). Petitioners allege that MWAA is a federal instrumentality for purposes of their constitutional claims and, therefore, jurisdiction in this court is proper under the Little Tucker Act.
>
> We must therefore determine whether MWAA is a federal instrumentality. "[T]here is no simple test for ascertaining whether an institution is so closely related to governmental activity as to become a [federal] instrumentality." *Dep't of Emp't v. United States*, 385 U.S. 355, 358–59 (1966). Nonetheless, "the Supreme Court has looked to several factors, including: whether the entity was created by the government; whether it was established to pursue governmental objectives; whether government officials handle and control its operations; and whether the officers of the entity are appointed by the government." *Augustine v. Dep't of Veterans Affairs*, 429 F.3d 1334, 1339 n.3 (Fed. Cir. 2005) (citing *Lebron v. Nat'l R.R. Passenger Corp.*, 513 U.S. 374 (1995)).

Corr, 702 F.3d at 1336–37. The Federal Circuit concluded that MWAA met none of the factors for jurisdiction under the Little Tucker Act and transferred the case to the Fourth Circuit, which had federal question jurisdiction.

3. In *Corr*, the Federal Circuit also concluded that the MWAA was not a federal agency pursuant to *Lebron v. Nat'l R.R. Passenger Corp.*, 513 U.S. 374 (1995), in which the Supreme Court concluded that entities may be considered federal entities if they are created and controlled by the federal government. The Fourth Circuit also adopted the *Lebron* framework in *Kerpen v. Metro. Wash. Airports Auth.*, 907 F.3d 152 (4th Cir. 2018), and similarly concluded that the MWAA, was neither created by, nor controlled by the federal government. The Fourth Circuit also concluded that the MWAA's lease of Ronald Reagan National Airport and the federal interest in ensuring that members of Congress and federal employees have access to the airport did not convert the MWAA into a federal entity.

4. Prior to the *Brooklyn Bridge Park Coalition* case, the Third Circuit concluded that the Delaware River Basin Commission was not subject to NEPA without any discussion of the Eleventh Amendment. *Delaware Water Emergency Group v. Hansler*, 536 F. Supp. 26 (E.D. Pa. 1981), *aff'd*, 681 F.2d 805 (3d Cir. 1982).

> That DRBC is a federal agency for purposes of NEPA is very doubtful. 42 U.S.C. § 4332(2)(C) requires that an environmental impact statement be prepared as to all "major Federal actions significantly affecting the quality of the human environment." The Commission, formed by a compact among four states and the United States Government as co-equal members, would not appear to be a federal agency, nor would actions of DRBC appear to be "Federal." Arguably, to the extent that the United States' member of the Commission votes in favor of an application or otherwise acquiesces in accordance with the Compact, such approval might be deemed "Federal action" which, if of sufficient importance, could constitute "major Federal action."
>
> In *Borough of Morrisville v. Delaware River Basin Comm'n*, 399 F. Supp. 469 (E.D. Pa. 1975), *aff'd*, 532 F.2d 745 (3d Cir. 1976), Judge Newcomer of this Court, without expressly ruling on the applicability of NEPA, determined that DRBC's resolution imposing a charge for use of surface water was adopted after full compliance with NEPA. Judge Newcomer thereby suggested, at least, that DRBC is subject to the provisions of NEPA.
>
> Because DRBC regulations in substance adopt all NEPA requirements, and possibly some additional procedural steps, the issue as to whether NEPA is applicable to DRBC need not be presently decided. In addition, defendants apparently concede that if the "negative declaration" is invalid, a full FEIS would be required.

Delaware Water Emergency Group v. Hansler, 536 F. Supp. at 35–36. Selective provisions of the Delaware River Basin Compact, however, suggest that the Delaware River Basin Commission seems to meet four or all five of the criteria in the *Brooklyn Bridge Park Coalition* case. Would the court's conclusion in *Hansler* continue to be correct after the *Brooklyn Bridge Park Coalition* case? In *New York v. U.S. Army Corps of Eng'rs*, 896 F. Supp. 2d 180 (E.D.N.Y. 2012), the court dismissed for lack of standing a case involving a question whether the Delaware River Basin Commission was a federal agency subject to NEPA. The court specifically noted that it was not addressing the claim that the DRBC was a federal agency. *Id.* at 197–98.

5. Relying on the text of the compact, *Colbert v. United States*, 601 A.2d 603 (D.C. 1992), established that the Washington Metropolitan Area Transit Authority (WMATA) is not a federal agency.

> Appellant's argument that the clause in the WMATA Compact approving the transportation agreement between the District of Columbia, Maryland and Virginia has transformed WMATA into a federal agency is without merit. Initially, it ignores the explicit language of the Washington Metropolitan Area Transit Authority Compact, which provides in pertinent part:
>
>> The purpose of this Title is to create a regional *instrumentality, as a common agency of each signatory party,* empowered, in the manner hereinafter set forth, (1) to plan, develop, finance and cause to be

> operated improved transit facilities * * *, (2) to coordinate the operation of the public and privately owned or controlled transit facilities,* * * and (3) to serve such other regional purposes and to perform such other regional functions as the signatories may authorize by appropriate legislation. (Emphasis supplied.)

D.C. CODE § 1-2431 (2). *See also* D.C. CODE § 1-2431 (4) (WMATA is "an instrumentality and agency of each of the signatory parties"). Moreover, our jurisprudence has explicitly acknowledged WMATA's status as an agency of the District of Columbia.

Colbert v. United States, 601 A.2d at 605. In this case, Colbert, a former employee of WMATA had been convicted of bribery under a District of Columbia statute. The court explained, "He contend[ed] that because WMATA is not an agency of the District of Columbia, he could not be a 'public servant' to whom the bribery statute applies." *Id.* at 603. A clever argument, but the court was not persuaded.

6. *Brooklyn Bridge Park Coalition* cited to *Lake Country Estates, Inc. v. Tahoe Reg'l Planning Agency*, noting the U.S. Supreme Court held that TRPA agency members were engaged in "state action." Was the Eastern District of New York hinting that TRPA might be a state agency? An excerpt of *Lake Country Estates* appears in Chapter 7.

7. Many of the compacts that have some of the factors mentioned in *Brooklyn Bridge Park Coalition* expressly state that they are not federal agencies. Should this disclaimer matter? In the next case, *Colbert v. Pac. States Marine Fisheries Comm'n*, the court paid careful attention to such a disclaimer.

Colbert v. Pac. States Marine Fisheries Comm'n

124 Wash. App. 821 (2004)

SWEENEY, JUDGE:

Federal courts have exclusive jurisdiction over disputes involving federal agencies. But mere consent by Congress to the creation of a multistate commission (consent required by the compact clause of the United States Constitution, article I, section 10) does not mean that the resulting commission is a federal agency. The trial court held in this personal injury suit that, absent an express disclaimer, any commission created by the consent of Congress was a federal agency. We disagree and therefore reverse the court's summary dismissal of Susan Colbert's damage suit against the Pacific States Marine Fisheries Commission.

Susan Colbert was injured when she fell through a trapdoor located on a platform at Lower Granite Dam. An employee of the Pacific States Marine Fisheries Commission (Commission) had left the trapdoor open. Ms. Colbert sued the employee and the Commission for damages claiming negligence. The Commission (we will refer to the employee and the Commission as the Commission) filed a motion to dismiss for lack of subject matter jurisdiction. The court granted the motion. It concluded that the Commission was a federal agency and that the suit was therefore subject to federal jurisdiction, exclusively.

Ms. Colbert challenges the trial court's essential characterization of the Commission as a federal agency.

. . . .

The compact clause of the United States Constitution requires that Congress approve agreements or compacts between or among states. But even then it is only those agreements which tend to concentrate political power in the states and thus encroach upon the supremacy of the United States. Congress does not actually create a compact entity by providing its consent. It simply provides the authority for the states to do so.

The consent of Congress causes the compact agreement itself to become federal law. Therefore, federal law applies to all litigation regarding the scope or construction of the language establishing the compact. State law may apply to matters within the language of the compact if the compact expressly provides for state law to apply.

But while compacts may be treated as federal law, it does not necessarily follow that the fruits of these compacts are federal agencies. *Old Town Trolley Tours of Wash., Inc. v. Wash. Metro. Area Transit Comm'n*, 129 F.3d 201, 204 (D.C. Cir. 1997). The agency created is an authority of the states creating it. This is not true, however, if the compact specifically incorporates federal law, unless the compact also includes a congressional disclaimer that the agency created is not a federal agency. *See Tucker v. Columbia River Gorge Comm'n*, 73 Wash. App. 74, 78 (1994); *Skamania County v. Woodall*, 104 Wash. App. 525 (2001); *Seattle Master Builders [Ass'n v. Pac. Nw. Elec. Power & Cons. Planning Council*, 786 F.2d 1359 (9th Cir. 1986)].

We can find no support for the Commission's position that all interstate compact entities are federal agencies absent such a disclaimer.

Tucker and *Skamania* dealt with questions generally related to the Columbia River Gorge Commission. It was formed by an interstate compact. And the compact creating that commission included more than simple congressional consent to the compact. 16 U.S.C. § 544c. There, the Columbia River Gorge Commission's operations were specifically spelled out by the federal government:

> (A) the States of Oregon and Washington shall establish by way of an interstate agreement a regional agency known as the Columbia River Gorge Commission, *and shall incorporate sections 544 to 544p of this title by specific reference in such agreement. The Commission shall carry out its functions and responsibilities in accordance with the provisions of the interstate agreement and of sections 544 to 544p of this title and shall not be considered an agency or instrumentality of the United States for the purpose of any Federal law.*

16 U.S.C. § 544c(a)(1)(A) (emphasis added). And the Washington statute ratifying the Columbia River Gorge Commission compact acknowledges as much:

> A compact is entered into by and between the states of Washington and Oregon, signatories hereto, with the consent of the Congress of the United

> States of America, *granted by an Act entitled, "The Columbia River Gorge National Scenic Area Act," P.L. 99-663.*
>
> ARTICLE I
>
> COLUMBIA GORGE COMMISSION ESTABLISHED
>
> a. The States of Oregon and Washington establish by way of this interstate compact a regional agency known as the Columbia River Gorge Commission. *The commission established in accordance with this compact shall have the power and authority to perform all functions and responsibilities in accordance with the provisions of this compact and of the Columbia River Gorge National Scenic Area Act (the federal Act), which is incorporated by this specific reference in this agreement.*

RCW 43.97.015 (emphasis added). And so a disclaimer expressly denying the federal character of the commission was necessary: "The Commission * * * *shall not be considered an agency or instrumentality of the United States for the purpose of any Federal law.*" 16 U.S.C. § 544c(a)(1)(A) (emphasis added).

The Pacific Northwest Electric Power and Conservation Planning Council is another example of the same problem. *Seattle Master Builders*, 786 F.2d at 1362–63. Again, specific federal laws for the Council's operation are set out in the compact by the federal government:

> (1) The purposes of this section are to provide for the prompt establishment and effective operation of the Pacific Northwest Electric Power and Conservation Planning Council, *to further the purposes of this chapter . . . and to otherwise expeditiously and effectively carry out the Council's responsibilities and functions under this chapter.*
>
> (2) To achieve such purposes and facilitate cooperation among the States of Idaho, Montana, Oregon, and Washington, and with the Bonneville Power Administration, the consent of Congress is given *for an agreement described in this paragraph and not in conflict with this chapter, pursuant to which -*
>
> (A) * * * the "Pacific Northwest Electric Power and Conservation Planning Council" * * * (ii) *shall carry out its functions and responsibilities in accordance with the provisions of this chapter* , (iii) *shall continue in force and effect in accordance with the provisions of this chapter, and* (iv) *except as otherwise provided in this chapter, shall not be considered an agency or instrumentality of the United States for the purpose of any Federal law.*

16 U.S.C. § 839b(a) (emphasis added). And again, the Washington statute for Washington's participation in the council also expressly incorporates the federal act: "The state of Washington agrees to participate in the Pacific Northwest Electric Power and Conservation Planning Council *pursuant to the Pacific Northwest Electric Power Planning and Conservation Act [federal Act]*." RCW 43.52A.010 (emphasis added).

So the disclaimer set out in 16 U.S.C. § 839b(a)(2)(A)(iv) of the federal act was necessary to specifically disclaim that the council was [not] a federal agency for the purposes of federal law. Without the disclaimer the agency appeared to be just that—a federal agency. Incidentally, the court noted the importance of maintaining the council as a multistate entity in several references to the legislative history. *Seattle Master Builders*, 786 F.2d at 1363 ("Congress wanted to avoid conflicts with state law and to maintain accountability through the application of federal substantive and procedural law, * * * but also wanted to avoid the potential constitutional problems of a federal agency composed of state appointees.").

We are led to conclude from these cases that where federal law is not expressly incorporated into the compact, a disclaimer that the agency is not a federal agency is unnecessary. *See Salmon for All [v. Dep't of Fisheries]*, 118 Wash. 2d 270 [1992]; RCW 77.75.010. The Columbia River Compact is an example of a compact controlled by state law:

> There exists between the states of Washington and Oregon a definite compact and agreement as follows:
>
> *All laws and regulations now existing or which may be necessary* for regulating, protecting or preserving fish in the waters of the Columbia river, or its tributaries, over which the states of Washington and Oregon have concurrent jurisdiction, or which would be affected by said concurrent jurisdiction, *shall be made, changed, altered and amended in whole or in part, only with the mutual consent and approbation of both states.*

RCW 77.75.010 (emphasis added).

Here, Congress provided nothing more than its consent: "To ratify the compact and agreement between the States of Oregon and Washington regarding concurrent jurisdiction over the waters of the Columbia River and its tributaries in connection with regulating, protecting, and preserving fish." Act of Apr. 8, 1918. The compact incorporates no federal law. *Id.* In fact, no federal statute forms the Columbia River Compact; this was left up to the states.

And our Supreme Court noted that the Columbia River Compact was not a federal agency: "The Columbia River Compact, *a multistate entity*, is the chief regulatory authority over non-Indian commercial salmon fishing on the Columbia River." *Salmon for All*, 118 Wash. 2d at 275 (emphasis added). The federal government did not disclaim the federal nature of the Columbia River Compact in *Salmon for All.* But any such disclaimer was unnecessary. *Id.* Nothing in Congress's consent implied that it was a federal agency.

The Commission relies on our Supreme Court's holding in *Tucker*: "the federal government must specifically disclaim the federal nature of an interstate compact agency for a commission to be considered an instrumentality of the states. *Tucker (vs) Columbia River Gorge Commission*, 73 Wash. App. 74." But this case is not *Tucker*.

Unlike the Columbia River Gorge Commission in *Tucker* and *Skamania*, state legislation creating the Commission did not expressly incorporate federal law. The compact here is completely governed by the member states: "This agreement shall become operative immediately as to those states executing it whenever the compacting states have executed it in the form that is *in accordance with the laws of the executing states* and the congress has given its consent." RCW 77.75.030, art. II (emphasis added). Article V states: "*Said commission shall adopt rules and regulations for the conduct of its business.*" RCW 77.75.030, art. V (emphasis added). Article VI states: "No action shall be taken by the commission except by the affirmative vote of a majority of the whole number of compacting states represented at any meeting." RCW 77.75.030, art. VI.

No federal statute directs that federal law is controlling. Unlike the Columbia River Gorge Commission, Congress simply consented to the interstate compact: "Granting the consent and approval of Congress to an interstate compact relating to the better utilization of the fisheries (marine, shell, and anadromous) of the Pacific coast and creating the Pacific Marine Fisheries Commission." Act of July 24, 1947, Pub. L. No. 80-232, 61 Stat. 419–422. The Commission here is similar to the Columbia River Compact in *Salmon for All.* Like the Columbia River Compact, Congress provided its consent to the interstate compact *without* incorporating federal laws. *Id.*

We conclude then that the Commission is a multistate entity, not a federal agency.

The Commission argues nonetheless that a state agency (or here a multistate agency) may be converted into a federal agency if it engages in contracts with the federal government where the federal government ultimately controls the agency's operations. But the question is not whether the agency "receives federal money and must comply with federal standards and regulations, but whether its day-to-day operations are supervised by the Federal Government." Congress finances many programs but that does not mean that it controls the details of their actual performance.

The Commission has contracts with the federal government and receives federal moneys. But we find nothing in this record to suggest that the federal government controls its daily operations. To the contrary, the Commission is run entirely by the participating states. Money is not the determining factor; control is. And we do not see that control here.

The Pacific States Marine Fisheries Commission is not a federal agency. And its employees are not, therefore, federal employees. Washington courts have subject matter jurisdiction over this dispute.

We reverse the trial court's decision to the contrary.

Notes & Questions

1. Here, the Washington Court of Appeals concluded that the Pacific States Marine Fisheries Commission is not a federal agency. Recall the Pacific States Marine Fisheries Commission case presented earlier in this chapter in which the Oregon court concluded that the commission is not a public corporation "in this state." How would you succinctly describe what the commission is to an average person or to a court that is unfamiliar with compacts?

2. Do you agree with the court's reasoning that a compact must affirmatively declare a compact agency is not a federal agency when the compact contains some reference to federal law? Should the mere presence or absence of a disclaimer be controlling? Should such a disclaimer be just another factor such as those from the *Brooklyn Bridge Park Coalition* case?

The court's reasoning relied heavily on the Columbia River Gorge Compact; however, Congress actually had a different reason for disclaiming the Gorge Commission as a federal agency. Congress's consent to the Columbia River Gorge Compact was just six months after the *Seattle Master Builders* decision. Both compacts involve the Columbia River in the Pacific Northwest. Archived records from Senator Dan Evans, who was one of the principal authors of the federal consent statute authorizing the Columbia River Gorge Compact, show that Judge Beezer's dissent (excerpted in Chapter 1) was fresh on the minds of the Oregon and Washington congressional delegation. The federal legislators added this provision and several others to ensure that the creation of the Gorge Commission would not violate the Appointments Clause of the U.S. Constitution. Memorandum from Joe Mentor and Mike Salsgiver to [Senator] Mark O. Hatfield (Nov. 7, 1986) (on file with author).

3. Why do parties argue that compact agencies are federal agencies? Are these arguments expeditious for the specific issues in the cases or part of a long-term strategy? What benefits would a compact agency gain by being classified as a federal agency? What burdens might the agency face?

4. In contrast to *Brooklyn Bridge Park Coalition* and *Colbert*, courts commonly apply federal law to compact agencies after concluding the agency is not a federal agency. In *Ingerman v. Del. River Port Auth.*, 630 F. Supp. 2d 426 (D.N.J. 2009), the Delaware River Port Authority argued that the federal Privacy Act of 1974 did not apply to it because it was not a federal agency. The court concluded that the Port Authority was not a federal agency, but that the Privacy Act applied broadly to government agencies and the DRPA is an agency to which the Privacy Act applied. Does the application of federal law depend on the terms of a federal law more than the terms of a compact and the characterization of the agency in the compact? Chapter 5 discusses the application of federal law in more detail.

In *Colbert*, the Washington Court of Appeals cited to a similar case, *Old Town Trolley Tours of Wash., Inc. v. Wash. Metro. Area Transit Comm'n*, 129 F.3d 201, 204 (D.C. Cir. 1997), which held that the Transit Commission was not a federal agency, but that the court should use the standards of review specified in the federal Administrative Procedure Act (APA) to review the Transit Commission's decision. In another line of cases, courts have asked whether a particular compact agency is so endowed with a "federal interest" that it should be considered a "quasi-federal agency" for the purpose of judicial review under the federal APA. The lead in this line of cases was *Seal & Co. v. Wash. Metro. Area Transit Auth.*, 768 F. Supp. 1150 (E.D. Va. 1991). However, in 2010, the Second Circuit expressed significant doubt about the validity of the "quasi-federal agency" doctrine for applying the federal APA to compact agencies. *New York v. Atl. States*

Marine Fisheries Comm'n, 609 F.3d 524, 533–35 (2d Cir. 2010). The Second Circuit concluded, "[I]n the absence of other factors not present in this case, the acts of Congress in approving the interstate Compact, in adopting the ACFCMA, and in providing funding to the Commission, did not transmogrify the ASMFC into a 'quasi-federal' agency." *Id.* at 535–36. Chapter 10 discusses the application of the federal APA to compact agencies and contains excerpts of the *Old Town Trolley* and *Atlantic States* cases.

5. Can a compact agency be considered a federal agency for one purpose, but a state agency for another? Compare *Seal* and *The Bootery, Inc. v. Wash. Metro. Area Transit Auth.*, 326 F. Supp. 794 (D.D.C. 1971) (holding that Congress's role as legislature for the District of Columbia supported a finding that the Transit Authority "should be treated like a federal agency subject to the [federal] APA") with *Morris v. Wash. Metro. Area Transit Auth.*, 781 F.2d 218 (D.C. Cir. 1986) (holding that the states (including the District of Columbia) conferred their Eleventh Amendment immunity on WMATA—essentially treating WMATA like a state agency).

After reading this section, how would you characterize an interstate compact agency? Should compact agencies be considered state agencies or federal agencies for some purposes? What analysis should courts use to determine how to characterize a compact agency? Should there be a different analysis for different purposes? What are the implications for characterizing compact agencies as separate and independent of the states and federal governments?

CHAPTER 5: COMPACTS AS FEDERAL LAW

The Supreme Court has long recognized the federal government's involvement in the compacting process; however, the implications of that federal involvement have fluctuated. Except for a few early decisions from the Supreme Court, congressional consent has always enabled federal court jurisdiction for enforcing compacts. In contrast, the Supreme Court originally held, then questioned whether, and then finally held again that consent transforms a compact into federal law. The Supreme Court's 1981 *Cuyler v. Adams* decision seems to have solidified that concept now, and several cases excerpted and cited in Chapters 1 through 4 have relied on this concept, citing *Cuyler*. The Supreme Court has used the term "law of the union" as a general reference to the compact-as-federal-law concept. Courts are still exploring and developing the implications of the "law of the union," which makes it an interesting study and an area with plenty of potential for new application or disagreement with current applications.

I. ORIGIN OF THE "LAW OF THE UNION" DOCTRINE

Cuyler v. Adams explained the history of the law of the union doctrine and reaffirmed the concept that a compact enacted with the consent of Congress becomes federal law. The dissent was understandably disturbed. Take the time to understand the reasoning in both opinions.

Cuyler v. Adams
449 U.S. 433 (1981)

BRENNAN, JUSTICE:

. . . .

In April 1976, respondent John Adams was convicted in Pennsylvania state court of robbery and was sentenced to 30 years in the State Correctional Institution at Graterford, Pa. The Camden County (New Jersey) prosecutor's office subsequently lodged a detainer against respondent and in May 1977 filed a "Request for Temporary Custody" pursuant to Art. IV of the Detainer Agreement in order to bring him to Camden for trial on charges of armed robbery and other offenses.

[Under the Detainer Agreement, a state or the federal government with an untried complaint or indictment against a person serving a term of imprisonment in another state may file a "detainer" and seek temporary custody of that person to resolve the complaint or indictment. A prisoner may also initiate final disposition of untried complaints or indictments in another state.]

In an effort to prevent his transfer, respondent filed a *pro se* class-action complaint in June 1977 in the United States District Court for the Eastern District of Pennsylvania. He sought declaratory, injunctive, and monetary relief under 42 U.S.C. §§ 1981 and 1983, alleging . . . that petitioners had violated the Due Process Clause by failing to inform him of his right pursuant to Art. IV(a) of the Detainer Agreement to petition Pennsylvania's Governor to disapprove New Jersey's request for custody. Respondent contended, *inter alia*, that had he been granted a hearing or advised of his right to petition the Governor, he would have been able to convince Pennsylvania authorities to deny the custody request.

The District Court, without reaching the class certification issue, dismissed respondent's complaint in October 1977 for failure to state a claim upon which relief could be granted. Respondent was then transferred to New Jersey, where he was convicted, sentenced to a 9 1/2-year prison term (to be served concurrently with his Pennsylvania sentence), and returned to Pennsylvania.

The Court of Appeals for the Third Circuit vacated the District Court judgment and remanded for further proceedings. Finding no need to reach respondent's constitutional claims, it concluded as a matter of statutory construction that respondent had a right under Art. IV(d) of the Detainer Agreement to the procedural safeguards, including a pretransfer "hearing," prescribed by § 10 of the Extradition Act. It made no finding with respect to respondent's argument that he was entitled to notification of his right to petition the Governor.

While this case was on appeal, a Pennsylvania state court held that state prisoners transferred under Art. IV of the Detainer Agreement have no constitutional right to a pretransfer hearing. Although the Court of Appeals did not reach this constitutional issue, it held that it was not bound by the state court's result because the Detainer Agreement is an interstate compact approved by Congress and is thus a federal law subject to federal rather than state construction. Before reaching the merits of the Third Circuit's decision, we must determine whether that conclusion was correct. We hold that it was.

The Compact Clause of the United States Constitution, Art. I, § 10, cl. 3, provides that "No State shall, without the Consent of the Congress, * * * enter into any Agreement or Compact with another State * * * ." Because congressional consent transforms an interstate compact within this Clause into a law of the United States, we have held that the construction of an interstate agreement sanctioned by Congress under the Compact Clause presents a federal question. *See Petty v. Tennessee-Missouri Bridge Comm'n*, 359 U.S. 275, 278 (1959); *West Virginia ex rel. Dyer v. Sims*, 341 U.S. 22, 28 (1951); *Delaware River Joint Toll Bridge Comm'n v. Colburn*, 310 U.S. 419, 427 (1940).[7] It thus remains to be determined

---

[7] The "law of the Union" doctrine upon which this principle is based had its origin in *Pennsylvania v. Wheeling & Belmont Bridge Co.*, 13 How. 518 (1852). In that case, a bridge construction company defended a nuisance suit on the ground that the state legislature had authorized construction of the offending bridge. The company argued that the state legislative authorization shielded it from the nuisance suit because "there is no act of Congress prohibiting obstructions on the Ohio River, and * * * until there shall be such a regulation, a State, in the construction of bridges, has a right to exercise its own discretion on the subject." This Court rejected that argument in light of a clause in the Virginia-Kentucky Compact of 1789, sanctioned by Congress, declaring that the use and navigation of the Ohio River shall be "free and common to the citizens of the United States." Even though there had been no Act of Congress explicitly regulating navigation on the river, the

whether the Detainer Agreement is a congressionally sanctioned interstate compact within Art I, § 10, of the Constitution.

The requirement of congressional consent is at the heart of the Compact Clause. By vesting in Congress the power to grant or withhold consent, or to condition consent on the States' compliance with specified conditions, the Framers sought to ensure that Congress would maintain ultimate supervisory power over cooperative state action that might otherwise interfere with the full and free exercise of federal authority. See Frankfurter & Landis, *The Compact Clause of the Constitution—A Study in Interstate Adjustments*, 34 YALE L.J. 685, 694–695 (1925).

Congressional consent is not required for interstate agreements that fall outside the scope of the Compact Clause. Where an agreement is not "directed to the formation of any combination tending to the increase of political power in the States, which may encroach upon or interfere with the just supremacy of the United States," it does not fall within the scope of the Clause and will not be invalidated for lack of congressional consent. *See, e.g.*, *United States Steel Corp. v. Multistate Tax Comm'n*, 434 U.S. 452, 468 (1978); *New Hampshire v. Maine*, 426 U.S. 363, 369–70 (1976). But where Congress has authorized the States to enter into a cooperative agreement, and where the subject matter of that agreement is an appropriate subject for congressional legislation, the consent of Congress transforms the States' agreement into federal law under the Compact Clause.[8]

Court stated that the prohibition in the Compact was controlling because "[t]his compact, by the sanction of Congress, has become a law of the Union. What further legislation can be desired for judicial action?

Although the law-of-the-Union doctrine was questioned in *People v. Central R. Co.*, 12 Wall. 455, 456 (1872) and in *Hinderlider v. La Plata River & Cherry Creek Ditch Co.*, 304 U.S. 92, 109 (1938), any doubts as to its continued vitality were put to rest in *Delaware River Joint Toll Bridge Comm'n v. Colburn*, where the Court stated:

> In *People v. Central Railroad*, . . . jurisdiction of this Court to review a judgment of a state court construing a compact between states was denied on the ground that the Compact was not a statute of the United States and that the construction of the Act of Congress giving consent was in no way drawn in question, nor was any right set up under it. This decision has long been doubted, . . . and we now conclude that the construction of such a compact sanctioned by Congress by virtue of Article I, § 10, Clause 3 of the Constitution, involves a federal "title, right, privilege or immunity" which when "specially set up and claimed' in a state court may be reviewed here on certiorari under § 237(b) of the Judicial Code, 28 U.S.C. § 344.

This holding reaffirmed the law-of-the-Union doctrine and the underlying principle that congressional consent can transform interstate compacts into federal law. *Accord, Petty v. Tennessee-Missouri Bridge Comm'n*, 359 U.S. at 278; *see also United States ex rel. Esola v. Groomes*, 520 F.2d 830, 841 (3d Cir. 1975) (Garth, J., concurring); *League to Save Lake Tahoe v. Tahoe Regional Planning Agency*, 507 F.2d 517 (9th Cir. 1974).

[8] See *West Virginia ex rel. Dyer v. Sims*, 341 U.S. 22, 26 (1951) (congressional consent given to compact to control pollution in interstate streams, "an appropriate subject for national legislation"); *Petty v. Tennessee-Missouri Bridge Comm'n*, *supra* at 281 (congressional consent given to compact affecting navigable waters and interstate commerce).

Congress may consent to an interstate compact by authorizing joint state action in advance or by giving expressed or implied approval to an agreement the States have already joined. *Virginia v. Tennessee*, *supra* at 521; *Green v. Biddle*, 8 Wheat. 1, 85–87 (1823). In the case of the Detainer Agreement, Congress gave its consent in advance by enacting the Crime Control Consent Act. . . .

. . . .

Because this Act was intended to be a grant of consent under the Compact Clause, and because the subject matter of the Act is an appropriate subject for congressional legislation, we conclude that the Detainer Agreement is a congressionally sanctioned interstate compact the interpretation of which presents a question of federal law.

REHNQUIST, JUSTICE, DISSENTING (WITH CHIEF JUSTICE BURGER AND JUSTICE STEWART):

In a remarkable feat of judicial alchemy the Court today transforms state law into federal law. It decides that the construction of an enactment of the Pennsylvania Legislature, for which the consent of Congress was not required under the Constitution, and to which Congress never consented at all save in the vaguest terms some 25 years prior to its passage, presents a federal question. Nothing in the prior decisions of this Court suggests, say nothing of compels, such an untoward result.

The cases relied upon by the Court establish, at most, that the interpretation of an interstate compact sanctioned by Congress pursuant to the Compact Clause will present a federal question. . . .

[Justice Rehnquist questioned whether the Detainer Agreement required consent].

What is most disturbing about the Court's analysis is its potential sweep. The statute books of the States are full of reciprocal legislation in the criminal area. As this Court made clear in *Multistate Tax Comm'n*, such reciprocal legislation is as subject to the Compact Clause as other more formal interstate agreements. In light of the Court's analysis in this case, it is not at all clear why the construction of each of the provisions in this broad array of state legislation is not a federal matter. It is apparently no answer that congressional consent was not required under the Compact Clause; the same is true with the Detainer Agreement. And the congressional "consent" in the Crime Control Consent Act of 1934 applies with the same force to all this reciprocal legislation as it does to the Detainer

---

As Justice WHITE stated, dissenting in *United States Steel Corp. v. Multistate Tax Comm'n*, 434 U.S. 452 (1978):

> Congress does not pass upon a submitted compact in the manner of a court of law deciding a question of constitutionality. Rather, the requirement that Congress approve a compact is to obtain its political judgment: Is the agreement likely to interfere with federal activity in the area, is it likely to disadvantage other States to an important extent, is it a matter that would better be left untouched by state and federal regulation? *Id.* at 485.

Agreement. Yet it has never been supposed that the construction of the terms of such reciprocal legislation is a matter on which federal courts could override the courts of the enacting State. Enough has been said to demonstrate that the Court's opinion threatens to become a judicial Midas meandering through the state statute books, turning everything it touches into federal law.

Since I view the Detainer Agreement as a state statute, I would defer to the state court's interpretation of it....

Notes & Questions

1. Did the Supreme Court need to state that consent transforms a compact into federal law to resolve Adams's claims? What might have caused the Court to include this reasoning in its decision? The Supreme Court did not discuss any implications of concluding that consent transforms a compact into federal law. Before continuing, consider what some of those implications might be.

2. The Supreme Court also did not discuss any practical reasons why consent transforms a compact into federal law. Consider reasons noted by the U.S. District Court in *Pievsky v. Ridge,* 921 F. Supp. 1335 (M.D. Pa. 1996) why a compact should present a federal question.

> The Supreme Court's conclusion that the interpretation of a congressionally approved interstate agreement presents a question of federal law rests upon the need to "safeguard * * * national interest[s]" that are necessarily affected when two or more states enter into agreements that potentially impact federal authority. In order to fully ensure the protection of federal interests, the interpretation of an interstate compact necessarily must comport with federal law. For the Supreme Court to have held otherwise would have resulted in states acting as the final arbiters in interstate disputes regarding the meaning of congressionally approved interstate agreements. States would have held the power to unilaterally nullify compacts, and their terms would have been subject to varying interpretations.

Id. at 1338. Does this reasoning sound like the Supreme Court's reasoning in *West Virginia ex rel. Dyer v. Sims*? In Chapter 2, you learned that the function of congressional consent is to protect the supremacy of the United States and to protect non-compacting states from compacting states. Is the transformation of a compact into federal law necessary to protect the United States or non-compacting states, or does it protect the compacting states from individual state actions that conflict with the collective interest of the compacting states, or both?

3. Recall *Kansas City Area Transp. Auth. v. Missouri*, 640 F.2d 173 (8th Cir. 1981) (excerpted in Chapter 3), in which the Eighth Circuit noted that a state may not enact a law "in reprobation of the compact." *Id.* at 174. In contrast, Chapter 2 discussed that Congress is not similarly restricted—it can enact new legislation that specifically targets a compact. Why is there a difference in state and federal legislative authority?

4. Justice Rehnquist noted in his dissent that "the construction of a compact not requiring consent even if Congress has consented will not present a federal

question." 449 U.S. at 452. The majority in *U.S. Steel* (excerpted in Chapter 2), decided three years before *Cuyler v. Adams*, also hinted at this issue, stating, "It is true that most multilateral compacts have been submitted for congressional approval. But this historical practice, which may simply reflect considerations of caution and convenience on the part of the submitting States, is not controlling." *U.S. Steel*, 434 U.S. at 471. Similarly, in *Wash. Metro. Area Transit Auth. v. One Parcel of Land*, 706 F.2d 1312 (4th Cir. 1983), the court stated, "Nor will a compact become federal law simply because Congress, in an excess of caution, enacts consent legislation." *Id.* at 1317. Why would a compact that receives congressional consent unnecessarily neither be considered federal law, nor present a federal question?

5. In *Bi-State Dev. Agency v. Dir. of Revenue,* 781 S.W.2d 80 (Mo. 1989) the Missouri Supreme Court stated, "Application of the law of the union doctrine, moreover, is limited to cases in which state law conflicts with federal law." *Id.* at 83. Why should compacts only be considered federal law when state law conflicts with federal law? How else may state action potentially impair the "just supremacy of the United States"?

6. The transformation into federal law is not unique to interstate compacts. For example, courts have held when the federal Environmental Protection Agency approves state implementation plans pursuant to the federal Clean Air Act and Clean Water Act, those state plans become federal law. *See Safe Air for Everyone v. EPA*, 488 F.3d 1088, 1091 (9th Cir. 2007) (Clean Air Act); *Trustees for Alaska v. Fink*, 17 F.3d 1209, 1210 n.3 (9th Cir. 1994) (same); *Arkansas v. Oklahoma*, 503 U.S. 91, 110 (1992) (Clean Water Act).

7. Justice Rehnquist's dissent questioned whether other reciprocal criminal laws (non-compact laws) would also be considered federal law. Was this a legitimate concern, or was the majority's opinion sufficiently narrow?

8. *California Dep't of Transp. v. City of South Lake Tahoe*, 466 F. Supp. 527 (E.D. Cal. 1978), involved the question whether NEPA applies to a compact agency, and predated the *Brooklyn Bridge Park Coalition* case from Chapter 4. The Eastern District of California concluded that NEPA did not apply, but consider its reasoning.

> Section 102(2)(C) of NEPA, 42 U.S.C. § 4332(2)(C) (1976), requires all "agencies of the Federal Government" to the fullest extent possible to "include in every recommendation or report on proposals for legislation and other major Federal actions significantly affecting the quality of the human environment" an environmental impact report (EIR) analyzing the consequences of, and alternatives to, the proposed action. A threshold question is thus whether TRPA is a federal agency within the meaning of this provision. This is a matter of first impression, and to determine the guiding principles we must analyze the other cases involving the implications of congressional consent to interstate compacts.
>
> The Supreme Court has long held that the construction of an interstate compact presents a federal question for the purpose of certiorari review of

judgments of the highest state court under 28 U.S.C. § 1257(3). *Delaware River Joint Toll Bridge Comm'n v. Colburn*, 310 U.S. 419 (1940); [*West Virginia ex rel.*] *Dyer v. Sims*, 341 U.S. 22 (1951). This position was based on the conclusion in *Colburn* that the construction of such a [bi-state] compact sanctioned by Congress by virtue of Article I, § 10, Clause 3 of the Constitution, involves a federal "title, right, privilege, or immunity" which when "specially set up or claimed" in a state court may be reviewed here on certiorari under [the predecessor of 28 U.S.C. § 1257(3)].

While the Supreme Court did not clearly articulate the rationale for its conclusion in *Colburn*, the decision appears to have been based on the "law of the Union" doctrine—i.e., on the theory that congressional consent transforms an interstate compact into a federal law. The Ninth Circuit's holding in *League to Save Lake Tahoe v. Tahoe Regional Planning Agency*, 507 F.2d 517, 519–22 (9th Cir. 1974), that construction of an interstate compact presents a federal question was based on this interpretation of *Colburn*. The Ninth Circuit has emphasized, however, that its holding was also supported by a strong policy favoring access to the federal courts where conflicts develop over the interpretation of interstate compacts. *Id.* at 522–24; *League to Save Lake Tahoe v. B.J.K. Corp.*, 547 F.2d 1072, 1074–75 (9th Cir. 1976). *See generally* Comment, *Federal Question Jurisdiction to Interpret Interstate Compacts*, 64 GEO. L.J. 87, 107–11 (1975).

As a logical implication of the law of the Union doctrine, plaintiff argues that TRPA, in administering the Compact, is a federal agency and is therefore subject to the provisions of NEPA. While such an interpretation is not inconsistent with *Colburn*, plaintiff has failed to cite a single modern case not involving a jurisdictional question in which courts have applied the law of the Union doctrine to interstate compacts. The Ninth Circuit impliedly declined to apply the doctrine in *Jacobson v. Tahoe Regional Planning Agency*, 566 F.2d 1353 (9th Cir. 1977), in which it held that landowners could not sue the United States although they had allegedly been deprived of the beneficial use of their property as a result of down-zoning mandated by a TRPA ordinance. The court stated: "We agree with the district court that the approval of the Compact by Congress and the limited appointment power of the President [to appoint a single non-voting representative to the governing body pursuant to Article VIII(d)(3) of the Compact] do not thereby establish the TRPA as an agency of the United States." *Id.* at 1362–63.

Jacobson reflects the strong policy reasons for not implicating the federal government in the operation of interstate compacts merely because of the constitutional requirement of congressional consent to such compacts. Indeed, giving the law of the Union doctrine expansive application would as a practical matter spell the death knell for interstate compacts, since states would understandably be reluctant to enter into agreements to solve regional problems if by doing so they would subject themselves to a host of federal regulations.

Thus we reject plaintiff's argument that, by virtue of the law of the Union doctrine, TRPA is a federal agency within the meaning of NEPA.

California Dep't of Transp. v. City of South Lake Tahoe, 466 F. Supp. at 534–36. Do you agree with the court's reasoning for keeping a narrow law of the union doctrine?

II. Implications of the "Law of the Union" Doctrine

California Dep't of Transp. v. City of South Lake Tahoe, excerpted above, is still the best direct discussion of the implications of the law of the union doctrine. Below are several additional implications that naturally flow from congressional consent or are related fallout of a compact being federal law. As you study these implications, keep in mind *Jacobson's* admonition that a broad application of the law of the union doctrine would be a death knell for compacts.

A compact that is federal law is treated as any other federal statute in a conflict-of-laws analysis. *See, e.g.*, *NYSA-ILA Vacation and Holiday Fund v. Waterfront Comm'n of N.Y. Harbor*, 732 F.2d 292 (2d Cir. 1984) (compact that had received congressional consent was not preempted or superseded by federal ERISA statute); *Am. Sugar Refining Co. v. Waterfront Comm'n of N.Y. Harbor*, 55 N.Y.2d 11, 29–30 (1982) (because a compact provision is "federal law," conflicts between compact provisions and federal statutes cannot be resolved by "preemption" analysis, but by an analysis of whether one "impliedly repeals" another); *Lake Tahoe Watercraft Recreation Ass'n v. Tahoe Reg'l Planning Agency*, 24 F. Supp. 2d 1062, 1073 (E.D. Cal. 1998) ("to the extent the two federal schemes [the Clean Water Act and the Tahoe Compact] conflict, the Compact should be given effect 'because it is a congressional enactment passed later in time and, is more specific than the [Clean Water Act] as it is limited to a very narrow geographical area.'"); *City of South Lake Tahoe v. Tahoe Reg'l Planning Agency*, 664 F. Supp. 1375, 1378 (E.D. Cal. 1987) ("The only common ground of the [Compact and the Airline Deregulation Act] is geographic and perhaps incidental but is not substantive. As for this geographic overlap, the Compact is clearly more specific and enacted later in time."). Compare these holdings to Judge Beezer's dissent in *Seattle Master Builders* (excerpted in Chapter 1), in which he argued that a compact could not guide actions of a federal agency.

A compact that is federal law also supersedes the party states' constitutions. The notes following *West Virginia ex rel. Dyer v. Sims* in Chapter 3 discuss several cases concluding that compacts supersede limits in state constitutions. In each of those cases, the courts specify that as federal law, the compact preempts state statutory and constitutional provisions. In contrast, a compact that has not received the consent of Congress may not supersede state constitutions. Consider this succinct reasoning from the *PacifiCorp v. Montana Dep't of Revenue*, 254 Mont. 387 (1992): "Because [the Multistate Tax Commission] derives powers from and on behalf of its member states, it exercises no more power than the states already possess. The MTC's audit information is not subject to any greater burden of confidentiality than Montana law commonly imposes on tax information gathered by the [Montana Department of Revenue]. Any further 'confidentiality' violates Montana's constitutional right to know provision." *Id.* at 394.

One scholar suggested that congressional consent to a compact may also abrogate a prior international treaty, noting, "whether the prior treaty or the subsequent compact would be of superior efficacy depends . . . upon whether the consent given by Congress to the compact is held to have the abrogatory effect of a statute. There may also be further restriction upon the power to disturb, by compact, rights resulting from guaranties recognized by the law of nations." Note, *Legal Problems Relating to Interstate Compacts*, 23 IOWA L. REV. 618 (1938).

A compact that is federal law can also make federal remedies available for violation of a compact. For example, the Interstate Agreement on Detainers (to which the United States is also a signatory) is considered a law of the United States whose violation is grounds for habeas corpus relief under 28 U.S.C. § 2254. *See, e.g.*, *Bush v. Muncy*, 659 F.2d 402, 407 (4th Cir. 1981), *cert. denied*, 455 U.S. 910 (1982). A federal civil rights claim pursuant to 42 U.S.C. § 1983 may also become available. *See Doe v. Pa. Bd. of Prob. and Parole*, 513 F.3d 95 (3d Cir. 2008) (stating such, but finding no claim allowed by the Interstate Compact for the Supervision of Adult Offenders). A not-so-surprising corollary is that a compact that is not federal law cannot be a basis for a section 1983 claim. *Ghana v. Pearce*, 159 F.3d 1206 (9th Cir. 1998) (Interstate Corrections Compact is not federal law and does not create a constitutionally protected liberty interest, and thus a violation of the compact could not be the basis for a section 1983 claim).

If a compact is federal law, and the *City of South Lake Tahoe* case suggested reasons for keeping a narrow law of the union doctrine, then to what extent should other federal law apply to that compact? For example, courts routinely apply federal law standards and methods when construing a compact. In *N.Y. State Dairy Foods, Inc. v. Ne. Dairy Compact Comm'n*, 26 F. Supp. 2d 249, 260 (D. Mass. 1998), the federal court applied the federal *Chevron* method for review of the compact agency's interpretation of federal law. In *Friends of the Columbia Gorge v. Columbia River Gorge Comm'n*, 346 Or. 366, 384 (2009), the Oregon Supreme Court similarly applied *Chevron* and applied the federal *Auer* deference for review of the compact agency's interpretation of its compact-required regulations.

In *Waterfront Comm'n of N.Y. Harbor v. Constr. & Marine Equip. Co.*, 928 F. Supp. 1388 (D.N.J. 1996), the court applied federal law to determine justiciability and some of the elements for issuing a preliminary injunction. For the first element of a preliminary injunction, whether the Waterfront Commission was likely to succeed on the merits, the court applied New Jersey state law. The court cited a provision of the compact, codified at N.J. STAT. § 32:23-51, which states,

> the action of the commission in denying any application for a license or in refusing to include any person in the longshoremen's register under this compact or in suspending or revoking such license or removing any person

> from the longshoremen's register or in reprimanding a licensee or registrant shall be subject to judicial review by a proceeding instituted in either State at the instance of the applicant, licensee or registrant in the manner provided by the law of such State for review of the final decision or action of administrative agencies of such State.

928 F. Supp. at 1400. The court then concluded:

> While the Commission's determinations here do not fall specifically within N.J. STAT. § 32:23-51, and, under *Cuyler,* the compact must generally be interpreted as federal law, the Court believes that it would be inappropriate to treat the Commission as a federal agency for purposes of deciding the standard of review. The Court considers that the application of state law here accords more with the intent of Congress and the purpose of the statute. Thus, the Court will rely on the law of New Jersey. It should be noted, however, that these decisions on these issues would be the same if determined under federal law.

Id. Do you agree that the court should have applied New Jersey law when the Waterfront Commission's actions did not fall within the compact's specific reservation of state law? Chapter 8 discusses the application of specific reservations of state law. Do you agree with the court's statement that it should not apply federal standards of review? Chapter 10 discusses the application of the standards of review in the federal Administrative Procedure Act to compact agencies.

In *Petty v. Tennessee-Missouri Bridge Comm'n,* 359 U.S. 275, 280 (1959), the U.S. Supreme Court observed, "Congress might of course adopt as federal law the law of either or both of the States." This raises an interesting issue; if Congress adopts state law in the compact (transforming the state law into federal law), then would federal law control construction of that state law in the context of the compact, but not for the general application of that law? Compact interpretation is covered in more detail in Chapter 9.

However, courts do not blindly apply federal law to compact disputes. In *California Tahoe Reg'l Planning Agency v. Jennings,* 594 F.2d 181 (9th Cir. 1979), the court stated, "We recognize that by consenting to the Compact, Congress transformed the agreement of California and Nevada into federal law. . . . But by consenting to the Compact, Congress did no more than incorporate the agreement of the two parties into the body of federal law; it did not make applicable to the agreement the entire panoply of Federal administrative and substantive standards." *Id.* at 190. The court gave no further explanation and there are few other cases with similar analysis. In the next case, the D.C. Circuit considered applying federal and state law when filling a gap in the compact:

Beebe v. Wash. Metro. Area Transit Auth.
129 F.3d 1283 (D.C. Cir. 1997)

TATEL, JUDGE:

. . . .

In 1966, acting pursuant to the Compact Clause of the Constitution, Congress approved the Washington Metropolitan Area Transit Authority Compact between Maryland, Virginia, and the District of Columbia to deal with growing traffic problems in the Washington area. Responsible for creating a coordinated public transportation system for the region, WMATA now operates an extensive Metrobus and Metrorail system running throughout Northern Virginia, the District, and two Maryland counties. . . .

Appellant Richard W. Beebe works for WMATA as an attorney, having served in both the Office of General Counsel and the Office of Procurement. In 1989, he became a Construction Engineer Negotiator in what was then the Office of Procurement's Final Decisions and Disputes Section, headed by appellee Narinder Kumar. In that job, Beebe investigated and analyzed contract claims and drafted final contracting decisions.

In 1992, by which time Beebe had reached a rank of TA-24, WMATA's Board of Directors approved a reorganization of the Office of Procurement, appointing appellee Robert Bearinger to oversee its implementation. The reorganization shrank the Final Decisions and Disputes Section from thirteen to six positions and transferred it to a new Construction Contract Management division. In this new office, Beebe's duties expanded from managing a single stage of the contracting process to "cradle-to-grave" contract administration.

During several personnel policy meetings with Bearinger and others and in a separate memorandum to Bearinger, Kumar criticized Beebe's performance, suggesting that he was unqualified for his broader responsibilities and that Beebe should return to the Office of General Counsel. Bearinger then abolished Beebe's job, replaced it with a new TA-24 Contract Administrator position, and appointed Kumar to head a selection committee to fill the new position. Beebe applied, but the committee selected him instead for a TA-22 Contract Administrator position.

In July, 1994, Beebe filed a ten-count complaint in the U.S. District Court for the District of Columbia . . . . [Beebe named WMATA, Bearinger, and Kumar in several of the counts.]

. . . .

In signing the WMATA Compact, Maryland, Virginia, and the District of Columbia conferred upon WMATA their respective sovereign immunities. Section 80 of the Compact waives this immunity for torts "committed in the conduct of any proprietary function," while retaining immunity for torts committed by its agents "in the performance of a governmental function."

[The D.C. Circuit concluded that WMATA was immune from Beebe's tort claims.]

. . . .

Because Beebe also asserts tort claims against Bearinger and Kumar in their individual capacities, we must determine whether, as the district court held, they too have immunity from suit. The scope of immunity of WMATA employees for torts committed in the course of governmental or discretionary functions is a road not well traveled.

Section 80 of the Compact provides that the "exclusive remedy" for any action for which WMATA is liable "shall be by suit against the Authority." In other words, for torts committed in the course of proprietary or ministerial functions, WMATA is liable and its employees immune. The Compact is silent on the question this case presents: whether WMATA employees have immunity from suit where WMATA itself has immunity because the alleged torts occurred in the exercise of governmental or discretionary functions.

To resolve this issue, we must first determine which law to rely on — those of the three signatories or federal common law? Where Congress wanted state law to govern a question under the WMATA Compact, such as in proprietary tort actions, it said so explicitly. *See* D.C. CODE ANN. § 1-2431(80) ("The Authority shall be liable for * * * torts * * * committed in the conduct of any proprietary function, in accordance with the law of the applicable signatory * * * ."). Where Congress has not so provided, federal law governs the interpretation of Compact terms. *Cuyler v. Adams* ("[W]here Congress has authorized the States to enter into a cooperative agreement, and where the subject matter of that agreement is an appropriate subject for congressional legislation, the consent of Congress transforms the States' agreement into federal law under the Compact Clause [of the Constitution]."). We thus regularly look to federal law when distinguishing between governmental and proprietary functions. Although the issue in this case requires us to interpret no specific Compact terms, but rather to fill in a gap left by those terms, we think the issue remains essentially federal, resolvable pursuant to federal common law.

While perhaps not the proper standard for interpreting *every* interstate compact, federal common law is particularly appropriate in WMATA's case. Not only does the Compact have its roots in congressionally authorized studies, but "Congress played a particularly active role" in WMATA's creation. From the very outset, the federal government has contributed significantly to the construction and operation of WMATA's transportation system. Moreover, although WMATA operates in three jurisdictions, it runs its core policy-making functions in one central District of Columbia headquarters. Resorting to the laws of the individual signatories could expose WMATA policymakers to different, possibly inconsistent immunity rules, a result that would run counter to the uniform interpretation of WMATA's governmental immunity, a uniformity which results from our reliance on federal law. . . .

. . . .

Notes & Questions

1. What do you think about filling gaps in compacts with federal law? Consider some of the complexities of using state law. Which party state's law should a court

use to fill the gap? *West Virginia ex rel. Dyer v. Sims* and *Kansas City Area Transp. Auth. v. Missouri* (both excerpted in Chapter 3) introduced the concept that a state cannot act unilaterally in a way that impairs administration of a compact. Does gap-filling with one state's law have the same unilateral effect that may impair administration of a compact? In *Texas Industries, Inc. v. Radclife Materials, Inc.*, 451 U.S. 630 (1981), an anti-trust case, the Supreme Court discussed the power of the federal courts to fashion common law, stating,

> absent some congressional authorization to formulate substantive rules of decision, federal common law exists only in such narrow areas as . . . interstate and international disputes implicating the conflicting rights of States . . . . In these instances, our federal system does not permit the controversy to be resolved under state law . . . because the interstate or international nature of the controversy makes it inappropriate for state law to control.

Id. at 641.

2. The D.C. Circuit noted that its reliance on federal law results in uniform interpretation of WMATA's governmental immunity. In contrast, in *Friends of the Columbia Gorge v. Columbia River Gorge Comm'n*, 346 Or. 366 (2009), the Oregon Supreme Court specifically rejected an argument that the court should use federal deference regimes when reviewing a compact agency's interpretation of the federal consent statute to ensure uniformity. The Court noted "interpretation of statutes arguably is a different matter" than judicial review of agency action. *Id.* at 380–81. Should uniformity always be the goal? Chapter 9 discusses the goal of uniformity when interpreting compacts.

3. Chapter 1 noted that states sometimes use compacts when the federal government has not acted in a particular policy area. Does a court's use of federal law to fill gaps and govern interpretation of compacts conflict with this intent? If not state law, and not federal law, then how should a court fill gaps in a compact? Chapter 9 discusses how the Supreme Court has used contract law principles to interpret compacts that are silent on a particular legal issue. Should courts consider an interstate compact agency's own interpretation of the compact through its rulemaking and other actions?

4. The D.C. Circuit observed that the Transit Compact specifies, "The Authority shall be liable for * * * torts * * * committed in the conduct of any proprietary function, in accordance with the law of the applicable signatory * * * ." *Beebe v. Wash. Metro. Area Transit Auth.*, 129 F.3d at 1288. How should a plaintiff determine which state's tort law applies to a specific claim? Should a court or WMATA be limited to applying the tort law from the state that the plaintiff selects? Could this text lead to forum shopping? Should courts attempt to harmonize the states' tort laws?

5. In a Washington Metropolitan Area Transit Compact case predating *Beebe*, the court summarized the Transit Compact as having "the force and effect of state law in each state, and the force and effect of federal law." *Strange v. Chumas*, 580 F. Supp. 160, 161 (D.D.C. 1983). With this description, should the court fill gaps in the compact with state law or federal law?

The law of the union doctrine also cures some other potential constitutional issues involving compacts, such as claims that a compact impairs interstate commerce. In *Intake Water Co. v. Yellowstone River Compact Comm'n*, 590 F. Supp. 293, 297 (D. Mont. 1983), *aff'd*, 769 F.2d 570 (9th Cir. 1985), the court concisely explained that a compact that has received the consent of Congress does not impermissibly impede interstate commerce because Congress may enact a law or give approval to a state law that interferes with interstate commerce, and because consent transforms a compact into federal law, which by definition is no longer a state law impeding commerce. For similar reasons, at least one court has held that a compact agency's regulation was not subject to limitation by the dormant commerce clause. *Lake Tahoe Watercraft Recreation Ass'n v. Tahoe Reg'l Planning Agency*, 24 F. Supp. 2d 1062, 1070 (E.D. Cal. 1998).

Still, much like any other state or federal statute, the subject matter of a compact or its implementation may raise questions involving other provisions of the U.S. Constitution. For example, in *Columbia River Gorge United v. Yeutter*, 960 F.2d 110 (9th Cir. 1992), the court rejected claims that Congress's consent and conditions of consent to the Columbia River Gorge Compact violated the Property Clause, the Commerce Clause and the Tenth Amendment. In *Smith v. Ill. Sec'y of State*, No. 01 C 1605, 2002 U.S. Dist. LEXIS 1318 (N.D. Ill. Jan. 28, 2002), the court concluded that procedural due process did not require providing a hearing prior to suspending a driver license due to out-of-state convictions and providing such hearings would undermine the Interstate Driver License Compact, which only requires administrative reporting. In *Delaware River Basin Comm'n v. Bucks Cty. Water & Sewer Auth.*, 641 F.2d 1087 (3d Cir. 1981), the court applied rational review to an equal protection claim. The Compact allowed the DRBC to collect charges for water, except for water drawn from the basin if the withdrawal "could lawfully have been made without charge on the effective date of the Compact [1961]." The DRBC enacted a resolution to collect charges beginning in 1974 and a prior case held that the DRBC acted within its authority to enact the resolution establishing the charges. This case held the resolution violated equal protection based on a pre-Compact/post-Compact distinction; but did not address whether the Compact provision violated equal protection.

State courts also consider questions arising under the U.S. Constitution. In *Kinnear v. Hertz Corp.*, 86 Wash. 2d 407 (1976), the Washington Supreme Court concluded that multistate audit provisions in the Multistate Tax Compact did not violate the Commerce Clause in the U.S. Constitution. What would have been the effect if the Washington Supreme Court had ruled the Multistate Tax Compact violated one or more provisions of the U.S. Constitution? Would the ruling have been effective to the other party states, such that it could have scuttled the entire compact?

Keep in mind that the Compact Clause applies differently than other provisions of the U.S. Constitution. For example, Justice White, in his dissent in *U.S.*

Steel, noted a distinction between how the Compact Clause and Commerce Clause apply.

> States may legislate in interstate commerce until an actual impact upon federal supremacy occurs. For individual States, the harm of potential impact is insufficiently upsetting to require prior congressional approval. For States acting in concert, however, whether through informal agreement, reciprocal legislation, or formal compact, "potential . . . impact upon federal supremacy" is enough to invoke the requirement of congressional approval.

U.S. Steel Corp. v. Multistate Tax Comm'n, 434 U.S. 452, 484 (1978).

III. Compact Agency Regulations as Federal Law

Compacts typically authorize the agency they create to write regulations governing that agency's own actions and governing persons and entities subject to the agency's jurisdiction. If a compact is a federal law, but compact agencies are not federal agencies, then are the regulations that a compact agency writes also federal regulations? Surprisingly, only a few courts have addressed this interesting question. In *Stephans v. Tahoe Reg'l Planning Agency*, 697 F. Supp. 1149, 1152 (D. Nev. 1988), the court expressly stated that the Tahoe Regional Planning Agency's regional land use plan is federal law. In *Rhode Island Fishermen's Alliance v. R.I. Dep't of Envtl. Mgmt.*, 585 F.3d 42 (1st Cir. 2009), the court similarly stated that an Atlantic States Marine Fisheries Commission management plan was federal law. Neither court gave any explanation for its statement. Another Tahoe case, *Lake Tahoe Watercraft Recreation Ass'n v. Tahoe Reg'l Planning Agency*, 24 F. Supp. 2d 1062 (E.D. Cal. 1998), provided only the barest explanation. Essentially, the court reasoned that because "the compact is federal law, it would seem that actions mandated thereunder would likewise have the force of federal laws." *Id.* at 1068. The court then expressly held that a Tahoe Regional Planning Agency ordinance prohibiting discharge of unburned fuel and oil by carbureted two-stroke boat engines is federal law.

Several other courts have treated compact agency regulations as if the regulations were federal law, but without expressly stating so. In *League to Save Lake Tahoe v. B.J.K. Corp.*, 547 F.2d 1072 (9th Cir. 1976), the Ninth Circuit observed, "Questions arising under the TRPA Land Use Ordinance enacted pursuant to the Compact do not automatically give rise to Section 1331(a) jurisdiction, because the Compact is not an ordinary federal statute and the Ordinance is not directly analogous to the Code of Federal Regulations. Interstate compacts occupy a unique position in our federal system." *Id.* at 1073. In *B.J.K.*, the court devised an interesting test for determining whether a question arising under an ordinance presented a federal question. Chapter 6 contains as excerpt and discussion of the case. In *Friends of the Columbia Gorge v. Columbia River Gorge Comm'n*, 215 Or. App. 557, 603 (2007), *aff'd in relevant part*, 346 Or. 366, 410 (2009), the Oregon appellate courts applied *Auer v. Robbins*, 519 U.S. 452 (1997), to the Columbia River Gorge Commission's interpretation of its own regulations. *Auer* specifies that federal courts give deference to a federal agency's interpretation of its own regulations. The Oregon Court of Appeals stated, "In construing the [Commission's land use] plan itself, we are mindful of the federal rules governing the interpretation of federal regulations. In particular, we note the rule that an agency's construction of its own regulations ordinarily is controlling unless it is 'plainly erroneous or inconsistent with the regulation.'" Interestingly, the Oregon Court of Appeals also cited Oregon case law specifying that Oregon courts similarly defer to Oregon state agencies' interpretations of their own regulations.

Other courts have simply noted that compact agency regulations are federally authorized or mandated. For example, in *City of South Lake Tahoe v. Tahoe Reg'l Planning Agency*, 664 F. Supp. 1375 (E.D. Cal. 1987), the court stated that TRPA regulations are part of a federally authorized regulatory scheme. Similarly, in *Klickitat Cty. v. State*, 71 Wash. App. 760 (1993), the court stated, "The [Columbia River Gorge] Commission's land management plan and the [federal] act's provisions relative to the plan are federally mandated, and do not constitute a state program." *Id.* at 767.

Notes & Questions

1. Are the arguments for treating compacts as federal law similarly compelling for treating compact agency regulations as federal regulations? What other factors should courts consider?

2. Should a compact's description of the agency be an important factor in determining the status of the agency's rules? For example, would the Washington Metropolitan Area Transit Commission, which is described as "an instrumentality of the compacting states," create state regulations? How about an agency that has no descriptor in the compact, or an agency that is merely described as a "body corporate and politic"? What about the Kansas City Area Transportation Authority, which is described as a "body corporate and politic and a political subdivision of the states"? What about the Columbia River Gorge Commission, for which Congress's consent specifies that it "shall not be considered an agency or instrumentality of the United States for the purpose of any Federal law"?

3. If compact agency regulations are "state regulations," then which state's regulations do they become? Do they become regulations of all the party states? How do you resolve the party states differing drafting conventions and numbering systems for state regulations? Does the compact agency need to adopt the regulations in accordance with all the party states' requirements for rulemaking? Can the states publish a compact agency's regulations in their state administrative regulation compilations?

4. If not state regulations and not federal regulations, then what are compact agency regulations? Does there need to be a unique set of standards for creating compact agency regulations, much like the rulemaking standards in the federal Administrative Procedure Act or the states' administrative procedure acts? Administrative procedure is discussed in Chapter 10.

5. If a compact agency's regulations are treated like federal law, should those regulations also supersede state constitutional restrictions? Should a compact agency have more power than the states that created it? Consider the *Amica Life Ins. Co. v. Wertz* case excerpted in Chapter 3.

IV. Supplemental State Legislation as Federal Law

States often enact legislation relating to their own implementation of a compact, and indeed many compacts specifically authorize such supplemental statutes. For example, article III of the Interstate Compact to Preserve Oil and Gas states, "Each State bound hereby agrees that within a reasonable time it will enact laws, or if the laws have been enacted, then it agrees to continue the same in force, to accomplish within reasonable limits the prevention of...." Supplemental statutes may serve many purposes. They may specify the relationship between the compact and other state law and state agencies, specify procedures for the compact agency or the role for other state agencies in the compact, or fill gaps left by the compact. The next case, *De Veau v. Braisted,* involved the relationship between federal law and a state statute enacted to supplement the compact.

De Veau v. Braisted
363 U.S. 144 (1960)

FRANKFURTER, JUSTICE:

....

The Waterfront Commission Act formulates a detailed scheme for governmental supervision of employment on the waterfront in the Port of New York. The relevant part of the specific provision, § 8, under attack follows:

> No person shall solicit, collect or receive any dues, assessments, levies, fines or contributions within the state from employees registered or licensed pursuant to the provisions of this act (pier superintendents, hiring agents, longshoremen and port watchmen) for or on behalf of any labor organization representing any such employees, if any officer or agent of such organization has been convicted by a court of the United States, or any state or territory thereof, of a felony unless he has been subsequently pardoned therefor by the governor or other appropriate authority of the state or jurisdiction in which such conviction was had or has received a certificate of good conduct from the board of parole pursuant to the provisions of the executive law to remove the disability.

[Section 8 is a part of New York law, not part of the bi-state compact].

The complaint upon which this action is based makes the following allegations. Appellant was a member, and beginning in 1950 had been Secretary-Treasurer, of Local 1346, International Longshoremen's Association, a labor organization with offices in Richmond County, New York, representing "employees registered or licensed pursuant to" the Waterfront Commission Act. As Secretary-Treasurer appellant had control of the Local's funds and also served as a bargaining representative. In 1920 appellant had pleaded guilty to a charge of grand larceny in New

York and had received a suspended sentence. It is not alleged that appellant has ever applied for or received a pardon or a "certificate of good conduct." Three years after the enactment of the Waterfront Commission Act, in 1956, the President of the International Longshoremen's Association was informed by the appellee, who was and is the District Attorney of Richmond County, New York, that because of appellant's conviction § 8 of the Act prohibited any person from collecting dues on behalf of Local 1346, so long as appellant remained its officer or agent. Appellee threatened to prosecute anyone collecting dues for the Local while appellant remained its officer. By reason of § 8 and this threat appellant was suspended as an officer of Local 1346, whereupon he brought this action.

The appellee moved to dismiss the complaint, and for judgment on the pleadings in his favor. This motion was granted. The court, holding that appellant's 1920 conviction was a conviction for a felony within the meaning of § 8, sustained the validity of that section. This judgment was affirmed by the Appellate Division of the Supreme Court and by the Court of Appeals of New York. Since a statute of a State has been upheld by the highest court of the State against a federal constitutional attack, the case is properly here on appeal.

Due consideration of the constitutional claims that are made requires that § 8 be placed in the context of the structure and history of the legislation of which it is a part. The New York Waterfront Commission Act was an endeavor by New York and New Jersey to cope with long-standing evils on their joint waterfront in the Port of New York. The solution which was evolved between the two States embodies not only legislation by each but also joint action by way of a constitutional compact between them, approved by Congress, including the establishment of a bi-state Waterfront Commission.

For years the New York waterfront presented a notoriously serious situation. Urgent need for drastic reform was generally recognized. Thoroughgoing investigations of the mounting abuses were begun in 1951 by the New York State Crime Commission and the Law Enforcement Council of New Jersey. After extensive hearings, the New York Crime Commission in May 1953 published a detailed report on the evils its investigation disclosed and the legislative remedies these were thought to require. The Commission reported that the skullduggeries on the waterfront were largely due to the domination over waterfront employment gained by the International Longshoremen's Association, as then conducted. Its employment practices easily led to corruption, and many of its officials participated in dishonesties. The presence on the waterfront of convicted felons in many influential positions was an important causative factor in this appalling situation. It was thus described to Congress in the compact submitted by New York and New Jersey for its consent:

> [T]he conditions under which waterfront labor is employed within the Port of New York district are depressing and degrading to such labor, resulting from the lack of any systematic method of hiring, the lack of adequate information as to the availability of employment, corrupt hiring practices and the fact that persons conducting such hiring are frequently criminals and

> persons notoriously lacking in moral character and integrity and neither responsive or responsible to the employers nor to the uncoerced will of the majority of the members of the labor organizations of the employees; that as a result waterfront laborers suffer from irregularity of employment, fear and insecurity, inadequate earnings, an unduly high accident rate, subjection to borrowing at usurious rates of interest, exploitation and extortion as the price of securing employment and a loss of respect for the law; that not only does there result a destruction of the dignity of an important segment of American labor, but a direct encouragement of crime which imposes a levy of greatly increased costs on food, fuel and other necessaries handled in and through the Port of New York district.
>
> [M]any of the evils above described result not only from the causes above described but from the practices of public loaders at piers and other waterfront terminals; that such public loaders serve no valid economic purpose and operate as parasites exacting a high and unwarranted toll on the flow of commerce in and through the Port of New York district, and have used force and engaged in discriminatory and coercive practices including extortion against persons not desiring to employ them; * * *
>
> [S]tevedores have engaged in corrupt practices to induce their hire by carriers of freight by water and to induce officers and representatives of labor organizations to betray their trust to the members of such labor organizations.

Shortly after the Crime Commission submitted its report, the Governor of New York conducted hearings based upon the Crime Commission report. As a result, a Waterfront Commission Act was introduced into and passed by the Legislatures of both States in June 1953.

Part I of both Acts constitutes what became the compact between the two States. This is the heart of the legislation. It establishes as a bi-state agency a Waterfront Commission of New York Harbor with power to license, register and regulate the waterfront employment of pier superintendents, hiring agents, longshoremen and port watchmen, and to license and regulate stevedores. It entirely prohibits one class of waterfront employment, public loading, found to be unnecessary and particularly infested with corruption. Manifestly, one of the main aims of the compact is to keep criminals away from the waterfront. The issue of licenses to engage in waterfront occupations, or the right to be registered, depends upon findings by the Commission of good character. In particular, past convictions for certain felonies constitute specific disabilities for each occupation, with discretion in the Commission to lift the disability, except in the case of port watchmen, where it constitutes an absolute bar to waterfront employment. A new procedure for the employment of longshoremen is also provided under the supervision of the Commission, replacing the archaic, corrupt "shape-up."

Under the requirement of Art. I, § 10, of the Constitution the compact was submitted to the Congress for its consent, and it was approved. This was no perfunctory consent. Congress had independently investigated the evils that gave rise to the Waterfront Commission Acts, and the Subcommittee of the Senate Committee on Interstate and Foreign Commerce had in a Report endorsed the state legislative solution embodied in these Acts. After the compact's submission to Congress, hearings were held upon it by the Committee on the Judiciary of the House of Representatives, at which arguments were made by interested parties for and against the compact. Approval was recommended by both the House Judiciary Committee and the Senate Committee on Interstate and Foreign Commerce. The House Committee concluded that "(t)he extensive evidence of crime, corruption, and racketeering on the waterfront of the port of New York, as disclosed by the State investigations reported to this committee at its hearings and by the recent report of the Senate Committee on Interstate and Foreign Commerce, has made it clear beyond all question that the plan proposed by the States of New York and New Jersey to eradicate those public evils is urgently needed." The Senate Committee Report stated its conclusion in similar terms. The compact was approved by Congress in August 1953.

In addition to the compact, New York enacted, as Parts II and III of its 1953 Waterfront Commission Act, supplementary legislation dealing, in most part, with the administration of New York's responsibility under the compact. This supplementary legislation also contains two substantive provisions in furtherance of the objectives of the compact, but not calling for bi-state enforcement, and thus not included in the compact. These are § 8, which is here challenged, and a prohibition against loitering on the waterfront. New Jersey enacted a supplementary provision essentially similar to § 8. Although § 8 does not require enforcement by the bi-state Waterfront Commission, and was therefore not formally submitted as part of the compact to Congress, in giving its approval to the compact Congress explicitly gave its authority to such supplementary legislation in accord with the objectives of the compact by providing in the clause granting consent "(t)hat the consent of Congress is hereby given to the compact set forth * * * and to the carrying out and effectuation of said compact, and enactments in furtherance thereof."

In giving this authorization Congress was fully mindful of the specific provisions of § 8. Not only had § 8 already been enacted by the States as part of the Waterfront Commission Acts when the compact was submitted to Congress, but, in the hearings held before the House Committee on the Judiciary, it was specifically urged by counsel for the International Longshoremen's Association, as a ground of opposition to congressional consent, that approval of the compact by Congress would carry with it sanction of § 8. See Hearing before Subcommittee No. 3 of the Committee on the Judiciary, House of Representatives. The ground of objection to the section which is appellant's primary reliance here, namely, that it conflicts with existing federal labor policy, was urged as ground for rejecting the compact. It is in light of this legislative history that the compact was approved, and that congressional consent was given to "enactments in furtherance thereof."

. . . .

Here the challenged state legislation was not in terms approved by Congress, but was part of the legislative history and of the revealed purpose of the compact which was approved. Formal inclusion of § 8 in the compact was not called for since its enforcement was to be unilateral on the part of each State. Both New York and New Jersey enacted § 8 at the time they enacted the proposed compact. Section 8 is the same kind of regulation as is contained in the compact: it effectively disqualifies ex-felons from waterfront union office, just as the compact makes prior conviction of certain felonies a bar to waterfront employment, unless there is a favorable exercise of executive discretion. The total state legislative program represents a drastic effort to rid the waterfront of criminal elements by generally excluding ex-felons. What sensible reason is there to suppose that Congress would approve the major part of this local effort, as it has expressly done through its approval of the compact, and disapprove its application to union officials who, as history proved, had emerged as a powerful and corrupting influence on the waterfront second to none?

This is not all. As we have seen, § 8 was brought to the attention of Congress as part of the legislation which would come into effect as an adjunct to the compact, and the objection was raised at that time and not heeded that § 8 unduly interfered with federal labor policy. Finally, it is of great significance that in approving the compact Congress did not merely remain silent regarding supplementary legislation by the States. Congress expressly gave its consent to such implementing legislation not formally part of the compact. This provision in the consent by Congress to a compact is so extraordinary as to be unique in the history of compacts. Of all the instances of congressional approval of state compacts—the process began in 1791, Act of Feb. 4, 1791, 1 Stat. 189, with more than one hundred compacts approved since—we have found no other in which Congress expressly gave its consent to implementing legislation. It is instructive that this unique provision has occurred in connection with approval of a compact dealing with the prevention of crime where, because of the peculiarly local nature of the problem, the inference is strongest that local policies are not to be thwarted.

The sum of these considerations is that it would offend reason to attribute to Congress a purpose to pre-empt the state regulation contained in § 8. . . .

. . . .

In disqualifying all convicted felons from union office unless executive discretion is exercised in their favor, § 8 may well be deemed drastic legislation. But in the view of Congress and the two States involved the situation on the New York waterfront regarding the presence and influence of ex-convicts called for drastic action. Legislative investigation had established that the presence of ex-convicts on the waterfront was not a minor episode but constituted a principal corrupting influence. The Senate Subcommittee which investigated for Congress conditions on the New York waterfront found that "(c)riminals whose long records belie any suggestion that they can be reformed have been monopolizing controlling positions in the International Longshoremen's Association and in local unions. Under their regimes gambling, the narcotics traffic, loansharking, shortganging, payroll 'phantoms,' the 'shakedown' in all its forms—and the brutal ultimate of murder have flourished, often virtually unchecked."

In light of these findings, and other evidence to the same effect, the Congress approved as appropriate if indeed not necessary a compact, one of the central devices of which was to bar convicted felons from waterfront employment, and from acting as stevedores employing others, either absolutely, or in the Waterfront Commission's discretion. No positions on the waterfront were more conducive to its criminal past than those of union officials, and none, if left unregulated, were felt to be more able to impede the waterfront's reform. Duly mindful as we are of the promising record of rehabilitation by ex-felons, and of the emphasis on rehabilitation by modern penological efforts, it is not for this Court to substitute its judgment for that of Congress and the Legislatures of New York and New Jersey regarding the social surgery required by a situation as gangrenous as exposure of the New York waterfront had revealed.

Barring convicted felons from certain employments is a familiar legislative device to insure against corruption in specified, vital areas. . . . State provisions disqualifying convicted felons from certain employments important to the public interest also have a long history. And it is to be noted that in § 504(a) of the 1959 Federal Labor Act, quoted earlier in this opinion, Congress adopted this same solution in its attempt to rid all unions of criminal elements. Just as New York and New Jersey have done, the 1959 Federal Act makes a prior felony conviction a bar to union office unless there is a favorable exercise of executive discretion. In the face of this wide utilization of disqualification of convicted felons for certain employments closely touching the public interest, remitting them to executive discretion to have the bar removed, we cannot say that it was not open to New York to clean up its waterfront in the way it has. New York was not guessing or indulging in airy assumptions that convicted felons constituted a deleterious influence on the waterfront. It was acting on impressive if mortifying evidence that the presence on the waterfront of ex-convicts was an important contributing factor to the corrupt waterfront situation.

. . . .

DOUGLAS, JUSTICE, DISSENTING (WITH CHIEF JUSTICE WARREN AND JUSTICE BLACK):

. . . .

. . . Much is made of the fact that Congress, when it approved the Waterfront Commission Compact between New York and New Jersey, knew of the restrictions contained in § 8 of the New York Waterfront Commission Act now in litigation. But that is an argument that comes to naught when Art. XV, § 1 of the Compact is read.

> This compact is not designed and shall not be construed to limit in any way any rights granted or derived from any other statute or any rule of law for employees to organize in labor organizations, to bargain collectively and to act in any other way individually, collectively, and through labor organizations or other representatives of their own choosing. Without limiting the generality of the foregoing, nothing contained in this compact shall be construed to limit in any way the right of employees to strike.

Yet how can employees maintain their right to act through "representatives of their own choosing" if New York can tell them whom they may not choose?

. . . .

Notes & Questions

1. The issue in *De Veau v. Braisted* was not whether the NLRA preempted the Waterfront Compact, but whether the NLRA preempted a New York state law that supplemented the compact. Regarding supplementary legislation in general, the Court observed:

> Finally, it is of great significance that in approving the compact Congress did not merely remain silent regarding supplementary legislation by the States. Congress expressly gave its consent to such implementing legislation not formally part of the compact. This provision in the consent by Congress to a compact is so extraordinary as to be unique in the history of compacts. Of all the instances of congressional approval of state compacts—the process began in 1791 with more than one hundred compacts approved since—we have found no other in which Congress expressly gave its consent to implementing legislation.

363 U.S. at 154. If Congress does not consent to implementing statutes, then where is the authority for states to enact implementing statutes? What if the states enact conflicting statutes?

2. The Court stated, "In giving [consent], Congress was fully mindful of the specific provisions of § 8." 363 U.S. at 151. Should Congress's mere knowledge of this provision of state law be sufficient to defeat a claim that the NLRA preempts it? Alternatively, was section 8 so intertwined with the Waterfront Commission compact that the Court effectively had to treat it like a part of the compact?

3. The Court also observed, "Here the challenged state legislation was not in terms approved by Congress, but was part of the legislative history and of the revealed purpose of the compact which was approved. Formal inclusion of § 8 in the compact was not called for since its enforcement was to be unilateral on the part of each State. Both New York and New Jersey enacted § 8 at the time they enacted the proposed compact. Section 8 is the same kind of regulation as is contained in the compact . . . ." 363 U.S. at 153. Why are these characteristics significant?

4. In *Bush v. Muncy*, 659 F.2d 402, 410–13 (4th Cir. 1981), the court concluded that supplementary provisions to the Interstate Agreement on Detainers authorized by that compact are to be interpreted as federal law as part of the compact. Must a compact authorize supplemental statutes before a court should treat those supplemental statutes as part of the compact?

Compare *Bush v. Muncy* to *Garey v. Neb. Dep't of Nat. Res.*, 277 Neb. 149 (2009), in which the Nebraska Supreme Court concluded that a property tax authorized in a Nebraska Law violated a provision of the Nebraska Constitution prohibiting the state from levying a property tax for state purposes. The introducer of the bill stated that it was "designed to address the water problem in the Republican River Basin" and "[p]rovide a way to guarantee that Nebraska stays in compliance with the . . . Compact . . . with Kansas on an annual basis." Do you agree with *Bush v. Muncy* or *Garey* and why? What if Kansas did not have such a constitutional limit? How would you apply *Garey* to a compact that expressly requires the states to enact supplemental statutes to administer them? In a later, related case, *Kiplinger v. Neb. Dep't of Nat. Res.*, 282 Neb. 237, 241 (2011), the court concluded that an occupation tax to help fund the compact did not violate the Nebraska Constitution because it was an excise tax on the activity of irrigation, and not a property tax for state purposes.

5. Should courts treat one state's supplemental statutes as part of a compact if other party states do not enact their own supplemental statutes? For example, Oregon enacted numerous statutes to supplement the Columbia River Gorge Compact. OR. REV. STAT. §§ 196.110 and 196.115 specify procedure and standards of review applicable only in Oregon state courts. Washington, the other party state, did not enact similar statutes, and neither Congress's consent nor the compact directed the states to enact such supplemental statutes.

CHAPTER 6: JURISDICTION IN THE VARIOUS COURTS

Like other government entities, compact entities may sue and be sued and states may be sued for their actions pursuant to a compact. But where should a compact agency initiate legal action, or an aggrieved person sue a compact agency or a state?

In many early compacts, the states and Congress did not specify jurisdiction or did not specify jurisdiction for new types of cases that were not common in the past. Now, Congress and the states nearly always specify jurisdiction. For example, the consent for compacts in the Clean Water Act specifies that the U.S. district courts share original jurisdiction with the Supreme Court and state courts:

> (a) The United States District Courts shall have original jurisdiction (concurrent with that of the Supreme Court of the United States, and concurrent with that of any other court of the United States or of any State of the United States in which the Supreme Court, or any other court, has original jurisdiction) of any case or controversy – (1) which involves the construction or application of an interstate compact which (A) in whole or in part relates to the pollution of the waters of the an interstate river system or any portion thereof, and (B) expresses the consent of the States signatory to said compact to be sued in a district court in any case or controversy involving the application or construction thereof....

33 U.S.C. § 466g-1. Some compacts and congressional consent actions specify a specific court and procedure for compact disputes. For example, article IV(o) of the Low-Level Radioactive Waste Policy Amendments Act of 1985, Pub. L. No. 99-240, 99 Stat. 1842, 1917 (1986) states, "The United States Court of Appeals for the District of Columbia Circuit shall have jurisdiction to review the final administrative decisions of the Commission."

Some compacts specify different courts for different types of cases or forms of relief. For example, the Waterfront Commission of New York Harbor Compact, art. XI, § 7 specifies judicial review of the Commission's licensing decisions in state court using the New York and New Jersey administrative procedure acts, but the Commission may seek injunctive relief in federal court to require persons to obtain a license. *See, e.g.*, *Waterfront Comm'n of N.Y. Harbor v. Constr. & Marine Equip. Co.*, 928 F. Supp. 1388 (D.N.J. 1996).

Where a compact does not specify jurisdiction, compact entities and aggrieved persons will consider the usual concerns of being in one court versus another. But the interstate nature of a compact makes this analysis more complicated. For example, when a compact "becomes" federal law through congressional consent, jurisdiction in the federal courts would seem obvious. But, as the Supreme Court noted in *Cuyler v. Adams*, federal court jurisdiction was in flux for a long time.

More recently, federal courts have started questioning whether a case merely involves a compact or compact agency, or really requires application or interpretation of a compact. Jurisdiction in state courts raises different issues, including whether judgment in one state's courts could apply to the application and interpretation of a compact in other states.

This chapter looks at jurisdiction in different courts, including legal and practical issues unique to compacts. The first section looks at jurisdiction in federal courts, focusing on certiorari jurisdiction in the U.S. Supreme Court and original jurisdiction in the U.S. district courts. The second section explores the unique issues for compacts that specify jurisdiction in state courts. The final section looks at original jurisdiction in the U.S. Supreme Court in which one state may sue another state.

I. Jurisdiction in the Federal Courts

Until 1940, the Supreme Court had issued conflicting decisions on whether interpretation of an interstate compact presented a federal question that would permit jurisdiction in federal court. In *Green v. Biddle*, 21 U.S. (8 Wheat.) 1, 90–91 (1823), the Supreme Court reviewed a case between private parties arising in the Kentucky courts. However, it noted that the case involved a dispute between sovereign states and the question whether a Kentucky law was constitutional. The Court did not analyze its jurisdiction.

Subsequently, the Court began considering whether consent converted a compact into federal law. Reread footnote 7 in *Cuyler v. Adams* (excerpted in Chapter 5), summarizing the evolution of this question from *Pennsylvania v. Wheeling and Belmont Bridge Co.*, 54 U.S. (13 How.) 518 (1851), to *People v. Central R.R.*, 79 U.S. 455 (1872), and *Hinderlider v. La Plata River & Cherry Creek Ditch Co.*, 304 U.S. 92 (1938). Two years later, *Delaware River Joint Toll Bridge Comm'n v. Colburn*, 310 U.S. 419 (1940), overruled *Central R.R.* and *Hinderlider*, holding that "the construction of such a compact sanctioned by Congress by virtue of Article I, § 10, Clause 3 of the Constitution, involves a federal 'title, right, privilege or immunity' which when 'specially set up and claimed' in a state court may be reviewed here on certiorari." *Id.* at 427–28. This is where the law relating to certiorari jurisdiction remains today.

In 1951, in *West Virginia ex rel. Dyer v. Sims* (excerpted in Chapter 3), the Supreme Court strongly reaffirmed its jurisdiction to review state court decisions involving interpretation of a compact. The Court's majority and two concurring opinions leave little question that the Supreme Court has decided once and for all that it has jurisdiction to review state court decisions relating to the states' obligations under compacts that have received consent; however, the opinions presented different reasoning. Justice Frankfurter, writing for the majority, presented a functional approach, stating: "Just as this Court has power to settle disputes between States where there is no compact, it must have final power to pass upon the meaning and validity of compacts. It requires no elaborate argument to reject the suggestion that an agreement solemnly entered into between States by those who alone have political authority to speak for a State can be unilaterally nullified, or given final meaning by an organ of one of the contracting States. A State cannot be its own ultimate judge in a controversy with a sister State." 341 U.S. at 28.

Justice Reed, in his concurrence, focused on the federal question that naturally arises when interpreting compacts: "Under the Compact Clause, however, the federal questions are the execution, validity, and meaning of federally approved state compacts. The interpretation of the meaning of the compact controls over a state's application of its own law through the Supremacy Clause and not by any implied federal power to construe state law." *Id.* at 33.

Justice Jackson, in his concurrence, focused on equitable principles in finding a federal question: "West Virginia officials induced sister States to contract with her and Congress to consent to the Compact. She now attempts to read herself out of this interstate Compact by reading into her Constitution a limitation upon the powers of her Governor and Legislature to contract. West Virginia, for internal affairs, is free to interpret her own Constitution as she will. But if the compact system is to have vitality and integrity, she may not raise an issue of *ultra vires*, decide it, and release herself from an interstate obligation. The legal consequences which flow from the formal participation in a compact consented to by Congress is a federal question for this Court." *Id.* at 35.

Thus by 1951, certiorari jurisdiction in the U.S. Supreme Court was firmly established, but courts had not yet determined whether the federal district courts had federal question jurisdiction for disputes involving compacts and compact entities with congressional consent. At the time, many cases were in federal court under diversity jurisdiction, which is discussed later in this chapter.

A. Federal Question Jurisdiction

Recall from your civil procedure classes that 28 U.S.C. § 1331 specifies original jurisdiction in federal court for "actions arising under the Constitution, laws, or treaties of the United States."

In 1974, the question arose whether federal district courts have federal question jurisdiction for cases involving interstate compacts. League to Save Lake Tahoe filed its case in the U.S. District Court for the Eastern District of California, which dismissed for lack of jurisdiction. The Ninth Circuit believed it was the first to address whether it had federal question jurisdiction. Take note where the court looks for precedent.

League to Save Lake Tahoe v. Tahoe Reg'l Planning Agency
507 F.2d 517 (9th Cir. 1974)

RENFREW, JUDGE:

In 1968 the states of California and Nevada entered into a compact to create a regional agency with extensive powers to regulate and control development within the Lake Tahoe Basin in order to protect the natural resources and ecological balance of the area. In December of 1969 Congress gave its consent to the compact as provided for in Article I, 10, cl. 3 of the United States Constitution.

The Tahoe Regional Planning Compact ("Compact") created Tahoe Regional Planning Agency ("TRPA") and charged it with responsibility for developing within ninety days a regional interim plan and, within eighteen months, a regional plan which would reflect a wide variety of economic, environmental and social considerations. The Compact also directed the TRPA to adopt all ordinances, rules, regulations and policies necessary to effectuate the regional interim plan and the regional plan.

The League to Save Lake Tahoe, the Sierra Club and two individuals who reside in the Tahoe area ("appellants") brought this action for declaratory and injunctive relief alleging, basically, that defendant TRPA has failed to comply with the legal requirements of the Compact. They contend that TRPA has failed to adopt a regional plan as required by the Compact, has failed to adopt certain implementing ordinances mandated by the Compact, has adopted other ordinances which are defective, and has failed to prepare a detailed environmental analysis as required by the Compact. In particular, appellants charge that defendant TRPA has granted "approval" to the development projects of defendants Thomas Raley, Park Cattle Company and Harvey's Wagon Wheel, Inc., in violation of the Compact.

Jurisdiction in the district court was predicated solely on 28 U.S.C. § 1331(a).[*] On defendants' motion, the District Court dismissed the action without prejudice on the ground that it lacked jurisdiction over the subject matter of plaintiffs' claims. Appellants now appeal that determination.

The appeal here presents but a single issue, yet one of first impression: whether a federal court has original jurisdiction over this suit as one arising under the Constitution, laws or treaties of the United States. For the reasons developed in this opinion, we hold that it does, and we reverse the decision below.

Appellants advance two arguments in support of their contention that the construction of a congressionally sanctioned interstate compact is a matter of federal law. First, they argue that congressional consent transforms the Compact into a law of the United States. Second, they urge that the construction of an interstate compact requires the application of federal "common law" which is law of the United States within the meaning of § 1331(a). Because we agree with the first argument asserted by appellants, we have no occasion to consider the second.

For this case to be within the purview of § 1331(a), a right or immunity created by the Constitution or laws of the United States must be an essential element of plaintiffs' claim. The gravamen of the complaint is the alleged failure of TRPA to comply with the requirements of the Compact in various particulars. To determine the nature and scope of these requirements requires a construction of the Compact. Such construction, therefore, forms an essential element of the complaint. Thus, if the Compact can properly be characterized as a "law" of the United States, then federal jurisdiction is established.

---

[*] [*Ed. Note*: At the time of this case, section 1331 had subsections, including an amount in controversy requirement. In 1980, Congress amended section 1331 to its current form.]

Counsel have not cited nor has independent research revealed any decision by the Supreme Court or any of the Circuit Courts of Appeals which deals directly with this issue.

The Supreme Court has, however, in a series of cases considered the status of interstate compacts in connection with its certiorari jurisdiction. *See Delaware River Comm'n v. Colburn*, 310 U.S. 419 (1940); *West Virginia ex rel. Dyer v. Sims*, 341 U.S. 22 (1951). In these cases the Court addressed the question of whether a claim based on an interstate compact is cognizable under the provision for Supreme Court review, by writ of certiorari, of judgments of the highest state court where "any title, right, privilege or immunity is specially set up or claimed under the Constitution, treaties or statutes of * * * the United States." 28 U.S.C. § 1257(3). In *Colburn* the Court unequivocally answered this question in the affirmative, holding that "the construction of such a (bi-state) compact sanctioned by Congress by virtue of Article I, 10 cl. 3 of the Constitution, involves a federal 'title, right, privilege or immunity' which when 'specially set up or claimed' in a state court may be reviewed here on certiorari under 237(b) of the Judicial Code (the predecessor of 1257(3))." 310 U.S. at 427. The Court has reaffirmed this holding in *Dyer*, 341 U.S. at 26.

In reaching this interpretation of the certiorari statute, *Colburn* and its progeny have firmly established that the construction of a compact, by virtue of congressional consent, presents a federal question. This result has its genesis in the case of *Pennsylvania v. The Wheeling & Belmont Bridge Co.*, 54 U.S. (13 How.) 518 (1851), wherein the court stated that "this compact (the Virginia-Kentucky Compact of 1789) by the sanction of Congress, has become a law of the Union. What further legislation can be desired for judicial action?" Although later decisions created considerable doubt as to the continued validity of that doctrine, *Colburn* has put these doubts to rest.

While the Court in *Colburn* felt it unnecessary to clearly articulate the basic premise of its decision, we conclude after careful investigation that the result there was based upon the implicit finding that the interstate compact involved was a "statute of the United States" within the meaning of 28 U.S.C. § 1257(3). Neither logic nor policy justifies a different interpretation of the substantially similar language in 28 U.S.C. § 1331(a). Therefore, a case involving the construction of an interstate compact which requires a judicial determination of the nature and scope of obligations set forth therein "arises" under the "laws" of the United States within the meaning of 1331(a).

We do not, of course, ignore the significant differences between original jurisdiction in the federal courts and certiorari jurisdiction in the Supreme Court. The test for determining whether a case involves substantial federal issues at the very outset of litigation differs from the test for making that determination after the case has passed through a state judicial system. For this reason in cases in which there is a claim of original jurisdiction, there is the *Gully* [*v. First National Bank*, 299 U.S. 109, 112 (1936)] requirement that the federal question form an "essential element" of the plaintiff's complaint. No such requirement exists with respect to certiorari jurisdiction. There it is the record in the state tribunal and not the original complaint which must support the claim of a federal question. To erect, in addition, a distinction between what constitutes a federal law for certiorari purposes and what constitutes a federal law for original jurisdiction purposes would be artificial, unnecessary and irrational; we decline, therefore, to do so. The Compact must be deemed a law of the United States under *Colburn* and the requirements of *Gully* have been satisfied in this case. Therefore, jurisdiction should have been sustained in the district court under 1331(a).

Furthermore, post-*Colburn* decisions of the Supreme Court and strong policy considerations support this result. Appellees have argued that the need for a final arbiter of compact disputes requires only certiorari jurisdiction, and that the desirability of having state courts decide matters of state law, such as zoning and land use control, before that arbitration is undertaken precludes original jurisdiction in the federal courts. We disagree. The Supreme Court has made it clear that the construction of an interstate compact is a matter of federal law, not the law of the party states. *Petty v. Tennessee-Missouri Bridge Comm'n*, 359 U.S. 275, 279–280 (1959). State court consideration, therefore, cannot constitute a necessary predicate to proper construction of a compact.

Moreover, interstate compacts frequently involve not only local concerns of the states involved, but also important national interests. [*West Virginia ex rel.*]*Dyer v. Sims*, 341 U.S. at 27. *See also Petty*, 359 U.S. at 282 n.1. The instant Compact deals with much more than mere local concerns such as zoning and land use. It addresses the environmental problems of an area not subject to the control of a single state. In addition to the specific congressional concern for the subject of this Compact, evidenced by the statement of purpose accompanying the consent, the national legislature has with increasing frequency evinced a strong interest in solving environmental problems, which by their very nature transcend state boundaries, through interstate cooperation. *See, e.g.*, The Clean Air Act and the National Environmental Policy Act. The result reached here serves those important national interests.

It is therefore most appropriate to sustain jurisdiction under 28 U.S.C. § 1331(a) over a case involving the construction of the Tahoe Regional Planning Compact.

. . . .

Notes & Questions

1. What do you think about the Ninth Circuit's consideration of certiorari jurisdiction in the U.S. Supreme Court when deciding that the federal court had original (federal question) jurisdiction? Did you notice that at the end of the opinion, the court discussed how certiorari and original jurisdiction differ? Perhaps the Ninth Circuit was signaling to the Supreme Court that it should consider this question. The Supreme Court denied review of this case. 420 U.S. 974 (1975).

2. Recall the discussion in *Green v. Biddle* and *Poole v. Lessee of Fleeger* (both excerpted in Chapter 3) concerning the nature of compacts as an affirmation of

state sovereignty. Does original jurisdiction in federal court defeat the concept of a compact as a state-based solution that is limited only by the requirement of congressional consent?

3. TRPA argued, "the need for a final arbiter of compact disputes requires only certiorari jurisdiction, and that the desirability of having state courts decide matters of state law, such as zoning and land use control, before that arbitration is undertaken precludes original jurisdiction in the federal courts." 507 F.2d at 522. Does the concept of a "compact as an affirmation of the states' sovereignty" explain why TRPA wanted to litigate in state court, or are there more prudential reasons that a compact agency might want to litigate in state court? Interestingly, TRPA now typically seeks to remove cases filed in state court to the federal courts.

4. Citing *Petty v. Tennessee-Missouri Bridge Comm'n*, the Ninth Circuit stated, "The Supreme Court has made it clear that the construction of an interstate compact is a matter of federal law, not the law of the party states." 507 F.2d at 523. As well, after *Cuyler v. Adams*, federal court jurisdiction seems almost certain. But are there situations in which a case involving a compact or compact agency would not involve a federal question? The next two case excerpts explore this question. The first case involved a related question whether construction of a TRPA regulation enacted pursuant to authority in the compact also presented a federal question. In the second case, the court disagreed that resolving the plaintiff's claim required construction of the compact.

League to Save Lake Tahoe v. B.J.K. Corp.
547 F.2d 1072 (9th Cir. 1976)

HUFSTEDLER, JUDGE:

This appeal is a sequel to *League to Save Lake Tahoe v. Tahoe Regional Planning Agency*, 507 F.2d 517 (9th Cir. 1974). The issue is whether this suit arising under the Tahoe Regional Planning Agency's ("TRPA") Land Use Ordinance raises a federal question permitting the League to invoke federal question jurisdiction. The district court dismissed the suit for lack of subject matter jurisdiction. We reverse because the suit raises serious issues that affect the effective functioning of the Tahoe Regional Planning Compact ("Compact").

The Compact was adopted in 1969, and in March, 1970, the TRPA was convened. Sometime in 1969, or 1970, the predecessors in interest to defendant B.J.K. Corporation applied to defendant Washoe County for a building permit. The corporation sought to construct a 15-story, 274-room hotel on the edge of Lake Tahoe adjacent to the stateline at North Lake Tahoe, Nevada. The building permit was granted on September 10, 1970, and construction commenced. At some point before 1972, construction was abandoned, with only the garage portion of the structure completed. On April 11, 1972, the TRPA Land Use Ordinance became effective. This ordinance included a "grandfather clause" that exempted existing uses including projects "upon which construction has commenced as allowed by * * * permit prior to February 10, 1972." However, the exemption does not apply "if any such use ceases for a period of one (1) year. The building permit was renewed on June 5, 1972, January 4, 1974, and January 2, 1975. Shortly after B.J.K. undertook to resume construction in May, 1975, this action was filed.

Plaintiffs alleged both violations of the TRPA Land Use Ordinance and, as a pendent claim, violations of the Washoe County Uniform Building Code. The district court granted defendants' motion to dismiss for lack of subject matter jurisdiction under 28 U.S.C. § 1331(a), and plaintiffs appeal. On appeal they urge three theories of jurisdiction: (1) that their case falls directly under *League to Save Lake Tahoe*, *supra*, because construction and enforcement of the Compact is an essential element of their claims; (2) that construction of the Land Use Ordinance presents a federal question; and (3) that enforcement of the Ordinance raises issues of federal common law.

The starting point for our analysis is *League to Save Lake Tahoe v. Tahoe Regional Planning Agency*, 507 F.2d 517 (9th Cir 1974), in which we held that the Tahoe Compact is a "law of the United States" within the meaning of Section 1331(a) by virtue of the congressional consent to that compact. Questions arising under the TRPA Land Use Ordinance enacted pursuant to the Compact do not automatically give rise to Section 1331(a) jurisdiction, because the Compact is not an ordinary federal statute and the Ordinance is not directly analogous to the Code of Federal Regulations. Interstate compacts occupy a unique position in our federal system.

Consent to an interstate compact is a way station on the road to exercise of congressional power under the commerce clause. By permitting a state-initiated response to regional matters, Congress has done something quite different from incorporating a state law into a federal statute or from enacting a federal regulatory statute. The very diversity among types of compacts alone suggests a more detailed approach.

. . . .

In addition to the well-pleaded complaint rule, federal question jurisdiction is available only when the claim arises "directly" under federal law. In determining which disputes contain federal issues that are "basic" and not "collateral" and that are "necessary" and not "merely possibly" at issue, it has been suggested that pragmatic considerations be utilized. We think that same considerations are relevant in deciding when construction of the Land Use Ordinance itself presents a federal question.[3]

The most important pragmatic considerations in this case are whether interstate conflicts in the interpretation and application of the Ordinance may arise that may substantially affect the effective functioning of the Compact and whether, absent a federal trial forum, existing judicial mechanisms supply a practical means for resolving such conflicts. If exclusive jurisdiction to interpret and to apply the Ordinance rests in the state courts of Nevada and California, we think

---

[3] The case arises directly under the Ordinance, and the only issue is the threshold inquiry whether the Ordinance is a "law of the United States" within the meaning of 28 U.S.C. § 1331(a).

that conflicting interpretations are inevitable. The legal questions that can be posed, including those in the case at bar, are knotty; reasonable judicial minds can be expected to differ in resolving them. Moreover, the history of the Compact and the Ordinance reveals that California and Nevada do not have identical views about the appropriate scope of land use regulation. In simplistic terms, California tends to favor strict controls, and Nevada is less inclined to inhibit development. To be sure, not every interpretation or application of the Ordinance would generate conflict, and not every conflict would involve questions of such substantiality that differing decisions by the courts of Nevada and California would impair the effective administration of the regional plan. But when a conflict develops over a substantial question, we have no judicial mechanism that can be invoked to resolve conflict. If the questions are deemed not federal enough to permit access to the federal district court in the first instance, it is difficult to find a path to the Supreme Court after a conflict has developed between the state courts of last resort.[5]

Even if certiorari jurisdiction were expanded to encompass such questions, resort to the Supreme Court is impractical. Increased access to the Supreme Court which is seriously overburdened cannot be justified absent compelling necessity. That necessity does not exist when the problem can be resolved by permitting access to the lower federal courts using Section 1331(a)(1) jurisdiction.

We hold that questions concerning the interpretation and application of TRPA ordinances present federal questions under Section 1331(a).[7] Differing interpretations by state courts of the impact of the grandfather clause on lapsed use or on interrupted construction of highrise buildings in the Tahoe basin could impair the effectiveness of the regional plan.

There may be future controversies involving the interpretation and application of TRPA ordinances that have little or no impact on the regional plan. Whether the district courts under such circumstances can abstain from exercising federal jurisdiction in favor of state court resolution of the issues is a question that for decision can await the event.

Collier v. Bi-State Dev. Agency[*]

No. 4:14-cv-1263 (E.D. Mo. Oct. 20, 2014)

HAMILTON, JUDGE:

Collier initiated this action by filing a Petition on January 15, 2014 in the Circuit Court for the City of St. Louis, State of Missouri. Defendants timely removed on July 16, 2014.

. . . .

---

[5] The present case is a good example of this difficulty. Because the dispute is among private parties and a local municipality, original Supreme Court jurisdiction over disputes between the States is not available. 28 U.S.C. § 1251(a)(1).

[7] Of course, state courts have concurrent jurisdiction over Section 1331 suits, but in deciding these cases the state courts must apply federal law.

[*] [*Ed. Note*: unattributed quotes in this case excerpt refer to the parties' court filings.]

Collier's Petition involves the alleged acceptance by Metro's Pension Committee, which is a named Defendant here and whose existence is not expressly established by the Compact, of a purported Qualified Domestic Relations Order ("QDRO"). The effect of the purported QDRO was "to immediately reduce the pension obligations of the pension plan to" Collier. . . . The Pension Committee is alleged, *inter alia*, to have had knowledge that the document presented to it had not been approved by the St. Louis City Circuit Court. While Collier does not explicitly state a legal theory, his claims appear to be breach of Metro's pension plan and breach of the Pension Committee's fiduciary duties.

Collier suggests that remand is necessary because the Court does not have subject-matter jurisdiction over the issues contained in the Petition. Defendants contend that the claims alleged in the Petition require construction of the Compact, which is a federal question.

DISCUSSION

. . . .

. . . One situation in which a claim can be said to arise under federal law is when "vindication of a right under state law necessarily turn[s] on some construction of federal law." [*Merrell Dow Pharm. Inc. v. Thompson*, 478 U.S. 804, 808 (1986)].

Defendants are correct to point out that "Federal courts have jurisdiction over state law claims alleged against a bi-state entity when interpretation of the interstate compact that created the entity is implicated." The Supreme Court has held that "where Congress has authorized the States to enter into a cooperative agreement, and where the subject matter of that agreement is an appropriate subject for congressional legislation, the consent of Congress transforms the States' agreement into federal law under the Compact Clause." *Cuyler v. Adams*, 449 U.S. 433, 440 (1981). Because the agreement itself is federal law, "the construction of an interstate agreement sanctioned by Congress under the Compact Clause presents a federal question." *Id.* at 438.

Defendants . . . contend that Compact interpretation is necessary because this case "(1) * * * implicates a uniquely internal function of Metro (*i.e.*, management of an employee pension plan), as opposed to an external function like transporting passengers on a bus; and (2) the compact is silent as to which law applies to the internal function of managing a pension plan." Therefore, according to Defendants, it is necessary to interpret the Compact to determine which law should apply. Collier contends that no federal question exists because "Defendants do not cite any term in the [C]ompact that calls for interpretation or application."

The specifics of Defendants' contention are somewhat confusing. The principle on which their contention seems to rest is that bi-state entities are "formed through each state's surrender of a portion of its sovereignty to the compact entity[,]" and that the terms of that surrender "are found in the compact agreement itself. . . ." They do not assert, however, that construction of the Compact is therefore necessary to understand the sovereignty issues inherent in a choice-of-law inquiry. Instead, they make the seemingly unconnected assertion that

> [t]he question of whether and to what extent the laws of the compacting states apply to a bi-state entity they create has been approached differently by various courts, but has been clarified in this Circuit which held that 'one party to an interstate compact may not enact legislation that would impose burdens upon the compact absent the concurrence of the other signatories.'

They contend further that this principle is broad enough to require the consent of both compacting states when either state wishes to apply its own common law to a matter involving the Compact. [W]hatever law that Plaintiff seeks to apply clearly creates a burden on Defendants and Illinois must have concurred in the laws' application."

There are several problems with Defendants' contention. The first is that the Defendants do not make clear why the question of whether Illinois has consented to the application of Missouri law, which Defendants have made central to their argument, is relevant to whether interpretation of the Compact is necessary. Even if the consent question is relevant to the choice-of-law determination, Defendants have presented nothing to suggest that interpretation of the Compact will provide an answer. They have not suggested, for example, that the required consent can be found in the Compact, that the methods for consenting are set forth in the Compact, or that a particular provision would shed light on any issue relevant to the existence of consent. In other words, Defendants have failed to link the question of consent with the issue at hand, which is whether interpretation of the Compact is necessary and therefore a basis for subject-matter jurisdiction.

There is a broader possible reading of Defendants' argument: that interpretation is necessary to resolve the sovereignty concerns inherent in all choice-of-law determinations. Compact interpretation would therefore be necessary because the parameters of each state's surrender of sovereignty are defined in the Compact. But even on this more generous reading, Defendants have failed to demonstrate which portion or portions of the Compact will assist the Court in understanding the sovereignty issues related to choice of law. A vague claim that interpretation of the entire Compact may be necessary to understand sovereignty issues that may be important is not a firm enough basis on which to establish federal question jurisdiction.

There is also a more fundamental shortcoming in Defendants' contention. Defendants have not shown, based on Collier's Petition, that a choice-of-law determination will be necessary to the outcome of this case. They speculate that Missouri law applies. But they do not show whether or how Missouri law conflicts with the law of the other two interested sovereigns, *i.e.* Illinois law and federal law. Nor do they put forward any other theory as to why the choice-of-law inquiry will impact the outcome. Defendants have therefore failed to show that a determination of which law applies is necessary in this matter. Thus, even if Compact interpretation is necessary to determine which law applies, it is not necessary to the outcome of the case and cannot serve as a jurisdictional basis.

In short, Defendants have not met their burden to show that interpretation of the Compact will more likely than not be necessary to decide the Collier's state law claims.

Notes & Questions

1. The *B.J.K.* decision presents a remarkably simple and understandable rule for determining whether interpretation of a compact agency's ordinance presents a federal question. What do you think of the rule? Interestingly, this case is infrequently cited. Consider whether the rule is too simplistic, too difficult to apply, too subjective, not generally applicable. Why else do you think the reasoning in this case did not stick?

2. The *B.J.K.* decision also mentions that state court interpretation of a TRPA ordinance would inevitably generate conflicting interpretations of the compact that could "impair the effective administration of the compact." 547 F.2d at 1074. How important should uniform interpretation of the compact be in determining whether a federal question exists? In the next section, you will study different ways that state courts in different states have used to interpret compacts uniformly.

3. The *B.J.K.* decision reserved the possibility that there could be "future controversies involving the interpretation and application of TRPA ordinances that have little or no impact on the regional plan." 547 F.2d at 1075. The regional plan is the central planning document for TRPA. What interpretation and application of a TRPA ordinance would have little or no impact on the regional plan?

4. The *B.J.K.* decision stated, "Questions arising under the TRPA Land Use Ordinance enacted pursuant to the Compact do not automatically give rise to Section 1331(a) jurisdiction, because the Compact is not an ordinary federal statute and the Ordinance is not directly analogous to the Code of Federal Regulations." 547 F.2d at 1073. Interestingly, just 12 years later, in *Stephans v. Tahoe Reg'l Planning Agency*, 697 F. Supp. 1149, 1152 (D. Nev. 1988), the court concluded that TRPA's Regional Plan was federal law and preempted state law and state constitutional provisions. If this apparent change in the federal status of TRPA authorities is the reason that the *B.J.K.* decision is no longer cited, then you would expect *Stephans* to be frequently cited, but it too is only rarely cited.

5. At the time of the *B.J.K.* case excerpted above, the Tahoe Regional Planning Compact did not specify jurisdiction. The compact has been amended to now specify that jurisdiction lies in the "appropriate courts of California and Nevada and of the United States." Tahoe Regional Planning Compact, art. VI(j). This specific statement of jurisdiction obviates the need to rely on 28 U.S.C. § 1331 and is most likely the reason the *B.J.K.* decision is no longer cited.

6. The *Collier* case illustrates that a compact agency cannot bootstrap federal question jurisdiction simply by arguing that some interpretation of the compact may be necessary. In another similar case, *Int'l Union of Operating Eng'rs, Local 542 v. Delaware River & Bay Auth.*, No. 13-3204 (RBK/JS), 2014 U.S. Dist. LEXIS 64879 (D.N.J. May 12, 2014), the court dismissed a complaint alleging the DRBA

circumvented its collective bargaining agreement with Local 542 by using seasonal vessel workers (who are not union employees) for painting vessels owned by the DRBA. An arbitrator found in favor of Local 542. The DRBA complied with the award but sought to vacate the portion of the award requiring the DRBA to recognize the former seasonal workers as permanent employees covered by the collective bargaining agreement. The court dismissed the complaint for lack of jurisdiction for two reasons, one of which was that the suit did not involve construction of the interstate compact creating the DRBA. The complaint only mentioned the compact once and the principal issue raised in the complaint was the scope of the collective bargaining agreement.

7. Federal question jurisdiction can be difficult to determine. For example, in *Mitskovski v. Buffalo & Fort Erie Public Bridge Auth.*, 435 F.3d 127 (2d Cir. 2004), Mitskovski had filed the case in New York state court, but the Bridge Authority removed the case to federal court, which would seem to make sense because the Bridge Authority was created pursuant to a compact between New York and the Government of Canada. Mitskovski moved to remand the case back to state court, and the Second Circuit observed, in part:

> The Plaintiffs have pleaded only state law violations. The Authority contends that determination of whether the state law obligations may be imposed on it will require construction of the compact, but the Plaintiffs respond by pointing out that to the extent that the Authority is relying on the compact as a defense, such defensive assertion of federal law does not invoke federal question jurisdiction. We need not decide whether the nominally defensive use of the compact is so inextricably connected to the validity of the Plaintiffs' substantive claims as to support federal question jurisdiction,[7] nor whether the allegedly preemptive force of the compact accomplishes that result because, apart from the allegations of substantive state law violations, the Plaintiffs have alleged that the Authority is a New York State agency, and sought a declaratory judgment to that effect. Adjudication of that affirmative contention and claim for relief will inevitably require construction of the compact.
>
> 7. In his decision granting a stay pending consideration of the petition for mandamus, Judge Hall observed:
>
>> By the very terms of the [Plaintiffs'] Verified Petition, they implicate such a nexus among the Buffalo and Fort Erie Public Bridge Authority, the Government of Canada and its agencies, the Government of the United States and its agencies, and the proper and necessary flow of commercial traffic over an international boundary, it is inconceivable that the entire set of issues pleaded and the relief sought do not raise questions "arising under the Constitution, laws[,] or treaties of the United States." *In re: Buffalo and Fort Erie Public Bridge Authority*, No. 04-5365-op, Order granting temporary stay (Oct. 20, 2004) (quoting 28 U.S.C. § 1331).

Id. at 135. The Second Circuit concluded that federal question jurisdiction was properly invoked. Should a legal question of how to characterize the Authority be enough of a federal question for the federal court to retain the matter and decide the substantive state law issues under supplemental jurisdiction?

B. Diversity Jurisdiction

As noted above, before the courts landed on compacts presenting a federal question for the purpose of original jurisdiction in federal district courts, many courts found jurisdiction under the diversity jurisdiction statute, 28 U.S.C. § 1332. In the following *Yancoskie v. Delaware River Port Authority* case, the federal court considers diversity jurisdiction after first holding that the claim did not involve a federal question. Recall that you read a later *Yancoskie* case in Chapter 4 in which the Pennsylvania Supreme Court held that the DRPA was not an agency of the state entitled to sovereign immunity and thus Pennsylvania state courts could hear Yancoskie's wrongful death claim.

Yancoskie v. Delaware River Port Auth.

528 F.2d 722 (3d Cir. 1975)

VAN DUSEN, JUDGE:

While helping to construct a bridge linking the State of New Jersey with the Commonwealth of Pennsylvania, and being built for the Delaware River Port Authority ("Authority"), Francis J. Yancoskie fell to his death on the Pennsylvania side of the bridge. Lorraine Yancoskie, decedent's wife, who is a Pennsylvania resident, commenced this suit in the United States District Court for the District of New Jersey on June 10, 1974. She sued as administratrix of decedent's estate, in her own right, and on behalf of her minor son, who is also a Pennsylvania resident. The complaint asserted a right to recover any and all damages they are entitled to receive "under any and all wrongful death or survival actions or under any other theory of law or recovery."

On September 20, 1974, defendant filed a motion to dismiss the complaint on the ground that there was no federal jurisdiction. On December 4, 1974, the district court filed an opinion in which it denied the motion and held that there was federal jurisdiction. The rationale of the opinion was that, since the Authority was created by an interstate compact pursuant to the Compact Clause of the Constitution, the construction of the compact creating the Authority was a federal question. From this, the district court concluded that there was federal jurisdiction, though the opinion did not specify the statute on which jurisdiction was based. Presumably the district court found jurisdiction on the basis of either 28 U.S.C. § 1331 or 28 U.S.C. § 1337.

On December 13, 1974, the district court amended the order to include a certification that "a controlling question of law as to which there is substantial ground for difference of opinion" was involved "and that an immediate appeal from the order may materially advance the ultimate termination of the litigation." By order dated January 7, 1975, this court granted the Authority leave to appeal. The instant appeal is the result.

We hold that the district court was without jurisdiction, and we therefore reverse the denial of the defendant's motion to dismiss.

. . . .

II. *Diversity Jurisdiction*

Because of the district court's decision that federal question jurisdiction did exist, it did not reach the question of the existence of diversity of citizenship jurisdiction, 28 U.S.C. § 1332. Our contrary decision requires us to consider § 1332 as an alternate basis for federal jurisdiction here.

The Authority contends that it is an alter ego of the Commonwealth of Pennsylvania, citing *Appeal of Lillian Anderson*, 408 Pa. 179 (1962), and therefore not a "citizen" of any state for purposes of diversity jurisdiction. In answer to this contention, the plaintiff relied on the financial independence of the Authority from the state, and argued that citizenship for diversity purposes is a federal, and not a state, question.

We need not resolve this issue, however. In the compact, the Authority is referred to as a "body corporate and politic * * * which shall constitute the public corporate instrumentality of the Commonwealth of Pennsylvania and the State of New Jersey * * * ." Further, the Supreme Court in *Petty* referred to a similar commission as a "bistate corporation * * * a joint or common agency of Tennessee and Missouri." 359 U.S. at 279. We conclude that for the purpose of determining the existence of diversity of citizenship jurisdiction the Authority, if it is not the alter ego of the state, should be treated as a corporation incorporated in both New Jersey and Pennsylvania. Section 1332(c) reads in part:

> For the purposes of this section * * *, a corporation shall be deemed a citizen of any State by which it has been incorporated * * * ."

Assuming, arguendo, that the Authority is not the alter ego of any state, we hold that the Authority is a citizen of both Pennsylvania and New Jersey, and since plaintiff is a citizen of Pennsylvania, there is no diversity of citizenship jurisdiction.[17]

Therefore, the district court order will be reversed and the case remanded so that the district court may enter an order of dismissal for want of subject matter jurisdiction.

Notes & Questions

1. The Delaware River Port Authority argued that as an "alter ego of the Commonwealth of Pennsylvania," it was not a citizen of any state for the purpose of diversity; the Third Circuit, however, held that the DRPA "should be treated as

[17] The treatment of multi-state corporations for purposes of diversity of citizenship is not free from doubt. Prior to 1958, a corporation incorporated in several states, one of which was the forum state, probably was treated as a citizen only of the forum state. *Railway v. Whitton's Administrator*, 80 U.S. (13 Wall.) 270, 283; *Seavey v. B & M R.R.*, 197 F.2d 485, 487 (1st Cir. 1952) (dictum). *See also Gavin v. Hudson & Manhattan Ry.*, 185 F.2d 104 (3d Cir. 1950). In 1958 Congress amended § 1332 by adding subsection c, the relevant portion of which is quoted in the text above. We hold that this 1958 amendment means that a multi-state corporation is deemed a citizen of every state in which it has been incorporated.

a corporation incorporated in both New Jersey and Pennsylvania." 528 F.2d at 727. Recall in *Pac. States Marine Fisheries Comm'n v. Dep't of Revenue*, 346 Or. 117 (2009) (discussed in Chapter 4), the court determined that the Commission was a public corporation, but not "in this state." Can you harmonize why a compact agency that is incorporated in all the party states for the purpose of diversity might not be "in" one of the party states for another purpose?

2. The Port Authority of New York and New Jersey compact contains a venue statute that expressly states the authority "shall be deemed to be * * * a citizen of both of said two States." N.J. STAT. ANN. § 32:1-171; MCKINNEY'S UNCONSOL. LAWS OF N.Y. § 7106 [as added by L. 1950 c 301, § 6]. There are only a few compacts that address the citizenship of the compact agency and *Yancoskie* is one of the last cases to address whether diversity jurisdiction is available for compact agencies. Footnote 17 in *Yancoskie* suggests why this is so.

Under former diversity jurisdiction jurisprudence, plaintiffs that were citizens of one state and plaintiffs that were incorporated in multiple states were treated differently. A single-state plaintiff could choose to treat an entity incorporated in multiple states as a citizen of another state for the purpose of diversity. However, a multi-state entity could not elect to treat itself as a citizen of only one state when it was the plaintiff to achieve diversity. In *Delaware River Joint Toll Bridge Comm'n v. Stults*, 146 F. Supp. 241 (D.N.J. 1956), the federal district court in New Jersey stated, "We are of the opinion that a multi-state corporation, organized under the laws of the state of the forum and another state, may not invoke the jurisdiction of the federal court on the ground of diversity of citizenship, where, as here, the action is one against citizens of the state of the forum. Such a corporation may not ignore its status as a corporation of the state of the forum and elect to maintain the action as a foreign corporation." *Id.* at 242. And, in *Delaware River Joint Toll Bridge Comm'n v. Miller*, 147 F. Supp. 270 (E.D. Pa. 1956), the court similarly denied jurisdiction under the diversity statute, noting that its decision "is not inconsistent with the underlying purpose of the diversity clause in Article III, Section 2, of the Constitution, which was to prevent the obstruction of the administration of justice by 'state attachments, state prejudices, state jealousies and state interests,' since plaintiff, as a creature of the Pennsylvania legislature, will clearly receive fair treatment in the Pennsylvania courts." *Id.* at 273.

With the recognition that cases involving compacts with consent may raise a federal question, and most compacts now have a provision that specifies jurisdiction, diversity issues rarely arise in compact cases. In one recent case, *Anderson v. Bi-State Dev. Agency*, No. 4:16CV908 JCH, 2016 U.S. Dist. LEXIS 101649 (E.D. Mo. Aug. 3, 2016), Bi-State removed the case to federal court, arguing the federal court had diversity jurisdiction, but the court concluded that both Bi-State and one of the plaintiffs are citizens of the State of Missouri and thus remanded back to state court. The court cited Bi-State's own filing stating that it is incorporated or has its principal place of business in Missouri.

As you read the next section, consider whether you agree with the federal court in *Delaware River Joint Toll Bridge Comm'n v. Miller*, cited above, that state courts are free of "state attachments, state prejudices, state jealousies, and state interests" when handling cases involving compacts.

II. Jurisdiction in the State Courts

Recall from your civil procedure classes that state courts are courts of general jurisdiction. State courts may resolve most disputes arising under federal law, with some exceptions. The U.S. Supreme Court has sole jurisdiction over certain cases, such as state versus state disputes (discussed in the next section); federal statutes may provide for sole jurisdiction in federal court; and federal courts may also exercise supplemental jurisdiction to resolve issues typically appropriate for state court.

Resolving cases involving interstate compacts in state court presents unique issues. Compact agencies are especially vulnerable to claims in multiple courts because jurisdiction often lies in multiple courts. One obvious problem is forum shopping between many possible courts. Should a plaintiff in a compact case have a broad ability to forum shop? Correspondingly, should a compact agency be stuck in the plaintiff's selected state court or should it be able to ask the court to dismiss the matter for refiling in another state or to "transfer" the matter to another state? For example, Congress's consent to the Columbia River Gorge Compact, 16 U.S.C. § 544m(b)(6), requires jurisdiction in the two states' courts, but does not specify venue to determine which state court should hear a particular matter. In Oregon, judicial review of the bi-state Commission's actions occurs in the single state court of appeals with appeal by petition to the state Supreme Court; in contrast in Washington, judicial review occurs in four different trial courts, feeding into two divisions of the courts of appeals, with appeal by petition to the state Supreme Court. How would you guard against forum shopping in this compact?

Another obvious problem is that different states' laws provide different remedies that might apply to a compact dispute. One compact agency has successfully avoided this problem by arguing that its compact provides the exclusive remedies available against the agency. In *W. Birkenfeld Trust v. Bailey*, 827 F. Supp. 651 (E.D. Wash. 1993), the court noted, "The [Columbia River Gorge National Scenic Area] Act provides an elaborate set of administrative and judicial remedies for parties adversely affected by a violation of the Act or by a final action or order of the [Columbia River Gorge] Commission . . . ." *Id.* at 665. The court then denied the plaintiff's claim for a declaratory judgment because it was not a remedy specified in the compact. This was a federal court decision; would a state court be more likely to apply its own state law remedies rather than only the remedies specified in the compact? Similarly, in *Klickitat County v. State*, 71 Wash. App. 760 (1993), the Washington Court of Appeals dismissed a declaratory judgment action, reasoning, "If Congress had intended state courts to have plenary jurisdiction over all kids of suits against the [Columbia River Gorge] Commission, it would not have included the descriptions of certain cases in [16 U.S.C. § 544m]." *Id.* at 765.

Another problem is that jurisdiction in the state courts of multiple states makes conflicting interpretations of a compact almost inevitable? Recall the three opinions in *West Virginia ex rel. Dyer v. Sims* (excerpted in Chapter 3). Each was concerned about one state being a judge in its own case against a sister state. Should the U.S. Supreme Court have the same concern where the compact specifies state court jurisdiction. In such a compact, did the states bargain for or understand that each state's courts might independently decide a conflict of laws issue, interpret a compact, or review an action of the compact agency based on local law? Did the states bargain for or understand that the states' courts use different statutory interpretive methods, which can lead to different interpretations of the same compact, destroying or making more difficult the uniform application of that compact.

The Virginia and District of Columbia statutes creating the Metropolitan Washington Airports Authority is one example of how to have state court jurisdiction, but avoid some of these issues. VA. CODE ANN. § 5.1-173 and D.C. CODE § 9-922(a) specify jurisdiction only in the Virginia Commonwealth courts. District of Columbia courts do not have jurisdiction.

Another concern with state court jurisdiction is that early decisions tend to anchor questions of law in later cases in the other party states' courts. The following case, *Coyle v. Port Auth. Transit Corp.*, illustrates this anchoring effect and other issues with litigating compact cases in state court.

Coyle v. Port Auth. Transit Corp.
438 Pa. 99 (1970)

COHEN, JUSTICE:

This is an action instituted by twenty individuals, members of Transport Workers Union, Local 234 (TWU) to require the Port Authority Transit Corporation (PATCO) to recognize and bargain with TWU based on a Memorandum of Agreement dated January 13, 1969. Prior to October, 1968, appellees' employer was the Philadelphia Transportation Company (PTC) and its predecessor corporations. The appellees and all other PTC employees similarly situated had as their exclusive bargaining representative, TWU. In October, 1968, the Southeastern Pennsylvania Transportation Authority (SEPTA) took over the operation and maintenance of the transit facilities owned and/or operated by PTC and assumed the obligations of the TWU collective bargaining agreement then in effect which was to continue until January 14, 1969. Part of the local mass transit facilities taken over by SEPTA from PTC was the high-speed operation from 16th and Locust Streets in Philadelphia to Camden, New Jersey (the Bridge Line). About 42 SEPTA employees covered by the TWU agreement were directly employed in the operation of the Bridge Line.

Appellant PATCO is a subsidiary corporation of the Delaware River Port Authority (DRPA) which is a bistate agency formed pursuant to 1951–52 Compact Legislation (including enabling legislation) by and between the Commonwealth of Pennsylvania and the State of New Jersey and pursuant to an Act of Congress of the United States. In 1963 the two states entered into a Supplemental Agreement to the Compact Agreement which provided, *inter alia*, that the Commission of the

DRPA could form a wholly owned subsidiary corporation to effectuate any of the authorized purposes of DRPA. Pursuant to this Supplemental Compact, PATCO was formed on September 20, 1967, for the purpose of operating the Bridge Line and a proposed extension to Lindenwold, New Jersey. Prior to the formation of PATCO, TWU informed DRPA of the seniority, pension representation and other rights of the appellee and further notified DRPA that it was obligated to continue to recognize all such rights when and if it took over the operation of the Bridge Line. Similar notification was given to PATCO upon its formation. On December 27, 1968, one day before DRPA terminated its lease to SEPTA to operate the Bridge Line, TWU and DRPA/PATCO orally agreed, among other things, that TWU was to continue as the exclusive bargaining representative for the hourly employees who were to operate the Bridge Line and its extension.

This oral agreement was reduced to writing on January 13, 1969, and that Memorandum of Understanding states that PATCO recognizes TWU as collective bargaining representatives for its hourly employees and that PATCO will give those SEPTA employees whose jobs were eliminated by the take-over (approximately 42) an opportunity to select comparable employment in PATCO. It also states that the parties agree to meet as soon as possible and work out terms of a contract covering wages, hours, pensions, fringe benefits and working conditions. This action has arisen because it is alleged that PATCO has employed only twelve of the forty-two former SEPTA employees, has refused to recognize TWU as bargaining representatives for PATCO employees, and had refused to negotiate a definitive agreement with TWU. The real basis of the controversy is the struggle between TWU and the Teamsters Local Union No. 676 over which will represent employees on the Bridge Line.

In order to avoid confusion, we list in chronological order the course this litigation has taken.

December 28, 1968 Oral agreement between PATCO and TWU.

January 13, 1969 Oral agreement reduced to writing.

January 27, 1969 Teamsters notify DRPA of intent to represent employees.

January 31, 1969 Teamsters petition the New Jersey Public Employment Relations Commission (PERC) to settle the representation question.

February 12 and 21, 1969 Hearings held by PERC hearing officer.

February 28, 1969 Appellees file equity suit in Common Pleas Court of Philadelphia County seeking enforcement of January 13 agreement.

March 13, 1969 Arthur Sills, New Jersey Attorney General, PERC, Teamsters Local 676 and TWU permitted to intervene in equity suit.

March 18, 1969 To preserve labor peace all parties stipulated that PATCO would immediately hire fourteen SEPTA employees who formerly operated the Bridge Line (TWU members) and that their seniority (with respect to nonformer SEPTA people PATCO had hired) would be slotted in proportionately; that within six months PATCO would employ 28 more such employees; and that the trial would proceed on a question of permanent and not preliminary relief.

April 18, 1969 New Jersey Superior Court orders PATCO not to recognize TWU as negotiating agent of its employees or negotiate with them until PERC resolves all issues as to which organization represents them.

April 23, 1969 PERC decides to continue holding hearings.

May 12, 1969 PERC orders hearings to resume June 6.

May 23, 1969 Appellees file motion in Common Pleas Court of Philadelphia County to restrain PERC from holding the hearings scheduled for June 6.

June 5, 1969 Judge Eiseman, presiding over this whole matter, denies the motion to restrain stating the court doubts its power to restrain a subdivision of another state. He does order appellants not to enforce or carry out any order or decree resulting from the PERC hearings until the equity action has been decided. He bases this on the March 18 stipulation and the fact that further hearings are to begin before him on June 23.

June 19, 1969 This appeal filed.

June 25, 1969 Taking of testimony in the equity action is completed.

July 22, 1969 PERC hearing officer files his report.

September 23, 1969 PERC orders an election to be held.

October 16, 1969 Court of Common Pleas enjoins (in Pennsylvania) the American Arbitration Association from conducting the election.

October 20, 1969 PERC conducts the election itself. Out of 112 eligible to vote, 93 vote for the Teamsters and 2 for TWU.

November 5, 1969 PERC certifies the Teamsters as exclusive representatives.

November 14, 1969 Judge Eiseman files an opinion dismissing appellant's objections to jurisdiction and venue and stating he will decide the merits as soon as this appeal is disposed of.

As the situation now stands, PATCO, by order of the New Jersey Superior Court, is not to recognize or bargain with TWU until the PERC has reached a final determination of all relevant questions. Now that PERC has certified the Teamsters as representing the employees, PATCO may run a serious risk of violating that order if it deals with anyone other than the Teamsters. Under [an order from the Pennsylvania Common Pleas] both PATCO and the Teamsters are enjoined from enforcing any PERC decree or order, and both may well be in violation of that order if they begin to bargain as it seems they must do according to the New Jersey decisions. There is no guarantee that any decision by this Court will finally settle the controversy. The New Jersey appellate courts may reach a different conclusion, and the parties will again be subject to conflicting orders.

The problem in this action is not exactly the same as the situation where the equity courts of one state enjoin a litigant from pursuing an action in another state, but the general principles relevant there are applicable. In certain situations, in the interests of comity, one state will recognize an equity decree of a sister state.

The principle of comity is extremely important in an action such as this where one party is the creation of a bi-state compact and neither state's law is clearly controlling. Rather than state that we will give recognition to a New Jersey decree, we hold that the lower court should have declined jurisdiction of this matter because New Jersey is the state with the most significant relationship with the parties and events. PATCO's principal offices are located in Camden; its maintenance center and headquarters are located in Lindenwold; eight of twelve stations are located in New Jersey; all the employees report to work there; 95% of the employees actually work there; it hires in New Jersey; a great majority of its investments are in New Jersey; and the majority of the patrons using the line are residents of the New Jersey area who commute to and from Philadelphia.

Helping us reach this conclusion is the fact that another forum is readily available. This is not an action in which convenience, in the sense of availability of witnesses and evidence, is involved as much as is the concept of appropriateness of exercising jurisdiction. The availability of another forum, however, is an element in determining appropriateness. When presented with cases, courts should be careful to weigh the costs of assuming jurisdiction, and after examining the long and complex history of this action, we feel it important that the controversy be finally settled by the jurisdiction that has the greatest interest in the matter. The conflicting orders of various courts and agencies indicate that the only way in which this result can be assured is for the courts of Pennsylvania to decline jurisdiction.

The order of the court below is vacated, and all proceedings are dismissed.

ROBERTS, JUSTICE, DISSENTING:

Saying that its decision is dictated by the principles of comity, the majority today declares that the trial court should never have taken jurisdiction over this suit. The result of this conclusion is that the courts of this Commonwealth will never be able to play any role in the resolution of this controversy. I must dissent for several interdependent reasons.

First, Pennsylvania's interest in this controversy, though probably quantitatively less than that of New Jersey, is still substantial. The contract upon which the appellees base their cause of action was signed in Pennsylvania by an employer created in part by the Commonwealth and by a union representing Pennsylvania-based employees. And although most of the PATCO-operated high-speed line lies in New Jersey, that section of the operation in which the affected employees used to work ran only between Philadelphia and Camden. This is therefore not a case where Pennsylvania's interest is truly insubstantial.

Secondly, even if both Pennsylvania and New Jersey assume jurisdiction, and even if both states attempt to resolve the controversy, it is not inconceivable that their actions will be compatible. Pennsylvania need not specifically enforce the TWU-PATCO agreement, but could grant such relief as damages or merely requiring PATCO to hire the affected employees without mandating their union affiliation. In fact, assuming that both states will apply intelligent conflicts-of-law rules, the likelihood of consistent and complimentary outcomes in both suits is high.

Thirdly, I believe that it is improper to dismiss a case on grounds of comity at the preliminary objection stage whenever there is the least doubt as to the propriety of such an action. All of the ends which are served by such a resolution can be equally well reached at a later stage in the litigation. The inconveniences of proceeding further seem slight when compared with the finality of dismissal. At the very least, the trial court could, if appropriate, stay the proceedings but retain jurisdiction pending the outcome of litigation in the other forum before deciding to divest itself of all jurisdiction over the matter.

Notes & Questions

1. What issues with litigating compact cases in state court are raised in *Coyle*?

2. Do you agree that the principle of comity is especially important in cases involving an interstate compact? Does this principle create a race to file suit in one state or another? Is there another principle that courts should consider?

3. The court observed that the real basis of the controversy was a power struggle between the Transport Workers Union and the Teamsters. In the chronology, the court noted that the PERC held the election and the workers overwhelmingly voted in favor of the Teamsters. Is this a type of dispute that the courts should get involved in, and could this be an unwritten explanation for the court's decision?

4. The dissent began with a statement that by dismissing the case the Commonwealth would not be able to play a role in the dispute. What important or necessary state interest does playing a role in disputes involving a compact fulfill? Recall, for example, that only Virginia courts have jurisdiction over suits brought by or against the Metropolitan Washington Airports Authority, and that Virginia courts must apply Virginia law.

5. The dissent also observed that if both states would apply intelligent conflicts-of-law rules, there would be a high likelihood of consistent and complimentary outcomes in both suits. How would you compare this likelihood to the likelihood of an inconsistent decision? Is there a greater possibility of inconsistent decisions from judges in different states than from different judges in the same state? Consider whether the states might have use different conflict-of-laws principles.

6. What do you think about the *Coyle* dissent's third objection that the court should not have dismissed the case because it appeared the case was properly before the court? Is comity just a prudential resolution that courts should use only cautiously? Chapter 9 looks at comity again in the context of interpreting compacts. The next case, *Gauntt Constr. Co. v. Delaware River and Bay Auth.*, also involved multiple concurrent lawsuits arising from the same set of facts filed in the different party states' courts.

Gauntt Constr. Co. v. Delaware River and Bay Auth.
241 N.J. Super. 310 (App. Div. 1990)

MICHAELS, JUDGE:

Pursuant to leave granted by this court, defendants Delaware River & Bay Authority (Authority) and John Lewis, Project Engineer, appeal from an order of the Law Division that declared that the laws of the State of New Jersey applied to the construction contract between plaintiff Gauntt Construction Company/Lott Electric Company, a joint venture, The Lott Group, Inc. (Lott Group) and the Authority, thereby making the proceedings before the Authority director and his conclusions null and void, and ordering the action to continue before the trial court for the purposes of adjudicating the breach of contract claims and all other issues involved in the proceeding.

The facts giving rise to this appeal are essentially uncontroverted. The Authority and the Lott Group [successor by merger to Gauntt] entered into a written contractual agreement for modifications and improvements to the maintenance building located at the Delaware Memorial Bridge Complex in New Castle, Delaware. Section 1.5.1 of the contract provides:

> The Director shall act as referee in all questions arising under the terms of the Contract between the parties hereto, and the decision of the Director shall be final and binding. On all questions concerning the interpretation of Plans and Specifications, the acceptability, quality and quantity of materials or machinery furnished and work performed, the classification of material, the execution of the work and the determination of payment due or to become due, the decision of the Director shall be final and binding.

A dispute arose between the parties concerning the performance of the work and the amount due and owing under the contract. Pursuant to section 1.5.1, the parties agreed to appear before the Director for an arbitration hearing to be conducted on January 25, 1988. However, on January 21, 1988, the Lott Group instituted this action in the Superior Court of New Jersey, Law Division, seeking compensatory damages for work performed under the contract. In addition to filing the complaint, the Lott Group's attorney certified to the trial court that "to [his] knowledge the matter in controversy is not the subject of any other action pending in any court or of a pending arbitration proceeding" and that "to [his] knowledge, no other action or arbitration procedure is contemplated."[2] Thereafter, the Lott Group, through counsel, notified the Authority of the filing of the lawsuit and advised the Authority that it would not appear at the hearing. The Director nevertheless proceeded, conducting the arbitration hearing as scheduled, and, at the conclusion thereof resolved all claims between the parties and awarded the Lott

---

[2] The trial court stated that this misrepresentation would be reported to the Office of Attorney Ethics. After review of this matter, the Secretary for the Supreme Court of New Jersey District IV Ethics Committee informed the trial court and counsel that he "determined that the matter should not proceed further to formal proceeding."

Group $175,463.16. The Lott Group considered this amount to be grossly inadequate.

The Authority raised the arbitration award as an affirmative defense, and moved for a judgment on the pleadings. The trial court denied the Authority's motion to dismiss, stating that "the contract clause permitting the resolution of disputes by one party to the contract, the [Authority] Director, was unenforceable under New Jersey law." The trial court also analyzed Delaware law and concluded that "the enforceability of the clause had not been addressed conclusively by any Delaware court."

On June 2, 1988, the Authority instituted suit in the Delaware Chancery Court, seeking enforcement of the arbitration award. The prosecution of that action was enjoined on the theory that "when suits are pending in two jurisdictions, the court first acquiring jurisdiction has precedence, although particular circumstances not present here, may dictate otherwise." The trial court then lifted the restraint against the prosecution of the Delaware suit "to the extent necessary to permit the [Authority] to obtain a ruling as to the validity of the dispute resolution clause."

On August 29, 1988, the Authority moved for summary judgment in Delaware on the issue of the validity of the arbitration provision. The Delaware court refused to decide the issue of whether the arbitration provision was valid, but opined that such clauses are generally enforceable under Delaware law. . . . Noting that the courts of Delaware and New Jersey have concurrent jurisdiction over this dispute, the Delaware court denied the Authority's motion for summary judgment because the suit was "first filed in the New Jersey court which has proceeded to consider the entire controversy." In so holding, the Delaware court noted: "Even if, however, the New Jersey court has in fact failed to correctly apply the correct conflict of law principles, as the Authority claims, there is an appropriate remedy in the courts of New Jersey." . . .

On January 23, 1989, the Lott Group moved to reinstate the restraint against further proceedings in the State of Delaware. The trial court, having retained jurisdiction, indicated that it would reconsider its earlier opinion regarding the choice of law issue. On May 3, 1989, the trial court issued a second opinion, affirming its initial opinion. The trial court held: "1) New Jersey law applies, making the proceedings before the [Authority] Director and his conclusions a nullity, and 2) this action shall continue for the purpose of adjudicating the breach of contract claims and all other issues involved in these proceedings." This appeal followed.

This appeal presents the difficult question of whether New Jersey or Delaware law should apply when both states have concurrent jurisdiction. The interstate compact between New Jersey and Delaware is silent on this issue and, thus, does not provide a method of resolving this type of dispute. The compact, in pertinent part, merely states:

> Judicial proceedings to review any by-law, rule, regulation, order or other action of the authority or to determine the meaning or effect thereof, may be brought in such court of each State, and pursuant to such law or rules

> thereof, as a similar proceeding with respect to any agency of such State might be brought.
>
> Each State may provide by law what penalty or penalties shall be imposed for violation of any lawful rule, regulation or order of the authority, and, by law or rule of court, for the manner of enforcing the same.

We begin our analysis with *Alaska Packers Ass'n v. Industrial Accident Comm'n*, 294 U.S. 532 (1935), where the United States Supreme Court was faced with a decision as to which state's law to apply where the laws of both states were applicable. There, the Supreme Court enunciated a balance of interest test to resolve conflict of law problems. In so doing, the Supreme Court stated:

> In the case of statutes, the extra-state effect of which Congress has not prescribed, where the policy of one state statute comes into conflict with that of another, the necessity of some accommodation of the conflicting interests of the two states is still more apparent. A rigid and literal enforcement of the full faith and credit clause, without regard to the statute of the forum, would lead to the absurd result that, wherever the conflict arises, the statute of each state must be enforced in the courts of the other, but cannot be in its own. Unless by force of that clause a greater effect is thus to be given to a state statute abroad than the clause permits it to have at home, it is unavoidable that this Court determine for itself the extent to which the statute of one state may qualify or deny rights asserted under the statute of another.
>
> The necessity is not any the less whether the statute and policy of the forum is set up as a defense to a suit brought under the foreign statute or the foreign statute is set up as a defense to a suit or proceedings under the local statute. In either case, the conflict is the same. In each, rights claimed under one statute prevail only by denying effect to the other. In both the conflict is to be resolved, not by giving automatic effect to the full faith and credit clause, compelling the courts of each state to subordinate its own statutes to those of the other, *but by appraising the governmental interests of each jurisdiction, and turning the scale of decision according to their weight.*
>
> The enactment of the present statute of California was within state power and infringes no constitutional provision. Prima facie every state is entitled to enforce in its own courts its own statutes, lawfully enacted. *One who challenges that right, because of the force given to a conflicting statute of another state by the full faith and credit clause, assumes the burden of showing, upon some rational basis, that of the conflicting interests involved those of the foreign state are superior to those of the forum.* (emphasis supplied)
>
> . . . .

In *State Farm Mutual Auto. Ins. Co. v. Simmons' Estate*, 84 N.J. 28 (1980), the New Jersey Supreme Court set forth the traditional conflict-of-law rule applicable in contract cases. There, the Court began its analysis by considering the relevant factors listed in the Restatement (Second) of Conflict of Laws (1971):

> The Restatement identifies seven general considerations germane to a court's conflict-of-law analysis, *viz.*: (1) the needs of the interstate and international system, (2) the relevant policies of the forum, (3) the relevant policies of other affected states and the relevant interests of those states in the determination of the particular issue, (4) the protection of justified expectations, (5) the basic policies underlying the particular field of law, (6) certainty, predictability, and uniformity of result, and (7) ease in the determination and application of the law to be applied.
>
> . . . .

In *Interstate Wrecking Co. v. Palisades Interstate Park Comm'n*, 57 N.J. 342 (1971), the Supreme Court resolved a conflict-of-law issue arising from a contract dispute between a private contractor and the Palisades Interstate Park Commission (Commission), created by an interstate compact between New Jersey and New York. The Commission "was established by the compact as the 'joint corporate municipal instrumentality of the States of New Jersey and New York.'" Certain buildings on Iona Island in New York were to be demolished so that the Island could be developed for recreational purposes. The Commission advertised for bids in New York. The contract was executed by the parties in New York. All of the work was performed in New York. The plaintiff was paid from the appropriations made by the New York legislature. The plaintiff wrecking company—the successful bidder—however, was a New Jersey corporation. The contract specifically provided that "the work would be done in compliance 'with all of the laws of the State of New York' and 'with the lawful directions of the officers, agents or representatives of the State.'" Additionally, "the contract set forth that the Commission was 'acting for and in behalf of the State of New York' and contained additional references to New York but none to New Jersey."

Although the Court found that New Jersey had "ample jurisdiction to entertain the plaintiff's action against the Commission and that any ensuing judgment would be entitled to full faith and credit in New York," the Court then decided the question of whether New Jersey's jurisdiction should be withheld under principles of comity or under the doctrine of *forum non conveniens*. In so doing, the Court noted that although the Commission had been

> designed in the compact as a "joint corporate municipal instrumentality" its operations have consistently recognized the territorial separations of the respective states; the park is divided into New York and New Jersey sections; employees are separated into New York and New Jersey employees with divided benefits; separate police and enforcement units are maintained; and there are separate controls for acquisitions and disbursements * * * . "To date, by interstate cooperation, litigation emanating from New York has been remitted to the New York Attorney General and, similarly, matters involving the New Jersey section have been serviced by the New Jersey Attorney General," and that since inception, "no attempt has been made to transpose or intertwine the several liabilities of the respective States."

When the Wrecking Company entered into its contract with the Commission it undoubtedly was aware that there were vital administrative separations between New York and New Jersey and that it was dealing entirely with New York.

The Court held that under the circumstances, it was evident that the plaintiff should have brought its action in New York rather than in New Jersey. Indeed, the Court emphasized that "[a]ll of the pertinent documents were drawn in New York, all of the demolition occurred in New York and all of the significant witnesses would presumably come from New York." Thus, the Court stated that "[d]ecent regard for the convenience of all those concerned as well as for the vital administrative separations in the Commission's operations would have dictated the choice of New York rather than New Jersey as the appropriate forum."

More recently, in *Eastern Paralyzed Veterans Ass'n v. Camden*, 111 N.J. 389 (1988), our Supreme Court resolved a conflict-of-law issue arising from a case involving a cooperative undertaking by a bi-state agency and a New Jersey municipal agency to create a downtown mass transportation center in New Jersey. The Association of handicapped persons filed suit to compel the city and the Delaware River Port Authority (DRPA) to install elevators in a mass transit terminal being constructed in New Jersey. . . .

. . . .

. . . [T]he Court concluded that "to hold that the DRPA is subject to [New Jersey's statutes] would result in the imposition, unauthorized by the bi-state compact, of substantial duties or responsibilities on that Authority." Thus, the Court held that the Department of Community Affairs could not unilaterally impose on the DRPA the obligations set forth in the New Jersey Uniform Construction Code and the New Jersey Law Against Discrimination.

. . . After considering state and federal policy, the Court concluded that:

> This State lacks the sovereign authority to direct the DRPA to cede jurisdiction to New Jersey. Just as "[a] State cannot be its own ultimate judge in a controversy with a sister State," *West Virginia ex rel. Dyer v. Sims*, 341 U.S. 22 (1951), so too a single state cannot dictate the policy of a bi-state agency. We hold that the State of New Jersey cannot exercise unilateral jurisdiction over the DRPA.

Analogously, in *Bell v. Bell*, 83 N.J. 417 (1980), the Supreme Court held that the New Jersey Tort Claims Act does not apply to a bi-state agency. There, the plaintiff sustained injuries when she struck an unmarked girder supporting a railroad bridge used and maintained jointly by Conrail and PATCO. The Court stated that "[t]he New Jersey Legislature does not have the power to modify by unilateral action the waiver of sovereign immunity set forth in the bi-state compact; yet that would be the result were the Tort Claims Act held to apply to DRPA."

Similarly, in *Delaware River & Bay Auth. v. New Jersey Pub. Employment Relations Comm'n*, 112 N.J. Super. Ct. App. Div. 160 (1970), New Jersey enacted its Employer-Employee Relations Act subsequent to the creation of the plaintiff authority, a bi-state agency of New Jersey and Delaware. There, we held that New

Jersey could not unilaterally vest the Public Employment Relations Commission with jurisdiction over the bi-state agency in violation of the compact which made no provision for such jurisdiction. In so holding, we emphasized that:

> Bi-state agencies exist by virtue of compacts between the states involved, entered into by their respective legislatures with the approval of Congress. When formed, they become a single agency of government of both states. Their primary purpose is to cooperate in advancing the mutual interests of the citizens of both states by joint action to overcome common problems. We fail to see how either state could enact laws involving and regulating the bi-state agency unless both states agree thereto. To sanction such practice would lead to discord and a destruction of the purposes for which such bi-state agencies are formed.

Likewise, in *Delaware River & Bay Auth. v. Carello*, 43 Del. Ch. 213 (1966), the Delaware court held that where an interstate compact exists, one state may not unilaterally legislate so as to place burdens on the compact. The court stated that "[b]y entering into a compact * * * a state surrenders *pro tanto* a portion of its own sovereignty."

Applying these fundamentally sound principles in this case, it is evident that the trial court's theory of jurisdiction cannot be sustained. Here, the contract in dispute was prepared, bid, accepted and executed in Delaware. Moreover, the subject matter of the contract—the maintenance building—was located in Delaware and the work was performed in Delaware. New Jersey's only connection in this matter concerns the citizenship of the parties. The Lott Group is a New Jersey corporation. The Authority is an agent of New Jersey and Delaware, and, therefore, is subject to the jurisdiction of both states. After carefully considering the circumstances surrounding the contract in question, we find that Delaware has greater contacts. Clearly, the Authority has met its burden of proving that Delaware's interests are superior to those of New Jersey. As such, the law of Delaware should have been applied to resolve this dispute.

Moreover, we are satisfied that it is not fundamentally unfair to enforce the arbitration provision in this contract if such provision is valid and enforceable under Delaware law. The trial court, on the other hand, after considering New Jersey state policies and governmental interests, concluded that public policy reflected in both states' arbitration statutes and in New Jersey decisional law prevents a biased party from acting as an arbitrator. Thus, the trial court applied New Jersey's public policy to resolve this dispute. In *Eastern Paralyzed Veterans Ass'n v. Camden*, however, the New Jersey Supreme Court expressly refused to allow a single state to "dictate the policy of a bi-state agency." That case involved an even more compelling policy question concerning handicapped individuals' access to public transportation. There, the Court held that New Jersey lacked the authority to direct the DRPA to cede jurisdiction to New Jersey. Consequently, New Jersey's public policy should not be the basis for the construction of this bi-state agency's contract.

Accordingly, the order under review is reversed and the matter is remanded to the trial court for further proceedings applying Delaware law to resolve the underlying contract dispute between the parties.

Notes & Questions

1. The New Jersey Superior Court mentioned that the Delaware Chancery Court enjoined prosecution of the case in Delaware courts because of the preexisting New Jersey litigation. That decision, *Delaware River and Bay Auth. v. Gauntt,* No. 9952, 1989 Del. Ch. LEXIS 5 (Del. Ch. Jan. 19, 1989), held:

> Although I do not find on the present record that any determination by this Court would be barred by the doctrines of res judicata, collateral estoppel or the Full Faith and Credit clause of the U.S. Constitution because no final judgment has apparently been entered in the New Jersey Court, in the interests of judicial comity and efficiency, I decline to rule on any motion duplicating issues already ruled upon by Judge Haines [in New Jersey]. The New Jersey litigation was commenced months prior to the filing of this Delaware action and no reason has been shown why the New Jersey Court cannot properly dispose of all the issues. *Coyle v. Port Authority Transit Corporation*, 438 Pa. 99 (1970). ('The principle of comity is extremely important in an action such as this where one party is the creation of a bi-state compact and neither state's law is clearly controlling.'). . . .

Id. at *9–10. Do you agree that the Delaware court properly dismissed this case because there was already another case pending in New Jersey? Does this reasoning promote forum shopping or a race to the courthouse to find the most favorable law? How else would you resolve the issue of two parallel cases?

2. Interestingly, the New Jersey court cited New Jersey, Delaware, and Pennsylvania cases, relying heavily on precedent prohibiting one state from applying its own law to the compact. In the last paragraph, the court specifically states that New Jersey's public policy should not be the basis for the construction of the DRBA's contract. But did the court's decision effectively mandate Delaware public policy as the basis for this decision. How can you reconcile a prohibition against applying a single state's law to a compact with the factors and methodology for a conflict of laws analysis? Chapter 8 explores the relationship between state law and compacts in more detail.

3. How similar are the *Coyle* and *Gauntt* methodologies? What factors distinguish the methodologies?

4. Three cases involving the Delaware River Port Authority illustrate the complexity of litigating in multiple courts. In the first case, *Textar Painting Corp v. Delaware River Port Auth.*, 296 N.J. Super. 251 (Law Div. 1996), a New Jersey trial court reviewed both New Jersey and Pennsylvania standards for judicial review in a competitive bid dispute and noted, ". . . New Jersey *and* Pennsylvania have each determined that a decision by a public agency, as to whether or not a particular bidder is qualified will not be set aside unless the decision of the public agency is arbitrary and unreasonable so as to constitute an abuse of discretion." *Id.* at 259.

In the second case, *Allied Painting, Inc. v. Delaware River Port Auth.*, No. 04-1032, 2004 U.S. Dist. LEXIS 13994 (E.D. Pa. July 20, 2004), a federal court similarly considered both states' laws and noted, "Here, given DRPA's unique position as a bi-state agency, the Court will consider whether Pennsylvania *or* New Jersey law creates a legitimate claim of entitlement in receiving a public contract for which a party is the low bidder." *Id.* at *6 (emphasis added).

In *Textar*, the court considered whether both states' laws created a claim, whereas in *Allied Painting*, the court considered whether just one of the states' laws created a claim. In both cases, the courts ultimately determined that there was no conflict in the states' laws, but what would have been the next step if the courts had found a conflict?

In the third case, *Alpha Painting & Constr. Co. v. Del. River Port Auth.*, 853 F.3d 671 (3d Cir. 2017), the Third Circuit noted that the DRPA has internal rules for competitive bids, yet it interpreted and applied those rules in accordance with federal APA case law as opposed to state law as in *Textar* and *Allied Painting.* The court reasoned:

> The parties rely on our previous bidding dispute cases without addressing a crucial distinction present here: nearly all of those cases involve challenges to contract awards by federal agencies brought under the Administrative Procedures Act. DRPA, however, is a bi-state corporate instrumentality created under the Compact Clause of the U.S. Constitution. For purposes of review in this diversity case, we do not think this distinction is material. Compare 5 U.S.C. § 706 (permitting federal courts to set aside agency action under the APA that is "arbitrary, capricious, [or] an abuse of discretion"), with *Textar* (noting, in bid dispute case, that "the actions of . . . DRPA are reviewable by [the] court," and applying "arbitrary and unreasonable" standard).

Id. at 684 n.15. The Third Circuit concluded that federal, Pennsylvania, and New Jersey courts nominally use the "arbitrary and capricious" standard, but it did not discuss *how* the state and federal courts apply the "arbitrary and capricious" standard. If there are differences, what manner of applying the "arbitrary and capricious" standard should the Third Circuit have used?

5. In *Lakeview Dev. Corp. v. City of South Lake Tahoe*, 915 F.2d 1290 (9th Cir. 1990), the Ninth Circuit suggested factors that it might have considered if it had discovered a conflict in state laws in a case involving the Tahoe Regional Planning Agency:

> Congress did no more than incorporate the agreement of the two parties into the body of federal law; it did not make applicable the entire panoply of federal administrative and substantive standards. We therefore must look to the laws of Nevada and California to resolve the question before us. If there were a conflict between California and Nevada law on the question of vested rights, this case would be more difficult. We would have to decide whether to apply the law of the jurisdiction where the land is situated and

the permit was granted or whether to apply some other principle to resolve the conflict.

Id. at 1295. How reasonable is the *Lakeview Dev. Corp.* method of resolving conflicts if the compact involves more than two states? Does this approach make more sense than the Delaware court's reasoning in *Delaware River and Bay Auth. v. Gauntt* in note 1?

6. Questions may also arise about which court within a state should hear a case. In *State ex rel. List v. Cty. of Douglas*, 90 Nev. 272 (1974), the Nevada Supreme Court decided to take a case in which it shared original jurisdiction with state district courts, reasoning, "The decision as to whether an application for a writ of mandate will be entertained lies within the discretion of the court. Usually, this court prefers that such an application be addressed to the discretion of the appropriate district court, since that court also is invested with the power of mandamus. NEV. CONST. art. 6, § 6; [NEV. REV. STAT. §] 34.160. However, since the counties of Washoe, Carson City (Ormsby), and Douglas border the Nevada side of Lake Tahoe, and since the district courts serving those counties may possibly have different views about the issue here tendered, we chose to entertain this application rather than to direct its filing in a district court." *Id.* at 276–77.

Compact cases often involve the same or similar claims in both state and federal courts. Several cases illustrate ways that federal and state courts handle cases where jurisdiction may be in multiple courts and issues that are unique to compact cases and claims.

In *Gonzalez v. Waterfront Comm'n of the N.Y. Harbor*, 755 F.3d 176 (3d Cir. 2014), the court applied the *Younger* abstention doctrine to the plaintiff's federal complaint. Under *Younger* abstention, federal courts will not consider a federal complaint when there is a related and parallel state proceeding that involves an important state interest and in which the plaintiff can raise the federal claims. Gonzalez's federal complaint sought to enjoin the Waterfront Commission from suspending him without pay and from scheduling a disciplinary hearing. The U.S. District Court denied a temporary restraining order, finding that the Commission's hearing involved an important state interest, "the regulation of the conduct of officers by Defendant." *Gonzalez v. Waterfront Comm'n of the N.Y. Harbor*, No. 2:13-cv-00978-FSH-PS, 2013 U.S. Dist. LEXIS 198177 (D.N.J. Mar. 13, 2013). Gonzales was a detective for the Waterfront Commission, and law enforcement officers for the Waterfront Commission are vested with powers of police officers in both New Jersey and New York.

The "important state interest" factor was relatively straightforward in the *Gonzales* case, but could be a difficult argument for compact agencies to make where a case involves the application or interpretation of the compact. This is because arguing an important "state" interest could conflict with arguments that the compact, compact regulations, or other authorities are federal law or have the force and effect of federal law. How would you advise a compact agency to raise *Younger* abstention?

In *Bey v. Port Auth. of N.Y. & N.J.*, No. 13-1399 (SRC), 2014 U.S. Dist. LEXIS 114985 (D.N.J. Aug. 19, 2014), the U.S. District Court applied state law prohibiting the plaintiff from filing the same claim in multiple courts. The plaintiff filed an action for replevin in U.S. District Court, but it had already filed the same claim in the Superior Court of New Jersey, which dismissed the claim with prejudice. In the U.S. District Court, the Port Authority argued that New Jersey's state law "entire controversy" doctrine barred the claim and the District Court agreed. Should this state common law apply if New York does not have the same law? Chapter 8 discusses the application of state common law to compacts and compact agencies.

In *GLW Ventures, LLC v. U.S. Dep't of Agriculture*, 261 F. Supp. 3d 1098 (W.D. Wash. 2016), the U.S. District Court simply stayed a federal case, allowing a state court case to proceed to conclusion. GLW had sought land use approval through the Columbia River Gorge Compact's regulatory program, which includes judicial review exclusively in state court. The U.S. Forest Service had previously purchased a conservation easement on the property at issue and claimed that GLW's application violated the easement. GLW sued the U.S. Forest Service in federal court and sought to have the federal court adjudicate its claims. In 2016, the federal court dismissed the federal court case, holding that the state court had adjudicated all GLW's claims and that the compact did not allow the federal court to adjudicate claims involving GLW's land use claims. If the court was without jurisdiction to adjudicate GLW's land use claims, why wouldn't the federal court have dismissed the case instead of staying it?

In *Pomales v. Hoke*, No. 1:11CV2616, 2012 U.S. Dist. LEXIS 88127 (N.D. Ohio June 26, 2012), the federal district court discussed its own jurisdiction: "The Supreme Court has reasoned that when Congress enacted § 2241, it never intended a 'federal judge familiar with the laws and practices of [his jurisdictional state * * * to be forced] to defend its action in a distant State and to preclude the resolution of the dispute by [that] federal judge.' Thus, as Petitioner brought this action in West Virginia, where he is confined, but attacks a detainer lodged by Ohio, the court in West Virginia 'acts as agent for the demanding State.' Because West Virginia has no vested interest in the resolution of the prisoner's attack on an Ohio detainer, it properly transferred the suit to this Court, the most convenient forum." *Id.* at *10.

In *Lizzie v. Wash. Metro. Area Transit Auth.*, 384 Md. 199 (2004), the Maryland Court of Appeals (the state's highest court) concluded that *res judicata* barred the plaintiff's claims because he had raised the identical claims in federal court and that court had already resolved the claims. Lizzie originally filed his complaint in Maryland state court, then more than one year later, filed his complaint in federal court. The state trial court ordered a stay of the state court proceedings pending a decision in the federal court case. After the Fourth Circuit ruled against the plaintiff, *see Lizzie v. Alexander*, 255 F.3d 128 (4th Cir. 2001), the transit authority moved the state trial court to lift the stay and dismiss the case arguing *res judicata*. Does this sequencing make more sense than the sequencing in *GLW Ventures* in which the federal court stayed its proceeding while the plaintiff prosecuted its claims in state court?

III. Original Jurisdiction in the Supreme Court

Original jurisdiction in the Supreme Court has its basis in Article III, Section 2 of the U.S. Constitution. The statute granting jurisdiction is 28 U.S.C. § 1251(a), which states, "The Supreme Court shall have original and exclusive jurisdiction of all controversies between two or more States."

The historical basis for original jurisdiction is an interesting study, primarily the result of colonial boundary disputes that existed prior to the Declaration of Independence and the Articles of Confederation.

Charles Warren, *The Supreme Court and Disputes Between States*, Bull. Coll. Wm. & Mary, Vol. 34, No. 5 (June 1940)*

. . .

The American Colonies were familiar with the power possessed by the King's Privy Council in England to settle boundary controversies arising under charters granted by the King. Such disputes were heard in England by one of the Council's political or executive committees, termed the Lord Commissioners of Trade and Plantations, or by Commissioners in America specially appointed from the residents of colonies adjacent to the disputants. . . . Three decisions in such boundary cases had been made by the Privy Council and were widely known in the colonies prior to the year 1776 . . . . It was natural, therefore, that within eight days after the colonies declared their independence as sovereign states, John Dickinson, on July 12, 1776, in the Continental Congress should draft a plan for a procedure to be set up by the new states to settle their quarrels, similar to that before the King in Council; and his proposal resulted in a provision of the Articles of Confederation in 1781, authorizing the Congress, as "the last resort on appeal" for "all disputes and differences . . . between two or more states concerning boundary, jurisdiction, or any other cause whatever," to constitute a court for each case as it arose and to appoint "commissioners or judges" with power to proceed to final judgment, even if a defendant state refused to appear . . . .

For various reasons, only three courts were ever appointed under the Articles of the Confederation . . . .

When the Federal Convention met in 1787 for the framing of the Constitution, serious interstate disputes over lands, boundaries, and river rights were pending, involving at least ten states, as well as Vermont which had declared its independence. It is little realized now to what a high degree the states of this country then regarded themselves as sovereign and independent, except so far as they might have surrendered certain rights of sovereignty to the United States under the Articles of Confederation. . . . Experience, therefore, had shown to the members of the Federal Convention that there was a grave need for a more satisfactory

* Available at http://scholarship.law.wm.edu/cutler/21.

method of adjusting these boundary and other interstate disputes, and that for their adjudication a permanent court with power to enforce its decrees was necessary. And it was out of such necessity that the convention finally decided to give to the new Supreme Court, which it was constituting, jurisdiction "in controversies between two or more states."

The fundamental reason for this jurisdiction was that there are only three ways of settling a dispute—by force, by treaty or agreement, and by judicial decision. Now the Constitution, by express provision forbade the States of the Union to wage war or to make treaties or alliances, or to make compacts without the consent of Congress. Some method of settlement of disputes had to be provided, and the only method left was settlement by a court.

States cannot simply initiate a case under the Supreme Court's original jurisdiction by filing a complaint. Original jurisdiction is not automatic; the Court has interpreted the Constitution and 28 U.S.C. § 1251(a) as making original jurisdiction "obligatory only in appropriate cases" and as providing "substantial discretion to make case-by-case judgments as to the practical necessity of an original forum in this Court." Supreme Court Rule 17 requires states to petition the Court to file a complaint to initiate an original-jurisdiction matter. In this section, we look at when the Court will consider a case justiciable under its original jurisdiction. The next case, *Mississippi v. Louisiana* did not involve a compact, but provides a good summary of what the Supreme Court looks for in deciding whether to accept a state-versus-state case under its original jurisdiction. Following this case is an excerpt of Justice Thomas's dissent from denial of a bill of complaint in *Nebraska v. Colorado*, in which he questions the Court's discretionary approach to original jurisdiction cases. The notes and questions include relatively recent jurisprudence concerning the ability of a compact agency to initiate an original jurisdiction case against a state and participate as a party in a state-versus-state case.

Mississippi v. Louisiana
506 U.S. 73 (1992)

REHNQUIST, CHIEF JUSTICE:

This action was originally commenced by private plaintiffs suing other private defendants in the District Court for the Southern District of Mississippi to quiet title to certain land riparian to the Mississippi River. The State of Louisiana intervened in the action and filed a third-party complaint against the State of Mississippi seeking to determine the boundary between the two States in the vicinity of the disputed land. We hold that 28 U.S.C. § 1251(a), granting to this Court original and exclusive jurisdiction of all controversies between two States, deprived the District Court of jurisdiction of Louisiana's third-party complaint against Mississippi.

The land in question lies along the west bank of the Mississippi River near Lake Providence, Louisiana. The private plaintiffs, known as the Houston Group, alleged that they own the land in fee simple as a result of a homestead patent issued by the United States in 1888 and a deed issued by Mississippi in 1933. Louisiana and the Lake Providence Port Commission intervened in the title dispute and filed a third-party complaint against Mississippi seeking a determination of the boundary between the States. Louisiana then sought leave to file a bill of complaint against Mississippi in this Court. Mississippi opposed the motion in view of the pendency of the District Court action, and also emphasized that the case was originally a dispute between private parties: "Houston brought the suit to establish the boundary line to their land. It is incidental that the boundary line is also alleged to be the State line." We denied leave to file.

The District Court thereafter found that the thalweg, frozen by an avulsive shift[*] in the river, was to the west of the disputed land and thus placed it within Mississippi. Alternatively, the District Court concluded that the disputed land was part of Mississippi because "Louisiana has acquiesced in the exercise of the exclusive jurisdiction over the island by * * * Mississippi." Having found the land to be part of Mississippi, the District Court then considered the ownership question and quieted title in the Houston Group.

The Court of Appeals reversed, rejecting the District Court's rulings both on the location of the thalweg and on acquiescence. We granted certiorari on these two questions and on a third that we formulated: "Did the District Court properly assert jurisdiction over respondent's third-party complaint against petitioner State of Mississippi?" We now reverse.

The constitutional and statutory provisions necessary to our decision are these:

> Article III, § 2, of the Constitution:
>
> The judicial Power [of the United States] shall extend * * * to controversies between two or more States; * * * .
>
> In all cases affecting ambassadors, other public ministers and consuls, and those in which a state shall be party, the Supreme Court shall have original jurisdiction.
>
> Title 28 U.S.C. § 1331: "The district courts shall have original jurisdiction of all civil actions arising under the Constitution, laws, or treaties of the United States."
>
> Title 28 U.S.C. § 1251(a): "The Supreme Court shall have original and exclusive jurisdiction of all controversies between two or more States."

Mississippi, even though its contentions as to the boundary between itself and Louisiana were rejected by the Court of Appeals, urges us to find that the District Court had jurisdiction of the third-party complaint that Louisiana brought against it. Mississippi argues that our refusal to allow Louisiana to file an original complaint to determine the boundary between the two States must, by implication,

[*] [*Ed. Note*: a *thalweg* is the line drawn to join the lowest parts of a streambed or valley, and an *avulsive shift* is a sudden shift of a river course to another location in the floodplain.]

have indicated that the District Court was a proper forum for the resolution of that question. This is particularly true, Mississippi argues, since its opposition to Louisiana's motion to file its complaint in this Court was premised in part on the contention that the boundary question could be determined in the then-pending action between the private landowners in the District Court. Mississippi asserts that that court had jurisdiction by virtue of 28 U.S.C. § 1331, which confers jurisdiction of all civil actions arising under federal law on the District Court.

If it were not for the existence of 28 U.S.C. § 1251(a), Mississippi's arguments would be quite plausible. We have said more than once that our original jurisdiction should be exercised only "sparingly." *Wyoming v. Oklahoma*, 502 U.S. 437, 450 (1992); *Maryland v. Louisiana*, 451 U.S. 725, 739 (1981); *Arizona v. New Mexico*, 425 U.S. 794, 796 (1976). Indeed, Chief Justice Fuller wrote nearly a century ago that our original "jurisdiction is of so delicate and grave a character that it was not contemplated that it would be exercised save when the necessity was absolute." *Louisiana v. Texas*, 176 U.S. 1, 15 (1900). Recognizing the "delicate and grave" character of our original jurisdiction, we have interpreted the Constitution and 28 U.S.C. § 1251(a) as making our original jurisdiction "obligatory only in appropriate cases," *Illinois v. City of Milwaukee*, 406 U.S. 91, 93 (1972), and as providing us "with substantial discretion to make case-by-case judgments as to the practical necessity of an original forum in this Court," *Texas v. New Mexico*, 462 U.S. 554, 570 (1983).

We first exercised this discretion not to accept original actions in cases within our nonexclusive original jurisdiction, such as actions by States against citizens of other States, and actions between the United States and a State. But we have since carried over its exercise to actions between two States, where our jurisdiction is exclusive. Determining whether a case is "appropriate" for our original jurisdiction involves an examination of two factors. First, we look to "the nature of the interest of the complaining State," *Massachusetts v. Missouri*, 308 U.S. 1 (1939), focusing on the "seriousness and dignity of the claim." *City of Milwaukee, supra*, at 93. "The model case for invocation of this Court's original jurisdiction is a dispute between States of such seriousness that it would amount to *casus belli*[*] if the States were fully sovereign." *Texas v. New Mexico, supra*, at 571. Second, we explore the availability of an alternative forum in which the issue tendered can be resolved. *City of Milwaukee, supra*, at 93. In *Arizona v. New Mexico*, for example, we declined to exercise original jurisdiction of an action by Arizona against New Mexico challenging a New Mexico electricity tax because of a pending state-court action by three Arizona utilities challenging the same tax: "We are persuaded that the pending state-court action provides an appropriate forum in which the issues tendered here may be litigated." 425 U.S. at 797.

But Mississippi's argument for jurisdiction in the District Court here founders on the uncompromising language of 28 U.S.C. § 1251(a), which gives to this Court "original and *exclusive* jurisdiction of all controversies between two or more States" (emphasis added). Though phrased in terms of a grant of jurisdiction to

* [*Ed. Note*: "a cause for war."]

this Court, the description of our jurisdiction as "exclusive" necessarily denies jurisdiction of such cases to any other federal court. This follows from the plain meaning of "exclusive," and has been remarked upon by opinions in our original jurisdiction cases.

Because the District Court lacked jurisdiction over Louisiana's third-party complaint against Mississippi, the judgment of the Court of Appeals is reversed insofar as it purports to grant any relief to Louisiana against Mississippi. The District Court is conceded to have had jurisdiction over the claims of the private plaintiffs against the private defendants, and in deciding questions of private title to riparian property, it may be necessary to decide where the boundary lies between the two States. Adjudicating such a question in a dispute between private parties does not violate § 1251(a), because that section speaks not in terms of claims or issues, but in terms of parties. The States, of course, are not bound by any decision as to the boundary between them which was rendered in a lawsuit between private litigants.

Because both the District Court and the Court of Appeals in this case intermixed the questions of title to real property and of the location of the state boundary, we are not in a position to say whether on this record the claims of title may fairly be decided without additional proceedings in the District Court. We therefore reverse the judgment of the Court of Appeals insofar as it adjudicated the complaint filed by Louisiana against Mississippi, with instructions that it direct the District Court to dismiss the complaint for want of jurisdiction. We remand the balance of the case to the Court of Appeals for the necessary inquiry as to whether further proceedings are required in order to adjudicate the claims of title in this action.

Nebraska v. Colorado

136 S. Ct. 1034 (2016)

The motion for leave to file a bill of complaint is denied.

THOMAS, JUSTICE, DISSENTING (WITH JUSTICE ALITO):

Federal law does not, on its face, give this Court discretion to decline to decide cases within its original jurisdiction. Yet the Court has long exercised such discretion, and does so again today in denying, without explanation, Nebraska and Oklahoma's motion for leave to file a complaint against Colorado. I would not dispose of the complaint so hastily. Because our discretionary approach to exercising our original jurisdiction is questionable, and because the plaintiff States have made a reasonable case that this dispute falls within our original and exclusive jurisdiction, I would grant the plaintiff States leave to file their complaint.

I

The Constitution provides that "[i]n all Cases . . . in which a State shall be [a] Party, the supreme Court shall have original Jurisdiction." Art. III, § 2, cl. 2. In accordance with Article III, Congress has long provided by statute that this Court "shall have original and exclusive jurisdiction of all controversies between two or more States." 28 U. S. C. §1251(a). Federal law is unambiguous: If there is a controversy between two States, this Court—and only this Court—has jurisdiction over it. Nothing in §1251(a) suggests that the Court can opt to decline jurisdiction over such a controversy. Context confirms that §1251(a) confers no such discretion. When Congress has chosen to give this Court discretion over its merits docket, it has done so clearly. Compare §1251(a) (the Court "shall have" jurisdiction over controversies between States) with §1254(1) (cases in the courts of appeals "may be reviewed" by this Court by writ of certiorari) and §1257(a) (final judgments of state courts "may be reviewed" by this Court by writ of certiorari).

The Court's lack of discretion is confirmed by the fact that, unlike other matters within our original jurisdiction, our jurisdiction over controversies between States is exclusive. Compare §1251(a) with §1251(b) (the Court "shall have original but not exclusive jurisdiction" of other cases over which Article III gives this Court original jurisdiction). If this Court does not exercise jurisdiction over a controversy between two States, then the complaining State has no judicial forum in which to seek relief. When presented with such a controversy, "[w]e have no more right to decline the exercise of jurisdiction which is given, than to usurp that which is not given." *Cohens v. Virginia*, 6 Wheat. 264, 404 (1821) (Marshall, C. J.).

. . . The Court's reasons for transforming its mandatory, original jurisdiction into discretionary jurisdiction have been rooted in policy considerations. The Court has, for example, cited its purported lack of "special competence in dealing with" many interstate disputes and emphasized its modern role "as an appellate tribunal." [*Ohio v. Wyandotte Chemicals Corp.*, 401 U.S. 493, 498 (1971)]; *see id.*, at 497–499.

I have previously applied the Court's precedents taking this discretionary approach to our original jurisdiction. *See Wyoming v. Oklahoma*, 502 U.S. 437, 474–475, n. (1992) (dissenting opinion) (acknowledging precedents, noting that they "have not been challenged here," and arguing against exercising jurisdiction). I have also acknowledged that "sound reasons" support that approach. *Id.*, at 475.

Because our discretionary approach appears to be at odds with the statutory text, it bears reconsideration. Moreover, the "reasons" we have given to support the discretionary approach are policy judgments that are in conflict with the policy choices that Congress made in the statutory text specifying the Court's original jurisdiction.

. . . .

Notes & Questions

1. *Mississippi v. Louisiana* shows how easy it is for litigants to confuse true state-to-state disputes with private disputes that involve state-to-state issues. Most disputes involving interstate compacts are not state-versus-state disputes; however, the U.S. Supreme Court seems to always have one or more pending original jurisdiction cases, most of which involve interstate water compacts.

2. In *Mississippi v. Louisiana,* the Court stated that it uses its original and exclusive jurisdiction "sparingly." Two articles chronicle the Court's original jurisdiction cases: one through 1959 and the other between 1961 and 1993. Note, *The Original Jurisdiction of the United States Supreme Court*, 11 STAN. L. REV. 665 (1959); Vincent L. McKusick, *Discretionary Gatekeeping: The Supreme Court's Management of its Original Jurisdiction Docket Since 1961*, 45 ME. L. REV. 185 (1993). The latter article notes that the Court accepted only about half of the petitions for leave to file a complaint in the Court's original jurisdiction where the complaint was filed by or against a state. *Id.* at 188–89. Regarding state-versus-state cases, the article noted:

> Historically, interstate boundary disputes are the paradigm subject matter for original jurisdiction cases. From the 1790s until 1900 all the State v. State cases producing Supreme Court opinions on the merits (thirteen in all) arose out of boundary disputes. At the start of the twentieth century, the Court entertained cases in four additional categories of subject matter: (1) water rights; (2) interstate pollution abatement; (3) enforcement of a contract between states; and (4) state regulation. As of 1939, the Court began to accept yet another category of State v. State suits, those involving interstate tax disputes, when in that year it accepted jurisdiction of *Texas v. Florida*, involving the question of the domicile of a decedent for state inheritance tax purposes.
>
> Since 1961, the only clearly new category of State v. State cases that the Court has entertained has involved interstate disputes over the escheat of uncashed checks or other unclaimed property. The Court has taken all escheat cases . . . . In the same period the Court has continued almost invariably to accept the traditional boundary and water-rights cases between two or more states: all but one of twenty-two boundary cases and all but two of sixteen water rights cases. Suits in three other subject matter categories, however, have met only a mixed reception, making future Supreme Court action difficult to predict. Those intermediate categories involve interstate pollution abatement (one denial out of two cases), challenges to state taxes (seven denials out of ten cases), and challenges to state regulation (six denials out of eight cases). Any State v. State case involving a subject matter beyond the six or seven categories here mentioned is, judging from past experience, certain to be rejected by the Supreme Court.

Id. at 198–200 (citations and footnotes omitted). Is this article suggesting that the Supreme Court is unlikely to grant leave to file a complaint in a state-versus-state compact case that does not involve the subjects described? If original jurisdiction is spare and certiorari is difficult too, is there a realistic review mechanism for disputes involving compacts? For additional reading on original jurisdiction from an author who served as a Special Master, see Kristin A. Linsley, *Original Intent: Understanding the Supreme Court's Original Jurisdiction in Controversies Between States*, 18 J. APP. PRAC. & PROCESS 21 (2017).

3. Another article suggests that the Supreme Court's handling of original jurisdiction cases causes states to engage in aggressive measure to protect themselves against a threat of suit and that the Supreme Court's resolution of cases causes states to choose suit over negotiation. *See* Jonathan Horne, *On Not Resolving Interstate Disputes*, 6 N.Y.U. J.L. & LIBERTY 95 (2011).

4. The Court considers two factors: the nature of the interest of the complaining state, focusing on the seriousness and dignity of the claim (whether the claim would be *casus belli* if states were fully sovereign), and the availability of an alternate forum in which the issues tendered can be resolved. *Oklahoma v. Texas*, 258 U.S. 574 (1922), presented a dispute over their common boundary along the Red River that met the *casus belli* requirement.

> After we acquired jurisdiction of the suit it developed that the State of Oklahoma was claiming title to the entire river bed from one bank to the other; that the State of Texas was claiming title to the southerly half; that the United States was disputing the claims of both States and asserting full proprietorship of the southerly half and an interest (because of its relation to Indian allottees) in portions of the northerly half; that a part of the bed, particularly of the southerly half, had been but recently discovered to be underlaid with strata bearing oil and gas and to be of great value by reason thereof; that many persons were proceeding to drill for, extract and appropriate these minerals with uncertain regard for the dispute over the title and for the true ownership; that possession of parts of the bed was being taken and held by intimidation and force; that in suits for injunction the courts of both States were assuming jurisdiction over the same areas; that armed conflicts between rival aspirants for the oil and gas had been but narrowly averted and still were imminent; that the militia of Texas had been called to support the orders of its courts and an effort was being made to have the militia of Oklahoma called for a like purpose; that these conflicting assertions of jurisdiction and the measures taken to sustain them were detrimental to the public tranquility . . .

Id. at 579–80. *New Jersey v. Delaware*, 552 U.S. 597 (2008), also presented a dispute that might fit the *casus belli* requirement. The states have a compact that preserves jurisdiction to each on its own shore of the Delaware River. British Petroleum (BP) wanted to build a facility to import, store, and vaporize foreign-source liquid natural gas. The project would have included a gasification plant, storage tanks, and other structures onshore in New Jersey, and a pier and related structures extending some 2,000 feet from New Jersey's shore. Construction would have required dredging, affecting the riverbed within Delaware's territory. In September 2004, BP sought permission from the Delaware Department of Natural Resources and Environmental Control (DNREC) to construct the unloading terminal. DNREC refused permission because Delaware's Coastal Zone Act barred the terminal. The Supreme Court noted:

> Reactions to DNREC's decision boiled over on both sides. New Jersey threatened to withdraw state pension funds from Delaware banks, and Delaware considered authorizing the National Guard to protect its border from encroachment. One New Jersey legislator looked into recommissioning the museum-piece battleship U. S. S. New Jersey, in the event that the vessel might be needed to repel an armed invasion by Delaware.

New Jersey v. Delaware, 552 U.S. at 607–08.

The construction of Parker Dam on the Colorado River beginning in 1934 had a similar history of near hostilities. When construction began, Arizona Governor Benjamin Moeur called up the National Guard, initially to observe and subsequently to prevent construction of a trestle bridge on the Arizona shore. After the second deployment, U.S. Secretary of Agriculture Harold Ickes intervened and halted construction of the dam. In *U.S. v. Arizona*, 295 U.S. 174 (1935), the Supreme Court concluded that the dam was not authorized and shortly after, Congress enacted the River and Harbors Bill, which authorized it. Arizona was a holdout in signing the Colorado River Compact in 1922, finally joining in 1944.

5. The early Supreme Court decision *Hinderlider v. La Plata River & Cherry Creek Ditch Co.*, 304 U.S. 92 (1938), involving a water allocation compact, noted that "resort to the judicial remedy is never essential to the adjustment of interstate controversies, unless the States are unable to agree upon the terms of a compact, or Congress refuses its consent." *Id.* at 105. As discussed at the beginning of this chapter, the Supreme Court overruled *Hinderlider*; nevertheless, the decision is provocative. There have not been any judicial cases in which a legal issue involved states not agreeing on drafting compact terms or Congress refusing to grant consent. Should the Supreme Court only allow original jurisdiction in cases involving these narrow subject matters?

6. Is creating a compact an "alternative forum" to original jurisdiction? In *Texas v. New Mexico*, 462 U.S. 554 (1983), the court stated, "[W]e shall not construe a compact to preclude a State from seeking judicial relief when the compact does not provide an equivalent method of vindicating the State's rights." *Id.* at 569–70. The Court then observed, "If authorized representatives of the compacting States have reached an agreement within the scope of their congressionally ratified powers, recourse to this Court when one State has second thoughts is hardly 'necessary for the State's protection.'" *Id.* at 570–71. Chapter 11 contains an excerpt of this case for its discussion of enforcement of compacts.

7. *New Jersey v. New York*, 345 U.S. 369 (1952) was the litigation that caused New York and New Jersey to create the Delaware River Basin Compact and Susquehanna River Basin Compact. In this case, the City of Philadelphia tried to intervene. The Court, however, rejected intervention under the *parens patriae* doctrine, in which the court recognizes that a state must be deemed to represent all of its citizens in a suit involving a matter of sovereign interest, and in this case, Pennsylvania was already a party. The court noted:

> The case before us demonstrates the wisdom of the rule. The City of Philadelphia represents only a part of the citizens of Pennsylvania who reside

> in the watershed area of the Delaware River and its tributaries and depend upon those waters. If we undertook to evaluate all the separate interests within Pennsylvania, we could, in effect, be drawn into an intramural dispute over the distribution of water within the Commonwealth. Furthermore, we are told by New Jersey that there are cities along the Delaware River in that State which, like Philadelphia, are responsible for their own water systems, and which will insist upon a right to intervene if Philadelphia is admitted. Nor is there any assurance that the list of intervenors could be closed with political subdivisions of the states. Large industrial plants which, like cities, are corporate creatures of the state may represent interests just as substantial.

Id. at 373.

8. Original jurisdiction cases take several years, sometimes more than a decade to resolve. There are multiple stages of a case including an initiating petition for leave to file a bill complaint, presentation of evidence and argument before a special master, and consideration of objections to a special master's report. One article suggested "that the Supreme Court has thoroughly realized the emollient influence of the lapse of years; and, while not countenancing unnecessary delays, it has regarded cases between States as susceptible of grave circumspection in the taking of each successive step by both counsel and the Court." CHARLES WARREN, THE SUPREME COURT AND SOVEREIGN STATES 86–87 (Princeton Univ. Press 1924).

9. Do you agree with Justices Thomas and Alito that the Court should not have discretion to decide whether to accept state-versus-state original jurisdiction cases? They are unlikely to prevail on changing the Supreme Court's practice. They again dissented from the Supreme Court's denial of a bill of complaint in *Arizona v. California*, 140 S. Ct. 684 (2020), but none of the other justices appointed since 2016 joined this latter dissent.

10. Can a compact agency sue a state in the original jurisdiction of the Supreme Court? The Supreme Court faced this question in *Se. Interstate Low-Level Radioactive Waste Mgmt. Comm'n v. North Carolina*, 533 U.S. 926 (2001). Before deciding whether to allow the Southeast Interstate Low Level Radioactive Waste Management Commission to file its complaint, the Supreme Court invited the U.S. Solicitor General to file a brief expressing the views of the United States. The Solicitor General made two arguments: (1) the compact commission is not a state and thus does not fall under the Court's original jurisdiction statute, 28 U.S.C. § 1251(a), and (2) the compact commission could seek a remedy in state court. Brief for the United States as *Amicus Curiae*, *Se. Interstate Low-Level Radioactive Waste Mgmt. Comm'n v. North Carolina*, 533 U.S. 926 (2001) (No. 131 Orig.). The Supreme Court denied the commission's motion for leave to file such a complaint.

Several of the states in the Southeast Compact and the Southeast Commission followed up this dismissal with another petition to file a complaint pursuant to the Supreme Court's original jurisdiction. That latter case was *Alabama v. North Carolina*. In 2003, the Supreme Court granted leave to file the complaint. In 2010 the

Court considered several exceptions to a Special Master's report, including whether the Southeast Commission was a proper party in the original jurisdiction action.

Alabama v. North Carolina
560 U.S. 330 (2010)

SCALIA, JUSTICE:

[This case involved a failed attempt to site a low-level radioactive waste disposal facility in North Carolina. After several years of work, and $80 million in financial aid from the Southeast Interstate Low-Level Radioactive Waste Management Commission, the Commission informed North Carolina that it could no longer provide financial assistance. North Carolina subsequently stopped work toward obtaining licenses for the facility. Florida and Tennessee, two of the several states to the compact that would have used the facility, filed with the Southeast Commission a complaint for sanctions against North Carolina, and following a sanctions hearing, the Commission concluded that North Carolina failed to fulfill its obligations under the compact. In 2000 the Southeast Commission moved for leave to file a bill of complaint under the Supreme Court's original jurisdiction to enforce the sanctions resolution, which the Court denied. Subsequently, in 2002, Alabama, Florida, Tennessee, Virginia, and the Southeast Commission, moved the Court for leave to file a bill of complaint against North Carolina alleging several counts, including violation of the states' rights under the compact, breach of contract, unjust enrichment, promissory estoppel, and money had and received. The Court appointed a Special Master, who issued a preliminary report, to which the parties filed several objections. One of the exceptions was from North Carolina.]

North Carolina takes exception to the Special Master's recommendation in his Preliminary Report to deny without prejudice its motion to dismiss the Commission's claims on the ground that they are barred by the Eleventh Amendment to the Constitution and by structural principles of state sovereign immunity. The Special Master assumed for the sake of argument that a State possesses sovereign immunity against a claim brought by an entity, like the Commission, created by an interstate compact.[5] But he recommended denying North Carolina's motion to dismiss "at this point in the proceedings."

The Special Master relied upon our decision in *Arizona v. California*, 460 U.S. 605 (1983), which held that the Eleventh Amendment did not bar the participation of several Indian Tribes in an original action concerning the allocation of rights to the waters of the Colorado River. The United States had already intervened, in its capacity as trustee for several Indian Tribes; but the Tribes moved

---

[5] We have held that an entity created through a valid exercise of the Interstate Compact Clause is not entitled to immunity from suit under the Eleventh Amendment, *see Hess v. Port Authority Trans-Hudson Corporation*, 513 U.S. 30 (1994), but we have not decided whether such an entity's suit against a State is barred by sovereign immunity.

to intervene as well, and the States opposed. We granted the Tribes' motion, stating that the States do not enjoy sovereign immunity against the United States, and "[t]he Tribes do not seek to bring new claims or issues against the States, but only ask leave to participate in an adjudication of their vital water rights that was commenced by the United States." *Id.*, at 614. Thus, "our judicial power over the controversy is not enlarged by granting leave to intervene, and the States' sovereign immunity protected by the Eleventh Amendment is not compromised." *Ibid.* Relying on this holding, the Special Master held that sovereign immunity does not bar the Commission's suit, so long as the Commission asserts the same claims and seeks the same relief as the other plaintiffs. Whether that is so, he said, "cannot be resolved without further factual and legal development[s]," and so North Carolina is free to renew its motion at a later point.

Assuming (as the Special Master did) that the Commission's claims against North Carolina implicate sovereign immunity, we agree with his disposition. North Carolina contends that making application of the Constitution's waiver of sovereign immunity turn upon whether a nonsovereign party seeks to expand the relief sought is inconsistent with our decisions construing state sovereign immunity as a "personal privilege." *College Savings Bank v. Florida Prepaid Postsecondary Ed. Expense Bd.*, 527 U.S. 666, 675 (1999) (internal quotation marks omitted); *see also Alden* [*v. Maine*], 527 U.S. [706,] 758 [(1999)]. But nothing in those cases suggests that *Arizona v. California* has been implicitly overruled.[6] Neither of them arose under our original jurisdiction, and neither cited *Arizona v. California* or discussed—at all—the sovereign immunity issue that case addressed. That sovereign immunity is a personal privilege of the States says nothing about whether that privilege "is not compromised," *Arizona v. California, supra*, at 614, by an additional, nonsovereign plaintiff's bringing an entirely overlapping claim for relief that burdens the State with no additional defense or liability.

North Carolina contends that *Arizona v. California* cannot apply to the Commission's claims, because the Commission does not—indeed, cannot—assert the same claims or seek the same relief as the plaintiff States. We disagree. In the bill of complaint, the States and the Commission assert the same claims and request the same relief. Their claim for restitution of $80 million cannot, given the other allegations of the complaint, be thought to be $80 million payable to each of the four plaintiff States and the Commission.

North Carolina argues, however, that summary judgment in its favor is appropriate because it is clear that the Commission, and not the plaintiff States, provided $80 million to North Carolina—wherefore, as a matter of law, only the Commission can claim entitlement to $80 million, either as a measure of damages for breach of the Compact under Counts I and II of the bill of complaint, or under

---

[6] North Carolina has not asked us to overrule *Arizona v. California*, 460 U.S. 605 (1983). We decline to do so on our own motion and without argument. We therefore do not address the merits of The Chief Justice's dissent.

the unjust enrichment, promissory estoppel, and money-had-and-received theories of recovery in Counts III, IV, and V. And, it contends, a stand-alone suit by the Commission is barred by sovereign immunity.

With regard to Counts I and II, at least, we disagree. The Commission's claims under those Compact-related Counts are wholly derivative of the States' claims. *See Arizona v. California*, *supra*, at 614. The Commission is "a legal entity separate and distinct from" the States that are parties to the Compact. Art. 4(M)(1), 99 Stat. 1877. Since it is not a party it has neither a contractual right to performance by the party States nor enforceable statutory rights under Article 5 of the Compact. The Compact does, however, authorize the Commission to "act or appear on behalf of any party [S]tate or [S]tates . . . as an intervenor or party in interest before . . . any court of law," Art. 4(E)(10), 99 Stat. 1875, and it is obviously in this capacity that the Commission seeks to vindicate the plaintiff States' statutory and contractual rights in Counts I and II. Its Count I and Count II claims therefore rise or fall with the claims of the States. While the Commission may not bring them in a stand-alone action under this Court's original jurisdiction, it may assert them in this Court alongside the plaintiff States, *see Arizona v. California*, 460 U.S., at 614. The summary judgment disallowing the underlying claims on their merits renders the sovereign immunity question with regard to any relief the Commission alone might have on those claims moot.

Counts III–V, which do not rely upon the Compact, stand on a different footing. As to them, while the Commission again seemingly makes the same claims and seeks the same relief as the States, it is conceivable that as a matter of law the Commission's claims are not identical. The Commission can claim restitution as the party that paid the money to North Carolina; the other plaintiffs cannot claim it on that basis. Whether this means that the claims are not identical for *Arizona v. California* purposes, and that the Commission's Counts III–V claims must be dismissed on sovereign immunity grounds, is a question that the Special Master declined to resolve until the merits issues were further clarified. We have approved his deferral of those issues, and we likewise approve his deferral of the related sovereign immunity issue.

. . . .

ROBERTS, CHIEF JUSTICE, CONCURRING IN PART AND DISSENTING IN PART (WITH JUSTICE THOMAS):

The parties to this case are Alabama, Florida, North Carolina, Tennessee, Virginia, and the Southeast Interstate Low-Level Radioactive Waste Management Commission. One of these things is not like the others: The Commission is not a sovereign State. The Court entertains its suit—despite North Carolina's sovereign immunity—because the Commission "asserts the same claims and seeks the same relief as the other plaintiffs." Our Constitution does not countenance such "no harm, no foul" jurisdiction, and I respectfully dissent.

The Court has made this mistake before. In *Arizona v. California*, 460 U.S. 605 (1983), we allowed Indian Tribes that could not sue sovereign States to piggyback on the claims of the United States, which could. We reasoned that once the

United States had initiated suit, the state defendants could "no longer * * * assert [their] immunity with respect to the subject matter of [the] action," so the Tribes were free to pile on and join the suit. *Id.*, at 614. Today the Court retraces *Arizona*'s steps, quoting that case for the proposition that when private plaintiffs "'do not seek to bring new claims or issues, . . . our judicial power over the controversy is not enlarged . . . , and the States' sovereign immunity protected by the Eleventh Amendment is not compromised.'"

That statement is contrary to the language of the Constitution. The Eleventh Amendment provides:

> "The Judicial power of the United States shall not be construed to extend to any suit in law or equity, commenced or prosecuted against one of the United States by Citizens of another State, or by Citizens or Subjects of any Foreign State."

The immunity conferred is against the "commence[ment] or prosecut[ion]" of "any suit in law or equity." There is no carve-out for suits "prosecuted" by private parties so long as those parties "'do not seek to bring new claims or issues.'"

Understandably, the Court's opinion leans heavily on *Arizona*, which has never been squarely overruled. But *Arizona* itself is built on sand. The relevant portion of that opinion is almost wholly unreasoned. It cites only a footnote in a prior case, the pertinent paragraph of which failed even to discuss the State's immunity from private suit. *See* 460 U.S., at 614 (citing *Maryland v. Louisiana*, 451 U.S. 725, 745, n.21 (1981)). That paragraph addressed only intervention, not sovereign immunity, and the two issues are distinct.

Most importantly, the subsequent development of our sovereign immunity jurisprudence has only undermined *Arizona*'s already weak foundations. We recognized in *Alden v. Maine*, 527 U.S. 706, 718 (1999), that the Constitution left intact the States' pre-existing "immunity from private suits"; as the Eleventh Amendment confirms, the States did not "'surrender . . . this immunity in the plan of the convention.'" *Id.*, at 717; 718–722, 755–756. There is no reason to suppose that the States, at the founding, made an exception for private suits that happen to mimic other plaintiffs' claims—and neither *Arizona* nor the Court today suggests otherwise.

Whether or not a plaintiff "seeks the same relief" or imposes any "additional defense or liability" simply does not matter in light of our recognition that sovereign immunity provides an "immunity from suit," not a "defense to . . . liability." *Federal Maritime Comm'n v. South Carolina Ports Authority*, 535 U.S. 743, 766 (2002). As we have explained, "the relief sought by a plaintiff suing a State is irrelevant to the question whether the suit is barred." *Seminole Tribe of Fla. v. Florida*, 517 U.S. 44, 58 (1996). Indeed, we have suggested that private parties may not sue even if a court is "precluded . . . from awarding them any relief." *Federal Maritime Comm'n, supra*, at 766 (dictum). It is the fact that a private party is allowed to sue a sovereign State—not the burden of litigation or the relief sought—that infringes the immunity of the State. "The Eleventh Amendment is concerned not only with the States' ability to withstand suit, but with their privilege not to be sued." *Puerto Rico Aqueduct and Sewer Authority v. Metcalf & Eddy, Inc.*, 506 U.S. 139, 147, n.5 (1993).

It is therefore impossible for the Court to hear private claims against a nonconsenting State without expanding "our judicial power over the controversy." *Arizona, supra*, at 614. Sovereign immunity is a limitation on that power. The similarity of claims may be relevant to joinder or intervention, but those are procedural means of processing claims, not fonts of judicial authority.

Nor may the Court entertain private claims without "compromis[ing]" "the States' sovereign immunity." *Arizona*, 460 U.S., at 614. As a party, the Commission enjoys legally enforceable rights against the defendant State: It may object to settlement, seek taxation of costs, advance arguments we are obliged to consider, and plead the judgment as res judicata in future litigation. If the Commission truly sought nothing for itself—other than "a full exposition of the issues,"—it could have participated as an *amicus*.

The Commission and North Carolina know that more is at stake if the Commission is allowed to sue the State. It is precisely the Commission's status as a party, its attempt to "prosecut[e]" a "suit in law or equity * * * against one of the United States," U.S. Const., Amdt. 11, that sovereign immunity forbids.

I would sustain North Carolina's first exception to the Special Master's reports.

Notes & Questions

1. Does Justice Scalia or Chief Justice Roberts have the better argument? What do you think about allowing a compact agency to participate as a plaintiff in a state-versus-state action? Does the test from *Arizona v. California*, which Justice Scalia explained, make sense for compact agencies? In that case, the United States had a trust relationship with the tribes. Is there a trust-like relationship between the United States and a compact agency? Is there a trust-like relationship between states and the compact agency they create? Could states adequately represent the interests of a compact agency in a state-verses-state action?

2. As mentioned at the end of Chapter 6, the Supreme Court allowed the Catawba River Water Supply Project, a bi-state entity, to intervene on the side of the plaintiff states in *South Carolina v. North Carolina*, 558 U.S. 256 (2010). How is participation as an original plaintiff different from allowing intervention on the side of the plaintiff states?

3. In *South Carolina v. North Carolina*, 558 U.S. 256 (2010), the Supreme Court allowed the Catawba River Water Supply Project, a bi-state entity, to intervene on the side of the petitioner in an existing state-versus-state original jurisdiction case. The Court concluded that the entity had "a compelling interest in protecting the viability of its operations, which are premised on a fine balance between the joint venture's two participating counties," *id.* at 270, and "neither state has sufficient interests in maintaining that balance to represent the full scope of the [entity's] interests." *Id.* Can any single state represent the interests of a bi-

state entity, such as the Catawba River Water Supply, especially when one party state is suing another party state? Should the *parens patriae* doctrine apply when a multistate entity seeks to intervene in an original jurisdiction matter?

CHAPTER 7: IMMUNITY FROM SUIT

Constitutional law is one of the key legs of interstate compact law. Chapter 2 looked closely at the Compact Clause, and several of the cases in the prior chapters have looked at how provisions of the U.S. Constitution arise in compact cases. *Seattle Master Builders* considered whether appointments to the Northwest Power Planning Council violated the Appointments Clause of the U.S. Constitution. *Columbia River Gorge United* considered whether the Columbia River Gorge Compact violated the Tenth Amendment, Property Clause, Commerce Clause and the Equal Protection Clause of the Fifth Amendment. *Alabama v. North Carolina* considered the limits of original jurisdiction. Other cases excerpted and cited throughout this book, including *Hess* and *Lake Country Estates*, have involved the Eleventh Amendment. Indeed, courts have cited these and other Eleventh Amendment cases as precedent for other legal principles. Much of this chapter looks directly at the application of the Eleventh Amendment. The end of the chapter considers other ways that courts have concluded that compact agencies or party states are immune from suit.

I. COMPACT AGENCY IMMUNITY

The Eleventh Amendment (1795) to the U.S. Constitution states, "The judicial power of the United States shall not be construed to extend to any suit in law or equity, commenced or prosecuted against one of the United States by citizens of another state, or by citizens or subjects of any foreign state." By its text, this amendment prohibits suit in federal court against a state by a citizen of another state. In *Hans v. Louisiana*, 134 U.S. 1 (1890), however, the Supreme Court concluded that the Eleventh Amendment guarantees state sovereign immunity from suit in federal court even when the suit is brought by a state's own citizen. But Congress may abrogate and states may waive this sovereign immunity. Thus, there are two significant questions concerning the application of the Eleventh Amendment to compact agencies: (1) whether a compact agency is a "state" such that it enjoys immunity under the Eleventh Amendment, and (2) if so, then did Congress abrogate immunity in its consent to the compact or did the states waive immunity in the compact?

Whether a compact agency enjoys immunity under the Eleventh Amendment was the focus of much litigation for a period of time, but not so in recent years. Two factors may explain this. First, compact drafters are drafting more precise compacts. New compacts more clearly specify jurisdiction in federal courts—a clear waiver by the party states. Second, the Supreme Court seems to have landed on a workable set of tests for determining whether a compact agency is a "state" and whether congressional consent, compact text, or other related state law abrogates or waives Eleventh Amendment immunity.

This section takes the significant cases in the order they arose. Eventually the Supreme Court completely addressed the two questions relating to compact agency immunity under the Eleventh Amendment. In the first case, *Petty v. Tennessee-Missouri Bridge Comm'n*, the Supreme Court considered whether the states waived their immunity from suit in federal court.

Petty v. Tennessee-Missouri Bridge Comm'n
359 U.S. 275 (1959)

DOUGLAS, JUSTICE:

When the Court in 1793 held that a State could be sued in the federal courts by a citizen of another State (*Chisholm v. Georgia*, 2 Dall. [2 U.S.] 419), the Eleventh Amendment was passed precluding it. But this is an immunity which a State may waive at its pleasure as by a general appearance in litigation in a federal court or by statute. The conclusion that there has been a waiver of immunity will not be lightly inferred. Nor will a waiver of immunity from suit in state courts do service for a waiver of immunity where the litigation is brought in the federal court. And where a public instrumentality is created with the right 'to sue and be sued' that waiver of immunity in the particular setting may be restricted to suits or proceedings of a special character in the state, not the federal, courts. *Cf. Delaware River Joint Toll Bridge Commission v. Colburn*, 310 U.S. 419 [(1940)]....

The question here is whether Tennessee and Missouri have waived their immunity under the facts of this case.

Congress, under conditions specified in 33 U.S.C. § 525 *et seq.*, gave its consent to the construction of bridges over the navigable waters in the United States. Respondent is a 'body corporate and politic' created by Missouri and Tennessee acting pursuant to the Compact Clause of the Constitution. The compact prepared by the two States and submitted to the Congress provided in Art. I, §§ 1 and 2 that respondent should have the power to build a bridge and operate ferries across the Mississippi at specified points and in Art. I, § 3, that it should have the power "to contract, to sue and be sued in its own name." Congress granted its consent to the compact, stating in a proviso:

> That nothing herein contained shall be construed to affect, impair, or diminish any right, power, or jurisdiction of the United States or of any court, department, board, bureau, officer, or official of the United States, over or in regard to any navigable waters, or any commerce between the States or with foreign countries, or any bridge, railroad, highway, pier, wharf, or other facility or improvement, or any other person, matter, or thing, forming the subject matter of the aforesaid compact or agreement or otherwise affected by the terms thereof.

The facts are that petitioner's husband was employed on a ferryboat operated by respondent as a common carrier across the Mississippi between a point in Missouri and one in Tennessee. He met his death when he was trapped in the pilothouse of the ferryboat as it sank, following a collision with another boat. Suit was brought under the Jones Act[*] charging respondent with negligence.

The District Court granted the motion to dismiss, holding that respondent is an agency of the States of Tennessee and Missouri and immune from suit in tort. The Court of Appeals, agreeing with that view, affirmed. The case is here on certiorari.

The construction of a compact sanctioned by Congress under Art. I, § 10, cl. 3, of the Constitution presents a federal question. *Delaware River Comm'n v. Colburn*, *supra* at 427. Moreover, the meaning of a compact is a question on which this Court has the final say. [*West Virginia ex rel.*] *Dyer v. Sims*, 341 U.S. 22, 28. The rule is no different when the contention is that a State has, by compact, waived its immunity from suit. Of course, when the alleged basis of waiver of the Eleventh Amendment's immunity is a state statute, the question to be answered is whether the State has intended to waive its immunity. But where the waiver is, as here, claimed to arise from a compact between several States, the Court is called on to interpret not unilateral state action but the terms of a consensual agreement, the meaning of which, because made by different States acting under the Constitution and with congressional approval, is a question of federal law. In making that interpretation we must treat the compact as a living interstate agreement which performs high functions in our federalism, including the operation of vast interstate enterprises.

The Court of Appeals laid emphasis on the law of Missouri, which, it said, construes a sue-and-be-sued provision as not authorizing a suit for negligence against a public corporation. It likewise cited Tennessee decisions strictly construing statutes permitting suits against the State. We assume arguendo that this suit must be considered as one against the States since this bi-state corporation is a joint or common agency of Tennessee and Missouri. But we disagree with the construction given by the Court of Appeals to the sue-and-be-sued clause. For the resolution of that question we turn to federal not state law. Congress might of course adopt as federal law the law of either or both of the States. *Delaware River Comm'n v. Colburn*, *supra*. But Congress took no such step here. It approved a sue-and-be-sued clause in a compact under conditions clause in a compact under conditions that make it clear that the States accepting it waived any immunity from suit which they otherwise might have.

. . . .

. . . Congress, when it approved this compact, attached a condition that "nothing herein contained shall be construed to affect, impair, or diminish any right, power, or jurisdiction of * * * any court * * * of the United States over or in regard to any navigable waters or any commerce between the States * * * ." We need not stop to catalogue all the ends that may be served by this proviso. It is argued that

* [*Ed. Note*: The Jones Act regulates commerce in U.S. waters and between U.S. ports and gives injured sailors a right to sue their employers for damages.]

the proviso was included to make plain that the bonds issued by the agency were taxable by the United States. We must go further however, to find a rational purpose since another proviso of the Act of Congress specifically stated: "That any obligations issued and outstanding, including the income derived therefrom, under the terms of the compact or agreement, and any amendments thereto, shall be subject to the tax laws of the United States." Whatever may be the several effects of the other proviso with which we are presently concerned, one result seems to us clear. This proviso, read in light of the sue-and-be-sued clause in the compact, reserves the jurisdiction of the federal courts to act in any matter arising under the compact over which they would have jurisdiction by virtue of the fact that the Mississippi is a navigable stream and that interstate commerce is involved. There is no more apt illustration of the involvement of the commerce power and the power over maritime matters than the Jones Act. This is not enlarging the jurisdiction of the federal courts but only recognizing as one of its appropriate applications the business activities of an agency active in commerce and maritime matters.

The States who are parties to the compact by accepting it and acting under it assume the conditions that Congress under the Constitution attached.[7] So if there be doubt as to the meaning of the sue-and-be-sued clause in the setting of the compact prior to approval by Congress, the doubt dissipates when the condition attached by Congress is accepted and acted upon by the two States.

. . . .

Reversed.

FRANKFURTER, JUSTICE, DISSENTING (WITH JUSTICE HARLAN AND JUSTICE WHITTAKER):

The Court, acknowledging the applicability of the provisions of the Eleventh Amendment to the Tennessee-Missouri Bridge Commission, states: "The question here is whether Tennessee and Missouri have waived their immunity under the facts of this case." The Court finds such a waiver in the words "sue and be sued" included in Art. I, § 3, of the Compact creating respondent Commission.

[7] Historically the consent of Congress, as a prerequisite to the validity of agreements by States, appears as the republican transformation of the needed approval by the Crown. But the Constitution plainly had two very practical objectives in view in conditioning agreement by States upon consent of Congress. For only Congress is the appropriate organ for determining what arrangements between States might fall within the prohibited class of "Treaty, Alliance, or Confederation", and what arrangements come within the permissive class of "Agreement or Compact." But even the permissive agreements may affect the interests of States other than those parties to the agreement: the national, and not merely a regional, interest may be involved. Therefore, Congress must exercise national supervision through its power to grant or withhold consent, or to grant it under appropriate conditions. The Framers thus astutely created a mechanism of legal control over affairs that are projected beyond State lines and yet may not call for, nor be capable of, national treatment. They allowed interstate adjustments but duly safeguarded the national interest.

The Supreme Court of Missouri has said: "A statutory provision that such a public corporation 'may sue and be sued' does not authorize a suit against it for negligence." The Tennessee courts have not ruled on the significance of this clause, but the Supreme Court of Tennessee has been emphatic in its holding that waivers of sovereign immunity from suit are to be narrowly construed. The Court of Appeals below held that in neither Missouri nor Tennessee would the language "sue and be sued" render a public corporation liable for suit in tort. Three times during this Term the Court followed its settled practice in dealing with a doubtful state statute by deferring to interpretations of local law rendered by the lower federal courts. We should not now disregard this settled practice but should accept the interpretation of Missouri and Tennessee law as found by the Court of Appeals for the Eighth Circuit.

Despite the fact that it has been authoritatively held that neither State waives sovereign immunity by the "sue and be sued" provision, this Court finds that those words constitute a waiver by the States of the immunity from suit, in the federal courts, afforded them by the Eleventh Amendment.

The legal consequences of the terms of a Compact are not, as a generalized proposition, for the originating construction of this Court. What was held in [*West Virginia ex rel.*] *Dyer v. Sims*, 341 U.S. 22 does not support such a claim. That case arose under a Compact among eight States to control pollution in the Ohio River System. Seven of the States asserted that under the Compact West Virginia was obligated to appropriate funds for administrative expenses of the Joint Commission formed under the Compact. By a self-serving construction of its duty under the Compact, West Virginia resisted the claims of the other States to the Compact. Here was a typical controversy among States, a controversy as to the undertaking of a Compact among States, for the peaceful solution of which the Constitution designed Art. III, § 2. The very nature of the controversy made it necessary for this Court to construe the terms of the Compact, that is, the contractual obligations assumed by West Virginia vis-à-vis the other parties to the Compact. The problem presented by this case has no kinship with that presented by [*West Virginia ex rel.*] *Dyer v. Sims*. This is a suit by an individual against the States over which the federal courts have jurisdiction only if the States have authorized such suits. Both States deny having given such authorization and the Court of Appeals, has justified their denial in its finding of their law. Since a Compact comes into being through an Act of Congress, its construction gives rise to a federal question. But a federal question does not require a federal answer by way of a blanket, nationwide substantive doctrine where essentially local interests are at stake. A Compact is, after all, a contract. Ordinarily, in the interpretation of a contract, the meaning the parties attribute to the words governs the obligations assumed in the agreement. Similarly, since these States had the freedom to waive or to refuse to waive immunity granted by the Eleventh Amendment, the language they employed in the Compact, not modified by Congress, should be limited to the legal significance that these States have placed upon such language, not to avoid the obligations they undertook, but to enforce the meaning of conventional language used in their law.

This Court, however, finds that Congress, in granting the necessary consent to the Compact, imposed suability in the federal courts upon the States as a condition to its consent. No doubt Congress could have insisted upon a provision waiving immunity from suit in the federal courts as the price of obtaining its consent to the Compact. The fact that this Court in *Keifer & Keifer v. Reconstruction Finance Corp.*, 306 U.S. 381, 389–391, indicated that governmental immunity from suit had fallen into disfavor may well have been a good reason why Congress should have done just this in passing upon the Tennessee-Missouri Compact. It is a bad reason for this Court to write in such a waiver when Congress has not done so. Surely the doctrine of sovereign immunity was not so obsolete that a waiver of immunity did not require a clear indication that Congress had exacted a waiver by the States as the price of consent. The disfavor which was referred to by this Court in *Keifer* has not attained such acceptance as to lead this Court to disregard the strictness with which States continue to enforce it. Moreover, the Court's conclusion that Congress must have understood the "sue and be sued" clause to be a waiver of the Eleventh Amendment and that therefore their consent must have been predicated on that understanding finds no support in the legislative history.

As the evidence from which the Court finds an implied imposed withdrawal of the States' immunity from suit is tenuous, the basis for its finding of an explicit imposition of waiver is non-existent. Such an explicit imposition is deemed to lie in the language in the Act which states that nothing in the Compact "shall be construed to affect, impair, or diminish any right, power, or jurisdiction of the United States or of any court, * * * over or in regard to any navigable waters, or any commerce between the States * * * ." Read as this should be read on the natural understanding of the phrasing, there is nothing to indicate that the subject of immunity from suit was in contemplation. In addition, this clause has a history of more than one hundred years which confirms and emphasizes the plain intendment of the language.

The use of clauses preserving "jurisdiction * * * of any court" dates back to a Compact between New York and New Jersey approved by Congress in 1834: "Provided, That nothing therein contained shall be construed to impair or in any manner affect, any right of jurisdiction of the United States in and over the islands or waters which form the subject of the said agreement." Substantially this same language may be found in other early congressional Acts consenting to interstate Compacts. An alternate but similar provision regarding federal jurisdiction is found in some other congressional consents: "Nothing herein contained shall be construed to affect the right of the United States to regulate commerce, or the jurisdiction of the United States over navigable waters." A third variation has been: "Provided, That nothing therein contained shall be construed as impairing or in any manner affecting any right or jurisdiction of the United States in and over the region which forms the subject of said agreement." In not one of the ten cited Compacts thus approved was there any language which could be construed as a waiver of the constitutional immunity granted to States from suits in the federal courts. And yet the language before us, in essence conveying the same meaning, is said to have that effect. Indeed, the identical clause upon which the Court today rests its finding of an imposed waiver of the Eleventh Amendment has appeared in at least two prior consents to Compacts. One of these Compacts contained a "sue and be sued" provision, but the other did not. The history of these federal jurisdiction provisions demonstrates beyond peradventure that the clause was unrelated to the question of waiver of Eleventh Amendment immunity.

The conclusion that what the language in the Act alone would not do it accomplishes when read "in light of the sue-and-be-sued clause," violates the very congressional language on which it relies. Had there been no "sue and be sued" clause in the Compact, this Bridge Commission could not have been sued in the federal courts despite the fact that it was operating a vessel on navigable water and in interstate commerce. The Eleventh Amendment would not have permitted it. By finding that language in the Compact permits this suit, the Court is construing the Compact to "affect," by enlarging, the jurisdiction of the United States courts over activities conducted interstate commerce.

The constitutional requirement of consent by Congress to a Compact between the States was designed for the protection of national interests by the power to withhold consent or to grant it on condition of appropriate safeguards of those interests. The Compact may impair the course of interstate commerce in a way found undesirable by Congress. Or the national interest may derive from the necessity of maintaining a properly balanced federal system by vetoing a Compact which would adversely affect States not parties to the Compact. To imply from a congressional consent changes in the law of the Compact States of merely local concern, such as dislodging a State's policy on suability for torts attributable to the administration of the bridge (while necessarily leaving unaffected the State's suability for torts not attributable to its administration), would constitute a complete disregard of the purpose of the Constitution in requiring congressional consent to Compacts. Such disregard would introduce a wholly irrational disharmony in the application of local policy.

In view of the authorities cited by the Court for the proposition that the Jones Act applies to the Commission, I assume that the Court is referring solely to the substantive applicability of that Act. Believing as I do that the federal courts have no jurisdiction over this suit, I do not reach that substantive question.

I would affirm the judgment of the Court of Appeals for the Eighth Circuit.

Notes & Questions

1. Remember from your civil procedure class that state courts are courts of general jurisdiction, but jurisdiction in federal courts requires authorization from the U.S. Constitution or a statute. Does the congressional condition stating the compact does not "affect, impair, or diminish any right, power, or jurisdiction of the United States or of any court" grant jurisdiction to federal court? If not, then under what authority would there be jurisdiction in federal court?

2. The Court stated, "The question here is whether Tennessee and Missouri have waived their immunity under the facts of this case." 359 U.S. at 277. But whether this case involves waiver or abrogation is not so clear. The Court first quoted a condition of Congress's consent: "Nothing herein contained shall be construed to affect, impair, or diminish any right, power, or jurisdiction of any court, department, board, bureau, officer, or official of the United States over or in regard to any navigable waters or any commerce between the States . . . ." *Id.* at 277–78. This would seem to be a congressional abrogation of immunity. But it then stated, "[Congress] approved a sue-and-be-sued clause in a compact under conditions that make it clear that the States accepting it waived any immunity from suit which they otherwise might have." *Id.* at 280. Is this "sue-and-be-sued" clause a waiver by the states that Congress accepted, or did Congress's acceptance of it constitute an abrogation of immunity, or both?

Perhaps the distinction between abrogation and waiver was not important in 1959, but in *Seminole Tribe of Florida v. Florida,* 517 U.S. 44 (1996), the Supreme Court held that Congress did have not the power under the Commerce Clause to abrogate the sovereign immunity of the states that is further protected under the Eleventh Amendment. If the issue in *Petty* was "abrogation," then would the congressional consent have satisfied the limit on Congress's authority specified in *Seminole Tribe*?

3. *Petty* contained a concurrence as well, which states in its entirety, "Mr. Justice Black, Mr. Justice Clark, and Mr. Justice Stewart concur in the judgment and opinion of the Court with the understanding that we do not reach the constitutional questions as to whether the Eleventh Amendment immunizes from suit agencies created by two or more states under state compacts which the Constitution requires to be approved by the Congress." 359 U.S. at 283. Why do you think the concurrence did not reach the Eleventh Amendment? Did the concurrence see compact agencies as something different from state agencies? Did the concurrence see this case as involving a simple interpretation of the compact?

4. In his dissent, Justice Frankfurter observed that the Court was deviating from its "settled practice in dealing with a doubtful state statute by deferring to interpretations of local law rendered by the lower federal courts." 359 U.S. at 283–84. In the next paragraph, he distinguished *West Virginia ex rel. Dyer v. Sims* and made a point of stating that both Tennessee and Missouri deny giving their authorization to suit in the federal courts. Do you think Justice Frankfurter would have been so anxious to defer to the Eighth Circuit's interpretation if the states were not in accord on this point? Is an interpretation regarding immunity from suit under a compact different from a direct controversy over the meaning of the compact? Consider that federal law may be more or less favorable than state law concerning liability.

5. Consider how the Court described the Bridge Commission. Justice Douglas first stated the Commission was a "body corporate and politic," but later began the Court's analysis by stating, "We assume *arguendo* that this suit must be considered as one against the States since this bi-state corporation is a joint or common agency of Tennessee and Missouri." 359 U.S. at 279.

Is a "joint or common agency" of the states the equivalent of the states? Recall the cases in Chapter 4 considering whether a compact agency is a state agency, and reread the notes following *Mississippi v. Louisiana* in Chapter 6 about compact agencies as parties in original jurisdiction cases. What do you think about this assumption? Justice Douglas did not base his presumption on any specific compact text or precedent. What bases would a court use today to make this presumption?

The Court's assumption that the case involved a suit against the states avoided the difficult question of whether a compact agency is a state for the purpose of the Eleventh Amendment, but the Court was forced to address it in *Lake Country Estates*, which is the next case.

Lake Country Estates, Inc. v. Tahoe Reg'l Planning Agency
440 U.S. 391 (1979)

STEVENS, JUSTICE:

We granted certiorari to decide whether the Tahoe Regional Planning Agency, an entity created by Compact between California and Nevada, is entitled to the immunity that the Eleventh Amendment provides to the compacting States themselves. . . .

Lake Tahoe, a unique mountain lake, is located partly in California and partly in Nevada. The Lake Tahoe Basin, an area comprising 500 square miles, is a popular resort area that has grown rapidly in recent years.

In 1968, the States of California and Nevada agreed to create a single agency to coordinate and regulate development in the Basin and to conserve its natural resources. As required by the Constitution, in 1969 Congress gave its consent to the Compact, and the Tahoe Regional Planning Agency (TRPA) was organized. The Compact authorized TRPA to adopt and to enforce a regional plan for land use, transportation, conservation, recreation, and public services.

Petitioners own property in the Lake Tahoe Basin. In 1973, they filed a complaint in the United States District Court for the Eastern District of California alleging that TRPA, the individual members of its governing body, and its executive officer had adopted a land-use ordinance and general plan, and engaged in other conduct, that destroyed the economic value of petitioners' property. Petitioners alleged that respondents had thereby taken their property without due process of law and without just compensation in violation of the Fifth and Fourteenth Amendments to the Constitution of the United States. They sought monetary and equitable relief.

. . . .

. . . Although the point had not been argued, the Court of Appeals decided that the Eleventh Amendment immunized TRPA from suit in a federal court. . . .

Petitioners ask this Court to hold that TRPA is not entitled to Eleventh Amendment immunity. . . .

. . . .

The Court of Appeals held that California and Nevada had delegated authority ordinarily residing in each of those States to TRPA. Because "the bi-state Authority serves as an agency of the participant states, exercising a specially aggregated slice of state power," the court concluded "that the TRPA is protected by sovereign immunity, preserved for the states by the Eleventh Amendment." 566 F.2d at 1359–60.

The reasoning of the Court of Appeals would extend Eleventh Amendment immunity to every bistate agency unless that immunity were expressly waived. TRPA argues that the propriety of this result is evidenced by the special constitutional requirement of congressional approval of any interstate compact. Any agency that is so important that it could not even be created by the States without a special Act of Congress should receive the same immunity that is accorded to the States themselves.

We cannot accept such an expansive reading of the Eleventh Amendment. By its terms, the protection afforded by that Amendment is only available to "one of the United States." It is true, of course, that some agencies exercising state power have been permitted to invoke the Amendment in order to protect the state treasury from liability that would have had essentially the same practical consequences as a judgment against the State itself. But the Court has consistently refused to construe the Amendment to afford protection to political subdivisions such as counties and municipalities, even though such entities exercise a "slice of state power."

If an interstate compact discloses that the compacting States created an agency comparable to a county or municipality, which has no Eleventh Amendment immunity, the Amendment should not be construed to immunize such an entity. Unless there is good reason to believe that the States structured the new agency to enable it to enjoy the special constitutional protection of the States themselves, and that Congress concurred in that purpose, there would appear to be no justification for reading additional meaning into the limited language of the Amendment.

California and Nevada have both filed briefs in this Court disclaiming any intent to confer immunity on TRPA. They point to provisions of their Compact that indicate that TRPA is to be regarded as a political subdivision rather than an arm of the State. Thus TRPA is described in Art. III(a) as a "separate legal entity" and in Art. VI(a) as a "political subdivision." Under the terms of the Compact, 6 of the 10 governing members of TRPA are appointed by counties and cities, and only 4 by the 2 States. Funding under the Compact must be provided by the counties, not the States. Finally, instead of the state treasury being directly responsible for judgments against TRPA, Art. VII(f) expressly provides that obligations of TRPA shall *not* be binding on either State.

The regulation of land use is traditionally a function performed by local governments. Concern with the proper performance of that function in the bistate area was a primary motivation for the creation of TRPA itself, and gave rise to the specific controversy at issue in this litigation. Moreover, while TRPA, like cities, towns, and counties, was originally created by the States, its authority to make rules within its jurisdiction is not subject to veto at the state level. Indeed, that TRPA is not in fact an arm of the State subject to its control is perhaps most forcefully demonstrated by the fact that California has resorted to litigation in an unsuccessful attempt to impose its will on TRPA.

The intentions of Nevada and California, the terms of the Compact, and the actual operation of TRPA make clear that nothing short of an absolute rule, such as that implicit in the holding of the Court of Appeals, would allow TRPA to claim the sovereign immunity provided by the Constitution to Nevada and California. Because the Eleventh Amendment prescribes no such rule, we hold that TRPA is subject to "the judicial power of the United States" within the meaning of that Amendment.

. . . .

Notes & Questions

1. TRPA argued, "Any agency that is so important that it could not even be created by the States without a special Act of Congress should receive the same immunity that is accorded to the States themselves." 440 U.S. at 400. Does this argument suggest that compact agencies are the same as or different from state agencies? Ultimately, how important was the requirement for congressional consent in the Court's reasoning?

2. The Supreme Court noted that the Eleventh Amendment is only available to "one of the United States," but it also applies to agencies exercising state power. What factors did the Court consider to determine whether TRPA exercised state power? What sources did the Court look to? Do you agree that a compact agency is like a county or municipality?

3. The majority looked to the states' intentions when they created TRPA. Reread Frankfurter's dissent in *Petty*, in which he too suggested that the Court look to the intentions of the party states. Did the majority in *Lake Country Estates* consider the same factors in looking for the states' intention as Justice Frankfurter did in *Petty*?

4. Note 5 following the *Colbert v. Pac. States Marine Fisheries Comm'n* case excerpt in Chapter 4 asked whether a compact agency should be considered a federal agency for one purpose, but a state agency for another. Consider a variation on that question here—should states be able to create an entity that is a "state agency" for one purpose, but not for another? One such entity is the Delaware Valley Regional Planning Commission. The Pennsylvania Commonwealth Court determined that the DVRPC is "a commonwealth agency" for the purpose of Commonwealth Court jurisdiction, but is not a "commonwealth agency" under the Pennsylvania Right-to-Know Act. *Safety, Agric., Vill. and Env't (S.A.V.E.) v. Delaware Valley Reg'l Planning Comm'n*, 819 A.2d 1235 (Pa. Commw. Ct. 2003).

5. The Supreme Court highlighted the Ninth Circuit's statement that "California and Nevada had delegated authority ordinarily residing in each of those States to TRPA." While each state certainly has authority to do land use planning,

didn't the states enact the compact to do something they couldn't have done alone—i.e., to jointly manage the Lake Tahoe region?

6. Courts have applied the *Lake Country Estates* factors to entities created by non-compact intergovernmental agreements. In *Nixon v. Smith*, No. 10-C-1382, 2011 U.S. Dist. LEXIS 82317 (N.D. Ill. July 26, 2011), the court applied *Lake Country Estates* to analyze whether a regional law enforcement entity, the Lake County Metropolitan Enforcement Group (LCMEG), was a separate legal entity that could be sued in federal court, or whether it was an arm of the state that enjoyed Eleventh Amendment immunity from suit in federal court. In *Simmons v. Sabine River Auth. of Louisiana*, 823 F. Supp. 2d 420 (W.D. La. 2011) the court also applied *Lake Country Estates.* The Sabine River Compact authorizes Louisiana and Texas to create a compact agency, the "Sabine River Compact Administration" for the purpose of the compact—allocation of water. The states also created their own independent state agencies to manage other aspects of the Sabine River Basin—economic development, recreation, and power development. In this case, the plaintiffs sued only the Sabine River Authority of Louisiana (i.e., one of the non-compact state entities) for flood damage from spilling from the reservoir. The court does not explain why it applied the *Lake Country Estates* factors when the defendant in the case was a state agency, not the compact agency.

The Supreme Court accepted the next case, *Port Auth. Trans-Hudson Corp. v. Feeney*, to address a split between the Second and Third circuits about whether PATH was created as a state agency. The majority opinion, however, avoided the question whether PATH is a state agency for the purpose of the Eleventh Amendment, just as it did in *Petty v. Tennessee-Missouri Bridge Comm'n*. The concurrence focused on the state agency issue, but only followed a bit of the *Lake Country Estates* analytical framework.

Port Auth. Trans-Hudson Corp. v. Feeney
495 U.S. 299 (1990)

O'CONNOR, JUSTICE:

These cases call upon the Court to determine whether the Eleventh Amendment bars respondents' suits in federal court against an entity created by New York and New Jersey to operate certain transportation and other facilities.

In 1921, New York and New Jersey entered a bistate compact creating the Port Authority of New York and New Jersey (Authority). In accord with the Constitution's Compact Clause, Congress consented to the compact. Through the compact, the States created the Authority to achieve "a better co-ordination of the terminal, transportation and other facilities of commerce in, about and through the port of New York," and lodged in the Authority "full power and authority to purchase, construct, lease and/or operate any terminal or transportation facility within [the port] district." The Port Authority Trans-Hudson Corp. (PATH), petitioner in these consolidated cases, is a wholly owned subsidiary of the Authority that operates an interstate railway system and other facilities. PATH is entitled to "all of the privileges, immunities, tax exemptions and other exemptions of the port authority" and is subject to suit to the same extent as the Authority.

Respondents Patrick Feeney and Charles Foster alleged injuries incurred during their employment with PATH. Both filed separate complaints against PATH in the United States District Court for the Southern District of New York to recover damages pursuant to the Federal Employers' Liability Act (FELA), the Boiler Inspection Act, and the Safety Appliance Act. PATH moved to dismiss both complaints, asserting that PATH enjoyed New York and New Jersey's sovereign immunity and thus that the Eleventh Amendment deprived the federal court of jurisdiction over the suits. Relying in part on *Port Authority Police Benevolent Assn., Inc. v. Port Authority of New York and New Jersey*, 819 F.2d 413 (3d Cir. 1987), the District Court concluded that the Eleventh Amendment deprived it of jurisdiction and dismissed respondents' complaints. In *Port Authority Police Benevolent Assn.*, the Court of Appeals for the Third Circuit reasoned that because the States had established the Authority as a state agency and continued to exercise extensive control over its operations, the Authority was entitled to Eleventh Amendment immunity. The court also found no waiver of that immunity.

The Court of Appeals for the Second Circuit held that the Eleventh Amendment did not bar Feeney's suit because "the Eleventh Amendment immunity either does not extend to [PATH] or has been waived." 873 F.2d 628, 628–29 (1989). The court concluded that PATH did not enjoy the States' sovereign immunity, principally because the treasuries of New York and New Jersey are largely insulated from PATH's liabilities. In reaching its conclusion that the States had waived any immunity that PATH possessed, the court relied upon two provisions of an Act governing suits against the Authority and its subsidiaries and passed by New York (in 1950) and New Jersey (in 1951). The first section provided that the States "consent to suits, actions or proceedings of any form or nature at law, in equity or otherwise * * * against the Port of New York Authority." Another section provided in part:

> The foregoing consent is granted upon the condition that venue in any suit, action or proceeding against the Port Authority shall be laid within a county or a judicial district, established by one of said States or by the United States, and situated wholly or partially within the Port of New York District. The Port Authority shall be deemed to be a resident of each such county or judicial district for the purpose of such suits, actions, or proceedings.

The court concluded that, despite the "somewhat anomalous" location of an indication of waiver in a venue provision, the statutory provisions demonstrated "an intent to allow the Port Authority to be sued in the designated federal courts and is thus an explicit waiver, albeit partial, of the Eleventh Amendment [immunity]." 873 F.2d at 633. The Second Circuit reversed the District Court's dismissal of Foster's complaint on identical grounds. Two days before the Second Circuit issued these decisions, the Third Circuit had reaffirmed and elaborated its conclusion that the States had not waived the sovereign immunity that extended to PATH. *See Leadbeater v. Port Authority Trans-Hudson Corp.*, 873 F.2d 45 (3d Cir. 1989). That court acknowledged that "[i]t is certainly arguable that the consent to suit statutes, read in light of this venue provision, create the 'overwhelming implication' of consent to suit in federal court," but held that "[n]ot without some unease, we conclude that the venue provision fails to constitute the requisite showing that the states intended to waive P.A.T.H.'s [E]leventh [A]mendment immunity." To resolve this conflict, we granted certiorari to review the consolidated decisions of the Second Circuit, and we now affirm.

The Eleventh Amendment states: "The Judicial power of the United States shall not be construed to extend to any suit in law or equity, commenced or prosecuted against one of the United States by Citizens of another State, or Citizens or Subjects of any Foreign State." This Court has drawn upon principles of sovereign immunity to construe the Amendment to "establish that 'an unconsenting State is immune from suits brought in federal courts by her own citizens as well as by citizens of another state.'" *Pennhurst State School and Hospital v. Halderman*, 465 U.S. 89, 100 (1984). The Eleventh Amendment bar to suit is not absolute. States may consent to suit in federal court, *see, e.g.*, *Atascadero State Hospital v. Scanlon*, 473 U.S. 234, 241 (1985), and, in certain cases, Congress may abrogate the States' sovereign immunity. *See, e.g.*, *Dellmuth v. Muth*, 491 U.S. 223 (1989).

Respondents challenge PATH's claim that it is a state agency entitled to the Eleventh Amendment immunity of New York and New Jersey. *Petty v. Tennessee-Missouri Bridge Comm'n*, 359 U.S. 275 (1959), guides our resolution of this issue. In *Petty*, the Court considered whether the Eleventh Amendment barred a federal court from entertaining an action under the Jones Act brought against the Tennessee-Missouri Bridge Commission. Similar to the Authority, the Commission constructed and operated transportation facilities pursuant to a bistate compact entered by Tennessee and Missouri and ratified by Congress. The Court "assume[d] arguendo that this suit must be considered as one against the States since this bi-state corporation is a joint or common agency of Tennessee and Missouri," 359 U.S. at 279, but concluded that the States had waived any immunity that the Commission possessed. Because we find that the States of New York and New Jersey have consented to suit against PATH in federal court, we conclude that a similar course is appropriate in this case.

Well-established law governs abrogation and waiver of Eleventh Amendment immunity. Because "abrogation of sovereign immunity upsets 'the fundamental constitutional balance between the Federal Government and the States,'" *Dellmuth v. Muth, supra,* at 227, and because States are unable directly to remedy a judicial misapprehension of that abrogation, the Court has adopted a particularly strict standard to evaluate claims that Congress has abrogated the States' sovereign immunity. *See Id.* at 242 ("Congress may abrogate the States' constitutionally secured immunity from suit in federal court only by making its intention unmistakably clear in the language of the statute"). Respondents do not assert that Congress has abrogated the States' sovereign immunity through any of the statutes that underlie their claims against PATH, and such arguments would be unavailing. Similar solicitude for States' sovereign immunity underlies the standard that this Court employs to determine whether a State has waived that immunity. The Court will give effect to a State's waiver of Eleventh Amendment immunity "'only where stated by the most express language or by such overwhelming implication from the text as [will] leave no room for any other reasonable construction.'" *Atascadero State Hospital, supra*, at 239–40. A State does not waive its Eleventh Amendment immunity by consenting to suit only in its own courts, and "[t]hus, in order for a state statute or constitutional provision to constitute a waiver of Eleventh Amendment immunity, it must specify the State's intention to subject itself to suit in federal court." *Atascadero State Hospital, supra*, at 241.

New York and New Jersey have expressly consented to suit in expansive terms. The statutory consent to suit provision, which provides that the States "consent to suits, actions, or proceedings of any form or nature at law, in equity or otherwise * * * against the Port of New York Authority," might be interpreted to encompass the States' consent to suit in federal court as well as state court. But such a broadly framed provision may also reflect only a State's consent to suit in its own courts. Sensitive to the values underlying the Eleventh Amendment, the Court has required that consent to suit in federal court be express and thus has construed such ambiguous and general consent to suit provisions, standing alone, as insufficient to waive Eleventh Amendment immunity. *See* [*Atascadero State Hospital*,] 473 U.S. at 241 (general consent to suit provision did not waive Eleventh Amendment immunity because the "provision does not specifically indicate the State's willingness to be sued in federal court"); *Great Northern Life Ins. Co. v. Read*, 322 U.S. 47 (1944) ("When a state authorizes a suit against itself * * *, it is not consonant with our dual system for the federal courts to be astute to read the consent to embrace federal as well as state courts"). Other textual evidence of consent to suit in federal courts may resolve that ambiguity and sufficiently clearly establish the scope of the State's more general consent to suit. In such circumstances, the Court must give effect to that clearly indicated consent to suit in federal court.

In this case, the statutory venue provision suffices to resolve any ambiguity contained in the States' general consent to suit provision by expressly indicating that the States' consent to suit extends to suit in federal court. The section provides that "[t]he foregoing consent is granted on the condition that venue * * * shall be laid within a county or judicial district, established by one of said States or by the United States, and situated wholly or partially within the Port of New York District." This provision eliminates the danger, identified in *Atascadero State Hospital, supra*, and *Great Northern Life Ins. Co., supra*, that federal courts may mistake a provision intended to allow suit in a State's own courts for a waiver of Eleventh Amendment immunity. Petitioner does not deny that the phrase "judicial district, established * * * by the United States" refers to the United States District Courts, but rather argues that the reference to venue cannot shape our construction of the general consent to suit provision. Although one might not look first to a venue provision to find evidence of waiver of sovereign immunity, we believe that the provision directly indicates the extent of the States' waiver embodied in the consent provision. The States passed the venue and consent to suit provisions as portions of the same Acts that set forth the nature, timing, and extent of the States' consent to suit. The venue provision expressly refers to and qualifies the more general consent to suit provision. Additionally, issues of venue are closely related to those concerning sovereign immunity, as this Court has indicated by emphasizing that "[a] State's constitutional interest in immunity encompasses not merely whether it may be sued, but where it may be sued." *Pennhurst State School and Hospital v. Halderman*, 465 U.S. at 99. Petitioner's related argument that a venue provision cannot broaden the consent to suit provision begs the question what the States intended through the consent provision. The venue provision elucidates rather than broadens the consent to suit provision: It provides persuasive textual evidence that the consent to suit provision encompasses suits in federal court, and broadens the effect of the consent provision only to the extent of removing an ambiguity that called forth this Court's prudential canon of construction. The venue provision would hardly qualify "[t]he foregoing consent" unless the States intended that consent to include suits in federal court.

. . . .

We conclude that the statutory consent to suit provision, elucidated by the venue provision, establishes the States' waiver of any Eleventh Amendment immunity that might otherwise bar respondents' suits against petitioner. The judgments of the Court of Appeals for the Second Circuit are therefore affirmed.

BRENNAN, JUSTICE, CONCURRING:

. . . .

Even under the Court's current interpretation of the Eleventh Amendment, I do not believe that PATH had any defense to waive. The Eleventh Amendment bars federal jurisdiction only over suits "commenced or prosecuted against one of the United States." PATH is a subsidiary of the Port Authority of New York and New Jersey (Port Authority) which is a bistate agency created by interstate compact; it is not "one of the United States." By its terms, then, the Eleventh Amendment would appear to be inapplicable. But this Court has created two very limited exceptions to a literal reading of the phrase "one of the United States," so that immunity applies: (1) where the entity being sued is so intricately intertwined with the State that it can best be understood as an "arm of the State"; and (2) where the State, though not a nominal party, is the real party in interest. I believe that no bistate agency falls within the first exception and that no bistate agency falls within the second exception if, like the Port Authority, it is independently and solely liable for any judgments levied against it.

The inherent nature of interstate agencies precludes their being found so intricately intertwined with the State as to constitute an "arm of the State." The Court developed the "arm-of-the-State" doctrine as a tool for determining which entities created by a State enjoy its Eleventh Amendment protection and which do not. This Court has found that a private suit against a state agency is barred by the Eleventh Amendment. *See Alabama v. Pugh*, 438 U.S. 781, 782 (1978) (reversing a lower court's decision to enjoin the State of Alabama and the Alabama Board of Corrections). Nonetheless, this Court has long held that counties and cities are not so integrally related to the State that they are shielded from suit in federal court. In *Lincoln County v. Luning*, 133 U.S. 529, 530 (1890), the Court held that the Eleventh Amendment does not bar suit against counties in federal court, noting that the "Eleventh Amendment limits the jurisdiction [of the federal courts] only as to suits against a State." The Court continued: "[W]hile the county is territorially a part of the State, yet politically it is also a corporation created by and with such powers as are given to it by the State. In this respect it is a part of the State only in that remote sense in which any city, town, or other municipal corporation may be said to be a part of the State."

In *Mt. Healthy City Board of Education v. Doyle*, 429 U.S. 274, 280 (1977), the Court noted that "[t]he bar of the Eleventh Amendment to suit in federal courts * * * does not extend to counties and similar municipal corporations" and looked to the "nature of the entity created by state law" to determine whether local school boards in Ohio appeared to be more like a county or city or more like an arm of the State. The Court concluded that the school boards' extensive powers to issue bonds and levy taxes, and their categorization under state law as a form of political subdivision, rendered them "[o]n balance * * * more like a county or city."

The rule to be derived from our cases is that the Eleventh Amendment shields an entity from suit in federal court only when it is so closely tied to the State as to be the direct means by which the State acts, for instance a state agency. In contrast, when a State creates subdivisions and imbues them with a significant measure of autonomy, such as the ability to levy taxes, issue bonds, or own land in their own name, these subdivisions are too separate from the State to be considered its "arms." This is so even though these political subdivisions exist solely at the whim and behest of their State.

Interstate agencies lack even this close link to any one State. While a State has plenary power to create and destroy its political subdivisions, a State enjoys no such hegemony over an interstate agency. To begin with, a State cannot create such an agency at will. In order to do so, it must persuade another State, or several other States, to join it. Moreover, the creation of an interstate agency requires each State to relinquish to one or more sister States a part of its sovereignty. The regulatory powers exercised by an interstate agency are powers no longer inhering in any one compacting State; they are powers shared. Likewise, no one State has complete dominion over property owned, and proprietary activities operated, by such an agency. For instance, in order to achieve the practical advantages of coordinated planning and administration through the Port Authority, New York and New Jersey each has ceded partial control over the regulation and operation of transportation facilities in its own State since 1921 and for the foreseeable future. In order to change the Port Authority's organization or powers, the legislatures of both States must pass a bill to that effect.

In addition, States may not create an interstate agency without the express approval of Congress; they surrendered their right to do so "in the plan of the Convention" when they accepted the Interstate Compact Clause.

The Constitution also prohibits States from entering into any "Treaty, Alliance, or Confederation" either with other States or with foreign governments. Art. I, § 10, cl. 1. The Interstate Compact Clause and the State Treaty Clause ensure that whatever sovereignty a State possesses within its own sphere of authority ends at its political border.

Thus, it is not within the autonomous power of any State to create and regulate an interstate agency. Each State's sovereign will is circumscribed by that of the other States in the compact and circumscribed further by the veto power relinquished to Congress in the Constitution. If counties are not "arms" of their States merely because the State conferred a certain autonomy on them—an autonomy it can withdraw at will—then an interstate agency, over which none of the compacting States exercises such untrammeled control, cannot be said to be an "arm" of any of them.

Although this Court has held that a suit in which the State, rather than the nominal defendant, is the real party in interest is a suit against "one of the United States" within the meaning of the Eleventh Amendment, a State is the real party in interest generally only when the State is directly liable for a money judgment. In *Ford Motor Co. v. Department of Treasury of Indiana*, 323 U.S. 459 (1945), the Court held that a suit against a state treasury department and the individuals constituting its board for a refund of taxes was a suit against the State because "when the action is in essence one for the recovery of money from the state, the state is the real, substantial party in interest and is entitled to invoke its sovereign immunity from suit even though individual officials are nominal defendants." This Court relied on that decision 30 years later in *Edelman v. Jordan*, 415 U.S. [651,] 677 [(1974)], in holding that the Eleventh Amendment barred a suit brought in federal court in which the nominal defendants were Illinois officials because the relief sought was an injunction ordering retroactive payments of benefits from the state treasury. The Court observed that "the rule has evolved that a suit [in federal court] by private parties seeking to impose a liability which must be paid from public funds in the state treasury is barred by the Eleventh Amendment." *Id.* at 663.

Conversely, when a State is not liable for the obligations of an interstate agency, it is not a real party in interest in a suit against that agency. The court below found that no State is liable for PATH's obligations. It concluded:

> We believe it clear that a judgment against PATH would not be enforceable against either New York or New Jersey. The Port Authority is explicitly barred from pledging the credit of either state or from borrowing money in any name but its own. Even the provision [permitting] the appropriation of moneys for administrative expenses up to $100,000 per year requires prior approval by the governor of each state and an actual appropriation [by the legislature] before obligations for such expenses may be incurred. Moreover, the [provision's] phrase 'salaries, office and other administrative expenses' clearly limits this essentially optional obligation of the two states to a very narrow category of expenses and thus also evidences an intent to

> insulate the states' treasuries from the vast bulk of the Port Authority's operating and capital expenses, including personal injury judgments. No provision commits the treasuries of the two states to satisfy judgments against the Port Authority.

Therefore neither New York nor New Jersey is a real party in interest in respondents' suits, as this Court has understood and applied the concept in the Eleventh Amendment area.

This is not to say that the only restriction on whether an interstate agency can be sued in federal court is the Eleventh Amendment. Congress may provide an interstate agency with an affirmative defense to its federal statutory obligations as Congress wishes, subject only to independent constitutional strictures such as the Equal Protection Clause. Congress would ordinarily be expected to address the matter through a specific statutory provision. It may also be that a court could legitimately infer Congress' intention to provide such a defense from its consent to an interstate compact the terms of which patently attempt to grant immunity from suit in federal court. *See Lake Country Estates, Inc. v. Tahoe Regional Planning Agency*, 440 U.S. 391 (1979).

But it cannot be disputed that there is no such showing here. Congress has not passed any law conferring any immunity on the Port Authority. Nor did the compact to which Congress consented include any provision attempting to grant immunity from suit in federal court. Consequently, I believe that this Court, following its current view of the Eleventh Amendment, could have rested its decision today on the absence of an Eleventh Amendment defense as well as on waiver.

Notes & Questions

1. The Supreme Court granted certiorari in this case to resolve a split between the Second and Third circuits. The Third Circuit previously "reasoned that because the States had established the Authority as a state agency and continued to exercise extensive control over its operations, the Authority was entitled to Eleventh Amendment immunity. The court also found no waiver of that immunity." 495 U.S. at 302. The Second Circuit "concluded that PATH did not enjoy the States' sovereign immunity, principally because the treasuries of New York and New Jersey are largely insulated from PATH's liabilities." *Id.* Alternatively, the Second Circuit concluded that immunity had been waived, even though that waiver was found in a "'somewhat anomalous' location," *id.* at 303, in a venue provision.

The Supreme Court considered two provisions of the compact. The first provision consented to suit or proceedings, "of any nature at law, in equity or otherwise, against the Port of New York Authority." This provision was not clear enough because it might have only reflected consent to suit in state court. The second provision specified venue within a "county or judicial district established by one of the states, or by the United States, and situated . . . within the Port of New York District." Why is this venue provision "anomalous"?

The majority followed elements from both *Petty* and *Lake Country Estates*. *Petty* involved a similar jurisdiction provision, which the Court interpreted as a waiver of Eleventh Amendment immunity. *Lake Country Estates* established the analytical framework for considering the impact on the state's finances. Here, New York and New Jersey provide only a tiny portion of the Port Authority's budget, so that any judgment against Port Authority would have an insignificant impact on the states.

2. Justice Brennan's concurrence focused on the nature of compact agencies as different from states, stating, "The inherent nature of interstate compact agencies precludes their being found so intricately intertwined with the State as to constitute an 'arm of the State.'" 495 U.S. at 312. He observed, "States may not create an interstate agency without the express approval of Congress." *Id.* at 314. Of course, some compacts do not require consent. Should compact agencies that did not receive congressional consent be subject to suit in federal court?

3. Justice Brennan also observed, "While a state has plenary power to create and destroy its political subdivisions, a State enjoys no such hegemony over an interstate agency." 495 U.S. at 314. He then followed with several characteristics of compact agencies. Do these characteristics persuade you that compact agencies are different from a typical state agency? Are there characteristics of compact agencies discussed at the beginning of Chapter 4 that Justice Brennan did not mention, or that contradict those in Justice Brennan's analysis?

In the last case in this section, *Hess v. Port Auth. Trans-Hudson Corp.*, a majority of the Court finally reached the question whether PATH was an "arm of the state" for the purpose of immunity. As you read the case, consider whether the majority opinion more closely followed *Lake Country Estates* or Justice Brennan's concurrence in *Feeney*.

Hess v. Port Auth. Trans-Hudson Corp.

513 U.S. 30 (1994)

GINSBURG, JUSTICE:

These paired cases arise out of work-related accidents in which a locomotive engineer and a train conductor, employees of a bistate railway authorized by interstate compact, sustained personal injuries. The courts below—the United States District Court for the District of New Jersey, and the United States Court of Appeals for the Third Circuit—rejected both complaints on the ground that the Eleventh Amendment sheltered the respondent railway from suit in federal court. We granted certiorari to resolve an intercircuit conflict on this issue. Concluding that the respondent bistate railway, the Port Authority Trans-Hudson Corporation (PATH), is not cloaked with the Eleventh Amendment immunity that a State enjoys, we reverse the judgment of the Third Circuit.

Petitioners Albert Hess and Charles F. Walsh, both railroad workers, were injured in unrelated incidents in the course of their employment by PATH. PATH, a wholly owned subsidiary of the Port Authority of New York and New Jersey, operates a commuter railroad connecting New York City to northern New Jersey. In separate personal injury actions commenced in the United States District Court for the District of New Jersey, petitioners sought to recover damages for PATH's alleged negligence; both claimed a right to compensation under the federal law governing injuries to railroad workers, the Federal Employers' Liability Act (FELA). Hess and Walsh filed their complaints within the 3-year time limit set by the FELA, but neither petitioner met the 1-year limit specified in the States' statutory consent to sue the Port Authority.

PATH moved to dismiss each action, asserting (1) PATH's qualification as a state agency entitled to the Eleventh Amendment immunity from suit in federal court enjoyed by New York and New Jersey, and (2) petitioners' failure to commence court proceedings within the 1-year limit prescribed by New York and New Jersey. Third Circuit precedent concerning the Port Authority supported PATH's plea. In *Port Authority Police Benevolent Assn., Inc. v. Port Authority of New York and New Jersey*, 819 F.2d 413 (3d Cir. 1987), the Court of Appeals for the Third Circuit held that the Port Authority is "an agency of the state and is thus entitled to Eleventh Amendment immunity." 819 F.2d at 418. In reaching this decision, the Court of Appeals acknowledged that "[g]iven the solvency and size of the [Port Authority's] General Reserve Fund, it is unlikely that the Authority would have to go to the state to get payment for any liabilities issued against it." *Id.* at 416. But the Third Circuit considered "crystal clear" the intentions of New York and New Jersey: "if the Authority is ever in need of financial support, the states will be there to provide it." *Ibid.*

In line with *Port Authority PBA*, the District Court held in the *Hess* and *Walsh* actions that PATH enjoys Eleventh Amendment immunity, and could be sued in federal court only within the 1-year time frame New York and New Jersey allowed. *See Walsh v. Port Authority Trans-Hudson Corp.*, 813 F. Supp. 1095 (D. NJ 1993); *Hess v. Port Authority Trans-Hudson Corp.*, 809 F. Supp. 1172 (D. NJ 1992). Accordingly, both actions were dismissed.

The District Court in Hess noted an anomaly: Had Hess sued in a New Jersey or New York state court the FELA's 3-year limitation period, not the States' 1-year prescription, would have applied. This followed from our reaffirmation in *Hilton v. South Carolina Public Railways Comm'n*, 502 U.S. 197 (1991), that the entire federal scheme of railroad regulation—including all FELA terms—applies to all railroads, even those wholly owned by one State. Time-bar rejection by a federal court of a federal statutory claim that federal prescription would have rendered timely, had the case been brought in state court, becomes comprehensible, the District Court explained, once it is recognized that "'the Eleventh Amendment does not apply in state courts.'"

Consolidating *Hess* and *Walsh* on appeal, the Third Circuit summarily affirmed the District Court's judgments.

The Port Authority, whose Eleventh Amendment immunity is at issue in these cases, was created in 1921, when Congress, pursuant to the Constitution's Interstate Compact Clause, consented to a compact between the Authority's parent States. Through the bistate compact, New York and New Jersey sought to achieve "a better co-ordination of the terminal, transportation and other facilities of commerce in, about and through the port of New York." The compact grants the Port Authority power to "purchase, construct, lease and/or operate any terminal or transportation facility within [the Port of New York D]istrict; and to make charges for the use thereof; and for any of such purposes to own, hold, lease and/or operate real or personal property, to borrow money and secure the same by bonds or by mortgages upon any property held or to be held by it."

. . . .

The Third Circuit's assessment of PATH's qualification for Eleventh Amendment immunity conflicts with the judgment of the Court of Appeals for the Second Circuit on the same matter. *See Feeney v. Port Authority Trans-Hudson Corporation*, 873 F.2d 628, (1989), *aff'd on other grounds*, 495 U.S. 299 (1990). The Second Circuit concluded:

> No provision [of the compact or of state legislation pursuant to the compact] commits the treasuries of the two states to satisfy judgments against the Port Authority * * * . We believe that this insulation of state treasuries from the liabilities of the Port Authority outweighs both the methods of appointment and gubernatorial veto so far as the Eleventh Amendment immunity is concerned. 873 F.2d at 631.

We affirmed the Second Circuit's judgment in *Feeney*, but we bypassed the question whether PATH enjoyed the States' Eleventh Amendment immunity. Assuming, arguendo, that the suit in *Feeney* was tantamount to a claim against the States, we ruled that New York and New Jersey had effectively consented to the litigation. Consent is not arguable here, because Hess and Walsh commenced suit too late to meet the 1-year prescription specified by the States. Accordingly, we confront directly the sole question petitioners Hess and Walsh present, and we hold that PATH is not entitled to Eleventh Amendment immunity from suit in federal court.

. . . .

Bistate entities occupy a significantly different position in our federal system than do the States themselves. The States, as separate sovereigns, are the constituent elements of the Union. Bistate entities, in contrast, typically are creations of three discrete sovereigns: two States and the federal government. Their mission is to address "'interests and problems that do not coincide nicely either with the national boundaries or with State lines'"—interests that "'may be badly served or not served at all by the ordinary channels of National or State political action.'" V. Thursby, *Interstate Cooperation: A Study of the Interstate Compact* 5 (1953) (quoting National Resources Committee, *Regional Factors in National Planning and Development* 34 (1935)); *see* Grad, *Federal-State Compact: A New Experiment in Coop-*

erative Federalism, 63 COLUM. L. REV. 825, 854–855 (1963) (Compact Clause entities formed to deal with "broad, region-wide problems" should not be regarded as "an affirmation of a narrow concept of state sovereignty," but as "independently functioning parts of a regional polity and of a national union.").

A compact accorded congressional consent "is more than a supple device for dealing with interests confined within a region. * * * It is also a means of safeguarding the national interest. * * *" *West Virginia ex rel. Dyer v. Sims*, 341 U.S. 22, 27 (1951). The Port Authority of New York and New Jersey exemplifies both the need for, and the utility of, Compact Clause entities:

> From the point of view of geography, commerce, and engineering, the Port of New York is an organic whole. Politically, the port is split between the law-making of two States, independent but futile in their respective spheres. The scarcity of land and mounting commerce have concentrated on the New York side of the Hudson River the bulk of the terminal facilities for foreign commerce, while it has made the Jersey side, to a substantial extent, the terminal and breaking-up yards for the east- and west-bound traffic. In addition, both sides of the Hudson are dotted with municipalities, who have sought to satisfy their interest in the general problem through a confusion of local regulations. In addition, the United States has been asserting its guardianship over interstate and foreign commerce. What in fact was one, in law was many. Plainly the situation could not be adequately dealt with except through the coordinated efforts of New York, New Jersey, and the United States. The facts presented a problem for the unified action of the law-making of these three governments, and law heeded facts. Frankfurter & Landis, *The Compact Clause of the Constitution—A Study in Interstate Adjustments*, 34 YALE L.J. 685, 697 (1925) (footnote omitted).

Suit in federal court is not an affront to the dignity of a Compact Clause entity, for the federal court, in relation to such an enterprise, is hardly the instrument of a distant, disconnected sovereign; rather, the federal court is ordained by one of the entity's founders. Nor is the integrity of the compacting States compromised when the Compact Clause entity is sued in federal court. As part of the federal plan prescribed by the Constitution, the States agreed to the power sharing, coordination, and unified action that typify Compact Clause creations. Again, the federal tribunal cannot be regarded as alien in this cooperative, trigovernmental arrangement. This is all the more apparent here, where the very claims in suit—the FELA claims of Hess and Walsh—arise under federal law.

Because Compact Clause entities owe their existence to state and federal sovereigns acting cooperatively, and not to any "one of the United States," their political accountability is diffuse; they lack the tight tie to the people of one State that an instrument of a single State has:

> An interstate compact, by its very nature, shifts a part of a state's authority to another state or states, or to the agency the several states jointly create to run the compact. Such an agency under the control of special interests or gubernatorially appointed representatives is two or more steps removed

from popular control, or even of control by a local government. M. RIDGEWAY, INTERSTATE COMPACTS: A QUESTION OF FEDERALISM 300 (1971).

In sum, within any single State in our representative democracy, voters may exercise their political will to direct state policy; bistate entities created by compact, however, are not subject to the unilateral control of any one of the States that compose the federal system.

Accordingly, there is good reason not to amalgamate Compact Clause entities with agencies of "one of the United States" for Eleventh Amendment purposes. This Court so recognized in *Lake Country Estates, Inc. v. Tahoe Regional Planning Agency*, 440 U.S. 391 (1979), the only case, prior to this one, in which we decided whether a bistate entity qualified for Eleventh Amendment immunity.

Lake Country rejected a plea that the Tahoe Regional Planning Agency (TRPA), an agency created by compact to which California and Nevada were parties, acquired the immunity which the Eleventh Amendment accords to each one of TRPA's parent States. TRPA had argued that if the Amendment shields each State, then surely it must shield an entity "so important that it could not be created by [two] States without a special Act of Congress." *Id.* at 400. That "expansive reading," we said, was not warranted, for the Amendment specifies "the State" as the entity protected:

> By its terms, the protection afforded by [the Eleventh] Amendment is only available to "one of the United States." It is true, of course, that some agencies exercising state power have been permitted to invoke the Amendment in order to protect the state treasury from liability that would have had essentially the same practical consequences as a judgment against the State itself. But the Court has consistently refused to construe the Amendment to afford protection to political subdivisions such as counties and municipalities, even though such entities exercise a "slice of state power." *Id.* at 400–01.

We then set out a general approach: we would presume the Compact Clause agency does not qualify for Eleventh Amendment immunity "[u]nless there is good reason to believe that the States structured the new agency to enable it to enjoy the special constitutional protection of the States themselves, and that Congress concurred in that purpose." *Id.* at 401.

The Court in *Lake Country* found "no justification for reading additional meaning into the limited language of the Amendment." Indeed, all relevant considerations in that case weighed against TRPA's plea. The compact called TRPA a "political subdivision," and required that the majority of the governing members be county and city appointees. Obligations of TRPA, the compact directed, "shall not be binding on either State." TRPA's prime function, we noted, was regulation of land use, a function traditionally performed by local governments. Further, the agency's performance of that function gave rise to the litigation. Moreover, rules made by TRPA were "not subject to veto at the state level."

This case is more complex. Indicators of immunity or the absence thereof do not, as they did in *Lake Country*, all point the same way. While 8 of the Port Authority's 12 commissioners must be resident voters of either New York City or other parts of the Port of New York District, this indicator of local governance is surely offset by the States' controls. All commissioners are state appointees. Acting alone, each State through its governor may block Port Authority measures; and acting together, both States, through their legislatures, may enlarge the Port Authority's powers and add to its responsibilities.

The compact and its implementing legislation do not type the Authority as a state agency; instead they use various terms: "joint or common agency"; "body corporate and politic"; "municipal corporate instrumentality of the two states for the purpose of developing the port and effectuating the pledge of the states in the * * * compact." State courts, however, repeatedly have typed the Port Authority an agency of the States rather than a municipal unit or local district. *See, e.g.*, *Whalen v. Wagner*, 4 N.Y.2d 575, 581–83 (1958) (legislation authorizing specific Port Authority projects does not pertain to the "property, affairs or government" of a city because "the matters over which the Port Authority has jurisdiction are of "State concern").

Port Authority functions are not readily classified as typically state or unquestionably local. States and municipalities alike own and operate bridges, tunnels, ferries, marine terminals, airports, bus terminals, industrial parks, also commuter railroads. This consideration, therefore, does not advance our Eleventh Amendment inquiry.

Pointing away from Eleventh Amendment immunity, the States lack financial responsibility for the Port Authority. Conceived as a fiscally independent entity financed predominantly by private funds, the Authority generates its own revenues, and for decades has received no money from the States. *See Commissioner v. Shamberg's Estate*, 144 F.2d 998, 1002 (2d Cir. 1944) ("In the compact * * * the states agreed to make annual appropriates (not in excess of $100,000 for each state) for expenses of the Authority until revenues from its operations were sufficient to meet its expenses. These annual appropriations were discontinued in 1934 because the revenues from the bridges, the Holland Tunnel and Inland Terminal had become sufficient.").

The States, as earlier observed, bear no legal liability for Port Authority debts; they are not responsible for the payment of judgments against the Port Authority or PATH. The Third Circuit, in *Port Authority PBA*, assumed that, "if the Authority is ever in need," the States would pay. But nothing in the compact or the laws of either State supports that assumption. As the Second Circuit concisely stated:

> The Port Authority is explicitly barred from pledging the credit of either state or from borrowing money in any name but its own. Even the provision for the appropriation of moneys for administrative expenses up to $100,000 per year requires prior approval by the governor of each state and

> an actual appropriation before obligations for such expenses may be incurred. Moreover, the phrase 'salaries, office and other administrative expenses' clearly limits this essentially optional obligation of the two states to a very narrow category of expenses and thus also evidences an intent to insulate the states' treasuries from the vast bulk of the Port Authority's operating and capital expenses, including personal injury judgments. *Feeney*, 873 F.2d at 631.

When indicators of immunity point in different directions, the Eleventh Amendment's twin reasons for being remain our prime guide. We have already pointed out that federal courts are not alien to a bistate entity Congress participated in creating. Nor is it disrespectful to one State to call upon the Compact Clause entity to answer complaints in federal court. Seeing no genuine threat to the dignity of New York or New Jersey in allowing Hess and Walsh to pursue FELA claims against PATH in federal court, we ask, as *Lake Country* instructed, whether there is here "good reason to believe" the States and Congress designed the Port Authority to enjoy Eleventh Amendment immunity.

PATH urges that we find good reason to classify the Port Authority as a state agency for Eleventh Amendment purposes based on the control New York and New Jersey wield over the Authority. The States appoint and can remove the commissioners, the governors can veto Port Authority actions, and the States' legislatures can determine the projects the Port Authority undertakes. But ultimate control of every state-created entity resides with the State, for the State may destroy or reshape any unit it creates. "[P]olitical subdivisions exist solely at the whim and behest of their State," *Feeney*, 495 U.S. at 313 (Brennan, J., concurring), yet cities and counties do not enjoy Eleventh Amendment immunity. Moreover, no one State alone can control the course of a Compact Clause entity. Gauging actual control, particularly when an entity has multiple creator-controllers, can be a "perilous inquiry," "an uncertain and unreliable exercise." *See* Note, 92 COLUM. L. REV. 1243, 1284 (1992).

Moreover, rendering control dispositive does not home in on the impetus for the Eleventh Amendment: the prevention of federal court judgments that must be paid out of a State's treasury. Accordingly, Courts of Appeals have recognized the vulnerability of the State's purse as the most salient factor in Eleventh Amendment determinations....

The Port Authority's anticipated and actual financial independence—its long history of paying its own way—contrasts with the situation of transit facilities that place heavy fiscal tolls on their founding States.... And in *Morris v. Washington Metropolitan Area Transit Authority*, 781 F.2d 218 (D.C. Cir. 1986), Eleventh Amendment immunity was accorded an interstate transit system whose revenue shortfall Congress and the cooperating States anticipated from the start, an enterprise constantly dependent on funds from the participating governments to meet its sizable operating deficits. As the *Morris* court concluded: "[W]here an agency is so structured that, as a practical matter, if the agency is to survive, a judgment must expend itself against state treasuries, common sense and the rationale of the eleventh amendment require that sovereign immunity attach to the agency." *Id.* at 227. . . .

. . . .

The conflict between the Second and Third Circuits, it bears emphasis, is no longer over the correct legal theory. Both Circuits, in accord with the prevailing view identify "the 'state treasury' criterion—whether any judgment must be satisfied out of the state treasury—as the most important consideration" in resolving an Eleventh Amendment immunity issue. The intercircuit division thus persists only because the Second and Third Circuits diverge in answering the question: Are the Port Authority's debts those of its parent States?

. . . .

A discrete entity created by constitutional compact among three sovereigns, the Port Authority is financially self-sufficient; it generates its own revenues, and it pays its own debts. Requiring the Port Authority to answer in federal court to injured railroad workers who assert a federal statutory right, under the FELA, to recover damages does not touch the concerns—the States' solvency and dignity—that underpin the Eleventh Amendment. The judgment of the Court of Appeals is accordingly reversed, and the *Hess* and *Walsh* cases are remanded for further proceedings consistent with this opinion.

O'CONNOR, JUSTICE, DISSENTING (WITH CHIEF JUSTICE REHNQUIST, JUSTICE SCALIA, AND JUSTICE THOMAS):

The Court's opinion, as I read it, makes two different points. First, an interstate compact entity is presumptively not entitled to immunity under the Eleventh Amendment, because the States surrendered any such entitlement "[a]s part of the federal plan prescribed by the Constitution." When States act in concert under the Interstate Compact Clause, they cede power to each other and to the Federal Government, which, by consenting to the state compact, becomes one of the compact entity's creators. As such, each individual State lacks meaningful control over the entity, and suits against the entity in federal court pose no affront to a State's "dignity." Second, in place of the various factors recognized in *Lake Country* for determining arm-of-the-state status, we may now substitute a single overriding criterion, vulnerability of the state treasury. If a State does not fund judgments against an entity, that entity is not within the ambit of the Eleventh Amendment, and suits in federal court may proceed unimpeded. By the Court's reckoning, the state treasury is not implicated on these facts. Neither, it follows, is the Eleventh Amendment.

I disagree with both of these propositions and with the ultimate conclusion the Court draws from them. The Eleventh Amendment, in my view, clothes this interstate entity with immunity from suit in federal courts.

Despite several invitations, this Court has not as yet had occasion to find an interstate entity shielded by the Eleventh Amendment from suit in federal court. As I read its opinion, the Court now builds upon language in *Lake Country* to create what looks very much like a per se rule that the Eleventh Amendment never applies when States act in concert. To be sure, the [majority opinion] leaves open the possibility that in certain undefined situations, we might find "good reason" to confer immunity where States structure an entity to enjoy immunity and we see evidence that "Congress concurred in that purpose." But the crux of the Court's analysis rests on its apparent belief that the States ceded their sovereignty in the interstate compact context in the plan of the convention. Such broad reasoning brooks few, if any, exceptions.

In reaching its conclusion, the Court attaches undue significance to the requirement that Congress consent to interstate compacts. Admittedly, the consent requirement performs an important function in our federal scheme. In *Cuyler v. Adams*, 449 U.S. 433 (1981) we observed that "the requirement that Congress approve a compact is to obtain its political judgment: Is the agreement likely to interfere with federal activity in the area, is it likely to disadvantage other States to an important extent, is it a matter that would better be left untouched by state and federal regulation?" *Id.* at 440. But the consent clause neither transforms the nature of state power nor makes Congress a full-fledged participant in the underlying agreement; it requires only that Congress "check any infringement of the rights of the national government." J. Story, *Commentaries on the Constitution of the United States* § 1403, p.264 (T. Cooley ed. 1873). In consenting, Congress certifies that the States are acting within their boundaries in our federal scheme and that the national interest is not offended. Once Congress consents to cooperative state activity, there is no reason to presume that immunity does not attach. Sovereign immunity, after all, inheres in the permissible exercise of state power. "If congress consent[s], then the states [are] in this respect restored to their original inherent sovereignty; such consent being the sole limitation imposed by the constitution, when given, [leaves] the states as they were before * * * ." *Rhode Island v. Massachusetts*, 12 Pet. 657, 725 (1838); *see also* L. Tribe, *American Constitutional Law* § 6-33, p. 523 (2d ed. 1988).

Even if the Court were correct that the States ceded a portion of their power to Congress in ratifying the consent provision, it would not logically or inevitably follow that any particular entity receives no immunity under the Eleventh Amendment. In *Fitzpatrick v. Bitzer*, 427 U.S. 445 (1976), we held that the States surrendered a portion of their sovereign authority to Congress in ratifying § 5 of the Fourteenth Amendment. Despite this, we have consistently required "an unequivocal expression of congressional intent to overturn the constitutionally guaranteed immunity of the several States" before allowing suits against States to proceed in federal court. *Atascadero State Hospital v. Scanlon*, 473 U.S. 234, 240 (1985). Assuming arguendo that States ceded power to Congress to abrogate States' Eleventh Amendment immunity in the interstate compact realm, our precedents caution that we should be reluctant to infer abrogation in the absence of clear signals from Congress that such a result was, in fact, intended. At the least, I would presume the applicability of the Eleventh Amendment to interstate entities unless Congress clearly and expressly indicates otherwise.

The Court ignores these abrogation cases, however, in favor of exactly the opposite presumption. By the Court's reckoning, the Eleventh Amendment is inapplicable unless we have "good reason" to believe that Congress affirmatively concurs in a finding of immunity. In other words, the baseline is no immunity, even if the State has structured the entity in the expectation that immunity will inhere. If, however, Congress manifests a contrary intent, the Eleventh Amendment shields an interstate entity from suit in federal court. Congress, therefore, effectively may dictate the applicability of the Eleventh Amendment in this context. The notion that Congress possesses this power, an extension of dictum in *Lake Country*, 440 U.S. at 401, has little basis in our precedents. Congress may indeed be able to confer on the States what in fact looks a lot like Eleventh Amendment immunity; but we have never held that Eleventh Amendment immunity itself attaches at the whim of Congress.

The Court shores up its analysis by observing that each State lacks meaningful power to control an interstate entity. As an initial matter, one wonders how important this insight actually is to the Court's conclusion, given that the opinion elsewhere disclaims reliance on a control inquiry. In any event, that we may sometimes, or even often, in the application of arm-of-the-state analysis, find too attenuated a basis for immunity does not mean we should presume such immunity altogether lacking in this context. Two sovereign States acting together may, in most situations, be as deserving of immunity as either State acting apart. I see no reason to vary the analysis for interstate and intrastate entities.

. . . .

An arm of the State, to my mind, is an entity that undertakes state functions and is politically accountable to the State, and by extension, to the electorate. The critical inquiry, then, should be whether and to what extent the elected state government exercises oversight over the entity. If the lines of oversight are clear and substantial—for example, if the State appoints and removes an entity's governing personnel and retains veto or approval power over an entity's undertakings—then the entity should be deemed an arm of the State for Eleventh Amendment purposes. This test is sufficiently elastic to encompass the Court's treasury factor. It will be a rare case indeed where the state treasury foots the bill for an entity's wrongs but fails to exercise a healthy degree of oversight over that entity. But the control test goes further than the Court's single factor in assuring state governments the critical flexibility in internal governance that is essential to sovereign authority.

The Court dismisses consideration of control altogether, noting that States wield ultimate power over cities and counties, units that have never been accorded Eleventh Amendment immunity. This criticism, based on a supposed line-drawing problem, is off the mark. That "political subdivisions exist solely at the whim and behest of their State," *Port Authority Trans-Hudson Corp. v. Feeney*, 495 U.S. at 313 (Brennan, J., concurring), does not mean that state governments actually exercise sufficient oversight to trigger Eleventh Amendment immunity under a control-centered formulation. The inquiry should turn on real, immediate control and oversight, rather than on the potentiality of a State taking action to seize the reins. Virtually every enterprise, municipal or private, flourishes in some sense at the behest of the State. But we have never found the Eleventh Amendment's protections to hinge on this sort of abstraction. The control-centered formulation necessarily looks to the structure and function of state law. If the State delegates control and oversight of an entity to municipalities under state law, the requisite state-level control is lacking, and the Eleventh Amendment does not shield the entity from suit in federal court.

Turning to the instant case, I believe that sufficient indicia of control exist to support a finding of immunity for the Port Authority, and hence, for the PATH. New Jersey and New York each select and may remove 6 of the Port Authority's 12 commissioners. The Governors of each State may veto the actions of that State's commissioners. The quorum requirements specify that "no action of the port authority shall be binding unless taken at a meeting at which at least three of the members from each state are present, and unless a majority of the members from each state present at such meeting but in any event at least three of the members from each state, shall vote in favor thereof." Accordingly, each Governor's veto power is tantamount to a full veto power over the actions of the Commission. The Port Authority must make annual reports to the state legislatures, which in turn must approve changes in the Port Authority's rules and any new projects. Each State, and by extension, each State's electorate, exercises ample authority over the Port Authority. Without setting forth a shopping list of considerations that govern the control inquiry, suffice it to say that in this case, the whole is exactly the sum of its parts. I would hold that the Eleventh Amendment shields the PATH and Port Authority from suits in federal court. I respectfully dissent.

Notes & Questions

1. The Court noted early in its decision that it granted certiorari to resolve a split between the Second and Third Circuits. This is the same split that the Court acknowledged in *Feeney*, but did not resolve because it concluded that the states had waived their Eleventh Amendment immunity. The split was over an interpretation of the compact—the state treasury factor from *Lake Country Estates.* Is there a risk of "self-serving" interpretation of a compact (using Justice Frankfurter's language describing West Virginia's action in *West Virginia ex rel. Dyer v. Sims*) where, as here, federal circuit courts differ in their interpretation of the compact?

2. In her dissent, Justice O'Connor stated, "But the consent clause neither transforms the nature of state power nor makes Congress a full-fledged participant in the underlying agreement." 513 U.S. at 57. Was Justice O'Connor disagreeing with the holding in *Cuyler v. Adams* that consent transforms a compact into federal law?

3. Justice O'Connor also noted that the Court "has not as yet had occasion to find an interstate entity shielded by the Eleventh Amendment from suit in federal court." 513 U.S. at 56. Was she suggesting that the *Lake Country Estates* test might not be appropriate? What other tests might be appropriate?

4. Justice O'Connor argued, "I would presume the applicability of the Eleventh Amendment to interstate entities unless Congress clearly and expressly indicates otherwise." 513 U.S. at 58. Is this presumption consistent with how the Court has treated other constitutional requirements concerning compacts, such as Congress impliedly consenting to a compact?

Justice O'Connor also stated that there is no reason to change the standard Eleventh Amendment immunity analysis for interstate agencies. But doesn't the Court treat compact agencies differently in so many ways? What is different about the Eleventh Amendment such that the dissent would treat interstate agencies the same as states?

5. The majority adopted much of the reasoning in Justice Brennan's concurrence in *Feeney* only four years earlier. Couldn't the Court have avoided reviewing this case if the *Feeney* majority had adopted Justice Brennan's reasoning. Was there anything in the *Feeney* case that prevented the Court from ruling on the "arm of the state" argument?

Between *Feeney* (1990) and *Hess* (1994), the Court saw a sizeable turnover: Justice Souter replaced Justice Brennan in 1990 (after *Feeney*); Justice Thomas replaced Justice Marshall in 1991; Justice Ginsburg replaced Justice White (who was not in the *Feeney* concurrence) in 1993; and Justice Breyer replaced Justice Blackmun in 1994 (before *Hess*). As well, Justice Kennedy, who had voted with the majority in *Feeney* (and not in support of Justice Brennan's concurrence), voted with Justice Ginsburg's majority in *Hess*.

6. Justice Ginsburg's majority opinion cited to Vincent V. Thursby, *Interstate Cooperation: A Study of the Interstate Compact* (1953), one of the few books about compacts published in the 1950s and 1960s. Ironically, the Harvard Law Review gave this book a poor review, stating in part, "it displays neither a firsthand acquaintance with the practice nor an imaginative grasp of the problems in the compact field," and "[a]lthough not without value, the present work appears rather pedestrian and may not prove very helpful in the continued use and future development of the compact device." Book Note, 68 HARV. L. REV. 567, 568 (1954). However, Professor Thursby seems to have had the last laugh; the U.S. Supreme Court has quoted his book twice; the New Hampshire and Vermont Supreme Courts, the Third Circuit, and one U.S. District Court have all also quoted his book; and the Library of Congress Legislative Research Service cited it in 1958 hearings on consent to the Great Lakes Basin Compact.

II. State Eleventh Amendment Immunity from Actions by Compact Agencies

In *Entergy, Arkansas, Inc. v. Nebraska*, 201 F.3d 887 (8th Cir. 2000), the Central Interstate Low-Level Radioactive Waste Commission and several utilities sued Nebraska in federal court, claiming that it had not fulfilled its compact obligation to license a low-level radioactive waste disposal facility. Nebraska raised several defenses, including sovereign immunity under the Eleventh Amendment. The Eighth Circuit concluded that the compact, which requires the Commission to enforce the obligations it imposes on the party states in "any court of law, or any Federal, state or local agency board or Commission that has jurisdiction over any matter arising under or relating to the terms of the provisions of this compact" was a waiver of sovereign immunity. Additionally, the Eighth Circuit concluded that the district court had jurisdiction under *Ex parte Young*, which allows suits against state officers in federal court for prospective relief to stop an ongoing violation of a federal right, noting, "The rights that the Commission seeks to enforce are federal rights which arise under the Compact." *Id.* at 897.

In contrast, in *Waterfront Comm'n of N.Y. Harbor v. Murphy*, 961 F.3d 234 (3d Cir. 2020), the Waterfront Commission sued the New Jersey Governor to enjoin him from implementing a state law that Governor Chris Christie signed on his last day in office that authorized the governor to terminate New Jersey's participation in the Waterfront Compact and transfer responsibilities and assets to the New Jersey State Police. The district court granted the injunction, but the Third Circuit concluded that the suit was against the state, which enjoyed sovereign immunity from suit in federal court. The Third Circuit concluded,

> This suit is no mere attempt to compel or forestall a state official's actions consistent with *Ex parte Young*'s holding. Rather, when we compare the Commission's allegations about [the state law] with the [law's] text, we observe that the Commission attempts to pry back its authority to assess employers, in direct conflict with [the law's] provisions. On these facts, where a judgment for the Commission would divert state treasury funding and thereby operate against the State, we conclude that New Jersey is the real, substantial party in interest." *Id.* at 241.

The court remanded the case back to the district court with an instruction to dismiss the case.

The Third and Eighth circuits appear to be in conflict on the right to sue a state official in federal court to prevent a violation of a compact. Where suit in federal court is unavailable, must a compact agency seeking to compel a state to perform the compact bring suit against the non-performing state in that state's own court? Can that state be objective in such a suit?

III. Non-Eleventh Amendment Immunity

When states create compact agencies, those agencies typically enjoy sovereign immunity from suit much like other government agencies; however, the source or scope of that immunity is not always clear. Most often, these questions arise when a plaintiff seeks a type of relief that a compact does not specify or when the nature of the compact agency action is unclear.

Tinsley v. Wash. Metro. Area Transit Auth.
429 Md. 217 (2012)

BATTAGLIA, JUDGE:

. . . .

The WMATA Compact is an interstate agreement among Maryland, Virginia, and the District of Columbia to create an interstate entity responsible for overseeing a mass transportation system in and around the District of Columbia. . . . By virtue of Congressional ratification, issues involving the interpretation of the Compact are questions of federal law. . . .

Central to this case is the doctrine of state sovereign immunity. Under this doctrine, courts do not have jurisdiction to hear cases involving claims for money damages against the State, absent the State's consent to such suit. . . .

In considering whether the doctrine of sovereign immunity prevents a court from exercising jurisdiction in a given suit, we ask "'(1) whether the entity asserting immunity qualifies for the protection; and, if so, (2) whether the legislature has waived immunity either directly or by necessary implication, in a manner that would render the defense of immunity unavailable.'" *Beka Indus. [v. Worcester County Bd. Of Educ.]*, 419 Md. [194,] 206 [(2011)].

WMATA enjoys sovereign immunity as a result of the Compact's signatories "confer[ring] their respective sovereign immunities upon it." *Morris v. Washington Metropolitan Transit Authority*, 781 F.2d 218, 219 (D.C. Cir. 1986). WMATA's sovereign immunity has been waived, under certain circumstances, by Section 80 of the Compact, which states:

> The Authority shall be liable for its contracts and for its torts and those of its directors, officers, employees and agents committed in the conduct of any proprietary function, in accordance with the law of the applicable signatory (including rules on conflict of laws), but shall not be liable for any torts occurring in the performance of a governmental function. The exclusive remedy for such breach of contracts and torts for which the Authority shall be liable, as herein provided, shall be by suit against the Authority. Nothing contained in this title shall be construed as a waiver by the District of Columbia, Maryland, Virginia and the counties and cities within the zone of any immunity from suit.

Section 10-204(80) of the Transportation Article, Md. Code (1977, 2008 Repl. Vol.).

Under Section 80 of the Compact, WMATA has waived immunity for proprietary functions but retained it for governmental functions. To determine whether a function is proprietary or governmental, courts, both federal and state, within the jurisdiction in which WMATA operates, employ a test in which the controlling inquiry is whether the challenged activity involves an element of discretion or choice that is "grounded in social, economic, and political policy." *Berkovitz v. United States*, 486 U.S. 531, 537 (1988) (internal quotations omitted). If the activity does involve an element of choice grounded in public policy, it is governmental and the agency is immune from suit; if the activity does not involve an exercise of discretion, or the discretion is not grounded in concerns of public policy, then the agency does not enjoy immunity for the action.

. . . .

Although we have considered very few cases involving the WMATA Compact, our colleagues on the United States Courts of Appeals for the Fourth and District of Columbia Circuits have issued a myriad of opinions involving WMATA's immunity. As was thoroughly explained by the United States Court of Appeals for the District of Columbia Circuit, when considering whether WMATA was entitled to immunity in *Morris* . . ., WMATA's immunity protects the States in which WMATA operates from money judgments against them. As that court wrote, "We think that, where an agency is so structured, that, as a practical matter, if the agency is to survive, a judgment must expend itself against state treasuries, common sense and the rationale of the eleventh amendment require that sovereign immunity attach to the agency." [*Morris*, 781 F.2d] at 227. As is evident, the purpose of WMATA's immunity is to shield the State from demands for money judgments. *See also Proctor v. Washington Metropolitan Area Transit Authority*, 412 Md. 691, 711 (2010) (stating that, under the general principle of sovereign immunity, "the State and its agencies [can] not be sued unless the General Assembly authorized suit and enabled State agencies to obtain funds necessary to satisfy judgments" (emphasis added) (internal quotations omitted)). WMATA's immunity, however, is not absolute. As Section 80 of the Compact makes clear, its immunity is limited to governmental functions rather than proprietary functions.

In considering the distinction between governmental and proprietary functions, both the United States Courts of Appeals for the Fourth and District of Columbia Circuits have employed a test, developed under the Federal Tort Claims Act, 28 U.S.C. § 2671 et seq. (2012), under which the court determines whether the activity is "discretionary" or "ministerial," *Smith v. Washington Metropolitan Area Transit Authority*, 290 F.3d 201 (4th Cir. 2002); *Sanders v. Washington Metropolitan Area Transit Authority*, 819 F.2d 1151, 1154–55 (D.C. Cir. 1987), rather than whether it is governmental or proprietary, as is expressed in the Compact. As the Fourth Circuit recognized, however, the discretionary/ministerial distinction is merely a tool for analysis:

Although these two tests—"governmental/proprietary" and "discretionary/ministerial"—are not coterminous, the discretionary acts of public officials are recognized as being "within a subset of governmental functions." . . .

The Court of Special Appeals,[*] in [this case], also employed the language used in the federal circuit courts' cases, because neither this court nor the United State Supreme Court had interpreted Section 80 with respect to what constitutes a governmental or proprietary function. We, however, prefer to rely on the lan-

---

[*] [*Ed. Note*: The Court of Special Appeals is the intermediate court in Maryland.]

guage of the Compact for the distinction, that being governmental and proprietary, rather than the Federal Tort Claims Act distinction, to conform with the Statute, although our evaluation necessarily will rely on federal cases involving the latter analysis.

. . . .

Notes & Questions

1. Note the court's quote from *Morris v. Wash. Metro. Transit Auth.*, 781 F.2d 218, 219 (D.C. Cir. 1986): "WMATA enjoys sovereign immunity as a result of the Compact's signatories 'confer[ring] their respective sovereign immunities upon it.'" Can the states confer "their" respective sovereign immunities on a compact (*i.e.*, a non-state) agency? Can Congress require the states confer their sovereign immunity as a condition of consent? What immunities would apply if the states' immunities differ under state law? Would one state's immunity apply if that immunity was not available in another party state? What immunity would apply if the states' immunities conflicted as to scope of the immunity?

2. *Jacobson v. Tahoe Reg'l Planning Agency*, 566 F.2d 1353 (9th Cir. 1977), considered whether compact agency officials are entitled to legislative immunity, that is, immunity of a legislator from civil liability when acting in a legislative capacity.

> "Absolute immunity is given to legislators for actions performed in their legislative function. . . .
>
> . . . The question of immunity for officers acting under the authority of an interstate compact has not been squarely addressed, but we believe that such compacts, by their very nature, establish regional legislatures. In an area such as the Lake Tahoe Basin the legislature of either state could not deal effectively with problems that demand the consideration of a body which can weigh regional interests and wisdom. We discern no reason why these 'regional legislators' should not be accorded the same immunity as their state and national counterparts.

Id. at 1365. The U.S. Supreme Court accepted review of *Jacobson* and issued its decision *sub nom, Lake Country Estates, Inc. v. Tahoe Reg'l Planning Agency*, 440 U.S. 391 (1979) which you read above. The Supreme Court affirmed the Ninth Circuit's decision that the TRPA officials enjoy legislative immunity.

3. In *Tinsley*, the Maryland Supreme Court distinguished between governmental and proprietary functions because section 80 of the Washington Metropolitan Area Transit Regulation Compact creates that distinction. Government functions include policy development, administration, and enforcement. Proprietary functions include other actions such as operating utilities and purchasing. Where courts use this distinction, they typically conclude that common governmental immunities apply for government functions, not for agreements involving proprietary endeavors. However, courts and scholars regularly criticize this distinction as unworkable. *E.g.*, *Hillerby v. Town of Colchester*, 167 Vt. 270, 285–87 (1997) (citing cases criticizing the distinction dating back to 1943); Hugh D. Spitzer, *Realigning the Governmental/Proprietary Distinction in Municipal Law*, 40 SEATTLE U.

L. REV. 173 (2016). Dissatisfied with the governmental/proprietary distinction, the D.C. Circuit Court of Appeals re-characterized the terms in section 80 of the Transit Regulation Compact as "discretionary" and "ministerial" functions. *See Dant v. Dist. of Columbia*, 829 F.2d 69, 74 (D.C. Cir. 1987).

4. In *Hubble v. Bi-State Dev. Agency of the Illinois-Missouri Metro. Dist.*, 238 Ill. 2d 262 (2002), the Illinois Supreme Court concluded that Bi-State, an agency created by an interstate compact is a "local public entity" as defined by the Illinois Local Governmental and Governmental Employees Tort Immunity Act because it falls within the catchall phrase in the Tort Act's definition of "local public entity": "or any not-for-profit corporation organized for the purpose of conducting other business." The effect of this holding was important because the Tort Immunity Act provides a one-year statute of limitations, whereas the general statute of limitations for personal injuries in Illinois is two years.

Compare this holding with the holding in the *Pacific States Marine Fisheries Commission* case discussed in Chapter 4. Recall in that case the Oregon Supreme Court concluded that the commission was not "in this state." It reasoned that the entities listed in the applicable statute—irrigation districts, drainage districts, water districts, and municipal corporations—refer to entities whose geographic boundaries are in Oregon and that serve geographic areas primarily within the state, whereas the Pacific States Marine Fisheries Commission serves several states. The Oregon Supreme Court also interpreted the statutory phrase, "all other public . . . corporations," a non-specific term, to share the same qualities as the specific terms that precede it.

By comparison, the applicable definition in *Hubble* is:

> "Local public entity" includes a county, township, municipality, municipal corporation, school district, school board, educational service region, regional board of school trustees, trustees of schools of townships, treasurers of schools of townships, community college district, community college board, forest preserve district, park district, fire protection district, sanitary district, museum district, emergency telephone system board, and all other local governmental bodies. "Local public entity" also includes library systems and any intergovernmental agency or similar entity formed pursuant to the Constitution of the State of Illinois or the Intergovernmental Cooperation Act as well as any not-for-profit corporation organized for the purpose of conducting public business. It does not include the State or any office, officer, department, division, bureau, board, commission, university or similar agency of the State.

745 ILL. COMP. STAT. 10/1-206. Is an interstate compact agency similar to the specific terms in this definition? Is a compact agency formed under the Illinois Constitution or the Illinois Intergovernmental Cooperation Act? Is it a state agency that the definition explicitly excludes?

CHAPTER 8: RELATIONSHIP BETWEEN STATE LAW AND COMPACTS

Because states enact compacts as statutes, the relationship between compacts and new or existing state law presents an interesting study. One scholar wrote long ago, "Once the Compact becomes effective, it is binding upon the legislatures of the compacting States, and the passage of statutes which are inconsistent, or any attempt by the State legislatures to repudiate, has been held void. It is also binding upon administrative officials, the Courts, and citizens of the signatory states." H.B. Rubenstein, *The Interstate Compact—A Survey*, 27 TEMP. L.Q. 320, 327 (1953) (citations omitted). *See also* FREDERICK L. ZIMMERMANN & MITCHELL WENDELL, THE LAW AND USE OF INTERSTATE COMPACTS 43 (1961). While this is an accurate statement of the law, neither the law nor its application is so straightforward. It wasn't then, and it has become more complicated since then. The texts of compacts may specifically allow states to apply their own law, or prohibit state law, and there is no single test that courts have used or continue to use for determining whether state law applies in the absence of compact language.

Some compacts specify the relationship between the compact and federal and state laws. For example, the former Southern Dairy Compact, art. II, § 3(a), stated, "This compact shall not be construed to displace existing federal milk orders or state dairy regulation in the region but to supplement them." Similarly, the Interstate Library Compact, art. III, similarly states, "Nothing in this compact or in any library agreement shall be construed to supersede, alter or otherwise impair any obligation imposed on any library by otherwise applicable law . . . ." In another example, Congress's consent to the Central Interstate Low-Level Radioactive Waste Compact, art. VI, §§ b, c, states, "No party state shall pass or enforce any law or regulation which is inconsistent with this compact" and "All laws and regulations or parts thereof of any party state which are inconsistent with this compact are hereby declared null and void for the purposes of this compact." Many new compacts have similar provisions; however, older compacts are typically silent about the relationship to state law.

Most of the cases about the relationship between a compact and state law involve compacts that have received Congress's consent, which would make them federal law under *Cuyler v. Adams*, and thus a simple federal supremacy analysis might have resolved them. Surprisingly, though, federal supremacy has played little role in this jurisprudence. More often, courts have analyzed these problems as contractual issues, occasionally using methods of statutory construction, for resolving conflicts of law. As you read the cases and notes in this chapter consider why courts have taken so many different directions when resolving the relationship between a specific compact and a specific state law.

I. Constitutional Restraint on Applying State Law

The now-familiar *Green v. Biddle* case leads off again. Recall that this case involved the question whether two Kentucky statutes violated the compact between Virginia and Kentucky, which preserved Virginia law upon the creation of Kentucky out of Virginia land in 1789. Excerpts of this case in Chapters 2 and 4 looked at the two principal objections to the compact—whether Congress properly gave its consent, and whether the compact was invalid because the states surrendered a slice of their individual sovereignty when enacting it. Here, we reread some of those materials and the Court's continuing discussion with an eye toward how the Court looks at the relationship between the compact and the statutes. Read carefully for the Court's discussion of a constitutional restraint on applying state law to a compact.

Green v. Biddle

21 U.S. (8 Wheat.) 1 (1823)

Story, Justice:

. . . .

Various objections were made to the literal construction of the compact, one only of which we deem it necessary particularly to notice. That was, that if it be so construed as to deny to the legislature of Kentucky the right to pass the act in question, it will follow, that that State cannot pass laws to affect lands, the title to which was derived under Virginia, although the same should be wanted for public use. If such a consequence grows necessarily out of this provision of the compact, still we can perceive no reason why the assent to it by the people of Kentucky should not be binding on the legislature of that State. Nor can we perceive, why the admission of the conclusion involved in the argument should invalidate an express article of the compact in relation to a quite different subject. The agreement, that the rights of claimants under Virginia should remain as valid and secure as they were under the laws of that State, contains a plain, intelligible proposition, about the meaning of which, it is impossible there can be two opinions. Can the government of Kentucky fly from this agreement, acceded to by the people in their sovereign capacity, because it involves a principle which might be inconvenient, or even pernicious to the State, in some other respect? The Court cannot perceive how this proposition could be maintained.

But the fact is, that the consequence drawn by counsel from a literal construction of this article of the compact, cannot be fairly deduced from the premises, because, by the common law of Virginia, if not by the universal law of all free governments, private property may be taken for public use, upon making to the individual a just compensation. The admission of this principle never has been imagined by any person as rendering his right to property less valid and secure than it would be were it excluded; and, consequently, it would be an unnatural and forced construction of this article of the compact, to say, that it included such a case.

We pass over the other observations of counsel upon the construction of this article, with the following remark: that where the words of a law, treaty, or contract, have a plain and obvious meaning, all construction, in hostility with such meaning, is excluded. This is a maxim of law, and a dictate of common sense; for were a different rule to be admitted, no man, however cautious and intelligent, could safely estimate the extent of his engagements, or rest upon his own understanding of a law, until a judicial construction of those instruments had been obtained.

We now come to the consideration of the question, whether this Court has authority to declare the act in question unconstitutional and void, upon the ground, that it impairs the obligation of the compact? This is denied for the following reasons: It is insisted, in the first place, that this Court has no such authority, where the objection to the validity of the law is founded upon its opposition to the constitution of Kentucky, as it was, in part, in this case. It will be a sufficient answer to this observation, that our opinion is founded exclusively upon the constitution of the United States.

2dly. It was objected, that Virginia and Kentucky, having fixed upon a tribunal to determine the meaning of the compact, the jurisdiction of this Court is excluded. If this be so, it must be admitted, that all controversies which involve a construction of the compact, are equally excluded from the jurisdiction of the State Courts of Virginia and Kentucky. How, then, are those controversies, which we were informed by the counsel on both sides crowded the Federal and State Courts of Kentucky, to be settled? The answer, we presume, would be, by Commissioners, to be appointed by those States. But none such have been appointed; what then? Suppose either of those States, Virginia for example, should refuse to appoint Commissioners? Are the occupants of lands, to which they have no title, to retain their possessions until this tribunal is appointed, and to enrich themselves, in the mean time, by the profits of them, not only to the injury of non-residents, but of the citizens of Kentucky? The supposition of such a state of things is too monstrous to be for a moment entertained. The best feelings of our nature revolt against a construction which leads to it.

But how happens it that the questions submitted to this Court have been entertained, and decided, by the Courts of Kentucky, for twenty-five years, as we were informed by the counsel? Have these Courts, cautious and learned as they must be acknowledged to be, committed the crime of usurping a jurisdiction which did not belong to them? We should feel very unwilling to come to such a conclusion.

The answer, in a few words, to the whole of the argument, is to be found in the explicit language of that provision of the compact, which respects the tribunal of the Commissioners. It is to be appointed in no case but where a complaint, or dispute shall arise, not between individuals, but between the Commonwealth of Virginia and the State of Kentucky, in their high sovereign characters.

Having thus endeavoured to clear the question of these preliminary objections, we have only to add, by way of conclusion, that the duty, not less than the power of this Court, as well as of every other Court in the Union, to declare a law unconstitutional, which impairs the obligation of contracts, whoever may be the parties to them, is too clearly enjoined by the constitution itself, and too firmly established by the decisions of this and other Courts, to be now shaken; and that those decisions entirely cover the present case.

A slight effort to prove that a compact between two States is not a case within the meaning of the constitution, which speaks of contracts, was made by the counsel for the tenant, but was not much pressed. If we attend to the definition of a contract, which is the agreement of two or more parties, to do, or not to do, certain acts, it must be obvious, that the propositions offered, and agreed to by Virginia, being accepted and ratified by Kentucky, is a contract. In fact, the terms compact and contract are synonymous: and in *Fletcher v. Peck*, the Chief Justice defines a contract to be a compact between two or more parties. The principles laid down in that case are, that the constitution of the United States embraces all contracts, executed or executory, whether between individuals, or between a State and individuals; and that a State has no more power to impair an obligation into which she herself has entered, than she can the contracts of individuals. Kentucky, therefore, being a party to the compact which guarantied to claimants of land lying in that State, under titles derived from Virginia, their rights, as they existed under the laws of Virginia, was incompetent to violate that contract, by passing any law which rendered those rights less valid and secure.

. . . .

Notes & Questions

1. The Supreme Court asked, "Can the government of Kentucky fly from this agreement, acceded to by the people in their sovereign capacity, because it involves a principle which might be inconvenient, or even pernicious to the State, in some other respect? The Court cannot perceive how this proposition could be maintained." 21 U.S. at 89. *Green v. Biddle* is the first time the Supreme Court considered the relationship between state law and a compact.

2. Reread this paragraph:

> We now come to the consideration of the question, whether this Court has authority to declare the act in question unconstitutional and void, upon the ground, that it impairs the obligation of the compact? This is denied for the following reasons: It is insisted, in the first place, that this Court has no such authority, where the objection to the validity of the law is founded upon its opposition to the constitution of Kentucky, as it was, in part, in this case. It will be a sufficient answer to this observation, that our opinion is founded exclusively upon the constitution of the United States.

21 U.S. at 90. Essentially, the Court held that a state law that violates the Kentucky Constitution (which was a product of the compact) violates the U.S. Constitution. But which clause of the Constitution was the Court's concern? The last two paragraphs of the excerpt seem to indicate the Court was considering the Contracts Clause.

3. Ten years later, in *Barron v. Baltimore,* 32 U.S. (7 Pet.) 243 (1833), the U.S. Supreme Court observed that if congressional consent is necessary, then the compact is a subject entrusted to the federal government, and hence, there is a constitutional restraint on state legislation:

> It is worthy of remark, too, that these inhibitions generally restrain state legislation on subjects intrusted to the general government, or in which the people of all the states feel an interest. A state is forbidden to enter into any treaty, alliance or confederation. If these compacts are with foreign nations, they interfere with the treaty-making power, which is conferred entirely on the general government; if with each other, for political purposes, they can scarcely fail to interfere with the general purpose and intent of the constitution.

Id. at 248. Why did the Supreme Court use this supremacy reasoning and not follow its recent precedent in *Green v. Biddle* and find a violation of the Contracts Clause? Curiously, there are few subsequent cases in which courts analyze conflicts between state law and a compact in supremacy terms. In 2013, the Supreme Court only mentioned supremacy in a footnote. *Tarrant Reg'l Water Dist. v. Herrmann*, 569 U.S. 614, 627 n.8 (2013).

4. More often, courts cite the Contracts Clause. For example, in *Aveline v. Pa. Bd. of Prob. and Parole*, 729 A.2d 1254 (Pa. Commw. Ct. 1999), the court noted, "the Contracts Clause of the United States Constitution protects compacts from impairment by the states. This means that upon enacting a compact, it takes precedence over the subsequent statutes of signatory states and, as such, a state may not unilaterally nullify, revoke or amend one of its compacts if the compact does not so provide." *Id.* at 1257 n.10 (citing Jill E. Hasday, *Interstate Compacts in a Democratic Society: The Problem of Permanence*, 49 FLA. L. REV. 1 (1997)). *Aveline* involved the Interstate Compact for Supervision of Parolees and Probationers, which had received congressional consent. Why didn't the supremacy of federal law control? When should a court use a Supremacy analysis versus a Contracts Clause analysis?

Traditionally, the court considers whether a statute impairs a contract and if so, then whether the change in law was reasonable and necessary to serve an important public purpose (intermediate scrutiny, neither rational nor strict). *See, e.g.*, *U.S. Trust Co. of N.Y. v. New Jersey*, 431 U.S. 1, 22, 25 (1976). Are compacts unique such that the Commonwealth Court in *Aveline* would not apply the full Contracts Clause analysis?

5. The dissent in *Wroblewski v. Pa. Dep't of Transp.*, 570 Pa. 249 (2002) (Zappala, J., dissenting), gave an enticingly simple contractual (but not Contracts Clause) analysis: "[I]n its essence, the Driver's License Compact is simply a contract between the forty party jurisdictions that have enacted the Driver's License Compact into law. I cannot discern any tenet of contract law which permits the unilateral modification of a contract by one of the contracting parties in the absence of specific language in the contract authorizing unilateral modification." *Id.* at 261. The Driver License Compact did not require consent, so the Supremacy

Clause analysis was unavailable, which may help explain why the court applied contract law. Not surprisingly, no compact allows just one state to unilaterally modify the compact. Should this reasoning apply to every case?

The majority in *Wroblewski* criticized Justice Zappala's focus on contract principles, stating, "Despite the effort expended in the dissenting opinion (an effort which exceeds that of the Appellant), respectfully, we cannot subscribe to Mr. Chief Justice Zappala's attempt to apply general contract principles to invalidate an act of the General Assembly." *Id.* at 256 n.6. The majority's criticism suggests that compacts without consent are fundamentally different from compacts with consent such that states should be able to more easily apply other state law. Other cases directly involving this issue are discussed in Section III below in this chapter.

6. Recall *West Virginia ex rel. Dyer v. Sims* from Chapter 3. In 1939, West Virginia ratified and approved the Ohio River Valley Water Sanitation Compact, managing water pollution. Article X of the compact provided that the states agreed "to appropriate for salaries, office and other administrative expenses, their proper proportion of the annual budget as determined by the Commission and approved by the Governors of the signatory states ...." In its 1949 session, the West Virginia Legislature appropriated its contribution; however, Edgar B. Sims, the state auditor, refused to pay it. The West Virginia members of the Compact Commission and the West Virginia State Water Commission sought direct relief in the West Virginia Supreme Court. The West Virginia Supreme Court found the Act ratifying the compact invalid under the West Virginia Constitution because it: (1) delegated West Virginia's police powers to other states and the federal government; (2) bound future legislatures to make appropriations for the compact; and (3) violated West Virginia's constitutional debt limitation provision. The U.S. Supreme Court reversed, with suggestions that it was analyzing West Virginia's unilateral actions in terms of a contract. The actions in this case were by a state official and the state Supreme Court. Read the quotes below and consider whether these concerns would still be valid if the case had involved action by the West Virginia Legislature enacting a new statute that conflicted with the compact.

> But a compact is after all a legal document. Though the circumstances of its drafting are likely to assure great care and deliberation, all avoidance of disputes as to scope and meaning is not within human gift. Just as this Court has power to settle disputes between States where there is no compact, it must have final power to pass upon the meaning and validity of compacts. It requires no elaborate argument to reject the suggestion that an agreement solemnly entered into between States by those who alone have political authority to speak for a State can be unilaterally nullified or given final meaning by an organ of one of the contracting States. A State cannot be its own ultimate judge in a controversy within a sister State.

341 U.S. at 28.

> Since the Constitution provided the compact for adjusting interstate relations, compacts may be enforced despite otherwise valid state restrictions on state action.

341 U.S. at 34 (Reed, J. concurring).

> West Virginia officials induced sister States to contract with her and Congress to consent to the Compact. She now attempts to read herself out of this interstate Compact by reading into her Constitution a limitation upon the powers of her Governor and Legislature to contract.
>
> West Virginia, for internal affairs, is free to interpret her own Constitution as she will. But if the compact system is to have vitality and integrity, she may not raise an issue of *ultra vires*, decide it, and release herself from an interstate obligation. The legal consequence which flow from the formal participation in a compact consented to by Congress is a federal question for this Court.
>
> . . . Whatever she now says her Constitution means, she may not apply retroactively that interpretation to place an unforeseeable construction upon what the other States to the Compact were entitled to believe was a fully authorized act.

341 U.S. at 35 (Jackson, J. concurring).

7. *Franchise Tax Board v. Hyatt*, 139 S. Ct. 1485 (2019), a non-compact case, suggested the prohibition against a state imposing its own law on a compact agency has another source. In that case, the Court decided that the U.S. Constitution does not permit a state to be sued by a private party without its consent in the courts of a different state. Justice Thomas, writing for the majority, stated that the "Constitution embeds interstate sovereign immunity within the constitutional design," *id.* at 1497, citing two provisions of the Constitution. One of those provisions was the Compact Clause, which Justice Thomas noted deprives states of the "independent power to . . . enter into treaties or compacts . . ." Justice Thomas also cited Court precedent illustrating that the "Constitution also reflects implicit alterations to the States' relationships with each other, confirming they are no longer fully independent nations." *Id.* Discussing those "alterations," Justice Thomas noted:

> For example, States may not supply rules of decision governing "disputes implicating the[ir] conflicting rights." *Texas Industries, Inc. v. Radcliff Materials, Inc.*, 451 U.S. 630, 641 (1981). Thus, no State can apply its own law to interstate disputes over borders, *Cissna v. Tennessee*, 246 U.S. 289, 295 (1918), water rights, *Hinderlider v. La Plata River & Cherry Creek Ditch Co.*, 304 U.S. 92, 110 (1938), or the interpretation of interstate compacts, *Petty v. Tennessee-Missouri Bridge Comm'n*, 359 U.S. 275, 278-279 (1959). The States would have had the raw power to apply their own law to such matters before they entered the Union, but the Constitution implicitly forbids that exercise of power because the

> "interstate . . . nature of the controversy makes it inappropriate for state law to control." *Texas Industries, supra,* at 641.

Id. at 1497–98 (parallel citations omitted). In citing the Compact Clause and *Hinderlider* and *Petty* (both compact law cases), was the Court suggesting that the prohibition against applying state law to an interstate compact is also embedded in the constitutional design?

8. In *Texas Industries, Inc. v. Radcliff Materials, Inc.*, 451 U.S. 630 (1981), the Supreme Court discussed the power of the federal courts to fashion common law, stating,

> absent some congressional authorization to formulate substantive rules of decision, federal common law exists only in such narrow areas as . . . interstate and international disputes implicating the conflicting rights of States . . . . In these instances, our federal system does not permit the controversy to be resolved under state law . . . because the interstate or international nature of the controversy makes it inappropriate for state law to control.

Id. at 641. Should all interstate compact disputes be inappropriate for state law to control? Certainly, disputes where two or more states dispute the meaning of a compact would seem inappropriate to resolve under state law; can you make an argument that a compact agency's action against a private party would also be inappropriate for state law to control? If the interstate nature of a controversy involving an interstate compact makes state law inappropriate for federal courts to apply, does the same reasoning apply to interstate compact controversies in state court?

9. Prior to *Green v. Biddle*, there were several cases concerning whether an adjudicated owner of land to which Virginia and Kentucky had granted to different people had to pay the occupant for the value of his improvements to the land. *E.g., Fowler v. Halbert*, 7 Ky. (4 Bibb) 52 (1815).

10. After *Green v. Biddle*, in *Hawkins v. Barney's Lessee*, 30 U.S. (5 Pet.) 457 (1831), the Supreme Court was concerned with the subservient relationship the compact would create if land in Kentucky that originated with Virginia land grants would always be subject to Virginia law.

> It can scarcely be supposed that Kentucky would have consented to accept a limited and crippled sovereignty: nor is it doing justice to Virginia to believe that she would have wished to reduce Kentucky to a state of vassalage. Yet it would be difficult, if the literal and rigid construction necessary to exclude her from passing this law were to be adopted; it would be difficult, I say, to assign her a position higher than that of a dependant on Virginia. Let the language of the compact be literally applied, and we have the anomaly presented of a sovereign state governed by the laws of another sovereign; of one half the territory of a sovereign state hopelessly and forever subjected to the laws of another state. Or a motley multiform administration of laws, under which A. would be subject to one class of laws, because holding under a Virginia grant; while B., his next door neighbour, claiming

> from Kentucky, would hardly be conscious of living under the same government.

Id. at 466–67.

Cases involving the application of state law generally fall into two categories. Section II discusses compacts that authorize modification of the compact through subsequent state statutes. Section III discusses when a state may apply its own law to a compact that does not expressly authorize the states to modify it. The cases in sections II and III typically involve statutory law, but cases involving the application of state law also involve common law. Section IV specifically considers cases where courts expressly applied one state's common law to the compact. For all the cases in this chapter, consider whether the principles also apply to state regulations and other forms of state law.

II. Compacts that Authorize Modification by State Law

Not surprisingly, compacts that expressly authorize the states to modify the compact through subsequent state law require that all states to the compact must concur in that subsequent state law. Examples of these compacts include the compacts creating the Port Authority of New York and New Jersey (art. VII), the Waterfront Commission of New York Harbor (art. XVI); the Delaware River Port Authority (art. IV(q)), and the Tahoe Regional Planning Agency (art. X(b)). A common question in cases involving the application of state law in these compacts is whether one of the party states has concurred in the law of the other state. Courts generally consider two factors—whether the laws are substantially similar and whether each state legislature has expressed some intent that the new state law would apply to the compact at issue. Not surprisingly, courts do not apply these factors uniformly.

Malverty v. Waterfront Comm'n of N.Y. Harbor
71 N.Y.2d 977 (1988)

Opinion of the Court:

Petitioner commenced this proceeding to review a determination of respondent Waterfront Commission of New York Harbor denying his application for restoration to the longshoremen's register as a checker, contending that respondent had erroneously ignored the relevant provisions of article 23-A of [New York's] Correction Law. Respondent denied the application, in part, because of the serious nature of petitioner's four felony convictions arising out of two schemes to defraud two Las Vegas casinos and because, as a result of these two deliberate schemes, petitioner lacked the good character and integrity needed for the sensitive position of checker. [The] Supreme Court granted the petition to annul respondent's determination but the Appellate Division reversed and dismissed, reasoning that a rational basis existed for denying petitioner's application.

We agree with the Appellate Division, for the reasons stated in its memorandum, that a rational basis exists for respondent's determination under the Waterfront Commission Act. We add, however, with respect to an issue not considered by that court, that the provisions of article 23-A of the Correction Law do not apply to the New York/New Jersey Waterfront Commission.

The Waterfront Commission was established by Interstate Compact, approved by Congress, contained in title 29 of McKinney's Unconsolidated Laws of NY. Part I of title 29 is the Interstate Compact between New York and New Jersey; parts II and III consist of implementing provisions which were not part of the Interstate Compact approved by Congress but which were enacted by both the New York and New Jersey Legislatures pursuant to explicit congressional authority to amend and supplement the Compact in the manner provided. Parts I and II of the Waterfront Commission Act contain provisions detailing the Commission's power to regulate the employment of longshoremen on the New York/New Jersey waterfront.

New York and New Jersey have agreed, and Congress has authorized the two States, to amend and supplement the Interstate Compact, to implement the purposes thereof, by legislative action of either State concurred in by legislative action of the other State. The "Compact" between the two States includes the Interstate Compact approved by Congress and any duly enacted amendments or any supplements thereto. In the past, the New York Legislature has expressly stated that certain legislation was amending a certain portion of the "Compact" and that the new law would take effect upon the enactment into law by New Jersey of legislation having an effect identical to New York's legislation, unless New Jersey had already done so, in which case the amendment would take effect immediately.

In the present case, the absence from the text and legislative history of article 23-A of any reference to the Waterfront Commission, coupled with the absence of an express statement that the Legislature was amending or supplementing the provisions of the "Compact" and that article 23-A would take effect upon the enactment by New Jersey of legislation of identical effect, if it had not already done so, indicates that the New York Legislature never intended article 23-A to apply to the Waterfront Commission. That the two States have evinced the same, or similar, public policy regarding employment opportunities for former inmates by enacting similar "antidiscrimination" laws is not sufficient under the express terms of the "Compact" to render it properly amended or supplemented such that the Commission would be subject to the provisions or article 23-A. Respondent, therefore, did not err in failing to apply article 23-A in denying petitioner's application for restoration of his checker registration.

Notes & Questions

1. What did the court say was necessary for the states to amend the Waterfront Commission Act (the compact)? Was there precedent for this legal conclusion or did the court make legal precedent of the legislatures' past practices? Chapter 9 discusses methods courts use to interpret and apply compacts, including contract law principles such as course of performance.

2. Courts do not always analyze whether the states' legislatures intend for a specific statute to apply to a compact agency. For example, in *In re Commission Proceeding on Revocation of License of Pontoriero*, 439 N.J. Super. 24 (App. Div. 2015), the court had to determine what standard of review to apply to its review of a Waterfront Commission of New York Harbor adjudication. Article XI of the Waterfront Commission compact expressly allows judicial review of adjudications, but the compact does not specify the standards for judicial review. The court reviewed the law of both New Jersey and New York and ultimately applied New Jersey law after concluding that New York law is in accord with New Jersey law. The court, however, did not analyze whether the states' legislatures expressed an intent to apply the standards of review in the states' APAs to review of the Waterfront Commission's adjudications.

3. Do you agree that even identical laws should not apply to the compact unless the legislatures "indicated" their intent to apply those laws to the compact? The next case explains the importance of this requirement. *Local 542* is the clearest summary of the jurisprudence relating to the application of state law to compacts that contain such a provision, even though the Delaware River Joint Toll Bridge compact does not contain such a provision.

Int'l Union of Operating Eng'rs, Local 542 v. Delaware River Joint Toll Bridge Comm'n

311 F.3d 273 (3d Cir. 2002)

RENDELL, JUDGE:

At issue is whether state law applies to a bi-state agency. The International Union of Operating Engineers, Local 542, petitioned for a court order compelling the Delaware River Joint Toll Bridge Commission to comply with New Jersey collective bargaining laws. In granting summary judgment to the Commission, the District Court held that neither New Jersey nor Pennsylvania collective bargaining laws apply because the state legislatures have not expressed a clear intent to impose their labor laws upon the Commission. We will affirm.

I. Background

Under the Compact Clause, Article I, Section 10, Clause 3 of the United States Constitution, states may enter into agreements regarding matters of common concern provided they obtain the consent of Congress. In 1934, the legislatures of New Jersey and Pennsylvania created the Delaware River Joint Toll Bridge Commission (the "Commission") to operate certain bridges spanning the Delaware River. The Commission was consented to by act of Congress the following year. The Compact has since been amended by the states, which amendments have been approved by Congress. The most current version is dated March 1986.

. . . .

The Compact is entirely silent regarding the rights of Commission employees to collectively bargain and the duty of the Commission to collectively bargain with unions. The Compact also contains no provision regarding procedures for its amendment, or, especially relevant here, enabling the states to modify it by passing legislation that is "concurred in" by the other state.

In June 2001, the International Union of Operating Engineers, Local 542, ("Local 542") advised the Commission that a majority of the full-time and regular part-time toll collectors, maintenance employees, bridge officers, and tellers employed by the Commission had selected Local 542 as their exclusive representative for collective bargaining purposes. The Commission refused to recognize Local 542 as the employees' representative, explaining that the Compact does not confer upon Commission employees the right to organize. Local 542 then petitioned a New Jersey state court to order a union election pursuant to the New Jersey Employer-Employee Relations Act and the Pennsylvania Public Employee Relations Act. Both acts provide for an election among public employees to determine whether they wish to be represented by a labor union and require public employers to bargain collectively with the selected union. Neither act specifically states that it applies to the Commission or is intended to amend the Compact.

The Commission removed the case to the U.S. District Court for the District of New Jersey. Both parties moved for summary judgment. Local 542 argued that New Jersey and Pennsylvania's "complementary and parallel" employee relations acts effectively amended the Compact and therefore require the Commission to engage in collective bargaining. The Commission countered that a bi-state compact cannot be modified unless both state legislatures expressly state an intention to alter the compact. In an oral opinion, the District Court granted summary judgment in favor of the Commission. Local 542 appeals.

. . . .

III. Discussion

In creating the Delaware River Joint Toll Bridge Commission, New Jersey and Pennsylvania agreed to "the power sharing, coordination, and unified action that typify Compact Clause creations." *Hess v. Port Authority Trans-Hudson Corp.*, 513 U.S. 40, 41 (1994). Bi-state entities like the Commission are intended to address "interests and problems that do not coincide nicely * * * with State lines." *Id.* at 40. They are to be regarded not as extensions of each compacting state's authority, but rather as "independently functioning parts of a regional polity and of a national union." *Id.* By compacting together to form the Commission, New Jersey and Pennsylvania have each surrendered a portion of their sovereignty over certain Delaware River bridge operations in order to better serve the regional interest. Such a surrender of state sovereignty should be treated with great care, and the Supreme Court has stated that courts should not find a surrender unless it has been "expressed in terms too plain to be mistaken." *Jefferson Branch Bank v. Skelly*, 66 U.S. 436, 446 (1861).

Our role in interpreting the Compact is, therefore, to effectuate the clear intent of both sovereign states, not to rewrite their agreement or order relief inconsistent with its express terms. *Texas v. New Mexico*, 462 U.S. 554 (1983) (declining to alter the voting structure of the Pecos River Commission to break an impasse); *see also New Jersey v. New York*, 523 U.S. 767 (1998) (declining to redraw the boundary between New Jersey and New York for reasons of practicality and convenience). Although we understand the desire to bring the Commission under the auspices of New Jersey and Pennsylvania's employee relations acts, we conclude that to do so would be an act of legislation, rather than interpretation or enforcement. We can find no legislative intent to subject the Compact to the collective bargaining schemes of New Jersey or Pennsylvania. We will therefore affirm the District Court's grant of summary judgment.

A. The Legal Landscape

Local 542 urges that states may amend a bi-state compact by passing legislation that is substantially similar, without an express statement, either in the legislation or otherwise, that they intend to apply that law to the bi-state entity. This issue has been treated differently by different courts. In nearly every one of these cases, courts have been presented with a compact that addresses the issue of modification by including language enabling one state to modify the compact through legislation "concurred in" by the other. Here, the Compact contains no "concurred in" language. Nonetheless, an overview of the relevant case law in this area assists in understanding the issue before us.

The most notable difference of opinion regarding the interpretation of "concurred in" language is between the courts of New York and those of New Jersey. New York courts have interpreted the "concurred in" language in a compact to permit application of states' laws to the compact if the states' legislation contains an express statement that they intend to amend the compact. New Jersey courts have held that this language will be effective to apply the states' laws that are "complementary or parallel" even where there is no stated intent to amend the compact. Federal courts, including those in our circuit, have at various times adopted both approaches.

i. New York View

The New York standard was most clearly articulated by the Court of Appeals of New York in *Malverty v. Waterfront Commission of New York Harbor*, 524 N.E.2d 421, 422 (N.Y. 1988). In *Malverty*, the petitioner sought to apply New York Corrections Law to the Waterfront Commission of New York Harbor, a bi-state agency established by New York and New Jersey and approved by Congress. *Id.* at 421. The compact creating the Waterfront Commission included authorization "to amend and supplement the Interstate Compact, to implement the purposes thereof, by legislative action of either State concurred in by legislative action of the other State." *Id.* at 422. The *Malverty* court found "the absence from the text and legislative history of [the Corrections Law] of any reference to the Waterfront Commission, coupled with the absence of an express statement that the Legislature was amending or supplementing the provisions of the 'Compact' and that [the Corrections Law] would take effect upon the enactment by New Jersey of legislation of identical effect," to indicate that the New York legislature had never intended the Corrections Law to apply to the Waterfront Commission. The court noted, "That the two States have evinced the same, or similar, public policy regarding employment opportunities for former inmates by enacting similar 'anti-discrimination' laws is not sufficient under the express terms of the 'Compact' to render it properly amended or supplemented such that the Commission would be subject to the provisions of [New York's Corrections Law]." *Id.* It thus viewed the "concurred in" language to require an express statement to that effect.

ii. New Jersey View

New Jersey courts have taken a different tack, finding the passage of similar legislation by compacting states to satisfy the "concurred in" test and be sufficient to imply an intent on the part of both states to apply the legislation to a bi-state entity. *Bunk v. Port Auth. of New York & New Jersey*, 144 N.J. 176 [, 184] (1996). In *Bunk*, the court applied New Jersey's workers' compensation laws to the Port Authority of New York and New Jersey, a bi-state entity whose compact contains "concurred in" language, without examining whether either state had expressly intended its workers' compensation laws to apply. The court reasoned that the "corollary of the proposition that neither state may unilaterally impose its legislative will on the bi-state agency is that the agency may be subject to complementary or parallel legislation." *Id.* The court then examined New York and New Jersey's workers' compensation laws and found them "somewhat similar." *Id.* According to the New Jersey view, then, a state may meet the requirements of "concurring in" the other's legislation merely by passing a somewhat similar statute of its own.

iii. Federal Courts

Federal courts have followed both lines of reasoning when interpreting compacts containing "concurred in" language. Courts in the Second Circuit have uniformly adopted the express intent standard, finding the New York view "more in line with the language" of the compacts before them. *Baron v. Port Auth. of New York & New Jersey*, 968 F. Supp. 924, 929 (S.D.N.Y. 1997).

Within our circuit, however, the district courts have espoused both views. The District Court for the District of New Jersey has applied the New Jersey complementary or parallel standard. *Moore v. Del. River Port Auth.*, 80 F. Supp. 2d 264, 268 (D.N.J. 1999). In *Moore*, the court refused to apply New Jersey common law regarding wrongful discharge and breach of contract to the Delaware River Port Authority, a bi-state entity whose compact includes "concurred in" language. *Id.* at 271. In arriving at the result, however, the court analyzed whether the common law of New Jersey was substantially similar to the common law of Pennsylvania, bypassing any discussion as to what was required in order for a law of one state to be "concurred in" by the other.

In contrast, in *Delaware River Port Authority v. Fraternal Order of Police, Penn-Jersey Lodge 30*, 135 F. Supp. 2d 596, 609 (E.D. Pa. 2001), Judge Robreno in the District Court for the Eastern District of Pennsylvania noted that "as a general rule of statutory interpretation, surrenders of sovereignty are to be strictly construed in terms of their scope," *id.* at 603, concluding that "the ambiguous term 'concurred in' of [the Delaware River Port Authority compact should] be interpreted to require the express consent of both legislatures before additional duties are imposed" upon the bi-state entity. *Id.* at 604. The court further noted that the weight of authority supported the express intent standard, and that the New Jersey complementary or parallel standard was based on a misreading of the law of compacts. *Id.* at 604–05. The court went on to hold that because neither New Jersey nor Pennsylvania had expressly stated that they intended to impose their collective bargaining laws on the Delaware River Port Authority, they had not "concurred in" the application of those laws. *Id.* at 609.

On appeal, we did not reach the merits of Judge Robreno's ruling, or of either the New York express intent or the New Jersey complementary or parallel views, but reversed on different grounds, concluding that the parties' litigation involved an attack on a New Jersey judgment entitled to preclusive effect. *[Delaware River Port Authority v. Fraternal Order of Police, Penn-Jersey]* *Lodge 30*, 290 F.3d [567,] 572 [(3d Cir. 2002)]. The parties to the *Lodge 30* litigation were in privity with the parties in a case resolved in the New Jersey courts; we were therefore required to give preclusive effect to the New Jersey court's ruling regarding the complementary or parallel test.[4] 290 F.3d at 577. In dicta, however, we noted, "Were we sitting on the New Jersey courts, we might have interpreted the respective statutes and the DRPA's obligations to its patrol officers differently. But we may not reconsider the New Jersey judgment."[5] *Id.*

iv. Bridge Commission Compact Before Us

The cases discussed above all address the interpretation of bi-state compacts that expressly authorize the compacting states to amend the compact through legislation "concurred in" by the other. As we have noted, the Compact before us contains no such language, nor did the relevant laws of each state evince an intent to apply to the Compact as such. The only case to address a bi-state compact in a similar setting is *International Union of Operating Engineers, Local 68 v. Delaware River & Bay Authority*, 147 N.J. 433 (1997). In *Local 68,* the New Jersey Supreme Court held that New Jersey and Delaware's collective bargaining laws were complementary and parallel with regard to collective negotiations for public employees and therefore applied to the Delaware River and Bay Authority. [*Id.* at 447.] The court so held in spite of the fact that the compact did not clearly authorize modification through legislation "concurred in" by both states, and neither New

---

[4] The fact that *Lodge 30* involved the interpretation of a bi-state compact, a question of federal law, by a state court made no difference to our preclusion analysis. As Judge Scirica explained:

State courts may answer federal questions. The unions and DRPA agreed to litigate this issue of federal law in New Jersey courts. If those courts answered federal questions erroneously, it remained for state appellate courts, and ultimately for the United States Supreme Court to correct any mistakes. *Lodge 30*, 290 F.3d at 576.

[5] Recently, the New Jersey Supreme Court characterized our ruling in *Lodge 30* as having endorsed New Jersey's view that express statements are not required to modify bi-state compacts. *Ballinger v. Del. River Port Auth.*, 172 N.J. 586 (2002). We do not read our ruling as having reached the merits issue.

Jersey nor Delaware had expressed any intent to amend the compact or apply state labor laws to the Authority.[6] The court found that because both states had a public policy endorsing collective bargaining, the legislatures had "in effect * * * modified the Compact." *Id.*

Here, Local 542 urged before the District Court that Local 68 was controlling and persuasive, but the Court rejected its reasoning. The District Court reviewed the New York and New Jersey views and the federal case law, and found that the New Jersey view has not been accepted as a matter of federal law. The District Court also considered Local 542's argument that the lack of "concurred in" language in the Compact provides a basis to distinguish it from, and therefore a basis to reject, the New York and Second Circuit approaches. But the District Court concluded that "rather than distinguishing those, it substantially weakens [Local 542]'s position, because absent concurred in, there would be no basis, whatsoever, to look to any parallel legislation." Since there had been "no showing that either the New Jersey or the Pennsylvania statutes were intended, by the legislatures, to be applicable to this particular commission," the court awarded summary judgment to the Commission.

Having reviewed the state of the law on this issue, we agree with the District Court that, given the facts of this case and the unique nature of this Compact, New Jersey and Pennsylvania have not exhibited any express intent to amend the Compact or apply their collective bargaining laws to the Commission's employees. We are persuaded, first, by the fact that the Compact does not contain any provision enabling either state to modify it through legislation "concurred in" by the other, and second, by the logic of the reasoning underpinning the New York express intent standard, which the District Court here found to be persuasive.

First, we can find no language in the Compact authorizing New Jersey and Pennsylvania to permit amendment of the terms of their agreement simply by each state's passing similar legislation. Judicial restraint dictates that we not divine a way for them to do so. Our "first and last order of business is interpreting the compact," *Texas v. New Mexico*, 462 U.S. at 567–68; we may not read into it language or intent that is simply not there. Principles of statutory interpretation also require us to strictly construe surrenders of sovereignty. As noted above, a party wishing to make a claim of right or entitlement against a state must prove that the state has expressly relinquished that measure of sovereignty "in terms too plain to be mistaken." *Skelly*, 66 U.S. at 446.

Neither New Jersey nor Pennsylvania has expressed any intent to allow the modification of this Compact through the passage of legislation concurred in by the other, let alone legislation of one state that bears a resemblance to the other.

---

[6] Curiously, earlier in the same opinion, the New Jersey Supreme Court held that the New Jersey PERC does not have jurisdiction over the Delaware River and Bay Authority because "such jurisdiction 'must be expressly given to the [PERC] by the Legislatures of New Jersey and Delaware, and not inferred by the courts.'" *Local 68*, 688 A.2d at 574. This view does not appear consistent with the court's later holding applying New Jersey and Delaware labor laws to the Authority when no expression of intent was present.

We cannot subscribe to the view espoused by the New Jersey Supreme Court in *Local 68* that the mere existence of similar public policies set forth in each state's collective bargaining laws is enough to imply an intent on the part of both states to amend the Compact and apply those laws to the Commission. Nor do we agree with Local 542 that the absence of a provision enabling the states to modify the Compact through legislation "concurred in" by the other means that no express intent is required. Rather, we agree with the District Court that the absence of "concurred in" language actually weakens Local 542's argument. This is because the "concurred in" provision introduces the issue of, and mechanism for, modification, without which there is absolutely no authority for, let alone specific means of accomplishing, a modification of the Compact by passing similar laws. Thus the absence of the "concurred in" language is fatal. We find that in this case New Jersey and Pennsylvania have not expressed any intent to amend the Compact. We will not amend it for them.

We find further support for our decision in the observation made by Judge Robreno in his *Local 30* decision, that the New Jersey complementary or parallel standard appears to be based on a misinterpretation of compact law. The New Jersey Supreme Court based the complementary or parallel test articulated in *Local 68* and *Bunk* on *Eastern Paralyzed Veterans Association, Inc. v. Camden*, 111 N.J. 389 (1988) and *Nardi v. Delaware River Port Authority*, 88 Pa. Cmwlth. 558 (1985). A closer reading of these two cases, however, reveals that neither stands for the proposition that express legislative intent is unnecessary. Rather, both cases lend further support to the New York express intent test governing the application of the "concurred in" language, asking first whether the two states have passed legislation that expressly applies to the bi-state entity, and then whether that legislation is substantially similar. *See Malverty*, 524 N.E.2d at 422.

In *Nardi*, the Pennsylvania Commonwealth Court examined Pennsylvania and New Jersey's employee benefits laws, both of which expressly stated that they applied to the Delaware River Port Authority (the bi-state agency at issue), to determine whether they were substantially similar. *Nardi*, 490 A.2d at 950–51. The court found that the laws were not identical and refused to apply either one. Similarly, in *Eastern Paralyzed*, the court refused to unilaterally impose New Jersey's Uniform Construction Code on the Delaware River Port Authority — even though the code expressly stated that it applied to all bi-state agencies — without "some showing of agreement by both states to the enforcement of the [Code]." *Eastern Paralyzed*, 545 A.2d at 133–34.

Principles of federalism further caution against inferring an intent to amend in this case. A bi-state entity, created by compact, is "not subject to the unilateral control of any one of the States that compose the federal system." *Hess* 513 U.S. at 42. Also, although Pennsylvania courts have not spoken on this specific issue, they have noted reluctance to equate the state's individual action with action on behalf of, or that binds, a bi-state agency. *See, e.g.*, *Aveline v. Penn. Bd. Of Probation & Parole*, 729 A.2d 1254, 1257 n.10 (Pa. Commw. Ct. 1999).

Looking to the relevant statutes and the plain language of the Compact, we find no intent on the part of either state legislature to amend the Compact and impose collective bargaining laws upon the Commission. The Compact grants the Commission the authority to appoint employees, determine their qualifications and duties, and fix their salaries. The Compact neither gives Commission employees the right to bargain collectively nor imposes any requirement on the Commission to bargain collectively with employee unions. Neither New Jersey nor Pennsylvania's collective bargaining laws mention the Commission or state that the legislation is intended to apply to bi-state agencies. To read into the Compact any collective bargaining requirements would be to rewrite the agreement between the two states without any express authorization to do so. That is simply not our role.

. . . .

Notes & Questions

1. The Third Circuit's holding was concise: "Although we understand the desire to bring the Commission under the auspices of New Jersey and Pennsylvania's employee relations acts, we conclude that to do so would be an act of legislation, rather than interpretation or enforcement. We can find no legislative intent to subject the Compact to the collective bargaining schemes of New Jersey or Pennsylvania." 311 F.3d at 276.

What did the Third Circuit mean when it stated that applying the states' laws would be an act of legislation? Why did the court look for legislative intent rather than simply stop when it did not find express language in the compact authorizing the states to apply their collective bargaining statutes to the compact?

2. *Local 542* cited several New Jersey and New York state court cases applying the states' laws. The court cited *Malverty*, which you read above, to explain New York's approach. New Jersey state courts do not follow *Malverty*. New Jersey state courts conclude that state law is "concurred in" when the party states have "complementary or parallel" state legislation. However, New Jersey courts do not apply this standard consistently. In one case., the New Jersey Supreme Court concluded that laws are "complementary or parallel "when they are "substantially similar." *E.g.*, *Int'l Union of Operating Eng'rs, Local 68 v. Delaware River & Bay Auth.*, 147 N.J. 433, 444 (1997). At the time of *Local 68*, Delaware's collective bargaining law allowed, but did not require, bargaining when requested by the employees, and New Jersey's law required bargaining. Are these laws "substantially similar" enough to apply to the compact? In other cases, New Jersey courts have described the "complimentary and parallel" standard in somewhat less rigorous terms. For example, in *Bunk v. Port Auth. of N.Y & N.J.*, 144 N.J. 176, 185 (1996), the New Jersey Supreme Court applied New Jersey's workers' compensation laws to the Port Authority of New York and New Jersey after finding the two states' workers' compensation laws were "somewhat similar." In *Ampro Fisheries v. Yaskin*, 127 N.J. 602, 611 (1992), the New Jersey Supreme Court applied fishing regulations that "do not directly conflict with any regulations enacted by the State of Delaware." In *Textar Painting Corp. v. Delaware River Port Auth.*, 296 N.J. Super. 251, 258 (Law Div. 1996), the court applied New Jersey public contracting law because it expressed similar public policy as Pennsylvania law. Should state

laws that are only "somewhat similar," that do not conflict with the other state's laws, or that express similar policy be applied to a compact?

Note that in *Ampro Fisheries*, the case involved the application of state regulations, not state legislation. How would the states' legislatures concur in the regulations of the others when state agencies, not state legislatures enact regulations.

3. In *Slack v. Wash. Metro. Area Transit Auth.*, 346 F. Supp. 3d 146 (D.D.C. 2018), the U.S. District Court for the District of Columbia gave as good an explanation as any court for why merely similar state statutes do not constitute express consent of the parties to apply each other's state law to a compact agency: "where each jurisdiction has enacted a different statute, the fact that the statutes address the same subject matter only increases the likelihood that applying one jurisdiction's laws to WMATA could upset the other jurisdictions' policy judgments." *Id.* at 156–57.

4. In *Chafin v. Delaware River and Bay Auth.*, No. 06-836 (RMB), 2006 U.S. Dist. LEXIS 94346 (D.N.J. Dec. 20, 2006), the federal court considered a variation on a "concurred in" provision. It compared the compact creating the Delaware River and Bay Authority and the compact creating the Delaware River Joint Toll Bridge Commission (at issue in *Local 542*):

> Additional differences exist between the DRBA's Compact and the one under review in *Local 542* that reinforce the conclusion that *Local 542* does not control. Specifically, in *Local 542* the compact did not contain any provision for amendment. Here, Article VIII of the Compact provides a mechanism for both increasing the Authority's powers and its duties, and does so in a manner consistent with *Local 542's* concern with principles of federalism and sovereignty:
>
> > Article VIII. Additional Powers
> >
> > For purposes of effectuating the authorized purposes of the authority, additional powers may be granted to the authority by legislation of either State without the concurrence of the other, and may be exercised within such State, or may be granted to the authority by Congress and exercised by it; but no additional duties or obligations shall be undertaken by the authority under the law of either State or of Congress without authorization by the law of both States.
>
> This Compact article reflects the compromise inherent in interstate compacts, and *Local 542's* concern with the integrity of sovereignty. Interstate compacts are a unique contract between at least three separate sovereigns. On the definite terms embodied in the Compact, each party—at least two states and Congress—has surrendered a degree of sovereignty and control over a subject within its exclusive purview. The result is an entity confined by those terms. Here, New Jersey and Delaware have surrendered their sovereign right to exclusive control over certain parts of their territory so that the Authority may operate crossings for the betterment of both states. Congress has, in turn, approved the Compact and has surrendered to a degree its otherwise exclusive control over that interstate conduct. The terms

> of that surrender of sovereignty cannot be altered without agreement from all the parties. *Local 542* holds that the new entity—the Authority—in which the surrendered sovereignty has been reposed cannot be imposed on without imposing on the sovereignty of the other parties. That imposition can only be by consent "expressed in terms too plain to be mistaken." [*Local 542* at 276]. Conversely, a party to a compact can unilaterally secede more power to the bi-state entity. But only such power as the sovereign possesses. This is the root of *Local 542's* concern that "[a] bi-state entity, created by compact, 'is not subject to the unilateral control of any one of the States that compose the federal system.'" [*Id.* at 281].
>
> This is exactly the scheme set out in Article VIII. In *Local 542* the compact contained no provision for amendment, thus even identical legislation passed by both member states could not be applied to the bi-state entity because that would alter the terms under which each party agreed to surrender a degree of sovereignty. Article VIII's terms, however, expressly permit additional powers unilaterally "by legislation of either State without the concurrence of the other, and may be exercised within such State"; or additional duties bi-laterally "with[] authorization by the law of both States." Whether complimentary and parallel law in both member states is sufficient authorization under Article VIII is unclear. *Local 542* suggests that such legislation would be insufficient. To be sure, the Third Circuit, in distinguishing the New Jersey Supreme Court's opinion in *Local 68*, noted that the DRBA's "compact did not clearly authorize modification through legislation 'concurred in' by both states * * * ." [*Local 542*] at 279. Article VIII's plain language speaks of authorizing legislation, not concurrent legislation. To authorize is a more express approval than to concur. Nonetheless, this provision differs from the compact in *Local 542* that did not provide for amendment at all. . . .

Chafin v. Delaware River and Bay Auth., 2006 U.S. Dist. LEXIS 94346 at *15–18. What do you think about a compact provision that specifically authorizes states to enact supplemental legislation for the purpose of implementing the compact? When could supplemental legislation become a de facto unilateral amendment of the compact? Consider also whether authorizing the DRBA to undertake additional responsibilities in one state would take time away from the DRBA handling business in the other state.

5. New Jersey state courts are not the only courts to apply a unique analytical approach. For cases involving the Port Authority of New York and New Jersey (which has a "concurred in" provision), New York state courts consider whether the state law regulates internal operations or conduct affecting external relations of Port Authority. According to the New York courts, the internal operations of a compact agency should be independent of the direct control of either state. New York courts have not applied this analytical approach to other compact agencies and no other state or federal court uses it. The next case was the first time the New York courts used this approach.

Agesen v. Catherwood
26 N.Y.2d 521 (1970)

BRIETEL, JUDGE:

Petitioners, direct employees of the Port of New York Authority engaged in the building and mechanical trades, appeal in consolidated proceedings under CPLR article 78, in which they urge the applicability to their employment of New York's prevailing rate of wage legislation (Labor Law, § 220).

The Industrial Commissioner, by order and determination dated August 4, 1967, dismissed petitioners' claims that they were receiving less than the prevailing rate of wage, on the ground that the Commissioner lacked jurisdiction. [The trial court] annulled the Commissioner's determination. The Appellate Division, however, unanimously reversed, confirmed the Commissioner's determination, and dismissed the petitions.

The problem is presented because of the special character of the Port of New York Authority, a public authority created by compact between two States and approved by Congress as required by the United States Constitution.

The facts and legal issues were succinctly presented at the Appellate Division in the opinion by the late Mr. Presiding Justice BELDOCK. Two variations must be noted, however, from that opinion.

First, article XIV of the applicable compact between the States of New York and New Jersey reads: "The port authority shall elect from its number a chairman, vice-chairman, and may appoint such officers and employees as it may require for the performance of its duties, and shall fix and determine their qualifications and duties" (L. 1921, ch. 154, § 1). This language does not expressly empower the Authority to fix salaries. The fixing of salaries, however, although not a power expressly granted to the Authority, is undoubtedly one of its implied powers. Certainly, as to employees not covered by prevailing wage statutes, there would otherwise be no power anywhere to fix their salaries, a consequence hardly conceivable and not tolerable.

Secondly, a disparate wage scale dependent upon the geographic location of work sites, although occasionally burdensome, is not necessarily "unworkable." Presumably, similar problems were involved, and surmounted, in the Authority's Workmen's Compensation coverage, since both New York and New Jersey each have independent statutes and agencies.

Consequently, the inapplicability of section 220 of the Labor Law results not from any express exclusion or inherent unworkability, but rather from a general intent, amply reflected in the compact, that the internal operations of the Authority be independent of the direct control of either State acting without the concurrence of the other. Section 220, enacted long before the creation of the Authority, should not be construed to impose a unilateral regulation of the wages of only a fraction of the Authority's employees, namely, those building and mechanical workers who, it is alleged, work solely on projects within the State of New York.

The distinction between the internal operations and conduct affecting external relations of the Authority is crucial in charting the areas permitting unilateral and requiring bilateral State action. New York and New Jersey have each undoubted power to regulate the external conduct of the Authority, and it may hardly be gainsaid that the Authority, albeit bistate, is subject to New York's laws involving health and safety, insofar as its activities may externally affect the public.

Indeed, given sufficient social or economic justification, the lines of external and internal operation may shift, justifying increased regulation as the impact outside the Authority becomes more pronounced. Finally, even as to internal matters, the two States, by bilateral action, may always regulate Authority action, when unilateral action is ineffective or impractical.

Although the Authority's participation in New York's Workmen's Compensation and State Employees' Retirement systems constitute qualified exceptions to the scheme of internal autonomy, these exceptions are not controlling. Participation in the retirement system is governed by a statutory clause most broad in scope, authorizing participation at the option of any "public or quasi-public organization" (Retirement and Social Security Law, § 31, subd. [a]). Although the basis for the application of the Workmen's Compensation statute is less clear, the administrative and legislative (see L. 1950, ch. 301, § 7) acceptance of the Authority as covered by the statute over many years constitutes, at most, a practical construction by the entities involved of markedly limited precedent or effect. Arguably, workmen's compensation is not quite as internal a matter as the adjustment of the wage level to prevailing wages.

In the instant matter, however, there is no showing of any sort that section 220 of the Labor Law was ever intended to apply to the Authority, or any justification, by way of practical construction or otherwise, for the unilateral imposition of such regulation on its internal operations.

Accordingly, the order of the Appellate Division should be affirmed . . . .

Notes & Questions

1. How would you explain the distinction between internal and external effects to a lay person? One article observed that the distinction between internal and external effects in not particularly clear. Matthew S. Tripolitsiotis, *Bridge Over Troubled Waters: The Application of State Law to Compact Clause Entities*, 23 YALE L. & POL'Y REV. 163, 182 (2005). More recently, federal courts have rejected the distinction altogether. In *HIP, Heightened Indep. & Progress, Inc. v. Port Auth. of N.Y. & N.J.*, 693 F.3d 345 (3d Cir. 2012), the Third Circuit rejected *Agesen* and New Jersey state courts' "complementary and parallel" approach, stating, ". . . even though we do not recognize implicit modifications of an interstate compact as the New Jersey Supreme Court might, both jurisdictions require evidence of mutual intent to alter a compact and regulate the bi-state agency, regardless of whether the action taken by the agency is 'external' or 'internal.'" *Id.* at 357 n.3.

2. In *Brust v. ACF Indus.*, No. 11-4839, 2011 U.S. Dist. LEXIS 147104 (D.N.J. Dec. 21, 2011), the court applied *Agesen* in a case involving the Delaware River

Port Authority in analyzing whether a common law claim implicated a bi-state compact, but also noted that analysis of statutory claims against a compact agency necessarily implicates the compact regardless of whether the effect is external. Should *Agesen* be limited to common law claims? How would you argue the rationale of such a limitation? *HIP* (in note 1 above) probably overruled *Brust*'s application of *Agesen*.

3. Note that the Labor Law in *Agesen* did not expressly conflict with the compact, rather the court considered the general intent of the compact. Should courts consider the general intent of a compact in deciding whether state law should apply, or should courts require an express conflict between a compact provision and state law before considering whether state law applies?

4. But for a few exceptions, only New Jersey state courts use the "complementary and parallel" standard and only New York state courts use the "internal/external effects" distinction and only in Port Authority of New York and Jersey cases. *Jordan v. Bi-State Dev. Agency*, 561 S.W.3d 57 (Mo. Ct. App. 2018), is one of those exceptions. In that case, the Missouri Court of Appeals noted that it had previously adopted New Jersey's complementary and parallel standard and acknowledged that the standard is less stringent than the standard used in most state and federal courts, but also noted that in Missouri, courts must find the laws identical for all intents and purposes, which is more stringent than New Jersey's application of its "complementary and parallel" standard.

5. In 2018 and 2019, the Port Authority of New York and New Jersey argued in several cases that the New York and New Jersey state courts should reject the *Agesen* approach and apply the express intent standard that the federal courts use (and that New York courts apply to other interstate compact agencies). The New York trial courts have consistently rejected these arguments. *See Granados v. Port Auth. of N.Y. & N.J.*, No. 714754/2017, 2018 N.Y. Misc. LEXIS 2995 (N.Y. Sup. Ct. Queens Cty. Mar. 9, 2018); *Ayars v. Port Auth. of N.Y. & N.J.*, No. 158178/2017, 2018 N.Y. Misc. LEXIS 2582 (N.Y. Sup. Ct. N.Y. Cty. Jun. 21, 2018); *Wortham v. Port Auth. of N.Y. & N.J.*, No. 155687/2017, 2018 N.Y. Misc. LEXIS 2190 (N.Y. Sup. Ct. N.Y. Cty. May 30, 2018); *Wortham v. Port Auth. of N.Y. & N.J.*, No. 155686/2017, 2018 N.Y. Misc. LEXIS 3978 (N.Y. Sup. Ct. N.Y. Cty. Sept. 17, 2018); *Rosario v. Port Auth. of N.Y. & N.J.*, No. 150040/2018, 2018 N.Y. Misc. LEXIS 6006 (N.Y. Sup. Ct. N.Y. Cty. Dec. 5, 2018). To date, appellate courts have also consistently rejected the Port Authority's arguments to try to develop a uniform manner of evaluating such claims. *See Matter of Lopez v. Port Auth. of N.Y. & N.J.*, 98 N.Y.S.3d (N.Y. App. Div. 2019); *Wortham v. Port Auth. of N.Y. & N.J.*, 110 N.Y.S.3d 539 (N.Y. App. Div. 2019); *Port Auth. of N.Y. & N.J. v. Port Auth. of N.Y. & N.J. Police Benevolent Ass'n*, 459 N.J. Super. 278 (App. Div. 2019).

6. Courts have long struggled with determining what laws a state can unilaterally apply to a compact without the concurrence of the other state. The next case presents a more common analytical approach than the "complementary and parallel" standard and the "internal/external effects" distinction.

C. T. Hellmuth & Assoc. v. Wash. Metro. Area Transit Auth.
414 F. Supp. 408 (D. Md. 1976)

WATKINS, JUDGE:

. . . .

The facts are essentially undisputed. Plaintiff C. T. Hellmuth & Associates, Inc., is a Maryland insurance concern; Defendant WMATA is an interstate agency, the result of an interstate compact between the State of Maryland, the Commonwealth of Virginia and the District of Columbia, entered into with the approval of Congress. The instant controversy apparently arose when WMATA awarded an insurance contract to the Prudential Life Insurance Company of America. Plaintiff, one of the unsuccessful bidders for that contract, seeks by this action to obtain copies of (1) the Prudential proposal, (2) the report prepared by a member of the Metro Insurance Administrators, WMATA's insurance consultant, recommending the Prudential proposal, and (3) any and all opinions, reports, and decisions relating to the selection of the Metro Insurance Administrators.

Plaintiff bases its right of access to these records upon the Maryland Public Information Act. Section 2(a) of that Act provides that all "public records" shall be available for inspection except as they are exempted from disclosure by the Act or as otherwise protected by law. The Act defines "public records" as including those records made or received by any state agency in connection with the transaction of public business except as they are privileged or confidential by law. Defendant WMATA maintains that by virtue of its status as an interstate agency, it is exempt from the Public Information Act; Plaintiff, on the other hand, contends that WMATA, as an agency of the state,[2] is subject to and must comply with the provisions of [the Act]. Thus, the only issue raised here, is whether WMATA falls within the purview of the Maryland Act.

Upon entering into an interstate compact, a state effectively surrenders a portion of its sovereignty; the compact governs the relations of the parties with respect to the subject matter of the agreement and is superior to both prior and subsequent law. Further, when enacted, a compact constitutes not only law, but a contract which may not be amended, modified, or otherwise altered without the consent of all parties. It, therefore, appears settled that one party may not enact legislation which would impose burdens upon the compact absent the concurrence of the other signatories.

While apparently conceding the validity of this principle where one party to a compact attempts to enact legislation which clearly would affect the other parties' interests, Plaintiff, nonetheless, argues that the rule is inapplicable where it is claimed the parties have equivalent legislation. This Court cannot agree. Clearly,

---

[2] Section 4 of the WMATA compact provides: "There is hereby created, as an instrumentality and *agency of each of the signatory parties* hereto, the Washington Metropolitan Area Transit Authority which shall be a body corporate and politic, and which shall have the powers and duties granted herein and such additional powers as may hereafter be conferred upon it pursuant to law." (Emphasis supplied)

the mere fact that Virginia and the District have adopted freedom of information laws can hardly be taken as a tacit agreement on their part that WMATA should be governed by the Maryland law, particularly in view of the fact that [the Maryland law] was enacted subsequent to the Virginia and District of Columbia laws. Moreover, the Court is not persuaded by the alternative premise implicit in Plaintiff's argument, that the existence of comparable legislation eliminates the possibility that one party may impinge upon the others' interests. Whatever force that contention may have in the situation in which the various laws involved are identical, it is plainly unmeritorious here, where the laws involved differ in not insignificant respects. Presumably these laws reflect considered policy decisions on the part of the respective jurisdictions as to the types of information which should be accessible to the public and the circumstances under which it will be made available. Regardless of how similar the laws may be, plainly Maryland may not impose its preferences in this regard upon Virginia and the District, for such an imposition, however minimal, is nonetheless an intrusion upon their interests and in derogation of the compact. Clearly then, Maryland may not unilaterally subject WMATA to the provisions of [its law], if indeed that is the portent of the Act. . . .

Notes & Questions

1. In *C. T. Hellmuth*, the court noted that it could apply state laws that don't burden the compact, but the burden test wasn't in the compact. The court was thus establishing a test to precede applying the "concurred-in" factors, much like the New York courts did with the external/internal distinction. Can you make arguments why such a pretest is necessary? How would you determine what constitutes a burden? Conversely, can you think of examples of state law that might not burden a compact if they applied in only one state?

2. Other courts apply essentially the same analytical approach but use slightly different terminology. For example, in *Hubble v. Bi-State Dev. Agency of Ill.-Mo. Metro. Dist.*, 238 Ill. 2d 262 (2010), the Illinois Supreme Court reasoned:

> [I]t is true that one party to an interstate compact may not enact legislation that would impose burdens upon the compact absent the concurrence of the other signatory states. However, the converse is widely recognized: "It is within the competency of a State, which is a party to a compact with another State, to legislate in respect of matters covered by the compact so long as such legislative action is in approbation and not in reprobation of the compact."

Id. at 278. In *Hubble*, the Illinois Supreme Court concluded that applying the Illinois Tort Immunity Act to the bi-state agency generally protects rather than burdens the compact. Similarly, in *Henderson v. Delaware River Joint Toll Bridge Comm'n*, 362 Pa. 475, 486 (1949), the Pennsylvania Supreme Court concluded that a statute eliminating the need for the bridge commission to obtain municipal consent to occupy a street or overpass a street was "in aid of the Commonwealth's expeditious fulfillment of its undertakings in the compact." In *Eastern Paralyzed Veterans Ass'n, Inc. v. City of Camden*, 111 N.J. 389, 407 (1988), the New Jersey Supreme Court remanded the case back to the trial court to take evidence on whether installing an elevator would burden or interfere with rail operation or whether both New Jersey and Pennsylvania have similar legislation obligating the DRPA to provide barrier-free access to its transit.

3. In *C. T. Hellmuth*, if the court had concluded that state law could apply, then which of the states' freedom of information laws would apply? Would such a decision have given power to the plaintiffs to determine which law it wanted to apply, or to determine which forum to appear in?

III. Compacts that Do Not Authorize Modification by State Law

Most compacts are silent about the application of other state law. When a compact is silent, courts have not usually permitted the states to apply state law that conflicts with the compact. A single statement in *Seattle Master Builders Ass'n v. Pac. Nw. Elec. Power and Cons. Planning Council*, 786 F.2d 1359, 1371 (9th Cir. 1986), is one of the most-frequently cited authorities in this situation: "A state can impose state law on a compact organization only if the compact specifically reserves its right to do so." Surprisingly, the Ninth Circuit provided no reasoning beyond a reference to *Cal. Dep't of Transp. v. City of South Lake Tahoe*, 466 F. Supp. 527, 537 (E.D. Cal. 1978), which also gave no reasoning.

As you read through the notes and questions below, consider why states and courts often seem to strive to apply state law where it conflicts with a compact.

Notes & Questions

1. What do you think of the "specifically reserves" test in *Seattle Master Builders*? Recall from Chapter 3 that amending a compact requires the action of all parties, and if the compact has consent, amending a compact requires congressional action as well. In other words, amending a compact can be difficult. Does this test put too much burden on the drafters and legislatures to draft the perfect agreement the first time? As a result, are compacts vulnerable to becoming outdated?

2. *Skamania Cty. v. Woodall*, 104 Wash. App. 525 (2001), reversed the presumption in *Seattle Master Builders* that a compact must reserve state law. The Washington Court of Appeals stated:

> Moreover, a state may reserve the right to have its laws apply to an interstate compact commission. *See Seattle Master Builders*. As noted, by statute and judicial decision, all Washington statutes are interpreted by Washington courts under Washington common law unless the Legislature expresses otherwise. *See* RCW 4.04.010. Nothing in the Compact or the Act can be interpreted as a clearly expressed intention of the Legislature to give the Commission the authority to ignore Washington common law when interpreting a Washington State county ordinance.

Skamania Cty. v. Woodall, 104 Wash. App. at 535. What do you think of a presumption that state law applies to the compact unless the compact specifically rejects it? Should courts presume that state legislatures are aware of state laws when enacting a compact, and that the compact is subject to those laws? How is one state's legislature to know the law of the other states? With this presumption, can a state too easily abrogate a compact? How would you handle this presumption when the party states could apply their own different state laws to the same compact?

The presumption that state law applies to a compact unless rejected in the compact also appeared in *Delaware River Joint Toll Bridge Comm'n v. Colburn*, 310 U.S. 419 (1940), which is most often cited for the proposition that construction of a compact that has received the consent of Congress presents a federal question that the Supreme Court may review. *Colburn* involved a landowner seeking damages against the commission pursuant to New Jersey law for interference with access to their land and with their light, air and view caused by the commission's construction of a bridge abutment on adjacent land. The Court noted:

> The Compact was explicit in its specifications of what property interests should be taken and compensated for, and of the right and authority of the Commission to acquire them by purchase or by eminent domain. By its silence it left the Commission subject to consequential damages only as was imposed by the laws of the state, including the Act of 1912, except in so far as the Compact restricted the application of the Act.

Id. at 431. *Colburn's* conclusion that state law should apply when the compact is silent did not last long. Eleven years later, in 1951, the Supreme Court issued its decision in *West Virginia ex rel. Dyer v. Sims*, which cast significant doubt that a state could apply its own conflicting law to a compact. Although *West Virginia ex rel. Dyer v. Sims* did not expressly overrule *Colburn* in this respect, perhaps the strong language in the multiple opinions had the effect of changing this aspect of compact jurisprudence because no other case until *Woodall* held that state law applies unless rejected in the compact.

3. If a compact reserves state law, does that state law remains static such that it applies to the compact as it existed as of the date of the compact, or does it apply as it may be amended over time. Applying state law as amended over time comes with its own concern—that a state may amend its reserved law in a manner that another party state objects to. How would you address this issue when drafting a compact?

4. Consider whether the any of the various tests for applying a "concurred in" provision should apply instead of the *Seattle Master Builders* test.

5. Even where state law is not applicable, some courts express direction to follow state law as much as possible. For example, in *Simpson v. Bijou Irrigation Co.*, 69 P.3d 50 (Colo. 2003), the court stated, "Given an irreconcilable conflict between intrastate priority administration and compliance with an interstate compact, it is compact compliance that must take precedence. . . . 'If interstate allocation is subordinate to individual rights, interstate compacts would be valueless.' This court has nevertheless recognized that the State Engineer, while enforcing compact delivery requirements, must simultaneously adhere, insofar as possible, to the [State's] constitutional and statutory provisions for priority administration." *Id.* at 69.

6. In *Campaign for Buffalo History, Architecture & Culture, Inc. v. Buffalo & Ft. Erie Pub. Bridge Auth.*, No. 12-CV-00605 M, 2013 U.S. Dist. LEXIS 25390 (W.D.N.Y. Feb. 22, 2013), the court denied a preliminary injunction that would have restrained the Buffalo and Fort Erie Public Bridge Authority from demolishing several vacant residential properties it owned. New York and Canada created the Bridge Authority by a compact, which Congress approved. H.R.J. Res. 315, 73rd Cong., 2d sess. (1934); H.R.J. Res. 342, 85th Cong., 1st sess. (1957) (reauthorizing a reconstituted compact with the Bridge Authority). Campaign for Buffalo History sought a preliminary injunction based on allegations that the Bridge Authority violated the New York State Environmental Quality Review Act. The court denied the motion, applying the principles of law from *Seattle Master Builders* and *Hess* stating that state law does not apply unless preserved in the compact "should apply with equal or even greater force to [the Bridge Authority,] an international compact." 2013 U.S. Dist. LEXIS 25390 at *19. Does the international nature of this compact complicate the question of whether state law (or Canadian province law) applies? Is the *Seattle Master Builders* standard more compelling in this situation? Chapter 12 contains materials on agreements between states and foreign powers.

7. Another way that state law can apply is when a court looks to prior interpretations of a compact by courts in another state. Chapter 6 discussed the principle of comity, and Chapter 9 covers this variation in more detail, but consider the following examples. In *Atl. Richfield Co. v. Dep't of Revenue,* 300 Or. 637 (1986), involving the Multistate Tax Compact, the Oregon Supreme Court concluded:

> If we were the first state to address this question, we likely would affirm the department and the Tax Court, for the department has some latitude in interpreting the phrase "original cost" in ORS 314.655(2). It appears, however, that those UDITPA jurisdictions that have considered the IDC question by rule or statute (no court or administrative decisions to the contrary have been cited to us) require that IDCs be included in the property factor. The department has not invited our attention to any decision concerning any UDITPA jurisdiction's counterpart of [Or. Admin. R. 150-314-655(2)-(A) that reaches a contrary result."

Id. at 646–47 (internal citations omitted). Note that the Oregon Supreme Court explained the other states considered the question "by rule or statute." The effect here is that Oregon is applying those other states' rules and statutes to its own administration of the Multistate Tax Compact.

In another example, *Proctor v. Wash. Metro. Area Transit Auth.*, 412 Md. 691 (2010), the Court of Appeals of Maryland (Maryland's highest court), answered two certified questions from the U.S. District Court. One question asked whether the sovereign immunity provision in the Maryland Tort Claim Act applied to the Washington Metropolitan Area Transit Authority. The Court concluded that the broad waiver of sovereign immunity in the Washington Metropolitan Area Transit Compact, not the waiver in Maryland's Tort Claim Act, applied to the Transit Authority. The other question asked whether the Maryland state law cap on noneconomic damages applied to actions against the Transit Authority. The Court concluded that the cap did apply.

This is a complex decision that cites to many prior Maryland cases involving the Transit Authority, intrastate application of the tort claim act, and other courts' decisions involving the Transit Compact's waiver of sovereign immunity. In the end, the Court of Appeals overruled a relatively recent decision from the Maryland Court of Special Appeals (Maryland's intermediate appellate court), *Wash. Metro. Area Transit Auth. v. Deschamps*, 183 Md. App. 279 (2008), that concluded the Maryland Tort Claims Act applied to the Transit Authority. In overruling *Deschamps*, the Maryland Court of Appeals harmonized Maryland, Virginia, and District of Columbia decisions involving the application and scope of the parties' tort liability acts and damages caps to the Transit Authority. The Court of Appeals noted that the importance of decisions from the other parties' courts and suggested that one state's interpretation of the compact may be understandably suspicious when it differs from all the other party states' interpretations. The Court of Appeals stated:

> The decisions of courts in Virginia and the District of Columbia have particular significance in this case because WMATA is a multi-jurisdiction agency governed by a compact to which Virginia and the District of Columbia are parties. Accordingly, the decisions of courts in Virginia and the District of Columbia are highly persuasive regarding matters related to WMATA. Because the rationale of *Deschamps* is inconsistent with the reasoning of other courts from the other two WMATA-related jurisdictions, the District Court, quite reasonably in our view, had reservations about whether *Deschamps* was decided correctly.

412 Md. at 705.

8. Recall the *Gauntt* case from Chapter 6 that required the court to determine which of the states' laws concerning the enforceability of arbitration agreements to apply. The court considered cases from New Jersey, Delaware, and Pennsylvania rejecting the application of state law to a compact and conflicts of laws principles. Similarly, in *Yancoskie v. Delaware River Port Auth.*, 155 N.J. Super. 1 (App. Div. 1977), the court stated, "Neither the compact nor the federal statutes evidencing congressional approval contains any provision requiring the giving of notice or limiting the time within which actions against the Authority must be commenced. Thus there is no inhibition against the application of the procedural requirements of the New Jersey Tort Claims Act." *Id.* at 4. Are conflict-of-laws principles helpful in determining whether to apply a state law to a compact?

9. In *Parkridge 6, LLC v. U.S. Dep't of Transp.*, 420 F. App'x 265 (4th Cir. 2011), the court considered whether a state law specifically applicable to state and local government also applied to a compact agency. It concluded, "The MWAA is 'a political subdivision constituted to operate and improve the Metropolitan airports,' and it exists 'independent of Virginia and its local governments, the District of Columbia, and the United States Government.' 49 U.S.C. § 49106(a)(2)–(3) (2006). As such, it is not subject to Virginia's FOIA." *Id.* at 268.

Using this reasoning, would a compact agency described as an agency of the party states be subject to each of the parties' law?

10. Some compacts preserve state law as an alternative. For example, the Interstate Insurance Product Regulation Compact allows the party states to determine whether to apply state law or the compact. Article III allows the party states to "opt out" of the uniform standards that the Interstate Insurance Product Regulation Commission enacts. In another example, the Multistate Tax Compact, art. III, § 1, allows multistate taxpayers to decide whether to apportion their income according to state law or to a formula specified in the compact. As discussed in prior chapters, several state courts have concluded the states could apply the Multistate Tax Compact inconsistent with the text of article III, section 1, and require taxpayers use only the state law apportionment formula.

11. Should consent be an important factor in determining whether state law applies to a compact? In *Gillette Co. v. Franchise Tax Bd.*, 209 Cal. App. 4th 938, 956 (2012), the court concluded that the Multistate Tax Compact superseded conflicting state law even though it did not receive nor require consent. The California Supreme Court reversed but avoided the question "whether an interstate compact not approved by Congress necessarily takes precedence over other state law" *Gillette Co. v. Franchise Tax Bd.*, 62 Cal. 4th 468 (2015). Review *Green v. Biddle* and the other cases excerpted and cited in this chapter. Does the application of state law depend on the compact as federal law—on supremacy? One example where a court did use supremacy reasoning is *Bush v. Muncy*, 659 F.2d 402, 410 (4th Cir. 1981) (stating the provisions of a compact with consent "interpreted as federal law, must prevail over any existing or subsequently created provisions of state law in direct conflict"). Curiously, the Fourth Circuit cited to *Delaware River Joint Toll Bridge Comm'n v. Colburn*, 310 U.S. 419, 429–30 (1940), which addressed only the terms of the compact, not supremacy, and as mentioned in note 2 above, suggested state law could apply because the compact was silent.

12. Two non-compact intergovernmental agreement cases suggest courts should presume legislators know about agreements relating to the subject matter of proposed legislation. In *Pioneer Coach Lines, Inc. v. City of Chicago*, No 1-10-2964, 2012 Ill. App. Unpub. LEXIS 776 (Ill. App. Ct. Mar. 30, 2012), the court did not invalidate a non-compact intergovernmental agreement after a change in the law, reasoning that under Illinois law, "the legislature is presumed to have known that the agreement was in effect when it amended the statute." *Id.* at *11. Similarly, in *DeFazio v. Wash. Pub. Power Supply Sys.*, 296 Or. 550, 562 (1984), the court assumed municipalities had authority to enter into agreements to operate power plants and held that enactment of new statutes that specifically authorized the agreements did not supersede or restrict the prior authority.

IV. Application of State Common Law to Compacts

Some form of common law exists in every case, such as how courts apply methods and standards for analysis of claims and defenses, interpret statutes and regulations, and apply standards for judicial review of agency actions. Like statutory law, common law differs among the states. Surprisingly few cases expressly question whether and how a compact agency, a state, or the court applies state common law in interstate compact cases. Should courts distinguish between applying statutory and common law to a compact? If common law applies only in the same manner as statutory law as discussed above, consider how a court can decide a compact case without considering common law and how states and compact agencies can administer a compact without following common law. The next case excerpt, *Ballinger v. Delaware River Port Authority*, discusses the direct application of state common law.

Ballinger v. Delaware River Port Auth.
172 N.J. 586 (2002)

COLEMAN, JUSTICE:

This appeal presents two issues of first impression: first, whether the Delaware River Port Authority (DRPA) and its employees are subject to the New Jersey Conscientious Employee Protection Act (CEPA); second, if they are not, whether they are subject to the New Jersey common law principle that protects employees from being discharged in violation of a clear mandate of public policy. Because DRPA is a bi-state agency, a unique creature of a federally approved compact between two states, this Court must determine as a threshold matter the proper methodology to apply in resolving when one state can impose obligations on a bi-state agency.

[The Court concluded that New Jersey's Conscientious Employee Protection Act and Pennsylvania's Whistleblower Law are not complementary and parallel because they differ in scope, filing period, damages and the right to trial by jury, and those differences reflect that the goals of the overriding legislative schemes are different.]

. . . .

We now address whether DRPA may be subject to the common law and, if so, to what extent. DRPA argues that since neither state may unilaterally impose additional duties on it, such obligations may be imposed only through legislation enacted by both states that expressly includes DRPA. To support that position, DRPA relies on the provision of the compact that states that DRPA "shall also have such additional powers as may hereafter be delegated to or imposed upon it from time to time by the action of either State concurred in by legislation of the other." N.J.S.A. 32:3-5; Pa. Stat. Ann. tit. 36, § 3503, art. IV(q). According to DRPA, because the two states never expressly agreed to the imposition of the common law, DRPA cannot now be subject to the common law absent express legislative consent. We disagree.

Under the compact, DRPA has the power to "sue and be sued." N.J.S.A. 32:3-5(b); Pa. Stat. Ann. tit. 36, § 3503, art. IV(b). The "sue and be sued" provision "is considered a waiver of sovereign immunity." *Bell* [*v. Bell*, 83 N.J. 417,] 423

[(1980)]. If DRPA's authority to institute common law suits against others is derived from the power to sue, then logically the power to be sued infers the corollary proposition: a plaintiff can sue DRPA to enforce a common law claim.

We reject DRPA's position that the "sue and be sued" clause operates only within the confines of the compact. That is, when DRPA is the party suing it apparently assumes it may take advantage of expanding common law, but when it is being sued it contends that it may not be subject to common law obligations without express legislative consent. Even if that were so, plaintiff correctly points out that the compact does not state that only a member state's Legislature may impose duties on DRPA contrary to defendant's argument. Subsection (m) of the enumerated powers section of the compact provides that DRPA may "exercise the powers, duties, authority and jurisdiction heretofore conferred and imposed on [it] by the Commonwealth of Pennsylvania or the State of New Jersey, or both of the said two States." N.J.S.A. 32:3-5(m). That subsection is not limited to legislative law; rather, it broadly applies to all the laws of the two states.

"Bi-state agencies such as the [DRPA] do not exist in a vacuum." *Del. River Port Auth. v. Commonwealth, State Ethics Comm'n,* [585 A.2d 587,] 588 ([Pa Commw. Ct.] 1991). As Chief Justice Weintraub once stated in a case involving a different bi-state agency whose compact also contained a "sue and be sued" provision:

> The [agency] is not a separate level of government somewhere between the federal government and the contracting states. It is part of the government of each of the states....
>
> ... [T]he states did not create a governmental authority and cut the umbilical cord.... As the agent of each state, the [agency] is subject to all of its laws, whether of statutory or common law origin, except insofar as the states agreed expressly or by fair implication to place it beyond them.

[*State v. Murphy*, [36 N.J. 172,] 186 [(1961)] (requiring agency to produce transcripts in a criminal case, notwithstanding internal agency rule that transcripts were confidential).]

We conclude that the common law can be applied to the extent it fills a void in the compact. *See, e.g.*, *New Jersey v. New York*, 523 U.S. 767, 784 (1998) (resolving territorial dispute between New York and New Jersey regarding Ellis Island by following "common-law rule [that] speaks in the silence of the Compact").

"[J]ust as a state through its legislature may deal with specific circumstances menacing the peace by an appropriately drawn act, so the law of a state may be fitted to a concrete situation through the authority given by the state to its courts." *Milk Wagon Drivers Union of Chicago, Local 753 v. Meadowmoor Dairies*, 312 U.S. 287, 297 (1941). The common law, unlike statutory law, is "flexible" and "adapts itself to varying conditions." *Funk v. United States*, 290 U.S. 371, 383 (1933). And, undoubtedly, the common law is as much a part of the law of a state as is statutory law. *Magnolia Petroleum Co. v. Hunt*, 320 U.S. 430, 445 (1943). In this case, a legislative agreement between the states created the compact, but the application of common law allows the compact to function in a manner that is consistent with public expectations.

In the past, DRPA has been both subject to and has asserted the common law. *See, e.g.*, *Kozikowski*, [397 F. Supp. 1115,] 1116–17 [D.N.J. 1975] (asserting third-party complaint in personal injury action for indemnification against defendant who designed and constructed bridge); *Bell, supra*, 83 N.J. at 425 (allowing tort action for personal injuries arising from alleged negligent maintenance of bridge); *Yancoskie v. Del. River Port Auth.*, 478 Pa. 396, 387 (1978) (allowing suit in trespass for personal injuries arising from alleged negligent failure to follow safety standards in constructing bridge); *Del. River Port Auth. v. Thornburgh*, 585 A.2d 1123, 1124 n.1 (Pa. Commw. Ct. 1991) (asserting claim and counterclaim for breach of contract against Pennsylvania Department of Transportation). In the process of asserting common law claims, the DRPA also has relied on changes in the common law since 1931 when the compact was formed. *See, e.g.*, *Thornburgh, supra*, 585 A.2d at 1128 (relying on Pennsylvania Supreme Court case from 1957 regarding oral modification, and two cases from the 1980s regarding agency principles as applied to defendant Department of Transportation). Indeed, DRPA undoubtedly has benefited from the evolution of the common law. *See, e.g.*, *Textar Painting Corp. v. Del. River Port Auth.*, 296 N.J. Super. 251, 258 (Law Div. 1996) (dismissing complaint against DRPA after finding substantially similar common law in New Jersey and Pennsylvania from the 1950s through 1990s that favored competitive bidding).

Although the common law may be a source of the imposition of duties on DRPA, the common law of those two states, like the statutory law, must be substantially similar so that its application not be deemed a unilateral imposition. *See* [*Int'l Union of Operating Eng'rs, Local 68 v. Del. River & Bay Auth.*, 147 N.J. 433, 444 (1997)]. . . . Since that time, the test has been recognized and applied by the federal courts. *See Moore v. Del. River Port Auth.*, 80 F. Supp. 2d 264, 266, 269 (D.N.J. 1999) (applying the "substantial similarity test" in analyzing a common law employment claim brought against the DRPA). We hold that the "substantial similarity" test applies to common law claims as well as statutory law claims . . . .

. . . .

Notes & Questions

1. At the end of the case excerpt, the New Jersey Supreme Court noted that New Jersey and Pennsylvania common law must be substantially similar—in essence, applying the same rule that it applies to state statutory law. Litigation in state court inevitably raises questions of common law in many forms. For example, the basic elements of a tort come from common law; thus, to defend itself, a compact agency would necessarily have to make arguments relating to those elements and the agency would have to rely on how the courts have applied those elements in the past. The agency would also have to rely on judicial decisions interpreting rules of civil procedure, such as for whether a plaintiff has properly plead his or her claims and how courts have applied summary judgment standards. Also, if the states allowed different forms of tort damages or used different jury

instructions, or used different procedures for determining the amount of damages, could a plaintiff receive any damages without violating the general compact law principle against applying state law to the compact?

As you recall from the *Local 542* excerpt above, New Jersey courts have a much lower threshold than Pennsylvania courts for determining when states' laws are "substantially similar. Does this make the application of common law more troubling than if the states applied the substantially similar standard in the same manner?

2. The New Jersey Supreme Court did not address the second requirement for when one state concurs with new law of another state—that the states' legislatures must give some indication that they intend for the law to apply to the compact. While skipping the second requirement seems like a significant oversight, perhaps it was intentional. How would the states' legislatures indicate intent to apply common law to the compact when common law is "created" by the judicial branch of state government?

3. The New Jersey Supreme Court emphasized that common law should apply in this case because the Delaware River Port Authority had relied on common law in cases that it brought in the past. Reread note 1 above and consider whether the DRPA could have handled past cases without relying on some common law. If common law is unavoidable, should the court have used DRPA's past practice as rationale to apply common law in *Ballinger*?

4. The Court also stated, ". . . plaintiff correctly points out that the compact does not state that only a member state's Legislature may impose duties on DRPA . . . ." 172 N.J. at 597. Presumably, the Court was suggesting that as an arm of the state, it too could impose duties on the DRPA. The Court considered one provision of the compact that allows the DRPA to "exercise the powers, duties, authority and jurisdiction heretofore conferred and imposed on [it] by the Commonwealth of Pennsylvania or the State of New Jersey, or both of the said two States." But the court also cited another provision of the compact that specifies the DRPA "shall also have such additional powers as may hereafter be delegated to or imposed upon it from time to time by the action of either State concurred in by legislation of the other." Is there a conflict between these two provisions of the compact? Did the Court's decision create a conflict?

5. In *Alpert v. Port Auth. of N.Y. & N.J.*, 442 N.J. Super. 146 (Law Div. 2015), the court concluded that New Jersey's Conscientious Employee Protection Act (CEPA) did not apply to a claim against the Port Authority of New York and New Jersey because CEPA and New York's Whistleblower Law differed as to the range of activities covered by the law, damages and the right to a jury trial. In this respect, it closely followed *Ballinger*. But the Superior Court further concluded that the plaintiff could not raise common law wrongful termination claims for retaliation against the Port Authority in New Jersey because New York does not recognize common law claims for wrongful termination of employees-at-will, and thus the common law of the states is not substantially similar.

6. Should common law apply through a state statute that a compact does not specifically preserve? In *Skamania Cty. v. Woodall*, 104 Wash. App. 525 (2001), involving the Columbia River Gorge Compact, the court stated,

> Congress's decision not to dictate that federal law apply suggests it intended the Commission to apply state law. When Congress placed jurisdiction almost exclusively in the state courts, it did not command the state courts to apply federal law. Congress had to know that absent such a command, Washington state courts are required to apply Washington state common law. *See* RCW 4.04.010 ('The common law, so far as it is not inconsistent with the Constitution and laws of the United States, or of the state of Washington nor incompatible with the institutions and condition of society in this state, shall be the rule of decision in all the courts of this state.') . . .

Id. at 535. The Columbia River Gorge Compact did not preserve RCW 4.04.010. Moreover, the Columbia River Gorge Compact postdated *Cuyler v. Adams*, in which the Supreme Court concluded that a compact with consent becomes federal law. Why would Congress need to specify that state courts must apply federal law to a compact when state courts routinely do so with other federal laws? Similarly, in *I.B.M. v. Dep't of Treasury*, No. 306618, 2012 Mich. App. LEXIS 2293 (Mich. Ct. App. Nov. 20, 2012), *rev'd*, 496 Mich. 462 (2014), the Michigan Court of Appeals concluded that the Michigan Legislature did not create a binding contract because it did not use specifically use the words "contract" or "covenant" or otherwise indicate that it intended to surrender its power to change state law after enacting the compact, which Michigan common law requires.

7. In *Proctor v. Wash. Metro. Area Transit Auth.*, 412 Md. 691 (2010), involving questions certified from the federal court, the Maryland Court of Appeals (Maryland's highest court) concluded that the federal court could apply state common law on non-economic damages under the Maryland Tort Claims Act where the compact incorporated Maryland's substantive tort law. Its reasoning was brief: when federal courts apply state law, they do so "whether the law of the State shall be declared by its Legislature or by the Highest court in a decision." *Id.* at 728 (citing *Erie R.R. v. Tompkins*, 304 U.S. 64, 78 (1938)).

8. *Tarrant Reg'l Water Dist. v. Sevenoaks,* 545 F.3d 906 (10th Cir. 2008), is an interesting variation on the application of state common law. The Tenth Circuit noted that Oklahoma Supreme Court precedent requires public officers to follow an attorney general's opinion until a court determines otherwise, and rejected an argument that the Red River Compact overruled the attorney general opinion because the compact was not a judicial action. *Id.* at 909 n.2. Should a legislatively enacted compact with congressional consent supersede the prior opinion of one state's attorney general? Should the opinion of one state's attorney general guide the actions of a multi-state compact?

9. Consider whether prior private actions pursuant to state law can vest third party rights that bind a compact agency. In *W. Highland Mortg. Fund I, LLC v. Tahoe Reg'l Planning Agency*, No. 3:11-CV-00444-RCJ, 2013 U.S. Dist. LEXIS

131955 (D. Nev. Sept. 16, 2013), the court considered whether an "orgy of encumbrances" created a legal parcel such that the Tahoe Regional Planning Agency must also recognize as a "parcel" under its own regulations for the purposes of development. The district court held that it did not, reasoning in part that the Tahoe Regional Planning Compact, having been approved by Congress, had the force of a federal statute. *Id.* at *4.

V. State Law as Implied Repeal of Compact

Occasionally, parties that would prefer the application of later-enacted state law instead of a compact argue that the later-enacted state law impliedly repealed a conflicting provision of the compact. Courts universally conclude that implied repeal is a disfavored approach to legislation and thus require the implied repealing text must be unmistakable. The next case, *Santiago v. Port Auth. of N.Y. & N.J.*, illustrates the typical approach courts use for implied repeal arguments in a compact case, mashing together implied repeal and application of state law jurisprudence.

Santiago v. Port Authority of N.Y. & N.J.

429 N.J. Super. 150 (App. Div. 2012)

Messano, P.J.A.D.

On October 12, 2010, plaintiff Enid Santiago filed a complaint against defendant the Port Authority of New York and New Jersey (the Port Authority), and one of its employees, Tunnel and Bridge Agent Gregory Noa. Plaintiff alleged: violations of the New Jersey Conscientious Employee Protection Act (CEPA); the New Jersey Law Against Discrimination (LAD); common law claims for abuse of process, interference with contractual rights, and defamation; and claims for violations under the State constitution. . . .

On April 12, 2011, prior to filing an answer and relying upon [New Jersey statutes codifying the compact], defendants moved to dismiss the complaint. That statute provides in relevant part:

> [A]ny suit, action or proceeding prosecuted or maintained under this act shall be commenced within one year after the cause of action therefor shall have accrued, and ... in the case of any suit, action or proceeding for the recovery or payment of money, prosecuted or maintained under this act, a notice of claim shall have been served upon the Port Authority by ... the plaintiff ... at least sixty days before such suit, action or proceeding is commenced.

Defendants contended that because plaintiff admittedly failed to serve any notice of claim prior to filing her complaint, the court lacked subject matter jurisdiction. The motion judge agreed and entered an order dismissing the complaint "because of [p]laintiff's failure to comply with the statutory prerequisites set forth in [the compact]."

On appeal, plaintiff argues that the judge erred as a matter of law because the Port Authority "has implicitly consented to New Jersey's jurisdiction" since both

New Jersey and New York have "enact[ed] similar legislation to eradic[ate] unlawful employment practices in the workplace," and "no notice of claim was required to be filed before ... filing ... suit." Additionally, plaintiff contends that her constitutional claims, cognizable under New Jersey's Civil Rights Act (the CRA), "appl[y] to the Port Authority." We have considered these arguments in light of the record and applicable legal standards. We affirm.

. . . .

The Port Authority was created by a bi-state compact enacted into law by the legislatures of New York and New Jersey and approved by Congress. Plaintiff does not contend that the compact has explicitly been modified to recognize her claims under the LAD, CEPA or the CRA. Instead she argues that, because the LAD and CEPA are substantially similar to legislation enacted by New York, the Port Authority has implicitly consented to being sued for such claims. As to the CRA, plaintiff contends that it, too, applies to the Port Authority because application "would not interfere with the operations of the Port Authority or its stated mission." She further contends that because New Jersey does not impose a notice requirement before filing a complaint alleging causes of action under these statutes, it was error to conclude that the court lacked subject matter jurisdiction because of plaintiff's failure to comply with [the compact].

We first look to the statutory framework governing the Port Authority, which has "the powers and jurisdiction * * * enumerated" in the compact, "and such other and additional powers as shall be conferred upon it by the Legislature of either State concurred in by the Legislature of the other, or by Act or Acts of Congress. * * *" N.J.S.A. 32:1-4. Therefore, "[t]he Port Authority is not the agency of a single state but rather a public corporate instrumentality of New Jersey and New York[,]" *Bunk v. Port Auth. of N.Y. & N.J.*, 144 N.J. 176, 184 (1996), and, "neither creator state may unilaterally impose additional duties, powers, or responsibility upon the [Port] Authority." *Ibid.* (citing *Nardi v. Del. River Port Auth.*, 490 A.2d 949, 950 ([Pa. Commw. Ct.] 1985)). Our Supreme Court has said that "[t]o sanction such practice would lead to discord and a destruction of the purposes for which such bi-state agencies are formed." *Bell v. Bell*, 83 N.J. 417, 424, (1980).

Nonetheless, "[t]he corollary of the proposition that neither state may unilaterally impose its legislative will on the bi-state agency is that the agency may be subject to complementary or parallel state legislation[,]" *Bunk*, supra, 144 N.J. at 184, "that does not intrude on the mission of the agency." *Ampro Fisheries v. Yaskin*, 127 N.J. 602, 610 (1992).

"Under the 'complementary or parallel legislation' principle, one compact state's statute can be applied to the bi-state agency if it is 'substantially similar' to an enactment of the other state." *Ballinger v. Del. River Port Auth.*, 172 N.J. 586, 594 (2002). "In order to be deemed substantially similar, the two laws at issue must evidence some showing of agreement." *Id.* at 600.

We need not decide whether the LAD or CEPA are substantially similar to New York's legislation such that the compact is violated by application of either statute to the Port Authority. Nor need we address whether the CRA applies to the Port Authority because the statute "does not intrude on the mission of the agency." Instead, assuming arguendo that these statutes do apply, we consider the necessary corollary to plaintiff's argument. She contends that because these statutes apply to the Port Authority, the notice requirement of N.J.S.A. 32:1-163 has been impliedly repealed because New Jersey does not require any pre-suit notification under the LAD, CEPA or the CRA. We disagree.

"Prior to 1951 the Port Authority was immune from suit." *Wood v. Dic/Underhill & Universal Builders Supply Co.*, 136 N.J. Super. 249, 252 (Law Div. 1975). [The compact] now provides that, with certain exceptions not applicable here, "the States of New York and New Jersey consent to suits, actions or proceedings of any form or nature at law, in equity or otherwise... against the [Port Authority], and to appeals therefrom and reviews thereof." *See Wood*, *supra*, 136 N.J. Super. at 252 ("By joint legislation which became effective June 13, 1951, sovereign immunity was waived and consent was given to suits against th[e] agency."). "[I]n the absence of the 1951 waiver the [Port] Authority would continue to enjoy the protection of sovereign immunity." *Port Auth. of N.Y. v. Ingram*, 232 N.J. Super. 401, 404 (App. Div. 1989).

The scope of the Port Authority's statutory consent, as set forth in [the compact], "is broader ... than that used for many other agencies." *Lieberman v. Port Auth. of N.Y. & N.J.*, 132 N.J. 76, 83 (1993). That statute provides that the "two States consent to liability on the part of the Port Authority in such suits, actions or proceedings for tortious acts committed by it and its agents to the same extent as though it were a private corporation." N.J.S.A. 32:1-162 [New Jersey's statutes enacting the compact]. The Lieberman Court concluded that the Port Authority's "amenability to suit in the exercise of non-governmental functions is broader than that of agencies authorized only to 'sue and be sued.'" *Lieberman*, 132 N.J. at 84.

. . . .

Facing this body of precedent, plaintiff has taken a different tack. She contends that because the notice provisions of the Tort Claims Act (TCA) do not apply to suits brought under the LAD, CEPA or the CRA, we should conclude that the notice provisions of [the compact] have been impliedly repealed whenever a complaint implicating those statutes is filed against the Port Authority. . . .

First, our courts have long-recognized that the TCA does not apply to the Port Authority. *See Lieberman, supra*, 132 N.J. at 82 (noting that even though the Port Authority statutorily consented to being sued, "it is not subject to the New Jersey Tort Claims Act"). We are, therefore, hard-pressed to accept plaintiff's argument by analogy to a statute that is inapplicable from the start.

Second, those cases cited by plaintiff that recognized the "complementary and parallel" legislation doctrine as impliedly amending the compact did so only with respect to the substantive nature of the claims. The Court in *Bunk*, *Ampro Fisheries*, *E. Paralyzed Veterans Ass'n* [*v. City of Camden*, 111 N.J. 389 (1988)], and *Int'l Union of Operating Eng'rs, Local 68 v. Del. River & Bay Auth.*, 147 N.J. 433, 445 (1997), utilized the "complementary and parallel" legislation doctrine to construe an implied modification of a bi-state compact so as to permit statutory or regulatory claims to be asserted. But, none of those cases considered implied repeal or modification of conditions precedent to establishing subject matter jurisdiction for the suits, i.e., in this case, the notice requirement of N.J.S.A. 32:1-163. Plaintiff has not cited any case for that proposition, nor did our research reveal one.

Third, modification of a statute by implication is disfavored, even when the intent of our Legislature alone is at issue. "[T]here is a strong presumption in the law against implied repealers and every reasonable construction should be applied to avoid such a finding." *In re Comm'r of Ins.'s Issuance of Orders A-92-189 & A-92-212*, 137 N.J. 93, 99 (1994) (citing *Mahwah Twp. v. Bergen Cnty. Bd. of Taxation*, 98 N.J. 268, 281 (1985). "[A] repeal by implication requires clear and compelling evidence of legislative intent, and such intent must be free from reasonable doubt." *Ibid.* (citing *Mahwah Twp., supra*, 98 N.J. at 280). We, therefore, reject plaintiff's implied modification or repeal argument as applied to the Port Authority, a bi-state agency created by a compact entered into by both New Jersey and New York, and its limited consent to be sued.

Lastly, we recognize our role as a court of intermediate appellate jurisdiction. It would be unwise for us to conclude that the notice provisions of [the compact] do not apply to plaintiff's statutory causes of action given the significant implications of such a holding. . . .

In sum, we affirm the dismissal of plaintiff's complaint because she failed to comply with the sixty-day notice provisions of [the compact].

Notes & Questions

1. The implied repeal issue also arises with compacts that are silent about modification by new state law. In *Gillette Co. v. Franchise Tax Bd.*, 209 Cal. App. 4th 938 (2012), *rev'd on other grounds*, *Gillette Co. v. Franchise Tax Bd.*, 62 Cal. 4th 468 (2015), the California Franchise Tax Board argued that a later-enacted state statute impliedly repealed a provision of the Multistate Tax Compact. The California Court of Appeal disagreed, holding that the effect of an implied repeal would have violated the California Constitution. *Id.* at 960.

2. In *I.B.M. v. Dep't of Treasury*, 496 Mich. 642 (2014), a case like *Gillette*, the Michigan Supreme Court concluded that Michigan's Business Tax Act (BTA), enacted in 2008, did not impliedly repeal Michigan's participation in the Multistate Tax Compact. The Court reasoned in part:

> Subsequent action by the Legislature indicates that it did not impliedly repeal the Compact's election provision when it enacted the BTA. On May 25, 2011, the Legislature expressly amended the Compact's election provision by adding the following language:
>
> > [E]xcept that beginning January 1, 2011 any taxpayer subject to the Michigan business tax act or the income tax act of 1967, shall, for purposes of that act, apportion and allocate in accordance with the provisions of that act and shall not apportion or allocate in accordance with article IV.

> There is no dispute that the Legislature specifically intended to retroactively repeal the Compact's election provision for taxpayers subject to the BTA beginning January 1, 2011. The Legislature could have—but did not—extend this retroactive repeal to the start date of the BTA. . . . [B]y only repealing the Compact's election provision starting January 1, 2011, the Legislature created a window in which it did not expressly preclude use of the Compact's election provision for BTA taxpayers. Further, we believe that the express repeal of the Compact's election provision effective January 1, 2011, is evidence that the Legislature had not impliedly repealed the provision when it enacted the BTA.

496 Mich. at 658–60. Note that the Court stated the Legislature expressly amended the Compact's election provision. Is a unilateral amendment of a compact through new state law the functional equivalent of an implied repeal of a compact through new state law? The Multistate Tax Compact does not expressly allow the states to amend the compact. Based on the material you have read so far in in this chapter, how could it have done so? Should repeal by implication occur when all parties to a compact subsequently enact a substantially similar conflicting statute? What if the parties enact statutes that differently amend the same provision of the compact? Would the states still have a compact of any kind?

Should a state ever be able to repeal a compact by implication? Consider two analogies. First, recall the *Riverside Irrigation Dist.* case in Chapter 2, suggesting that Congress may enact generally applicable legislation that may affect a compact, but may not be able to enact legislation directed at changing the obligations of a compact. Second, Recall the *Sullivan v. Pa. Dep't of Transp.* case in Chapter 3 holding that Pennsylvania did not properly enact a compact by executive action when the compact requires withdrawal by statute. Article X.2 of the Multistate Tax Compact similarly specifies that a state may withdraw from the compact by enacting a statute repealing its enactment of the compact. Does this withdrawal provision require an express repeal? Does an implied repeal by enacting a conflicting statute fulfill this requirement? How would other parties to the compact know that Michigan is no longer a member if its repeal is merely implied?

3. *Universal Interpretive Shuttle Corp. v. Wash. Metro. Area Transit Comm'n*, 393 U.S. 186 (1968) (excerpted in Chapter 2), is a variation on state law acting as an implied repeal of a compact—the Supreme Court concluded that a compact (with consent) did not impliedly repeal other federal law, stating, "There is thus no reason to ignore the principle that repeals by implication are not favored . . ." and thus concluding that the Washington Metropolitan Area Transit Compact did not "disturb the exclusivity of the Secretary [of Interior's] control over the Mall . . . ." *Id.* at 193.

4. If states have different implied repeal jurisprudence, then could provisions of a compact be considered repealed in one state but not another? With different compact provisions applicable to the party states, would the states still have a valid compact? Would there still be a meeting of the minds?

VI. Compact Agency Consent to State Law

Finally, state law may apply to a compact when a compact agency has consented to the application of state law. Compact agencies may expressly consent in different ways. Some compact agencies adopt state law as part of their own regulations. For example, the Tahoe Regional Planning Agency Code incorporates California standards for certain types of signs. TRPA Code §§ 34.3.2.D, 38.5.2, 38.6.1.A. Compact agencies may also comply with requests from a party state to follow a particular state law requirement. In the next case, the court considered how a compact agency could impliedly consent to the application of state law.

E. Paralyzed Veterans Assoc. v. Camden
111 N.J. 389 (1988)

O'HERN, J.

This case presents a troublesome dilemma for resolution. It involves a cooperative undertaking by a bi-state agency and a New Jersey municipal agency to create in New Jersey a downtown mass transportation center. Such a center will serve the laudable public goals of reducing dependence on automobiles, improving public transportation, and strengthening an inner city area. Both the Camden Housing Authority and the Delaware River Port Authority (DRPA), a bi-state agency of New Jersey and Pennsylvania, had the best of intentions. Under their cooperative plan, the Camden Housing Authority was to erect and construct a mass transit terminal in which DRPA's subsidiary Port Authority Transportation Corporation (PATCO) train service would operate.

The issue in this appeal has been presented as whether New Jersey's barrier-free design requirements in aid of the handicapped may be applied to the DRPA's operations or facilities. The trial court, differentiating between independent state regulation of the "external" operations of bi-state agencies and states' common regulations of their "internal" operations, concluded that the DRPA was required by New Jersey's Handicapped-Access Law to grant the municipality permission to install an elevator in the facility. *Eastern Paralyzed Veterans Ass'n, Inc. v. Camden*, 220 N.J. Super. 573, 582-85 (Ch. Div. 1986). The Appellate Division affirmed that judgment, but did so primarily on the ground that the portion of the building in which the elevator is located is "not exempt from the operation and effect of the applicable New Jersey statutes and regulations by virtue of the contractual arrangements and property conveyances made among and between the Delaware River Port Authority, Camden and the Housing Authority of Camden." *Eastern Paralyzed Veterans Ass'n, Inc. v. Camden*, 220 N.J. Super. 528, 531 (1987).

We hold that the trial court's theory of jurisdiction cannot be sustained, and we believe that before a court can conclude that the agency impliedly consented to New Jersey's design requirements, it must consider the question of whether the structural change would significantly affect PATCO's operations. On remand to consider that question, the Chancery Division may also consider whether the requirement may be justified as one of "complementary" regulation in each of the enabling states.

. . . .

If the New Jersey regulatory system is not "complementary" to Pennsylvania's, then we believe that additional findings must be made before we can conclude that the DRPA has impliedly consented to provide elevator access to its train platform. As noted, the Appellate Division concluded that the DRPA had implicitly consented to the plenary exercise of jurisdiction by New Jersey. This would be a critical finding indeed, because as an independent agency possessing the power to sue and be sued, *Bell v. Bell, supra,* 83 N.J. 417, the DRPA could waive its rights under the compact and cede jurisdiction to the New Jersey regulatory agencies. We surmise that in almost all circumstances such as these, an agency would have its construction plans reviewed by the state in which the construction was planned. We were informed at oral argument that the Port Authority of New York and New Jersey has voluntarily cooperated with New Jersey agencies to provide handicapped access to planned new facilities. We do not, however, find that the DRPA offered such cooperation here: it is quite clear from the record that from the outset the DRPA resisted the exercise of jurisdiction by the State of New Jersey and limited its own efforts to providing the shaft for future installation of the elevator.

. . . .

Notes & Questions

1. If the New Jersey Supreme Court had affirmed the trial court's conclusion that by simply entering into a contract, the DRPA had impliedly consented to follow state law, then would any interaction between a compact agency and another party, whether state government or private party, suggest consent to apply state law because those other parties are independently subject to state law? What could be a limiting principle for the trial court's holding?

2. If a compact agency chooses to follow one state law, then is it impliedly consenting to follow any other state law? What about state laws that are related in some way to the law the compact agency has chosen to follow? For example, if a compact agency chooses to follow one state's rulemaking procedure, then has it impliedly consented to judicial review in that state's courts using that state's jurisprudence? How would you analyze whether a different state law is related to the state law that the compact agency has chosen to follow?

3. How can a compact agency that has impliedly consented to state law for a period of years change its policy or practice to not follow the state law? Does the contract law principle of "course of performance" apply? Chapter 9 discussed course of performance and other contract and statutory interpretation principles to a compact.

CHAPTER 9: INTERPRETATION OF COMPACTS

Interpretation of compacts has the same goal as interpretation of statutes and contracts—to find the intent of the legislatures as the parties to the compact. Courts frequently apply principles that they have developed for interpreting statutes and commercial contracts; however, courts sometimes also apply unique interpretive principles not relevant to traditional statutes and contracts. For example, as you have read throughout this book, the goal of uniformly applying a compact throughout the party states sometimes conflicts with the states' internal priorities, such as funding problems and changing public opinion, which force legislatures and agencies to choose whether and how to honor their compact obligations.

Recall *West Virginia ex rel. Dyer v. Sims* (excerpted in Chapter 3), in which the Supreme Court discussed how one state could not be the last word on its obligations under the compact, and *Beebe v. Wash. Metro. Transit Auth.* (excerpted in Chapter 5), in which the Third Circuit filled a gap in the compact using federal law because using state law could result in applying "different, possibly inconsistent" rules to the agency. The ability to seek review at the Supreme Court is one way that courts can provide uniform application of a compact. This chapter, however, looks specifically at interpretative methods that courts use when interpreting compacts.

Courts often recognize that different interpretive methods in the states may create different outcomes but struggle with whether their long-established methods of statutory construction allow them to consider the goal of uniformity. As a result, some courts interpret compact texts or congressional consent actions to mean that the states may not have intended uniform interpretations of the compact. The task of finding legislative intent within a single Congress or a single state legislature is complicated. That task is even more difficult when trying to find a single intent of Congress *and* multiple state legislatures.

I. APPLYING TREATY INTERPRETATION PRINCIPLES

International treaties share many of the same challenges as compacts; both have multiple sovereigns whose courts interpret the agreement. For example, undefined terms in a compact may have different or unanticipated meanings in the states' jurisprudence just as treaties that are authenticated in multiple languages may result in terms that have unanticipated meanings. The Vienna Convention on the Law of Treaties, which has 45 contracting states and 116 parties, includes principles for the interpretation of treaties, and is authenticated in English, French, Chinese, Russian, and Spanish. Consider how the Vienna Convention's principles might apply to the interpretation of compacts between states.

Vienna Convention on the Law of Treaties, 1155 U.N.T.S. 331 (May 23, 1969)

PART III.

OBSERVANCE, APPLICATION AND INTERPRETATION OF TREATIES

SECTION 1. OBSERVANCE OF TREATIES

Article 26

"Pacta sunt servanda"

Every treaty in force is binding upon the parties to it and must be performed by them in good faith.

Article 27

Internal law and observance of treaties

A party may not invoke the provisions of its internal law as justification for its failure to perform a treaty. . . .

. . . .

SECTION 3. INTERPRETATION OF TREATIES

Article 31

General rule of interpretation

1. A treaty shall be interpreted in good faith in accordance with the ordinary meaning to be given to the terms of the treaty in their context and in the light of its object and purpose.

2. The context for the purpose of the interpretation of a treaty shall comprise, in addition to the text, including its preamble and annexes:

(a) any agreement relating to the treaty which was made between all the parties in connection with the conclusion of the treaty;

(b) any instrument which was made by one or more parties in connection with the conclusion of the treaty and accepted by the other parties as an instrument related to the treaty.

3. There shall be taken into account, together with the context:

(a) any subsequent agreement between the parties regarding the interpretation of the treaty or the application of its provisions;

(b) any subsequent practice in the application of the treaty which establishes the agreement of the parties regarding its interpretation;

(c) any relevant rules of international law applicable in the relations between the parties.

4. A special meaning shall be given to a term if it is established that the parties so intended.

Article 32

Supplementary means of interpretation

Recourse may be had to supplementary means of interpretation, including the preparatory work of the treaty and the circumstances of its conclusion, in order to confirm the meaning resulting from the application of article 31, or to determine the meaning when the interpretation according to article 31:

(a) leaves the meaning ambiguous or obscure; or

(b) leads to a result which is manifestly absurd or unreasonable.

Article 33

Interpretation of treaties authenticated in two or more languages

1. When a treaty has been authenticated in two or more languages, the text is equally authoritative in each language, unless the treaty provides or the parties agree that, in case of divergence, a particular text shall prevail.

2. A version of the treaty in a language other than one of those in which the text was authenticated shall be considered an authentic text only if the treaty so provides or the parties so agree.

3. The terms of the treaty are presumed to have the same meaning in each authentic text.

4. Except where a particular text prevails in accordance with paragraph 1, when a comparison of the authentic texts discloses a difference of meaning which the application of articles 31 and 32 does not remove, the meaning which best reconciles the texts, having regard to the object and purpose of the treaty, shall be adopted.

Notes & Questions

1. What principles of compact law are like the principle stated in Article 27?

2. The principles stated in Article 31.3 are like principles used when interpreting an ordinary contract. Should these principles also apply when interpreting a compact? Would a "subsequent agreement" between the parties stated in subsection (3)(a) be a permissible amendment of the compact? Would subsection (3)(c) refer to federal law in the compact context, and would applying it conflict with any other principles of compact law?

3. What does Article 33.1 mean when it says that the text of a treaty is equally authoritative in each language? Compacts are similarly authoritative in each state, but courts in the compacting states may give different meanings to the same text. This most often arises when courts have already interpreted a term in another context, or when courts use different means for statutory construction. Some courts give terms their meaning as found in a dictionary of common usage. Some courts expressly look to interpretations that will lead to uniform application of the

compact, and some courts consider the prior decisions of other courts relating to the compact. Consider these approaches in the cases throughout this chapter.

4. Is treaty law an appropriate analogy for interstate compacts? A few courts have hinted that treaties and compacts are conceptually similar. In *Rhode Island v. Massachusetts*, 37 U.S. (12 Pet.) 657 (1838), the Supreme Court stated, "If congress consented, then the states were in this respect restored to their original inherent sovereignty; such consent being the sole limitation imposed by the constitution, when given, left the states as they were before, as held by this Court in *Poole v. Fleeger*, 11 Peters, 209; whereby their compacts became of binding force, and finally settled the boundary between them; operating with the same effect as a treaty between sovereign powers." *Id.* at 725. More recently, *New Jersey v. New York*, 523 U.S. 767 (1998), involved a question whether filled portions of New York Harbor increasing the size of Ellis Island belonged to New Jersey or New York pursuant to an 1834 boundary compact between the states. Justice Scalia, in a dissent, observed, "the Compact here is of course a treaty." *Id.* at 831. In *Alabama v. North Carolina*, 560 U.S. 330 (2010), Justice Kennedy, in a concurrence, similarly used a treaty analogy, stating, "Like a treaty, a compact represents an agreement between parties" and cited cases interpreting treaties. *Id.* at 359. In *State ex rel. Intake Water Co. v Bd. of Nat. Res. and Cons.*, 197 Mont. 482 (1982), the Montana Supreme Court observed, "The [Yellowstone] Compact, signed by Wyoming, Montana, and North Dakota and ratified by congress has the status of a treaty and state law is subordinate to it." *Id.* at 489.

In *Arizona v. California*, 292 U.S. 341 (1934), the Supreme Court applied the "traditional rule" for interpreting treaties "that when the meaning of a treaty is not clear, recourse may be had to the negotiations, preparatory works, and diplomatic correspondence of the contracting parties to establish its meaning. But that rule has no application to oral statements made by those engaged in negotiating the treaty which were not embodied in any writing and were not communicated to the government of the negotiator or to its ratifying body." *Id.* at 359–60. In *Oklahoma v. New Mexico*, 501 U.S. 221 (1991), the Supreme Court cited this passage from *Arizona v. California* in concluding that a letter from the New Mexico compact commissioner to a single legislator, but not transmitted to other commissioners, the governor, or the legislature was "of little use in ascertaining the meaning of compact provisions." *Id.* at 236 n.6.

5. One scholar argues that treaties are distinct from "compacts" and "agreements" for the purpose of determining when consent is necessary under the Compact Clause. David E. Engdahl, *Characterization of Interstate Arrangements: When is a Compact Not a Compact?*, 64 MICH. L. REV. 63 (1965). Should courts use principles of treaty law to interpret compacts if requirements for consent under the Compact Clause differ for treaties and compacts?

6. Article I, section 1, clause 1 of the U.S. Constitution prohibits states from entering into "any Treaty, Alliance, or Confederation . . . ." Should courts use principles of treaty law to interpret compacts if states may not enter into treaties? Chapter 12 discusses this Article I treaty clause.

II. Court Interpretation of Compacts

Should courts interpret a compact as they would any other federal or state statute or commercial contract? Consider that courts use different interpretive principles for statutes and contracts. For example, as a statute, courts may give deference to a state's interpretation of a compact that it drafted, but as a contract, courts would construe the compact against the drafter. Another difference is that, unlike commercial contracts, courts may not imply a duty of good faith and fair dealing in compacts with congressional consent. The Supreme Court explained:

> We have never held that an interstate compact approved by Congress includes an implied duty of good faith and fair dealing. Of course "[e]very contract imposes upon each party a duty of good faith and fair dealing in its performance and its enforcement." But an interstate compact is not just a contract; it is a federal statute enacted by Congress. If courts were authorized to add a fairness requirement to the implementation of federal statutes, judges would be potent lawmakers indeed. We do not—we cannot—add provisions to a federal statute.

Alabama v. North Carolina, 560 U.S. 330, 351–52 (2010). But courts also use some similar principles for interpreting statutes and contracts. For example, courts may also defer to state agencies, associations, or compact agencies' interpretation of statutes that they administer, which is similar in concept to using course of performance to interpret contracts.

The next three case excerpts discuss two themes in interpreting compacts: plain text and uniformity. You should be familiar with the plain text approach from your contracts and statutory interpretation classes; courts typically start with the plain text to determine the meaning that the parties or legislature intended. A desire to seek a uniform interpretation of the compact and the use of federal law or one state's law as you studied in Chapters 5 and 8, however, may conflict with the plain text approach. The notes following these excerpts explore this tension, and the complexity of achieving a uniform interpretation of a compact when multiple state and federal courts have jurisdiction to hear cases involving the compact.

A. Consideration of Plain Text

Pievsky v. Ridge
98 F.3d 730 (3d Cir. 1996)

COWEN, JUDGE:

. . . .

The issue we must decide is strictly one of statutory construction. Does the DRPA Compact allow the Governor of Pennsylvania to remove a commissioner to the DRPA at will and prior to the expiration of his term?

Since the Compact is an interstate agreement which requires the consent of Congress, such congressional consent transforms the Compact into an agreement pursuant to federal law. Our interpretation of the terms and conditions of the Compact is, therefore, governed by federal law.

. . . .

The Compact is merely an agreement between states that has received the imprimatur of Congress. The interpretation of the Compact must be grounded and based upon the very language of the instrument. *Texas v. New Mexico*, 482 U.S. 124, 128 (1987). The Compact between Pennsylvania and New Jersey states that "six of the eight commissioners for the Commonwealth of Pennsylvania shall be appointed by the Governor of Pennsylvania for terms of five years." It does not explicitly state whether the commissioners may be removed by the governor prior to the expiration of their term.

The long-standing rule in the context of federal appointments is that "in the absence of specific provision to the contrary, the power of removal from office is incident to the power of appointment." *Keim v. United States*, 177 U.S. 290, 293 (1900). Pennsylvania has also adopted this principle of law. The Compact explicitly gives the Governor of Pennsylvania the power to appoint six commissioners to the DRPA. Accordingly, pursuant to federal law, there is a presumption that the Governor also has the authority to remove those six commissioners prior to the end of their terms.

Pievsky argues that since the DRPA Commissioner's term of office is five years, as compared to the Governor's four year term of office, the Pennsylvania legislature and Congress intended to limit the Governor's power of removal. We disagree. The fact that the Governor's term of office is shorter than that of the commissioners does not indicate an intent on the part of the legislature to limit the Governor's ability to remove his appointees. If the Pennsylvania legislature intended such a limitation, it would have stated so in the Compact. Instead, the Compact simply reads that the Governor of Pennsylvania shall appoint a DRPA Commissioner for a term of five years. Since the power to remove is incident to the power to appoint, we hold that under the terms of the Compact the Governor of Pennsylvania has the authority to remove a DRPA Commissioner at will.

We believe that the difference in the length of terms of office is irrelevant. Since the Compact provides that commissioners may hold office after the expiration of the term for which they are appointed, and "no period during which any commissioner shall hold over shall be deemed to be an extension of this term of office for the purpose of computing the date on which his successor's term expires," a commissioner's term of office may in fact be for four years or less. This would occur if a commissioner is succeeding a prior commissioner who has continued to hold office after the expiration of his term of office.

Pievsky also contends that interpreting the Compact to permit the Governor to remove a commissioner at will vitiates the plain language of the Compact which provides that six of the Commonwealth's commissioners "shall be appointed by the Governor of Pennsylvania for terms of five years." He asserts that five years means five years, and not less than five years. We are not persuaded. It is a long-standing rule in the federal courts that a fixed term merely provides a time for the term to end. The fixed term is merely a "cap" with the appointee removable at will. We read the term "five years" as a means of limiting the length of the term of office, not as a prohibition on the Governor's removal authority.

. . . .

Notes & Questions

1. The Third Circuit stated that federal law governed its interpretation of the compact. Why didn't the court adopt Pievsky's plain language argument? Why did the court also mention Pennsylvania law? Why did the court not also consider New Jersey law? What would the court have done if New Jersey, Pennsylvania, and federal law had differed in any material way?

The Third Circuit also stated, "The Compact is merely an agreement between states that has received the imprimatur of Congress. The interpretation of the Compact must be grounded and based upon the very language of the instrument." 98 F.3d at 733. Could multiple courts find different meaning from the same "plain language"?

2. Plain language is a long-standing principle. *Green v. Biddle*, the first compact case at the U.S. Supreme Court, mentioned it, stating, "that where the words of a law, treaty, or contract, have a plain and obvious meaning, all construction, in hostility with such meaning, is excluded. This is a maxim of law, and a dictate of common sense; for were a different rule to be admitted, no man, however cautious and intelligent, could safely estimate the extent of his engagements, or rest upon his own understanding of a law, until a judicial construction of those instruments had been obtained." *Green v. Biddle*, 21 U.S. (8 Wheat.) 1, 89–90 (1823).

3. *Pievsky v. Ridge* has an interesting background. Chapter 10 contains a longer excerpt of the case relating to appointment and removal of compact officials, and the notes following that latter excerpt fill in some of the rest of the story not mentioned in the court's opinion.

B. Uniform Interpretation of Compacts

In re Application of Waterfront Comm'n of N.Y. Harbor
39 N.J. 436 (1963)

PROCTOR, JUSTICE:

[The Waterfront Commission of New York Harbor instituted contempt proceedings against John Moody and William Murphy for failure to testify pursuant to subpoenas. The Waterfront Commission had granted the defendants immunity from prosecution in the states of New York and New Jersey.]

On this appeal, the defendants first point out that under the [New Jersey] Evidence Act, 1960, the privilege against self-incrimination expressly extends to federal incrimination. They argue that since the Waterfront Commission declared that its grant of immunity to the defendants did not and could not extend to federal prosecutions, the Commission's orders to answer were in violation of the aforesaid act.

. . . .

. . . The Waterfront Commission Act is an interstate compact, enacted by the States of New York and New Jersey in 1953 with the consent of Congress in order to eliminate evil conditions on the waterfront in the Port of New York Harbor. The Compact creates the Waterfront Commission as an agency of both States, with authority to license or register workers, and for good cause to refuse licenses and registrations, and to regulate labor and hiring practices on the waterfront. In order to further the elimination of waterfront evils, the Commission is empowered to investigate waterfront practices and other matters bearing on the objectives of the Compact, and to make recommendations to the two States for the improvement of waterfront conditions and for the effectuation of the purposes of the Compact. The members of the Commission and its properly designated officers may administer oaths and issue subpoenas throughout both States to compel the attendance of witnesses, the giving of testimony, and the production of other evidence. . . .

. . . .

. . . The question before us [is whether under the Evidence Act, 1960] the privilege against self-incrimination to include incrimination under federal law was intended by the Legislature to immediately impair the powers of the Waterfront Commission to investigate evil waterfront practices and to compel testimony after a grant of immunity from statewide prosecution in New York and New Jersey. We think the Legislature had no such intention in mind when it passed the Evidence Act, 1960.

It is clear that in the formation of the Compact our Legislature, together with the Legislature of New York, intended to deal with joint problems existing throughout a single port area situated partly in New York and partly in New Jersey, and not with separate problems in separate ports of each State. From the standpoint of geography, commerce, and waterfront working conditions, New York Harbor is an organic whole, although politically the harbor is split between the law-making authority of the two States. Plainly, these joint problems could not be adequately dealt with except through the coordinated efforts of the two States and the United States. The situation called for unified action. As a consequence, the Waterfront Commission, a single bistate agency, was established with the consent of Congress to administer a joint legislative program throughout the Port of New York District, embracing the New York-New Jersey waterfront. Both States ceded certain governmental powers to this autonomous bistate agency. These powers, as mentioned earlier in this opinion, include the power to make appropriate investigations, subpoena witnesses, and compel testimony after a grant of immunity against prosecution in both States. The objectives of the Compact were to provide for uniform treatment of a unique, bistate problem. Such uniformity, in order to be effective, must be maintained throughout the life of the Compact. *See* Frankfurter & Landis, *The Compact Clause of the Constitution—A Study in Interstate Adjustments*, 34 YALE L.J. 685, 698 (1925). In short, the Waterfront Commission, when acting within the orbit of the governmental responsibility which the States have expressly or by fair implication agreed to vest in it, was intended to be free from any unilateral restraint by either State which might thwart the Commission in its efforts to eliminate evil conditions in an area where there is extensive activity in international and interstate commerce. Indeed, it is doubtful whether a single legislature could unilaterally impair the powers of the Waterfront Commission, even if it so desired. *See Green v. Biddle*, 8 Wheat. 1 (1823); *President, Managers &c., v. Trenton City Bridge Co.*, 13 N.J. Eq. 46 (Ch. 1860).

If, as defendants contend, a witness may claim the privilege against self-incrimination with respect to federal crimes notwithstanding a conferral of bistate immunity by the Commission, it would follow that there could be no effective investigation not only of the state aspects of such crimes but even of the non-criminal aspects of waterfront conditions since possible federal criminal overtones are frequently present. This is so because of the nature of waterfront activity and its constant involvement with interstate commerce and other such areas of federal jurisdiction. Since the Commission cannot grant immunity as to the federal crimes it will remain helpless. The difficulty is not merely fanciful; it might well result that investigations by the Commission would be seriously hampered and, in many cases, frustrated.

Moreover, an interpretation of the Compact which is not uniform in both States would lead to results disruptive of the investigative process of the Commission. It might mean that different witnesses would have different rights depending on which side of the Hudson River they lived, or on which side the events in question took place. It might also mean that the same witnesses would have different rights depending on which side of the River they appear for examination or are prosecuted for contempt. Certainly, our Legislature in adopting the Evidence Act, 1960 never intended such results.

. . . .

Notes & Questions

1. At base, this *Waterfront Commission* case involves the application of New Jersey's Evidence Act to the Waterfront Commission. Article XVI, § 1 of the Waterfront Commission Compact authorizes the states to amend and implement the compact through legislative action of either State concurred in by legislative action of the other State. What is the appropriate analysis from Chapter 8? Why did the New Jersey Supreme Court delve into the purposes of the compact?

2. The New Jersey Supreme Court expressly sought a uniform interpretation of the compact. Would the *Pievsky v. Ridge* method of statutory interpretation result in uniform interpretation of the compact? If not, then is there a reason to value uniformity in one compact, but not the other?

3. Should uniformity always be a goal when interpreting compacts? In the *Waterfront Commission* case, the New Jersey court cited to Frankfurter and Landis's seminal 1925 article (excerpted in Chapter 1). The full discussion of uniformity from that cited portion of the article is:

> Diversity of legislation among the several states as to some matters is inevitable and desirable. We have all too few social experiments carried on "in

> the insulated chambers afforded by the several States." But in other fields uniformity is being pursued with marked achievement through the National Conference of Commissioners on Uniform State Laws by securing the independent enactment by the individual States of the same measure. In one instance, at least, the Compact Clause had been relied on for uniformity. Attaining this end through compact assures maintenance of uniformity during the life of the compact.

Felix Frankfurter & James M. Landis, *The Compact Clause of the Constitution—A Study in Interstate Adjustments*, 34 YALE L.J. 685, 698 (1925). In contrast, another scholar questioned the characterization of compacts with consent as federal law and argued that qualities of federal law are not essential to a compact. One such quality would be receiving the benefit of uniform application of the compact. However, he argued:

> There appears no special reason to value uniformity more in the compact context than in the context of interpretation of identical state statutes. Even if uniformity is sought, however, that goal can be achieved through other means. One simple alternative would be to specify the choice of procedural or other governing laws within the compact itself. Another option would be for the compact agency to specify the choice of law for suits arising under compact agency law, just as many contracts between individuals or corporations specify choice of law.

L. Mark Eichorn, NOTE: *Cuyler v. Adams and the Characterization of Compact Law*, 77 VA. L. REV. 1387, 1407 (1991).

4. The last paragraph of the *Waterfront Commission* excerpt explained the implications of a non-uniform interpretation of the compact. These concerns relate to the subject matter of the compact. Should courts be concerned where non-uniform interpretation of a compact is only tangential to the implementation of a compact, such as different standards of review in different courts?

5. The New Jersey Court also questioned the ability of the state to unilaterally impair the powers of the Waterfront Commission, citing *Green v. Biddle*, and an 1860 New Jersey case. In that 1860 case, a corporation built one bridge over the Delaware River from Trenton, New Jersey to Pennsylvania pursuant to concurrent legislation from the two states. Subsequently, New Jersey enacted legislation amending the original legislation to allow another bridge within three miles of the first. Pennsylvania did not amend its legislation. A New Jersey court concluded that New Jersey could not unilaterally grant a franchise to a corporation to build another bridge over and on land within Pennsylvania. *President, Managers, & Co. for Erecting a Bridge Over the River Delaware at or Near Trenton v. Trenton City Bridge Co.*, 13 N.J. Eq. 46 (N.J. Ch. 1860). *Green v. Biddle* and this early *Trenton City Bridge* case involved interpreting and applying compacts to avoid unilateral impairment of compacts. How does this compare to more recent New Jersey cases discussed in the *Local 542* case from Chapter 8, which applied New Jersey legislation that is only "somewhat similar" to other party states' legislation? Would

two states applying "somewhat similar" state laws predictably have uniform interpretations of a compact?

6. The *Waterfront Commission* case went on to be an important U.S. Supreme Court case, *Murphy v. Waterfront Comm'n of N.Y. Harbor*, 378 U.S. 52 (1964). It was argued on the same day and decided on the same day as *Malloy v. Hogan*, 378 U.S. 1 (1964), in which the Supreme Court held for the first time that the Fifth Amendment privilege against self-incrimination is applicable to the states through the Fourteenth Amendment. *Murphy* held that a jurisdiction could compel a witness to give testimony after it had granted that witness immunity from prosecution under its laws, even if another jurisdiction might use the testimony to convict the witness under that other jurisdiction's laws.

7. Early boundary compacts that lacked precision have required on-going interpretation. For example, in *North Carolina v. Tennessee*, 235 U.S. 1 (1914), the Supreme Court essentially deferred to the state boundary that commissioners from both states determined. Tennessee had claimed that the commissioners located the line inconsistent with the cession act in which North Carolina ceded land to Tennessee and inconsistent with the federal act consenting to the cession act. Tennessee argued that the line violated the Compact Clause because it did not have congressional consent. The Supreme Court disagreed, noting, "The cession act is very general and necessarily demanded definition to satisfy the requirements of a boundary line, a line not only necessary to mark private land, but political jurisdiction." *Id.* at 16.

McComb v. Wambaugh
934 F.2d 474 (3d Cir. 1991)

WEIS, JUDGE:

As a result of parental abuse, the minor plaintiff suffered severe injuries for which he seeks damages against a municipality and its employees because of their failure to protect him. We conclude that a protective order issued by a Virginia court purportedly in accordance with the Interstate Compact for Placement of Children did not establish a special relationship between the plaintiff and the Pennsylvania defendants. . . .

. . . .

The Interstate Compact on Placement of Children has not received congressional consent. Rather than altering the balance of power between the states and the federal government, this Compact focuses wholly on adoption and foster care of children—areas of jurisdiction historically retained by the states. Congressional consent, therefore, was not necessary for the Compact's legitimacy.

Because congressional consent was neither given nor required, the Compact does not express federal law. Consequently, this Compact must be construed as state law. *See* Engdahl, *Construction of Interstate Compacts: A Questionable Federal Question*, 51 VA. L. REV. 987, 1017 (1965) ("The construction of a compact not requiring consent * * * will not present a federal question. * * *").

Nevertheless, uniformity of interpretation is important in the construction of a Compact because in some contexts it is a contract between the participating states. *See West Virginia ex rel. Dyer v. Sims*, 341 U.S. 22 (1951). Having entered into a contract, a participant state may not unilaterally change its terms. A Compact also takes precedence over statutory law in member states.

The crucial question here is whether the Interstate Compact on the Placement of Children applies when a court in one state directs that a child be taken from foster care and sent to a natural parent in another participating state. Mindful of the need for uniform interpretation, we have not only searched for Pennsylvania cases discussing the Compact, but for those of other states as well. The results, however, have not been helpful. No state Supreme Court has analyzed the question in a reasoned opinion, nor has any state intermediate appellate court.

[The court then reviewed the history and text of the compact, regulations implementing the compact that the Association of Administrators of the Compact adopted, and decisions from courts in several states.]

. . . .

Notes & Questions

1. *McComb v. Wambaugh* is only one of many cases involving the question whether the Interstate Compact on the Placement of Children applies to placements with a natural parent in another state. Since the *McComb* decision, many state appellate courts have interpreted the compact, but they do not interpret it uniformly, and several decisions acknowledge this difference. In one case, the California Court of Appeal strongly lamented the states' inconsistent decisions:

> One of the key elements of any interstate compact is uniformity in interpretation. Uniformity, however, is lacking with respect to the issue of whether the [Interstate Compact on the Placement of Children (ICPC)] applies to the placement of a child with a natural parent * * * ." (Butler, *Child Welfare—Outside the Interstate Compact on the Placement of Children—Placement of a Child with a Natural Parent* (1992) 37 VILLANOVA L. REV. 896, 916.)
>
> As we will discuss, California cases have consistently held that the ICPC does not apply to an out-of-state placement with a parent. They have even gone so far as to invalidate statewide rules and regulations that purported to make the ICPC apply. Other jurisdictions that have taken the same position include Arkansas, New Hampshire, New Jersey, Washington, and the Third Circuit.
>
> This brings California into conflict with those jurisdictions holding that the ICPC does apply to an out-of-state placement with a parent. These include Alabama, Arizona, Delaware, Massachusetts, Mississippi, New York, and Oregon.
>
> We find the decisions in California and elsewhere holding that the ICPC does not apply to be far better reasoned than those holding that it does. Accordingly, we see no reason not to follow our sister California courts.

> We are publishing this opinion, however, to point out that the resulting lack of uniformity is dysfunctional, that courts and rule makers have not been able to fix it, and hence that it may call for a multistate legislative response.

In re C.B., 116 Cal. Rptr. 3d. 294, 295–96 (2010); *see also State v. Springer*, 406 S.W.3d 526 (Tenn. 2013) (also considering multiple states' application of the Interstate Agreement on Detainers and finding no consistency). In situations where courts split on the application of a compact, the options for achieving uniformity may be very limited. The ICPC does not have congressional consent and thus its interpretation does not raise a federal question that may be reviewed by the U.S. Supreme Court.

2. In *In re J.D.M.-J.*, 260 N.C. App. 56 (2018), the North Carolina Court of Appeals identified two conflicting lines of cases within North Carolina, one applying the ICPC to an out-of-state placement with a relative, and the other not applying the ICPC. To resolve the conflict, the court applied North Carolina's common law principle of applying the older of the two lines of cases. Does using this first-in-time approach anchor a state's early interpretation of a compact? How can the state change that interpretation if the states form a later consensus on a different interpretation? Does applying common law in this situation raise the same issues of applying state law as discussed in Chapter 8?

3. In states where the ICPC does not apply to out-of-state parents, there remains a question of how to get information prior to placement with that out-of-state parent. Ironically, courts have used the ICPC even though it is not legally required. For example, *In re I.G.*, No. C078248, 2015 Cal. App. Unpub. LEXIS 7763 (Cal. Ct. App. Oct. 27, 2015), noted that in California the ICPC does not apply to out-of-state parents, but concluded that the states did not err in requesting an ICPC study before placing a child with a parent in Washington State. The court cited one of its court rules, which stated that "the court has discretion to take the steps it deems necessary to ensure the child's safety and well-being in that placement. Those steps may include: '(1) Directing the child welfare agency to request an independent, non-ICPC home study or courtesy check;' . . . ." *Id.* at *13–14. Nevertheless, the court concluded, "While . . . ICPC compliance is not required for an out-of-state placement with a parent, nothing in the ICPC prevents the use of an ICPC evaluation as a means of gathering information before placing a child with such a parent." *Id.* at *14–15. So, while not formally applying the ICPC, the court recognized that it was a standard means of obtaining information before placing a child with an out-of-state parent.

Coincidentally, on the same day as the California Court of Appeal's *In re I.G.* decision, the Washington Court of Appeals reached the same holding in a similar case, stating, "An ICPC approval is needed so that the State of Nevada will provide oversight of the family if [Ca.R.] is placed in the home." *In re Welfare of Ca.R.*, 191 Wash. App. 601, 611 (2015). The court reasoned that even though the ICPC does not apply to parental placements, that limit "does not eliminate cooperation between the two states as the parties work toward reunification." *Id.* at

612. This decision elicited a strong dissent, stating the majority ordered Nevada's involvement contrary to the ICPC. The dissent continued:

> The majority also writes that any prohibition of employing ICPC for a parental placement does not eliminate cooperation between the two states as the parties work toward reunification. The majority does not explain what cooperation is needed or permissible and why two states would cooperate outside their authority to act. Again, the trial court ordered an ICPC placement review in Nevada contrary to the interstate compact, state statute, and this court's decision. A court's sanctioning of extralegal and unauthorized conduct by a state agency against the will of the legislature creates a dangerous precedence.

Id. at 634. The Washington Supreme Court denied review. 185 Wash. 2d 1026 (2016). What do you think about applying a compact where it is not legally required simply because it creates a useful administrative structure for non-compact cooperation?

4. When interpreting a compact, most courts look to decisions from other state or federal courts that previously interpreted the compact at issue. For example, the notes in Chapter 8 cited *Atl. Richfield Co. v. Dep't of Revenue*, 300 Or. 637 (1986), in which the Oregon Supreme Court stated, "If we were the first state to address this question, we likely would affirm the department and the Tax Court, for the department has some latitude in interpreting the phrase 'original cost' in ORS 314.655(2). It appears, however, that those UDITPA jurisdictions that have considered the IDC question by rule or statute. . . ." *Id.* at 646–47. Note that the Oregon Supreme Court stated the Department of Revenue has "some latitude" in interpreting terms in the Multistate Tax Compact. How much latitude should compact administrators or a compact agency have? Is that latitude constrained by how other states have already interpreted the compact?

In another example, in *State v. Sweet*, No. E2010-00729-CCA-R3-CD, 2011 Tenn. Crim. App. LEXIS 947 (Tenn. Crim. App. Feb. 15, 2011), the court stated:

> The next issue we must address is whether the Defendant's trial in this case was also timely as defined by the Interstate Compact [on Detainers]. . . . While this issue is one of first impression in this state, it has been addressed by multiple courts in other states. The seemingly unanimous conclusion is that. . . .

Id. at *23. Luckily, the court did not find a difference in the states' application of the compact. However, in *State v. Springer*, 406 S.W.3d 526 (Tenn. 2013), the court observed, "A split of authority exists as to whether the IAD applies to a convicted and sentenced prisoner who is held in temporary custody pending a transfer to permanent incarceration." *Id.* at 535. The court reviewed decisions from many states and explained why it selected one interpretation over the other. *Id.* at 535–38. How should a court decide between many states' interpretations of a compact?

5. *Ex parte Uniroyal Tire Co.*, 779 So. 2d 227 (Ala. 2000), took a different approach when faced with conflicting precedent from other courts. The Alabama

Supreme Court acknowledged, but mostly ignored the precedent rather than choose between it, and conducted a statutory interpretation analysis using Alabama law (and cited the cases that supported Alabama law), ultimately holding that the Alabama regulation was inapplicable to the extent it was inconsistent with a statutory provision that is identical to a provision of the MTC.

6. In *Oracle Corp. v. Dep't of Revenue*, No. TC-MD 070762C, 2010 Ore. Tax LEXIS 32 (Or. Tax Feb. 11, 2010), the Oregon Tax Court also chose to ignore other states' interpretation of a compact. It acknowledged the Oregon Supreme Court's *Atlantic Richfield* decision (see note 4) that considered other state court decisions, but questioned whether it must apply the Multistate Tax Compact in a way that creates uniformity:

> What Defendant seeks is for the court to fashion an equitable doctrine to achieve the goal of uniformity. It is not entirely clear how such a doctrine would operate, but it would apparently be aimed at achieving uniformity and consistency in the reporting of business income in states that have adopted the UDITPA business income definition. Defendant acknowledges that no clear precedent exists and that this would be "a decision of first impression in the UDITPA states." The court declines Defendant's invitation to declare the equitable doctrine it seeks. The court is not opposed to fairness and equity. In fact, it embraces those principles, but only as shaped and informed by the law, and where the result would, in fact, be fair and equitable.
>
> The court agrees that UDITPA is premised on a goal of uniformity, and that the Oregon Supreme Court has sanctioned consideration of uniformity in the cases cited by Defendant. Further, the Multistate Tax Compact is intended to promote uniformity. However, aspirational goals and "consideration" of such goals represent matters of policy, not law. As to the question of whether California and Oregon have identical (or nearly identical) definitions of business income, that is a matter better left for another day. Moreover, regardless of whether the two states' definitions of business income are essentially identical, there are practical reasons that militate against granting the relief Defendant seeks.
>
> A favorable ruling for Defendant would require the court to become an expert in the laws of 49 other states as they pertain to the definition of business and nonbusiness income, not only as set forth in the various states' statutes, but as those statutes are refined and clarified by years of judicial opinions. Moreover, the whole notion of federalism and state's rights would be compromised. As Plaintiffs note in their brief, "[t]he right of each state to have its own tax laws and interpret them in its own fashion is fundamental to our federal system of government." . . .

Id. at *6–8. Are the Oregon Tax Court's concerns problematic enough that courts should not try to give uniform interpretations to compact provisions? Would the same problems exist if the compact involves only two states?

7. In *Proctor v. Wash. Metro. Area Transit Auth.*, 412 Md. 691 (2010), a case involving the application of state tort liability statutes first mentioned in Chapter 8, the Maryland Court of Appeals (Maryland's highest court) expressly noted that prior decisions in other courts are "highly persuasive" and overruled a Maryland Court of Special Appeals (Maryland's intermediate appellate court) decision that was contrary to decisions from Virginia and District of Columbia courts. The Court of Appeals harmonized Maryland, Virginia, and District of Columbia decisions involving the application and scope of the parties' tort liability acts and damages caps to the Washington Metropolitan Area Transit Authority. The Court of Appeals noted the importance of decisions from the other parties' courts and suggested that one state's interpretation of the compact may be understandably suspicious when it differs from all the other party states' interpretations. The Court of Appeals stated:

> The decisions of courts in Virginia and the District of Columbia have particular significance in this case because WMATA is a multi-jurisdiction agency governed by a compact to which Virginia and the District of Columbia are parties. Accordingly, the decisions of courts in Virginia and the District of Columbia are highly persuasive regarding matters related to WMATA. Because the rationale of *Deschamps* is inconsistent with the reasoning of other courts from the other two WMATA-related jurisdictions, the District Court, quite reasonably in our view, had reservations about whether *Deschamps* was decided correctly.

Id. at 705.

8. What do you think of courts looking for precedent in how other states interpret a compact provision? Could this lead to forum shopping or a race to get a decision from a specific court (such as by setting up cases for declaratory judgment)? What if the first decision was unfavorable? Can you think of a better approach to ensuring uniform court decisions?

9. In some cases, courts have concluded that uniformity is not a goal in interpreting interstate compacts. For example, the Oregon Supreme Court concluded that the goal of uniformity was not relevant in determining whether it should review the Columbia River Gorge Commission's interpretation of the Columbia River Gorge Compact in accordance with federal deference standards. The Oregon court specifically noted that inconsistent interpretation could undermine the uniform application of the compact regulations, but it concluded that the compact's requirement of jurisdiction in the state courts suggested that Congress did not intend uniform treatment of Commission actions in the party states' courts. *Friends of the Columbia Gorge v. Columbia River Gorge Comm'n*, 346 Or. 366, 380 (2009). Do you agree that the political decision to place judicial review only in state courts suggests that Congress did not intend uniform interpretation and administering of a compact? The end of this chapter looks at judicial review of a compact agency's interpretation of a compact with an excerpt of this case.

10. In *State v. Eldert*, 199 Vt. 520, 532–33 (2015), the Vermont Supreme Court concluded that records from the Interstate Compact Offender Tracking System

(ICOTS) were hearsay and not reliable enough for a court to deny a right to confrontation and rely on the documents. Article V of the Interstate Compact for the Supervision of Adult Offenders specifically authorizes the Interstate Commission for Adult Offender Supervision "[t]o establish uniform standards for the reporting, collecting, and exchanging of data." While neither the compact nor the Interstate Commission's rules specifically require states to admit ICOTS documents as reliable, can you make an argument that doing so ensures uniform administration of the compact?

11. Several recent compacts have authorized their compact agency to provide guidance on compact responsibilities and interpretation of compact provisions. One example of this is the Interstate Compact for the Supervision of Adult Offenders (ICAOS), art. XIV.B, which provides "Upon the request of a party to a conflict over meaning or interpretation of Interstate Commission actions, and upon a majority vote of the Compacting States, the Interstate Commission may issue advisory opinions regarding such meaning or interpretation." The Interstate Commission for Adult Offender Supervision also issues an annual "Bench Book for Judges," which explains principles of compact law and prior interpretations of the compact from the Commission and courts. Courts commonly cite to ICAOS advisory opinions and the ICAOS Bench Book. *E.g., State v. Brown*, 140 A.3d 768, 776, 777 n.5 (R.I. 2016). Courts' willingness to apply advisory opinions and the Bench Book suggests these may be effective ways to help courts uniformly interpret and apply a compact.

The ICAOS also contains a provision requiring parties to serve the interstate commission when a litigation matter involves the powers, responsibilities or actions of the interstate commission and provides that the commission has standing to intervene in the proceeding. This serves two important purposes. First, it allows the interstate commission to present its views on the matter and promote a single uniform interpretation and application of the compact. Second, it allows the interstate commission to track litigation and interpretations of the compact so the commission can determine whether to clarify a state responsibility or address inconsistent court decisions through rulemaking.

Interstate compact agencies may also develop policies for addressing inconsistent interpretation or application of a compact. For example, the Ohio River Valley Water Sanitation Commission has a *Protocol for Addressing Interstate Inconsistencies*, which specifies several alternative courses of action:

a. *Staff work with the states involved to resolve the inconsistency*- This might be the best alternative if the inconsistency involves a difference in approach (not specified in regulation) by two states.

b. *Resolve through the Technical Committee*- This would be the preferred course when more than two states are involved, and the difference results from agency policies. It would also be the initial approach to differences among EPA Regions.

c. *Resolve at the Commission level-* This would be the probable course if the inconsistency results from differences in state regulations. The Commission might choose to recommend changes to the states, or might adopt its own regulation.

d. *Resolve through Commission-level contacts with state government-* Article VIII of the Compact includes a directive to the Commission to recommend state legislation necessary to advance the objectives of the Compact.

e. *Take no action-* It is conceivable that, after careful consideration, it might be concluded that the effort needed to resolve the inconsistency outweighs the benefit that might be gained. If this is the chosen course of action, the particular inconsistency should not be raised for consideration again unless there is some change in one or more of the factors that led to this decision.

Ohio River Valley Water Sanitation Comm'n, *Protocol for Addressing Interstate Inconsistencies*, http://www.orsanco.org/orsanco-library/ (search for title).

12. Although not a compact case, consider the methods the Oregon Court of Appeals used for interpreting the Uniform Arbitration Act in *Prime Properties v. Leahy*, 234 Or. App. 439, 445 (2010):

> The statute is part of a statutory scheme that derived from the Uniform Arbitration Act, which was promulgated by the National Conference of Commissioners on Uniform State Laws (NCCUSL). ORS 36.735 provides that, "[i]n applying and construing [the Uniform Arbitration Act], consideration must be given to the need to promote uniformity of the law with respect to its subject matter among states that enact it." The NCCUSL's commentary to the uniform act helps to explicate the meaning of the statutory terms, so it provides a useful tool for promoting uniformity of the law, and we consider it where appropriate.

Should Congress and the states be more diligent in providing commentary or detailed legislative history to help courts that want to take this approach? Different courts give varying weight to legislative history when interpreting statutes. How could drafters be assured that courts would consider commentary and legislative history?

13. Reread the excerpt from the Vienna Convention on the Law of Treaties. What factors would you consider in determining how to interpret a compact to achieve uniformity no matter which party state or which court is interpreting the compact?

14. Reread Justice Frankfurter's dissent in *Petty v. Tennessee-Missouri Bridge Comm'n* (excerpted in Chapter 7), in which he stated that the compacting states' mutual understanding of compact language should take precedence over congressional intent, particularly when Congress has not altered the compact language in giving its consent to the compact, and the Supreme Court should impose its interpretation of the compact only when one of the compacting states attempts to impose its views on the other. What do you think of this proposition as a general rule? Does this enable the states to modify their obligations under a compact by

mutual interpretation even without an express provision allowing the state to do so? Is this concept of judicial intervention found in common contracts analysis?

Consider Justice Frankfurter's statement: "But a federal question does not require a federal answer by way of a blanket, nationwide substantive doctrine where essentially local interests are at stake." *Petty v. Tenn.-Mo. Bridge Comm'n*, 359 U.S. at 285. Was he saying that uniformity does not need to be the goal of compact interpretation, or that uniformity could be accomplished without resorting to federal law?

15. In *I.B.M. v. Dep't of Treasury*, 496 Mich. 642 (2014), the dissent stated that the *McComb* decision is internally inconsistent—that the compact cannot by construed as state law yet take precedence over a member state's statutory law. *Id.* at 679. Do you agree that these statements conflict?

The next case, *State v. Morris*, provides an interesting twist on ensuring uniform treatment of prisoners within the state where some of the prisoners are incarcerated under the Interstate Agreement on Detainers. The Washington Supreme Court used a widely accepted interpretation of a term in the Interstate Agreement on Detainers to guide its interpretation of its own state law outside of the compact.

State v. Morris
126 Wash. 2d 306 (1995)

DURHAM, JUSTICE:

At issue is the proper interpretation of Washington's intrastate detainers statute, RCW 9.98. Under RCW 9.98.010, prisoners incarcerated within the state have a right to trial within 120 days on unrelated charges pending within the state. The statute requires this speedy disposition upon a prisoner's request for trial. We must decide at what point the 120-day period commences—when the prisoner transmits a request for trial to the superintendent having custody of the prisoner, or when the prosecutor and superior court actually receive the request for trial.

The Court of Appeals adopted the delivery-to-the-superintendent theory, which resulted in dismissal of a theft charge against the defendant, Clark Morris. The United States Supreme Court has adopted the receipt-by-the-prosecutor theory for the Interstate Agreement on Detainers (IAD), which employs language nearly identical to Washington's intrastate statute. *Fex v. Michigan*, 507 U.S. 43 (1993). Washington is a signatory to the IAD.

The State urges reversal of the Court of Appeals in order to ensure a uniform measuring event governing the speedy disposition periods for both detainer statutes. We agree, but affirm the dismissal of this case on other grounds.

....

We will first decide whether the 120-day time-for-trial period under RCW 9.98.010 commences upon transmittal of a request for trial by the prisoner to prison authorities or upon actual receipt of the request by the prosecutor and superior court.

The statute directly at issue is Washington's intrastate detainers act. RCW 9.98. This statute gives prisoners within Washington the right to request trial on "any untried indictment, information or complaint" within 120 days of the request. RCW 9.98.010(1). The IAD is an interstate compact with parallel language which applies to prisoners who have untried charges lodged against them by other states or the federal government. See RCW 9.100 (codifying the IAD).

Both statutes set up a 2-stage process. First, a prisoner makes a request for speedy and final disposition of untried charges. This request "shall be given or sent by the prisoner to the superintendent having custody of him." Second, the superintendent forwards the request (together with a certificate stating the term of confinement, the time remaining to be served, and other details) to the appropriate prosecuting attorney and superior court. If the case is not brought to trial within 120 days, no court of this state shall any longer have jurisdiction thereof, nor shall the untried indictment, information or complaint be of any further force or effect, and the court shall enter an order dismissing the same with prejudice.

The intrastate statute dictates that a prisoner "shall be brought to trial within one hundred twenty days after he shall have caused to be delivered to the prosecuting attorney and the superior court" a written request for a speedy disposition of any untried indictment, information, or complaint. The IAD has nearly identical language, except that period is 180 days, and request is delivered to "the prosecuting officer and the appropriate court" rather than "the prosecuting attorney and the superior court."

The United States Supreme Court recently considered the question of when the IAD's 180-day period commences. *Fex v. Michigan*, 507 U.S. 43 (1993). The Court conceded the statutory language supports either the theory that the period commences with delivery of the request by the prisoner to the warden or the theory that it begins only with the actual receipt of the request by the prosecutor and court.... Nevertheless, the Court examined textual and contextual clues and concluded that the period for trial "does not commence until the prisoner's request for final disposition of the charges against him has actually been delivered to the court and prosecuting attorney." *Fex,* 507 U.S. at 52. The Court noted that actual delivery is a determinate event, whereas when the prisoner "caused" the request to be delivered is less easily determined. *Fex*, 507 U.S. at 49–51.

Moreover, the statute provides for verification of when actual delivery takes place. Both the IAD and the intrastate detainers statute require the warden to forward the prisoner's request and accompanying documents by registered mail, return receipt requested. In contrast, there is no provision for verifying when the prisoner "caused" the request to be delivered to the warden. Instead, the statutes leave open two possible modes of delivery to the warden. The statutes specify that the request "shall be given or sent by the prisoner" to the warden or superintendent. The United States Supreme Court concluded that the context supports the theory that the period commences with actual receipt by the prosecutor and court rather than with delivery to the warden.

. . . .

The Court of Appeals found Justice Blackmun's dissent in *Fex* more persuasive than the majority opinion. In adopting the dissent's position, the Court of Appeals stressed that the analysis in *Fex* of the IAD is persuasive but not controlling authority for the interpretation of the similarly worded Washington intrastate detainers statute. *Hoffer v. State*, 113 Wash. 2d 148, 151 (1989) ("it is well settled that the Supreme Court's construction of a similarly worded federal statute, although often persuasive, does not control this court's interpretation of a state statute). The court reasoned that its reading of the statute accorded with the plain meaning of the words and furthered the purpose of the statute. The court agreed with the dissent in *Fex* that the focus of the relevant language is on the prisoner's act, which is complete when he transmits his request to the warden.

Regardless of how convincing one finds the *Fex* majority, its interpretation now governs the IAD for prisoners subject to the IAD in this state. Prisoners subject to the IAD exist side by side in our state's prisons with prisoners subject to the Washington intrastate detainers statute. As the State argues, it is unnecessarily confusing to create two different sets of rules governing the commencement of speedy disposition periods for prisoners in the same system.

Consistency seems more desirable here than confusion. There is no utility in creating a potentially confusing situation in which identical statutory language is read two different ways to create two different means of measuring the commencement of the speedy disposition period. Furthermore, a precise measuring event is more desirable than an unverifiable or indeterminate one. Of the two different interpretations, the *Fex* majority adopts the more verifiable and easily ascertained measuring event. Accordingly, we hold that actual receipt by the prosecuting attorney and superior court of the county in which the indictment, information, or complaint is pending commences the 120-day period.

. . . .

Notes & Questions

1. What do you think of the Washington Supreme Court using the U.S. Supreme Court interpretation of a compact to govern interpretation of a non-compact state statute? Other courts have done so too. *See, e.g.*, *State v. Moore*, 23 N.E.3d 206 (Ohio Ct. App. 2014), and *Bower v. Eaton Corp.*, 301 Neb. 311, 328 (2018). But other courts have rejected doing so. *See, e.g.*, *State v. Witham*, No. 112,729, 2016 Kan. App. Unpub. LEXIS 94 (Kan. Ct. App. Feb. 5, 2016). In *Witham*, the state argued that the Kansas Court of Appeals should adopt the Interstate Compact for Adult Offender Supervision definition of "abscond," which was broader than a prior court of appeals decision defining the term. The Court of Appeals stated, "The State further suggests that dual definitions for absconding in the two probation regimens reflects a shortsighted public policy. Maybe.

But the fix for that kind of problem is a legislative correction, not a judicial one." *Id.* at *4.

How important is consistency between similar compact and non-compact statutory schemes? Should enacting a compact trigger the states to review their internal statutes and conform similar but not related requirements to the provisions of a compact?

2. In *Reed v. Farley,* 512 U.S. 339 (1994), the Supreme Court recognized the need for uniform interpretation of the Interstate Agreement on Detainers: "The [Interstate Agreement on Detainers'] purpose—providing a nationally uniform means of transferring prisoners between jurisdictions—can be effectuated only by nationally uniform interpretation. Therefore, the argument that the compact would be undermined if a State's courts resisted steadfast enforcement, with total insulation from [federal habeas corpus] review, is not without force." *Id.* at 348–49.

In denying relief, the Court used the federal law standards it would consider in other federal habeas corpus cases: "We see no reason to afford habeas review to a state prisoner like Reed, who let a time clock run without alerting the trial court, yet deny collateral review to a federal prisoner similarly situated." *Id.* at 354–55. Is applying a prior interpretation of related federal law to a compact an appropriate means of achieving uniformity in applying an agreement between 48 states? If not federal law, then what factors could all the states' courts use?

Indeed, courts do not interpret the IAD uniformly. Article III of the IAD provides that a prisoner serving a term of imprisonment may request a trial within 180 days after being delivered to another state. Article IV provides that an official of one jurisdiction may seek custody of a prisoner serving a term of imprisonment in another jurisdiction. However, the prisoner must be tried within 120 days of arrival in that jurisdiction and cannot be "shuttled" back to the original place of imprisonment before the trial. Violating Article III or IV results in a mandatory dismissal of the indictment. In *State v. Galiano*, No. A-1865-11T1, 2014 N.J. Super. Unpub. LEXIS 780 (N.J. Super. Ct. App. Div. Apr. 8, 2014), the court explained, "Some courts have ruled that, by invoking Article III, the defendant waives the protections of Article IV; some courts have ruled that the case is governed by the article which was invoked first; and other courts apply the time periods of both articles." *Id.* at *11–12. Another case involving this issue is *State v. Springer*, 406 S.W.3d 526 (Tenn. 2013), in which the Court interpreted the compact consistent with the U.S. Supreme Court's holding in *Alabama v. Bozeman*, 533 U.S. 146 (2001) which held that "every prisoner arrival in the receiving state, whether followed by a very brief stay or a very long stay in the receiving state, triggers [Article] IV(e)'s 'no return' requirement." *Id.* at 154.

3. Courts may also consider other compacts when interpreting a compact. In *EnergySolutions, LLC v. Nw. Interstate Compact on Low-Level Radioactive Waste Mgmt.*, No. 2:08-CV-352 TS, 2009 U.S. Dist. LEXIS 41209 (D. Utah May 15, 2009), the district court held that a definition used by the Northwest Compact was overbroad and inconsistent with an original grant of consent even though

Congress later amended that consent. The Northwest Compact appealed to the Tenth Circuit. The Rocky Mountain Low-Level Radioactive Waste Compact intervened, and six other low-level radioactive waste compacts participated as *amici curiae*. The Tenth Circuit reversed, citing *Alabama v. North Carolina*, in which the Court looked to the course of performance of other low-level radioactive waste compacts. The Tenth Circuit stated, "This indicates the Court viewed the entire [low-level radioactive waste] interstate compact system as allowing for great flexibility in determining each compact's specific authority, which is defined by each compact's language." *EnergySolutions, LLC v. Utah*, 625 F.3d 1261, 1276 (10th Cir. 2010). This reasoning suggests that the interpretation of one compact may be considered when interpreting a different compact that shares the same grant of consent, but the interpretation should still be based on the text of the specific compact at issue. The next case, *Tarrant*, seems to have solidified the practice of looking at other compacts when interpreting an ambiguous term, but not limited to only those compacts that share the same grant of consent.

C. Applying Traditional Contract Interpretation Principles

Tarrant Reg'l Water Dist. v. Herrmann
569 U.S. 614 (2013)

SOTOMAYOR, JUSTICE:

. . . .

Tarrant claims that under § 5.05(b)(1) of the [Red River] Compact, it has the right to cross state lines and divert water from Oklahoma located in subbasin 5 of Reach II and that the Oklahoma water statutes interfere with its ability to exercise that right. Section 5.05(b)(1) provides:

> "The Signatory States shall have equal rights to the use of runoff originating in subbasin 5 and undesignated water following into subbasin 5, so long as the flow of the Red River at the Arkansas-Louisiana state boundary is 3,000 [CFS] or more, provided no state is entitled to more than 25 percent of the water in excess of 3,000 [CFS]."

In Tarrant's view, this provision essentially creates a borderless common in which each of the four signatory States may cross each other's boundaries to access a shared pool of water. Tarrant reaches this interpretation in two steps. First, it observes that § 5.05(b)(1)'s "equal rights" language grants each State an equal entitlement to the waters of subbasin 5, subject to a 25 percent cap. Second, Tarrant argues § 5.05(b)(1)'s silence concerning state lines indicates that the Compact's drafters did not intend to allocate water according to state borders in this section. . . .

The [Oklahoma Water Resources Board] disputes this reading. In its view, the "equal rights" promised by § 5.05(b)(1) afford each State an equal opportunity to make use of the excess water within subbasin 5 of Reach II but only within each State's own borders. This is because the OWRB reads § 5.05(b)(1)'s silence differently from Tarrant. The OWRB interprets that provision's absence of language granting any cross-border rights to indicate that the Compact's drafters had no intention to create any such rights in the signatory States.

Unraveling the meaning of § 5.05(b)(1)'s silence with respect to state lines is the key to resolving whether the Compact pre-empts the Oklahoma water statutes. If § 5.05(b)(1)'s silence means that state borders are irrelevant to the allocation of water in subbasin 5 of Reach II, then the Oklahoma water laws at issue conflict with the cross-border rights created by federal law in the form of the Compact and must be pre-empted. But if § 5.05(b)(1)'s silence instead reflects a background understanding on the part of the Compact's drafters that state borders were to be respected within the Compact's allocation, then the Oklahoma statutes do not conflict with the Compact's allocation of water.

Interstate compacts are construed as contracts under the principles of contract law. *Texas v. New Mexico*, 482 U.S. 124, 128 (1987). So, as with any contract, we begin by examining the express terms of the Compact as the best indication of the intent of the parties, *see also Montana v. Wyoming*, [563 U.S. 368, 375 and n.4 (2011)]; Restatement (Second) of Contracts § 203(b) (1979).

Tarrant argues that because other provisions of the Compact reference state borders, § 5.05(b)(1)'s silence with respect to state lines must mean that the Compact's drafters intended to permit cross-border diversions. . . .

. . . .

At the very least, the problems that arise from Tarrant's proposed reading suggest that § 5.05(b)(1)'s silence is ambiguous regarding cross-border rights under the Compact. We therefore turn to other interpretive tools to shed light on the intent of the Compact's drafters. *See Oklahoma v. New Mexico*, 501 U.S. 221, 235, n.5, (1991). Three things persuade us that cross-border rights were not granted by the Compact: the well-established principle that States do not easily cede their sovereign powers, including their control over waters within their own territories; the fact that other interstate water compacts have treated cross-border rights explicitly; and the parties' course of dealing.

. . . .

Looking to the customary practices employed in other interstate compacts also helps us to ascertain the intent of the parties to this Compact. *See Alabama v. North Carolina*, 130 S. Ct. 2295 (2010); *Oklahoma*, 501 U.S., at 235, n.5; *Texas v. New Mexico*, 462 U.S. 554, 565 (1983). *See also* Restatement (Second) of Contracts § 203(b) (explaining that "usage of trade" may be relevant in interpreting a contract). Many of these other compacts feature language that unambiguously permits signatory States to cross each other's borders to fulfill obligations under the compacts. *See, e.g.*, Amended Bear River Compact, Art. VIII(A), 94 Stat. 12 ("[N]o State shall deny the right of another signatory State ... to acquire rights to the use of water ... in one State for use of water in another"). The absence of comparable language in the Red River Compact counts heavily against Tarrant's reading of it.

Tellingly, many of these compacts provide for the terms and mechanics of how such cross-border relationships will operate, including who can assert such cross-border rights, *see, e.g.*, Kansas-Nebraska Big Blue River Compact, Art. VII(1), 86 Stat. 198, who should bear the costs of any cross-border diversions, *see, e.g.*, Belle Fourche River Compact, Art. VI, 58 Stat. 96–97, and how such diversions should be administered, Arkansas River Basin Compact, Kansas-Oklahoma, Art. VII(A), 80 Stat. 1411.

Provisions like these are critical for managing the complexities that ensue from cross-border diversions. Consider the mechanics of a cross-border diversion or taking of water in this case. If Tarrant were correct, then applicants from Arkansas, Texas, and Louisiana could all apply to the OWRB for permits to take water from Oklahoma. The OWRB would then be obligated to determine the total amount of water in Oklahoma beyond the 25 percent cap created in § 5.05(b)(1), given that the Compact would only obligate Oklahoma to deliver water beyond its quarter share. This alone would be a herculean task because the Compact does not require ongoing monitoring or accounting and not all of the water in subbasin 5 is located or originates in Oklahoma. Moreover, the OWRB would be tasked with determining the priority under the Compact of applicants from other States. This would almost certainly require the OWRB to not only determine whether Oklahoma had received more or less than its 25 percent allotment, but whether other States had as well. Put plainly, the end result would be a jurisdictional and administrative quagmire. The provisions in the other interstate water compacts resolve these complications. The absence of comparable provisions in the Red River Compact strongly suggests that cross-border rights were never intended to be part of the States' agreement.

. . . .

The parties' conduct under the Compact also undermines Tarrant's position. A "part[y's] course of performance under the Compact is highly significant" evidence of its understanding of the compact's terms. *Alabama v. North Carolina*, [560 U.S. 330, 346 (2010)]. Since the Compact was approved by Congress in 1980, no signatory State had pressed for a cross-border diversion under the Compact until Tarrant filed its suit in 2007. Indeed, Tarrant attempted to purchase water from Oklahoma over the course of 2000 until 2002, a strange offer if Tarrant believed it was entitled to demand such water without payment under the Compact.

. . . .

Notes & Questions

1. *Tarrant* is mostly an unremarkable case, except for its consideration of whether and how other water compacts allow cross-border diversions. In contract interpretation terms, this is "usage of trade." Looking to other compacts is not usually a straightforward practice because most compacts are uniquely written texts; however, some compacts use very similar language. For example, the Susquehanna River Basin Compact is substantially similar in form as the Delaware River Basin Compact.

The Court cited three of its prior cases as precedent for considering usage of trade. In two of those cases, *Alabama v. North Carolina* and *Texas v. New Mexico*, the Court compared the text of the compacts at issue to the texts of other compacts that Congress granted consent to contemporaneously. In *Tarrant*, none of the compacts that the Court considered as relevant for interpreting the Red River Compact received contemporaneous consent. In the third case, *Oklahoma v. New Mexico*, the Court only considered the negotiating history of the compact at issue. *Tarrant* represents a shift in the Court's interpretation of compacts—that is, the Court used the "usage of trade" principle more broadly to include compacts that did not receive contemporaneous congressional consent. Still, the Court only considered other water allocation compacts.

Are contemporaneous consent and similar subject matter compacts logical limiting principles? Should courts have limiting principles for applying the "usage of trade" principle? Can you think of other logical limiting principles for which a court might consider when addressing usage of trade: for example, should a court consider only compacts that predated the compact at issue; compacts that the party state at issue is a member of, or compacts that may have used the same drafting entity, such as The Council of State Governments, which has assisted with drafting nearly 20 compacts in the past several years.

Curiously, Justice Sotomayor did not cite to the Court's then-most recent water compact case, *Montana v. Wyoming*, 563 U.S. 368 (2011), for the usage of trade principle. In that 2011 case, the Court stated, ". . . if [the Yellowstone River Compact] were intended to guarantee Montana a set quantity of water, it could have done so as plainly as other compacts that do just that." *Id.* at 388 (citing the Colorado River Compact and the Republican River Compact).

2. Are new compact drafting practices helpful in interpreting previously drafted compacts? In *Health Net, Inc. v. Dep't of Revenue*, 22 Or. Tax 128 (2015), *aff'd on other grounds*, 362 Or. 700 (2018), the Oregon Tax Court held that Oregon tax statutes applied where those statutes altered the Multistate Tax Compact. One reason the tax court discussed is that in contrast to other compacts, "no provision of the Multistate Tax Compact provides that it supersedes any Oregon law." *Id.* at 164. The tax court cited the Interstate Compact for Juveniles, art. XIII, which expressly states that the compact supersedes conflicting state law. *Id.* The Multistate Tax Compact became effective in 1967, 40 years prior to the Interstate Compact for Juveniles, which became effective in 2008. Is citing to a compact that had not yet been drafted an appropriate contract interpretation principle?

3. *Tarrant* was also the second case in three years that the Supreme Court considered the states' course of performance of the compact at issue. In *Alabama v. North Carolina*, 560 U.S. 330 (2010), the Court noted that course of performance is "highly significant." *Id.* at 346. In an earlier case, *New Jersey v. New York*, 523 U.S. 767 (1998), Justice Scalia's dissent applied "hornbook contract law that the practical construction of an ambiguous agreement revealed by later conduct of the parties is good indication of its meaning." *Id.* at 831.

4. Just since *Alabama v. North Carolina* in 2010, the Supreme Court seems to be emphasizing traditional contract interpretation principles—negotiation history, course of performance, and usage of trade—when a compact is ambiguous. But this focus on contract principles may not be the preferred interpretive method for all compact cases. In each of the cases discussed in these notes, one of the parties was arguing that the compact was ambiguous because its terms did not expressly authorize or prohibit some specific conduct. Do the same interpretive principles apply when there is an express term that one or both parties believe is ambiguous? What other traditional contract interpretation principles could apply?

5. In *Wayne Land and Mineral Group v. Delaware River Basin Comm'n*, 894 F.3d 509 (3d Cir. 2018) the court stated in a rather absolute manner that even though congressional consent transforms a compact into federal law, courts review compacts using contract law principles. The Third Circuit cited to *Tarrant* without harmonizing other Supreme Court authority in which the Court did not apply contract law principles. For example, in *Alabama v. North Carolina*, 560 U.S. 330 (2010), decided just three years earlier, the Supreme Court suggested that it should not blindly apply contract law principles and should also apply federal statutory construction principles. The Court stated,

> We have never held that an interstate compact approved by Congress includes an implied duty of good faith and fair dealing. Of course "[e]very contract imposes upon each party a duty of good faith and fair dealing in its performance and its enforcement." [Restatement (Second) of Contracts § 205 (1979)]. But an interstate compact is not just a contract; it is a federal statute enacted by Congress. If courts were authorized to add a fairness requirement to the implementation of federal statutes, judges would be potent lawmakers indeed. We do not—we cannot—add provisions to a federal statute. And in that regard a statute which is a valid interstate compact is no different."

Id. at 351–52. How do you reconcile the Third Circuit's firm statement that it must use compact law with the well-established analysis of compacts as both contracts <u>and</u> statutes as discussed in Chapter 1? There are significant differences in contract and statutory interpretive methods; for example, courts use various deference regimes when an agency interprets its own statute, but, in contrast, courts generally construe contracts against the drafter. No court has explained why it chooses a contract or statutory analysis over the other and there is no discernible pattern in the cases.

6. Are interstate compacts fundamentally different from commercial contracts such that courts should not apply contract interpretation principles to compacts? In *Entergy Arkansas, Inc. v. Nebraska*, 358 F.3d 528, 541–42 (8th Cir. 2004), the Eighth Circuit explained:

> Although the Supreme Court has acknowledged that an interstate compact is like a contract to the extent that it is "a legal document that must be construed and applied in accordance with its terms," *Texas v. New Mexico*,

482 U.S. 124, 128 (1987), the Court has also recognized the unique features and functions of such a compact. An interstate compact is one "of two methods under our Constitution of settling controversies between States," *Petty v. Tennessee-Missouri Bridge Comm'n*, 359 U.S. 275, 279 n.5 (1959), and it "performs high functions in our federalism," *id.* at 279. *See also* Felix Frankfurter & James M. Landis, *The Compact Clause of the Constitution — A Study in Interstate Adjustments*, 34 YALE L.J. 685, 691–95 (1925) (discussing history of Compact Clause). An interstate compact represents a political compromise between "constituent elements of the Union," as opposed to a commercial transaction. *Hess v. Port Auth. Trans-Hudson Corp.*, 513 U.S. 30, 40 (1994). Such an agreement is made to "address interests and problems that do not coincide nicely either with the national boundaries or with State lines—interests that may be badly served or not served at all by the ordinary channels of National or State political action." *Id.*

While a common law contract directly affects only the rights and obligations of the individual parties to it, an interstate compact may directly impact the population, the economy, and the physical environment in the whole of the compact area. A suit alleging that a state has breached an obligation owed to its sister states under a congressionally approved interstate compact also raises delicate questions bearing upon the relationship among separate sovereign polities with respect to matters of both regional and national import.

In *Commonwealth ex rel. Smith v. Clark*, 331 Pa. 405 (1938), the Pennsylvania Supreme Court considered whether the Pennsylvania Legislature could lawfully remove members of the Delaware River Joint Commission (now the Delaware River Port Authority) when the compact required a term of five years. The Court concluded that the compact unambiguously did not allow such removal, but, "even if there was ambiguity a state should be reluctant to interpret ambiguous language in its favor. Scrupulous care should be exercised by a sovereign state to comply with the terms of its contract." *Id.* at 415. Is "scrupulous care" similarly required in commercial contracts?

7. Non-compact intergovernmental agreements are not enacted as statutes, so courts apply contract principles when interpreting them, including giving effect to the agreement as written, using parol evidence on when the terms of the agreement are ambiguous, and construing the agreement against the drafter. *See, e.g.*, *Town of Marana v. Pima Cty.*, 281 P.3d 1010 (Ariz. Ct. App. 2012). Courts also consider course of performance when interpreting non-compact intergovernmental agreements. *See, e.g.*, *Tarrant Cty. v. Denton Cty.*, 87 S.W.3d 159 (Tex. Ct. App. 2002) (in concluding that an interlocal agreement establishing a boundary between two counties was binding, the court considered the text of the agreement, the implementation of the agreement and counties' action accepting of the agreement).

Courts also look to how other state and federal courts have interpreted similar provisions in non-compact intergovernmental agreements, and not necessarily agreements of the same subject. For example, in *Parker Excavating, Inc. v. City & Cty. of Denver*, 303 P.3d 1222 (Colo. App. 2012), the court stated:

> "No Colorado appellate court has reviewed, under Colorado law, an award of an equitable adjustment for unanticipated site conditions. The language of the equitable adjustment provision in the contract between Parker and Denver Water is commonly found in similar provisions in federal contracts. Therefore, we look to federal cases reviewing similar equitable adjustment provisions for guidance." *See Colo. Intergovernmental Risk Sharing Agency v. Northfield Ins. Co.*, 207 P.3d 839, 843 (Colo. App. 2008) (looking to other jurisdictions that have directly addressed similar contract provisions).

Id. at 1225. Similarly, in *City of Arvada v. Colo. Intergovernmental Risk Sharing Agency*, 19 P.3d 10 (Colo. 2001), the court cited cases from Missouri and California, and in *Durango Transp., Inc. v. City of Durango*, 824 P.2d 48 (Colo. App. 1991), the court cited cases from California, Missouri, Minnesota, and Indiana.

8. How would you interpret a compact in which one state seeks to apply its own law, arguing that doing so is consistent with the parties' course of performance or the usage of trade? Would you apply the *Seattle Master Builders* principle (state law applies only when specifically reserved in the compact) alone; would you apply course of performance and usage of trade principles? Could you apply both? How would you resolve a difference in interpretation using the different principles?

III. Compact Agency Interpretation of Compacts

Like other federal and state agencies, compact agencies must interpret compacts as part of administering them. What is the legal status of a compact agency's interpretation? Is it binding, only persuasive, merely helpful, or of no legal significance? What is the legal status if the party states treat agency interpretations differently?

Many courts apply federal law methods and standards to review a compact agency's interpretation of the compact and the federal law granting consent. *Chevron USA, Inc. v. Nat. Res. Def. Council,* 467 U.S. 837 (1984), has long provided the two-step process that federal courts use to review a federal agency's interpretation of a federal statute. Over time, courts have expanded and contracted the use of *Chevron*, but that is a topic for your administrative law class. Without the myriad tests and caveats grafted onto *Chevron* over time, the basic *Chevron* approach considers first whether the statute is unambiguous. If so, then the court simply applies it. But if the statute is ambiguous, then the court's second step is to determine whether the agency's interpretation is reasonable. If so, the court is required to defer to the agency's interpretation. Most of the courts that have applied *Chevron* to compact agencies have been federal courts. However, the most completely reasoned opinion about why *Chevron* applies comes from the Oregon Supreme Court in the following case.

Friends of the Columbia Gorge v. Columbia River Gorge Comm'n
346 Or. 366 (2009)

GILLETTE, JUSTICE:

Petitioners, who are individuals, businesses and conservation organizations with connections to the Columbia River Gorge, sought judicial review by the Court of Appeals of the Columbia River Gorge Commission's (commission) 2004 revision of its management plan for the Columbia River Gorge National Scenic Area. Before that court, petitioners argued, in numerous assignments and subassignments of error, that various aspects of the 2004 revision violated the Columbia River Gorge National Scenic Area Act, 16 U.S.C. §§ 544–544p. The Court of Appeals rejected all but one of petitioners' subassignments of error. We allowed petitioners' petition for review, which challenges the various standards of review that the Court of Appeals employed in considering petitioners' claims, as well as a number of the Court of Appeals' substantive holdings. For the reasons that follow, we affirm the Court of Appeals decision in part, reverse it in part, and remand the case to the commission for further proceedings.

. . . .

As noted, petitioners contend that the management plan is inconsistent, in various respects, with the requirements of the Act. To assess the validity of those claims, it is necessary to determine what the Act requires. Consequently, our review of petitioner's claims generally will involve some interpretation of the Act.

In interpreting the Act, we follow the methodology that federal courts have prescribed for interpreting federal statutes, just as we would do in interpreting any other federal statute. *Corp. of Presiding Bishop v. City of West Linn,* 338 Or. 453, 463 (2005). In general, that means examining the text, context, and legislative history of the statute. However, there is an additional methodological wrinkle when, as in the present case, one of the parties before the court is the agency that has been charged with implementing the statute that is to be interpreted. A long line of federal cases, beginning with *Chevron U.S.A. v. Natural Res. Def. Council,* 467 U.S. 837, 842–44 (1984), holds that, when Congress has charged a federal agency with implementing a federal statute, courts should defer to that agency's interpretation of the statute, treating that interpretation as controlling as long as it is reasonable. Although that sort of deference is foreign to the administrative law of this state,[8] we are bound to apply it in our interpretation of federal statutes if the federal interpretive methodology so demands.

The remaining methodological question in this case, however, is whether the federal methodology would require deference by a federal court to the commission's interpretation of the Act, given the fact, among others, that the commission is not, strictly speaking, a federal agency charged by Congress with implementing

---

[8] The *Chevron* doctrine has been widely criticized. *See, e.g.,* Laurence H. Tribe, I American Constitutional Law 997–1002 (3d ed. 2000) (*Chevron,* in combination with relaxation of nondelegation doctrine, threatens to "cede large areas of the legal landscape to relatively unaccountable federal agencies.").

a federal law. The Court of Appeals concluded that, although the commission is not a federal agency, *Chevron* deference to its interpretations of the Act is appropriate because the commission is "a creation of federal law," it is authorized to implement federal law, and "the usual rationales for deference to agency construction" therefore should apply to its interpretations of the Act.

Petitioners argue, however, that the commission is not a creation of federal law but, instead, is the creation of an interstate compact that Congress authorized but did not require Oregon and Washington to adopt. From that premise, petitioners argue that the commission is not the recipient of delegated authority from Congress but, instead, derives its authority from state law, insofar as Washington and Oregon chose to create the commission and to assign to it its present powers. Finally, petitioners observe that the Act expressly states that the commission "shall not be considered an agency or instrumentality of the United States for the purpose of any federal law," 16 U.S.C. § 544c(a)(1)(A), including (they argue) the federal judicially created law relating to deference to agencies' statutory constructions.

For its part, the commission argues that, even if it is not directly a creature of federal law, the interstate compact that created it is more federal in nature than not, insofar as it incorporates federal law (the Act), pertains to subject matter of national interest, and required Congress's express consent. The commission concludes that *Chevron* deference therefore is appropriate. The commission also argues that applying *Chevron* deference in Oregon courts to the commission's interpretations of the Act is desirable because it "brings a degree of consistency and uniformity to the states' judicial review of commission actions involving interpretation of the federal Scenic Area Act that would not occur if the state courts use their own state law." The commission notes, in that regard, that federal and Washington state courts have applied *Chevron* to the commission's interpretations of the Act. Finally, the commission points to what it characterizes as a "solid history" in federal courts of applying *Chevron* deference to interstate compact agencies' interpretations of their own organic statutes. The commission suggests that this court should follow suit.

The commission's last two points are unpersuasive. First, given that *Chevron* is a mainstay in the federal courts, the fact that federal courts have applied *Chevron* deference to compact agencies' interpretations of federal statute may simply have been reflexive. In the absence of any explicit and authoritative holding that all courts should defer to compact agencies' interpretations of their (federal) organic statutes, regardless of differences between the particular compact agencies' powers, the review provisions in the statutes at issue, and the reviewing courts' ordinary practices, we are not inclined to follow the cited cases without conducting our own analysis of the question.

The commission's argument for applying *Chevron* as a means of ensuring uniformity in judicial review also is unpersuasive. Although we agree with the commission that variation in judicial review methodologies could undermine uniformity of land use standards within the scenic area, such variation appears entirely consistent with, and may even be contemplated by, the Act. We note, in that regard, that the Act specifically places jurisdiction to review appeals taken from commission actions in the state courts of Washington and Oregon, but does not specify any standard of review. One Washington court has responded to that circumstance by applying the standards of review set out in its own administrative procedures act when it is called upon to review a commission action, while Oregon courts use a standard of review that the legislature specifically adopted for review of commission actions, now codified at ORS 196.115(3)(c) to (e). Although we acknowledge that the interpretation of statutes arguably is a different matter, the fact that the Act by omission creates a situation in which Oregon and Washington are free to apply different standards of review to commission actions suggests that uniform treatment may not be the objective that Congress sought to achieve under the Act, as the commission suggests.

In the end, we think that the applicability of *Chevron* turns on a single question— whether the federal interpretive methodology (which, as discussed, we are bound to apply) would require it. And the answer to that question, as it turns out, is itself a function of congressional intent: The United States Supreme Court, which first announced the *Chevron* standard, has explained the standard in terms of a congressional intent or expectation—specifically, a congressional expectation, implied from the agency's "general conferred authority" and other circumstances, that the agency will "be able to speak with the force of law when it addresses ambiguity in the statute or fills a space in the enacted law." *United States v. Mead Corp.*, 533 U.S. 218, 229 (2001). According to the Court, when circumstances suggest that such intent or expectation exists,

> "A reviewing court has no business rejecting an agency's exercise of its generally conferred authority to resolve a particular statutory ambiguity simply because the agency's chosen resolution seems unwise, but is obliged to accept the agency's position if Congress has not previously spoken to the point at issue and the agency's interpretation is reasonable."

Mead Corp., 533 U.S. at 229 (citations omitted).

It follows that, to resolve whether the commission's interpretations of the Act are entitled to *Chevron* deference, we must determine whether the commission's "generally conferred authority" or other aspects of the Act imply a congressional expectation that the commission will "speak with the force of law" when it addresses ambiguities and gaps in the statute.[12] A strong indicator of such an expectation, according to the cases, is express congressional authorization to engage in rulemaking and adjudication with respect to the matters under review. That inference is particularly strong when that authorization provides for formal administrative procedures designed to "foster the fairness and deliberation that should underlie a pronouncement of such force." *Mead Corp.,* 533 U.S. at 230.

---

[12] Of course, Oregon courts do not operate on the same set of assumptions about the intentions of the Oregon legislature. *See generally Springfield Education Assn. v. School Dist.*, 290 Or. 217, 221–30 (1980) (explaining how authority to construe statutes is allocated between agencies and courts depending on type of statutory term that is at issue).

Applying the foregoing considerations to the present case, it appears that, to the extent that the management plan purports to carry out the purposes of the Act in a way that includes resolving ambiguities in or filling in gaps in the Act, the commission is entitled to *Chevron* deference. The Act clearly contains gaps that the commission is charged with filling. Indeed, Congress has directed the commission to "adopt a management plan for the scenic area," which must be based on resource inventories and land use designations that the Act requires the commission to develop, which must be "consistent with" certain specified statutory standards, and which, once adopted, will effectively control land use actions within the scenic area. That would seem to be the precise sort of delegation of authority that, according to *Mead* and similar cases, indicates a congressional expectation that the commission will "speak with the force of law" in filling the significant gaps left open by the statute. Moreover, to the extent that the Act authorizes the commission to develop and adopt a management plan (a documentary product that in every relevant sense is a rule or a compilation of rules), requires the commission to conduct public hearings and solicit public comment before adopting a final management plan, and requires the commission to adopt and follow other administrative procedures that would appear to be designed to foster fairness and deliberation, the commission stands well within the mainstream of agencies whose interpretations of their organic statutes have been deemed worthy of *Chevron* deference.

Petitioners argue that *Chevron* is a federal doctrine that applies only to agencies and instrumentalities of the United States, and that, whatever else it may be, the commission is not a federal agency. Petitioners note, in that regard, that the Act expressly provides that the commission "shall not be considered an agency or instrumentality of the United States for the purpose of any Federal Law." However, none of the federal cases that discusses and applies *Chevron* to agency actions appears to focus on the agency's status as a federal agency. Although the cases, of necessity, generally do pertain to federal agencies, their focus is on the nature of Congress's delegation of authority to the agency, rather than the agency's federal status.

Petitioners also argue that the commission is not a recipient of a congressional delegation of authority but, instead, derives its authority from an interstate agreement and, thus, from the two member states. Petitioners acknowledge that Congress gave consent for Oregon and Washington to enter into an interstate compact, but it notes that Congress did not require the states to do so. Petitioners contend that, under those circumstances, Oregon and Washington must be deemed to have created the commission and to be the source of its authority to develop and implement the management plan.

We disagree. The Act reveals a far greater Congressional role in the creation of the commission and the development of the management plan than petitioners' argument acknowledges. In addition to memorializing Congress's consent to an interstate compact, the Act provides for the formation of an interstate commission to administer that compact, describes in relatively fine detail the structure of that body and how its members will be appointed, requires the commission to adopt a management plan, describes the process that the commission must use for developing the management plan, and provides standards to which the resulting management plan must adhere. In short, even if Oregon and Washington are the parties who enter into the compact, it is a compact of Congress's design. Of particular relevance here, it is Congress—not the states—that determined what powers and responsibilities would be delegated to the commission and what procedures the commission must follow in carrying out its responsibilities.

In the end, we conclude that, in 16 U.S.C. §§ 544–544p, Congress delegated authority to the commission that, under the federal methodology that we are bound to apply, implies a congressional expectation that the commission will "speak with the force of law" when it addresses ambiguities and gaps in the statutory scheme. The commission's interpretations of the Act therefore are entitled to the level of deference that the *Chevron* doctrine prescribes. That means that, if the Act is ambiguous with respect to some matter, the commission's construction must be upheld, unless it is unreasonable.

. . . .

Notes & Questions

1. This decision is the most complete analysis of whether courts should apply *Chevron* to review of compact agency actions. Most opinions have applied *Chevron* without explaining the reason for doing so. For example, the Ninth Circuit stated,

> TRPA is an interstate agency empowered to administer the 1980 Compact by way of ETCC's, an amended regional plan, and ordinances, rules, and regulations. Necessarily, administration of the Compact requires its interpretation. . . . Interpretation given a statute by the agency charged with its administration is entitled to deference from the courts, and the courts are the final authority on questions of statutory construction. Generally this means that the court must review the controlling legislation and the agency's interpretation and determine two things. *Chevron* . . . .

California ex rel. Van de Kamp v. Tahoe Reg'l Planning Agency, 766 F.2d 1308, 1313 (9th Cir. 1985). Despite expressly stating that TRPA is an "interstate agency," the question whether the court should apply *Chevron* never arose, perhaps because this case was just one year after *Chevron*. The Ninth Circuit also applied *Chevron* to the Pacific Northwest Electric Power and Conservation Planning Council, reasoning that it should apply *Chevron* to the Council because it would apply *Chevron* to the federal Bonneville Power Administration that the Council oversees:

> For the same reasons that we defer to BPA expertise in construing other sections of the [Northwest Power] Act, therefore, we will defer to the Council's interpretations of [the Act] if reasonable.

Seattle Master Builders Ass'n v. Pac. Nw. Elec. Power & Cons. Planning Council, 786 F.2d 1359, 1367 (9th Cir. 1986). Perhaps the court's reasoning was so cursory because the case involved the Northwest Power Act, which granted consent to the compact, states that "judicial review of Council functions and actions under this Act, and related matters, the Federal laws applicable to such matters in the case of the Bonneville Power Administration shall apply to the Council to the extent appropriate . . . ." 16 U.S.C. § 839b(a)(4).

2. Several other courts have applied *Chevron* to compact agencies. For example, the U.S. district courts for Massachusetts and Vermont both applied *Chevron* to the Northeast Dairy Compact Commission, a compact that expired in 2001. Congress's consent to the Northeast Interstate Dairy Compact required that the commission use the federal APA for its rulemaking. 7 U.S.C. § 7256 (consent to compact text contained in S.J. Res. 28, 104th Cong. (1995)). Nevertheless, in deciding to apply *Chevron*, the courts did not rely on this provision, rather both courts recognized the commission was a compact agency and relied on the principle that a compact with consent is federal law.

The U.S. District Court for Massachusetts stated, "Just as if a court were addressing a federal statute, then, the first and last order of business of a court addressing an approved interstate compact is interpreting the compact. . . ." *N.Y. State Dairy Foods, Inc. v. Ne. Dairy Compact Comm'n*, 26 F. Supp. 2d 249, 260 (D. Mass. 1998) (quoting *New Jersey v. New York*, 523 U.S. 767 (1998)).

Just as briefly, the federal district court of Vermont stated, "Congressional consent has transformed the Compact into a law of the United States. Although the Compact is the equivalent of a federal law, the Commission is not the equivalent of a federal agency governed by the Administrative Procedures Act. The Commission is an authority of the six New England states, not the United States government." *The Organic Cow, LLC v. Ne. Dairy Compact Comm'n*, 164 F. Supp. 2d 412, 419–20 (D. Vt. 2001).

3. The Oregon Supreme Court rejected the Gorge Commission's argument that application of *Chevron* was necessary to achieve a uniform interpretation of the compact. In contrast, in *Am. Sugar Refining Co. v. Waterfront Comm'n of N.Y. Harbor*, 55 N.Y.2d 11 (1982), the New York Court of Appeals observed that uniformity of interpretation comes from the party states expounding federal law:

> Somewhat more complex is the determination of what law governs, the complicating factor being that the legislation to be construed is the product of not one but three legislative bodies. Our determination in *Bell v Waterfront Comm. of N.Y. Harbor,* 20 N.Y.2d 54, 61, that construction of an interstate compact (indeed, the very compact now under consideration) is "a matter of Federal rather than State law" accords with the Supreme Court's recent holding in *Cuyler v Adams* that interpretation of a compact the subject matter of which is appropriate as a subject of congressional legislation (as of course is waterfront governance, closely related as it is to interstate and foreign commerce) presents a question of Federal law. Thus, while uniformity of interpretation by the courts of New York and New Jersey is to be desired, it is a uniformity born not of comity but of the fact that each, in interpreting the Compact, is expounding Federal not State law. Thus, also,

> while State legislative history has bearing and is not to be ignored, the history of the Compact before the Congress is an essential of interpretation.

Am. Sugar Refining Co., 55 N.Y.2d at 25–26.

4. Chapter 5 mentioned that the *Friends of the Columbia Gorge* case also applied *Auer v. Robbins,* 519 U.S. 452 (1997), in which the Court deferred to an agency's interpretation of its own regulations. Both the Oregon Court of Appeals and the Oregon Supreme Court applied *Auer*. Applying *Auer* was an issue of first impression, but neither court explained why it is appropriately applied to compact agencies. What do you think? Should courts use federal methods to review compact agency interpretations of their own rules?

CHAPTER 10: ADMINISTRATION OF COMPACTS

Administering a compact involves many of the same tasks as administering state and federal statutes, but there are special problems and considerations because of the bi- or multi-state nature of compacts and compact entities. Chapter 3 looked at the authority of states to enter into compacts; this chapter looks at on-the-ground problems of when a compact should become effective, oversight of the compact, and withdrawal and winding up. Chapter 4 considered whether a compact agency is like a state or federal agency; this chapter looks at appointment and removal of officials and operational issues of the agency. Many of the cases in earlier chapters involved judicial review of compact agency decisions; this chapter looks more closely at the administrative procedures that the agency might have used when making the decision under review.

I. WHEN DOES A COMPACT BECOME EFFECTIVE?

Determining when a compact becomes effective seems like a simple task; after all, legislation typically sets an effective date or becomes effective by operation of law at a specified time. Compacts present a more difficult problem because multiple states must enact the compact through legislation. Not only do states have different default dates for when legislation becomes effective by operation of law, but they may also enact the compact during different legislative sessions over a period of years. For example, states began enacting the Interstate Wildlife Violator Compact in 1989 and continue to adopt it; as of mid-2020, there were 49 member states. In another example, in 2017, Idaho joined the Interstate Oil and Gas Compact as a full member 82 years after the original states negotiated the compact in 1935. Consider some of the following compact provisions, specifying when the compacts would become effective.

The Interstate Compact for the Supervision of Adult Offenders, art. XI, provides: "The Compact shall become effective and binding upon legislative enactment of the Compact into law by no less than 35 of the States. The initial effective date shall be the later of July 1, 2001, or upon enactment into law by the 35th jurisdiction. Thereafter it shall become effective and binding, as to any other Compacting State, upon enactment of the Compact into law by that State." The 35th state enacted the compact in 2002, just 2 1/2 years after the compact became ready for the states' consideration. Why would a compact specify alternative dates such as in the Adult Offender Compact?

In contrast to the experience with the Adult Offender Compact, the revised Interstate Compact for the Placement of Children also requires 35 states to enact it before it becomes effective, but as of mid-2020, only 12 states have enacted it since it became ready for the states in 2009. Trying to give a boost to membership, the Conference of Chief Justices enacted a resolution in 2018 encouraging states to enact the revised ICPC and urging the new interstate commission to include a representative of the Conference of Chief Justices and Conference of State Court

Administrators. Conference of Chief Justices, *Resolution 6, In Support of the Revised Interstate Compact for the Placement of Children* (Jan. 31, 2018). Why would a compact specify such a high threshold to become effective?

In another example, the Boating Offense Compact, art. IV(1), provides: "This compact shall enter into force and become effective as to any state when it has enacted the same into law." Does this clause mean that the compact is effective when only one state has enacted it?

The Columbia River Gorge Compact, art III provides: "This compact shall take effect, and the commission may exercise its authorities . . . when it has been ratified by both states and upon the appointment of four initial members from each state. The date of this compact shall be the date of the establishment of the commission." The Gorge Compact requires six members from each state and certain actions of the commission require a majority of members from each state, so making the compact effective upon ratification in both states and requiring the minimum number to take all possible actions in the compact makes sense. But does it make sense that the compact should be effective if one state has appointed all six members, but the other state has appointed only four members?

The Kansas and Missouri Metropolitan Cultural Compact, art. VIII(a), provides: "This compact shall enter into force and become effective and binding upon the states of Kansas and Missouri when it has been enacted into law by the legislatures of the respective states." Additionally, article IV(a) specifies, "The counties in Kansas and Missouri eligible to create and initially compose the metropolitan culture district shall be those counties which meet one or more of the following criteria . . . . The counties of Johnson in Kansas and Jackson in Missouri shall be *sine qua non*[*] to the creation and initial composition of the district. Additional counties in Kansas and Missouri shall be eligible to become a part of the metropolitan culture district if such counties are contiguous to any one or more of the counties which compose the district and within 60 miles of the counties required by this article to establish the district." Here, while the compact nominally states that it becomes effective when the states enact it into law, its creation is of no consequence until the requisite local governments create the culture district.

Surprisingly, many compacts do not have any provision specifying a time or conditions to become effective, but a reasonable effective date may be inferred from the language of the compact. For example, the Tahoe Regional Planning Compact did not contain an effective date clause, but in *Lake Country Estates, Inc. v. Tahoe Reg'l Planning Agency*, 440 U.S. 391 (1979), the Supreme Court noted, "The actual implementation of TRPA, after federal approval was obtained, depended upon the appointment of governing members and executives by the two States and their subdivisions and upon mandatory financing secured, by the terms of the Compact, from the counties." *Id.* at 399.

---

[*] [*Ed. Note*: *Sine qua non* means "without which not." In this context, it means that Johnson County, Kansas, and Jackson County, Missouri, are required to be part of the metropolitan cultural district.]

II. Appointment and Removal of Compact Agency Officials

All compacts that create an agency contain some provisions for appointment of the agency's officials—typically, who appoints the officials, their terms of office, and voting rights. Compacts that specify one or more Presidential appointees typically also require advice and consent of the Senate and allow removal only for cause. *E.g.*, Congress's consent to the Metropolitan Washington Airports Authority, 49 U.S.C. §§ 49106(c)(1)(D), 49106(c)(6)(C). Surprisingly however, few compacts specify whether compact agency officials must be confirmed by the state legislatures, continue to hold office after their term of appointment has expired if there is no new appointee, or are removeable at will or for cause. These are important issues because when a compact is silent about confirmation, governors may have more flexibility in who they would appoint, new state officials may want to replace appointees from a prior administration, and states may have different rules relating to holdover or what justifies cause. These factors may allow one state to steer the compact agency more than another state.

In Chapter 9, you read a short excerpt from *Pievsky v. Ridge* illustrating how courts look to federal law when interpreting a compact. Here, we look at a governor's authority to remove a compact agency official before the end of his appointed term.

Pievsky v. Ridge
98 F.3d 730 (3d Cir. 1996)

Cowen, Judge:

Former Commissioner of the Delaware River Port Authority of Pennsylvania and New Jersey ("DRPA"), Max Pievsky, filed a complaint challenging the Governor of Pennsylvania's power to remove him without cause under the terms of the DRPA Compact, an interstate agreement between the Commonwealth of Pennsylvania and the State of New Jersey. The district court dismissed the complaint on summary judgment, concluding that the Governor of Pennsylvania had the power to remove DRPA Commissioners prior to the expiration of their terms. Because we agree that, under the terms of the DRPA Compact, the Governor of Pennsylvania has the power to remove the appointed DRPA Commissioners at will, we will affirm the April 12, 1996 order of the district court.

. . . .

The parties stipulated to the following facts. The DRPA derives its authority from the DRPA Compact, an interstate agreement between the Commonwealth of Pennsylvania and the State of New Jersey. The Compact was originally enacted by the Pennsylvania and New Jersey legislatures in 1931 and is codified in reciprocal statutes. As required by the Compact Clause of the United States Constitution, Congress originally consented to the terms of the Compact in 1932 and thereafter consented to amendments in 1952 and 1992.

The DRPA was created, among other things, to construct and operate bridges across the Delaware River, to construct and maintain facilities for the transportation of passengers between Pennsylvania and New Jersey, and to improve and develop the ports of Philadelphia and Camden. The DRPA has sixteen commissioners, eight of whom are appointed from Pennsylvania and eight of whom are appointed from New Jersey. The Compact establishes the procedure for the appointment of the eight commissioners from Pennsylvania as follows:

> [S]ix of the eight commissioners for the Commonwealth of Pennsylvania shall be appointed by the Governor of Pennsylvania for terms of five years. The Auditor General and the State Treasurer of said Commonwealth shall, ex-officio, be commissioners for said Commonwealth, each having the privilege of appointing a representative to serve in his place at any meeting of the commission which he does not attend personally.
>
> All commissioners shall continue to hold office after the expiration of the terms for which they are appointed or elected until their respective successors are appointed and qualify, but no period during which any commissioner shall hold over shall be deemed to be an extension of his term of office for the purpose of computing the date on which his successor's terms expire.

DRPA Compact, Article II. Article II of the Compact states that the New Jersey appointees must be confirmed by the Senate of New Jersey, but does not require legislative confirmation of Pennsylvania's appointees.

The states have significant control over the DRPA. The Compact provides that the Board may act only by way of a majority of each state's commissioners voting in favor of the action. In 1992, the state legislatures amended the Compact to allow each state to pass legislation authorizing its Governor to veto the action of any of the state's commissioners within ten days of receipt of the minutes of the meeting at which the vote was taken.

On December 28, 1994, former Governor of Pennsylvania Robert Casey appointed Max Pievsky as a commissioner of the DRPA. The commission, signed by the Governor, states that Pievsky shall hold office until December 28, 1999. On January 22, 1996, Pievsky received a telephone call from Leslie Gromis, Director of Governor Ridge's Office of Public Liaison. Gromis informed Pievsky that the Governor was disappointed in Pievsky's vote for a new chairperson for the DRPA Board on January 17, 1996. Gromis further stated that if Pievsky did not resign the next day, the Governor would make an appointment to the DRPA to replace him.

. . . .

The issue we must decide is strictly one of statutory construction. Does the DRPA Compact allow the Governor of Pennsylvania to remove a commissioner to the DRPA at will and prior to the expiration of his term?

Since the Compact is an interstate agreement which requires the consent of Congress, such congressional consent transforms the Compact into an agreement pursuant to federal law. Our interpretation of the terms and conditions of the Compact is, therefore, governed by federal law.

Though state law is not binding, federal courts show deference to prior state adjudications and rulings in construing an interstate compact. *See [West Virginia] ex rel. Dyer v. Sims*, 341 U.S. 22, 28 (1951) ("To determine the nature and scope of obligations as between States [when] they arise through the legislative mean of compact * * * is the function and duty of the Supreme Court of the Nation. Of course every deference will be shown to what the highest court of a State deems to be the law and policy of its State * * *"); *see also Petty [*v. Tennessee-Missouri Bridge Comm'n], 359 U.S. [275,] 278 n.4 [(1959)] ("While we show deference to state law in construing a compact, state law as pronounced in prior adjudications and rulings is not binding"); *Seattle Master Builders Ass'n v. Pac. Nw. Elec. Power & Cons. Planning Council*, 786 F.2d 1359, 1365 (9th Cir. 1986) ("While congressional consent gives an interstate compact some attributes of federal law, the Council members' appointment, salaries, and administrative operations are pursuant to the laws of the four individual states, within parameters set by the Act.").

The Compact is merely an agreement between states that has received the imprimatur of Congress. The interpretation of the Compact must be grounded and based upon the very language of the instrument. *See Texas v. New Mexico*, 482 U.S. 124 (1987). The Compact between Pennsylvania and New Jersey states that "[s]ix of the eight commissioners for the Commonwealth of Pennsylvania shall be appointed by the Governor of Pennsylvania for terms of five years." It does not explicitly state whether the commissioners may be removed by the governor prior to the expiration of their term.

The long-standing rule in the context of federal appointments is that "[i]n the absence of specific provision to the contrary, the power of removal from office is incident to the power of appointment." *Keim v. United States*, 177 U.S. 290, 293 (1900). Pennsylvania has also adopted this principle of law. The Compact explicitly gives the Governor of Pennsylvania the power to appoint six commissioners to the DRPA. Accordingly, pursuant to federal law, there is a presumption that the Governor also has the authority to remove those six commissioners prior to the end of their terms.

Pievsky argues that since the DRPA Commissioner's term of office is five years, as compared to the Governor's four year term of office, the Pennsylvania legislature and Congress intended to limit the Governor's power of removal. We disagree. The fact that the Governor's term of office is shorter than that of the commissioners does not indicate an intent on the part of the legislature to limit the Governor's ability to remove his appointees. If the Pennsylvania legislature intended such a limitation, it would have stated so in the Compact. Instead, the Compact simply reads that the Governor of Pennsylvania shall appoint a DRPA Commissioner for a term of five years. Since the power to remove is incident to the power to appoint, we hold that under the terms of the Compact the Governor of Pennsylvania has the authority to remove a DRPA Commissioner at will.

We believe that the difference in the length of terms of office is irrelevant. Since the Compact provides that commissioners may hold office after the expiration of the term for which they are appointed, and "no period during which any commissioner shall hold over shall be deemed to be an extension of this term of office for the purpose of computing the date on which his successor's term expires," a commissioner's term of office may in fact be for four years or less. This would occur if a commissioner is succeeding a prior commissioner who has continued to hold office after the expiration of his term of office.

Pievsky also contends that interpreting the Compact to permit the Governor to remove a commissioner at will vitiates the plain language of the Compact which provides that six of the Commonwealth's commissioners "shall be appointed by the Governor of Pennsylvania for terms of five years." He asserts that five years means five years, and not less than five years. We are not persuaded. It is a longstanding rule in the federal courts that a fixed term merely provides a time for the term to end. The fixed term is merely a "cap" with the appointee removable at will. We read the term "five years" as a means of limiting the length of the term of office, not as a prohibition on the Governor's removal authority.

Pievsky next maintains that under federal law the terms of the DRPA Compact evidence an intent by the legislatures to limit the Governor's removal power because the Compact states that six of Pennsylvania's commissioners "shall be appointed by the Governor * * * for terms of five years." The case law cited by Pievsky in support of his argument are readily distinguishable. In *Humphrey's Executor v. United States*, 295 U.S. 602 (1935), the Supreme Court reviewed President Roosevelt's attempt to remove a member of the Federal Trade Commission ("FTC"). Pursuant to the Federal Trade Commission Act, commissioners of the FTC were appointed for fixed rotating terms. The Federal Trade Commission Act provides that "[a]ny commissioner may be removed by the President for inefficiency, neglect of duty, or malfeasance in office." The Supreme Court held that in light of the statutory language limiting removal, "the fixing of a definite term subject to removal for cause, unless there be some countervailing provision or circumstance indicating the contrary, which here we are unable to find, is enough to establish the legislative intent that the term is not to be curtailed in the absence of such cause." *Humphrey's Executor*, 295 U.S. at 624. The statute at issue in *Humphrey's Executor* contained clear language limiting the removal authority of the President—such language is absent from the Compact.

Moreover, the Supreme Court in *Humphrey's Executor* considered the character of the commission as an essential basis for its holding. The Court determined that the FTC was a nonpartisan body, charged "with the enforcement of no policy except the policy of the law", and that "[i]ts duties are neither political nor executive, but predominantly quasi judicial and quasi legislative." 295 U.S. at 624. The *Humphrey's Executor* court noted that

> [I]t is quite evident that one who holds his office only during the pleasure of another, cannot be depended upon to maintain an attitude of independence against the latter's will.

295 U.S. at 629. Accordingly, the *Humphrey's Executor* court concluded that the President did not have the authority to remove a member of the FTC prior to the expiration of that member's term of office for reasons in addition to those specifically stated in the statute. In contrast, the DRPA is neither a quasi legislative or quasi judicial body. Also, in contrast to the character of the FTC, the DRPA is a politically sensitive body that must be responsive to the programs and policies of the administration presently in office.

We have previously discussed how the DRPA officers must be politically accountable in *Peters v. Delaware River Port Authority*, 16 F.3d 1346 (3d Cir. 1994). In *Peters*, the Secretary of the DRPA brought suit claiming that the DRPA infringed his constitutional rights of free speech and association by failing to reappoint him as its Secretary solely because he was a member of the New Jersey Republican Party. We rejected his claim, finding that party affiliation of the officers of the DRPA was relevant to the effective functioning of the DRPA. We stated,

> The DRPA has broad powers, leaving much room for principled disagreement on policy goals or their implementation.
>
> * * *
>
> The policy and political issues, including economic considerations, arising in an entity such as the DRPA are many. If tolls are raised, bridges fall into disrepair, or traffic is congested, there are surely political consequences. Whether decent roads and transit systems will be made available to all segments of the communities, or will be provided in a manner perceived as favoring some or excluding others, raises important and sensitive social, economic and political questions. * * * Since the governors of New Jersey and Pennsylvania directly appoint fourteen of the sixteen member Board of Commissioners, political responsibility for the DRPA's successes and failures can be expected to fall on the ruling administration of each state.
>
> * * *
>
> Obviously, the party affiliation or policy views of the officers in the DRPA could be relevant to the effective presentation and implementation of particular policy goals. If the states preferred huge increases in spending for the construction of bridges, for example, they might legitimately prefer that high positions in the DRPA not be filled with individuals belonging to a party which advocates decreased government spending.

16 F.3d at 1355. Therefore, the DRPA Commissioners must be accountable to the administration in office in order for the DRPA to function properly.

The goals of each state are accomplished only through the DRPA's responsiveness to each state. In order to ensure such responsiveness, the Governor must have the authority to remove Pennsylvania's appointed commissioners. The fact that Pennsylvania's representation on the Commission is comprised exclusively of Executive Department appointees and officials lends support to the conclusion that the DRPA is meant to be responsive to the Executive Branch of the Commonwealth of Pennsylvania. Six of Pennsylvania's eight commissioners are appointed by the governor, and the remaining two members who serve ex-officio are the State Treasurer and the Auditor General, both of whom are officers of the Executive Department. The ability of the Governor to remove DRPA Commissioners ensures that the commissioners are politically accountable to each state's administration. This case is clearly distinguishable from the Supreme Court's holding in *Humphrey's Executor*.

. . . .

We also find that *Borders v. Reagan*, 518 F. Supp. 250 (D.D.C. 1981) is distinguishable. In *Borders*, the district court held that President Reagan could not remove at will a member of the District of Columbia Judicial Nominating Commission that President Carter had appointed. The District of Columbia Self-Government and Governmental Reorganization Act ("Act") provides that the Commission would consist of seven members who "shall serve" for terms of six years, except for the member appointed by the President who "shall serve" for a term of five. The Act made no provision for the removal of commission members.

The district court in *Borders* held the language of the statute made clear that Congress did not intend a member of the commission would serve only at the pleasure of the appointing authority; rather, once an appointment was made it anticipated that the member would serve a complete term. The plain language of the Act provides that a member "shall serve" for the term of years. The Act makes no provision for the removal of a member, but does provide for the appointment of a member when a vacancy occurs. The district court noted that the Act contemplated that vacancies would occur only at the expiration of a given term: The Act provides that for vacancies occurring "other than [upon] the expiration of a prior term," the new member would serve only for the "remainder of the unexpired term of his predecessor." Thus, even if *Borders* were binding on us, the district court's conclusion in that matter that Congress did not intend a commissioner to be removed at will is distinguishable.

The plain language of the DRPA Compact does not indicate, as the language of the statute in *Borders* did, that the state legislatures contemplated vacancies on the DRPA Board would occur only at the expiration of DRPA members' expired terms. Moreover, the court's decision in *Borders* rested on additional grounds that are not present in this case. The Act provided for staggered terms for six of the commissioners, which the court determined was evidence of congressional intent that the members be isolated from political considerations and political changes.

Pievsky also asserts that the DRPA is an interstate entity which is not under the control of the Commonwealth of Pennsylvania or the State of New Jersey. He cites *Hess v. Port Authority Trans-Hudson Corp.*, 513 U.S. 30 (1994), for the proposition that "[b]ecause Compact Clause entities owe their existence to state and federal sovereigns acting cooperatively, and not to any 'one of the United States,' * * * their political accountability is diffuse; they lack the tight tie to the people of one State that an instrument of a single State has." 115 S. Ct. at 401. We agree that the DRPA is not under the control of any one state. As we stated in *Peters* the

DRPA is "not designed to further the political agenda of any one state or administration." 16 F.3d at 1355. Nevertheless, pursuant to the appointing process, Pennsylvania-appointed DRPA officials are under the control of the Pennsylvania Governor, just as New Jersey-appointed DRPA Commissioners must be politically accountable to the Governor of New Jersey.

. . . .

. . . Because the Compact does not limit the Governor's removal power, the Governor may exercise his power under the Pennsylvania Constitution to remove appointed officials to the DRPA Board. We agree with Pievsky's contention that the Compact is in the nature of federal law, and, under the Supremacy Clause of the U.S. Constitution, could limit the Governor's ability to remove his appointed officials. However, as discussed above, we conclude under a federal law analysis that the legislatures which passed the Compact did not intend to restrict the Governor's ability to remove DRPA Commissioners in this manner.

The appointed members of the DRPA are "policy makers" who exercise executive powers and are expected to carry out the policies of the current administration of each state . . . . Far from needing independent appointees, "the DRPA needs officers who are capable of efficiently, effectively, and loyally accessing the political channels that influence the DRPA's agenda and direction." *Peters*, 16 F.3d at 1356. Considering the mission of the DRPA, and the burden that interstate conflicts place on the effective functioning of this bi-state authority, the legislatures could not have intended to create a board on which Pennsylvania's members are independent of the current Governor.

Though state law is not binding, federal courts show deference to prior state adjudications and rulings in construing an interstate compact. *See* [*West Virginia*] *ex rel. Dyer v. Sims*, 341 U.S. 22, 28 (1951). Pennsylvania law is in accord with federal law that the Pennsylvania Governor may remove a DRPA commissioner at will and prior to the expiration of the term. The removal of state officers in Pennsylvania is governed by the Commonwealth's Constitution which provides that "[a]ppointed civil officers, other than the judges of the courts of record, may be removed at the pleasure of the power by which they shall have been appointed." In the absence of statutory language providing otherwise this constitutional provision governs the removal of appointed officials. The legislature may "impose such terms and limitations with reference to the tenure and removal of an incumbent [state official] as it sees fit." [*Watson v. Pa. Tpk. Comm'n*, 125 A.2d 354, 356 (Pa. 1956).]

The Pennsylvania Supreme Court has held that where a statute provides for fixed terms with staggered expiration dates, the legislature intended that those appointed shall not be removable at the will of the appointing authority. However, the mere fixing of a definite term does not override the dictates of Article VI, § 7 of the Constitution which gives removal power to the appointing authority. Pennsylvania case law provides that the staggering of terms, not the mere fixing of a definite term in office, bars the Governor from removing an appointed official at will. Therefore, in light of the fact that the DRPA Commissioners' terms are fixed and not staggered, the Pennsylvania Constitution, as interpreted by the Pennsylvania Supreme Court, does not preclude the Governor from removing Pievsky prior to the expiration of his term.

We note that the Pennsylvania Attorney General has officially opined that Pennsylvania's appointees to the DRPA are removable at will. *See* Pennsylvania Attorney General's Official Opinion, No. 280 issued on March 24, 1939.... We note that the Attorney General of New Jersey has also issued an opinion that the Pennsylvania appointees to the DRPA Board are removable at will by the Governor of Pennsylvania. Memorandum from Attorney General George F. Kugler, Jr. to Governor William T. Cahill, October 6, 1971. We need not decide the extent of deference due in this situation in light of all the other convincing bases for our conclusion that by reason of the state constitutional provisions governing the removal of appointed officials, and given that the DRPA commissioners' terms are fixed and not staggered, the Governor has the power to remove appointed DRPA Commissioners at will.

For the foregoing reasons, we conclude that the Governor of Pennsylvania has the power to remove an appointed DRPA Commissioner at will and prior to the expiration of the term. Accordingly, we will affirm the order of the district court entered on April 12, 1996.

Notes & Questions

1. This case has an interesting history. Governor Ridge, a Republican, had been working to disempower a bloc of Democrats that Governor Casey, a Democrat, appointed in the week prior to transferring power to Governor Ridge. Governor Ridge's action may not have been a purely political move; the *Philadelphia Inquirer* published a series of exposés in November 1995 disclosing a pattern of patronage, one-bid contracts, and mismanagement, essentially squandering most of the agency's reserves at the instigation of or with the support of the Democrats.

2. The Third Circuit noted that Governor Ridge's attorneys removed the case originally filed in state court to federal court because interpretation of the compact presents a federal question. However, the *Philadelphia Inquirer* reported, "[Governor] Ridge's advisers want the case in federal court because, they assert privately, some of the state's elected judges may be susceptible to pressure from Democratic Party leaders." *Ridge Takes DRPA Battle Into Court,* A01, The Philadelphia Inquirer, Jan. 25, 1996 SF Ed.

3. The Third Circuit also noted that the DRPA compact specifies New Jersey appointees must be confirmed by the state Senate, but Pennsylvania appointees do not. Why might a compact specify a different appointments process for the member states?

4. What do you think about the Third Circuit's statement, "the DRPA Commissioners must be accountable to the administration in office in order for the DRPA to function properly"? Does this apply to all compacts, or is there something special about the DRPA? *Peters v. Delaware River Port Auth.*, 16 F.3d 1346

(3d Cir. 1994), mentioned in the *Pievsky* case, involved a claim that "DRPA infringed his constitutional rights of free speech and association by failing to reappoint him as its Secretary solely because he is a member of the New Jersey Republican Party." *Id.* at 1352. In rejecting Peters's claim, the Third Circuit stated:

> Because the DRPA serves at least two different states' interests, it is forced to deal with more than one administration and a complex group of political interests. The DRPA needs officers who are capable of efficiently, effectively and loyally accessing the political channels that influence the DRPA's agenda and direction. The DRPA may choose to retain employees who can be knowledgeable of and be trusted by each state's executive and legislative political infrastructures. Party affiliation can be expected to be an important requirement to effectively carry out these tasks.
>
> . . . [W]hile the DRPA was created to achieve mutually beneficial goals, it did not compel each state to abandon all partisan political considerations and interests. In fact, the New Jersey and Pennsylvania delegations to the DRPA, as would be expected, continue to act as economic competitors.[12] The district court assumed that in governing the DRPA, this competition and the likelihood that there will be political differences between New Jersey and Pennsylvania concerning DRPA governance and policies will result in a situation that will minimize any need for the expertise of staff members who are politically sophisticated. We think the court erred in this respect. In fact, either state alone, or both states working together, might choose to accomplish broad economic goals at the DRPA through partisan or bipartisan means. Moreover, because the governor from each state appoints members of the Board, and because the Board in turn elects the positions of Chairman, Vice-Chairman, Secretary, and Treasurer, it can be expected that at various times particular members of the Board and the officers they elect will be partial to one particular state, administration or political party.

---

[12] We take judicial notice of newspaper accounts indicating that the New Jersey and Pennsylvania delegations within the DRPA are at times in competition with one another. For example, the *Philadelphia Business Journal* reported:

> After 10 years without a fare increase, and as the DRPA's monthly subsidies to PATCO, its subsidiary, have snowballed in the last few years, commissioners appeared to reach a consensus that rates will have to rise. * * *
>
> The subject has long been a volatile one, pitting the Pennsylvania and New Jersey delegations against each other, because the line's customers are overwhelmingly New Jersey residents commuting to work in Philadelphia.

David M. Halbfinger, *No Blockbusters From Secret DRPA Meeting,* Philadelphia Bus. J., March 29–April 4, 1993, at 3, 12.

Another article stated, "both [New Jersey and Pennsylvania] have tried to tap the [DRPA's] funds to develop piers, but every attempt has been thwarted by the state that enjoyed a competitive advantage at the shipping docks at the time." Michael Fabey, *DRPA Intends to Exert Its Influence Far From Riverfront,* Philadelphia Bus. J., Sept. 23–29, 1991, at 1, 26.

> Indeed, such loyalty among the individual members of the DRPA, in light of political reality, may be appropriate in order for each state to maintain a balance of power within the DRPA. The Compact itself provides that the Secretary and Treasurer "need not be members of the [Board]." Compact art. IV(d). Thus, the Compact allows, but does not require, the Board to elect their own members (who are political appointments) to act as Secretary and Treasurer. Contrary to the lower court's assumption, the Compact thus specifically considers and allows the possibility that the position of Secretary would be filled by individuals who are loyal to a particular state's governing administration, a particular political party, or to a particular group within the Board. Therefore, party affiliation can be expected to be an important requirement for the effective performance of the higher positions within the DRPA, including that of Secretary.

Id. at 1356.

5. The Third Circuit also cited a short excerpt from the Supreme Court's decision in *Hess v. Port Auth. Trans-Hudson Corp.*: "[b]ecause Compact Clause entities owe their existence to state and federal sovereigns acting cooperatively, and not to any 'one of the United States,' * * * their political accountability is diffuse; they lack the tight tie to the people of one State that an instrument of a single State has." The Third Circuit's quote, however, was incomplete and does not reflect the Supreme Court's decision in context. The Supreme Court continued

> "An interstate compact, by its very nature, shifts a part of a state's authority to another state or states, or to the agency the several states jointly create to run the compact. Such an agency under the control of special interests or gubernatorially appointed representatives is two or more steps removed from popular control, or even of control by a local government." M. RIDGEWAY, INTERSTATE COMPACTS: A QUESTION OF FEDERALISM 300 (1971). In sum, within any single State in our representative democracy, voters may exercise their political will to direct state policy; bistate entities created by compact, however, are not subject to the unilateral control of any one of the States that compose the federal system.

Hess, 513 U.S. at 401–02. As mentioned in Note 1, it was no secret that Governor Ridge was attempting to make big changes at the Delaware River Port Authority, but was he trying to unilaterally control the DRPA through his appointments? Does it make a difference that the compact authorized the governors to veto their appointees' votes, or that New Jersey Governor Whitman could have exerted the same level of influence as Governor Ridge?

6. The Delaware River Port Authority has had several cases involving appointment and removal of its board members. In *Crisconi v. Shapp*, 5 Pa. Commw. 375 (1972), the court noted that the compact creating the Delaware River Port Authority contained a requirement for New Jersey Senate consent of New Jersey Governor appointees, but the compact did not contain any similar requirement for Pennsylvania appointees. John Crisconi, a Pennsylvania Governor appointee who was being replaced before his term expired, argued that the Pennsylvania

Constitution required the Pennsylvania Senate's consent to Governor Shapp's new appointee. The court cited to several compacts that specifically required legislative consent and several that did not, along with several Pennsylvania agencies that required consent and several that did not. From this, the court concluded that legislative consent to DRPA officials was not required.

In *Commonwealth ex rel. Smith v. Clark*, 331 Pa. 405 (1938), the Pennsylvania Supreme Court considered whether the Pennsylvania Legislature could lawfully remove members of the Delaware River Joint Commission (the former name of the Delaware River Port Authority) when the compact required a term of five years. The Court concluded that the compact unambiguously did not allow such removal, but, "even if there was ambiguity a state should be reluctant to interpret ambiguous language in its favor. Scrupulous care should be exercised by a sovereign state to comply with the terms of its contract." *Id.* at 415.

7. The Supreme Court has not directly addressed the removal issue in compact agencies, but did observe in *Lake Country Estates, Inc. v. Tahoe Reg'l Planning Agency*, 440 U.S. 391, 399 (1979), that in discharging duties as officials of TRPA, the state and county appointees necessarily have also served the interests of the political units that appointed them. Does this give a hint as to whether compact officials are removable at will unless otherwise specified in the compact?

8. How does one individual being politically accountable to his or her appointing authority relate to the principles that you have studied so far that limit or prohibit one state from unilaterally controlling the actions of a compact agency? In *Pievsky v. Ridge*, the compact specifically authorized the governor to veto a decision of his or her appointee, but doesn't that place the ultimate control in the hands of the states individually rather than their joint action? One Law Review note suggests that this level of control is not appropriate.

> Rather than leave [problems that require continuous joint effort] to bilateral negotiation, the states have compacted to establish independent authorities, whose expansive powers and corporate form are designed for operating flexibility. Typically, the authority's powers include borrowing money and selling services for profit. To allow for expert planning and to exclude 'political' influences, it is freed from the pressures to which legislatures subject ordinary state agencies.

Note, *Congressional Supervision of Interstate Compacts*, 75 YALE L.J. 1416, 1426 (1966).

The authority for each governor to veto a decision of his or her appointee was added to the DRPA compact in 1992 at the same time the states added authority for the DRPA to take on economic development projects. This new economic development authority was quite controversial, and the veto was one way to ensure accountability and to quell the controversy. More recently, however, the DRPA's economic development projects themselves became very controversial. In 2012, the New Jersey Comptroller issued a scathing report concerning the DRPA's use of its funds for economic development projects and specific instances of misuse of funds. New Jersey Office of the State Comptroller, *Investigative Report, Delaware River Port Authority* (Mar. 29, 2012), https://www.state.nj.us/comptroller/news/docs/report_drpa_032912.pdf. In response to the controversy, the DRPA contracted for an internal management audit, CGR Management Consultants, *Yellow Book Management Audit Final Report: Delaware River Port Authority of Pennsylvania and New Jersey* (Jan. 14, 2013), http://www.drpa.org/pdfs/ManagementAudit_2012_DRPA.pdf; created its own Office of the Inspector General, *id.* at 52 (citing DRPA Resolution 12-007 (Jan. 18, 2012)); and the DRPA Board directed the general counsel office to develop and implement a public records policy that adopts the strictest provisions from both states. *Id.* at 133.

9. In *Seattle Master Builders, Inc. v. Pac. Nw. Elec. Power & Cons. Planning Council*, 786 F.2d 1359 (9th Cir. 1986) (excerpted in Chapter 1), the plaintiff argued that the President should appoint the compact officials because the Council was effectively a federal agency. The majority opinion rejected that argument noting that requiring the President to appoint members to a compact agency would "outlaw virtually all compacts because all or most of them impact federal activities and all or most of them have members appointed by the participating states." *Id.* at 1365. Other courts also rejected similar arguments in other cases. *Columbia River Gorge United v. Yeutter*, CV No. 88-1319-PA, 1990 U.S. Dist. LEXIS 15447, at *31–35 (D. Or. May 23, 1990); *Corr v. Metro. Wash. Airports Auth.*, 800 F. Supp. 2d 743, 758 (E.D. Va. 2011), *aff'd on other grounds*, 740 F.3d 295 (4th Cir. 2014), *cert. denied*, 136 S. Ct. 29 (2015).

10. *Alcorn v. Wolfe,* the next case, presents the opposite view from *Pievsky v. Ridge*, concluding that the need for independence from political influence is implicit in a compact.

Alcorn v. Wolfe

827 F. Supp. 47 (D.D.C. 1993)

GREEN, JUDGE:

Plaintiff Daniel S. Alcorn ("Alcorn"), appointed to the Board of Directors of the Metropolitan Washington Airports Authority ("MWAA") by Governor L. Douglas Wilder ("Wilder" or "the Governor") on November 28, 1990, commenced this suit against Gregory D. Wolfe ("Wolfe"), Secretary of the MWAA, on May 27, 1993. Plaintiff seeks a judgment declaring, *inter alia*, that he remains a bona fide member in good standing of the MWAA and its Board of Directors....

[Through a clerical error, Alcorn was not confirmed by the Virginia General Assembly. While serving on the Board of the MWAA, Alcorn had several politically related differences with the Governor. When the error was discovered more than two years later, the Governor appointed James M. DeFrancia to Alcorn's position].

The Governor relies on the Virginia enabling act's confirmation requirement and Article V, § 7 of the Virginia Constitution as the sources of his authority to appoint DeFrancia to the seat held by Alcorn. Article V, § 7 states in relevant part:

> The Governor shall have power to fill vacancies in all offices of the Commonwealth for the filling of which the Constitution and laws make no other provision. . . .
>
> Gubernatorial appointments to fill vacancies in offices which are filled by election by the General Assembly or by appointment by the Governor which is subject to confirmation by the Senate or the General Assembly, made during the recess of the General Assembly, shall expire at the end of thirty days after the commencement of the next session of the General Assembly.

According to the Governor, because 1985 Va. Acts, ch. 598 § 4(A) provides that "Members representing the Commonwealth of Virginia shall be subject to confirmation by the Virginia Assembly," and because Alcorn was never confirmed by the General Assembly, Alcorn's November 28, 1990 appointment expired in early 1991 and Alcorn served merely in a de facto capacity from the time of expiration until DeFrancia took his oath of office approximately two and one-half years later. Alcorn disagrees with Wilder that § 7 applies to his appointment, contending that the term "offices" in the last sentence of the provision refers to "offices of the Commonwealth" as that phrase is used in the preceding paragraph and that members of the MWAA, an independent authority, cannot be considered to hold Virginia offices. Alcorn posits that if any provision of the Virginia Constitution applies to his appointment, it should be Article V, § 11, which states:

> No person appointed to any office by the Governor, whose appointment is subject to confirmation by the General Assembly, under the provisions of this Constitution or any statute, shall enter upon, or continue in, office after the General Assembly shall have refused to confirm his appointment, nor shall such person be eligible for reappointment during the recess of the General Assembly to fill the vacancy caused by such refusal to confirm.

Because the General Assembly has not voted against his confirmation, Alcorn contends that he is still a valid member of the MWAA. In the alternative, Alcorn argues that in the event § 7 is interpreted to apply to this case, that provision is preempted by the terms of the compact and the federal Transfer Act.

Whether or not the language of Article V, § 7 should be interpreted to apply to offices created by a congressionally approved compact is a difficult issue of first impression, and the intervenor has requested that the question be referred to the Virginia Supreme Court for resolution. Because Article V, § 7 would be preempted by the terms of the compact creating the MWAA even if it were interpreted to apply to Alcorn's appointment, however, the issue need not be determined by this or any other Court for purposes of resolving this case.

Under the Compact Clause of the United States Constitution, "No State shall, without the Consent of Congress, * * * enter into any Agreement or Compact with another State * * * ." Because the compact creating the MWAA was congressionally sanctioned in accordance with the Compact Clause, it is a federal law subject to federal construction, notwithstanding its genesis in the enabling acts of Virginia and the District of Columbia. In light of the Supremacy Clause to the

United States Constitution and because compacts are analogous to contracts between states, the terms of the MWAA compact cannot be modified unilaterally by state legislation and take precedence over conflicting state law.

Assuming arguendo that Article V, § 7 of the Virginia Constitution can be interpreted to address appointments made by the Governor to the MWAA, application of that section to the circumstances of this case would clearly conflict with two provisions of the MWAA compact: namely, the provision expressly mandating the MWAA's independence from Virginia, its local subdivisions, the District of Columbia, and the federal government, and the provision requiring appointments to be for six-year terms. There can be no doubt that the independence of the MWAA from political influence is of critical importance. The legislation enacted by the United States, Virginia, and the District of Columbia make that point clear, as does the testimony of defendant Wolfe, who has been intimately involved with the MWAA since he served as the executive director of the Holton Commission. By attempting to replace Alcorn with DeFrancia based on his purported authority under § 7 and because of disputes concerning an election of the MWAA's Chairman of the Board, the possible effects of a new Redskins stadium on the operations of National Airport, and intra-party rivalries, Governor Wilder has attempted to inject his political influence into the operations of the MWAA. Such action significantly jeopardizes the independence of the MWAA and clearly frustrates one of the most important objectives of the compact.

The Governor's attempt to use § 7 to replace Alcorn also clashes with the compact provision requiring that members of the MWAA serve in staggered six-year terms. That requirement is significant to secure the independence of the MWAA and to ensure that its members possess a certain level of experience and expertise. By contending that § 7 authorizes him to interrupt the tenure of Alcorn, Wilder seeks in effect to transform Alcorn's commission into an appointment at will. Were § 7 allowed to operate in that manner, both goals of the six-year term requirement would be thwarted; the MWAA would be deprived of the substantial knowledge and experience Alcorn has obtained while serving on the Board, and the MWAA's insulation from outside political influence would be substantially reduced.

Accordingly, because Article V, § 7 of the Virginia Constitution as applied to Alcorn's appointment would be inconsistent with the terms and purposes of two separate provisions of the MWAA compact, § 7 is held to be preempted under the Supremacy Clause and case law governing the construction of interstate compacts.

For the reasons stated above, the Court concludes that Daniel S. Alcorn's appointment to the MWAA did not lapse for lack of confirmation and that Governor Wilder's attempt to appoint James DeFrancia to the seat held by Alcorn had no legal effect. . . .

Notes & Questions

1. *Alcorn v. Wolfe*, *Pievsky v. Ridge*, and *Peters v. Delaware River Port Auth.* all involved politically motivated removals and appointments. Why did *Alcorn v.*

Wolfe turn out differently? Consider the terms of the compact and the purpose of the compact.

2. Recall *De Veau v. Braisted* and the Supreme Court's discussion of the problems of political influence and corruption in the New York Harbor, and that the purpose of the Waterfront compact was to eliminate these problems. Should such a legislative history make a difference in the question whether an appointing authority may remove an appointee at will?

3. Did you pick up on the court's mention that Alcorn suggested the U.S. District Court refer to the Virginia Supreme Court the question whether the compact supersedes Virginia's constitution? Why might Alcorn suggest this? Would the Virginia Supreme Court be likely to determine that the compact supersedes the state's constitution? Why might he prefer to argue his case in state court rather than federal court?

Delaware ex rel. Gebelein v. Killen, 454 A.2d 737 (Del. 1982), involved the question whether a holdover appointee's appointment to the Delaware River and Bay Authority had expired under the Delaware Constitution. Does the question when a holdover's term expires involve the same considerations as the politically motivated removals in *Pievsky* or *Alcorn*?

4. The court described the makeup of MWAA Board of Directors as "eleven members serving staggered six-year terms, five members to be appointed by the Governor of Virginia, three by the Mayor of the District of Columbia, two by the Governor of Maryland, and one by the President of the United States with the advice and consent of the United States Senate." Why would a compact establish an uneven number of members from the compacting states? The makeup of MWAA Board of Directors was originally more complicated, involving a Board of Review with nine Members of Congress. *Metro. Wash. Airports Auth. v. Citizens for the Abatement of Aircraft Noise*, 501 U.S. 252 (1991), excerpted below, held that makeup of the MWAA Board of Review to be unconstitutional. The membership of the MWAA Board of Directors has changed several times over the years in response to court decisions holding the Board of Review unconstitutional and in an effort to give the states and District of Columbia more control. Most recently, in 2011, Congress amended its consent to the MWAA compact to require 17 directors and still with different numbers of members from each party state. Pub. L. No. 112-55, div. C, tit. I, § 191, 125 Stat. 552, 671 (2011).

III. Oversight of Compacts

When a governor, a state legislature, or the Congress is unhappy with the actions of a state or federal agency, it can act to take some control over that agency. Control of compact agencies, however, is different. Many of the case excerpts and notes you have studied in prior chapters and immediately above in the *Pievsky* and *Alcorn* cases have been about control of a compact or compact agency. For example, the inability of one state to enact new legislation that would burden the compact limits state control, but the power to remove a commissioner at will allows that governor some measure of control.

Many compacts also provide for other means of state oversight. For example, the DRPA compact that you just read about in *Pievsky* allows the governors to veto votes of their appointees. Similarly, article XVI of the Port Authority of New York and New Jersey compact provides, "Each state reserves the right to provide by law for the exercise of a veto power by the governor thereof over any action of any commissioner appointed therefrom." Interestingly, this provision allows the states to fix their own veto authority, which may differ.

Another means of oversight is a state-created oversight board for intrastate activities implementing a compact. For example, the Interstate Compact for the Supervision of Adult Offenders requires each state to create a "State Council" to oversee a state's implementation of the compact. *See, e.g.*, Kentucky's intrastate board created at KY. REV. STAT. § 439.562. This board may only make recommendations, but this advisory power can influence how a state participates in a compact.

Absent such a provision in a compact, oversight typically begins with information gathering about an agency, which inevitably leads to directing an agency to take or restrain from taking specific actions. For example, a governor may ask his or her appointees to report on the actions of an agency or a state legislature or Congress may want to conduct hearings about an agency's actions or lack of action. Oversight reporting and hearings are common in government, but how can a single governor, a single legislature, or Congress oversee a compact agency without violating legal principles studied in the prior chapters?

Tobin first appeared in Chapter 2 for its discussion of Congress's authority to retain the right to alter, amend, or repeal a compact. The D.C. Circuit concluded that authority was not an express power in the U.S. Constitution and did not reach the question whether that authority was an implied power. The facts and court's framing of the issues are repeated here, but this excerpt then jumps to the court's discussion of whether Congress gave the Judiciary Committee sufficient authority to investigate the Port Authority.

Tobin v. United States

306 F.2d 270 (D.C. Cir. 1962)

BASTIAN, JUDGE:

Austin J. Tobin, the Executive Director of the Port of New York Authority, was charged by information and convicted in the District Court of criminal contempt of Congress for refusing to produce certain documents called for by a subpoena issued by Subcommittee No. 5 of the Committee on the Judiciary of the United States House of Representatives.

The Port of New York Authority is a bi-state agency established in 1921 and 1922 by compacts between the States of New York and New Jersey to provide for the efficient administration of the New York harbor, which is divided geographically between the two states. Pursuant to the compact clause of the Constitution, Congress consented to the compacts but expressly retained, among other matters, "the right to alter, amend or repeal" its resolutions of approval. Over the years, the Port Authority has been remarkably successful in achieving its goals. As of 1959, it had investments of nearly one billion dollars and gross annual operating revenue in excess of one hundred million dollars.

In February of 1960, the Judiciary Committee initiated an investigation of the Authority on an informal basis. The Authority cooperated with the Committee investigators except as to disclosing certain documents alleged to relate exclusively to the internal administration of the Authority. After this refusal events moved swiftly to a climax.

On June 1, 1960, the Chairman of the Committee obtained from the House subpoena power in connection with matters "involving the activities and operations of interstate compacts." What little floor discussion there was preceding this grant of subpoena power was not very enlightening; it certainly provided no lucid analysis of what was soon to follow. On June 8, 1960, Subcommittee No. 5 of the Judiciary Committee instituted a formal inquiry into the Authority.

Appellant conferred with the Board of Commissioners of the Authority, as well as with the Governors of both New York and New Jersey, and the consensus of their opinion was that the investigation being attempted was too broad to be valid. The Subcommittee was informed of their objections and the reasons therefor. Discounting these objections, the Subcommittee issued the subpoena in question. Appellant requested postponement of the return date of the subpoena in order to give the Governors an opportunity to meet with the Subcommittee and discuss their objections but the Subcommittee refused the postponement.

After being denied the opportunity to appear before the Subcommittee, the Governors wrote identical letters to their respective representatives on the Board of Commissioners of the Authority, instructing them to direct appellant not to comply with the subpoena. The Board of Commissioners so directed appellant on June 27, 1960. Two days later, on June 29, 1960, the Subcommittee met to receive the return of the subpoena. It was against this background that appellant refused to comply with the demands of the subpoena and was ruled in default by the Chairman of the Subcommittee. Thereafter, the Subcommittee recommended to the full Committee that appellant be cited by the House for contempt. This recommendation was adopted by the Judiciary Committee, two members dissenting, and subsequently by the House itself. Charged by information, appellant waived his right to jury trial and was convicted of contempt of Congress by District Judge Youngdahl.

Appellant advances several arguments in support of the position that his conviction cannot stand. For present purposes, to illustrate the constitutional issues we would have to decide in order to affirm the conviction, we list but two of his arguments:

1. That Congress does not have the power, under the compact clause of the Constitution, to "alter, amend or repeal" its consent to an interstate compact, which was the stated purpose of the Subcommittee's investigation.

2. That "the subpoena issued by the Subcommittee, demanding documents relating to the internal administration of the Port Authority which

> the Governors of New York and New Jersey ordered appellant not to produce, [was] an unconstitutional invasion of powers reserved to the States under the Tenth Amendment to the Constitution."
>
> ....

Appellant is no criminal and no one seriously considers him one. He stands before us convicted of crime merely because no method has been provided for testing the merits of his contentions save that of a prosecution for contempt of Congress. It is truly unfortunate that his choice was so restricted as to the presentation of his case, for it places us in the posture of being asked to answer broad questions of civil law within the framework of reviewing a criminal conviction. Undoubtedly the questions presented to us properly demand resolution, but we should not and cannot permit this appeal for answers to blind us to our duty of administering criminal justice according to traditional concepts. It must be remembered that what we decide in this case will be precedent for another, and far too often has the rashness of today begotten the regrets of tomorrow to induce us to tread unsanctioned by-ways of criminal adjudication merely because the setting of a particular appeal suggests the expediency of such a course. In short, we decide this case as we would any other criminal appeal. It is with these considerations in mind, therefore, that we approach the disposition of the present controversy.

A contempt of Congress prosecution is not the most practical method of inducing courts to answer broad questions broadly. Especially is this so when the answers sought necessarily demand far-reaching constitutional adjudications. To avoid such constitutional holdings is our duty, particularly in the area of the right of Congress to inform itself. Consequently, when Congress authorizes a committee to conduct an investigation, the courts have adopted the policy of construing such resolutions of authority narrowly, in order to obviate the necessity of passing on serious constitutional questions.

Accordingly, the first issue we must decide is whether Congress gave the Judiciary Committee of the House (and therefore its Subcommittee No. 5) authority sufficient to permit the Subcommittee to conduct the sweeping investigation undertaken in the instant case. The authority pointed to as validating the present investigation was conferred by the House upon the Judiciary Committee in piecemeal fashion:

The Legislative Reorganization Act of 1946 granted to the Judiciary Committee authority over nineteen subjects, including "interstate compacts generally." In 1959 the Committee was given subpoena power to conduct "full and complete investigations and studies relating to (certain stated matters) coming within the jurisdiction of the Committee." As this last grant of authority did not encompass interstate compacts, it was amended on June 1, 1960, to include "the activities and operations of interstate compacts." Putting these resolutions of authority together, we find that the Committee was given jurisdiction over "interstate compacts generally," and the power "to conduct full and complete investigations and studies relating to * * * the activities and operations of interstate compacts."

The authority thus granted to the Committee is couched in general terms. In the present case, the Committee stretched these general terms in order to justify about as specific an investigation of the Port of New York Authority as can be envisaged. We are inclined to believe the House did not intend these general terms to be stretched quite so far. While it is true that the Judiciary Committee for many years did have specific jurisdiction over "interstate compacts generally," its traditional activity with respect to this jurisdiction was entirely foreign to an investigation of the kind and scope attempted here. . . .

In the present case, the very fact that Congress had never before attempted such an expansive investigation of an interstate compact agency—an investigation, by its very nature, sure to provoke the serious and difficult constitutional questions involved here—leads to the conclusion that if Congress had intended the Judiciary Committee to conduct such a novel investigation it would have spelled out this intention in words more explicit than the general terms found in the authorizing resolutions under consideration. In any event, general terms are usually susceptible of differing interpretations. And so, in view of the fact that we consider it our duty to avoid, if possible, constitutional adjudication, we read these authorizing resolutions to mean that the Judiciary Committee was empowered to conduct an investigation calling for documents relating to actual "activities and operations" of the Authority rather than for all of the administrative communications, internal memoranda, and other intra-Authority documents demanded by the subpoena in question. Therefore, we think the Subcommittee's investigative authority, as thus construed, was exhausted by the information actually tendered by appellant in compliance with the subpoena, for such information adequately disclosed all that the Authority had done in the areas under inquiry. The information refused to the Subcommittee related only to the why of Authority activity and, consequently, was outside the scope of the Subcommittee's authority to investigate.

We feel inclined to add a few words in conclusion. If Congress should adopt a resolution which in express terms authorizes and empowers the Committee and its duly authorized Subcommittee to initiate an investigation of the Port of New York Authority as deep and as penetrating as the one attempted here, a challenge of the congressional power so to provide would of course present constitutional issues which we should have to meet and decide. Therefore, we emphasize that all we are saying here is that a due regard for the responsibility of administering justice prompts us to avoid serious constitutional adjudications until such time as Congress clearly manifests its intention of putting such a decisional burden upon us.

Especially do we say this in view of the unusual nature of the present case, where we are asked to decide essentially civil and jurisdictional issues at the same time that we establish criminal precedent. The conflicting duality inherent in a request of this nature is not particularly conducive to the giving of any satisfactory answer, no matter what the answer should prove to be. Should this controversy be resumed, it is hoped that Congress will first give sympathetic consideration to Judge Youngdahl's eloquent plea:

> During the House debate on the contempt citation, the Committee inserted in the congressional Record a memorandum purporting to show that declaratory judgment procedures were not an available means for procuring judicial resolution of the basic issues in dispute in this case. Although this question is not before the Court, it does feel that if contempt is, indeed, the only existing method, Congress should consider creating a method of allowing these issues to be settled by declaratory judgment. Even though it may be constitutional to put a man to guessing how a court will rule on difficult questions like those raised in good faith in this suit, what is constitutional is not necessarily most desirable. Especially where the contest is between different governmental units, the representative of one unit in conflict with another should not have to risk jail to vindicate his constituency's rights. Moreover, to raise these issues in the context of a contempt case is to force the courts to decide many questions that are not really relevant to the underlying problem of accommodating the interest of two sovereigns. [*United States v. Tobin*,] 195 F. Supp. [588,] 616–617 (1961).
>
> Reversed.

Notes & Questions

1. Ultimately, this case doesn't really resolve how deeply Congress may investigate the operations of a compact. What do you think? Does Congress's role in the creation of a compact give it sufficient constitutional authority to investigate the agency that compact creates or the states' implementation of that compact?

2. This case did not end Congress's oversight of compacts. Congress simply began writing explicit reservations in its consent actions, although surprisingly, Congress did not do so for all compacts. In the 15 years after *Tobin*, Congress granted consent to 19 compacts (not including general consent statutes that did not result in a compact), but Congress only reserved its rights to oversee and amend or repeal the compact in four of those 19 consent actions. Ross Caldwell, untitled, unpublished manuscript 7 (May 6, 2012) (on file with author).

The Tahoe Regional Planning Compact, Pub. L. No. 96-551, §§ 6 & 7, 94 Stat. 3233, 3253 (1980), contains typical language that Congress uses when reserving its rights at issue in *Tobin*:

> SEC 6. The right is hereby reserved by the Congress or any of its standing committees to require the disclosure and furnishing of such information and date by or concerning the Tahoe Regional Planning Agency as is deemed appropriate by the Congress or such committee.
>
> SEC 7. The right to alter, amend, or repeal this Act is hereby expressly reserved.

3. Can a single state or federal legislator attempt oversight of a specific compact? In 2007, the U.S. GAO issued a report on natural resource compacts in response to congressional requesters, which followed a series of opinion editorials in 2005 in the *Tahoe Daily Tribune* from California Assemblyman Tim Leslie ridiculing decisions by the Tahoe Regional Planning Agency and claiming that it was

an unaccountable agency. Contrary to those opinion pieces, the U.S. GAO report demonstrated the organization and procedures of the TRPA and other natural resource compacts generally follow good government transparency practices and administrative procedures found in federal and state government even without express applicable procedures in those compacts. U.S. Gov't Accountability Office, No. GAO-07-519, *Interstate Compacts: An Overview of the Structure and Governance of Environment and Natural Resource Compacts* (2007).

One hallmark of good government is openness and transparency, and perhaps the most familiar and most used statutes are the federal Freedom of Information Act and the states' freedom of information acts. You have read a few cases involving public records already—the *S.A.V.E.* case in Chapter 7 and the *C.T. Hellmuth* case in Chapter 8. *Scott v. Delaware Valley Reg'l Planning Comm'n*, 56 A.3d 40 (Pa. Commw. Ct. 2012), is another such case. In *Scott*, the court concluded that the Delaware Valley Regional Planning Commission was not a Pennsylvania Commonwealth Agency and thus not subject to Pennsylvania's Right-to-Know Law. New Jersey is the other party to the compact, and a federal court had already concluded that New Jersey's Open Public Records Act does not apply to compact agencies, but for a different reason—that applying the open records law would have unilaterally imposed a duty on the compact agency in violation of the compact. That New Jersey case was *Pardo v. Port Auth. of N.Y. & N.J.*, No. 08-1311 (JLL), 2009 U.S. Dist. LEXIS 18192, at *28 (D.N.J. Mar. 10, 2009). The Delaware Valley Regional Planning Commission has its own open public records policy, as do many other compact agencies, but this policy is not required by the compact. Should a compact agency operate without having to make its records open to public inspection?

Even when a compact requires a compact agency to comply with an existing open public records law, should one state be able to unilaterally order the agency to disclose a record that the compact agency believes is confidential? Congress's consent to the Columbia River Gorge Compact requires the Columbia River Gorge Commission to adopt an open public records rule consistent with the more restrictive of Oregon and Washington's own public records statutes. 16 U.S.C. § 544c(b). Both states' public records laws include a procedure where a dissatisfied requestor can seek the assistance of the state Attorney General's office to obtain withheld records. OR. REV. STAT. § 192.450; WASH. REV. CODE § 42.56.530. However, both states have declined to involve themselves in requests for assistance from requestors that are dissatisfied with a Gorge Commission response. Is this a good compromise between transparency and the general principle prohibiting states from unilaterally directing compact agency actions?

In 2013, the U.S. Supreme Court upheld Virginia's Freedom of Information Act restriction allowing only Virginia residents access to information under the act. *McBurney v. Young*, 569 U.S. 221 (2013). If a Virginia Court concludes that the Virginia FOIA applies to a compact agency, then would requestors from other party states be able to obtain documents from a compact agency pursuant to the Virginia FOIA?

4. The notes following *Pievsky v. Ridge*, mentioned that the New Jersey Comptroller investigated and issued a report concerning the Delaware River Port Authority's economic development program. That unilateral report resulted in significant changes to the management, structure, and policies of the DRPA. Ironically, New Jersey cried foul when New York created a new Inspector General of New York for Transportation in its 2018 state budget. 2017 N.Y. LAWS c 59, part PPP. The responsibilities of the new Inspector General include overseeing transportation entities in cities over 1 million population. The only such entity is the Port Authority of New York and New Jersey, which has its own Office of Inspector General. New Jersey legislators enacted a resolution, A.R. 226, 2017 Leg., 2d Reg. Sess. (N.J. 2017), urging Port Authority not to recognize the legitimacy of New York's new Inspector General, relying in part on the compact creating Port Authority that only allows new state law to be effective for Port Authority with the concurrence of New Jersey and calling on the New Jersey Attorney General to seek a declaratory judgment that New York's new Inspector General for Transportation does not have authority to oversee Port Authority. Should one state be able to unilaterally oversee a compact agency or conduct an investigation that could result in how an interstate entity operates?

Even more ironically, in 2017, New Jersey enacted legislation that would unilaterally withdraw from the Waterfront Commission of New York Harbor compact. Chapter 11 discusses this case in detail.

5. One law review note that followed the *Tobin* decision suggested that congressional investigation of interstate compact agencies is desirable, listing several reasons:

> Congressional investigation of interstate agencies such as the Port Authority may be desirable in view of their relative freedom from both state and federal regulation. States take the initiative in creating these agencies, and assume responsibility for their direction and control. Opportunity for regulation is afforded by usual controls such as the appropriations power, the appointment power, and gubernatorial veto. But because of the compact agency's unfamiliar character and lack of integration into the state administrative structure, little control is imposed in practice. Moreover, modification of existing policy may be hindered by the need for joint action of two or more state legislatures. Nor can judicial control be relied upon to protect the national interest. Whereas both state and federal courts take responsibility for weighing the burden of state legislation on interstate commerce, they appear to be reluctant to engage in an analogous examination of the national interest when an interstate compact is involved.

Note, *Congress and the Port of New York Authority: Federal Supervision of Interstate Compacts*, 70 YALE L.J. 812, 818 (1961). Do you agree that congressional oversight is desirable for these reasons? What are some reasons why congressional oversight may not be desirable? What are alternatives to congressional oversight? Another article from the Chairman of the House Judiciary Committee at the time of the

Tobin events gives a more detailed history of those events. Emanuel Celler, *Congress, Compacts, and Interstate Authorities*, 26 LAW & CONTEMP. PROBS. 682 (1961). Another account of Celler's relationship to the Port Authority suggested that Chairman Celler initiated the hearings after the Port Authority rejected pressure from Celler to award contracts to three of his private clients, a claim that Celler denied. *See* JAMESON W. DOIG, EMPIRE ON THE HUDSON 339 (Columbia Univ. Press 2001).

In the next case, the Supreme Court considered whether members of Congress could properly serve on a board that oversaw the Metropolitan Washington Airports Authority. While the Supreme Court did not object to the concept of a review board, it was concerned about the details of how Congress structured the review board.

Metro. Wash. Airports Auth. v. Citizens for the Abatement of Aircraft Noise
501 U.S. 252 (1991)

STEVENS, JUSTICE:

An Act of Congress authorizing the transfer of operating control of two major airports from the Federal Government to the Metropolitan Washington Airports Authority (MWAA) conditioned the transfer on the creation by MWAA of a unique "Board of Review" composed of nine Members of Congress and vested with veto power over decisions made by MWAA's Board of Directors. The principal question presented is whether this unusual statutory condition violates the constitutional principle of separation of powers . . . .

In 1940, Congress authorized the Executive Branch to acquire a tract of land a few miles from the Capitol and to construct what is now Washington National Airport (National). From the time it opened until 1987, National was owned and operated by the Federal Government. . . .

. . . .

Despite the FAA's history of profitable operation of National and excellent management of [National and Dulles], the Secretary of Transportation concluded that necessary capital improvements could not be financed for either National or Dulles unless control of the airports was transferred to a regional authority with power to raise money by selling tax-exempt bonds. In 1984, she therefore appointed an advisory commission to develop a plan for the creation of such a regional authority.

The Commission recommended that the proposed authority be created by a congressionally approved compact between Virginia and the District, and that its Board of Directors be composed of 11 members serving staggered 6-year terms, with 5 members to be appointed by the Governor of Virginia, 3 by the Mayor of the District, 2 by the Governor of Maryland, and 1 by the President, with the advice and consent of the Senate. Emphasizing the importance of a "non-political, independent authority," the Commission recommended that members of the board "should not hold elective or appointive political office." To allay concerns that local interests would not be adequately represented, the Commission recommended a requirement that all board members except the Presidential appointee reside in the Washington metropolitan area.

In 1985, Virginia and the District both passed legislation authorizing the establishment of the recommended regional authority. A bill embodying the advisory commission's recommendations passed the Senate. In the House of Representatives, however, the legislation encountered strong opposition from Members who expressed concern that the surrender of federal control of the airports might result in the transfer of a significant amount of traffic from National to Dulles.

Substitute bills were therefore drafted to provide for the establishment of a review board with veto power over major actions of MWAA's Board of Directors. Under two of the proposals, the board of review would clearly have acted as an agent of the Congress. After Congress received an opinion from the Department of Justice that a veto of MWAA action by such a board of review "would plainly be legislative action that must conform to the requirements of Article 1, section 7 of the Constitution," the Senate adopted a version of the review board that required Members of Congress to serve in their individual capacities as representatives of users of the airports. The provision was further amended in the House, and the Senate concurred. Ultimately, § 2456(f) of the Transfer Act, as enacted, defined the composition and powers of the Board of Review in much greater detail than the Board of Directors.

Subparagraph (1) of § 2456(f) specifies that the Board of Review "shall consist" of nine Members of the Congress, eight of whom serve on committees with jurisdiction over transportation issues and none of whom may be a Member from Maryland, Virginia, or the District of Columbia. Subparagraph (4)(B) details the actions that must be submitted to the Board of Review for approval, which include adoption of a budget, authorization of bonds, promulgation of regulations, endorsement of a master plan, and appointment of the chief executive officer of the Authority. Subparagraph (4)(D) explains that disapproval by the Board will prevent submitted actions from taking effect. Other significant provisions of the Act include subparagraph (5), which authorizes the Board of Review to require Authority directors to consider any action relating to the airports; subsection (g), which requires that any action changing the hours of operation at either National or Dulles be taken by regulation and therefore be subject to veto by the Board of Review; and subsection (h), which contains a provision disabling MWAA's Board of Directors from performing any action subject to the veto power if a court should hold that the Board of Review provisions of the Act are invalid.

On March 2, 1987, the Secretary of Transportation and MWAA entered into a long-term lease complying with all of the conditions specified in the then recently enacted Transfer Act....

On March 16, 1988, MWAA's Board of Directors adopted a master plan providing for the construction of a new terminal at National with gates capable of handling larger aircraft, an additional taxiway turnoff to reduce aircraft time on the runway and thereby improve airport capacity, a new dual-level roadway system, and new parking facilities. On April 13, the Board of Review met and voted not to disapprove the master plan.

In November 1988, Citizens for the Abatement of Aircraft Noise, Inc., and two individuals who reside under flight paths of aircraft departing from, and arriving at, National (collectively CAAN) brought this action. CAAN sought a declaration that the Board of Review's power to veto actions of MWAA's Board of Directors is unconstitutional and an injunction against any action by the Board of Review as well as any action by the Board of Directors that is subject to Board of Review approval. . . .

Petitioners argue that this case does not raise any separation-of-powers issue because the Board of Review neither exercises federal power nor acts as an agent of Congress. Examining the origin and structure of the Board, we conclude that petitioners are incorrect.

Petitioners lay great stress on the fact that the Board of Review was established by the bylaws of MWAA, which was created by legislation enacted by the Commonwealth of Virginia and the District of Columbia. Putting aside the unsettled question whether the District of Columbia acts as a State or as an agent of the Federal Government for separation-of powers purposes, we believe the fact that the Board of Review was created by state enactments is not enough to immunize it from separation-of-powers review. Several factors combine to mandate this result.

Control over National and Dulles was originally in federal hands, and was transferred to MWAA only subject to the condition that the States create the Board of Review. Congress placed such significance on the Board that it required that the Board's invalidation prevent MWAA from taking any action that would have been subject to Board oversight. Moreover, the Federal Government has a strong and continuing interest in the efficient operation of the airports, which are vital to the smooth conduct of Government business, especially to the work of Congress, whose Members must maintain offices in both Washington and the districts that they represent and must shuttle back and forth according to the dictates of busy and often unpredictable schedules. This federal interest was identified in the preamble to the Transfer Act, justified a Presidential appointee on the Board of Directors, and motivated the creation of the Board of Review, the structure and the powers of which Congress mandated in detail. Most significant, membership on the Board of Review is limited to federal officials, specifically members of congressional committees charged with authority over air transportation.

That the Members of Congress who serve on the Board nominally serve "in their individual capacities, as representatives of users" of the airports, does not prevent this group of officials from qualifying as a congressional agent exercising federal authority for separation-of-powers purposes. As we recently held, "separation-of-powers analysis does not turn on the labeling of an activity," *Mistretta v. United States*, 488 U.S. 361, 393 (1989). The Transfer Act imposes no requirement that the Members of Congress who are appointed to the Board actually be users of the airports. Rather, the Act imposes the requirement that the Board members have congressional responsibilities related to the federal regulation of air transportation. These facts belie the *ipse dixit* that the Board members will act "in their individual capacities."

Although the legislative history is not necessary to our conclusion that the Board members act in their official congressional capacities, the floor debates in the House confirm our view. *See, e.g.*, 132 Cong. Rec. 32135 (1986) (The bill "also provides for continuing congressional review over the major decisions of the new airport authority. A Congressional Board will still have veto power over the new airport authority's: annual budget; issuance of bonds; regulations; master plan; and the naming of the Chief Executive Officer") (Rep. Lehman); *Id.* at 32136 ("In addition, the motion provides continued congressional control over both airports. Congress would retain oversight through a Board of Review made up of nine Members of Congress. This Board would have the right to overturn major decisions of the airport authority") (Rep. Coughlin); *Id.* at 32137 ("Under this plan, Congress retains enough control of the airports to deal with any unseen pitfalls resulting from this transfer of authority. * * * We are getting our cake and eating it too. * * * The beauty of the deal is that Congress retains its control without spending a dime") (Rep. Smith); *Id.* at 32141 ("There is, however, a congressional board which is established by this. * * * [T]hat board has been established to make sure that the Nation's interest, the congressional interest was attended to in the consideration of how these two airports are operated") (Rep. Hoyer); *Id.* at 32142 (The bill does "not give up congressional control and oversight—that remains in a Congressional Board of review") (Rep. Conte); *Id.* at 32143 ("I understand that one concern of Members is that by leasing these airports to a local authority, we would be losing control over them. But, in fact, under this bill exactly the opposite is true. We will have more control than before") (Rep. Hammerschmidt).

Congress as a body also exercises substantial power over the appointment and removal of the particular Members of Congress who serve on the Board. The Transfer Act provides that the Board "shall consist" of "two members of the Public Works and Transportation Committee and two members of the Appropriations Committee of the House of Representatives from a list provided by the Speaker of the House," "two members of the Commerce, Science, and Transportation Committee and two members of the Appropriations Committee of the Senate from a list provided by the President pro tempore of the Senate," and "one member chosen alternately * * * from a list provided by the Speaker of the House or the President pro tempore of the Senate, respectively." Significantly, appointments must be made from the lists, and there is no requirement that the lists contain more recommendations than the number of Board openings. The list system, combined with congressional authority over committee assignments, guarantees Congress effective control over appointments. Control over committee assignments also gives Congress effective removal power over Board members because depriving a Board member of membership in the relevant committees deprives the member of authority to sit on the Board.

We thus confront an entity created at the initiative of Congress, the powers of which Congress has delineated, the purpose of which is to protect an acknowledged federal interest, and membership in which is restricted to congressional officials. Such an entity necessarily exercises sufficient federal power as an agent of Congress to mandate separation-of-powers scrutiny. Any other conclusion would permit Congress to evade the "carefully crafted" constraints of the Constitution, *INS v. Chadha* 462 U.S. 919, 959 (1983), simply by delegating primary responsibility for execution of national policy to the States, subject to the veto power of Members of Congress acting "in their individual capacities." *Cf. Bowsher v. Synar*, 478 U.S. [714,] 755 (Stevens, J., concurring).

. . . .

Because National and Dulles are the property of the Federal Government and their operations directly affect interstate commerce, there is no doubt concerning the ultimate power of Congress to enact legislation defining the policies that govern those operations. Congress itself can formulate the details, or it can enact general standards and assign to the Executive Branch the responsibility for making necessary managerial decisions in conformance with those standards. The question presented is only whether the Legislature has followed a constitutionally acceptable procedure in delegating decisionmaking authority to the Board of Review.

. . . .

To forestall the danger of encroachment "beyond the legislative sphere," the Constitution imposes two basic and related constraints on the Congress. It may not "invest itself or its Members with either executive power or judicial power." *J.W. Hampton, Jr. & Co. v. United States*, 276 U.S. 394, 406 (1928). And, when it exercises its legislative power, it must follow the "single, finely wrought and exhaustively considered, procedures" specified in Article I. *INS v. Chadha*, 462 U.S. at 951.

The first constraint is illustrated by the Court's holdings in *Springer v. Philippine Islands*, 277 U.S. 189 (1928) and *Bowsher v. Synar*, 478 U.S. 714 (1986). *Springer* involved the validity of Acts of the Philippine Legislature that authorized a committee of three—two legislators and one executive—to vote corporate stock owned by the Philippine Government. Because the Organic Act of the Philippine Islands incorporated the separation-of-powers principle, and because the challenged statute authorized two legislators to perform the executive function of controlling the management of the government-owned corporations, the Court held the statutes invalid. Our more recent decision in *Bowsher* involved a delegation of authority to the Comptroller General to revise the federal budget. After concluding that the Comptroller General was in effect an agent of Congress, the Court held that he could not exercise executive powers:

> To permit the execution of the laws to be vested in an officer answerable only to Congress would, in practical terms, reserve in Congress control over the execution of the laws. . . . The structure of the Constitution does

not permit Congress to execute the laws; it follows that Congress cannot grant to an officer under its control what it does not possess.

The second constraint is illustrated by our decision in *Chadha.* That case involved the validity of a statute that authorized either House of Congress by resolution to invalidate a decision by the Attorney General to allow a deportable alien to remain in the United States. Congress had the power to achieve that result through legislation, but the statute was nevertheless invalid because Congress cannot exercise its legislative power to enact laws without following the bicameral and presentment procedures specified in Article I. For the same reason, an attempt to characterize the budgetary action of the Comptroller General in *Bowsher* as legislative action would not have saved its constitutionality because Congress may not delegate the power to legislate to its own agents or to its own Members.

. . . If the power is executive, the Constitution does not permit an agent of Congress to exercise it. If the power is legislative, Congress must exercise it in conformity with the bicameralism and presentment requirements of Art. I, § 7. In short, when Congress "[takes] action that ha[s] the purpose and effect of altering the legal rights, duties, and relations of persons . . . outside the Legislative Branch," it must take that action by the procedures authorized in the Constitution. *See Chadha*, 462 U.S. at 952–955.

One might argue that the provision for a Board of Review is the kind of practical accommodation between the Legislature and the Executive that should be permitted in a "workable government." Admittedly, Congress imposed its will on the regional authority created by the District of Columbia and the Commonwealth of Virginia by means that are unique and that might prove to be innocuous. However, the statutory scheme challenged today provides a blueprint for extensive expansion of the legislative power beyond its constitutionally confined role. Given the scope of the federal power to dispense benefits to the States in a variety of forms and subject to a host of statutory conditions, Congress could, if this Board of Review were valid, use similar expedients to enable its Members or its agents to retain control, outside the ordinary legislative process, of the activities of state grant recipients charged with executing virtually every aspect of national policy. As James Madison presciently observed, the legislature "can with greater facility, mask under complicated and indirect measures, the encroachments which it makes on the coordinate departments." *The Federalist* No. 48, at 334. Heeding his warning that legislative "power is of an encroaching nature," we conclude that the Board of Review is an impermissible encroachment.

Notes & Questions

1. What are the similarities and differences between the Board of Review's veto power here and the New Jersey and Pennsylvania governors' power to veto decisions by their appointees to the Delaware River Port Authority? What is significant about the differences between these two powers?

Reread Judge Beezer's dissent in *Seattle Master Builders* in Chapter 1. What are the similarities and differences between Justice Stevens's concerns with the

Board of Review and Judge Beezer's perspective of the Northwest Power and Conservation Council?

2. Shortly after the Supreme Court's decision, Congress enacted amendments to the Transfer Act that changed the composition and powers of the Board of Review. The amendments permitted Congress to remove members of the Board for cause and eliminated the Board's veto authority, but the amendments also expanded the Board's authority by expanding the list of actions requiring the Board's review and changing the review process. The D.C. Circuit held the Board's structure, as amended, still violated the separation of powers doctrine. *Hechinger v. Metro. Wash. Airports Auth.*, 36 F.3d 97 (D.C. Cir. 1994). What other changes would you consider for Congress to oversee a compact agency that would withstand scrutiny under the Constitution?

In 2014, Congress provided authority for the U.S. Department of Transportation Inspector General to audit and investigate MWAA. Congress required MWAA Board Members, employees, contractors, and subcontractors to cooperate and comply with requests from the Inspector General, including providing testimony and other information, and required MWAA to permit the Inspector General to observe closed executive sessions of the MWAA Board of Directors. Consolidated Appropriations Act of 2014, Pub. L. No. 113-76, Div. L, Tit. I, § 171, 128 Stat. 5, 600. If, as *Tobin* suggests, Congress is limited in its ability to directly oversee a compact agency, then can it authorize a federal agency to do so and require the compact agency to cooperate?

Also, at Congress's direction, the Federal Transit Administration (FTA) assumed safety oversight over the Washington Metropolitan Area Transit Authority's (WMATA) rail system. To wrest oversight back, in 2017, Maryland, Virginia, and the District of Columbia enacted a new interstate compact—the Metrorail Safety Commission Interstate Compact, MD. CODE ANN., TRANSP. §§ 7-709, 10-208; VA. CODE ANN. § 33.2-3101; D.C. CODE § 9-1109-1.1, and Congress granted its consent. Pub. L. No. 115-54, § 1, 131 Stat. 1093 (2017).

3. If Congress is limited in its ability to oversee a compact agency, then is oversight left to the states under the Tenth Amendment? Justice Brennan's concurrence in *Port Auth. Trans-Hudson Corp. v. Feeney,* 495 U.S. 299 (1990) (excerpted in Chapter 7), seems to question the authority of a state to oversee the operations of a compact:

> . . . The Interstate Compact Clause and the State Treaty Clause ensure that whatever sovereignty a State possesses within its own sphere of authority ends at its political border.
>
> Thus, it is not within the autonomous power of any State to create and regulate an interstate agency. Each State's sovereign will is circumscribed by that of the other States in the compact and circumscribed further by the veto power relinquished to Congress in the Constitution. If counties are not "arms" of their States merely because the State conferred a certain

> autonomy on them—an autonomy it can withdraw at will—then an interstate agency, over which none of the compacting States exercises such untrammeled control, cannot be said to be an "arm" of any of them.

Id. at 315–16. Of course, *Feeney* arose in the context of the Eleventh Amendment and Justice Brennan's opinion relates to that context. But, consider whether Justice Brennan was thinking about a compact being an arm of a single state. Justice Brennan's reasoning may impose a constitutional disability in a case asking whether a state may unilaterally regulate or oversee a compact agency.

What would Justice Brennan think about Justice Ginsburg's statement only four years later in *Hess v. Port Auth. Trans-Hudson Corp.*, 513 U.S. 30 (1994): "An interstate compact, by its very nature, shifts a part of a state's sovereignty to another state or states or to the agency the several states jointly create to run the compact."? *Id.* at 42. Do you think oversight by the states acting jointly, such as a joint (multi-state) legislative committee, would withstand constitutional scrutiny? Would this be feasible for a compact that is national in scope?

4. Consider some of these other methods that are commonly used to oversee federal and state agencies: legislative review of agency rules; legislative hearings to influence policy; separation of agency officials' duties; state strategic planning and performance goals requirements; financial audits; and Attorney General supervision of litigation. Are these proper for Congress or states to require for compact agencies?

IV. Withdrawal, Termination and Winding Up

Cooperation under compacts may fail for many reasons. One reason is that original assumptions forming the obligations written into a compact were faulty, such as in the Pecos River Compact, the subject of the *Texas v. New Mexico* case (excerpted in Chapter 11). Consider also the Virginia-Kentucky compact that was at issue in *Green v. Biddle*. There, Kentucky landowners enjoyed ownership rights under Virginia law. But how long could those rights be preserved as both Virginia and Kentucky real property law evolved?

Another problem is that *sui generis* agencies are difficult to create and maintain. Compact agencies have difficult relationships with states—by their nature, they are independent of the states that created by them, yet dependent on those states for funding, appointments, and adjunct authority. Compact agencies also require entirely new infrastructure, such as office space and staff that may be located in only one of the states; the adage of "out of sight, out of mind" may loom true in the other states. Compacts are also difficult to create and maintain because they require a fresh perspective on governance. Recall from the preface and some of the notes and questions in early chapters that most legislators, governors, and other government officials are unfamiliar with compacts. Disputes may arise because states may have enacted compacts without realizing the binding and enforceable effect of those agreements, or after many years or decades, the institutional memories have faded and new officials may not share prior officials' allegiance to the agreement. Would legislators enact compacts if they had full information about the legal implications of the compact?

Compacts may also fail because they don't achieve the parties' intent. Courts may conclude that text imposes different obligations than the states intended, or officials may discover that they cannot resolve foundational problems. While the compact and compact agency may still exist and carry on daily business, they may not achieve original intent.

Compacts may also fail because their governance structure is inadequate to manage the problem the states originally devised the compact to resolve. For example, in the Pecos River Compact discussed in *Texas v. New Mexico*, the two states each had one vote on the governing body with no way to resolve tie votes. Similarly, the Southeast Low-Level Radioactive Waste Commission, discussed in *Alabama v. North Carolina* (excerpted in Chapter 7) was unable to get permits for and construct the waste facility specified in the compact. The Pest Control Compact dissolved in 2012 after the parties realized that the funding structure for the compact was.

Neglect is another very real problem. There are many compacts that the parties seem to have forgotten about. Without some champion of the compact, states may fail to appoint new members as current members' terms expire, or agency officials may fail to meet for a long time and then become disinterested in reinvigorating the compact. State officials may also not be aware that new statewide obligations or restrictions may conflict with and be improper to apply to the compact. As well, through accretion or evolution of other state legislation and regulation, states may make compact requirements less important.

Surprisingly, many compacts do not contain provisions for one state to orderly withdraw, or for all the party states to terminate and orderly wind up the compact's affairs. The next two readings address the issue of how a state may withdraw and from and wind up a compact that does not contain withdrawal or winding up provisions. First, the Vienna Convention on the Law of Treaties gives default provisions for terminating international treaties. Consider whether these would be appropriate for interstate compacts. Second, *The Organic Cow* case illustrates that in the absence of provisions for orderly winding up a compact, the compact agency may be limited in its ability to provide for succession.

Vienna Convention on the Law of Treaties, 1155 U.N.T.S. 331 (May 23, 1969)

PART V. INVALIDITY, TERMINATION AND SUSPENSION OF THE OPERATION OF TREATIES

SECTION 3. TERMINATION AND SUSPENSION

OF THE OPERATION OF TREATIES

Article 54

Termination of or withdrawal from a treaty under its provisions or by consent of the parties

The termination of a treaty or the withdrawal of a party may take place:

(a) in conformity with the provisions of the treaty; or

(b) at any time by consent of all the parties after consultation with the other contracting States.

Article 55

Reduction of the parties to a multilateral treaty below the number necessary for its entry into force

Unless the treaty otherwise provides, a multilateral treaty does not terminate by reason only of the fact that the number of the parties falls below the number necessary for its entry into force.

Article 56

Denunciation of or withdrawal from a treaty containing no provision regarding termination, denunciation or withdrawal

1. A treaty which contains no provision regarding its termination and which does not provide for denunciation or withdrawal is not subject to denunciation or withdrawal unless:

(a) it is established that the parties intended to admit the possibility of denunciation or withdrawal; or

(b) a right of denunciation or withdrawal may be implied by the nature of the treaty.

2. A party shall give not less than twelve months' notice of its intention to denounce or withdraw from a treaty under paragraph 1.

. . . .

Notes & Questions

1. Compacts that allow a state to withdraw typically allow withdrawal by enacting a statute, notifying the other parties and waiting for a specified period to allow an orderly transfer. The Tahoe Regional Planning Compact, art. X(c), contains a typical withdrawal provision:

> A State party to this compact may withdraw therefrom by enacting a statute repealing the compact. Notice of withdrawal shall be communicated officially and in writing to the Governor of the other State and to the agency administrators. This provision is not severable, and if it is held to be unconstitutional or invalid, no other provision of this compact shall be binding upon the State of Nevada or the State of California.

The Tahoe compact is only a bi-state compact. Should bi-state compacts have such a liberal withdrawal provision? Is the ability for one state to withdraw from a two-party compact a form of improper unilateral control of the compact?

2. Does the ability for a state to withdraw from the compact with no restriction and no waiting period create a binding compact? In *Health Net, Inc. v. Dep't of Revenue*, 22 Or. Tax 128 (2015), *aff'd on other grounds*, 362 Or. 700 (2018), the Oregon Tax Court held that the lack of a waiting period in the withdrawal provision of the Multistate Tax Compact meant that there was no consideration between the states and the states had created an illusory and thus unenforceable contract. Consider *Burford v. Accounting Practice Sales, Inc.*, 786 F.3d 582 (7th Cir. 2015), a non-compact case in which the Seventh Circuit applied Illinois law disfavoring contracts of indefinite duration and held that such a contract is terminable at will by any party. Should a compact be terminable at will if it permits a state to unconditionally withdraw or does not contain a withdrawal provision?

3. The Southern Regional Education Compact, art. VIII, contains a provision that seems to address salient withdrawal issues:

> After becoming effective this compact shall thereafter continue without limitation of time; provided, however, that it may be terminated at any time by unanimous action of the states and provided further that any state may withdraw from this compact if such withdrawal is approved by its legislature, such withdrawal to become effective two (2) years after written notice thereof to the board accompanied by a certified copy of the requisite legislative action, but such withdrawal shall not relieve the withdrawing state from its obligations hereunder accruing up to the effective date of such withdrawal. Any state so withdrawing shall ipso facto cease to have any claim to or ownership of any of the property held or vested in the board or to any of the funds of the board held under the terms of this compact.

4. Two articles in the Interstate Insurance Product Regulation Compact provide a framework for the party states to develop a termination or withdrawal plan. Article XII.7 (relating to finance) provides, "No Compacting State shall have any claim to or ownership of any property held by or vested in the Commission or to any Commission funds held pursuant to the provisions of this Compact." Article XIV.3.b (relating to dissolution of the compact) provides, "any surplus funds shall be distributed in accordance with the Bylaws." Article XI of the interstate commission's bylaws specifies that a majority of the members of the commission may amend the bylaws, which is much easier than amending the compact itself, which requires action by all the parties, which as of mid-2020 has membership of 45 states. Does this flexibility make sense?

The drafters of the Insurance Product Regulation Compact, negotiated in 2003, were probably aware of the then-current litigation over property and funds following the termination of the Northeast Interstate Dairy Compact. Congress's consent to the Northeast Interstate Dairy Compact was valid for only a limited period; it expired in 2001 and did not have any winding up provision. The Dairy

Compact Commission issued a press release explaining its orderly transfer of the Commission's interests:

> At the meeting in Concord, the Commission acted to transfer ownership of its administrative records and remaining assets and equipment to the Center for New England Dairy Compact Research. The Center is a not-for-profit corporation, incorporated in the state of Vermont. For purposes of winding up the affairs of the Commission, the transfer of assets is contingent on the Center paying the debts of the Commission and conducting a final annual audit of the Commission's accounts. The Center has as its corporate purposes research, dissemination and education on the economic and social impacts of the Northeast Interstate Dairy Compact.

Press Release from Ne. Dairy Compact Comm'n, *Compact Commission Meets to Wind Up* (Sept. 28, 2001), http://www.dairycompact.org/sept_28_press.htm. The following case explains what happened next.

The Organic Cow, LLC v. Center For New England Dairy Compact Research

335 F.3d 66 (2d Cir. 2003)

CALABRESI, JUDGE:

The Organic Cow, LLC ("Organic Cow"), an organic dairy in Vermont, appeals from an order of the United States District Court for the District of Vermont, which granted summary judgment to the substituted Appellee, The Center for New England Dairy Compact Research ("the Center"). The Center became a party to this suit when the district court allowed it to take the place of the original appellee, The Northeast Dairy Compact Commission ("the Commission"). The Commission had been the governing body of an interstate dairy compact, whose congressional authorization had expired about three weeks before the Center filed a motion to substitute for the Commission, pursuant to Fed. R. Civ. P. 25.

We find that the district court erred in granting the Center's motion for substitution. Because the Commission no longer exists and there is currently no entity duly authorized to conduct the Commission's affairs, we vacate the district court's order granting the substitution and its summary judgment order, and we remand the case to the district court with instructions to dismiss the suit.

In the late 1980s and early 1990s, six northeastern states—Connecticut, Maine, Massachusetts, New Hampshire, Rhode Island, and Vermont—negotiated an interstate agreement to regulate milk prices, and sought congressional approval of the agreement, as required by the Compact Clause of the United States Constitution. Congress consented to the Northeast Interstate Dairy Compact subject to certain conditions. Congress originally provided that its consent to the Compact would expire concurrently with the reform of the federal milk pricing scheme, no later than April 4, 1999. Congress later adjusted the expiry date to September 30, 2001.

The Compact established the Northeast Interstate Dairy Compact Commission ("the Commission"), which was made up of delegations from each of the

Compact states. The Commission had authority to administer the Compact. The Compact, in turn, defined and limited the Commission and its authority. . . .

On May 30, 1997, the Commission promulgated a regulatory scheme that was effective July 1997. The scheme established an "over-order price" of $16.94 per hundred-weight (cwt) of Class I milk. This was the minimum price required to be paid for Class I milk, and was higher than the price set by the U.S. Secretary of Agriculture through the Federal Milk Marketing Orders. The difference between the Commission's over-order price and the Federal Milk Marketing Order price was called the "over-order obligation." The Commission was authorized to collect the over-order obligation from all milk handlers that sold Class I milk within the Compact region. The collected funds were then returned to the handlers, i.e. processors, according to a complex allocation formula, for distribution to the producers.

Organic Cow is a "pool plant"—a milk handler and processor in Vermont—which, by 1997, processed milk from sixty certified organic dairy farmers, pursuant to two-year, automatically renewable, output contracts. Under the contracts, Organic Cow guaranteed a price to its organic dairy farmers of $18.00 per cwt ($18.25 in Maine). Given the additional fees paid by Organic Cow, including premiums for certain butterfat and trucking charges, the organic farmers who contracted with Organic Cow were paid an effective price of between $19.36 and $24.00 per cwt.

When this action began, Organic Cow was selling more than 1,000,000 pounds (10,380 cwt) per month of Class I organic milk within the Compact region. In August 1997, soon after the Commission's regulatory scheme was enacted, Organic Cow petitioned the Commission for an exemption from the over-order obligation. Organic Cow argued that, because it was already paying its producers rates far in excess of the over-order price, it should not be assessed the "over-order obligation" as were the average processors (most of whom were then paying the federal market order minimum price of $13.95 per cwt). In March 1998, the Commission denied Organic Cow's petition for an exemption, and ordered Organic Cow to pay to it, in escrow pending any appeal, the amounts it owed the Commission under the over-order obligation.

Meanwhile, in December 1997, the Commission had instituted an enforcement proceeding in the Federal District Court in Vermont to collect the amounts due from Organic Cow under the regulation, and sought a preliminary injunction requiring Organic Cow to pay its over-order obligation. In March 1998, the district court stayed the order with respect to past due payments (about $152,000), but ordered that Organic Cow pay all future assessments into an escrow account, established with the Commission, pending resolution of the enforcement action.

In April 1998, Organic Cow appealed to the federal district court the Commission's denial of its request for an exemption from the assessment. . . . The court concluded that the record did not indicate "whether the Commission considered Organic Cow's argument that organic milk producers and handlers should be treated differently than non-organic producers and handlers under the Compact;

[or,] if it did consider the argument, on what basis it rejected it," and that, therefore, the court was "unable to conclude that the Commission's decision on this point is supported by substantial evidence."

Following the remand and after further proceedings, the Commission issued a final report in June 2000. In it, Organic Cow's request for an exemption from the over-order obligation again was denied. . . .

Organic Cow again appealed the Commission's denial to the federal court in Vermont and the Commission filed a counterclaim for the assessments it alleged to be due. . . . The district court . . . ordered that the funds in escrow be released for disbursement by the Commission pursuant to the Compact and its regulations. The district court's ruling was entered on September 24, 2001, but the court did not then resolve the Commission's counterclaim. As a result, it did not enter a final judgment in the suit.

Congress's consent to the Compact expired six days later, on September 30, 2001. Shortly before the expiration and in anticipation of it, the Commission held a special meeting at which its members voted to transfer and donate all "right, title, and interest in any and all records and assets of the Commission" to the Center for New England Dairy Compact Research, Inc., a not-for-profit Vermont corporation that had been formed on September 20, 2001. The Commission's resolution also directed that the Center "pay the outstanding just debts incurred by the Commission on or before September 20, 2001." The legal basis for this transfer is anything but clear.

In October 2001, the Center, claiming to be the successor-in-interest to the Commission, filed a motion for substitution of parties, pursuant to Fed. R. Civ. P. 25(c). The motion also asked (1) that the court certify and enter a final judgment with respect to its September 24 decision, (2) that it certify and enter a final judgment with respect to the Commission's counterclaim, and (3) that it make a finding that the amount due from Organic Cow to the Commission (now to the Center) was $152,778.40.

Over Organic Cow's objections, the district court granted the Center's motion for substitution. The court refused, however, to certify and enter a final judgment with respect to the (now) Center's counterclaim. Instead, it directed the Center to file a motion for summary judgment, and it established an expedited briefing schedule to allow for speedy resolution of the claim. Thereafter, the Center filed its motion for summary judgment, which Organic Cow opposed. In the same motion, the Center requested permission to amend the counterclaim to make a minor adjustment in the amount claimed in light of an audit, and otherwise to modify the relief sought. While this motion was pending, Organic Cow filed a countermotion to dismiss for lack of subject matter jurisdiction. The countermotion claimed that, because the federal court's jurisdiction was based exclusively on the Compact, that jurisdiction disappeared with the Compact's expiration.

. . . .

Organic Cow argues that the district court erred in granting the Center's motion for substitution of parties. We agree.

. . . .

"Substitution of a successor in interest or its joinder as an additional party under Rule 25(c) is generally within the sound discretion of the trial court." *Prop-Jets, Inc. v. Chandler*, 575 F.2d 1322, 1324 (10th Cir. 1978). However, the determination of "whether an entity is a transferee of interest" so as to warrant exercise of Rule 25(c) involves "application of law to facts." *Luxliner [P.L. Export, Co. v. RDI/Luxliner, Inc.*, 13 F.3d 69, 71–72 (3d Cir. 1993)]. . . .

Organic Cow asserts that the Center is not a legitimate successor in interest to the Commission because there is no legal basis for the transfer to the Center, in the Compact or in any other law. In particular, Organic Cow argues (1) that the Compact was silent on the subject of its own termination, (2) that Congress did not elsewhere provide a mechanism for the Commission to "wind down" its affairs or to transfer its assets to a separate entity; and (3) that the attempted transfer, made as it was to a private party with no legal obligations and subject to no oversight akin to that which constrained the Commission, finds no support in the Compact and hence cannot be justified.

The Center responds that "as a matter of common sense," there needed to be some procedure, for example, to pay the final phone bill, and otherwise bring the Commission's business to an orderly close. As authority for the Commission's transfer of its assets to the Center—allegedly for the purpose of concluding the Commission's outstanding business—the Center points to a provision in the Compact that authorizes the Commission "to acquire, hold, and dispose of real and personal property by gift, purchase, lease, license, or other similar manner, for its corporate purposes." But assuming arguendo that this clause permits a winding down of Commission affairs, we do not believe that the provision can be read so broadly as to authorize the Commission to transfer to the Center—an entity that is free from any of the restrictions to which the Commission was subject—its interest in this suit and the disputed funds. Even assuming further that the Compact allowed the Commission to make significant gifts to third parties, it did so only for the Commission's "corporate purposes." It is hard to see how such purposes could be served after the Compact had ended, and especially by a body like the Center that is not bound by any of the restrictions imposed on the Commission by the Compact.[4]

Generally, when a government agency, commission, or corporation expires, Congress (or the state legislature) appoints a successor in interest or establishes a

---

[4] For example, although the Commission was subject to oversight by the Secretary of Agriculture, was obligated to notify the participating states of its activities, and was required to distribute the funds it collected pursuant to regulations that had been established through specific rulemaking proceedings, the Center operates under none of these constraints. Thus, if the Compact had not expired and the Commission had prevailed in this case, it would have been obligated by its own rules, properly promulgated under the Compact, to distribute the funds obtained in the suit to dairy producers in the Compact region according to a specific formula. Yet there is nothing in the record to suggest that the Center would be similarly obligated.

method for identifying such a successor. In other cases, the governmental unit responsible for creating the entity is deemed the successor in interest. Where, however, a government entity terminates with no provision for naming a successor and with no appropriate governmental body to stand in its shoes for purposes of litigation, at least one circuit court has held that there can be no substitution of parties under Rule 25.[5] Similarly, in the instant case, Congress allowed the Compact to expire. It thereby withdrew congressional authorization for the Compact's scheme of price regulation, and the Commission became, in effect, *functus officio*.

We are not, of course, holding that the Compact must itself identify a successor, or that a valid successor cannot be a private entity. As noted above, when Congress intends to transfer assets and liabilities of an expiring federal entity, it often will do so by statute. . . . In this case, however, there is no statute providing for a transfer of the suit to anyone, let alone the Center. And, of course, the Center cites no precedent for the substitution under Rule 25(c) of a private corporation for a lapsed government agency in the absence of such a statute.

Congress saw fit to let the Compact expire without enacting any provision for winding down the Commission's affairs or transferring its assets or liabilities to another entity. This being so, and, especially, given the Center's own characteristics as a private, unregulated body, we find that the Center does not meet the requirements for substitution of parties under Rule 25. Accordingly, the district court erred in granting the Center's motion for substitution. We therefore VACATE both the court's order allowing the substitution and the court's grant of summary judgment in favor of the Center, and we REMAND the case to the district court with instructions that it dismiss the suit.

Notes & Questions

1. Before considering whether to extend its consent to the Northeast Dairy Compact, Senator Herbert Kohl from Wisconsin requested the U.S. Government Accountability Office conduct a study of the economic impacts of dairy compacts. Senator Kohl was on record as being opposed to dairy compacts. In one congressional session, he stated, "Now, as most in the Senate know by now, I am committed to fighting the creation, expansion, or continuation of the price fixing cartels known as dairy compacts. They embody bad national policy, bad economic policy, bad precedent, and disastrous implications for farmers who are forced to operate outside the protectionist walls these compacts throw up." Statement of Sen. Kohl, 145 Cong. Rec. 19321 (Aug. 4, 1999). The U.S. GAO study discusses the history of the dairy compact and how it works, and concludes, "[i]t is likely that the Northeast Compact affected dairy sector indicators within the six New England states, but determining the extent to which it has done so is difficult."

---

[5] We do not here decide whether an appropriate governmental unit might exist on the facts before us, since it is clear that the Center has none of the attributes of such a public agency. We note in passing, however, that because the Commission was a hybrid entity, formed by state agreement and congressional consent, there is no single government entity that can readily be held liable for the Commission's debts or, more to the point, lay claim to its assets.

U.S. Gov't Accountability Office, No. GAO-01-866, *Dairy Industry: Estimated Economic Impacts of Dairy Compacts* 4 (2001).

2. When the Dairy Compact expired and the commission ceased to exist, should it have ceased all functions (as it did), or implicitly retained enough life to wind up its affairs? When a state agency terminates, it typically winds up its own affairs or another agency handles winding up issues. When a compact ends, who should be responsible for winding up? Where would the funding come from? Should there be public notice to allow creditors and claimants to file claims and where should it be filed? Who should be responsible for getting the key and cleaning out the office? Who should get title to the office equipment and furnishings? Where do the records get archived? Are the regulated persons still subject to authorizations, permits, and enforcement actions that the compact agency issued? Who would enforce those actions? As of mid-2020, the Commission's website and the contents up to the date of termination are still available on the Internet: www.dairycompact.org. Who should maintain and monitor this website; who should own and renew the domain name? In comparison, the Pest Control Compact, which dissolved in 2012 no longer has any web presence.

3. If a compact does not designate a successor, why shouldn't a compact agency be able to do so without statutory authorization? After all, the states vested power in that agency to administer the compact. Is winding up a compact part of administering a compact?

4. If the states had authorized the New England Center for Dairy Research as the successor entity, it could have reserved prior claims. This was the case for the Ogdensburg Bridge and Port Authority. When New York created the Bridge and Port Authority as the successor to the Ogdensburg Bridge Authority, it specified, "No existing right or remedy of any character shall be lost or otherwise affected by reason of the enactment of this title" *See Tarbell v. Ogdensburg Bridge and Port Auth.*, 261 N.Y.S.2d 429, 430 (1965).

5. What would have happened in *The Organic Cow* if all six party states had jointly sought substitution in place of the Dairy Commission? What if fewer than all six had sought substitution?

6. Michigan retroactively repealed its participation in the Multistate Tax Compact. 2014 Mich. Pub. Act No. 282. During the retroactive period, Michigan paid its dues and actively participated in the compact by having an appointee who voted on compact matter and served as the Treasurer of the Multistate Tax Commission. Should Michigan's retroactive repeal nullify its appointees' votes and actions as Treasurer and what are the effects of doing so? What could be fiscal implications to the Commission of nullifying the Treasurer's actions years later? The Multistate Tax Compact also allows for joint audits of multistate taxpayers; would a retroactive repeal leave questions whether joint audits of taxpayers based in Michigan are valid in other states and whether audits of taxpayers based in other states are valid in Michigan?

Consider the effect of retroactive repeal of other compacts that handle more than fiscal policy. In briefing this issue to the Michigan Supreme Court, one amicus brief explained:

> For example, if Wisconsin would retroactively repeal the Interstate Compact on the Supervision of Adult Offenders, Michigan's parolees and probationers residing in Wisconsin would be unmanaged; Michigan could lose management of Wisconsin's parolees and probationers residing in Michigan, and those previously incarcerated for parole or probation violations under the authority of the compact could be set free or to have those "retroactively unauthorized" incarcerations expunged.

Brief for Amici Curiae Interstate Comm'n for Juveniles, et al. at 16, *Anheuser-Busch, Inc. v. Dep't of Treasury*, No. 316743 (Mich. Ct. App. Jan. 27, 2015) (order vacating and remanding). The Michigan Court of Appeals subsequently affirmed the retroactive repeal. *Gillette Commercial Operations N. Am. & Subsidiaries v. Dep't of Treasury*, 312 Mich. App. 394 (2015), *application for leave to appeal denied*, 499 Mich. 960 (2016). Should retroactive repeal of a compact be allowed when it creates legal uncertainty or controls the effect of the compact in other states? Should there be a blanket rule against retroactive repeals or should courts conduct a case-by-case analysis? Should a party be able to retroactively repeal a compact when a compact is silent about retroactive repeal?

7. For an example of a repeal that addressed salient issues, consider the 2008 repeal of the Maine-New Hampshire Interstate Bridge Compact. 2008 N.H. Laws c. 3; 2007 Me. Laws c. 306 § 10. Maine repealed the compact in a single sentence. New Hampshire's repeal was more comprehensive, referencing the need for Maine to jointly repeal the compact and for Congress to ratify the repeal. It also specified use of new funds received, a time for winding up, and disposition of remaining assets:

> Be it Enacted by the Senate and House of Representatives in General Court convened:
>
> 3:1 Ratification. The United States Congress expressly reserved the right to alter, amend, or repeal the provisions of the compact described in RSA 234:43. The state of New Hampshire contemplates that corresponding and concurrent legislation shall be enacted by the legislature of the state of Maine. Thereafter, the respective state enactments contemplate an act by the United States Congress to ratify the provisions of the state enactments.
>
> 3:2 Repeal. RSA 234:43-65, relative to the Maine-New Hampshire Interstate Bridge Authority and the Portsmouth-Kittery Bridge, also known as the Sarah Mildred Long Bridge, are repealed.
>
> 3:3 New Section; Fund Established. Amend RSA 234 by inserting after section 65 the following new section:
>
> 234:66 Fund Established. Any and all funds received by the department of transportation relative to the Portsmouth-Kittery Bridge, also known as the Sarah Mildred Long Bridge, shall be deposited with the state treasurer who

shall keep such funds in a special nonlapsing account known as the Portsmouth-Kittery Bridge fund, to be continuously appropriated and expended by the department of transportation for the purpose of operations, maintenance, and repairs of the Portsmouth-Kittery Bridge.

3:4 New Subparagraph; Portsmouth-Kittery Bridge Fund. Amend RSA 6:12, I(b) by inserting after subparagraph (268) the following new subparagraph:

(269) Moneys deposited in the Portsmouth-Kittery Bridge fund under RSA 234:66.

3:5 Betterment Fund Use. The department of transportation may expend betterment funds for repairs to the Sarah Mildred Long Bridge.

3:6 Dissolution of the Maine-New Hampshire Interstate Bridge Authority. The Maine-New Hampshire Interstate Bridge Authority shall dissolve 6 months after the United States Congress approves this act during which time it shall wind up all its affairs.

3:7 Assignment of Assets. The Maine-New Hampshire Interstate Bridge Authority shall assign all assets to the state of Maine and the state of New Hampshire in common. All funds assigned shall be deposited in accordance with RSA 234:66 after the United States Congress approves this act. Thereafter, the respective state transportation agencies shall assume all maintenance, operation, and repair responsibilities from the Maine-New Hampshire Interstate Bridge Authority.

3:8 Effective Date. This act shall take effect upon its passage.

V. Administrative Procedure

Few compacts specify comprehensive administrative procedures in the way that federal and state laws do for federal and state agencies. Many compacts are silent about administrative procedure, and the compacts that do specify some administrative procedure vary greatly in the procedure they require. Some compacts specify applying only some traditional administrative procedure, such as for rulemaking, but not for licensing or adjudication; some specify applying provisions of the federal Administrative Procedure Act (APA); and some specify applying provisions of the states' administrative procedure acts. As you read this section, consider why some compacts are silent about administrative procedure—is this absence by oversight or deliberate drafting?

Also consider what administrative procedure makes sense for a compact agency to use. Does the federal APA make sense if a compact has consent; do the states' APAs make sense? Should a compact use the model state APA as a way of avoiding favoring any one party state's law? If none of these make sense, should a compact specify procedural requirements, such as Article VIII of the 2015 enhanced Nurse Licensure Compact, which specifies rulemaking requirements? Consider what procedures make sense as you study the remainder of this chapter.

A. Applying Federal Administrative Procedure

The federal APA applies to an "agency," which the APA defines as "each authority of the Government of the United States, whether or not it is within or subject to review by another agency . . . ." 5 U.S.C. § 551(1). Chapter 4 discussed that compact agencies are not federal agencies for the purpose of NEPA and other federal statutes. Similarly, compact agencies are not included within the federal APA definition of agency. Some compacts, however, specify that compact agencies must comply with portions of the federal APA. For example, the Interstate Compact for the Supervision of Adult Offenders, art. VIII, specifies: "Such rulemaking shall substantially conform to the principles of the federal Administrative Procedure Act, 5 U.S.C.S. section 551 et seq., and the Federal Advisory Committee Act, 5 U.S.C.S. app. 2, section 1 et seq., as may be amended (hereinafter 'APA')." Congress's consent to the now-defunct Northeast Interstate Dairy Compact similarly required that the commission use the federal APA for its rulemaking. 7 U.S.C. § 7256 (consenting to compact text contained in S.J. Res. 28, 104th Cong. (1995)).

In another example, Congress's consent to the Northwest Power and Conservation Council specified that the Council should apply numerous federal administrative procedural laws applicable to the Bonneville Power Administration and FERC to the extent appropriate:

> For the purpose of providing a uniform system of laws, in addition to this Act, applicable to the Council relating to the making of contracts, conflicts-of-interest, financial disclosure, open meetings of the Council, advisory committees, disclosure of information, judicial review of Council functions and actions under this Act, and related matters, the Federal laws applicable to such matters in the case of the Bonneville Power Administration shall apply to the Council *to the extent appropriate*, except that with respect to open meetings, the Federal laws applicable to open meetings in the case of the Federal Energy Regulatory Commission shall apply to the Council *to the extent appropriate.*"

16 U.S.C. § 839b(a)(4) (emphasis added). Note this provision does not specify who determines "the extent appropriate." Should the Council, the party states, or the courts do so? If the parties make this determination, then in what form should they do so if not in the compact? In *Seattle Master Builders Ass'n v. Pac. Nw. Elec. Power and Cons. Planning Council,* 786 F.2d 1359 (9th Cir. 1986), the Ninth Circuit interpreted this provision, noting that Congress directed the federal APA govern review of the Council's actions. *Id.* at 1366.

In the absence of any compact language mentioning the federal APA, courts have had to determine whether the federal APA applies. Some courts have concluded that congressionally approved compact agencies are not automatically subject to the federal APA, and others have determined that compact agencies may be subject to the federal APA even without being a federal agency. Consider the following cases involving the applicability of the federal APA.

Old Town Trolley Tours of Wash., Inc. v. Wash. Metro. Area Transit Comm'n
129 F.3d 201 (D.C. Cir. 1997)

RANDOLPH, JUDGE:

Old Town Trolley operates buses modeled after turn-of-the-century trolleys. The buses take visitors to and from tourist attractions around the nation's capital. Double Decker, wanting to do the same with open-air, double decker buses, applied to the Washington Metropolitan Area Transit Commission for a certificate of authority. Over Old Town's protest, the Commission granted the certificate for a probationary period and attached conditions. Old Town then filed this petition for judicial review.

. . . .

. . . A preliminary question presents itself: what standard of review applies? To answer this question, some background is needed. The Commission was established by the Washington Metropolitan Area Transit Regulation Compact. Maryland, Virginia, and the District of Columbia entered into the Compact in 1960, with the consent of Congress, in order to regulate private transportation service in the metropolitan area. In 1990, the signatories amended the Compact, in large part for the purpose of "lower[ing] barriers to market entry * * * while maintaining a regional approach to transportation and keeping those controls necessary for the security of the public." To this end, the amended Compact replaced certificates of public convenience and necessity with certificates of authority. This is the first case in which our court has been asked to pass on a Commission order granting a certificate of authority.

Congress consented to the Compact pursuant to its authority under Article I, § 10, clause 3 of the Constitution. Although an early Supreme Court decision suggested that interstate compacts could not be considered federal laws, the Court abandoned this position in *Delaware River Comm'n v. Colburn*, 310 U.S. 419, 427 (1940), holding that the "construction of such a compact sanctioned by Congress" involves a federal question. congressional consent thus "transforms an interstate compact * * * into a law of the United States." *Cuyler v. Adams*, 449 U.S. 433, 438 (1981). As to the Compact before us, the "judicial Power of the United States" therefore extends to cases arising under it.

While the Compact may be treated as a federal law, it does not follow that the Commission is a federal agency governed by the Administrative Procedure Act. An "agency," according to the APA's definition, "means each authority of the Government of the United States * * * ." The Commission is an authority, not of the federal government, but of Virginia, Maryland, and the District of Columbia. As a result there is a gap in need of filling. The amended Compact provides for judicial review of Commission orders here or in the Court of Appeals for the Fourth Circuit, but it does not specify any standards of review:

> 5. (a) Any party to a proceeding under this Act may obtain a review of the Commission's order in the United States Court of Appeals for the Fourth

Circuit, or in the United States Court of Appeals for the District of Columbia Circuit, by filing within 60 days after Commission determination of an application for reconsideration, a written petition praying that the order of the Commission be modified or set aside.

(b) A copy of the petition shall be delivered to the office of the Commission and the Commission shall certify and file with the court a transcript of the record upon which the Commission order was entered.

(c) The Court shall have exclusive jurisdiction to affirm, modify, remand for reconsideration, or set aside the Commission's order.

(d) The court's judgment shall be final, subject to review by the Supreme Court of the United States upon certiorari or certification as provided in Title 28 U.S.C. §§ 1254 and 2350.

Of one thing we can be fairly confident—that our review should not be *de novo*. That would deprive the Commission's judgment of importance and would, in effect, place the court in the position of the licensing authority. Yet the granting of licenses may be a non-judicial function, outside Article III of the Constitution. We may also say with some assurance that the "substantial evidence" test, at least in its APA formulation, does not fit this case. The Compact requires the Commission neither to hold hearings in these licensing proceedings nor to make findings on the record of the hearings. Even if the APA covered the Commission, the substantial evidence standard contained in 5 U.S.C. § 706(2)(E) would therefore be inapplicable.

Of the remaining standard-of-review options, we have decided to adopt by reference the standards contained in 5 U.S.C. § 706(2)(A)–(D) [of the federal APA], which provide that reviewing courts shall:

(2) hold unlawful and set aside agency action, findings, and conclusions found to be—

(A) arbitrary, capricious, an abuse of discretion, or otherwise not in accordance with law;

(B) contrary to constitutional right, power, privilege, or immunity;

(C) in excess of statutory jurisdiction, authority, or limitations, or short of statutory right;

(D) without observance of procedure required by law . . . .

We do so because this court had basically been following those standards in reviewing Commission actions under the pre-amended Compact. Anyone familiar with these decisions—that is, anyone involved in drafting and approving revisions to the Commission's licensing authority—would likely have taken it for granted that we would follow the same course in cases arising under the amended Compact. For another thing, federal judicial review of agency action according to the standards just quoted is so commonplace that, wholly aside from our past practice, it would have been natural to assume that courts would treat Commission decisions in the same manner. Finally, it is worth remembering that subsections (A) through (D) of APA § 706(2) contained no innovations. When signed into law in 1946, these provisions merely "restate[d] the present law as to the scope of judicial review.

. . . .

Notes & Questions

1. What do you think about the D.C. Circuit's reasoning? Why didn't the court use the "compact as federal law" concept more forcefully? If not the standards of review expressed in the federal APA, what standards should the court have applied?

2. The D.C. Circuit cited to cases in which it says it "had basically been following [the federal APA] standards in reviewing Commission actions" before the 1990 amendments to the compact. 129 F.3d at 204–05. Of the three cases that the D.C. Circuit cited, one involved a motion for attorney fees and not any of the APA standards for review of agency action; the other two cases used the term "arbitrary and capricious," but without citing the federal APA. Do these citations compel the D.C. Circuit's conclusion that it should apply the federal APA standards of review after the compact amendments?

Old Town Trolley was not the first case in which the D.C. Circuit considered borrowing standards of review from a federal statute to apply to a compact agency action. In *Office & Prof. Emps. Int'l Union, Local 2 v. Wash. Metro. Area Transit Auth.*, 724 F.2d 133, 139 (D.C. Cir. 1983), the D.C. Circuit concluded that the district court erred in applying the standards of review from the federal Railway Labor Act (RLA). The district court concluded, "Because both the RLA and the Compact provide for compulsory arbitration and both denominate the resulting award as 'final and binding,' the court adopts the standards of the RLA for its review of the award at issue here." *Id.* at 138. However, the D.C. Circuit concluded, "Because the statutory framework of the RLA and of the Compact are substantially dissimilar, we cannot assume, without any supporting evidence of legislative intent, that the mere presence in both statutes of the words 'final and binding' permits a court to superimpose the RLA's congressionally-enacted standard of review onto the Compact." *Id.* at 139. The *Old Town Trolley* decision did not cite to the *Office & Prof. Emps.* decision; nevertheless, do you believe it followed the same reasoning? If not, did *Old Town Trolley* implicitly overrule *Office & Prof. Emps*?

Subsequent decisions involving the Transit Compact and other compacts have borrowed from the federal APA or case law applying the federal APA. For example, in *Exec. Tech. Servs., LLC v. Wash. Metro. Area Transit Comm'n*, No. 13-1239 (D.C. Cir. Feb. 27, 2014) (Doc. No. 1478905) (unpublished order granting motion to dismiss case for lack of jurisdiction), the D.C. Circuit relied on its definition of finality in *Blue Ridge Envtl. Def. League v. Nuclear Regulatory Comm'n*, 668 F.3d 747, 755–56 (D.C. Cir. 2012), which in turn relied on the definition of what constitutes final agency action under section 704 of the federal APA as announced in *Bennett v. Spear*, 520 U.S. 154, 178 (1997). In another example, in *League to Save*

Lake Tahoe v. Tahoe Reg'l Planning Agency, 739 F. Supp. 2d 1260, 1271 (E.D. Cal. 2010), *aff'd in relevant part & vacated in part*, 469 F. App'x 621 (9th Cir. 2012), the court relied on the seminal administrative law decision *Motor Vehicle Mfrs. Ass'n v. State Farm Mut. Auto. Ins. Co.*, 463 U.S. 29 (1983), in determining that it must rely on the basis that TRPA articulated.

3. *The Organic Cow, LLC v. Ne. Dairy Compact Comm'n*, 164 F. Supp. 2d 412 (D. Vt. 2001), the predecessor to the Second Circuit's decision excerpted above in this chapter, followed similar reasoning as *Old Town Trolley*. The Second Circuit, however, avoided determining whether the district court applied the correct standard of review by deciding the case on the issue of substitution of parties.

4. Is the D.C. Circuit's decision consistent with Judge Beezer's dissent in *Seattle Master Builders* (excerpted in Chapter 1)? Are there factors that Judge Beezer cited that this court did not, or that this court cited that Judge Beezer missed?

5. Related to the issue whether a compact agency must apply the federal APA is an issue whether courts must apply federal principles of justiciability—that is whether there is a reason that the court cannot or should not review a particular compact agency action. These are principles you probably studied in an administrative law class, and include standing, ripeness, exhaustion of administrative remedies and finality. For example, the Columbia River Gorge Compact specifies the bi-state Gorge Commission must enact an administrative procedure rule consistent with the more restrictive of Oregon and Washington law; nevertheless, federal courts have applied federal justiciability standards. *See Klickitat Cty. v. Columbia River Gorge Comm'n*, 770 F. Supp. 1419, 1423–24 (E.D. Wash. 1991) (applying federal jurisprudence standards for 60-day notice of intent to sue); *W. Birkenfeld Trust v. Bailey*, 827 F. Supp. 651, 660–61 (E.D. Wash. 1993) (same and also applying federal legislative immunity jurisprudence to compact commissioners and federal standing and ripeness jurisprudence); *Columbia River Gorge United v. Columbia River Gorge Comm'n*, CV No. 88-1319-PA, 1990 U.S. Dist. LEXIS 15447 (D. Or. May 23, 1990) (applying federal standing jurisprudence), *aff'd*, 960 F.2d 110 (9th Cir. 1992). However, the one state court to consider the issue for the Gorge Compact rejected federal ripeness jurisprudence because it differs significantly from state ripeness jurisprudence. *Friends of the Columbia Gorge v. Columbia River Gorge Comm'n*, 215 Or. App. 557, 571–74 (2007).

6. In another example of a compact where federal court jurisdiction does not equate to applying the federal APA, article IV(o) of the Low-Level Radioactive Waste Policy Amendments Act of 1985, Pub. L. No. 99-240, 99 Stat. 1842, 1917 (1986) states:

> 2. In the event that review is sought of the Commission's decision relative to the designation of a host state, the Court of Appeals shall accord the matter an expedited review, and, if the Court does not rule within 90 days after a petition for review has been filed, the Commission's decision shall be deemed to be affirmed.

For a critique of the automatic approval provision in the Low-Level Radioactive Waste Policy Amendments while it was still proposed legislation, see *Constitutionality of a Judicial Review Provision Providing for Automatic Affirmance of Agency Decisions*, 9 Op. O.L.C. 118 (1985), https://www.justice.gov/olc/opinions-volume. The Office of Legal Counsel noted, "this provision is virtually unprecedented. We are not aware of any comparable provision in statutes authorizing judicial review of administrative actions." *Id.* at 120. The opinion concluded that the automatic affirmance provision raises serious constitutional problems arising from the doctrine of separation of powers. *Id.* at 125.

7. In contrast to *Old Town Trolley*, the next case rejects claims under the federal APA because the court concludes the APA does not apply to compact agencies, even indirectly.

New York v. Atl. States Marine Fisheries Comm'n
609 F.3d 524 (2d Cir. 2010)

WESLEY, JUDGE:

For 68 years, the Atlantic States Marine Fisheries Commission ("ASMFC" or the "Commission") has endeavored to promote the utilization and protection of the fisheries of the Atlantic seaboard. The Commission is the product of a congressionally approved interstate compact authorized by Article I, § 10, clause 3 of the United States Constitution. This interlocutory appeal requires us to determine whether the intervenor-plaintiffs, United Boatmen of New York, Inc., New York Fishing Tackle Trade Association, Inc., and the Fishermen's Conservation Association (collectively "intervenor-plaintiffs" or "United Boatmen"), may assert a claim under section 702 of the Administrative Procedure Act, 5 U.S.C. § 702 (the "APA"), to seek judicial review of the Commission's decisions.

In essence, the premise of United Boatmen's complaint in intervention is a simple one: intervenor-plaintiffs maintain that the Commission is more than a congressionally authorized state cooperative agreement. In the view of the intervenor-plaintiffs, ASMFC is a federal agency, or at least acts so much like one that we should treat it as one for purposes of the APA.

. . . .

This case arises from disputes over the management of the summer flounder fishery off of the Atlantic coast. In response to a decrease in the stock of summer flounder, also known as fluke, regulatory "efforts have been made to conserve and restore the population." *Connecticut v. U.S. Dep't of Commerce,* 204 F.3d 413, 414 (2d Cir. 2000). . . .

. . . .

. . . . [P]laintiffs contend that the final management rule for the 2008 recreational summer flounder fishery violates the Magnuson-Stevens Fishery Conservation and Management Act and the APA, 5 U.S.C. § 706(2)(A).

Intervenor-plaintiffs in this action are private groups who maintain that the New York State plaintiffs failed to adequately represent their interests in defining the scope of their suit. United Boatmen of New York, Inc. is a professional trade organization that represents the for-hire fishing vessel industry in New York. Members of United Boatmen derive a substantial portion of their revenue from sport fishing for summer flounder. The New York Fishing Tackle Trade Association, Inc. is a professional trade organization that represents the wholesale and retail bait and tackle dealer industry in New York. The Fishermen's Conservation Association is a non-profit organization whose members are individual recreational anglers who target, among other species, summer flounder in state and federal waters contiguous to New York State.

In 1942, the ASMFC was created by a congressionally approved interstate compact. The purpose of the Compact "is to promote the better utilization of the fisheries * * * of the Atlantic seaboard" through a "joint program for the promotion and protection of such fisheries." ASMFC Compact, art. I. The Compact specifically provides that it shall not "be construed to limit the powers of any signatory state or to repeal or prevent the enactment of any legislation or the enforcement of any requirement by any signatory state imposing additional conditions and restrictions to conserve its fisheries." ASMFC Compact, art. IX.

. . . .

In 1993, Congress adopted the Atlantic Coastal Fisheries Cooperative Management Act (the "ACFCMA") in order to give the ASMFC some "teeth." Congress sought to accomplish this goal by mandating state participation in the interstate fishery management plans promulgated by the Commission. Pursuant to the ACFCMA, a plan must "specify the requirements necessary for [s]tates to be in compliance," and the ASMFC must "identify each [s]tate that is required to implement and enforce that plan." *Id.* The Commission is obligated to review member states' "implementation and enforcement of coastal fishery management plans" and "report the results of the reviews" to the Secretary of Commerce.

Under the ACFCMA, the Secretary of Commerce is empowered to make an independent finding regarding whether a state has failed to implement management measures and, if so, "whether the measures that the [s]tate has failed to implement and enforce are necessary for the conservation of the fishery in question." If the Secretary makes a determination of noncompliance with respect to "necessary" measures, he or she "shall declare a moratorium on fishing in the fishery in question within the waters of the noncomplying [s]tate."

The congressional findings accompanying the ACFCMA note that "[b]ecause no single governmental entity has exclusive management authority for Atlantic coastal fishery resources, harvesting of such resources is frequently subject to disparate, inconsistent, and intermittent [s]tate and [f]ederal regulation that has been detrimental to the conservation and sustainable use of such resources." The ACFCMA explicitly affirms, however, that the "responsibility for managing Atlantic coastal fisheries rests with the [s]tates, which carry out a cooperative program of fishery oversight and management through the Atlantic States Marine Fisheries Commission."

On July 16, 2008, United Boatmen moved to intervene in the action commenced by the New York State plaintiffs and to join the Commission as a defendant. The court granted United Boatmen's motion and "decline[d] to limit the scope of [United Boatmen's] intervention to the parties and issues asserted in [the New York] plaintiffs' complaint." The court concluded that the New York State plaintiffs' "failure to join ASMFC as a defendant constituted nonfeasance" sufficient to rebut the presumption of adequate representation present when a state brings suit in its capacity as parens patriae. Following the district court's decision, intervenor-plaintiffs filed their complaint in intervention on December 19, 2008.

ASMFC brought a motion to dismiss United Boatmen's complaint in intervention for failure to state a claim. [*New York v. Gutierrez*, 623 F. Supp. 2d 301, 305 (E.D.N.Y. 2009)]. In support of its motion to dismiss, ASMFC pointed out that neither its governing Compact[5] nor any federal statute provide a private right of action to seek judicial review of its regulatory decisions. More importantly for purposes of this litigation, the Commission maintained that the provisions of the APA, which provide a right of action against federal agencies, 5 U.S.C. §§ 701(b)(1), 702, do not apply to action by an interstate compact entity.

The district court denied ASMFC's motion to dismiss. 623 F. Supp. 2d at 305. The court concluded that intervenor-plaintiffs could maintain a claim against the Commission under section 702 of the APA based on the theory that the Commission is a "quasi-federal" agency. *Id.* at 311. In so holding, the district court concluded that "allowing ASMFC['s] actions essentially to escape judicial review [would be] inappropriate." *Id.* at 312. The district court then granted the Commission's request for certification of its order for interlocutory appeal. A panel of this Court granted leave to appeal the interlocutory order of the district court.

On appeal, the Commission advances largely the same arguments that it did before the district court. Essentially, ASMFC argues that intervenor-plaintiffs' complaint should be dismissed as it pertains to the Commission because it is not a federal agency; therefore, intervenor-plaintiffs may not seek review of the Commission's fishery management decisions under the APA. By contrast, intervenor-plaintiffs urge us to affirm the district court's determination that the Commission is a "quasi-federal" agency subject to suit under the APA. Intervenor-plaintiffs also suggest that this Court take an even stronger position than the one adopted by the district court and find that the Commission is actually a federal agency for the purpose of regulating coastal fishing activities. We hold that the Commission is not subject to suit by United Boatmen under the APA.

The coverage of the APA, including its judicial review provisions, is governed by the statutory definition of the term "agency." Thus, we must first look to the

---

[5] By contrast, other interstate compacts do provide for judicial review. E.g., Washington Metropolitan Transit Regulation Compact, Pub. L. No. 101-505, art. XIII, § 5(a), 104 Stat. 1300, 1312 (1990); Tahoe Regional Planning Compact, Pub. L. No. 96-551, art. VI(j)(3), 94 Stat. 3233, 3247 (1980); Northeast Dairy Compact, § 16(C), S.J. Res. 28, 104th Cong. (1995).

text, which provides a definition of this term. Other authorities have "characteriz[ed] the APA definition as 'not very satisfactory.'" *Lee Constr. Co., Inc. v. Fed. Reserve Bank*, 558 F. Supp. 165, 173 (D. Md. 1982). We agree that we cannot say that the meaning of agency as defined by the APA is so "plain on its face" as to end our inquiry. While this may not be a case where our "inquiry should end" with the text, the text of the APA does provide significant guidance.

. . . .

The provisions of the APA "provide[] the statutory structure upon which federal administrative law is built." *Cornejo-Barreto v. Seifert*, 218 F.3d 1004, 1012 (9th Cir. 2000). The APA states that "[a] person suffering legal wrong because of agency action, or adversely affected or aggrieved by agency action * * * is entitled to judicial review thereof." 5 U.S.C. § 702. Under the APA the term "agency" is defined as an "authority of the [g]overnment of the United States." 5 U.S.C. § 701(b)(1). Despite this express definition, courts that have wrestled with its application have declared that the "law on the simple question of what is an agency is quite complex." *McKinney v. Caldera,* 141 F. Supp. 2d 25, 31 (D.D.C. 2001). These courts have emphasized "the need to examine the structure, function, and mandate" of the entity in question in determining whether it falls within the definition set out in the APA. *Id.* at 33.

The APA definition expressly excludes certain entities, such as Congress and the federal courts. Although an interstate compact entity is not specifically exempted from the definition, this "textual silence, when read against the backdrop of * * * the canons of construction applicable to statutes that implicate the separation of powers, points," *Armstrong v. Bush*, 924 F.2d 282, 289 (D.C. Cir. 1991), to the conclusion that the ASMFC is not a federal agency within the meaning of the APA. "It is axiomatic that the statutory definition of the term excludes unstated meanings of that term." *Meese v. Keene*, 481 U.S. 465, 484 (1987). In any event, the statutory exclusions from the coverage of the APA applies only to bodies that would otherwise be "authorit[ies] of the [g]overnment of the United States." 5 U.S.C. § 701(b)(1). We find that the Commission is not such an authority.

. . . .

The fact that the ASMFC was created by an interstate compact and approved by Congress does not alter this analysis. We find that the APA's definition of a federal agency does not fit the Commission. The ASMFC Compact states that the "Commission shall be a body corporate, with the powers and duties set forth" in the Compact. ASMFC Compact, art. III. Although the Commission acts in parallel with the federal government in managing the stock of summer flounder off of the Atlantic coast, it exists outside the federal administrative law framework. And, it would upset the "federal-state balance," *Armstrong,* 924 F.2d at 289, to subject its actions to accountability measures devised to restrain the actions of federal authorities.

. . . .

Although interstate compacts are contemplated by the Constitution, U.S. CONST. art. I, § 10, cl. 3, and subject to congressional approval, we cannot escape the fact that the entity itself is an aggregation of states. While "an interstate compact or agreement becomes federal law if it is a congressionally sanctioned interstate compact within the meaning of the Compact Clause of the Constitution," *NYSA-ILA Vacation & Holiday Fund v. Waterfront Comm'n*, 732 F.2d 292, 297 (2d Cir. 1984), it does not follow that the Commission is a federal agency. To hold otherwise would have the effect of treating every congressionally authorized interstate compact entity, regardless of the body's structure and function, as a federal "agency" for purposes of the APA. For reasons explained below, we do not think this result was intended by Congress.

The authority exercised by ASMFC under the Compact is not federal in nature. The signatory states have agreed to coordinate their regulatory activity in order to "promote the better utilization of the fisheries." ASMFC Compact, art. I. But, there is no indication that the contracting states understood themselves to be compacting to create a federal agency. "Interstate compacts * * * are presumed to be the subject of careful consideration before they are entered into, and are drawn by persons competent to express their meaning, and to choose apt words in which to embody the purposes of the * * * contracting parties." *New Jersey v. Delaware*, 552 U.S. 597, 615–16 (2008). We therefore decline to find that ASMFC is anything other than a state cooperative agreement, from which states are free to withdraw upon notice to the other member states.

While it is true that there is a "strong presumption that Congress intends judicial review of administrative action," *Sharkey v. Quarantillo*, 541 F.3d 75, 84 (2d Cir. 2008), that presumption is only available with regard to the administrative acts of federal agencies as defined in the APA. United Boatmen maintain that their claim should be accorded this presumption because the enactment of the ACFCMA rendered ASMFC a federal agency. We disagree. United Boatmen assume the conclusion they seek to reach. ASMFC is simply not an authority of the United States. The "primary purpose," of the APA is not to reach contracts between states. And, the language of the ACFCMA makes it clear that the authority to regulate the summer flounder fishery within the territorial sea remains with the states and that the federal government plays only a supporting role in this endeavor. Therefore, we hold that ASMFC does not satisfy the definition of an agency as set forth in § 701(b)(1) of the APA.

The court below maintained that "whether Congress designates an entity as a federal agency does not end the inquiry as to whether the entity in fact operates as a federal agency." *Gutierrez,* 623 F. Supp. 2d at 307. The district judge opined that if the ASMFC "had become so federal in character" that it should be regarded as a "quasi-federal" agency, then it would be amenable to suit by the intervenor-plaintiffs under the APA. *Id.* at 308. Thus, the court found that, "[i]n light of [the] substantial federal involvement in the Commission, it is not unreasonable to conclude that, despite state sovereignty concerns, ASMFC should be treated as a 'quasi-federal agency' and subjected to a private right of action under the APA." *Id.* at 312.

The district court relied on decisions of several other courts that have acknowledged this doctrine. See *Am. Trucking Ass'n, Inc. v. Del. River Joint Toll Bridge Comm'n*, 458 F.3d 291, 304 n.10 (3d Cir. 2006); *Heard Commc'ns, Inc. v. Bi-State Dev. Agency*, 18 Fed. Appx. 438, 439–40 (8th Cir. 2001); *Elcon Enters., Inc. v. Wash. Metro. Area Transit Auth.*, 977 F.2d 1472, 1479–80 (D.C. Cir. 1992).[10] We find these decisions unpersuasive. Taken together, this authority provides scant support for the "quasi-federal" agency doctrine. Indeed, we are skeptical of the validity of this judge-created concept.

It is clear to us, at the very least, that the "quasi-federal" agency doctrine—whatever its merit—does not apply to the Commission. The lower court was of the view that the "quasi-federal" agency cases identify "three factors relevant to whether a compact authority warrants the quasi-federal agency classification." 623 F. Supp. 2d at 308 (internal quotation marks omitted). However, the court forthrightly acknowledged that two of the three factors do not apply to the ASMFC. With that concession, the court implicitly recognized that, given the facts of this case, designation as a "quasi-federal" agency is an ill-fitting means by which to describe the ASMFC. Nonetheless, the district court concluded that, irrespective of other considerations, federal involvement in the activities of the Commission warranted a finding that it is a "quasi-federal" agency. We disagree.

By its nature, there will always be federal involvement in a congressionally approved interstate compact. We are unpersuaded, however, that this requires us to subject what is, at its core, a contract between states to the judicial review provisions of the APA. The ASMFC is a body comprised "only of its constituent" states. A finding that the ASMFC is a "quasi-federal" agency would be in tension with its governing Compact, which serves as a contractual agreement between the

---

[10] No circuit court of appeals has adopted the "quasi-agency" doctrine in a published decision. Only the Eighth Circuit Court of Appeals has endorsed the analysis that underpins the "quasi-agency" doctrine. *Heard Commc'ns*, 18 F. App'x at 440. In any event, for the reasons expressed in this opinion, we are not persuaded that the doctrine—even as expressed by the courts that have accepted it—is properly invoked here. Indeed, no circuit court has applied the doctrine to bring an entity that does not otherwise meet the definition of an agency under § 701(b)(1) within the judicial review provisions of the APA. In *American Trucking Association*, the Third Circuit concluded that the appellants had waived the issue of whether or not review under the APA was available; therefore, it did not decide the issue. 458 F.3d at 304 n.10. Thus, this case cannot properly be read as an endorsement of the "quasi-federal" agency doctrine. The Eighth Circuit expressly held that the bi-state compact that was the subject of the litigation in *Heard Communications* was "not a quasi-federal agency subject to the APA." 18 F. App'x at 439. In *Elcon*, the Court of Appeals for the District of Columbia simply assumed, without deciding, that the Washington Metropolitan Transit Authority was a federal agency. 977 F.2d at 1480. It appears that this doctrine is the creation of several district courts. E.g., *Seal & Co., Inc. v. Wash. Metro. Area Transit Auth.*, 768 F. Supp. 1150, 1154-56 (E.D. Va. 1991); *Coal. for Safe Transit, Inc. v. Bi-State Dev. Agency*, 778 F. Supp. 464, 467–68 (E.D. Mo. 1991) (citing *Union Switch & Signal, Inc. v. Bi-State Dev. Agency*, No. 91-1401C (7) (E.D. Mo. Oct. 23, 1991) (unpublished disposition)).

member states. The structure and composition of the ASMFC weigh against characterizing it as a "quasi-federal" agency. We may infer that congressional approval of the ASMFC was granted as a means of aiding the contracting states in their regulatory activities. And, Congress chose to endorse the creation of this regulatory body comprised of states rather than preempt the area by creating an *actual* federal agency.

Beyond federal involvement, the fact that federal interests are implicated by the activities of the Commission does not transform ASMFC into a federal entity subject to suit under the APA. "An interstate compact represents a political compromise between constituent elements of the Union." *Entergy Arkansas, Inc. v. Nebraska*, 358 F.3d 528, 542 (8th Cir. 2004). Congress may often have an interest in the terms of such a compromise, but this does not lead us to conclude that private parties are therefore entitled to assert a claim against the compact as if it were a federal agency.

. . . The basis for the district court's observation that the Commission "closely resembl[es]" a federal agency eludes us. And, regardless of whether or not it would be desirable, as a policy matter, to extend the reach of the APA to the ASMFC, we see no basis to expand the definition of "agency" so as to allow it to reach the ASMFC. Congress and the states may work in partnership in the interest of a common regulatory goal without subjecting an interstate body to review provisions designed to apply to federal agencies.

. . . We hold that, in the absence of other factors not present in this case, the acts of Congress in approving the interstate Compact, in adopting the ACFCMA, and in providing funding to the Commission, did not transmogrify the ASMFC into a "quasi-federal" agency.

The APA is designed, at least in part, to ensure that federal actors are held accountable to the public. This concern is not a salient one here. There are other checks on the Commission's actions, which rest primarily within the authority of the states that comprise the Commission and the state-level officials that represent ASMFC's member states.

The fact that the ASMFC is an interstate compact entity provides an inherent restraint on its decision making process. "No action shall be taken by the Commission in regard to its general affairs except by the affirmative vote of a majority of the whole number of compacting states present at any meeting." ASMFC Compact, art. VI. And, "[n]o recommendation shall be made by the Commission in regard to any species of fish except by the affirmative vote of a majority of the compacting states which have an interest in such species." ASMFC Compact, art. VI. Each state is obligated to carry out the terms of the ASMFC Compact, and member states may seek judicial relief to enforce rights under the agreement. Further, member states may avail themselves of an internal appeal mechanism; states may appeal decisions of a management board to the full membership of the Commission.

Although its actions are not subject to review under § 702 of the APA, the Commission is a politically accountable body. ASMFC is composed of state conservation agency directors, state legislators, and public citizens appointed by the governors of the member states. ASMFC Compact, art. III. The actions of the ASMFC involve the coordinate exercise of the states' sovereign policy-making powers. In this regard, the Commission is more akin to a legislative body than to a federal agency. The Commission's decisions are implemented through rule-making by the individual states, which affords an opportunity for public participation in the management process. In addition, the ASMFC makes its decisions public.

Finally, the ACFCMA provides a check on the actions of the Commission; it requires that the Secretary of Commerce review a finding that a state has failed to comply with a fishery management plan. 16 U.S.C. § 5106(a). The Compact provides that, if the Secretary determines a state has failed to comply with measures that are "necessary for the conservation" of a fishery, the Secretary shall impose a moratorium. If the Secretary imposes and enforces a federal moratorium based on his or her independent findings of noncompliance, a party that is allegedly aggrieved by the Secretary's action can obtain APA review of that federal "agency action."

The Commission is designed to address concerns that are traditionally within the province of the states. That the Commission seeks to address these concerns with support from the federal government, and in a manner that is harmonious with federal regulations, does not alter its essential nature. The fact that federal interests are implicated by the activities of the ASMFC does not transform it into a federal agency for purposes of seeking judicial review of its actions.

Notes & Questions

1. The Second Circuit cited *Old Town Trolley* only for its citation of the federal APA definition of "agency." The Second Circuit also strongly rejected the "quasi-federal agency" approach to giving a cause of action under the federal APA that several district courts used. What might account for this stark contrast with these decisions? Is there a split between the Second Circuit and the D.C. Circuit as to the application of the federal APA?

2. In *Seal & Co., Inc. v. Wash. Metro. Area Transit Auth.*, 768 F. Supp. 1150 (E.D. Va. 1991) (cited in footnote 10), the court noted that the Transit Authority had replaced a previously existing federal agency, the National Capital Transportation Agency, and reasoned that because the prior agency was subject to the APA, Congress must have intended the Transit Authority to be subject to the APA as well. *Id.* at 1157. Compare this reasoning to the *Yancoskie* case that you read in Chapter 4, in which the court noted that the Delaware River Port Authority replaced a previously existing state agency and reasoned that fact suggested the DRPA was not a state agency. Wouldn't the reasoning in *Yancoskie* suggest that the federal APA does not apply to the Transit Authority?

3. In *Seal*, the court also stated that a cause of action pursuant to the federal APA was necessary to monitor and enforce the regulation at issue. 768 F. Supp.

at 1156. In *Atlantic States*, the court rejected the same point, which United Boatmen argued, concluding instead that the Atlantic States Marine Fisheries Commission was politically accountable. The commission has three appointees from each of the 15 members (including states, the District of Columbia, the Potomac River Fisheries Commission, and two federal agencies) for a total of 45 commissioners. Voting is done by membership; two commissioners decide a party's sole vote. How "accountable" is the commission? Compare the effect of one state's objection to a decision by the Atlantic State Marine Fisheries Commission to the governors' veto authority described in *Pievsky v. Ridge*. Is a single veto as effective when there are 14 other votes?

4. After *Atlantic States*, how can an affected trade association or environmental organization challenge a commission fisheries plan before the commission transmits the plan to the states for implementation? Should the states be concerned that they may become defendants in litigation over the substance of plans that they didn't write? Could affected industry individuals even challenge the substance of the plans in litigation against the states?

5. Despite the Second Circuit's sound rejection of *Seal* and application of the federal APA to compact agencies, other courts outside of the Second Circuit continue to cite *Seal* and apply the federal APA. For example, in *Challenger Transp., Inc. v. Wash. Metro. Area Transit Auth.*, No. TDC-14-3322, 2015 U.S. Dist. LEXIS 100004 (D. Md. July 30, 2015), the court expressly treated the Transit Authority as a federal agency for the purpose of applying the federal APA. Challenger filed a bid protest after the Transit Authority awarded contracts for paratransit services to three other bidders. The Transit Authority denied the protest and Challenger filed suit, alleging that the Transit Authority acted arbitrarily and capriciously by violating its own procurement policies and procedures. Although the case was not clear whether Challenger specifically alleged a violation of section 706 of the federal APA, the court focused on Challenger's "arbitrary and capricious" allegation and stated that this was a challenge under the APA. Citing *Seal*, the court reasoned, "Courts have treated WMATA as a federal agency when a party seeks to challenge WMATA's procurement decisions in federal court." *Id.* at *12.

B. Applying State Administrative Procedure

Some compacts require the use of state administrative procedure and may do so broadly, or for a specific purpose. For example, the Waterfront Commission of New York Harbor Compact, art. XI, § 7, specifies judicial review of the Commission's licensing decisions:

> The action of the commission in denying any application for a license or in refusing to include any person in the longshoremen's register under this compact or in suspending or revoking such license or removing any person from the longshoremen's register or in reprimanding a licensee or registrant shall be subject to judicial review by a proceeding instituted in either State at the instance of the applicant, licensee or registrant in the manner provided by the law of such State for review of the final decision or action of administrative agencies of such State . . . .

In the absence of a clear provision requiring the use of a state APA, determining whether state APAs apply to a compact agency is often similar to determining whether other state law applies to a compact, which was the focus of Chapter 8; however, the ubiquity and text of the states' APAs can make the application of state APAs more complicated. All state agencies apply state administrative law; thus, states and other persons naturally expect that compact agencies, which the states create, must also apply state administrative procedure. Additionally, the text of the states' APAs, other legislation, and the text of the compact may specify that a compact agency must use all or a portion of the states' APAs.

One state, Oklahoma, expressly applies its APA to compact agencies. OKLA. STAT. tit. 75, § 250.3 ("'Agency' includes but is not limited to any constitutionally or statutorily created state board, bureau, commission, office, authority, public trust in which the state is a beneficiary, or interstate commission, . . ."). Pennsylvania and the District of Columbia include "independent" commissions in their definitions of agency. 1 PA. CONSOL. STAT. ANN. § 31.3; D.C. CODE § 2-502. Chapter 4 discussed how compact agencies are typically independent of the states. No court has opined whether the Pennsylvania APA covers compact agencies, but the D.C. Circuit has held that one compact agency was not an "agency within the meaning of the D.C. APA." *KiSKA Constr. Corp. v. Wash. Metro. Area Transit Auth.*, 167 F.3d 608, 610 (D.C. Cir. 1999). The court principally relied on testimony by one of the principal drafters of the DC-APA, who testified during the adoption of the DC-APA that "the intention of this bill was to cover only agencies of the District of Columbia * * * It was not intended to cover agencies—joint agencies—but [rather] only agencies within the framework of the District of Columbia government." *Id.* at 611. Similarly, one state, South Dakota, defines "agency" to include, ". . . or other agent of the state vested with the authority to exercise any portion of the state's sovereignty." S.D. CODIFIED LAWS § 1-26-1(1). Chapter 2 discussed how compacts occupy a slice of each states' sovereignty.

Two states, Delaware and New York, expressly exclude compact agencies from their APA definition of "agency." DEL. CODE ANN. tit. 29, § 10101(1) ("Agency does not include . . . joint state-federal, interstate or intermunicipal authorities and their agencies."); N.Y. A.P.A. LAW § 102.1 ("'Agency' . . . shall not include the governor, agencies in the legislative and judicial branches, [or] agencies created by interstate compact or international agreement"). The Montana APA does not define agency to exclude compact agencies, but expressly excludes uniform rules of a compact agency from the definition of "Rule." MONT. CODE ANN. § 2-4-102(11)(b)(v). This ensures that compact agencies do not need to specifically enact compact rules in Montana or in accordance with Montana law.

The Delaware River Basin Compact, an agreement between Delaware, New Jersey, New York, Pennsylvania, and the United States, illustrates the potential for puzzling results in determining which APAs might apply to a compact agency. The compact states, "The Delaware River Basin Commission is hereby created as a body corporate and politic, with succession for the duration of this compact, as an agency and instrumentality of the governments of the respective signatory parties." Delaware River Basin Compact, art. 2, § 1. If the Delaware River Basin

Commission (DRBC) is "an agency and instrumentality" of the United States, then the federal APA would seem to be applicable, and if the DRBC is "an agency and instrumentality" of each state individually, then the New Jersey APA and Pennsylvania APAs could also apply. But the Delaware and New York APA would not apply because their APAs expressly exclude interstate agencies.

In 1981, the federal court determined that it could not apply the federal APA to judicial review of DRBC actions because the compact contained a provision stating that the DRBC was not to be considered a federal agency for the purpose of certain laws, including the predecessor to the APA. *Delaware Water Emergency Group v. Hansler*, 536 F. Supp. 26 (E.D. Pa. 1981), *aff'd,* 681 F.2d 805 (3d Cir. 1982). The district court filled this gap in administrative procedure using other federal law, stating,

> Since the Compact gives no hint of the scope of review and the APA is expressly not applicable, the case of *United States v. Bianchi & Co.*, 373 U.S. 709, 715, (1963), gives some guidance. That case, as I understand it, strongly suggests that in the absence of statutory standards the test is either "arbitrary and capricious" or "not substantial evidence," and, more importantly, that review should be limited to the administrative record.

536 F. Supp. at 36–40. In 1982, the states amended the compact, and the provision at issue in *Hansler* no longer appears in the compact.

The text of some compacts specifically or impliedly the federal or a state APA to the agencies authorized in those compacts. For example, the Susquehanna River Basin Compact has Maryland, New York, Pennsylvania, and the United States as its members. Article 2.2 of the compact requires that the commission's rules "shall not be effective unless and until filed in accordance with the law of the respective signatory parties applicable to administrative rules and regulations generally . . . ." In this case, the compact text suggests the agency must conduct its rulemaking in accordance with the federal APA and all the member states' APAs; however, the SRBC files its rulemaking notices in the federal register, but not in the states' notice registries. What would the agency do if there were conflicting requirements in the parties' APAs such that the agency cannot comply with all the APAs?

A handful of compacts specify that a compact agency must apply the more restrictive provisions of the signatory states' APAs. For example, Congress imposed the following condition when granting consent to the Columbia River Gorge Compact:

> . . . the Commission shall adopt regulations relating to administrative procedure, the making of contracts, conflicts-of-interest, financial disclosure, open meetings of the Commission, advisory committees, and disclosure of information consistent with the more restrictive statutory provisions of either State.

16 U.S.C. § 544(c)(b). The Tahoe Regional Planning Compact, art. III(d), similarly requires:

all meetings shall be open to the public to the same extent required by the law of the State of California or the State of Nevada, whichever imposes the greater requirements, applicable to local governments at the time such meeting is held.

Notes & Questions

1. What do the terms "more restrictive" or "greater requirements" in the Gorge and Tahoe compacts mean? How should an agency determine which law is "more restrictive"? Should the agency apply the more restrictive provision of each state's law or the more restrictive of each state's administrative procedure acts as a whole? What if one state law contains a provision that the other state law does not? For example, in 2008, the Tahoe Regional Planning Agency (TRPA) adopted a new Rule of Procedure to allow teleconferencing for Governing Board and Advisory Planning Commission meetings and associated committee proceedings. TRPA had long before determined that it must apply Nevada's open meeting law (NEV. REV. STAT. §§ 241.010 *et seq.*); however, Nevada law does not expressly allow or prohibit meetings by teleconference. In contrast, California's law (CAL. GOV'T CODE § 54953) does allow teleconference meetings. TRPA determined that because Nevada's law was silent, it could supplement the law as applied to TRPA. Is this reasoning correct? How would you argue that TRPA should not have applied California law?

2. Would a compact supersede the state APAs that define "agency" broadly enough to encompass interstate compact agencies? Would states that attempt to apply their own state APA without authorization in the compact be taking unilateral action that burdens administration of the compact? How would you resolve conflicts between the requirements of the multiple states' APAs?

3. The ABA Section of Administrative Law and Regulatory Practice studied the various ways that compacts specify administrative procedure, how compact agencies actually practice administrative procedure, and how courts address administrative law questions relating to compact agencies. In 2008, the ABA House of Delegates adopted the following resolution urging Congress, the states and territories, and compact agencies to specify the administrative procedures that compact agencies use.

American Bar Association, House of Delegates Resolution No. 111B, Adopted Aug. 2008

RESOLVED, That the American Bar Association urges Congress, when it consents to the creation of an interstate compact agency under Article I, Section 10, clause 3 of the U.S. Constitution, to prescribe the administrative procedures to be employed by the agency, provide for judicial review of agency action, and specify the standards of judicial review.

FURTHER RESOLVED, That the American Bar Association urges states and territories that are parties to an existing congressionally approved interstate compact to jointly review the administrative procedures employed by the agency created by the compact, if any, and, consistent with Congress's consent, enact necessary legislation to prescribe the administrative procedures to be employed by the agency, provide for judicial review of agency action, and specify the standards of judicial review.

FURTHER RESOLVED, That the American Bar Association urges existing compact agencies, in the absence of procedures specified by Congress or the states and territories, to review their administrative procedures and adopt appropriate administrative procedures to govern their functions.

FURTHER RESOLVED, That the American Bar Association urges that provisions concerning administrative procedure and judicial review for compact agencies should be consistent with fundamental administrative law norms:

1. In the case of adjudication, parties should be able to present their positions orally or in writing and challenge positions of opposing witnesses orally or in writing; the adjudicatory decision should be rendered by an impartial decision-maker; and, a statement of reasons should accompany each decision.

2. In the case of rulemaking, there should be an opportunity, following notice, for the public to comment on proposed regulations.

3. Statutory provisions relating to judicial review of agency decisions should assure that those adversely affected by an agency decision should receive an appropriate form of judicial review, and should specify standards of review that do not vary depending on the court that reviews an action of the compact agency.

Notes & Questions

1. Why did the ABA make multiple recommendations directed at Congress, the states, and compact agencies?

2. The resolution hints at recommending that Congress enact an APA specifically applicable to compact agencies. Is an interstate compact APA a "state-based" solution in the spirit of compacts? How might Congress write legislation that takes account of the variations in the myriad compacts? Some compacts are bi-state, others are multi-state, some cover all 50 states plus the territories, and some include Canadian provinces. There is also great diversity in the membership, authorities, and operation of the compact agencies. For example, many compacts have a governing board appointed entirely by the member states, but many compacts have a more diverse governing board, including members appointed by local governments or the federal government. Some compacts reserve the governors' right to veto actions taken by board members that they have appointed. Would a congressionally drafted interstate compact APA apply to compacts without congressional consent? Would states choose to impose such an APA?

3. An alternative to Congress enacting a compact APA would be to require each compact agency that conducts rulemaking or adjudications must enact procedures that make sense for that compact. But can a compact agency write APA provisions that govern the functions of other arms of the government? For example, is there a separation of powers concern with a compact agency specifying standards and justiciability requirements for judicial review of its own actions?

4. The Interstate Medical Licensure Compact § 15 (2015) requires that rulemaking must substantially conform to the procedures in the 2010 Model State APA. The Medical Licensure compact is national in scope, all 50 states and territories are eligible to join the compact. Reference to a single APA alleviates the complexities of trying to comply with multiple state APAs; however, there are possible limitations with using the Model State APA. One limitation is that the Model State APA does not anticipate applying to multistate entities, so it does not address issues such as where to file rulemaking notices—for example, should rulemaking notices be filed in each member state, in which there may be substantial differences in filing requirements, or should rulemaking notices be filed only the state where the compact commission has its principal office? Another issue with specifying the 2010 Model State APA is that no state has enacted it in substantial part, so judicial interpretation of the rules may be uncertain.

C. Compact Agency Rulemaking

Compact entities commonly enact rules to guide their internal operation, establish uniform standards for states, and directly regulate persons and entities. Compact agency rulemaking raises some unique issues. One issue is that some older compacts do not have a clear and complete statement of rulemaking authority. For example, article VII of the Interstate Compact on the Placement of Children states in its entirety:

> The executive head of each jurisdiction party to this compact shall designate an officer who shall be general coordinator of activities under this compact in his jurisdiction and who, acting jointly with like officers of other party jurisdictions, shall have power to promulgate rules and regulations to carry out more effectively the terms and provisions of this compact.

The Association of Administrators of the ICPC (AAICPC) enacts compact rules, but the ICPC does not expressly designate the AAICPC as the rulemaking entity and does not specify that the AAICPC rules are binding.

Some state courts and state legislatures have begun imposing a requirement for a party state to enact compact agency rules internally to make them effective. For example, in *In re* S.R.C-Q, 52 Kan. App. 454 (2016), the court opined that the ICPC Regulation 3 (stating that the ICPC applies to out-of-state natural parents) was not validly adopted in Kansas.

> The Kansas version of the ICPC as enacted by the legislature expressly states that it applies to out-of-state placements of children with foster care or as a preliminary to a possible adoption. The statute does not state that it applies to such placements with parents. Also, even if we were to assume that Regulation 3 promulgated by the AAICPC was validly enacted—which we doubt given that we have been unable to find any regulations issued by the Kansas coordinator of the ICPC—the language in Regulation 3 impermissibly enlarges the application of the ICPC to out-of-state placements with parents beyond the plain language of the statute.

Id. at 463. Similarly, in *In re Alexis O.*, 157 N.H. 781 (2008), the court concluded that it was not bound by an interpretative rule of the compact administrator for the Interstate Compact on the Placement of Children. The court concluded that the interpretive rule was not adopted in New Hampshire and was not promulgated pursuant to New Hampshire statutes governing the adoption of regulations. *Id.* at 184. Do you agree that a compact administrator's rule should only be effective when adopted within the state where it would apply and pursuant to that state's requirements for adoption of regulations? All 50 states and some territories are members of the ICPC; should the compact administrator for the ICPC or a state agency need to enact each of its interpretive rules separately in each state and territory?

In another example, in a memo to an Oregon legislative committee that was considering enactment of the Physical Therapist Licensure Compact, an Assistant Attorney General for the Oregon Department of Justice opined that the state could not delegate its rulemaking function to an interstate commission, but that the state Physical Therapist Licensing Board could adopt the interstate commission's rules, thereby making them effective. Memorandum from Joanna Tucker Davis, Senior Ass't Attorney Gen., Oregon Dep't of Justice, Office of the Attorney Gen. (Feb. 2, 2016), https://olis.leg.state.or.us/liz/-2016R1/Downloads/CommitteeMeetingDocument/84135. The Oregon Legislature enacted the compact with this additional requirement for state enactment of the interstate commission's rules. As of mid-2020, no other state adopting the Physical Therapist Licensure Compact has similarly required state readoption of the interstate commission's rules.

Compacts may permit member states to reject a compact agency rule. This may be on a state-by-state basis or all member state acting together. For example, the Interstate Insurance Product Regulation Compact, art. VII(3)-(5), allows each state to individually opt out of a uniform standard for an insurance product. In contrast, the Interstate Compact for Adult Offender Supervision, art. VII(d), allows that a majority of state legislatures can reject a compact agency rule promulgated by the interstate commission by enacting a statute or resolution in the same manner used to adopt the compact. Such clauses have been added to ameliorate legislative concern about rulemaking authority of compact commissions Many states have opted out of many standards adopted by the Interstate Insurance Product Regulation Commission. *See* https://www.insurancecompact.org/compact_rlmkng_record.htm. In contrast, to date, the states have not jointly rejected any rule of the Interstate Commission for Adult Offender Supervision.

Notes & Questions

1. Requiring a state to readopt a compact agency's rule approach raises several legal questions. Consider the following potential issues with Oregon's requirement that it must adopt the Physical Therapist Licensure Compact commission's rules: Did Oregon properly enact the compact when it added the additional rulemaking requirement not authorized in the compact? Can Oregon unilaterally reject or modify an interstate commission rule when section 9.B of the compact only

specifies that a majority of states can reject a rule? Should Oregon still be a member of the compact if it fails to adopt the interstate commission's rules? Will Oregon be in violation of the compact during the time between the interstate commission's adoption of a rule and Oregon's adoption of the rule? What will happen to the licensees that used the compact to obtain permission to practice in Oregon if a court rules against Oregon in any of these legal questions?

2. In *West Virginia ex rel. Dyer v. Sims*, 341 U.S. 22 (1951) (which you read in Chapter 3), the U.S. Supreme Court rejected the argument that a compact obligation was an unlawful delegation to an entity outside of the state in violation of the state constitution. The court held and reasoned:

> The West Virginia [Supreme] court . . . objects to the delegation here involved because it is to a body outside the State and because its Legislature may not be free, at any time, to withdraw the power delegated. We are not here concerned, and so need not deal, with specific language in a State constitution requiring that the State settle its problems with other States without delegating power to an interstate agency. What is involved is the conventional grant of legislative power. We find nothing in that to indicate that West Virginia may not solve a problem such as the control of river pollution by compact and by the delegation, if such it be, necessary to effectuate such solution by compact.

Id. at 30–31. Does this case satisfy legal questions about whether states may properly implement compact agency rules without readopting them?

CHAPTER 11: ENFORCEMENT OF COMPACTS

Prior chapters have already discussed many of the issues that arise with enforcement of compacts. Chapters 1 and 6 discussed original jurisdiction, which is the method frequently used by states seeking to enforce a compact against another state. Chapter 6 also discussed that compact agencies are not "states" for the purpose of original jurisdiction, which limits options for enforcement of compact obligations. Chapter 3 included *West Virginia ex rel. Dyer v. Sims*, which involved compact commissioners and a state agency seeking mandamus against West Virginia's auditor to fulfill the state's obligation to fund the compact. Chapter 8 explored the problems of states enacting conflicting legislation. This chapter looks at enforcement issues that arise in suits by the party states, compact agencies and third party beneficiaries.

Few early compacts specify internal enforcement mechanisms, such as procedures and remedies for legal enforcement or processes for alternative dispute resolution. Most newer compacts, from the 1980s and later, however, specify some means of enforcement.

Enforcement issues arise regardless of whether the compact specifies a means for dispute resolution and enforcement. As you read through these materials, consider how part states, compact agencies or third party beneficiaries can enforce compacts that do not specify a means of enforcement. For example, party states may always seek relief against other party states by using the U.S. Supreme Court's original jurisdiction specified in the U.S. Constitution. But non-state-versus-state disputes can be more challenging to bring pursuant to an administrative procedure act or tort, contract, or equitable principles unless a compact authorizes specific types of judicial actions and remedies.

I. ENFORCEMENT BY THE PARTY STATES

Few state-versus-state cases have been as contentious or long lasting as *Texas v. New Mexico*, a dispute over allocation of water from the Pecos River brought pursuant to the Supreme Court's original jurisdiction. As you read this case, think about the tension between the Court's preference for the states to resolve their issues on their own and the states' inability to do so, which has resulted in decades of dispute and litigation.

Texas v. New Mexico
462 U.S. 554 (1983)

BRENNAN, JUSTICE:

For the second time we consider exceptions to a report of the Special Master in this case. The States of Texas and New Mexico and the United States have filed exceptions to a report submitted by the Special Master on September 10, 1982 (1982 Report). We sustain an exception in which both New Mexico and the

United States concur, overrule all other exceptions, and return the case to the Special Master for a final decision on the basic issue in dispute—whether New Mexico is in compliance with obligations imposed by the Pecos River Compact.

The Pecos River rises in north-central New Mexico and flows in a southerly direction into Texas until it joins the Rio Grande near Langtry, Tex. It is the principal river in eastern New Mexico, draining roughly one-fifth of the State, and it is a major tributary of the Rio Grande.

. . . .

After 20 years of false starts,[3] in 1945 Texas and New Mexico commenced negotiations on a compact to allocate the waters of the Pecos Basin. A Compact Commission was formed, consisting of three Commissioners, representing the two States and the United States. In January 1948, the Compact Commission's engineering advisory committee submitted a lengthy report (1947 Study), the central portion of which was a set of river routing studies describing six "conditions" of the Pecos, one of which consisted of the actual conditions as of the beginning of 1947. Each of the studies was embodied in a 41-column table accounting for all known inflows and outflows of water on the river during each of the years between 1905 and 1946. The engineering advisory committee also drafted a Manual of Inflow-Outflow Methods of Measuring Changes in Stream-Flow Depletion (1948) (Inflow-Outflow Manual), which contained charts and tables, derived from data in the 1947 Study, to be used in determining how much water Texas should expect to receive over any particular period for any particular levels of precipitation, under the consumption conditions prevailing in New Mexico in 1947.

On the basis of the 1947 Study and the Inflow-Outflow Manual, the two States successfully negotiated the Pecos River Compact. It was signed by the Commissioners from both States on December 3, 1948, and thereafter ratified by both state legislatures and—as required under the Compact Clause of the Constitution—approved by Congress. The 1947 Study and the Inflow-Outflow Manual were incorporated into [a Senate document], and they unquestionably provided the basis upon which Congress approved the Compact.

The crucial substantive provision of the Pecos River Compact is found at Art. III(a): "New Mexico shall not deplete by man's activities the flow of the Pecos River at the New Mexico-Texas state line below an amount which will give to

---

[3] In 1925, the States negotiated a compact for regulating the river. It was approved by both state legislatures, but the Governor of New Mexico vetoed its bill. In the early 1930's, the Texas congressional delegation succeeded in holding up federal funding for construction of the Alamogordo Dam until New Mexico agreed to ensure that Texas received the same portion of flood flows originating above Avalon Dam that it had received during the period from 1905 to 1935. This agreement was signed in 1935 by the Secretary of the Interior, the United States Senators from both States, and representatives of the irrigation districts concerned, and it was formally ratified by the Texas Legislature but never by the New Mexico Legislature. New Mexico did, however, sharply restrict groundwater pumping in the Roswell area in 1937, thus restoring to some extent the base flow of the river.

Texas a quantity of water equivalent to that available to Texas under the 1947 condition." . . .

The Compact also established the Pecos River Commission as a permanent body, in more or less the same form that it had during the negotiations on the Compact. It was to have three Commissioners, one from each State and one representing the United States, but the United States representative could not vote. Accordingly, the Commission could take official action only with the concurrence of both state Commissioners. The Commission was given broad powers to make all findings of fact necessary to administer the Compact, as well as to "[engage] in studies of water supplies of the Pecos River" and to "[collect], analyze, correlate, preserve and report on data as to the stream flows, storage, diversions, salvage, and use of the waters of the Pecos River and its tributaries."

For roughly 15 years, the Pecos River Commission functioned more or less as had been contemplated in the Compact. It met regularly, passed resolutions, and undertook studies of various questions of importance to those who use the waters of the Pecos. The apparent harmony that characterized the Commission in those years, however, seems largely to have been the result of a tacit agreement to defer disagreement on a problem of serious magnitude. For it became clear soon after the Compact went into effect that the 1947 Study and, more importantly, the tables in the Inflow-Outflow Manual did not describe the actual state of the river. In almost every year following adoption of the Compact, state-line flows were significantly below the amount that one would have predicted on the basis of the Inflow-Outflow Manual, with no obvious change either in natural conditions along the river or in "man's activities."

The initial response of the Commission to this problem was to authorize, in 1957, an ambitious "Review of Basic Data," which would essentially retrace the steps of the engineering committee's 1947 Study to provide a more accurate description of the "1947 condition." The Review of Basic Data was presented to the Commission in 1960; it essentially duplicated the 1947 Study, but using different periods of time, revised records, a number of different assumptions, and different hydrological and mathematical procedures. The Commission took no action on the Review of Basic Data until two years later, when it directed the engineering committee to proceed with a draft of a new Inflow-Outflow Manual, and adopted as findings of fact a set of figures derived from the new study showing that the cumulative shortfall of state-line flows for the years 1950–1961 was approximately 53,000 acre-feet.

This was essentially the Commission's last action with respect to the all-important question of Texas' right under the Compact to receive as much water as it would have received under the "1947 condition."[9] Disputes that had been deferred and avoided in the past now surfaced. They came to a head at a special

[9] The Commission did not meet at all between January 1967 and November 1968, during which period the identities of four key persons changed. Both the Texas Commissioner (first appointed immediately after the Compact was ratified) and the Engineering Advisor

meeting of the Commission in July 1970, at which the Texas Commissioner stated his position that, calculated according to the original Inflow-Outflow Manual, there had been a cumulative shortfall in state-line flows of 1.1 million acre-feet for the years 1950–1969, that the Review of Basic Data was "incomplete and replete with errors," and that Texas had a right to an annual determination of departures in state-line flows under the original assumptions of the 1947 Study until the Commission adopted a different method. Thereafter, the Texas and New Mexico staffs prepared different reports in 1971 and 1974 on cumulative shortfalls under the "1947 condition," with Texas relying on the original Inflow-Outflow Manual and New Mexico on the Review of Basic Data. Attempts to mediate between the two positions failed, and the Commission took no action for lack of agreement between the two voting Commissioners.

In June 1974, Texas invoked the original jurisdiction of this Court . . . . Its bill of complaint alleged that New Mexico had breached its obligations under Art. III(a) of the Compact "by countenancing and permitting depletions by man's activities within New Mexico to the extent that from 1950 through 1972 there has occurred a cumulative departure of the quantity of water available from the flow of the Pecos River at the Texas-New Mexico State Line in excess of 1,200,000 acre-feet from the equivalent available under the 1947 condition * * * ." Texas sought a decree commanding New Mexico to deliver water in accordance with the Compact. The United States intervened to protect its own claims on the waters of the Pecos River, which had been preserved in Arts. XI–XII of the Compact. We granted leave to file the complaint and appointed a Special Master.

In 1979, the Special Master made his first report to this Court. In that report, he recommended that we reject Texas' position that the phrase "1947 condition" in the Compact should be taken to mean an artificial condition as described by the 1947 Study, however erroneous the data in that study might have been. Instead, he concluded that "[the] 1947 condition is that situation in the Pecos River Basin which produced in New Mexico the man-made depletions resulting from the stage of development existing at the beginning of the year 1947 * * * ," and that a new Inflow-Outflow Manual was required. We approved the report in full.

Over the following two years, the Special Master received evidence on the question of what corrections to the 1947 Study and the Inflow-Outflow Manual were required to produce an accurate description of the 1947 condition, and thus of New Mexico's obligations under Art. III(a) of the Compact. In his 1982 Report, however, he concluded that resolution of these issues would require that we "exercise administrative powers delegated to the [Pecos River Commission]" and that "such exercise of administrative power is beyond the judicial function." Recognizing that the Commission would be unlikely to act by unanimous vote of both

---

to the United States Commissioner (also chairman of the engineering committee and principal author of the 1947 Study and Inflow-Outflow Manual) died. The New Mexico and United States Commissioners (the latter an important force in the original compact negotiations) retired. Thus, by late 1968, administration of the Compact was largely in the hands of people with no personal connection to the Commission's early work.

State Commissioners, and that continued impasse favored the upstream State, the Special Master recommended:

> [The] equity powers of the Court are adequate to provide a remedy. If within a reasonable time * * * the States do not agree on a tie-breaking procedure, the Court would be justified in ordering * * * that either the representative of the United States, or some other third-party, be designated and empowered to participate in all Commission deliberations and act decisively when the States are not in agreement. The order should provide that the decision of the tie-breaker is final, subject only to appropriate review by the Court. Upon the selection of a tie-breaker, the States should be ordered to return to the Commission for determination of this long-standing controversy.

At the same time, the Special Master rejected two pending motions, one by New Mexico for dismissal of the case altogether, and one by Texas to adopt a simpler method than the Inflow-Outflow Manual provides for determining the extent of shortfalls in state-line water deliveries.

Both the United States and New Mexico have filed exceptions to the Special Master's key recommendation—that either the United States Commissioner or some other third party be given a vote on the Pecos River Commission and empowered to participate in all Commission deliberations. We sustain their exceptions.

Under the Compact Clause, two States may not conclude an agreement such as the Pecos River Compact without the consent of the United States Congress. However, once given, "congressional consent transforms an interstate compact within this Clause into a law of the United States." One consequence of this metamorphosis is that, unless the compact to which Congress has consented is somehow unconstitutional, no court may order relief inconsistent with its express terms. Yet that is precisely what the Special Master has recommended. The Pecos River Compact clearly delimits the role of the United States Commissioner. Although the United States Commissioner must be present at a Commission meeting in order to provide a quorum and serves as its presiding officer, and although the engineering advisers to the United States Commissioner have consistently participated fully in the work of the various engineering committees and subcommittees, the Compact specifies that "the Commissioner representing the United States * * * shall not have the right to vote in any of the deliberations of the Commission." No other third party is given the right to vote on matters before the Commission. To provide a third, tie-breaking vote on regular Commission business would be to alter fundamentally the structure of the Commission.

Congress may vest a federal official with the responsibility to administer the division of interstate streams. Other interstate compacts, approved by Congress contemporaneously with the Pecos River Compact, allow federal representatives a vote on compact-created commissions, or expressly provide for arbitration by federal officials of commission disputes. *E.g.*, Upper Colorado Basin Compact, 63 Stat. 31, 35–37; Arkansas River Compact, 63 Stat. 145, 149–151; Yellowstone

River Compact, 65 Stat. 663, 665–666. The Pecos River Compact clearly lacks the features of these other compacts, and we are not free to rewrite it.

Without doubt, the structural likelihood of impasse on the Pecos River Commission is a serious matter. In light of other States' experience, Texas and New Mexico might well consider amending their Compact to provide for some mutually acceptable method for resolving paralyzing impasses such as the one that gave rise to this suit. Nevertheless, the States' failure to agree on one issue, however important, does not render the Compact void, nor does it provide a justification for altering its structure by judicial decree. The Commission has acted on many matters by unanimous vote. We cannot say whether unanimity would have been achieved had a tie breaker stood ready to endorse one State's position over the other's. Under the Compact as it now stands, the solution for impasse is judicial resolution of such disputes as are amenable to judicial resolution, and further negotiation for those disputes that are not.

Texas, in support of the Special Master's recommendation, argues that reformation of the Compact is within this Court's equitable powers. Indeed, in its complaint Texas specifically requested that we appoint a Master "to control the diversion, storage and use of [the] Pecos River Basin waters within the State of New Mexico"; given the scope of the Commission's mandate, a tie breaker on the Commission would be the functional equivalent of such a Master. Texas has not, however, identified a single instance where we have granted similar relief.[11] We have expressly refused to make indefinite appointments of quasi-administrative officials to control the division of interstate waters on a day-to-day basis, even with the consent of the States involved. Continuing supervision by this Court of water decrees would test the limits of proper judicial functions, and we have thought it wise not to undertake such a project.

In the alternative, the Special Master recommends "continuance of [this] suit as presently postured." New Mexico excepts to this recommendation insofar as it embodies a certain conception of this Court's role in resolving the present dispute. It contends that this Court may do nothing more than review official actions of the Pecos River Commission, on the deferential model of judicial review of administrative action by a federal agency, and that this case should be dismissed if we find either that there is no Commission action to review or that the actions the Commission has taken were not arbitrary or capricious. Thus, in New Mexico's view, this suit may be maintained only as one for judicial review of the Commission's quantification of the 1950–1961 shortfall, and the implied acceptance of the Review of Basic Data which, New Mexico argues, that entailed. According to

[11] On occasion in the past, before the device of appointing special masters in original jurisdiction cases became common, we have gone so far as to appoint a commission with broad powers to resolve factual questions in a controversy between two States, *see Iowa v. Illinois*, 147 U.S. 1 (1893), but even then we declined to accept the commission's decisions without providing the States an opportunity to challenge them, *see Iowa v. Illinois*, 151 U.S. 238 (1894). We have, however, been willing to appoint a River Master solely to perform ministerial tasks. *New Jersey v. New York*, 347 U.S. 995 (1954).

New Mexico, "[this] Court has no authority to act *de novo* or assume the powers of the Pecos River Commission." We disagree.

There is no doubt that this Court's jurisdiction to resolve controversies between two States extends to a properly framed suit to apportion the waters of an interstate stream between States through which it flows, or to a suit to enforce a prior apportionment. It also extends to a suit by one State to enforce its compact with another State or to declare rights under a compact. If there is a compact, it is a law of the United States and our first and last order of business is interpreting the compact. "Where Congress has so exercised its constitutional power over waters, courts have no power to substitute their own notions of an 'equitable apportionment' for the apportionment chosen by Congress." Nevertheless, the mere existence of a compact does not foreclose the possibility that we will be required to resolve a dispute between the compacting States.

The question for decision, therefore, is what role the Pecos River Compact leaves to this Court. The Compact itself does not expressly address the rights of the States to seek relief in the Supreme Court, although it clearly contemplates some independent exercise of judicial authority.[14] Fundamental structural considerations, however, militate against New Mexico's theory. First, if all questions under the Compact had to be decided by the Commission in the first instance, New Mexico could indefinitely prevent authoritative Commission action solely by exercising its veto on the Commission. As New Mexico is the upstream State, with effective power to deny water altogether to Texas except under extreme flood conditions, the Commission's failure to take action to enforce New Mexico's obligations would invariably work to New Mexico's benefit. Under New Mexico's interpretation, this Court would be powerless to grant Texas relief on its claim under the Compact.

If it were clear that the Pecos River Commission was intended to be the exclusive forum for disputes between the States, then we would withdraw. But the express terms of the Pecos River Compact do not constitute the Commission as the sole arbiter of disputes between the States over New Mexico's Art. III obligations. Our equitable power to apportion interstate streams and the power of the States and Congress acting in concert to accomplish the same result are to a large extent

[14] Article V(f) provides: "Findings of fact made by the Commission shall not be conclusive in any court, or before any agency or tribunal, but shall constitute prima facie evidence of the facts found." That language is ambiguous as to the role of the Supreme Court, but an earlier version of Art. V(f)—one that was proposed by New Mexico—sheds further light: "The findings of the Commission shall not be conclusive in any court or tribunal which may be called upon to interpret or enforce this Compact." Since the only parties with rights and duties to be enforced under any draft of the Compact were the United States and the two signatory States, it is clear that the New Mexico draft reflected the assumption that this Court might be called upon to enforce the Compact. Article V(f) assumed its present from at a late stage in the negotiations and with no discussion on the record; its change was most likely due to the efforts of a federal drafting expert brought in after all significant disputes had been resolved. In the light of the other factors discussed in text, we need not consider whether, standing alone, this history would be dispositive.

complementary. Texas' right to invoke the original jurisdiction of this Court was an important part of the context in which the Compact was framed; indeed, the threat of such litigation undoubtedly contributed to New Mexico's willingness to enter into a compact. It is difficult to conceive that Texas would trade away its right to seek an equitable apportionment of the river in return for a promise that New Mexico could, for all practical purposes, avoid at will.[16] In the absence of an explicit provision or other clear indications that a bargain to that effect was made, we shall not construe a compact to preclude a State from seeking judicial relief when the compact does not provide an equivalent method of vindicating the State's rights.

Considerations outside the Compact itself also render New Mexico's theory of the role of this Court untenable. According to New Mexico, Texas *may* seek judicial review in this Court of decisions actually made by the Commission—presumably on the votes of both States' Commissioners. That is not the proper function of our original jurisdiction to decide controversies between two States. In recent years, we have consistently interpreted 28 U.S.C. § 1251(a) as providing us with substantial discretion to make case-by-case judgments as to the practical necessity of an original forum in this Court for particular disputes within our constitutional original jurisdiction. We exercise that discretion with an eye to promoting the most effective functioning of this Court within the overall federal system. If authorized representatives of the compacting States have reached an agreement within the scope of their congressionally ratified powers, recourse to this Court when one State has second thoughts is hardly "necessary for the State's protection." *Massachusetts v. Missouri*, 308 U.S. 1, 18 (1939).[18] Absent extraordinary cause, we shall not review the Pecos River Commission's actions without a more precise mandate from Congress than either the Compact or 28 U.S.C. § 1251 provides.

Therefore, we accept the Special Master's alternative recommendation that this suit continue as presently framed.

. . . .

Time and again we have counseled States engaged in litigation with one another before this Court that their dispute "is one more likely to be wisely solved by co-operative study and by conference and mutual concession on the part of representatives of the States so vitally interested in it than by proceedings in any court however constituted." *New York v. New Jersey*, 256 U.S. 296, 313 (1921); *cf. Vermont v. New York*, 417 U.S. [270,] 277–278 [(1974)]; *Minnesota v. Wisconsin*, 252 U.S. 273, 283 (1920); *Washington v. Oregon*, 214 U.S. 205, 218 (1909). It is within this Court's power to determine whether New Mexico is in compliance with Art. III(a) of the Pecos River Compact, but it is difficult to believe that the

---

[16] Note that under Art. XIV of the Compact Texas may withdraw from the Compact only with the concurrence of the New Mexico State Legislature.

[18] . . . When it is able to act, the Commission is a completely adequate means for vindicating either State's interests. The need for burdensome original jurisdiction litigation, which prevents this Court from attending to its appellate docket, would seem slight.

bona fide differences in the two States' views of how much water Texas is entitled to receive justify the expense and time necessary to obtain a judicial resolution of this controversy. With that observation, we return this case to the Special Master for determination of the unresolved issues framed in his pretrial order, in a manner consistent with this opinion.

Notes & Questions

1. *Texas v. New Mexico* is most often cited for holding that the court cannot order relief inconsistent with the compact. However, it was not the first case to suggest this legal principle. As early as 1823, in *Green v. Biddle*, the Supreme Court was uncomfortable modifying the terms of a compact, stating:

> Various objections were made to the literal construction of the compact, one only of which we deem it necessary particularly to notice. That was, that if it be so construed as to deny to the legislature of Kentucky the right to pass the act in question, it will follow, that that State cannot pass laws to affect lands, the title to which was derived under Virginia, although the same should be wanted for public use. If such a consequence grows necessarily out of this provision of the compact, still we can perceive no reason why the assent to it by the people of Kentucky should not be binding on the legislature of that State.

21 U.S. at 88–89. In *Texas v. New Mexico*, the Supreme Court invoked *Green v. Biddle* addressing the Supreme Court's jurisdiction:

> An argument was made [in *Green v. Biddle*]—similar to New Mexico's argument in this case—that disputes concerning the compact could only be resolved by a commission to be appointed under the terms of the agreement, and not by the courts that would ordinarily resolve questions of title to land. We rejected the argument because the possibility that one State could defeat the rights of the other's citizens or allow the occupants of the land to enrich themselves without title simply by refusing to appoint commissioners "is too monstrous to be for a moment entertained. The best feelings of our nature revolt against a construction which leads to it." [*Green v. Biddle*, 21 U.S.] at 91.

462 U.S. at 570 n.17. Why shouldn't the Supreme Court fashion an equitable remedy in a case that was serious enough for the Supreme Court to allow an original action in the first place, and for which there is no alternative judicial forum?

2. New Mexico's argument, referred to in the above quote of footnote 17, was that the Supreme Court could do "nothing more than review official actions of the Pecos River Commission, on the deferential model of judicial review of administrative action by a federal agency . . . ." *Id.* at 566–67. The Court succinctly responded, "There is no doubt that this Court's jurisdiction to resolve controversies between two States . . . extends to a properly framed suit to apportion the waters of an interstate stream between States through which it flows. . . . It also extends to a suit by one State to enforce its compact with another State or to de-

clare rights under a compact." *Id.* at 567. Finally, the Court noted that the "express terms of the Pecos River Compact do not constitute the Commission as the sole arbiter of disputes between the States over New Mexico's Art. III obligations." *Id.* at 569. The Supreme Court had already granted leave for Texas to file the complaint under the Court's original jurisdiction, so this may not have been one of New Mexico's better arguments.

In *Alabama v. North Carolina*, 560 U.S. 330 (2010), Alabama and the other plaintiff states surprisingly made the same argument as New Mexico did in *Texas v. New Mexico*—that the Southeast Interstate Compact for Low-Level Radioactive Waste Management made the compact commission the "sole arbiter" regarding North Carolina's compliance with the compact, and thus the Court must defer to the commission's finding that North Carolina violated the compact. The Supreme Court reviewed numerous provisions of the compact and concluded that while the commission had "authority to interpret the Compact or to say whether a party State has violated its terms," the compact did not make the commission the sole arbiter of compliance. *Id.* at 344. Alabama made this argument after initiating the original jurisdiction action, which might have made the Supreme Court hostile to that argument.

3. In *Alabama v. North Carolina*, the Supreme Court also expressly addressed for the first time whether there is an implied duty of good faith and fair dealing between parties to a compact. The Court concluded there was not:

> "We have never held that an interstate compact approved by Congress includes an implied duty of good faith and fair dealing. Of course "[e]very contract imposes upon each party a duty of good faith and fair dealing in its performance and its enforcement." [Restatement (Second) of Contracts § 205 (1979)]. But an interstate compact is not just a contract; it is a federal statute enacted by Congress. If court were authorized to add a fairness requirement to the implementation of federal statutes, judges would be potent lawmakers indeed. We do not—we cannot—add provisions to a federal statute. And in that regard a statute which is a valid interstate compact is no different."

560 U.S. at 351–52. Few compacts have such a good faith and fair dealings provision. The Great Lakes-St. Lawrence River Basin Water Resources Compact is an example of a compact that specifically requires good faith. Article 7, section 7.1 is titled, "Good Faith Implementation" and states, "Each of the Parties pledges to support implementation of all provisions of this Compact, and covenants that its officers and agencies shall not hinder, impair, or prevent any other Party carrying out any provision of this Compact." Do you agree with the Supreme Court that there is no implied duty of good faith and fair dealing in compacts that qualify as federal law? What about compacts that do not require consent?

4. In 1987, the Supreme Court accepted a recommendation for resolution from the Special Master.

> [T]he Master has recommended that because applying the approved apportionment formula is not entirely mechanical and involves a degree of

> judgment, an additional enforcement mechanism be supplied. We accept his recommendation and also his preferred solution: the appointment of a River Master to make the required periodic calculations. In 1983, because we thought the Compact foreclosed it, we declined to order a tie breaker in order that the Commission itself could arrive at a method to allocate water. We accordingly proceeded in the litigative mode to construe and enforce the Compact, asserting our authority to do so in unequivocal terms. We have arrived at what we deem to be a fair and equitable solution that is consistent with the Compact terms, and we are quite sure that our jurisdiction over original actions like this provides us with ample authority to appoint a master and to enforce our judgment.
>
> In exercising this power, we have taken a distinctly jaundiced view of appointing an agent or functionary to implement our decrees. *Vermont v. New York*, 417 U.S. 270 (1974), emphatically expressed this reluctance. But as we recognized, that solution, or a like one, has been employed when the occasion demands. *New Jersey v. New York*, 283 U.S. 805 (1931); *Wisconsin v. Illinois*, 281 U.S. 179 (1930). This is one of those occasions when such a mechanism should be employed. The natural propensity of these two States to disagree if an allocation formula leaves room to do so cannot be ignored. Absent some disinterested authority to make determinations binding on the parties, we could anticipate a series of original actions to determine the periodic division of the water flowing in the Pecos.

Texas v. New Mexico, 482 U.S. 124, 134 (1987).

5. In 1988, the Supreme Court issued its final order in this *Texas v. New Mexico* proceeding. The introductory paragraphs state:

> Last Term we issued a decree in this case which enjoined the State of New Mexico "to comply with its Article III(a) obligation under the Pecos River Compact and to determine the extent of its obligation in accordance with the formula approved by the decisions of this Court." *Texas v. New Mexico*, 482 U.S. 124, 133 (1987). We retained jurisdiction for the purpose of any order, direction, or modification of the decree as might be deemed proper. In particular, we approved the Special Master's recommendation that a River Master be appointed in this case, and requested that on remand the Special Master "recommend an amendment to the decree, specifying as he deems necessary the duties of the River Master and the consequences of his determinations. Any other suggestions for amendments should also be called to our attention." *Id.* at 135.
>
> The Special Master has now submitted a report, which includes a proposed amended decree. New Mexico's motion for leave to file a reply brief is granted. New Mexico's exceptions to the report are overruled. The report is approved and an amended decree will issue forthwith. The Special Master has also recommended a person to serve as River Master. We accept that recommendation.

Texas v. New Mexico, 485 U.S. 388, 388–89 (1988). The decree sets out the duties of the river master, which, consistent with the Supreme Court's admonition in the 1983 case, are ministerial in nature. The decree also specifically states that its provisions do not displace the authority of the Pecos River Commission. Disputes between the states continue to this date. In April 2020, the Supreme Court was scheduled to hear objections to the River Master's calculation of delivery credits for evaporation losses under the Compact. The Supreme Court postponed the argument to its October 2020 term.

6. If Texas and New Mexico could never agree on a new model for allocation, and the Supreme Court was unwilling to apply an equitable remedy, then is the only option for the states to repeal the compact? What would be New Mexico's incentive to repeal the compact when it had been the beneficiary of the faulty modeling? If Texas could not breach the compact by withdrawing, then should the court allow an equitable remedy of allowing Texas to withdraw in the absence of any withdrawal provision in the compact?

7. In *Texas v. New* Mexico, neither party had breached the compact. Where a state does breach a compact, what equitable remedies (other than those specified in the compact) should a court be able to impose? The Court considered this question in *Kansas v. Nebraska*, the next case excerpt.

Kansas v. Nebraska
574 U.S. 445 (2015)

KAGAN, JUSTICE:

For the second time in little more than a decade, Kansas and Nebraska ask this Court to settle a dispute over the States' rights to the waters of the Republican River Basin, as set out in an interstate compact. The first round of litigation ended with a settlement agreement designed to elaborate on, and promote future compliance with, the Compact's terms. The States now bring new claims against each other arising from the implementation of that settlement. Kansas seeks exceptional relief—both partial disgorgement of gains and an injunction—for Nebraska's conceded overconsumption of water. For its part, Nebraska requests amendment of a technical appendix to the settlement, so that allocations of water will faithfully reflect the parties' intent as expressed in both the body of that agreement and the Compact itself. We referred the case to a Special Master and now accept his recommendations as to appropriate equitable remedies: for Kansas, partial disgorgement but no injunction; and for Nebraska, reform of the appendix.

. . . .

After two years of conducting hearings, receiving evidence, and entertaining legal arguments, the Special Master issued his report and recommendations. The Master concluded that Nebraska had "knowingly failed" to comply with the Compact in the 2005–2006 accounting period, by consuming 70,869 acre-feet of water in excess of its prescribed share. To remedy that breach, the Master proposed awarding Kansas $3.7 million for its loss, and another $1.8 million in partial disgorgement of Nebraska's still greater gains. The Master, however, thought that an injunction against Nebraska was not warranted. . . .

. . . .

The Constitution gives this Court original jurisdiction to hear suits between the States. Proceedings under that grant of jurisdiction are "basically equitable in nature." *Ohio v. Kentucky*, 410 U.S. 641, 648 (1973). When the Court exercises its original jurisdiction over a controversy between two States, it serves "as a substitute for the diplomatic settlement of controversies between sovereigns and a possible resort to force." *North Dakota v. Minnesota*, 263 U.S. 365, 372–373 (1923). That role significantly "differ[s] from" the one the Court undertakes "in suits between private parties." *Id.* at 372; *see* Frankfurter & Landis, *The Compact Clause of the Constitution—A Study in Interstate Adjustments*, 34 YALE L.J. 685, 705 (1925) (When a "controversy concerns two States we are at once in a world wholly different from that of a law-suit between John Doe and Richard Roe over the metes and bounds of Blackacre"). In this singular sphere, "the court may regulate and mould the process it uses in such a manner as in its judgment will best promote the purposes of justice." *Kentucky v. Dennison*, 24 How. 66, 98 (1861).

Two particular features of this interstate controversy further distinguish it from a run-of-the-mill private suit and highlight the essentially equitable character of our charge. The first relates to the subject matter of the Compact and Settlement: rights to an interstate waterway. The second concerns the Compact's status as not just an agreement, but a federal law. Before proceeding to the merits of this dispute, we say a few words about each.

This Court has recognized for more than a century its inherent authority, as part of the Constitution's grant of original jurisdiction, to equitably apportion interstate streams between States. In *Kansas v. Colorado*, 185 U.S. 125, 145 (1902), we confronted a simple consequence of geography: An upstream State can appropriate all water from a river, thus "wholly depriv[ing]" a downstream State "of the benefit of water" that "by nature" would flow into its territory. In such a circumstance, the downstream State lacks the sovereign's usual power to respond—the capacity to "make war[,] . . . grant letters of marque and reprisal," or even enter into agreements without the consent of Congress. *Id.* at 143 (internal quotation marks omitted). "Bound hand and foot by the prohibitions of the Constitution, . . . a resort to the judicial power is the only means left" for stopping an inequitable taking of water. *Id.* at 144 (quoting *Rhode Island v. Massachusetts*, 12 Pet. 657, 726 (1838)).

This Court's authority to apportion interstate streams encourages States to enter into compacts with each other. When the division of water is not "left to the pleasure" of the upstream State, but States instead "know[] that some tribunal can decide on the right," then "controversies will [probably] be settled by compact." *Kansas v. Colorado*, 185 U.S. at 144. And that, of course, is what happened here: Kansas and Nebraska negotiated a compact to divide the waters of the Republican River and its tributaries. Our role thus shifts: It is now to declare rights under the Compact and enforce its terms. *See Texas v. New Mexico*, 462 U.S. 554, 567 (1983).

But in doing so, we remain aware that the States bargained for those rights in the shadow of our equitable apportionment power—that is, our capacity to prevent one State from taking advantage of another. Each State's "right to invoke the original jurisdiction of this Court [is] an important part of the context" in which any compact is made. *Id.* at 569. And it is "difficult to conceive" that a downstream State "would trade away its right" to our equitable apportionment if, under such an agreement, an upstream State could avoid its obligations or otherwise continue overreaching. *Id.* Accordingly, our enforcement authority includes the ability to provide the remedies necessary to prevent abuse. We may invoke equitable principles, so long as consistent with the compact itself, to devise "fair . . . solution[s]" to the state-parties' disputes and provide effective relief for their violations. *Texas v. New Mexico*, 482 U.S. 124, 134 (1987) (supplying an "additional enforcement mechanism" to ensure an upstream State's compliance with a compact).

And that remedial authority gains still greater force because the Compact, having received Congress's blessing, counts as federal law. *See Cuyler v. Adams*, 449 U.S. 433, 438 (1981) ("[C]ongressional consent transforms an interstate compact . . . into a law of the United States"). Of course, that legal status underscores a limit on our enforcement power: We may not "order relief inconsistent with [a compact's] express terms." *Texas v. New Mexico*, 462 U.S. at 564. But within those limits, the Court may exercise its full authority to remedy violations of and promote compliance with the agreement, so as to give complete effect to public law. As we have previously put the point: When federal law is at issue and "the public interest is involved," a federal court's "equitable powers assume an even broader and more flexible character than when only a private controversy is at stake." *Porter v. Warner Holding Co.*, 328 U.S. 395, 398 (1946); *see Virginian R. Co. v. Railway Employees*, 300 U.S. 515, 552 (1937) ("Courts of equity may, and frequently do, go much farther" to give "relief in furtherance of the public interest than they are accustomed to go when only private interests are involved exercising our jurisdiction, we may "mould each decree to the necessities of the particular case" and "accord full justice" to all parties. *Porter*, 328 U.S. at 398 (internal quotation marks omitted); see *Kentucky v. Dennison*, 65 U.S. at 98. These principles inform our consideration of the dispute before us.

. . . .

. . . [T]he case for disgorgement becomes still stronger when one State gambles with another State's rights to a scarce natural resource. From the time this Court began to apportion interstate rivers, it has recognized part of its role as guarding against upstream States' inequitable takings of water. And as we have noted, that concern persists even after States enter into a compact: This Court may then exercise remedial authority to ensure compliance with the compact's terms—thus preventing a geographically favored State from appropriating more than its share of a river. Indeed, the formation of such a compact provides this Court with enhanced remedial power because, as we have described, the agreement is also an

Act of Congress, and its breach a violation of federal law. *See Porter*, 328 U.S. 395 (exercising equitable power to disgorge profits gained from violating a federal statute). Consistent with those principles, we have stated that awarding actual damages for a compact's infringement may be inadequate, because that remedy alone "would permit [an upstream State] to ignore its obligation to deliver water as long as it is willing" to pay that amount. *Texas v. New Mexico*, 482 U.S. at 132. And as the Solicitor General noted in argument here, "[i]t is important that water flows down the river, not just money." Tr. of Oral Arg. 24. Accordingly, this Court may order disgorgement of gains, if needed to stabilize a compact and deter future breaches, when a State has demonstrated reckless disregard of another, more vulnerable State's rights under that instrument.

Assessed in this light, a disgorgement order constitutes a "fair and equitable" remedy for Nebraska's breach. *Texas v. New Mexico*, 482 U.S. at 134. "Possessing the privilege of being upstream," Nebraska can (physically, though not legally) drain all the water it wants from the Republican River. Report 130. And the higher value of water on Nebraska's farmland than on Kansas's means that Nebraska can take water that under the Compact should go to Kansas, pay Kansas actual damages, and still come out ahead. That is nearly a recipe for breach—for an upstream State to refuse to deliver to its downstream neighbor the water to which the latter is entitled. And through 2006, Nebraska took full advantage of its favorable position, eschewing steps that would effectively control groundwater pumping and thus exceeding its allotment. In such circumstances, a disgorgement award appropriately reminds Nebraska of its legal obligations, deters future violations, and promotes the Compact's successful administration. *See Porter*, 328 U.S. at 400 ("Future compliance may be more definitely assured if one is compelled to restore one's illegal gains"). We thus reject Nebraska's exception to the Master's proposed remedy.

. . .

Notes & Questions

1. Do you agree that the Supreme Court should impose equitable remedies that the compact did not specify? The Supreme Court reconciled its action with its prior direction in *Texas v. New Mexico* that a court may not order relief inconsistent with a compact? Does it make sense that a court can order a remedy not specified in a compact after finding a breach of the compact, but not to prevent a state from breaching a compact?

2. In *Texas v. New Mexico*, the Court stated, "In the absence of an explicit provision or other clear indications that a bargain to that effect was made, we shall not construe a compact to preclude a State from seeking judicial review when the compact does not provide an equivalent method of vindicating the State's rights." 462 U.S. at 569–70. In *New York v. Atl. States Marine Fisheries Comm'n* (excerpted in Chapter 10), the Second Circuit's decision effectively eliminated judicial review of fishery management plans at the time of their adoption. Should the Second Circuit have construed the compact governing the commission to have allowed regulated persons some ability to seek judicial review?

3. In *Texas v. New Mexico*, the Supreme Court disagreed with the special master, but in *Kansas v. Nebraska*, the Court generally deferred to the special master. Deference to special masters is common because the Court uses special masters to conduct factfinding and appellate courts typically defer to lower courts' determinations of facts. However, one recent article suggests that deference to special masters in water disputes leads to unpredictable and unstructured process and outcomes. *See* L. Elizabeth Sarine, *The Supreme Court's Problematic Deference to Special Masters in Interstate Water Disputes*, 39 ECOL. L.Q. 535 (2012).

4. Enforcement actions between the parties can take many forms. In *Illinois v. Chicago,* 137 F.3d 474 (7th Cir. 1998), Illinois and Indiana granted authority for the cities of Chicago, Illinois and Gary, Indiana to enter into a regional airport agreement. Illinois's suit claimed that the agreement was not a compact between "states." The court observed that this could also be a claim that Chicago acted beyond the scope of its authority (which would need to have been brought in state court). The court dismissed the case for lack of standing because Illinois could not sue to enforce its own interpretation of its own statute.

5. Should courts give special consideration to compact implementation records maintained by a compact agency? In *State v. Eldert*, 199 Vt. 520, 532–33 (2015), the Vermont Supreme Court concluded that records from the Interstate Compact Offender Tracking System (ICOTS) were not reliable enough for a court to deny a right to confrontation and to rely on the documents even though they are hearsay. This is a curious result because article V of the Interstate Compact for Adult Offender Supervision specifically authorizes the Interstate Commission for Adult Offender Supervision (Interstate Commission), "To establish uniform standards for the reporting, collecting, and exchanging of data." If neither the compact nor the Interstate Commission's rules specifically require states to admit ICOTS documents as reliable, should courts do so anyway as natural part of compact administration?

II. Enforcement by the Compact Agency

Not all compact enforcement must be by state-versus-state litigation. Many newer compacts specify detailed means for a compact agency to enforce the compact and resolve interstate disputes that could otherwise result in litigation, including taking enforcement action against persons and party states. The 2002 Interstate Compact for the Supervision of Adult Offenders contains several such provisions.

Interstate Compact for the Supervision of Adult Offenders

ARTICLE IX

OVERSIGHT, ENFORCEMENT, AND DISPUTE RESOLUTION BY THE INTERSTATE COMMISSION

. . . .

Section B. Dispute Resolution

The Compacting States shall report to the Interstate Commission on issues or activities of concern to them, and cooperate with and support the Interstate Commission in the discharge of its duties and responsibilities.

The Interstate Commission shall attempt to resolve any disputes or other issues which are subject to the Compact and which may arise among Compacting States and Non-compacting States.

The Interstate Commission shall enact a By-law or promulgate a Rule providing for both mediation and binding dispute resolution for disputes among the Compacting States.

. . . .

ARTICLE XII

WITHDRAWAL, DEFAULT, TERMINATION, AND JUDICIAL ENFORCEMENT

. . . .

Section B. Default

If the Interstate Commission determines that any Compacting State has at any time defaulted ("Defaulting State") in the performance of any of its obligations or responsibilities under this Compact, the By-laws or any duly promulgated Rules the Interstate Commission may impose any or all of the following penalties: Fines, fees and costs in such amounts as are deemed to be reasonable as fixed by the Interstate Commission; Remedial training and technical assistance as directed by the Interstate Commission; Suspension and termination of membership in the compact. Suspension shall be imposed only after all other reasonable means of securing compliance under the By-laws and Rules have been exhausted. Immediate notice of suspension shall be given by the Interstate Commission to the Governor, the Chief Justice or Chief Judicial Officer of the state; the majority and minority leaders of the defaulting state's legislature, and the State Council.

The grounds for default include, but are not limited to, failure of a Compacting State to perform such obligations or responsibilities imposed upon it by this compact, Interstate Commission By-laws, or duly promulgated Rules. The Interstate Commission shall immediately notify the Defaulting State in writing of the penalty imposed by the Interstate Commission on the Defaulting State pending a cure of the default. The Interstate Commission shall stipulate the conditions and the time period within which the Defaulting State must cure its default. If the Defaulting State fails to cure the default within the time period specified by the Interstate Commission, in addition to any other penalties imposed herein, the Defaulting State may be terminated from the Compact upon an affirmative vote of a majority of the Compacting States and all rights, privileges and benefits conferred by this Compact shall be terminated from the effective date of suspension. Within sixty days of the effective date of termination of a Defaulting State, the Interstate Commission shall notify the Governor, the Chief Justice or Chief Judicial Officer and the Majority and Minority Leaders of the Defaulting State's legislature and the state council of such termination.

The Defaulting State is responsible for all assessments, obligations and liabilities incurred through the effective date of termination including any obligations, the performance of which extends beyond the effective date of termination. The Interstate Commission shall not bear any costs relating to the Defaulting State unless otherwise mutually agreed upon between the Interstate Commission and the Defaulting State. Reinstatement following termination of any Compacting State requires both a reenactment of the Compact by the Defaulting State and the approval of the Interstate Commission pursuant to the Rules.

Section C. Judicial Enforcement

The Interstate Commission may, by majority vote of the Members, initiate legal action in the United States District Court for the District of Columbia or, at the discretion of the Interstate Commission, in the Federal District where the Interstate Commission has its offices to enforce compliance with the provisions of the Compact, its duly promulgated Rules and By-laws, against any Compacting State in default. In the event judicial enforcement is necessary the prevailing party shall be awarded all costs of such litigation including reasonable attorneys fees.

. . . .

ARTICLE XIV

BINDING EFFECT OF COMPACT AND OTHER LAWS

. . . .

Section B. Binding Effect of the Compact

. . . .

Upon the request of a party to a conflict over meaning or interpretation of Interstate Commission actions, and upon a majority vote of the Compacting States, the Interstate Commission may issue advisory opinions regarding such meaning or interpretation.

. . . .

Notes & Questions

1. What do you think about these different ways of facilitating or ensuring compliance with the compact? To help the party states and regulated persons comply with the compact and commission rules, the website for the Interstate Commission for Adult Offender Supervision, www.interstatecompact.org, contains copies of the commission's internal dispute resolution actions, court actions, and advisory opinions. To assist courts in enforcing compliance with the compact, the

commission prepared and regularly updates a "Bench Book for Judges and Court Personnel" explaining the compact and containing discussion of its dispute resolution actions. Courts routinely cite and enforce the commission's rules, advisory opinions, and Bench Book. *See, e.g.*, *Longson v. Nebraska*, No. 4:18CV3036, 2018 U.S. Dist. LEXIS 46874 (D. Nev. Mar. 22, 2018) (taking judicial notice of "all the information" in the interstate compact, commission's rules, and Bench Book); *State v. Brown*, 140 A.3d 768, 776–77 n.5 (R.I. 2016) (citing ICAOS rule, advisory opinion, and Bench Book); *Johnson v. State*, 957 N.E.2d 660, 663 (Ind. Ct. App. 2011) (citing ICAOS rule); *Voerding v. Mahoney*, No. CV 09-73-H-DWM-RKS, 2010 U.S. Dist. LEXIS 32059 (D. Mont. Apr. 1, 2010) (citing ICAOS rule and advisory opinion); *In re Paul*, No. A-3905-08T2, 2010 N.J. Super. Unpub. LEXIS 1729 (N.J. Super. Ct. App. Div. Apr. 10, 2010) (citing ICAOS advisory opinion).

2. Courts tend to uphold dispute resolution actions from compact commissions that have followed a process established by bylaw or rule, even if a court has some reservations about the process. In *Oklahoma v. Int'l Registration Plan*, 455 F.3d 1107 (10th Cir. 2006), Oklahoma established that several members of the IRP's Dispute Resolution Committee were biased because they represented some of the states that had sought enforcement against Oklahoma. However, the court concluded that the compact did not require an unbiased dispute resolution process:

> [M]ember jurisdictions agreed to have disputes decided by persons with an interest in the operation and administration of the Plan, not neutral third parties. In adopting this form of dispute resolution, member jurisdictions must have expected—and accepted—that representatives from different regions might carry with them certain biases and or predispositions. Thus, unlike an adjudication in a court of law or by an arbitration panel, decision-making by a disinterested third-party is not a fundamental characteristic of the dispute resolution structure agreed to by member jurisdictions.

Id. at 1115. Why might parties to a multi-state agreement design a dispute resolution process such as in the International Registration Plan?

3. Should all compacts have robust authority for the compact agency to resolve disputes and take enforcement actions? The Interstate Commission for Adult Offender Supervision has never had to take enforcement action against any of the party states.

4. Chapter 7, Section II discussed two cases, *Entergy, Arkansas, Inc. v. Nebraska*, 201 F.3d 887 (8th Cir. 2000), and *Waterfront Comm'n of N.Y. Harbor v. Murphy*, 961 F.3d 234 (3d Cir. 2020), in which the compact agencies sued one of the member states in federal court to enforce the compact. In both cases, the district courts imposed remedies sought by the compact agencies. The Eighth Circuit affirmed the district court's jurisdiction and the remedy, but the Third Circuit concluded that the district court was without jurisdiction because New Jersey enjoyed immunity from suit in federal court. Should compact agencies be able to bring suit in federal court, or must they seek remedies against a state in that state's own courts?

III. Enforcement by Third Parties

As a contract, compacts may offer opportunities for third parties to seek enforcement of the compact. Many of the early cases were third party cases, although the issue of whether a third party properly brought the case did not arise. For example, *Green v. Biddle* involved a private-party claim that a statute violated the Virginia-Kentucky compact. That was, at base, a compact enforcement claim by a landowner who was benefiting from the continuing application of Virginia law. Few cases have directly addressed the question whether a third party may enforce the compact. Most cases arise under some statutory authorization—the compact itself, an adjunct statute, or the federal APA. In the next case excerpt, *Doe v. Pennsylvania Board of Probation and Parole*, the court concluded there was no right for a probationer to sue for violation of the U.S. Constitution; it then turned to a third party beneficiary analysis under contract law.

Doe v. Pa. Bd. of Prob. and Parole

513 F.3d 95 (3d Cir. 2008)

NYGAARD, JUDGE:

John Doe, an anonymous plaintiff, sued under 42 U.S.C. § 1983, seeking declaratory and injunctive relief from aspects of Pennsylvania's Registration of Sexual Offenders Act ("Megan's Law"). Pennsylvania's Megan's Law requires all convicted sex offenders to register with state and local police, and subjects certain offenders to community notification. The suit involves the application of these requirements to a Pennsylvania resident who was convicted of a sexual offense in New Jersey, and sought to return to his home state to serve his parole. Under the provisions of Pennsylvania's Megan's Law, any out-of-state sex offender who transfers his supervision to Pennsylvania is subject to community notification. By contrast, an individual who was convicted of the same offense in Pennsylvania would only be subject to community notification if, after a civil hearing, he had been designated a "sexually violent predator due to a mental abnormality or personality disorder that makes the person likely to engage in predatory sexually violent offenses." The District Court concluded that the disparate treatment of out-of-state offenders violates the Equal Protection Clause of the Fourteenth Amendment to the Constitution. The Commonwealth of Pennsylvania has appealed. We will affirm.

. . . .

The first avenue by which we may divert our decision from Constitutional issues, is to see whether a private cause of action (and remedy) exists within the Interstate Compact itself. *See Cannon v. Univ. of Chicago*, 441 U.S. 677, 688 (1979) ("[T]he fact that a federal statute has been violated and some person harmed does not automatically give rise to a private cause of action in favor of that person."). The District Court opined that Congress did not intend to create an enforceable federal right under 42 U.S.C. § 1983 for probationers and parolees through the Compact. We agree.

In *Gonzaga Univ. v. Doe*, 536 U.S. 273 (2002), the Supreme Court took up the question of whether the Family Educational Rights and Privacy Act of 1974 (FERPA) created an enforceable right under Section 1983. The Court held that an act of Congress must "unambiguously confer" individual rights upon a particular class of beneficiaries for a right of action under Section 1983 to exist. *Gonzaga*, 536 U.S. at 282–283.

To determine whether a statute creates enforceable rights, we consider two indicia of legislative intent. First, we look to statutory text for "rights creating language." *Alexander v. Sandoval*, 532 U.S. 275, 288 (2001). Such language has generally "been the most accurate indicator of the propriety of implication of a cause of action." *Cannon*, 441 U.S. at 690 n 13. Statutory language that is "rights-creating" is explicit in conferring a right directly on a class of persons that includes the plaintiff in a particular case. *Id.* In contrast, general regulatory language or "statutory language customarily found in criminal statutes * * * and other laws enacted for the protection of the general public" provide "far less reason to infer a remedy in favor of individual persons." *Cannon,* 441 U.S. at 693. That is to say, "statutes that focus on the person regulated rather than the individuals protected create 'no implication of an intent to confer rights on a particular class of persons.'" *Sandoval*, 532 U.S. at 289

Absent "rights creating" language, we look to whether the statutory structure evinces an internal enforcement scheme. The Supreme Court advises that, where a statute provides an administrative review process, but does not provide judicial sanctions, the "express provision of one method of enforcing a substantive rule suggests that Congress intended to preclude others." *Sandoval*, 532 U.S. at 290.

Because the Compact does not manifest either expressly or indirectly an intent to create a federal right or remedy, we hold that the Compact itself does not create an enforceable right. The language of the Compact itself creates rights for the various states who are signatories to it. It does not create rights for probationers or parolees. Notably, the title under which Congress approved the Compact—"An act granting the consent of Congress to any two or more states to enter into agreements or compacts for cooperative effort and mutual assistance in the prevention of crime and for other purposes"—supports our inference that Congress approved the Compact as a means of aiding the states in crime prevention, not as a vehicle to provide procedural rights for probationers and parolees.

At the second point of inquiry, the Probation Compact regulates interactions among the states, delineating one state's rights and responsibilities to another. Regarding the strictures imposed by one state on probationers from another, the Compact described such requirements as duties that will be "governed by the same standards that prevail for its own probationers and parolees." As was the case in *Sandoval*, the Compact here focuses upon the State entities regulated by the standards, "rather than the individuals protected." *Sandoval,* 532 U.S. at 289. The Compact, we conclude, creates "no implication of an intent to confer rights on a particular class of persons." *Id.*

Lastly, the Compact has no mechanism by which to enforce the alleged "rights" of probationers or parolees. The Compact mentions neither court adjudication nor administrative proceedings. These omissions further lead us to conclude that Congress did not intend to create an enforceable federal right for probationers or parolees under this Compact.

We hold that Doe does not have a private right of action under Section 1983 to enforce the provisions of the Interstate Compact because one cannot be inferred from its terms.

However, that does not end our contractual inquiry. Interstate compacts are formal agreements between states, and hence, are contracts subject to the principles of contract law. "[A] Compact is, after all, a contract." *Petty v. Tennessee-Missouri Bridge Comm'n*, 359 U.S. 275, 285 (1959) (Frankfurter, dissenting). It remains a legal document that must be construed and applied in accordance with its terms. *Texas v. New Mexico*, 462 U.S. [554, 564 (1983)]; *West Virginia ex rel. Dyer v. Sims*, 341 U.S. 22, 28 (1951). Interstate compacts may be considered contracts because of the manner in which they are enacted: there is an offer (the presentation of a reciprocal law to state legislatures), an acceptance (the actual enactment of the law) and consideration (the settlement of a dispute or the creation of a regulatory scheme). *See Aveline v. Pa. Bd. of Prob. & Parole*, 729 A.2d 1254, 1257 n.10 (Pa. Commw. Ct. 1999).

Although a common law contract directly affects only the rights and obligations of the individual parties to it, an interstate compact may have a direct impact upon the larger population, the economy, and the physical environment in the whole of the compact area. Therefore, although Pennsylvania and New Jersey are the obvious parties to the Compact, we must decide whether Doe has any rights under this contract as a third-party beneficiary. This is an issue of first impression.

The Supreme Court has held that an interstate compact is like a contract to the extent that it is "a legal document that must be construed and applied in accordance with its terms," *Texas v. New Mexico*, 482 U.S. 124, 128 (1987). Because a compact is a contract, and must be enforced according to its terms, we do not have authority to provide relief that is inconsistent with its terms. *Texas v. New Mexico*, 462 U.S. 554, 564 (1983). When interpreting an interstate compact, we must address disputes under the compact just as if we were addressing a federal statute or a federal contract. Absent a federal statute making state statutory or common law applicable, federal law controls, and absent federal statutory guidance, the governing rule of decision must be fashioned by the federal court in the mode of the common law.

In addition to the parties to a contract, "third-party beneficiaries" of the contract can also enforce its terms. For either Pennsylvania or federal law on third-party beneficiaries we look to the Restatement of Contracts' definition. Under the Restatement, a third party can claim rights under a contract, even if not stated expressly, if it is consonant with the intention of the contracting parties. [The Restatement] states as follows:

> Intended and Incidental Beneficiaries
>
> (1) Unless otherwise agreed between promisor and promisee, a beneficiary of a promise is an intended beneficiary if recognition of a right to performance in the beneficiary is appropriate to effectuate the intentions of the parties and either
>
> (a) the performance of the promise will satisfy an obligation of the promisee to pay money to the beneficiary; or
>
> (b) the circumstances indicate that the promisee intends to give the beneficiary the benefit of the promised performance.
>
> (2) An incidental beneficiary is a beneficiary who is not an intended beneficiary.

Restatement (Second) of Contracts § 302 (1979).

Thus, we have two tests for determining third-party beneficiary status. The first one requires the parties to indicate in the agreement itself that the third party is a beneficiary. The second test does not require that the purported beneficiary be adverted to directly in the contract; but, if not, third-party status will be conferred only if circumstances compel us to recognize such a status in order to effectuate the intention of the parties.

The first test offers Doe no relief. The Interstate Compact does not specifically indicate that Doe, or for that matter any parolee, is a third-party beneficiary. Under the second test he fares no better. Here, the "intentions of the parties" must be discerned from the document itself.

The parties to this Compact have set forth their intentions quite clearly:

> It is the purpose of this compact and the Interstate Commission created hereunder, through means of joint and cooperative action among the compacting states: to provide the framework for the promotion of public safety and protection of the rights of victims through the control and regulation of the interstate movement of offenders in the community; to provide for the effective tracking, supervision, and rehabilitation of these offenders by the sending and receiving states; and to equitably distribute the costs, benefits and obligations of the compact among the compacting states.

The Compact speaks of cooperation between states, protection of the rights of victims, regulation and control of offenders across state borders and the tracking, supervision and rehabilitation of these offenders. In short, no explicit third-party obligation appears in the Compact and there is no compelling evidence that, by entering into the Compact, Pennsylvania and New Jersey implicitly intended to give legally enforceable rights to Doe. Doe and similarly situated parolees are not beneficiaries of this Compact; they are merely the subjects of it.

. . . .

Notes & Questions

1. *Doe* is one of the few cases that hold a third party beneficiary may not enforce the compact. Following *Doe*, the Second Circuit Court of Appeals subsequently held the Interstate Compact for the Supervision of Adult Offenders (the successor to the Probation Compact at issue in *Doe*) did not provide a private right of action for a probationer to claim that a state violated the compact. *M.F. v. N.Y. Exec. Dep't, Div. of Parole*, 640 F.3d 491 (2d Cir. 2011). In *Buckingham Twp. v. Wykle*, 157 F. Supp. 2d 457 (E.D. Pa. 2001), the court stated there was no private right of action conferred by the Delaware Valley Regional Planning Compact, but without any of the detailed analysis in *Doe* and without citation to any authority. *Id.* at 466.

2. Many cases mention that a compact is a contract, but few treat a compact as a contract as explicitly as the Third Circuit here. Why would that be? Do the cases typically involve statutory construction issues? Is the method for interpretation of a statute similar enough to the method for interpretation of a contract that the courts stop after applying only one interpretative methodology?

3. In setting up its third party beneficiary analysis, the Third Circuit cited to *Texas v. New Mexico*, which, as you read above, involved a state seeking to enforce a compact against another state, and to *West Virginia ex rel. Dyer v. Sims*, which as you read in Chapter 3, involved a state seeking to mandate that one of its own state officials comply with a compact. Is a third party beneficiary case similar to these situations?

4. There is rarely any question whether non-parties to a compact, *i.e.*, third parties, may seek to enforce a compact. For example, in *Borough of Morrisville v. Delaware River Basin Comm'n*, 399 F. Supp. 469 (E.D. Pa. 1975), the court considered whether several municipalities had standing to challenge a DRBC resolution that imposed a charge for consumptive use of water (that is, water used but not replaced). The court reasoned, "to hold that the Compact is an agreement between political signatories imputing only to those signatories standing to challenge actions pursuant to it would be unduly narrow in view of the direct impact on plaintiffs and other taxpayers." *Id.* at 472 n.3.

In *Texas v. New Mexico*, 138 S. Ct. 954 (2018), the Supreme Court concluded that the United States could intervene in a case involving Texas's claim that New Mexico was violating the Rio Grande Compact. The United States is not a party to the Rio Grande Compact, but the compact has consent. The Supreme Court did not analyze the United States as a third party beneficiary, but the Supreme Court recognized the unique interest of the United States in the litigation, in part because if the states did not fulfill their compact obligations, the United States might not be able to fulfill a treaty obligation with Mexico. In this situation, should the United States be considered a third party beneficiary that may initiate enforcement of the compact as opposed to merely participating in the states' existing litigation? Consider the Supreme Court's decision in *Se. Interstate Low-Level Radioactive Waste Mgmt. Comm'n v. North Carolina*, 533 U.S. 926 (2001), discussed in

Chapter 6, holding that the Southeast Commission could only intervene in an existing state-versus-state action; it could not be a co-plaintiff with a state. Should Mexico also be considered a third party beneficiary?

5. Most cases do not address whether a third party beneficiary can enforce a compact. For example, the issue never arose in *Medieros v. Vincent*, 431 F.3d 25 (1st Cir. 2005), in which a commercial fisherman sought to enforce the Atlantic States Marine Fisheries Compact against a state.

Few scholars have written about third parties asserting rights conferred by a compact. Compact scholarship from the 1960s and 1970s assumed that where a compact provided for private rights, private parties could assert those rights. *See, e.g.*, FREDERICK L. ZIMMERMANN & MITCHELL WENDELL, THE LAW AND USE OF INTERSTATE COMPACTS (1961).

> For the most part, interstate compacts have not created any privately assertable rights. Customarily, their subject matter has been cooperative governmental administration or the rights of governmental units as such rather than the specific rights of private person. However, this is not invariably the case. For example, water allocation compacts, while they apportion water among states, may affect the rights of individual water users in such a way as to make them proper parties to suits. In such situations, the governing fact is that compacts are statutory law. Consequently, the assertion of private rights created or otherwise affected by a compact is procedurally similar to the assertion of such rights conferred by other statutes of the jurisdiction dealing with similar subject matter.

Id. at 14–15. Zimmermann and Wendell updated their book in 1976, keeping this same passage. *See also* Jerome C. Muys, Nat'l Water Comm'n, Report No. NWC-L-71-011, *Interstate Water Compacts—The Interstate Compact and Federal-Interstate Compact* 310 (1971) (stating "Since an interstate compact is considered to be a law of each of the compacting states, actions thereunder may be challenged just as any other state action," citing *Hinderlider v. La Plata River & Cherry Creek Ditch Co.*, 304 U.S. 92 (1938) as an example).

6. Is there any difference between third party beneficiaries enforcing a compact that the states have not terminated and requiring the states continue a compact that the states wish to terminate? In *The Mayor, Recorder, Alderman & Common Council of Georgetown v. Alexandria Canal Co.*, 37 U.S. (12 Pet.) 91 (1838), the Court concluded that citizens of a state were not parties to a compact and could not object to termination of a compact by mutual consent of the states. There has not been any more recent case law involving this issue.

7. Most courts that have considered the availability of a claim to remedy violation of a constitutional right pursuant to 42 U.S.C. § 1983 against a compact agency have concluded that it is not available. In *Ghana v. Pearce*, 159 F.3d 1206 (9th Cir. 1998), the Ninth Circuit concluded that the Interstate Corrections Compact is not federal law, and thus a violation of the compact could not be the basis for a section 1983 action. In *Doe*, the Third Circuit held that under a compact that is federal law, there is still no right to a section 1983 claim. Similarly, there are

many decisions dismissing section 1983 claims against the Washington Metropolitan Area Transit Authority, which was created under a compact that received congressional consent. *See, e.g.*, *Lucero-Nelson v. Wash. Metro. Area Transit Auth.*, 1 F. Supp. 2d 1, 7–8 (D.D.C. 1998).

8. Recall in *Green v. Biddle*, the Supreme Court concluded that Kentucky's enactment of new legislation that conflicted with the compact violated the Contract Clause of the U.S. Constitution. In its jurisprudence long after *Green v. Biddle*, the Supreme Court has established three factors for Contract Clause claims: first, there must be a substantial impairment, second, the State must have a significant and legitimate public purpose for the regulation, and third, whether the impairment is based on reasonable conditions and is of a character appropriate to the public purpose. *See Energy Reserves Group, Inc. v. Kansas Power & Light Co.*, 459 U.S. 400, 410–13 (1983).

Energy Reserves Group cited to *United States Trust Co. of N.J. v. New Jersey*, 431 U.S. 1 (1977), stating that *U.S. Trust* and one other case "clarify the appropriate Contract Clause standard." *Energy Reserves Group*, 459 U.S. at 411. Interestingly, *U.S. Trust* was a compact case, in which the Supreme Court invalidated a New Jersey state covenant (also adopted by New York) to protect the Port Authority of New York and New Jersey from "greater involvement in deficit mass transportation." *U.S. Trust*, 431 U.S. at 32. Much of the Court's discussion involved the Contract Clause, and the Court noted that Contract Clause jurisprudence has long allowed a state to "bind itself in the future exercise of the taxing and spending powers." *Id.* at 23–24. In support, the Court cited a holding from 1812, which it observed, "has never been repudiated." *Id.* at 24 n.21.

Similarly, the early compact law cases finding violations of the Contract Clause, including *Green v. Biddle* and *Pennsylvania v. Wheeling and Belmont Bridge Co.*, have never been repudiated. Is the Contract Clause jurisprudence from *Green v. Biddle* and other early compact cases still good law after *Energy Reserves Group*, such that the prohibition against impairment of compacts is a different standard than for commercial contracts? Are compacts, as agreements between states in their sovereign nature as states, fundamentally different from contracts between private parties or states acting in commerce? Reread the following excerpt from the Eighth Circuit (which first appeared in Chapter 9).

> Although the Supreme Court has acknowledged that an interstate compact is like a contract to the extent that it is "a legal document that must be construed and applied in accordance with its terms," *Texas v. New Mexico*, 482 U.S. 124, 128 (1987), the Court has also recognized the unique features and functions of such a compact. An interstate compact is one "of two methods under our Constitution of settling controversies between States," *Petty v. Tennessee-Missouri Bridge Comm'n*, 359 U.S. 275, 279 n.5 (1959), and it "performs high functions in our federalism," *id.* at 279. *See also* Felix Frankfurter & James M. Landis, *The Compact Clause of the Constitution — A Study in Interstate Adjustments*, 34 YALE L.J. 685, 691–95 (1925) (discuss-

> ing history of Compact Clause). An interstate compact represents a political compromise between "constituent elements of the Union," as opposed to a commercial transaction. *Hess v. Port Auth. Trans-Hudson Corp.*, 513 U.S. 30, 40 (1994). Such an agreement is made to "address interests and problems that do not coincide nicely either with the national boundaries or with State lines—interests that may be badly served or not served at all by the ordinary channels of National or State political action." *Id.*
>
> While a common law contract directly affects only the rights and obligations of the individual parties to it, an interstate compact may directly impact the population, the economy, and the physical environment in the whole of the compact area. A suit alleging that a state has breached an obligation owed to its sister states under a congressionally approved interstate compact also raises delicate questions bearing upon the relationship among separate sovereign polities with respect to matters of both regional and national import.

Entergy Arkansas, Inc. v. Nebraska, 358 F.3d 528, 541–42 (8th Cir. 2004). Given the special nature of an interstate compact, should the law require a more facially absolute proscription against impairment than for commercial contracts? Consider also the following quote from a former compact agency staffer and scholar:

> All interstate organizations in the U.S. are threatened species using the parlance of the Federal Endangered Species Act. They often are considered rivals by existing federal and state governmental agencies. Their viability depends on the political and financial support of all of their signatory parties and the continued recognition by the parties, including their constituents of common problems and resource dependencies requiring regional solutions. Absent these conditions, they are highly vulnerable to atrophy and extinction.

Jeffrey Featherstone, *Existing Compacts, the Law and Lessons*, 4 TOL. J. GREAT LAKES' L. SCI. & POL'Y 271, 282 (2001). Given these threats, should the law require a more facially absolute proscription against impairment of compacts than for commercial contracts?

CHAPTER 12: STATE-FOREIGN POWER COMPACTS

So far, you have studied agreements between two or more of the United States. The Compact Clause, however, also requires congressional consent for agreements between a state and a foreign power. Again the Compact Clause states, "No State shall, without the Consent of Congress, . . . enter into any Agreement or Compact with another state, *or with a foreign Power* . . . ." U.S. CONST. art. I, § 10, cl. 3 (emphasis added). This requirement for consent in the Compact Clause is potentially in tension with the State Treaty Clause in Article I of the U.S. Constitution, which states, "No State shall enter into any Treaty, Alliance, or Confederation . . ." U.S. CONST. art. I, § 10, cl. 1.

The Compact Clause and State Treaty Clause are separate from the Treaty Clause in article II, section 2, clause 2 of the U.S. Constitution, which authorizes the President to make treaties with foreign nations. There are several differences between states enacting agreements or compacts with foreign powers pursuant to the Compact Clause and the President enacting treaties with foreign nations. For example, the requirement for Congress to grant consent pursuant to the Compact Clause is bicameral, necessarily requiring action by the House of Representatives. In contrast, there is no role for the U.S. House of Representatives under the Treaty Clause, which requires only the advice and consent of the Senate. The Compact Clause also does not require any supermajority vote in Congress. In contrast, the Treaty Clause requires concurrence of "two-third of the Senators present."

The availability of a higher court to resolve disputes also differs between compacts and treaties. As you studied in Chapters 6 and 11, the U.S. Supreme Court has exclusive jurisdiction for a state to sue another state to enforce an interstate compact. In contrast, the International Court of Justice does not have jurisdiction to enforce disputes between nations over treaties; a treaty must confer jurisdiction on the International Court of Justice or the parties must enact a special agreement conferring jurisdiction before a party may seek enforcement of that treaty at the Court. Additionally, only nations may use the International Court of Justice. A U.S. state may not enforce an agreement or compact with a foreign power at the International Court of Justice.

This chapter does not further address the Article II Treaty Clause. This chapter contains materials concerning the terms "Agreement or Compact" in the Compact Clause and "Treaty, Alliance, or Confederation" in the State Treaty Clause; domestic interstate compacts that also involve Canadian provinces; and agreements between a state and a foreign power where there is no domestic interstate compact.

I. Agreements, Compacts, Treaties, Alliances, and Confederations

The State Treaty Clause, which again states, "No State shall enter into any Treaty, Alliance, or Confederation . . ." is a strict prohibition; there is no opportunity for congressional consent. This raises the question what are agreements and compacts that are permissible pursuant to the Compact Clause and what are treaties, alliances, and confederations that are prohibited pursuant to the State Treaty Clause. Only one Supreme Court case has applied the State Treaty Clause. *See Williams v. Bruffy*, 96 U.S. 176, 182 (1877). In that case, the Supreme Court concluded that a Civil War Confederacy law sequestering property and credits within confederate states was invalid under the State Treaty Clause and thus a debtor who paid to the Confederate government a debt owed to a creditor in a union state did not satisfy that debt with the creditor. Other than the Civil War Confederacy, which was an obvious violation of the State Treaty Clause, the Supreme Court has not provided any direct guidance on what types of multilateral or binational state actions fall within the prohibition of the State Treaty Clause.

The *U.S. Steel* case, which you read in Chapter 2 when studying the need for congressional consent to an interstate compact, is the most complete Supreme Court discussion and historical review of the terms "treaty," "compact" and "agreement." The Court's discussion is just two paragraphs but contains extensive footnotes.

U.S. Steel Corp. v. Multistate Tax Comm'n
434 U.S. 452 (1978)

POWELL, JUSTICE:

. . . .

Article I, § 10, cl. 1, of the Constitution—the Treaty Clause—declares: "No State, shall enter into Any Treaty, Alliance or Confederation . . . ." Yet Art. I, § 10, cl. 3—the Compact Clause—permits the States to enter into "agreements" or "compacts," so long as congressional consent is obtained. The Framers clearly perceived compacts and agreements as differing from treaties.[10] The records of

---

[10] The history of interstate agreements under the Articles of Confederation suggests the same distinction between "treaties, alliances, and confederations" on the one hand, and "agreements and compacts" on the other. Article VI provided in part as follows:

> No State without the consent of the United States, in Congress assembled, shall send any embassy to, or receive any embassy from, or enter into any confe[r]ence, agreement, alliance or treaty, with any king, prince or state . . . .
>
> No two or more States shall enter into any treaty, confederation, or alliance whatever, between them, without the consent of the United States, in Congress assembled, specifying accurately the purposes for which the same is to be entered into, and how long it shall continue.

Congressional consent clearly was required before a State could enter into an "agreement" with a foreign state or power or before two or more States could enter into "treaties, alliances, or confederations." Apparently, however, consent was not required for mere

the Constitutional Convention, however, are barren of any clue as to the precise contours of the agreements and compacts governed by the Compact Clause.[11] This suggests that the Framers used the words "treaty," "compact," and "agreement" as terms of art, for which no explanation was required[12] and with

---

"agreements" between States. "The articles inhibiting any treaty, confederation, or alliance between the States without the consent of Congress . . . were not designed to prevent arrangements between adjoining States to facilitate the free intercourse of their citizens, or remove barriers to their peace and prosperity . . . ." *Wharton v. Wise*, 154 U.S. 155, 167 (1894).

For example, the Virginia-Maryland Compact of 1785, which governed navigation and fishing rights in the Potomac River, the Pocomoke River, and the Chesapeake Bay, did not receive congressional approval, yet no question concerning its validity under Art. VI ever arose. As the Court noted in *Wharton v. Wise*, in reference to the 1785 Compact, "looking at the object evidently intended by the prohibition of the Articles of Confederation, we are clear they were not directed against agreements of the character expressed by the compact under consideration. Its execution could in no respect encroach upon or weaken the general authority of Congress under those articles. Various compacts were entered into between Pennsylvania and New Jersey and between Pennsylvania and Virginia, during the Confederation, in reference to boundaries between them, and to rights of fishery in their waters, and to titles to land in their respective States, without the consent of Congress, which indicated that such consent was not deemed essential to their validity." 153 U.S. at 170–71.

[11] On July 25, 1787, the Convention created a Committee of Detail composed of John Rutledge, James Wilson, Edmund Randolph, Nathaniel Gorham, and Oliver Elsworth. The Convention then adjourned until August 6 to allow the Committee to prepare a draft. 2 M. FARRAND, RECORDS OF THE FEDERAL CONVENTION OF 1787, pp. 97, 128 (1911). Section 10 of the Committee's first draft provided in part: "No State shall enter into any Treaty, Alliance or Confederation with any foreign Power nor witht. Const. of U. S. into any agreement. or compact wh another State or Power . . . ." *Id.* at 169 (abbreviations in original). On August 6, the Committee submitted a draft to the Convention containing the following articles:

> XII No State shall . . . enter into any treaty, alliance, or confederation. . . .
> XIII No State, without the consent of the Legislature of the United States, shall . . . enter into any agreement or compact with another State, or with any foreign power . . . . *Id.* at 187.

The Committee of Style, created to revise the draft, reported on September 12, *id.* at 590, but nothing appears to have been said about Art. I, § 10, which contained the treaty and compact language incorporated into the Constitution as approved on September 17. The records of the state ratification conventions also shed no light. Publius declared only that the prohibition against treaties, alliances, and confederation, "for reasons which need no explanation, is copied into the new Constitution," while the portion of Art. I, § 10, containing the Compact Clause fell "within reasonings which are either so obvious, or have been so fully developed, that they may be passed over without remark." THE FEDERALIST, NO. 44 (J. Madison).

[12] Some commentators have theorized that the Framers understood those terms in relation to the precisely defined categories, fashionable in the contemporary literature of international law, of accords between sovereigns. *See, e.g.*, David E. Engdahl, *Characterization of Interstate Arrangements: When Is a Compact Not a Compact?*, 64 MICH. L. REV. 63 (1965);

which we are unfamiliar. Further evidence that the Framers ascribed precise meanings to these words appears in contemporary commentary.[13]

Whatever distinct meanings the Framers attributed to the terms in Art. I, § 10, those meanings were soon lost. In 1833, Mr. Justice Story perceived no clear distinction among any of the terms.[14] Lacking any clue as to the categorical definitions the Framers has ascribed to them, Mr. Justice Story developed his own

---

Abraham C. Weinfeld, *What Did the Framers of the Federal Constitution Mean by "Agreements or Compacts"?*, 3 U. CHI. L. REV. 453 (1936). The international jurist most widely cited in the first 50 years after the Revolution was Emmerich de Vattel. 1 J. KENT, COMMENTARIES ON AMERICAN LAW 18 (1826). In 1775, Benjamin Franklin acknowledged receipt of three copies of a new edition, in French, of Vattel's Law of Nations and remarked that the book "has been continually in the hands of the members of our Congress now sitting . . . ." 2 F. WHARTON, UNITED STATES REVOLUTIONARY DIPLOMATIC CORRESPONDENCE 64 (1889), cited in Weinfeld, *supra*, at 458.

Vattel differentiated between "treaties," which were made either for perpetuity or for a considerable period, and "agreements, conventions, and pactions," which "are perfected in their execution once for all." EMMERICH DE VATTEL, LAW OF NATIONS 192 (J. Chitty ed. 1883). Unlike a "treaty" or "alliance," an "agreement" or "paction" was perfected upon execution:

> [T]hose compacts, which are accomplished once for all, and not by successive acts,—are no sooner executed then they are completed and perfected. If they are valid, they have in their own nature a perpetual and irrevocable effect . . . . *Id.* at 208.

This distinction between supposedly ongoing accords, such as military alliances, and instantaneously executed, though perpetually effective, agreements, such as boundary settlements, may have informed the drafting in Art. I, § 10. The Framers clearly recognized the necessity for amicable resolution of boundary disputes and related grievances. *See Virginia v. West Virginia*, 246 U.S. 565, 597-600 (1918); Felix Frankfurter & James M. Landis, *The Compact Clause of the Constitution—A Study in Interstate Adjustments*, 34 YALE L.J. 685, 692-695 (1925). Interstate agreements were a method with which they were familiar. *Id.* at 694, 732-34. Although these dispositive compacts affected the interests of the States involved, they did not represent the continuing threat to the other States embodied in a "treaty of alliance," to use Vattel's words. Vattel, *supra*, at 192.

[13] St. George Tucker, who along with Madison and Edmund Randolph was a Virginia commissioner to the Annapolis Convention of 1786, drew a distinction between "treaties, alliances, and confederations" on the one hand, and "agreements or compacts" on the other:

> The former relate ordinarily to subjects of great national magnitude and importance, and are often perpetual, or made for a considerable period of time; the power of making these is altogether prohibited to the individual states; but agreements, or compacts, concerning transitory or local affairs, or such as cannot possibly affect any other interest but that of the parties, may still be entered into by the respective states, with the consent of congress. 1 W. BLACKSTONE, COMMENTARIES, Appendix 310 (S. Tucker ed. 1803) (footnotes omitted).

Tucker cited Vattel as authority for his interpretation of Art. I, § 10.

[14] Mr. Justice Story found Tucker's view, *see* n.13, *supra*, unilluminating:

> What precise distinction is here intended to be taken between *treaties*, and *agreements*, and *compacts*, is nowhere explained, and has never as yet been subjected to any exact judicial or other examination. A learned commentator, however,

theory. Treaties, alliances, and confederations, he wrote, generally connote military and political accords and are forbidden to the States. Compacts and agreements, on the other hand, embrace "mere private rights of sovereignty; such as questions of boundary; interests in land situate in the territory of each other; and other internal regulations for the mutual comfort and convenience of States bordering on each other." 2 J. Story, Commentaries on the Constitution of the United States § 1403, p. 264 (T. Cooley ed. 1873). In the latter situations, congressional consent was required, Story felt, "in order to check any infringement of the rights of the national government." *Id.*

. . . .

Notes & Questions

1. In the *U.S. Steel* excerpt in Chapter 2, you studied that the purpose of the Compact Clause is to protect the just supremacy of the federal government by giving Congress an opportunity to ensure that that state-to-state agreements do not upset the proper balance between states and the federal government. The State Treaty Clause also seeks to preserve the federal government, but the purpose was apparently different. Joseph Story, in his *Commentaries on the Constitution of the United States* § 1349, stated that the State Treaty Clause ensures "the preservation of any national government" and described the Founders' concerns that states might enter into agreements that are "utterly hostile to the interests of neighbouring or distant states; and thus the internal peace and harmony of the Union might be destroyed, or put in jeopardy" and that allowing agreements between states and foreign powers would create a "perpetual source of foreign corrupt influence." Other sources contemporary to the drafting of the Constitution raised different concerns. For example, *The Federalist* No. 4 (James Madison) describes how the country is stronger under one national government than if it would remain divided in its colonies or "split into a number of confederacies,"

---

supposes, that the former ordinarily relate to subjects of great national magnitude and importance, and are often perpetual, or for a great length of time; but that the latter relate to transitory or local concerns, or such as cannot possibly affect any other interests but those of the parties [citing Tucker]. But this is at best a very loose and unsatisfactory exposition, leaving the whole matter open to the most latitudinarian construction. What are subjects of great national magnitude and importance? Why may not a compact or agreement between States be perpetual? If it may not, what shall be its duration? Are not treaties often made for short periods, and upon questions of local interest, and for temporary objects? 2 J. STORY, COMMENTARIES ON THE CONSTITUTION OF THE UNITED STATES § 1402, p. 263 (T. Cooley ed. 1873) (footnotes omitted).

In *Green v. Biddle*, 21 U.S (8 Wheat.) 1 (1823), the Court, including Mr. Justice Story, had been presented with a question of the validity of the Virginia-Kentucky Compact of 1789, to which Congress had never expressly assented. Henry Clay argued to the Court that the Compact Clause extended "to all agreements or compacts, no matter what is the subject of them. It is immaterial, therefore, whether that subject be harmless or dangerous to the Union." *Id.* at 39. The Court did not address that issue, however, for it held that Congress' consent could be implied. *Id.* at 87.

specifically that a divided country could not rely on the constituent parts to assist each other in times of war and would have no single organizer or arbiter of such assistance. Curiously, *The Federalist* No. 44 (James Madison), which discusses the entirety of Article I, section 1, clause 1, contains only one sentence about the State Treaty Clause: "The prohibition against treaties, alliances, and confederations makes a part of the existing articles of Union [the Articles of Confederation]; and for reasons which need no explanation, is copied into the new Constitution."

2. Frankfurter and Landis's 1925 seminal article on the Compact Clause suggested that instead of defining differences between a treaty and a compact, Congress should use its political judgment on a case-by-case basis to determine whether an agreement is a compact that may be permitted with consent or a prohibited treaty.

> There is no self-executing test differentiating "compact" from "treaty." Story and other writers have attempted an analytical classification. The attempt is bound to go shipwreck for we are in a field in which political judgment is, to say the least, one of the important factors. The considerations that led the Supreme Court to leave Congress the determination of what constitutes a republican form of government as guaranteed by the Constitution are equally controlling in leaving to Congress to circumscribe the area of agreement open to the States.

Felix Frankfurter & James M. Landis, *The Compact Clause of the Constitution—A Study in Interstate Adjustments*, 34 YALE L.J. 685, 695 n.31 (1925).

3. The footnotes in *U.S. Steel* cite to many articles in the years following Frankfurter and Landis' article in which scholars suggested differences between agreements, compacts and treaties, all of which generally cited to the same original documents from the Constitutional Convention, Justice Story's Commentaries, and Emmerich de Vattel. These are still the best sources about the history and intersection of the State Treaty Clause and Compact Clause.

4. A more recent scholar suggested an approach similar to Frankfurter and Landis's approach, stating, "Under existing case law and contemporary practice, the 'treaties' proscribed to the states by the Compact Clause effectively comprise those pacts to which Congress has not consented, and 'compacts' are anything to which it has consented." Edward T. Swaine, *Does Federalism Constrain the Treaty Power*, 103 COLUM. L. REV. 403, 503–04 (2003).

While a distinction based on the receipt of congressional consent is enticingly simple, it does not reflect that the states' practice has long been to not submit every state-foreign agreement to Congress for consent, nor Congress's practice to not demand submission of such agreements for consideration. *See* Duncan B. Hollis, *The Elusive Foreign Compact,* 73 MO. L. REV. 1071, 1078–79 (2008). This distinction also differs from Professor Hollis's observation that the State Department, the Restatement (Third) of the Foreign Relations Law of the United States, and numerous scholars assume that courts would apply the Compact Clause test for when consent is needed to state-foreign power agreements. *Id.* at 1088. The effect of Frankfurter and Landis's and Professor Swaine's approach could anomalously be that agreements that do not impair the just Supremacy of the federal government would be considered impermissible treaties.

Professor Swaine also noted that in one early compact case, the Supreme Court suggested a strict application of the State Treaty Clause.

> In *Holmes v. Jennison*, 39 U.S. (14 Pet.) 540, 572 (1840), the Supreme Court wrote that the Framers' desire "to cut off all connection or communication between a state and a foreign power" requires giving the broadest possible construction to the term "agreement"); *id.* at 574 (describing the Framers' intention that "there would be no occasion for negotiation or intercourse between the state authorities and a foreign government"); *id.* at 575–76 (claiming that "[e]very part of [the Constitution] shows, that our whole foreign intercourse was intended to be committed to the hands of the general government," it being "one of the main objects of the constitution to make us, so far as regarded our foreign relations, one people, and one nation; and to cut off all communications between foreign governments, and the several state authorities").

Swaine, *supra*, at 506–07. The Supreme Court discussed *Holmes v. Jennison* in *U.S. Steel*, noting that Justice Catron "expressed disquiet over what he viewed as Mr. Chief Justice Taney's literal reading of the Compact Clause, noting that it might threaten agreements between States theretofore considered lawful." *U.S. Steel*, 434 U.S. at 465. The *U.S. Steel* decision continued, "Despite Mr. Justice Catron's fears, courts faced with the task of applying the Compact Clause appeared reluctant to strike down newly emerging forms of interstate cooperation." *Id.*

II. Interstate Compacts Involving Canadian Provinces*

There are five interstate compacts between U.S. states that also involve Canadian provinces. All five of the compacts that involve Canadian provinces have congressional consent to some degree. Two of the compacts involve management of the Great Lakes—the Great Lakes Basin Compact, partial consent granted by Pub. L. No. 90-419, 82 Stat. 414 (1968), and the Great Lakes-St. Lawrence River Basin Water Resources Compact, consent granted by Pub. L. No. 110-342, 122 Stat. 3739 (2008). The other three are regional emergency management assistance compacts—the International Emergency Management Assistance Compact (Maine, New Hampshire, Vermont, Massachusetts, Rhode Island, and Connecticut and the provinces of Québec, New Brunswick, Prince Edward Island, Nova Scotia and Newfoundland), consent granted by Pub. L. No. 110-171, 121 Stat. 2467 (2007); the State and Province Emergency Management Assistance Compact (Illinois, Indiana, Ohio, Michigan, Minnesota, Montana, North Dakota,

* As of 2020, the date of this edition of this book, there are no interstate compacts that also involve Mexican states or other foreign governments.

Pennsylvania, New York, and Wisconsin, and the provinces of Alberta, Manitoba, Ontario, and Saskatchewan), consent granted by Pub. L. No. 112-282, 126 Stat. 2486 (2013); and the Pacific Northwest Emergency Management Arrangement (Alaska, Idaho, Oregon, and Washington, the province of British Columbia, and the Yukon Territory), consent granted by S.J. Res. No. 35, Pub. L. No. 105-381 (1998).

The provinces participate in the two Great Lakes compacts through supplemental agreements between the states and provinces, not through authority in the actual compacts and do not vote on decisions made pursuant to the compacts. The provinces participate in the Great Lakes Basin Compact through a 1999 "Declaration of Partnership," signed 31 years after Congress granted its partial consent to the compact. The provinces participate in the Great Lakes-St. Lawrence River Basin Water Resources Compact through the "Great Lakes-St. Lawrence River Basin Sustainable Water Resources Agreement," which the states and provinces enacted concurrently with the states' enactment of the Water Resource Compact. Bi-national coordination at the state and province level through supplemental agreements works because the states allow the provinces to participate in deliberations and the states give equal consideration to the provinces interests, concerns, and limitations in their compact decisions even absent the provinces' formal right to vote on compact actions.

In contrast to the Great Lakes compacts, the provinces participate in the three emergency management agreements through authority granted in the compacts with the same participation and voting rights as the states. Each agreement has only a single administrative agency comprised of U.S. states and Canadian provinces. For example, the International Emergency Management Group (IEMG) manages the International Emergency Management Assistance Compact (IEMAC) The IEMG bylaws specify that the Board of Directors consists of the directors of emergency management or their designee from each party. There are co-chairs—one from a United States party and one from a Canada party; and both co-chairs must sign documents requiring the signature of the IEMG. Int'l Emergency Mgmt. Group, Bylaws, arts. III, § 1, IV, § 2, and VIII, § 1.

The Great Lakes Basin Compact is an interesting study of congressional consent and the states and provinces finding effective ways to work together. Congress considered several consent bills between 1955 and 1968. In 1968, Congress granted a limited consent to the compact. It did not fully consent to the Great Lakes Commission making recommendations to or cooperating with Canadian provinces, such that the provinces could not become full members of the compact.

The Great Lakes Basin Compact and Great Lakes Commission: A Case Study*

The Great Lakes Basin Compact is an interstate compact between the eight Great Lakes states (Illinois, Indiana, Michigan, Minnesota, New York, Ohio, Pennsylvania, and Wisconsin) and has two Canadian provinces (Ontario and Québec) as associate members. Through the Compact, the states created the Great Lakes Commission. The states negotiated the Compact in 1954 and 1955. Article II.A of the Compact specifies it would become effective and binding when it had been enacted by the legislatures of any four of the Great Lakes states. Five states enacted the Compact in 1955; the remaining states enacted the Compact in 1956, 1960, and 1963.

The Great Lakes Basin Compact creates a structure for the states to cooperate on Great Lakes policy involving several policy areas, including development and conservation, public works improvements relating to water resources in the Great Lakes Basin, navigation, fisheries, flood plains, zoning, pollution, lake levels, hydroelectric power development, soil and bank erosion, and diversions of water from and into the basin. *See* Great Lakes Basin Compact, arts. VI & VII.

Drafters of the original Compact seemed to believe that consent would not be necessary for the Compact because it is solely consultative, but that consent would be needed (and readily obtained) if it would involve a Canadian province, stating,

> I imagine that an agreement of this character would be considered of such importance by Congress that they would insist upon explicit consent being secured. . . . It would be farfetched for Congress to withhold approval of a compact of this kind through which officials of our Great Lakes states could sit around a table and talk and consult with officials of the Province of Ontario on matters which affect their common interests.

Nicholas V. Olds, Statement Presented to The Council of State Governments at its meeting held in Chicago, Illinois on August 26, 1954 8–9 (unpublished manuscript).

There were bills in Congress to grant consent to the Compact in 1955, 1957, 1958, 1959, 1961, 1965, 1966, and 1968. Congress granted partial consent to the Compact in 1968. Act of July 24, 1968, Pub. L. No. 90-419, 82 Stat. 414. Congress's consent contained three conditions roughly summarized as: (1) Congress did not fully consent to the Great Lakes Commission making recommendations to or cooperating with foreign governments, and the Commission must cooperate with and send reports to U.S. federal agencies; (2) nothing in the Compact affects the authority of U.S. federal agencies or any international commission; and

* Adapted from The Council of State Gov'ts Nat'l Ctr. for Interstate Compacts, *Legal Assessment of the Great Lakes Basin Compact and Great Lakes Commission* (Nov. 2019), available at https://www.glc.org/news/glc-legal-assessment-20191125. Used with permission of the Great Lakes Commission.

(3) Congress reserved the right to alter, amend, or repeal its consent to the Compact. *Id.* at §§ 2, 3, 4.

Despite Congress's limited consent, Ontario and Québec became associate members in 1999 after the states and provinces signed a Declaration of Partnership, which establishes and defines the provinces' participation in the Compact. The Declaration of Partnership does not identify which provisions of the Compact are applicable or inapplicable to the provinces. The Declaration of Partnership is not a binding element of the Compact. For example, article VII of the compact specifies, "Each party state agrees to consider the action the Commission recommends in respect to" several policy subjects. Given the silence in and non-binding nature of the Declaration of Partnership, this important implementation provision of the compact may not apply to the provinces.

Curiously, Congress has subsequently encouraged international cooperation in the Great Lakes Basin through consultation and other non-binding means. For example, The Water Resources Development Act of 2000 encouraged the Great Lakes states to work with Ontario and Québec, stating,

> [T]o encourage the Great Lakes States, in consultation with the Provinces of Ontario and Québec, to develop and implement a mechanism that provides a common conservation standard embodying the principles of water conservation and resource improvement for making decisions concerning the withdrawal and use of water from the Great Lakes Basin.

Pub. L. No. 106-541, § 504, 114 Stat. 2572, 2644–45 (2000), codified at 42 U.S.C. § 1962d-20(b)(2).

Notes & Questions

1. When Congress granted its partial consent to the Great Lakes Basin Compact in 1968, the compact had been operating for 13 years. Could Congress have abrogated past actions of the Commission that were inconsistent with the scope of Congress's consent? Because the states had enacted the compact before Congress granted its partial consent, should the states have reenacted the compact to accept Congress's conditions and limits? Did the states impliedly accept those conditions and limits by acting in accordance with them? If Congress may impliedly consent to a compact, can states impliedly accept conditions of consent?

2. Testimony and discussion in the federal legislative history shows that different entities had different reasons for wanting Congress to grant or withhold consent to the Great Lakes Basin Compact, but only two were related to the constitutional need for consent that you studied in Chapter 2. First, the U.S. Department of Justice testified that consent was necessary because the Great Lakes are a navigable waterway and because the Commission's recommendations may significantly influence the legislative actions of the party states and thus shape the future development of the Basin. Second, most of the legislative history shows that the Department of State and Congress were concerned about the states' and Commission's communications with Ontario and Québec interfering with existing treaties and bi-national entities (at that time, the Boundary Waters Treaty,

Jan. 11, 1909, 36 Stat. 2448, and its agency, the International Joint Commission; and the Convention on Great Lakes Fisheries, Sept. 10, 1954, 6 U.S.T. 2836, and its agency, the Great Lakes Fishery Commission) and future federal negotiations and cooperative efforts with the Canadian federal government and provinces. The New York Power Authority originally shared this latter concern because it believed the Great Lakes Commission might affect power development of the St. Lawrence River and that consent would enable the Great Lakes Commission to act with the appearance of federal authority.

3. Since 1999 when the states and provinces entered into their Declaration of Partnership, Congress has assigned new tasks to the Great Lakes Commission. For example, the Frank LoBiondo Coast Guard Authorization Act of 2018, Pub. L. No. 115-282, § 903(a)(1), 132 Stat. 4192, 4344–50, authorizes a Great Lakes state governor to request an enhanced ballast water standard, and potentially requires the Great Lakes Commission to study and make a recommendation on such a request. Notwithstanding this provision, the Act states "Nothing in this subsection limits, alters, or amends the Great Lakes Basin Compact." *Id.* at 4349–50. How does assigning a new task not alter or amend the compact?

In another example, the Farm Security and Rural Investment Act of 2008, Pub. L. No. 110-234, 122 Stat. 923, requires the U.S. Secretary of Agriculture to carry out a Great Lakes Basin program for soil erosion and sediment control in consultation with the Great Lakes Commission and to implement the Great Lakes Regional Collaboration Strategy to Restore and Protect the Great Lakes (2005)). *Id.* at § 2604, repealed, Pub. L. No. 113-79, tit. II, § 2708, 128 Stat. 770 (2014).

In Chapter 2, you read about how Congress may impliedly consent to an interstate compact through subsequent legislation and proceedings, such as recognizing a state boundary for the purpose of federal court districts, revenue collection, federal elections and federal appointments. Should Congress's new mandated tasks for the Great Lakes Commission (imposed after the Declaration of Partnership) suggest that Congress has impliedly amended its consent to allow the states and provinces to cooperate through the compact or the Declaration of Partnership?

4. The Great Lakes-St. Lawrence River Basin Water Resources Compact is the other Great Lakes compact that involves Canadian provinces. This compact regulates diversions into and out of the Great Lakes Basin. Similar to the Great Lakes Basin Compact, the Water Resources Compact is one of two agreements that constitutes the cross-border administration of the goals of the compact. The compact is solely between the U.S. States and there is a companion Great Lakes-St.-Lawrence River Basin Sustainable Water Resources Agreement that the U.S. States and Canadian provinces enacted concurrently with the compact. The "Compact" and the "Agreement" are separate and major decisions require action by both.

> The key to this two-part strategy was the development of a parallel, good-faith "agreement" between the eight states and two provinces that share the Great Lakes Basin, the terms of which mirrored the substance of the

> proposed compact between the U.S. states. While ultimately dependent on the goodwill of the parties, since such an international agreement between states and provinces lacks the mutual enforceability of a compact between states (and because there is no direct analog to the interstate compact mechanism in Canada), the proposed Great Lakes-St. Lawrence River Basin Sustainable Water Resources Agreement expressed a voluntary commitment by the states and provinces of the Great Lakes Basin to essentially play by the same set of rules to which the states were prepared to legally bind themselves under the proposed compact.

MICHAEL L. BUENGER, ET AL., THE EVOLVING LAW AND USE OF INTERSTATE COMPACTS 224 (2d ed. 2016).

5. The three international emergency management assistance compacts that have Canadian provinces as full members operate without companion agreements. For discussion of their effectiveness, see R. Bruce Sackinger, *Paradiplomatic Maneuvers on the Longest Undefended Border: National and Subnational Fire Protection Agreements Between Canada and the United States*, 13 WILLAMETTE J. INT'L L. & DISP. RESOL. 319 (2005).

6. The Pacific Northwest Economic Region (PNWER) (Alaska, Idaho, Oregon, Montana and Washington and the provinces of Alberta, British Columbia, the Yukon Territory, Saskatchewan and the Northwest Territories) illustrates another model of multistate bi-national cooperation with Canadian provinces. PNWER was created by the states and provinces enacting statutes or taking another form of legislative action. There is no reciprocity. PNWER refers to itself as a public-private organization. The states' statutes refer to the PNWER as an agreement. The parties do not refer to it as an interstate compact and they have never sought congressional consent.

III. Agreements Between States and Foreign Powers

Agreements between states and foreign powers that do not involve domestic compacts are common and address a wide range of policy areas, such as international bridges, trade, environmental protection, border security, mutual recognition of driver licenses, emergency response, regional economic cooperation and marketing. One scholar wrote in 1998 that more than 400 agreements existed between U.S. states and Canadian provinces and those agreements involved 46 states. EARL H. FRY, THE EXPANDING ROLE OF STATE AND LOCAL GOVERNMENTS IN U.S. FOREIGN AFFAIRS 5 (1998).

A. When Consent is Needed

The Supreme Court has not given any guidance for evaluating when an agreement between a state and a foreign power requires consent. However, as described in note 4 following the *U.S. Steel* excerpt in this Chapter, the State Department, the Restatement (Third) of the Foreign Relations Law of the United States and numerous scholars assume that Congress would apply the Compact

Clause if such an issue arose before the Supreme Court. The U.S. Court of Appeals for the First Circuit has applied a variation of the Compact Clause formulation of when consent is needed first expressed in *Virginia v. Tennessee* and discussed in Chapter 2 above.

> Federal dominion over foreign affairs does not mean that there is no role for the states. A limited role is granted by the Constitution .... *See* Restatement (Third) of Foreign Relations Law of the United States § 201 reporters' note 9 (commenting that "[u]nder the United States Constitution, a State of the United States may make compacts or agreements with a foreign power with the consent of Congress (Article I, Section 10, clause [3]), but such agreements are limited in scope and subject matter" and that "[a] State may make some agreements with foreign governments without the consent of Congress so long as they do not impinge upon the authority or the foreign relations of the United States").

National Foreign Trade Council v. Natsios, 181 F.3d 38, 50 (1st Cir. 1999). This use of the Compact Clause analysis has been courts' practice for a long time. For example, in 1917, the North Dakota Supreme Court applied the Compact Clause test for consent to an agreement between a county drainage board and Canada. *McHenry County v. Brady*, 37 N.D. 59 (1917). In contrast, the Eleventh Circuit concluded that certain types of international commercial agreements constitute treaties, requiring Senate ratification, but held that the question whether any specific agreement constitutes a treaty is a non-justiciable political question. *Made in the USA Found. v. U.S.*, 242 F.3d 1300 (11th Cir. 2001).

The next case excerpt is perhaps the most comprehensive judicial analysis of what types of state-foreign power agreements require consent under the State Treaty Clause and the Compact Clause.

U.S. v. California

No. 2:19-cv-02142, 2020 U.S. Dist. LEXIS 43422 (E.D. Cal. Mar. 13, 2020)

SHUBB, DISTRICT JUDGE:

Plaintiff United States of America ("United States") brought this action against the State of California and other related individuals and entities alleging California's cap-and-trade program violates, inter alia, the Treaty Clause and the Compact Clause of the United States Constitution....

....

[After California and Québec linked their cap-and-trade programs in 2013] the parties signed an agreement memorializing their commitment "to work jointly and collaboratively toward the harmonization and integration of [their] cap-and-trade programs for reducing greenhouse gas emissions." The 2013 Agreement provided in part that the parties would "consult each other regularly and notify each other of "any proposed changes or additions to [their individual] programs," including if either wished to discontinue using WCI, Inc.'s services. [WCI is a non-profit corporation. WCI, Inc. provides technical support to its member jurisdictions by hosting joint auctions and maintaining a computer system that tracks emissions allowances and other compliance instruments. These administrative and technological support services are provided under contract and for remuneration.]. Additionally, the parties agreed to "endeavor to provide" the other with 12 months notice if one wished to withdraw from the Agreement and to terminate the agreement only upon "unanimous consent of the Parties" in writing.

[In 2017, California also linked its cap-and-trade program with Ontario's cap-and-trade program. In 2018, Ontario repealed its cap-and-trade program with no notice to California or Québec, withdrawing Ontario from the Agreement].

. . . .

A. The Treaty Clause

The . . . challenge under the Treaty Clause relates only to the Agreement itself. In relevant part, Article I, Section 10, Clause 1 of the United States Constitution provides:

No State shall enter into any Treaty, Alliance, or Confederation . . .

U.S. Const. Art. I, § 10, cl. 1.

The Constitution does not provide a definition of a "treaty," nor does it distinguish a "treaty" from "alliance" or "confederation." The records of the Constitutional Convention do not include any discussion of Article I, § 10, nor do the state ratification conventions. *See U.S. Steel Corp. v. Multistate Tax Comm'n*, 434 U.S. 452, 461 n.11 (1978); *see also* 3 Joseph Story, *Commentaries on the Constitution of the United States* § 1396, 270 (1833) ("What precise distinction is here intended to be taken between treaties, and agreements, and compacts is no-where explained; and has never as yet been subjected to any exact judicial, or other examination.").

Indeed, only a handful of Supreme Court cases have grappled with the meaning of the Treaty Clause, and often the Treaty Clause is only considered in relation to the Compact Clause of Article I, Section 10, Clause 3. *See U.S. Steel Corp.*, 434 U.S. at 460-61 (comparing the two clauses and describing how "[t]he Framers clearly perceived compacts and agreements as differing from treaties," although unsure as to what extent).

[In *Holmes v. Jennison*, 39 U.S. (14 Pet.) 540 (1840)], [w]riting for a plurality, Chief Justice Taney rejected the proposition that "treaty," "alliance," and "confederation" "meant merely the same thing" and instead suggested a "treaty" is "an instrument written and executed with the formalities customary among nations." *Id.* at 571. Relying on Emerich de Vattel's *The Law of Nations*, Justice Taney found treaties can "only be made by the 'supreme power, by sovereigns who contract in the name of the state'" to serve "the public welfare" for "a considerable time" through "successive execution." *Id.* at 570.

Justice Story largely agreed with this view. In *Commentaries*, Justice Story suggested the "sound policy" behind the Treaty Clause was to prevent subverting the power of the national government. 3 Story, *Commentaries* § 1349, 217-18. In Story's view, treaties "ordinarily relate to subjects of great national magnitude and importance, and are often perpetual, or for a great length of time." *Id.* § 1401,

274. Story's pontifications were given precedential effect when the Supreme Court quoted Story's *Commentaries* in *Virginia* [*v. Tennessee*, 148 U.S. 503, 519 (1893)], explaining "treaties" were "of a political character; such as treaties of alliance for purposes of peace and war . . . in which the parties are leagued for mutual government, political co-operation, and the exercise of political sovereignty; and treaties of cession of sovereignty, or conferring internal political jurisdiction, or external political dependence, or general commercial privileges."

Consequently, the Supreme Court has come to understand that, not all "international agreements . . . constitute treaties in the constitutional sense." While agreements may be referred to colloquially as "treaties," they are not necessarily "treaties" violative of Article I.

The United States argues the Agreement is an "emissions treaty" prohibited by the Treaty Clause. The United States claims it is "of a political character" because it is binding and it "confederates the laws of the two jurisdictions in an important area of commercial policy."

Conversely, California argues the Agreement does not rise to the level of an Article I treaty because it "does not address a matter of substantial consequence to our federal structure, much less one implicating national unity." California claims the Agreement is not binding, and "merely expresses California's and Québec's good-faith intentions to continue communicating and collaborating . . . so that the link between the two cap-and-trade programs may continue to function properly." California primarily relies upon the provisions of the Agreement that permit the parties to make changes to their regulatory schemes and offers Ontario's unencumbered withdrawal as evidence that California could do the same.

. . . .

As the Supreme Court has taught in other cases, in the Article I context, "treaty" is a term of art. Not all international agreements may be "treaties" in the constitutional sense. In *Virginia [v. Tennessee*], the Supreme Court explained that "treaties" within the meaning of Article I are "of a political character." The Court provided examples of agreements that qualified as "treaties", including "treaties of alliance for purposes of peace and war," "mutual government," the "cession of sovereignty," and "general commercial privileges." By any metric, the Agreement between California and Quebec falls short of these consequential agreements.

This Agreement is not a treaty creating an alliance for purposes of peace and war. *See Williams v. Bruffy*, 96 U.S. 176, 182 (1877) (finding the Confederate States of America unconstitutional under the Treaty Clause). Nor does it constitute a treaty for "mutual government" or represent a "cession of sovereignty." To the contrary, the Agreement explicitly recognizes that Québec and California adopted "their own greenhouse gas emissions reduction targets, their own regulation on greenhouse gas emissions reporting programs and their own regulation(s) on their cap-and-trade programs. These programs are not identical, and their different aims and structures undercut any mutuality argument.

The programs, adopted independently and informed by each jurisdiction's policy objectives, could (and have) run independently of each other. Furthermore, the Agreement provides it is "each Party's sovereign right and authority to adopt, maintain, modify, repeal, or revoke any of their respective program regulations or enabling legislation." The Agreement does not "modify any existing statutes and regulations[,] nor does it require or commit the Parties or their respective regulatory or statutory bodies to create new statutes or regulations." Indeed, [the California Air Resources Board] has modified the regulations governing California's cap-and-trade program more than five times since it linked its program with Québec in 2013, without consulting with the province. Accordingly, there is no "mutual government" or "cession of sovereignty" representative of a treaty.

. . . .

B. The Compact Clause

. . . The Compact Clause of Article I, Section 10, Clause 3 provides:

> No State shall, without the Consent of Congress . . . enter into any Agreement or Compact with another State, or with a foreign Power . . .

U.S. Const. Art. I, § 10.

"Read literally, the Compact Clause would require the States to obtain congressional approval before entering into any agreement among themselves, irrespective of form, subject, duration, or interest to the United States." *U.S. Steel Corp.*, 434 U.S. at 459. Rather than adopt that interpretation, the Supreme Court has limited its application to agreements that encroach upon federal sovereignty. Accordingly, the court must first ascertain whether the Agreement falls within Article I's scope.

In *Northeast Bancorp* [*v. Bd. of Governors of Fed. Reserve Sys.*, 472 U.S. 159 (1985)], the Court was tasked with determining whether there was an agreement between a collection of New England states that amounted to a "compact." To do so, the Court considered whether the arrangement had the "classic indicia of a compact," including: (1) provisions that required reciprocal action for the agreement's effectiveness; (2) a regional limitation; (3) a joint organization or body for regulatory purposes; and (4) a prohibition on the agreement's unilateral modification or termination. It is indisputable that there is an agreement between the parties. However, the court must ascertain whether that Agreement "amount[s] to a compact" first.

The Agreement does not contain the first indicium of a compact because it does not require reciprocal action to take effect. Article 14 explicitly states that "this Agreement does not modify any existing statutes and regulations nor does it require or commit the Parties to their respective regulatory or statutory bodies to create new statutes or regulations in relation to this Agreement." While California requires linking jurisdictions to have equivalent or stricter enforcement goals than it does, the efficacy of the program does not rise or fall with other jurisdictions adopting similar enforcement goals; indeed, the program could operate independently of any other jurisdiction.

The Agreement also lacks the second indicium of a compact because it does not impose a regional limitation. While each cap-and-trade program can trace its roots back the recommendations for a "regional" cap-and-trade program promulgated by Western Climate Initiative, nothing in the Agreement or California's law limits the program's efficacy to a particular region. Quite the contrary --the Agreement's "Accession" provision is written without regard to geographical location.

The third indicium of a compact is also absent. While California has adopted a "joint organization or body" in WCI, Inc. to facilitate its linkage with Québec, WCI, Inc. exercises no regulatory authority under the Agreement or California law.

While WCI, Inc. admittedly provides "administrative and technical support" to both jurisdictions, it "plays no role in the enforcement of the cap-and-trade program of any participating jurisdictions" and "exercises no regulatory powers at all. Indeed, it does not exercise any policymaking, regulatory, or enforcement authority emblematic of other "joint bodies" found to be indicative of a compact under the Compact Clause. Consequently, while it is a "joint organization" it serves no "regulatory purpose" indicative of a compact.

Finally, there is no enforceable prohibition on unilateral modification or termination. As in *Northeast Bancorp*, "each [jurisdiction] is free to modify or repeal its law unilaterally." 472 U.S. at 175. Québec and California retain their "sovereign right and authority to adopt, maintain, modify, repeal, or revoke any of their respective program regulations or enabling legislation." California has modified its regulations without consulting Québec on multiple occasions. While modifications to and termination of the Agreement require the consent of all parties, the simple fact that California retains the power to modify its enacting regulations means unilateral termination of California's participation in the Agreement is possible. ([*See*] . . . Ontario's withdrawal from the Agreement and unilateral termination of its cap-and-trade program).)

The United States argues that the amount of money invested in the cap-and-trade program would prohibit a unilateral withdrawal. But while the practical consequences of withdrawal may be steep, caselaw shows this is not the relevant inquiry. California is "free to withdraw at any time," and this freedom defeats any characterization that the Agreement is binding. For the foregoing reasons, all of the "classic indicia" of a compact from Northeastern Bancorp are missing from the Agreement and California law as applied. But "[e]ven if all these indicia of compacts [were] present," only agreements that tend to "increase political power in the states," such that they "may encroach upon or interfere with the just supremacy of the United States" fall within the scope of the Compact Clause.

. . . .

What is before the court now is . . . the question of whether California's power has been increased such that it encroaches upon or interferes with the just supremacy of the United States. For that, the Supreme Court has offered guidance in *United States Steel Corporation v. Multistate Tax Commission.*

In *U.S. Steel*, the Supreme Court offered three factors which, if present in an agreement between states, could "enhance state power quoad the National Government": (1) if the agreement in question authorized member states to "exercise any powers they could not exercise in its absence"; (2) if there was any "delegation of sovereign power" to an outside organization; and (3) if each state was "free to withdraw at any time." 434 U.S.at 473. Factors two and three are not present in the Agreement, as described in the court's analysis of the Northeast Bancorp factors. The only question remaining is whether the Agreement and California law as applied authorized California to "exercise any powers [it] could not exercise in [the Agreement's] absence."

"[W]hatever else may be said of the revolutionary colonists who framed our Constitution, it cannot be doubted that they respected the rights of individual states to pass laws that protected human welfare, and recognized their broad police powers to accomplish this goal." *Rocky Mountain Farmers Union v. Corey*, 913 F.3d 940, 945-46 (9th Cir. 2019). As the Supreme Court has acknowledged, "[l]egislation designed to free from pollution the very air that people breathe clearly falls within the exercise of even the most traditional concept of what is compendiously known as the police power." *Huron Portland Cement Co. v. City of Detroit*, 362 U.S. 440, 442 (1960) (internal citations omitted). It is well within California's police powers to enact legislation to regulate greenhouse gas emissions and air pollution. Accordingly, the Agreement does not allow California to exercise any power it would not normally have.

Because each of the *U.S. Steel* factors weigh against finding the Agreement and California law as applied enhances California's power over that of the federal government, the Agreement does not fall within the scope of the Compact Clause.

Notes & Questions

1. The court's State Treaty Clause analysis largely followed the Supreme Court's analysis in *U.S. Steel*, citing the same sources. The discussion of the State Treaty Clause in *U.S. Steel* was largely dicta. Here, the court effectively adopted that dicta as its reasoning for rejecting the State Treaty Clause argument.

2. Note that the Court used a traditional Compact Clause analysis in analyzing the California-Québec Agreement just as Professor Hollis discussed the State Department, the Restatement (Third) of the Foreign Relations Law of the United States and numerous scholars assumed. *See* Duncan B. Hollis, *The Elusive Foreign Compact*, 73 MO. L. REV. 1071, 1088 (2008).

3. The court emphasized elements of the agreement that make it non-binding; however, California and Québec seem committed to implementing the agreement by enacting regulations, using WCI as secretariat, and actually having joint auctions. U.S. states and Canadian provinces have many other agreements that are

technically not binding, but that the parties are implementing as if they are binding. For example, one scholar described a 1988 Memorandum of Understanding on Environmental Cooperation on Lake Champlain between New York, Vermont, and Québec.

> [The MOU] contains no provision expressly indicating the nonbinding nature of the arrangement, unlike most other MOUs. Some argue that this is implicit within the MOU format, but while not strictly obligated to comply with the tenants of the arrangement, "in practice, the three jurisdictions treat them as 'binding covenants.' Although this agreement is called an MOU, it functionally serves as a near-binding arrangement because it represents the strongest legal arrangement these subnational actors could enter, and reflects a sincere desire by the parties to strongly bind their interests together.

Aaron Messing, *Nonbinding Subnational International Agreements: A Landscape Defined*, 30 GEO. INT'L ENVTL. L. REV. 173, 187 (2017).

4. Following the court's decision in the *U.S. v. California* opinion excerpted above, the United States filed a second motion for summary judgment on its claim that the agreement violates the Foreign Affairs Doctrine, in which foreign affairs and international relations are matters reserved to the federal government. As of the date of publication of this edition, the court had not decided this motion.

5. For an introduction to the law of agreements between Canadian provinces and foreign governments, including U.S. states, see Fabien Gélinas, *The Constitution of Agreement: A Brief Look at Sub-Federal Cross Border Cooperation*, 2006 MICH. ST. L. REV. 1179 (2006). Professor Gélinas summarized his comparison of the law of agreements between Canadian provinces and U.S. states as:

> The law on both sides of the [U.S.-Canada] border has striking similarities, at least if one cares to cast it at a sufficiently abstract level. Binding sub-federal agreements range from a formal treaty that purports to be binding under public international law, and which is off-limits for sub-entities on both sides of the border, to a contract with the attributes of an ordinary commercial contract, which is likely beyond challenge everywhere.
>
> Within that range there are countless possibilities, including agreements that are obviously not treaties but clearly engage matters of state policy and cannot be easily assimilated to an ordinary contract over a strictly commercial matter. One is naturally drawn to ask what it is that distinguishes a binding agreement that is valid from one that is off-limits. One could think of a number of criteria and use them to place each agreement on a sliding scale between contract and treaty. One could imagine that the name of the agreement, the kinds of obligations or commitments it contains, the existence of a consideration, the term, the financial components, and the creation of a joint body and its powers would all be useful in devising a means to decide on the validity of a sub-federal international agreement. The task seems difficult and would have to be informed by a more thorough empirical study than has been undertaken to date.

> .... [Regarding Canadian law,] [t]here is currently no available workable criterion to assess the validity of binding sub-federal international agreements. The only bright line we have is the law governing the agreement. If the sub-federal agreement is purportedly governed by public international law, it will almost certainly be considered a treaty—which the constitution does not allow....

Id. at 1189.

6. For more discussion of other agreements between U.S. states and Canadian provinces, see U.S. Dep't of Homeland Security and Public Safety Canada, *Compendium of U.S. Canada Emergency Management Assistance Mechanisms* (June 2012), available at http://www.dhs.gov/xlibrary/assets/policy/btb-compendium-of-us-canada-emergency-management-assistance-mechanisms.pdf; R. Bruce Sackinger, *Paradiplomatic Maneuvers on the Longest Undefended Border: National and Subnational Fire Protection Agreements Between Canada and the United States*, 13 WILLAMETTE J. INT'L L. & DISP. RESOL. 319 (2005); and Peter R. Jennetten, *State Environmental Agreements with Foreign Powers: The Compact Clause and the Foreign Affairs Power of the States*, 8 GEO. INT'L ENVTL. L. REV. 141 (1995).

B. State-Foreign Power Compact Entities

How a state-foreign power entity "fits" into the United States' federalist system of government raises similar issues as interstate compact entities. For example, how would you characterize such an entity? The New York legislation authorizing the Buffalo and Fort Erie Public Bridge Authority states that it "shall be a body corporate and politic, constituting a public benefit corporation" and "the municipal corporate instrumentality of the state of New York for the purpose of carrying out the provisions of this act." 1933 N.Y. Laws c 824, §§ 1, 2. The New York Court of Appeals described the Bridge Authority as "the creation of a new body corporate and politic with a board appointed by the State, responsible to the State and acting for the State." *People ex rel. Buffalo & Ft. Erie Public Bridge Auth. v. Davis*, 277 N.Y. 292, 299 (1938). Does "a board appointed by the state, responsible to the State and acting for the State" mean that the Authority is a New York State agency? Should the entity also be considered an agency of the government of Canada? The Canada Legislation creating the Bridge Authority did not use any similar descriptive terms. Act Respecting the Buffalo and Fort Erie Public Bridge Co., S.C. 1934, c 63 (Can.).

Should state law apply to a state-foreign power agency? In *Sklarski v. Niagara Falls Bridge Comm'n*, No. 09-cv-633(MAT), 2010 U.S. Dist. LEXIS 29035 (W.D.N.Y. Mar. 26, 2010), the federal court concluded that the New York State Freedom of Information Law does not apply to Niagara Falls Bridge Commission, an agency between New York State and Canada that operates three bridges. In *Sklarski*, the court dismissed the complaint, but granted leave to amend the complaint. The plaintiff amended the complaint to allege a violation of the federal Freedom of Information Act. The court subsequently concluded that the federal FOIA does not apply to the Niagara Falls Bridge Commission. *Sklarski v. Niagara*

Falls Bridge Comm'n, No. 09-cv-633(MAT), 2016 U.S. Dist. LEXIS 162756 (W.D.N.Y. Nov. 23, 2016).

Prior to the *Sklarski* cases, a New York state court concluded that New York's Labor Law applies to the Niagara Falls Bridge Commission. *Stephens & Rankin, Inc. v. Hartnett*, 160 A.D.2d 1201, 1202–03 (N.Y. App. Div. 1990). The state court reasoned:

> The prevailing wage requirement of the Labor Law reflects a strong public policy in this State, embodied in the State Constitution, and the statute is to be liberally construed to carry out its beneficent purposes. Thus, in our view, the statute's coverage was properly interpreted to include laborers involved in public works projects within the State pursuant to contracts with public or governmental entities. Moreover, we note that the NFBC functions with significant State involvement in that half of its members are appointed by the Governor, its members are bonded by the Comptroller, and disputes with the NFBC may be litigated in New York courts.
>
> Petitioner also contends that the application of the Labor Law to NFBC projects conflicts with the intent expressed in the Joint Resolution that the operations of NFBC be independent of State control. We disagree. The regulated party in this instance is petitioner, a private contractor, and demanding petitioner's compliance with the prevailing wage requirement is neither the regulation of the NFBC's internal operations (*cf.*, *Matter of Agesen v Catherwood*, 26 NY2d 521, 525) nor inconsistent with any provision of the Joint Resolution. Moreover, at oral argument petitioner expressly conceded that it was not claiming a preemption of Labor Law § 220 by the Joint Resolution of Congress creating the NFBC.

The Niagara Falls Bridge Commission operates the Rainbow Bridge, the Whirlpool Rapids Bridge, and the Lewiston-Queenston Bridge, each of which are toll bridges crossing the Niagara River between the United States and Canada that received individualized express consent. H.R.J. Res. 688, 75th Cong., 52 Stat. 767 (1938), as amended by Act of July 25, 1939, Pub. L. No. 76-222, 53 Stat. 1083, and by Act of Apr. 12, 1940, Pub. L. No. 76-453, 54 Stat. 107. Many of the International Bridges between the United States and Canada were built under similar authority. In 1972, Congress enacted the International Bridge Act, which granted advanced consent for a state or subdivision of a state to enter into agreements with the Government of Canada, a Canadian province, or a subdivision of a province, and with the Government of Mexico, a Mexican state, or subdivision of a state. 33 U.S.C. §§ 535–535i. Presidential approval is required for construction of international bridges pursuant to the International Bridge Act.

C. Enforcement of State-Foreign Power Agreements

There are few cases involving enforcement of a state-foreign power agreement. What little we know from court decisions largely involves the ability of a foreign power to enforce an agreement with one of the United States in U.S. federal court.

In *Martelli v. Niagara Falls Bridge Comm'n*, No. 13-CV-652-A, 2013 U.S. Dist. LEXIS 99134 (W.D.N.Y. July 16, 2013), the federal court questioned whether the Bridge Commission properly removed the case from state court to the federal court. The federal court considered federal question and diversity jurisdiction and the court's original jurisdiction pursuant to 28 U.S.C. § 1330(a) over actions brought against foreign states. In questioning whether the case was brought against a foreign state, the court cited provisions of the Bridge Commission's enabling legislation stating that it was a public agency or public authority of the State of New York, for the purposes of all Federal law and that the Bridge Commission is licensed in Ontario as a foreign entity. *Id.* at *14.

In *Principality of Monaco v. Mississippi*, 292 U.S. 313 (1934), the U.S. Supreme Court extended the Eleventh Amendment to suits by a foreign power against one of the United States, citing the State Treaty Clause and the Compact Clause, effectively making federal court unavailable unless the domestic state consented to suit.

> . . . . Controversies between a State and a foreign State may involve international questions in relation to which the United States has a sovereign prerogative. One of the most frequent occasions for the exercise of the jurisdiction granted by the Constitution over controversies between States of the Union has been found in disputes over territorial boundaries. Questions have also arisen with respect to the obstruction of navigation; the pollution of streams; and the diversion of navigable waters. But in the case of such a controversy with a foreign power, a State has no prerogative of adjustment. No State can enter "into any Treaty, Alliance, or Confederation" or, without the consent of Congress, "into any Agreement or Compact with a foreign Power." U.S. CONST. art. I, § 10. The National Government, by virtue of its control of our foreign relations is entitled to employ the resources of diplomatic negotiations and to effect such an international settlement as may be found to be appropriate, through treaty, agreement of arbitration, or otherwise. It cannot be supposed that it was the intention that a controversy growing out of the action of a State, which involves a matter of national concern and which is said to affect injuriously the interests of a foreign State, or a dispute arising from conflicting claims of a State of the Union and a foreign State as to territorial boundaries, should be taken out of the sphere of international negotiations and adjustment through a resort by the foreign State to a suit under the provisions of § 2 of Article III. In such a case, the State has immunity from suit without her consent and the National Government is protected by the provision prohibiting agreements between States and foreign powers in the absence of the consent of the Congress. While, in this instance, the proposed suit does not raise a question of national concern, the constitutional provision which is said to confer jurisdiction should be construed in the light of all its applications.

Principality of Monaco, 292 U.S. at 331–32. The Court seemed to reason that a state enjoys immunity because the Constitution prohibits agreements between a state and a foreign power' thus a state cannot be a proper party in such an action. But the Supreme Court also left open that a state may consent to suit, suggesting that the Constitution does not prohibit all agreements between a state and a foreign power without the consent of Congress. *Principality of Monaco* is still good law and still gets cited.

A Few Final Notes and Questions

You have studied examples of more than 50 compacts and excerpts, quotes, or cites from more than 150 cases. If you were advising a state considering a new compact, how would you draft compact provisions to avoid some of the difficult problems illustrated in existing compacts and past court decisions? How would you ensure multiple courts treat the compact in a uniform manner? How would you address the application of state law? How would you incorporate administrative procedures into compact administration? What would you tell a state legislator that wants to terminate a compact? How would you argue a compact law question to a court that has little or no experience with compact law and where there is a dearth of precedent? How would you talk to opposing counsel with similarly little experience?

You have also studied similarities between compacts and other forms of intergovernmental interaction. How would you apply concepts of compact law in other contexts? To gaming compacts between state governors and tribal governments under the Indian Gaming Regulatory Act? To interlocal agreements between local governments within the same state? To drafting, enacting, and interpreting uniform and model law? To drafting contracts between private parties? To drafting new legislation?

Throughout the book, you have also read about how congressional consent transforms a compact into federal law and the implications of the transformation. What would you think about state legislatures approving intergovernmental agreements thus transforming them into state law? Are there some intergovernmental agreements that should supersede state statutes governing municipalities or local government ordinances and charters? Should states be restricted in altering, amending, or repealing their approval of such a "super-intergovernmental agreement"?

Should Congress continue to encourage states to enact compacts? Should states enact more of the compacts that Congress encourages? Recall that Congress provided carrots and sticks for states to enact low-level radioactive waste management compacts in the 1980s; states have spent hundreds of millions of dollars and there are no new disposal facilities. Would federal legislation and management of such thorny interstate problems be more effective? Why does Congress encourage states to enact compacts when it could legislate in those policy areas?

Finally, when faced with the need for an interstate solution, consider whether a formal compact is the best solution. Do the states really have the political will to enact and maintain a compact over time? Is there a need for a compact that supersedes state law? Do the state legislatures and governors understand the implications of enacting a compact? Is a different form of cooperation a better solution?

Made in United States
Orlando, FL
04 November 2026

90201381R00254